My love to Hugh and Sierdu.

Margaret

THIRD EDITION

Marriage

BOB & MARGARET BLOOD

 THE FREE PRESS
A Division of Macmillan Publishing Co., Inc.
NEW YORK

Collier Macmillan Publishers
LONDON

The Free Press
A Division of Macmillan Publishing Co., Inc.
866 Third Avenue, New York, N.Y. 10022

Collier Macmillan Canada, Ltd.

Library of Congress Catalog Card Number: 77–3847

Printed in the United States of America

printing number

1 2 3 4 5 6 7 8 9 10

Library of Congress Cataloging in Publication Data

Blood, Robert O
  Marriage.

  Includes index.
  1. Marriage. I. Blood, Margaret, joint author.
II. Title.
HQ728.B6 1978   301.42   77–3847
ISBN 0-02-904180-5

Contents

1 BEFORE MARRIAGE

3 FAMILY LIVING

Preface to the Third Edition

In the decade since the completion of the previous edition of *Marriage* in the summer of 1967, a lot has happened to American marriages and a lot has happened to us. These have been years of women's liberation and the revolt against sexism; of sexual revolution and the revolt against traditional morality; of open marriage and the revolt against exclusivism and possessiveness; of the legalization of abortion and emancipation from unwanted childbearing; and of living together unmarried and the revolt against marriage itself. During these same years, our four sons have grown up and left home. Through their lives and our own we have confronted or lived through many of these revolutionary changes. Anything we have not experienced in our own family we have encountered through clients after leaving academia to devote ourselves to teamwork in the private practice of marriage and divorce counseling and giving weekend workshops on interpersonal relationships.

These experiences have shaped our writing. For the first time, the two of us have joined forces in co-authoring a book. Bob has been responsible for reviewing the research that has been done in the intervening years and pulling together relevant findings from 300 new books and articles. Margaret has critiqued Bob's old and new writing and has written numerous vignettes out of our own and our friends' and acquaintances' experiences that have humanized the book. Together, we have striven to eliminate sexist language from our writing to produce a book that treats men and women as true equals.

Chapters on "Living Together Unmarried" and on "Extramarital Involvement" are entirely new. Many other chapters have been almost entirely rewritten: the one on premarital "Sexual Involvement," to recognize that sexual intercourse is now a typical premarital experience; the one on "Getting Married," to take account of the "new wedding"; the one on "Occupational Involvement," to reflect the wholesale movement of married women into careers and the struggle to balance the roles of husband and wife inside and outside the home. There are whole new sections on massage, sterilization, abortion, adoption, the divorce process, and other topics too numerous to mention.

The result is a book more drastically changed from its predecessor than any of the previous revisions, from *Anticipating Your Marriage* (1955) to the First Edition of *Marriage* (1962) to the Second Edition, published in 1969. It is a new book that excites us, and we are eager to share it with you.

1

BEFORE MARRIAGE

Chapter 1 analyzes dating, which may provide a wealth of experience in personal relations and lays the experiential foundation on which marriage is built. The next two chapters portray the processes of affectional and sexual involvement that, sometimes jointly and sometimes separately, bring increased emotional and physical intimacy between persons. Chapter 4 explores an optional bypath on the way to marriage—living together in a quasi-marital state. Chapters 5 and 6 deal with choosing a marriage partner, the former with the personal qualities that attract people to each other and the latter with the social characteristics that may present special difficulties in mixed marriages. Although most couples move into marriage fairly swiftly once they have decided they are compatible, they are not necessarily ready for marriage, so Chapter 7 deals with the nature and consequences of being ready or not. Finally, Chapter 8 deals with the engagement, wedding, and honeymoon, which mark the transition from being single to being married.

Together, these chapters portray the process of growing interest in persons of the opposite sex, gradual involvement and increasing intimacy with a few partners, and the final decision to undertake the adventure of marriage with one special person.

1 Dating/Getting Together

In an earlier book one of us defined *dating* as "paired association between persons of the opposite sex for the purpose of companionship with no necessary intention of marrying" (Blood, 1972). This definition does not say what the couple will do when they get together. In the minds of some people, dating means going out to eat and watching a film or going dancing. For people who don't like these traditional activities, the alternate title of this chapter may be more comfortable.

Getting together is a less formal term that implies such activities as eating a homecooked meal, sitting around watching television, chatting, playing the guitar, or making love. It has the virtue of emphasizing the companionship derived from dating, with or without prearrangement. Dating emphasizes prearrangement in setting a time for getting together. As far as we are concerned, the terms mean essentially the same thing although their connotations may differ. In this chapter we will use the word "dating" most often, because it is simpler. But any reader who is turned off by it is cordially invited to substitute "getting together" or any other term s/he prefers.

We begin this book with activities that have no necessary connection with marriage. We will conclude this chapter with a discussion of ways in which dating prepares people for marriage. Dating more broadly enables the participants to learn how to interact in one-to-one relationships, regardless of whether marriage ever results. To view each date as an attempt to find a spouse would ruin it. Except in the later stages of involvement, dating is an end in itself.

MOTIVES FOR DATING

If the purpose of dating is not primarily to find a marriage partner or to prepare for marriage, what are the motives of those who date? At Harvard College, freshman and senior men were asked their chief reason for dating. Table 1–1 shows that their most common motive was to develop a friendship with someone of the opposite sex. This was the only motive that was more popular among the freshmen than the seniors, perhaps because the most accessible dating partners (Radcliffe students) were outnumbered eight to one by the Harvard student body, leaving first-year men particularly hard pressed to make women friends. Vreeland and Austin (1971) discovered that finding a friend and finding a good listener were closely correlated elements of a "companion dating pattern." This pattern emphasizes the personal-relationship quality in dating.

Dating for recreation emphasizes having fun apart from developing a friendship with the particular person. In that sense it is relatively impersonal. Vreeland and Austin found that it correlated negatively with the companion dating pattern.

Vreeland and Austin found that the desire for sexual intimacy was part of an exploitive dating pattern that they labeled "instrumental." But most of the increase in sexually motivated dating between the freshman and senior years paralleled an increased affectional involvement with the women whom they were dating. So a considerable proportion of this sexual motivation reflected a more general search for love rather than a tendency to treat the partner simply as a sex object.

To us, the most exploitive motive for dating would be to enhance the dater's reputation in the eyes of his peers. Not a single student in either class listed this as his primary reason for dating.

In general, then, dating is not usually intended to find a marriage partner. Nevertheless, insofar as dating involves making friends with

Table 1–1   Chief Motive for Dating, for Freshman and Senior Men

Motive	Freshmen	Seniors
Finding an opposite-sex friend	49%	34%
Recreation	26	29
Sexual intimacy	10	21
Finding a good listener	9	12
Finding a wife	5	6
Enhancing my reputation	0	0
Total	99%	102%
Number of cases		205

Adapted from Vreeland, 1971. *Source:* Random samples of Harvard classes of 1970 and 1973, questioned in 1970.

persons of the opposite sex, it paves the way to the eventual decision to focus on a long-term relationship with one's best friend.

PREFERRED PARTNERS

If the primary purpose of dating is to find a friend, that motive should be reflected in the characteristics people look for when they consider whom they would like to date. Of all the persons I know, which ones do I choose to date and why? What qualities turn me on and make me want to spend some time with persons who have them?

Vreeland gave the Harvard men a long list of characteristics and asked them to indicate which they considered essential in a dating partner. Table 1–2 shows that a woman who is a good conversationalist, is intellectually sophisticated, and is highly intelligent was particularly prized. Since Harvard ranks at the top of American colleges, these men were in effect saying that they wanted to date women who were like themselves.

Several times as many men were attracted by women who are intelligent and show it as were attracted by women who are intelligent and hide it. On that particular campus, women who exercise their intellectual capacities were especially attractive to many men. Similarly, Komarovsky (1973) found that 70 percent of the Princeton men she interviewed never felt that their intellectual relationships with dates were a problem, even though a number of them acknowledged that their partners were intellectually superior to them. From her exhaustive study of these students, Komarovsky concluded that the traditional norm "of male superiority is giving way to the ideal of companionship between equals."

However, in American society generally, there are still enough men who date down the intelligence scale to leave their feminine equals stranded. (Scott, 1965, called this "the Brahmin problem.") Such women face a difficult choice: Whether to attempt to hide their intellectuality so

Table 1–2 Essential Characteristics of Women as a Date, for Freshman and Senior Men

Characteristic	Freshmen	Seniors
Good conversationalist	49%	40%
Sexually attractive	49%	40%
Well dressed	14%	5%
Sexually liberated	12%	11%
Effervescent personality	12%	11%
Intellectually sophisticated	10%	17%
Highly intelligent and shows it	5%	11%

Adapted from Vreeland, 1971. Totals add up to more than 100% because students could rate any number of characteristics as essential.

as to attract dates, or to affirm their intellectual powers and content themselves with the companionship of other women or of nobody at all. For participants in the women's movement, the preferred choice is apt to be to preserve their personal integrity rather than to degrade themselves in an appeal for dates based on pretense. Indeed, in a Barnard College class that Komarovsky believed "probably recruited a relatively high proportion of feminists," more than half the women said that they had never pretended to be intellectually inferior to a man they were dating.

The second major cluster of preferences for Harvard men was that their dates be sexually attractive and sexually liberated. Choosing a dating partner is partly a matter of body chemistry, of being turned on emotionally and physically by factors of taste and appearance that are not intellectual at all but have to do with largely unconscious forces. Although a large proportion of the men felt sexual attractiveness was essential, fewer insisted that the woman be uninhibited. Vreeland and Austin (1971) found that those who were looking for a sexually liberated woman were also apt to be searching for an unconventional life-style that included taking drugs and engaging in radical political activity.

Women with effervescent personalities were presumably seen as easy to get along with because they share the burden of initiating activities. Well-dressed women ranked high on the freshman list but were relatively low for the senior men.

In general, these preferred qualities emphasize meaningful interchanges of conversation, physical intimacy, and emotional energy. From this perspective, a good date is not someone to show off to others but someone with whom a one-to-one experience is significant and enjoyable.

INITIATING DATING

Once I have noticed someone whom I would like to get to know, I must reach out to that person or nothing will ever happen. For some self-confident people, making new friends comes easily. But for those with less experience, getting started in a new relationship is frightening. How do I know I won't be rejected? How do I know the person will turn out to be as pleasant as I hope s/he will be? The answer, of course, is that I don't There is no guarantee in advance—only the chance that something may be gained if I try.

These uncertainties deter those who lack self-assurance. Zerface (1968) found that students who seldom dated tended to be "self-conscious about their physical appearance, to worry over humiliating experiences, to remain in the background in social situations, to experience recurrent loneliness, to desire solitude frequently, to lack self-confidence, to become discouraged easily and to daydream rather often." For such persons, doing nothing often seems preferable to risking a rebuff.

If I want a relationship the ball starts in my court. If I see you as an attractive, interesting person whom I'd like to know better, I've got to let you in on my fantasy. The action starts where the interest is. If I wait and hope for you to notice me or "sense" my interest in you, I may wait forever. I can't lose *unless* I invest too much in my expectation, putting my own self-worth on the line. You may have other plans or other priorities that have nothing to do with how interesting or okay I am. I lose only if I treat your refusal as devaluing me.

First dates have an excitement that reflects underlying tensions and anxieties. Each partner may strive to impress the other. The first impression has to be good or there won't be another chance. Sometimes anxiety is so intense that it paralyzes both partners. Nothing is said for fear of saying the wrong thing. Or both may choose the safety of saying the expected. If we say the same things everyone else does, surely we can't go far wrong. The relationship will not be very personal as long as it is so undistinctive, but the conventional pattern may provide a secure framework until we begin to move below the surface amenities.

One way of dealing with initial self-consciousness is to remember that both of us share this anxiety. To admit honestly my uneasiness or lack of certainty may disarm us both:

> I saw him as a bigwig on campus and he saw me as the smartest person in the geology class. When we both admitted our fear of not measuring up, we laughed and were off to a better start. *

The chief source of anxiety between new partners is uncertainty about whether we will be compatible. Mutual stereotyping occurs when people feed the first information received into the available slots in their computers. Openness to the fact that there is always more in each of us than is evident at first glance prevents immediate disillusionment.

On further acquaintance you may be very different from my earlier impression of you. If I can let go of my eagerness for compatibility I can use this occasion to get to know and understand someone different from myself. Although we may feel disappointed about not meshing, neither one of us is to blame for that.

Ways of Reducing Initial Strain

Certain types of dates create less strain. Structuring the dating situation to take the emphasis off the weak, new pair relationship reduces anxiety.

---

*Case materials are adapted from a wide variety of sources. Identifying data such as names have been changed to protect those involved except where permission has been specifically received to use personal materials.

This can be achieved in group parties and double-dating. If one couple's morale suffers from incompatible pairing, the group offers distraction and compensation. Strain is diffused over a larger set of relationships.

Strain is limited when the first date offers a chance to get acquainted over coffee rather than plunging blind into a whole evening or weekend. Tension is reduced by guaranteeing in advance as much compatibility as possible. Anxiety about the unknown is less when dates are chosen from among old friends and acquaintances. If dating must be arranged, the ideal matchmaker knows both partners well enough to assure their compatibility. Least satisfactory of all is a truly "blind" date where nothing but chance brings two people together.

Films, concerts, and ball games provide programed activities. When something goes on around the couple, the conversational resources of the two individuals are only marginally tested. Instead of having to entertain each other all the time, they need to do so only during intermission. There is a certain wisdom in the conventional coffee-and-movies pattern for first dates. Informal, private dates can come later. After a couple get to know each other, they can explore their special preferences.

Uncertainty about compatibility creates anxiety for both of us. The sooner we give and receive feedback of reassuring information, the better. The end of a date is a long time to wait to learn that the partner enjoyed the occasion. Some feedback comes from facial expressions and other nonverbal cues. But the sooner appreciation can be expressed, the sooner we will be able to relax, knowing each of us is accepted. Mere flattery is hollow and produces a false sense of compatibility from which the two may later have to extricate themselves. Genuine enthusiasm puts the partner at ease.

It takes self-confidence to ask a new person for a date. Those most lacking in self-confidence are also, unfortunately, those who suffer most from rejection. For such persons, it is better to make friendships first. Church groups, hobbies, and clubs allow familiarity to grow around common interests. Personal friendships among the members of such groups provide a basis for eventual dating.

For some, the inhibitions to dating go deep into past emotional conditioning that only professional therapy seems likely to overcome:

> I am the youngest of three children and the only girl. I never played with my brothers though they often teased me. I played by myself except when my cousin Carole and I were together. I was very shy, afraid of people in general but particularly of boys who were rough. They were always running, not caring who they ran into, yelling, fighting, and I was afraid of getting hurt. I never had any real dates until I was out of high school. I think I was asked a couple of times but I didn't care for the men who asked me. It is strange that though I wanted very much to have dates, I was more scared to have them. I never spoke to men unless I had to—I was afraid of them.

Some men view women as seductive. Because of negative parental attitudes toward sex, expressiveness and touching may be frightening. The loner plays it safe by avoiding social contacts that might expose his inadequacies and arouse his fears:

> *My mother always taught me, "Never kiss a girl until you are almost engaged." Therefore, my general attitudes were very prudish. As a result of this I developed a brotherly relationship with most women. They tell me their troubles and ask my advice. Most of the time I am satisfied with this.*

Persons who feel uptight about relating to the opposite sex often have dominating and overprotective parents who actively discouraged their dating. Claiming disinterest in "that stuff," they may immerse themselves in studies, sports, and organizations, allowing only platonic friendships with the opposite sex. Working through inhibitions with a counselor may increase self-awareness and self-respect and allow more freedom of response.

Passivity does not invite dates. For men who hesitate to initiate contacts, women can pave the way by being warm, outgoing, and friendly. The fear of reaching out may result in endless waiting for someone to come my way. There is nothing shameful in wanting to have warm relationships. Taking my own needs and desires seriously is important. If I really want a friendship, I've got to spend the time and energy it takes to make it come about. Brainstorming and planning strategy seem crude and "unnatural," but may be a part of being at the right place at a time when it is easiest to ask for what I'd like:

> *In high school I was pretty lonely. Finally in college I came to my senses and realized I'd been wasting time. Here in the university were men galore. I began to see that to make myself available I had to do more than sit by the telephone and wait for a call. I had to go halfway in being friendly, to be genuinely interested in men, to care enough about their interests, to show a little warmth and enthusiasm. When I started treating them like human beings, it was like magic. As I warmed up, they did, too.*

For women to initiate dates is still easier to say than to do. Practice lends courage. Consciousness-raising groups and classes in preparation for marriage are a good place to role-play telephoning a man. In our Singles workshops, men express enormous relief over women's sharing the burden of initiating relationships:

> *I don't know why you women think it's any easier for us to take the risk of calling up a woman for a date. There's the same chance she'll say no and that's just as scary for me as it is for you.*
> *I'm flattered to have someone want to have a date with me. And I*

don't like making myself vulnerable any more than you, which is what asking someone for a date amounts to.

Another problem is how to get a "raincheck" when you can't accept a first invitation. Because unwanted dates are frequently declined with polite excuses, a legitimate excuse is liable to be misinterpreted as a rebuff. Hence, a new inquirer needs to be explicitly encouraged to try again. The surest foundation for dating is the friendliness out of which intimate relationships grow.

Joel and Suzanne Springer (1972) noted that American college campuses were still difficult places to meet members of the opposite sex. Their research at California State University at Long Beach indicated that 61 percent of the men and 46 percent of the women were dating less than once a week. Most of these low-frequency daters wished they were dating more but felt handicapped by their inability to meet and communicate with others at dances or parties.

Low-frequency daters characterized themselves as lonely, shy, lacking in self-confidence, self-conscious, easily discouraged, frequently daydreaming. To cope with these problems, the Springers offered a dating class using experiential techniques that facilitated group unity and expression of feelings. These techniques included relaxation and nonverbal sensory-awareness exercises, meditation, Bach pairing exercises (1971), and role-training and psychodramatic techniques (Haskel, 1973). Through discussion and role training, the participants practiced meeting, initiating a conversation, making a date, developing and ending a dating relationship. This group practice was more helpful than one-to-one counseling.

Our own Singles workshops also have shown the value of a supportive group in providing an environment where persons dissatisfied with their dating experiences can practice and gain courage.

Co-op housing, communes, and other small living units offer environments where skills in interpersonal processes can be learned. Men's and women's consciousness-raising groups, transactional analysis, assertiveness training, and awareness and growth groups are available within and at the edge of college campuses and offer group environments for human relations training.

Group Solidarity and Pairing Off. A group of congenial persons is stimulating and less demanding than a one-to-one encounter. Group morale can soar in response to the dynamic input of a small minority or even one. As the group fosters greater ease in relating, pairing off begins and "the group" is threatened. The last two years of high school, our older sons belonged to what they called just "Group":

We met every Saturday night to talk politics, the war and civil rights, and to folk-dance and play our guitars—a very like-minded group that really clicked. I remember how hurt I was when the girl I liked best began to sit with the same boy every time. A lot of us felt cut off and betrayed by both of them. I continued to get angry at the coupling off in corners and outdoors until I found someone to be close with myself.

Within such a group, persons begin to dare to reach out. This is especially apparent in adolescence, but even for older men and women, classes, clubs, conferences, retreats, and workshops offer meeting grounds for unattached persons.

Computer Dating

For students who don't belong to social organizations and who attend large universities or commuter campuses where it is difficult to make acquaintances, computer dating offers an entree. Especially when students first arrive on campus, the computer offers something better than random selection of dating partners. The effectiveness of computer pairing depends on (1) the meaningfulness of the questionnaire used, (2) the honesty with which the questions are answered, and (3) the diversity of the pool of potential partners who have fed their data into the machine.

Whichever sex is in short supply has the selective advantage. For both sexes, however, the computer rules out the most obviously ineligible partners and selects eligibles who are at least minimally compatible. (Computers sometimes demonstrate their competence by incestuously pairing brothers and sisters because their family backgrounds are so similar!) Knowing that the prospective partner is interested in dating someone new and has been machine-selected for similarity of interests makes computer dating more comfortable than stab-in-the-dark dating.

At the University of Alabama, twice as many men students preferred their date with a woman with whom they had been computer-matched on social characteristics such as age, height, religion, social class, and grade-point average as preferred a woman drawn at random from those participating in the matching program (Strong, Wallace, and Wilson, 1969).

Iowa State University students were generally enthusiastic about their computer-selected partners at a dance. Of the men, 52 percent (and 43 percent of the women) felt the computer had matched them "quite successfully." Although a single event seldom generates long-term relationships, half a year later 20 percent of the men and 13 percent of the women still felt that they would enjoy additional dates with their computer partners "a great deal" or "quite a bit" (Coombs and Kendall, 1966).

A computer can bring together lonely individuals in our increasingly anonymous society. It is likely to be even more useful off-campus than on. People who move to a large metropolis may find a computer particularly strategic for beginning dating in a new environment.

Advertising

For persons who lack a sufficient number of contacts with the opposite sex, advertising is an unusual means of increasing the number of potential dating partners. Manheim (1961) described the experiences of a woman who was an administrator of a public school system in a large Western city and was also working on her doctorate at a large university. She placed the following classified ad in the personal columns of a newspaper for one week:

> Attractive professional woman in her thirties, warm outgoing personality, lively sense of humor, interested in the fine arts as well as more mundane things, desires to meet gentleman with compatible interests. Box No. ————, c/o this newspaper.

She received a total of 95 responses in the next few weeks and faced the task of choosing the ones whom she was most interested in meeting. She rejected 50 out of hand as offensive or uninteresting. Thirty-two were of borderline interest, and the remaining 13 were definitely interesting. After writing to each of the latter, she received telephone calls from 12 of the 13 and arranged to get together with them. With 11 of the 12, the first date was pleasant, but neither partner seemed sufficiently interested to want to get together any further. With one of the 12, however, both partners found in the other person things for which they had been looking, so the first date led to subsequent ones, and they were still seeing each other a year later. Had this not been the case among the first dozen, the woman could have explored the next 32 men who had written to her.

Advertising may speed up the process of making contact with potential dating partners. It seems especially useful for persons who lack an adequate number of personal acquaintances. With the waning of computer dating services, advertising may assume a new importance for persons who wish to increase their pool of eligible dating partners.

DATING ACTIVITIES

We have already described activities that may lessen the strain on first dates. But what kinds of things do people usually do when they get together?

Vreeland gave her Harvard students a list of 22 activities and asked them which ones they sometimes engaged in and which was their main activity on dates. Table 1–3 lists the dating activities that were most often reported as "primary or important."

Table 1-3   Primary and Occasional Dating Activities, for Freshman and Senior Men

Activity	PRIMARY ACTIVITIES		OCCASIONAL ACTIVITIES	
	Freshmen	Seniors	Freshmen	Seniors
Sitting in room talking	43%	32%	86%	93%
Making love	9%	21%	50%	80%
Going to movies	6%	5%	77%	92%
Taking walks	4%	2%	73%	80%
Attending private parties	4%	2%	60%	87%
Playing cards, etc. in a room	2%	4%	69%	83%

Adapted from Vreeland, 1971.

Remembering that these same students felt that being a good conversationalist was an essential characteristic of a date, we are not surprised to find how much of their dating was spent sitting around talking. Noteworthy by their absence from this list are such traditional activities as dancing and eating out. Indeed, only a third of these students ever went dancing, much less made it their main activity.

Notable also is that only one of the six activities costs any money—namely, the movies. All six are informal. Even the parties were private ones, unsponsored by any organization. Most of the activities involved only the man and the woman—talking, walking, or making love.

If "getting together" implies informality, it fits these activities. "Let's get together tonight and see what happens" seems an appropriate introduction to most of these unplanned, unorganized, noncommercial activities. All it takes to have this kind of a date is two people and a place where they can have some privacy. The necessary equipment is provided by the people—their brains, their feelings, their bodies—in short, themselves.

SOCIALLY EXPECTED VERSUS PERSONALLY NEGOTIATED PATTERNS

Since most dating activities are private, they are not subject to public scrutiny and are exempt from direct outside pressure. Nevertheless, because we have been conditioned by our society to expect certain behavior of one another, we bring to our initial dating experiences corresponding expectations of how you and I will behave.

Formality and Informality

Early dates tend to emphasize the niceties of social behavior. Dates with a new partner rely on fulfilling social expectations in the absence of knowledge about the individual.

As acquaintance increases, behavior becomes more individuated. As a relationship develops, both partners adapt their behavior to the other's needs. The danger in unconventional conduct is that it may abandon the spirit of considerateness along with the form. The essence of a personal relationship lies in concern and sympathy for the partner.

It would be wrong to assume that social conventions and personal needs necessarily conflict. For well-socialized people they usually coincide. But if one partner needs to be unconventional and the other to be conventional, it is difficult to satisfy both. Then, at least one partner must adapt his/her behavior to the other's counterneed if the relationship is to develop.

Making Decisions

Traditional sex roles called for men to dominate and women to submit. Some couples still adhere to this pattern in early dating but conform less as they get to know each other better. At the University of Connecticut 46 percent of casual couples exhibited traditional role behavior, but only 33 percent of serious couples and 10 percent of committed couples (Heiss, 1962).

The longer couples date, the more they turn from conventional behavior to patterns that express their personal value systems. The more committed they become, the more they dare to be themselves. The more honest they are with each other, the more meaningful the relationship becomes. So, although early dating involves a good deal of culturally prescribed pretense (whether "traditional" or "liberated"), this is abandoned as couples lay aside their masks.

After couples have dated enough to accept each other as people, they become more "realistic" about money. The longer they go together, the less likely they are to let tradition or liberation stand in the way of a good time. Sharing or even total financing by the woman may be appropriate if she has as much money as he or more.

The Effect of Liberation on Dating

Although it's still easier to talk about than to do, women are overthrowing the traditional patterns of male dominance in initiating dates, planning the activity, and paying the bill. Many men welcome this sharing of the burden of responsibility. From men in our Singles workshops the women hear:

> Of course I like to be invited out. It flatters me to have someone interested in me enough to stop and talk and to ask me to do something with them. I'm human, too!

And from women the men hear:

> *Talking about all this has made me realize that we don't have to let you men be in charge of our social lives, of whether we get asked out or not.*

Daring to develop an acquaintance is hardest the first few times. The acquaintance may not work out for either you or me. That's part of the chance we take. We may not hit it off, but if we do, the risk will have been worth it.

Men don't have to call the shots as to the degree of intimacy either:

> *Right now I am caught in the dilemma between my fear of being a prude and fear of being pushed past the limits I feel comfortable with. Because I don't know what I really want, I frequently go along when I'm not clear. Then I suddenly flip and accuse my date of exploiting me. Several of my friends tell me I give them double messages.*

The balance between what feels right for me and you can be found only by dealing directly and honestly about what each of us would like to give and receive:

> *I've come to realize we have to negotiate how much physical affection we are ready for just as we have to negotiate which movie or which restaurant we want to go to.*

DATING CAREERS

Most Americans begin dating in junior high and marry in their early twenties, so their dating career covers six to eight years. Since college students marry later than average, their premarital dating may span a whole decade.

Extensity

More significant than the number of years from first to last date is the number of dating partners. The college students in Table 1–4 had typically dated 21 to 30 members of the opposite sex, but the number varied widely. Presumably, those who dated fewer than a dozen partners had less perspective for choosing a marriage partner:

> *We both had such a need to be loved and for a while we picked each other up. Looking back on it I wish I'd gotten to know more women before Joan and I got so deeply involved that we couldn't pull out. I don't want to hurt her but I feel caught.*

Table 1–4   Number of Partners Ever Dated by College Men and Women

Number Ever Dated	Men	Women
0–10	8%	12%
11–20	23	20
21–30	22	18
31–50	25	21
Over 50	23	28
Total	101%	99%
Number of cases	160	174

Source: Students enrolled in the University of Michigan marriage course (sophomores-seniors) in 1956.

> *Jim was just right for me those first few months of school and then Tom was there when my father died. Rick and Tim appealed to my flamboyant streak and Rob to my vanity. Each was special for a while but then someone else would come along and seem more compatible. Am I too fussy? I wonder if I'll ever settle down.*

Some become involved quickly and get "stuck." Others dance gingerly through one relationship after another. There's no one rule to be followed. Each friendship is unique and has its own meanings, positive and negative. Each is a learning ground for future relationships. But experience with a variety of persons provides self-awareness and interpersonal knowhow that limited experience does not allow. Bell (1967) found that the estimated number of different individuals ever dated by college men and women was 53 and 43, respectively. Apparently most Americans date enough different persons prior to marriage to give them an extraordinarily broad acquaintance with persons of the opposite sex.

Intensity

Dating a wide range of partners is no substitute for thorough acquaintance with a few. Intensive relationships are not necessarily serious (in the sense of being oriented toward marriage), but they tend to focus on one partner for the time being. Dating the same person repeatedly offers new depths of understanding. Steady dating fosters the growth of a more personal relationship.

Steady dating offers intensified doses of the values provided by dating in general:

> *I took dating very seriously and never went with a woman I truly was not interested in. From each new woman I learned something more about the members of the opposite sex as well as more about myself. I*

learned what it felt like to be stood up, made a fool of, dominated, thrown over, and strung along; as well as being loved, cared for, admired, respected, trusted, and made secure. I dated each one long enough to learn her good and bad points, my mistakes, how they treated me, and how they expected me to treat them.

Extensity plus Intensity

It would be easy to assume that extensive and intensive dating are mutually incompatible. Probably, in extreme cases, they are. One can imagine someone dating so many people that s/he never has time to date the same one twice.

The opposite extreme is a college senior who dated only one person in his life:

I didn't get around to dating in high school. When I got to college I met Alice in my freshman English class and we started going together. We've been going together ever since and get along pretty well. But now that we're scheduled to get married in August, I'm suddenly full of doubts. I feel as though I don't know for sure if she's the right one for me. She wouldn't like it one bit, but I sometimes wonder whether I shouldn't start dating some other girls just to help me make up my mind.

Table 1–5 shows, however, that steady dating is not generally incompatible with a wide variety of partners. Quite the opposite: Those with the most steady partners had the most casual partners. Turned around the other way, the larger the number of casual partners, the greater the chances of going steady with some of them.

DATING AS PREPARATION FOR MARRIAGE

Thinking about marriage too soon may prevent a person from deriving the full range of values from dating:

Table 1–5   Steady Dating and Total Number of Dating Partners

	NUMBER OF STEADY RELATIONSHIPS					
	None	*One*	*Two*	*Three*	*Four +*	*Total*
Median number of individuals ever dated	18	22	34	35	44	30
Percentage of total cases	15%	26%	28%	16%	15%	100%

Source: 264 men and women students enrolled in the University of Michigan marriage course, 1960–61.

Dating for me began about the beginning of seventh grade. This dating took the form of steady relationships very early. My dominant motive was for close relationships to satisfy my emotional needs. I looked forward to marriage as a goal from my earliest experiences. As I look back on this time I see that my parents were right about this early dating being rushed too much, but what neither they nor I realized was that it was serving a vital need which my parents did not meet.

The great error in my dating was that it became marriage oriented at an unrealistic age. I considered qualities in dates on the basis of my marriage ideals almost from the very beginning. This pushed me into involvement at too early an age. As a result, I dated too few partners and my dating span was cut short by early marriage.

Dating is most often an end in itself, pure recreation. But, regardless of the motives of the participants, dating has two consequences for marriage: (1) knowledge of the opposite sex, and (2) development of interpersonal skills.

Knowledge of the Opposite Sex

Dating is not the only way of getting to know persons of the opposite sex. Coeducation provides classroom and extracurricular contact. These contacts tend to be unemotional and uninvolved. Dating provides an opportunity for intimate, personal acquaintance.

All members of the opposite sex are not alike. I need to discover what sort of partner is best for me. Each new date provides an experiment in latent matchmaking, a chance to discover what makes for compatibility and incompatibility. No matter how disappointing a date turns out to be, it adds to my wisdom about my own requirements. Without necessarily realizing it, I sharpen my ability to discriminate between good combinations and poor ones.

Development of Interpersonal Skills

Dating provides opportunities to develop interpersonal skills that are essential in marriage. Even a "bad date" with a person I wouldn't think of marrying tests my maturity in coping with frustration. This does not mean that I should go out of my way to date difficult partners for practice. It does mean that whenever I run into problems, my experience trains me for marriage—for better or for worse.

If such lessons can be learned from casual dating, even more can be gained from serious dating. The longer a couple date, the more their interaction pattern reveals and shapes their behavior in marriage, to each other or to others. Since the continuity between casual dating and marriage is less obvious, it may be useful to illustrate how casual dates provide opportunities for learning skills relevant to marriage.

Directness.   One of the biggest problems in early dating is difficulty in communication. A shy man or woman may be adept in talking to persons of his/her own sex but afraid on a date of saying the wrong thing, or making a bad impression, or boring the partner. To date means to take responsibility for holding up one end of the conversation—an appalling responsibility for the uninitiated. but with experience comes relief from being tongue-tied. Self-confidence grows with conversational expertise. The opposite sex turns out to be hardly more difficult to talk to than one's own, and offers new topics of conversation as each tells the other about the world s/he inhabits.

Empathy.   Communication is a two-way process. It begins with self-expression but is completed only if the partner receives the message. Empathy is the ability to perceive the partner's attitudes and feelings. It differs from sympathy because it doesn't necessarily involve agreement. Empathy is a skill that can be acquired and developed through practice. Dating provides opportunities for practice.

Lack of empathy impedes self-expression. If I am afraid that I'll "put my foot in my mouth" when I open it, I am too much concerned about myself and too little about my partner. If dating is to work best, both partners must express their own needs and be sensitive to the other's. Dating thrives on empathy in understanding the partner's moods even when they are contradictory to one's own. Skill depends not only on listening to what the partner says but on sensitivity to body language. A skillful empathizer appreciates the feelings behind the stumbling words. Empathy is a goal, not a given, in any particular relationship. It takes time and effort to learn to check out the feelings and wants of both partners. So empathy between two people grows over time.

Decision Making.   The expressed needs of two persons often conflict. When choices must be made between mutually exclusive preferences, new skills are called upon. Altruism under these circumstances is no solution. If I want to go swimming when you would rather go to a concert, it doesn't help for both of us to say, "After you, Alphonse." (Such dilemmas provide practice for settling problems in marriage.)

Learning to level on the simplest issues pays off and is better ground for getting to know the other as a real person than overeagerness to please the other:

> When a man asked me out to do a particular thing I tended to think there were only two alternatives—yes I will or no I won't. I'm beginning to learn that I can suggest other possibilities which indicate my interests.

Sometimes he actually likes my idea better and sometimes we take turns doing what we each like best. But we're not playing politeness games any more.

Commitment. People sometimes think of commitment as a once-and-for-all affair that occurs at marriage. But commitment, too, takes practice. To jump all at once from self-involvement to marital commitment is impossible. The growth of love creates progressive commitment. Even before affectional involvement, dating provides opportunities for tentative commitments. But those opportunities are not always exploited. Students at two Florida universities complained that the partner's lack of involvement was the chief obstacle to enjoying a date. They had several words for the same thing, "the date's lack of interest, uncooperativeness, or being in a bad mood" (Connor and Hall, 1952).

I prefer casual friendships and dating a number of different men rather than going out exclusively with one. For this reason I like group activities more than spending an evening entirely with one person. I seldom share my inner thoughts and feelings. I feel that this leads to a greater involvement with the person in whom I might confide; and this is the type of relationship I am trying to avoid. If I get the impression that a man I am dating is becoming serious, I quickly end the relationship.

This woman needed to commit herself to her partner, not irrevocably as in marriage but temporarily for the duration of the date. In a rudimentary way this resembles a willingness to love, not in the sense of "falling for" each new person but in the sense of participating fully in the relationship as long as it lasts.

Directness, empathy, decision making, and commitment are only a few of the skills that can be learned through dating. They illustrate the opportunities for developing interpersonal skills. The more they are acquired, the greater the preparation for marriage. Other benefits from dating are so closely related to readiness for marriage that they will be saved for a later chapter: emotional weaning from parents, and a sense of having "been around" enough to settle down with a long-term partner.

2 Affectional Involvement

In discussing dating, we saw that the chief reason men and women get together is because they want to make friends. Save in those rare instances of love at first sight, first dates seldom create much emotional involvement. But when first dates are mutually enjoyed and are followed by getting together repeatedly, feelings of affection grow between the partners.

The purpose of this chapter is to describe the process by which love and affection arise. We will use those terms interchangeably, making no attempt to distinguish between them. If there is any distinction, it may be one of degree, with love the stronger of the two. For our purposes, the difference is not important. All that matters is that emotional ties bind couples together increasingly until at some point they may want to commit themselves to marriage.

THE NATURE OF LOVE

Love may be defined as *an intense emotional attachment between people.* Intensity is a matter of degree. The minimum intensity cannot be precisely defined—many couples cannot pinpoint when their friendship changed to love. All we can say is that love is more intense than friendship.

The emotionality of love creates a dynamic force. Lovers yearn to be together. Loving enlarges their emotional capacity. Each time their hearts are stretched a bit, they become more perceptive and aware than before. The more they learn to feel, the more they can express compassion.

Love is an attachment between people, not a "free-floating" feeling.

One might call it an attraction, since sexual attraction is one of its ingredients. But attraction may be unreciprocated, and one-sided love is only a crush. "Attachment" is a better word than "attraction" because it reflects the relationship between the partners. They are involved with each other, related by ties of interdependence.

But attachment can be too close. The love that grows into a lasting marriage needs both attachment and independence. After the partners learn to be close, to be companions, and to care for each other, releasing control expresses trust, respect, and acceptance. Can the partners allow each other freedom to grow as individuals? Someone who delights in a partner's separate blooming will sense his/her gratitude and satisfaction. If one partner is afraid to let go and tries to control the other, love will be strangled.

Elements of Love

Love is a blend of many elements: sexual attraction, companionship, caring, and confirmation.

Sexual Attraction. Love between a man and a woman is seldom platonic. The partners enjoy each other's presence, are excited by the sight and touch of the other, are physically impelled toward each other.

Adults who have come to terms with their sexual feelings can express them and enjoy them. Sexual attraction is frequently the strongest element in the coming together of two persons and the quickest to fade if other ties do not develop. There is an infinite variety of physical expression. Some couples are reserved while others are more demonstrative.

Companionship. This is the social element in love: the enjoyment of doing things together. It is the basic element in friendship and is intensified in love. Companionship in leisure is the organizing framework of the dating from which love springs.

> *Caring. I enjoy being with Bert unless he's in a bad mood, though I've found a good deal of pleasure in helping him snap out of those moods. Even if he gets mad at me, I like the evidence it gives that he cares about me. I'm happy when I'm with him and enjoy doing things with him and trying to make him happy.*

Caring is altruistic. It involves concern for the partner, interest in his/her welfare, and effort to meet his/her needs. Caring is intensely personal. Awareness of the partner's needs is enough to bring response.

Caring rewards not only the recipient but the giver. To meet the partner's needs is to be needed oneself. To be useful is to be alive and growing. Love is like water: dammed up, it becomes stagnant; only when it flows is it fresh. My partner not only meets my needs but in depending on me allows me to give myself to him/her. In the words of Erich Fromm (1956: 23):

> Giving is the highest expression of potency. In the very act of giving, I experience my strength, my wealth, my power. This experience of heightened vitality and potency fills me with joy. I experience myself as overflowing, spending, alive, hence as joyous. Giving is more joyous than receiving, not because it is a deprivation, but because in the act of giving lies the expression of my aliveness.

The caring element in love corresponds to the responsibility parents assume for their children's welfare. The ultimate in tenderness is symbolized by a parent holding a baby. In marriage, husbands and wives care for each other just as earlier they were cared for by their parents. For me (Margaret):

> *A whole new stage in our love began the day I realized that this husband who I thought could take anything was as vulnerable as anyone. I knew how hurt he was as he put his head in my lap like a baby. I refrained from giving "advice." I just held him and listened, and was quiet.*

In every marriage there are times when each partner nurtures the other. In some marriages, nurturance flows mostly one way. Where one partner's need for succorance is complemented by the other's need to nurture, love takes on a parent-child emphasis. The "parent" may be of either sex, there are "mother-son" marriages and "father-daughter" marriages. Because they emphasize care and protection, they tend to neglect the other elements of love. As long as that neglect is not complete, they are normal variations of love:

> *Caring for Bob when he is sick is a whole different bag from relating to him when he is feeling vigorous. When he gets sick he's entirely different. I [Margaret] remember what a shock it was when he had his first really bad cold—not talking, depressed, no gratitude for my serving him. No physical energy made all the difference in the personality I knew. Being well, I had to be the objective parent who could accept his need and inability to meet me halfway.*

Confirmation.   Beyond the reciprocal attractiveness of sex and companionship, beyond caring responsiveness to the needs of the other, lies confirmation of the other as a person.

This goes beyond appreciation of the elements that bind the couple together to acceptance of even the elements that divide them. To confirm the otherness of the partner is to acknowledge the partner's right to be him/herself as s/he sees fit. I respect your being in all its complexity. I know that no one else can be exactly like me. I do not define the ways we are different as ways in which you are wrong.

When I confirm your right to be different from me, I look forward to your accepting my differentness from you. If our relationship is to be healthy, each of us must be an authentic person. In confirming your otherness, I appreciate the vitality and the energy with which you take charge of your life and make it into what you feel led to become. We may have to negotiate around some of the conflicts this creates between us. But those negotiations will be based on the necessity of finding a modus vivendi, not on the need to put either of us down or to prove that I am "right" or you are where we differ.

Confirmation at best becomes gratitude for the other's existence, including his/her differences. This is the point at which love transcends mere coziness and becomes mature.

There are many ingredients of love; sexual attraction, companionship, caring, and confirmation are simply the most prominent. Unlike a recipe, love has no fixed proportions of ingredients. It differs from couple to couple. For some, the sexual element is dominant, whereas for others, sexual attraction is unconscious. Love also changes over time. The caring element grows as partners come to understand each other's needs.

Love differs most from friendship in the strength of the sexual element. But it is not composed of unique ingredients so much as it is a unique combination of elements in an intense relationship with a particular person.

Variations in Intensity

Although love is by definition intense, its strength varies from couple to couple. Among Burgess and Wallin's engaged couples (1953), 24 percent described themselves as "head over heels" in love, 70 percent "very much" in love, and 7 percent only "somewhat" or "mildly" in love. What causes such differences?

High Intensity.   Although some people laugh at the idea of feverish romance, it can happen, although not as often in real life as in fiction.

1.   The greater the impact of a love affair on the individuals involved, the greater the emotional intensity. This is partly a question of speed. Sudden, unexpected changes arouse more emotion than gradual, long-term transitions. This makes summer romances exciting. A stranger comes suddenly into my life—and if I am vacationing with nothing else to do, intrudes intensively. Impact also reflects the attractiveness of the partner. The greater the compatibility, the more exciting the discovery. Finally,

impact reflects the individual's needs. Those who are insecure and lonely with no one to love (or be loved by) respond most eagerly.

2.   The more insecure the relationship, the greater the excitement. To discover gold and not know whether one can keep it is maddening. The danger may be my uncertainty about my partner, or it may come from outside the relationship. Summer romances are intensified by the knowledge that autumn will bring separation. Separation often heightens feeling as long as there is hope of reunion. Parental opposition may also increase desire.

3.   The more temperamental a person is, the higher his/her temperature rises in love. Some individuals are more sensitive than others. Their feelings are volatile and easily stirred. For them, love is a more searching experience than for matter-of-fact persons.

Low Intensity.   Those who don't have cardiac-respiratory symptoms fear something is wrong:

> *Other men have given me more of a rose-colored feeling than Louie. Does this show that I don't have the proper basis for marrying him? Or am I just getting too old at twenty-five for such an adolescent reaction to any man? We're engaged because I think being married to him will be very rewarding. But being engaged is not nearly as exciting as I expected it to be.*

Failure to feel as strongly as expected is disappointing. Skepticism calls for extra testing to be sure the lack of enthusiasm does not result from incompatibility. But a distinction must be drawn between doubts about the soundness of a relationship and calm, unruffled certainty.

Certainty, indeed, is one cause of calmness. In old friendships and long engagements, love may pass its peak intensity. The more gradual the involvement, the less earthshaking it is, especially for couples who were casual friends long before falling in love. For lifelong acquaintances, years of preadolescent familiarity make sudden excitement unlikely. For instance, young people who grow up in the same kibbutz in Israel rarely fall in love with each other and, if they do, rarely love passionately. As Talmon relates (1964), they know each other too well for that:

> "We are like an open book to each other. We have read the story in the book over and over again and know all about it." . . . They refer to the curiosity, excitement, and anticipation that unfamiliar people evoke in them and to the exhilarating sense of discovery and triumph they get when they establish a relationship with them. They describe the unfolding of their affair as an exchange of confidences and emphasize the importance of relating and comparing different life histories. The af-

fair with the outsider is experienced as an *overcoming of distance between persons* and as a growth of a newly won and unfamiliar sense of intimacy.

Some loves are fated by circumstance to be calm. Others reflect the dispositions of the participants. People who never get ruffled in crises or triumphs are not likely to get excited in love. While some people are predisposed to be easygoing from birth, most people become more philosophical as they grow older. The insecurity of adolescence gives early loves an urgency that later ones may lack. As people grow in self-acceptance and emotional independence, they often become less passionate. Hence the woman quoted above may have been right in thinking that she was too old for the excitability of adolescence. For reasons of maturity, then, or temperament or long acquaintance, low intensity is sometimes inevitable.

Multiple Involvements

Can I love more than one person at a time? Traditionally, no. Love is supposed to be so absorbing that one "doesn't even notice" others. People who claim to be in love with two people simultaneously are ipso facto not in love at all; they just think they are.

One study of college women showed, however, that one fourth had already been in love with multiple partners simultaneously (Ellis, 1949). What happens if two men date the same woman? Short of engagement, there is no reason she must choose between them. Though no two men are exactly alike, they can be equally compatible with a woman, in different ways. Personal relationships and emotional attachments can develop with both.

Whether both attachments can be intense enough to be called love is the crux of the problem. We would say yes, it can be love, even though simultaneous involvement in two deeply personal relationships is so demanding that it limits the ultimate possibilities for either one. Eventually the choice must be made since two men/women can't wait forever for the object of their affection to decide who is the primary partner.

Some Pseudoloves

When any element of love is missing, the others are correspondingly distorted. Although the participants may think they are in love, they are deluded. The resemblance to love is more apparent than real.

Infatuation. An affair based on sexual attraction to the exclusion of companionship and care is an infatuation. The dictionary defines infatuation as "an extravagant or foolish passion." Human beings can be attracted physically by countless persons. But sex appeal is no proof of love. When excitement is merely sexual, "passion" is a better word:

> *Usually we make up by a kiss–it's sort of sex. I think Sam's man-handling is sex too. I considered breaking up with him but I can't stay away from him when he lives so close and we have classes together. He's real fierce when he's mushy. He grabs me passionately and says, "Would you ever let another man do this to you?" I can't reason with him. I can't keep saying, no, no, no! I'd miss him too much to be able to drop him now.*

If sex holds two people together against their better judgment, their feeling is pretty sure to be pseudolove. If they marry, only a lucky coincidence would produce the other elements of love. Without those elements, marriage would become empty and likely to ebb with time.

Infatuations are dangerous but not inevitably disastrous. The fact that a relationship starts out as an infatuation does not mean it is doomed. Initial interest in face and physique does not prohibit the growth of other facets of love. But whether infatuation turns into love depends on whether the relationship broadens to embrace the entire personality of the partner—not just the body.

Idealization.   Infatuation responds to a limited object; idealization to an imagined one. If I see you through the proverbial rose-colored glasses, my enthusiasm for what I want to find in you may delude me into thinking you are exactly like that. I may project onto you my own ideals of what you *should* be. Since the process is unconscious, I may believe you are perfect even though you are not.

Lack of compatibility is masked when both partners engage in idealization simultaneously. This frequently happens in love at first sight (though occasionally that is caused by the sudden discovery of unusual compatibility). The boost to the ego from being idealized by another provides an illusion of compatibility without the substance. An image of destined choice balloons from the interplay of separate enthusiasms (Solomon, 1955). After an excited beginning it is difficult to admit failure, especially if one's need for love is great. Unfortunately, the very persons most prone to idealization are the least capable of recognizing it.

Idealization thrives in the absence of interaction. That is why it is so prominent in love at first sight. As real interaction occurs, knowledge converts the dream image into awareness of the real partner. Awareness punctures the dream bubble and brings the relationship down to earth. That earthy reality is by definition less attractive than the idealized image.

At Oklahoma State University, Pollis (1969) found that students who were only casually involved with their dating partners idealized them the most, whereas those who were more seriously involved saw their partners more realistically. In this study, idealization was defined as overrating the dating partner's personal characteristics (such as his/her dependability, self-confidence, sense of humor, sensitivity, emotional maturity, and friendliness) in comparison to friends' ratings of the same person. The more involved men and women tended to see their partners more nearly as their friends saw them. Thus idealization decreased with increasing involvement.

Immediately after the computer dance at Iowa State referred to earlier, many participants were enthusiastic about their new partners: they felt romantic attraction, liked their partner's personality and appearance, and felt a happy marriage might be possible—after just one date! Six months later, they had generally revised their estimates downward. Presumably, they were then past idealization and more solidly grounded (Coombs and Kenkel, 1966).

Only those too immature to accept any shortcomings in the partner go on indefinitely living in a dream world. Indeed, one characteristic of real love is that both partners drop their defenses and reveal themselves, no longer hiding their faults and weaknesses (Maslow, 1953).

By themselves, infatuation and idealization are respectively a snare and a delusion. But as parts of the total experience of involvement, they may serve useful functions. Fascination with the other weans the individual from his/her parents. The attraction of idealization helps me break out of the accustomed security of family and friends. Moreover, idealizing you may become a self-fulfilling prophecy if you respond to my hopes by becoming the kind of person I want you to be.

CONDITIONS FOR LOVE

The conditions under which love arises can be stated very simply: *love is the sentiment that men and women feel who have a fully personal relationship with another.* Their relationship provides the combustibles that are ignited in love.

Readiness for Involvement

Some people are not ready to enter into personal relationships. For them, only the appearance of love is possible. They may think they are in love because they are sexually aroused in an infatuation or they have discovered a love object whom they idealize from afar. But they are not ready for involvement with a whole, real person.

Involvement may be frightening for someone who has never experienced it before or whose previous experience has been disappointing.

I may have a need to belong somewhere. I may want to give myself to a relationship without playing games, without having to worry about whether I am worthy of your love, whether I'm okay, whether I'm measuring up. But I'm scared of what may happen if I allow myself to get involved. I am afraid of being enveloped—of losing myself in you, in your needs, in your demands.

Afraid that I am not strong enough to stand my own ground with you.

Afraid that you will use me, ask more than I can give.

Afraid that I can't say no, that I am weak and will give in.

I am afraid of your becoming too dependent on me, that I may let you down. If I encourage you, you are liable to come on strong and enmesh yourself in my life before I am sure. Yesterday it was okay; but maybe today my love and focus are elsewhere. Knowing that I can hurt people so easily, I fear your doing this to me. My fear of being hurt is tied to my fear of hurting you, betraying you—not being able to return the openness and caring you have for me.

Some people are afraid to let others see them as they really are. Menninger (1935) described this barrier to love:

> Love is impaired less by the feeling that we are not appreciated than by a dread, more or less dimly felt by everyone, lest others see through our masks, the masks of repression that have been forced upon us by convention and culture. It is this that leads us to shun intimacy, to maintain friendships on a superficial level, to underestimate and fail to appreciate others lest they come to appreciate us too well.

In daring to share intimately, I risk the pain of losing the relationship. After I have shared myself with you and you have accepted me as I am, if you later reject me I will feel betrayed, ashamed, and vulnerable. I will hurt because I have opened myself up to you emotionally and physically, I have shown you my strong and my weak, my beautiful and my ugly, sides. I have found safety and then you leave and go away. "If I tell you who I am you may not like who I am and it is all I have" (Powell, 1969: 21).

I am afraid of getting involved because my need for our relationship to continue is so strong. I need a safe place for sharing, for opening myself up, for a sense of belonging.

I am afraid of commitment. I might change and that would hurt you. You might change and that would hurt me. Suppose one of us changes. Could you endure me for long? Could I love you forever?

These fears of hurting and being hurt are closely tied together. Whenever one fear comes to the surface, the other is there also:

How can I develop the courage to be myself in my full strength with you? Will I break? Will you? How can I come to experience my own toughness and yours? I want to believe that you and I are not such fragile creatures that we will fall apart in the pulling and hauling. We can test our strength with each other, not holding back. I want to wrestle with you in this relationship. You are not a child and neither am I. I want to feel your power and my power. Power is aliveness. I want to dare to share our strong feelings, our feelings of resistance and of difference.

As long as I am paralyzed by fear, I cannot give myself to becoming affectionally involved with anyone. One of the conditions for love is that both partners must be emotionally ready for involvement.

Interaction

To say that love occurs within personal relations emphasizes that it does not occur in a vacuum. Love requires coming to grips with another person, not just dreaming about him/her. It requires mutual involvement and interdependence.

The value of interacting depends heavily on its realism. If I hide my faults from you, our love will be built on an unreal foundation. We have already seen that relationships tend to become increasingly realistic with increasing involvement. Maslow's self-actualizing persons (1953) excelled in their willingness to drop their defenses, to quit playing conventional roles with each other, and to deal openly and honestly with each other. He found that "this honesty also includes allowing one's faults, weaknesses, and physical and psychological shortcomings to be freely seen by the partner."

Such openness is no guarantee that love will flourish. It risks the possibility that my partner will not like what I reveal about myself. But emotionally healthy persons would rather risk the death of love than allow love to develop on an unreal foundation.

Autonomy

Interaction is a necessary, but not a sufficient, condition for love. The other condition is autonomy. Even after marriage, the partners are still separate human beings. Autonomy requires respect for the other's right to differ in his/her life goals and immediate concerns. It requires freedom of expression, freedom to make demands. More subtly, it requires recognition that the other person is the only one who knows his/her own feelings and needs:

Roger makes me furious. Just because he is a psychologist he thinks he knows better than I do how I feel. He never accepts what I say but twists it around into his own jargon. But I know enough about psychology myself to be able to recognize that the things he says about how I "really" feel are just projections of his own imagination. I wish he could see the difference between his feelings about me and my own feelings about myself.

When a man and woman respect each other as individuals, love becomes a releasing force. Without respect, it becomes a prison:

"You're not just there for me" is one of the mottoes on my mirror.

If autonomy is missing, love turns into mutual exploitation. The satisfaction of a few needs is no guarantee of love:

We've broken up many times but we just can't stay apart. I'm sure we both would get along better with others, but whenever we break up she always comes running back to me. We've had three really bad fights. She cries and says she hates the way I push her around. I'm terribly involved with her and I just don't have the strength to stay away from her.

Love must be given and received freely—not compulsively. Each partner must respect the dignity of the other. Property can be possessed—not people. Each still carries the primary responsibility for his/her own life.

Loving is risky without autonomy. The child in me says that if I give myself to you and you hurt me or reject me I will be destroyed. But my life can never totally depend on you. I have an identity of my own and I will always have this whether you respond to it or not. I will always be me. If I lose my lover I still have myself to love me. I do not intend to allow you to establish my identity for me.

The same is true for you. If you give yourself to me and I hurt you or differ with you or seem to reject you, you will not be destroyed. Your life can never totally depend on me. You have your own identity and this exists regardless of my treatment of you. You will always be you. If I go away you will still have yourself to love you. I do not intend to allow you to convince me that your identity depends on my loving you.

In order to be prepared for a relationship, I must allow myself the space to be alone, apart from all personal contact, to come to know myself. To be apart in solitude enables me to know my own meaning, to clarify my goals, to know who I am at this time. Thus I develop inner strength that does not have to suck another's strength.

To move directly from dependence on parents and teachers and counselors (any external authority) into a very intimate relationship is to run the risk of carrying over childhood roles into the new relationship. I may depend on you because I am still dependent on my parents. If I have not yet finished this task, I will have a need to complete this relationship in relating to you. Rejected, unsure of that basic security of being loved by my mother, I will go on compulsively needing mother love from you or from many women until I am satisfied that I am loved, until I have integrated this essential need of mine into my developing self. In my case (Margaret):

My father was too busy by the time I came along. I know now that he loved me, but we spent so little time together. I needed that support and care from a man who was not bent on using me for his pleasure. Our early married life was a period of having that kind of father through you. I never had a chance to test my own strength before I married you. I was always safe and well protected as a child and in college and graduate school by my community of good friends. There was always someone to love and advise me. I think I needed to be on my own, to live alone, to have a job and prove to myself that I could make my own decisions, take care of myself.

I skipped that period in my development and slid into your shelter, finding it easy to let you care for me and make my decisions. It may have satisfied a need for you to father me. But it kept me from growing up. I have always had an image of being the little sister (which I was in my family), enjoying the role of follower/assistant. Now I would like to explore and experience another identity, to be strong in my sense of my worth, truly accepting my intuition, believing in my own skills because I have proved them on my own apart from "family" support.

Like the child who skips the crawling stage and must go back and go through that stage, I need to find my own identity apart from you.

Effort

Love cannot be commanded. But does this mean one cannot resolve to love? Must it be completely spontaneous?

To be sure, spontaneous love is the most delightful. Responding effortlessly to the discovery of compatibility is pure joy. The faster love develops and the higher its intensity, the more the emotional capacities of the partners are mobilized. But not all loves begin so enthusiastically or maintain such vigorous momentum. These other loves suggest the value of conscious effort in supplementing the natural momentum of love. Our own case shows how one may deliberately deepen a relationship:

I [Margaret] dated Bob on and off for a year. We had good times folk-dancing, going to concerts, talking politics. I was sure he was the man for me. Though I knew he liked me, it didn't look like love since he never told me how he felt about me. Soon school would be over and we would go our separate ways. Dared I be the one to speak first? I became a "scheming woman," planning when and how it might be done. The right moment came and I found courage to say that despite all the fun we'd had doing things, we really didn't know how we felt about each other. By morning the stars were in his eyes too. If I had waited for him to start things moving, I probably would be waiting still!

A relationship can go only so far spontaneously. Beyond that its potentialities will remain untapped unless effort is expended. Couples do not have to transcend spontaneity. But those who don't are not likely to experience love to its fullest.

Erich Fromm (1956) wrote about "the art of loving," an art capable of being perfected with practice. The requirements, he believed, were self-discipline, concentration on the task at hand, patience with the slowness of achieving mastery, and supreme concern to achieve that mastery. Love is enhanced the more people concentrate on meeting each other's needs. The more rewarding activities a couple undertake together and the more thoughtfully each ministers to the other, the greater their love will grow. The major achievements in life require hard work, and love is no exception. Casual affairs may be nice, but those who wish to experience the deepest relationships must be more than dilettantes.

THE COURSE OF LOVE

So far we have discussed the emotional aspects of love. From here on we will deal with the rise and fall of affectional involvements.

Starting Points

To become interested in another person means far less than falling in love. Yet Table 2–1 shows that even such minimal attraction didn't happen at first for most of the Burgess-Wallin respondents. Most couples get acquainted first and only gradually become interested in each other. Love seldom begins at first sight. It usually emerges within the context of a growing relationship.

The starting point for love varies from couple to couple. The typical couple in Table 2–1 became interested after becoming acquainted, but some began to be interested earlier and others much later. Normally, love grows by intensification from mildly positive experiences, or at least neutral contacts. Occasionally, however, the first encounter is inauspicious:

> June and I first met on a blind date. I wasn't much impressed. She looked gawky to me. However, I was hard up for a date to the house dance the next weekend, so I asked her to go with me. She didn't exactly

Table 2–1 Degree of Acquaintance at First Becoming Interested in the Partner, for Men and Women

Degree of Acquaintance	Men	Women
On first meeting	46%	34%
After becoming acquainted	34	37
After becoming friends	20	29
Total	100%	100%
Number of cases	226	226

Adapted from Burgess and Wallin, 1953: 160.

bowl me over that time either, but we had a good time and I began to appreciate her sense of humor. It got so we were seeing each other fairly regularly after that and we gradually discovered that we were in love.

Table 2–2 describes more precisely the point at which feelings of love were first experienced by men and women students at Purdue University. The typical Purdue man began to feel affectionally involved with his partner on their twelfth date and the typical woman after some sixteen dates. So, while love blooms at first sight for a small minority, it typically takes considerably more time to develop.

The fact that love at first sight is rare does not mean it is necessarily unreliable. Slater and Woodside (1951) found that first impressions in their British working-class sample rather accurately predicted how happy the marriages would be. Seventy percent of those who experienced love at first sight were happily married, whereas only 33 percent of those who disliked their spouses at first sight became happy after marriage.

The Pace of Involvement

Love seldom develops suddenly. It takes effort and interaction to build a solid relationship. Except in cases of idealization, love takes time to develop:

My first date with Sandra was the night before Christmas vacation. We were pushing a taxi out of a snowdrift in front of the Administration building and the man asked us if we wanted a free ride downtown for the work. Naturally we accepted and went down to a show. This was the start of a friendship that has grown into companionship and finally love. We talked together some that spring and did many things, but it was purely on a friendly basis and actually we didn't mean much to each other. We

Table 2–2   Number of Dates prior to Experiencing Love for the Partner, for Men and Women

Number of Dates prior to Experiencing Love	*Men*	*Women*
1–4	27%	15%
5–19	43	42
20+	30	43
Total	100%	100%
Number of cases	250	429

Adapted from Kanin, Davidson, and Scheck, 1970: 66. *Source:* Students at Purdue University describing their current or most recent experience of love.

began to talk more about religion and our philosophy of life. As we talked we found we were drawn closer together. It wasn't until this fall that we found we were sure of our love for each other. It has not been "falling" in love but "growing" in love.

Because the whole next chapter is devoted to sexual involvement, we will not deal with the development of that element of love here, but skip to the remaining elements.

Companionship.   Since dates are joint recreation, companionship tends to grow fastest. The partner is increasingly appreciated as more experiences and more of the self are shared.

Caring.   Caring often lags behind the other components of love. One basis for caring is empathy—understanding the partner's point of view. Empathy presupposes knowledge that can be acquired only through continuing interaction.

Vernon and Stewart (1957) found that as time went by, couples improved their ability to judge the partner's satisfaction with various aspects of their relationship. The more they dated each other and the more committed they became, the more accurately they assessed the partner's satisfaction. Similarly, Hobart (1956) found that knowledge of the partner's views about marriage increased as couples progressed from casual dating to going steady and into engagement.

Commitment.   Commitment sounds like a once-and-for-all affair, but it isn't. It develops gradually as couples move from casual to steady dating to engagement. For some it develops subconsciously. Others move consciously into increasing involvement. By the time couples get engaged, commitment has necessarily become a conscious process.

Presumably, commitment is the last element of love to develop. Attraction comes first—then commitment. But the relationship between commitment and the other elements of love is reciprocal. Once a commitment is made, it provides a basis for the further growth of other elements.

The pace of love is usually slow and uneven. Relationships reach plateaus and then break through to greater intimacy. Love, like marriage, has moments for better and for worse.

The course of love leads ultimately to a personal relationship that provides the foundation of marriage. Gradually the relationship grows in strength and comprehensiveness. The richer the relationship becomes before marriage, the richer it will be after marriage.

Among young middle-class married couples in Tokyo, I (Blood, 1967) found marked continuity between pre-engagement interaction patterns and marital interaction patterns. Couples who told each other their troubles before engagement relied most often on each other for therapeutic relief after marriage. Those who shared more of their personal news with each other early in their relationship were more open with each other in later years. Such continuity from premarital to marital love is not surprising. Vital relationships grow from year to year; weak ones tend to shrivel.

Like the married years themselves, the months before marriage provide opportunities for creating a mutually rewarding relationship or for allowing it to deteriorate.

THE DEATH OF LOVE

So far we have assumed that affectional involvement moves progressively toward marriage. Often, however, it dies either a quick or a lingering death. When love dies, the empty shell sometimes remains.

Loss of Interest

Many involvements die quietly and unmourned. When both partners lose interest simultaneously, both are glad to extricate themselves from a relationship that has lost its momentum. Ordinarily, we would expect the poverty of a relationship to be apparent to both partners. As one partner loses enthusiasm, the declining energy invested in the relationship should be infectious. It isn't much fun going with a person who has lost interest.

Table 2–3 shows that nearly half of the affectional involvements experienced by students at the University of Minnesota ended bilaterally. No one had to make an effort to terminate the relationship because the partners simply drifted apart.

The major exception was where one partner became interested in a

Table 2–3   Cause of Termination of Affectional Involvement, for Men and Women

Cause of Termination	Men	Women
Mutual loss of interest	47%	38%
Subject's interest in another person	15	32
Partner's interest in another person	30	15
External pressure (parents, friends)	8	14
Total	100%	99%
Number of respondents	230	414

Adapted from Kirkpatrick and Caplow, 1945: 123. *Source:* University of Minnesota sociology students reporting on their previous affectional involvements.

new person while the other still felt involved in the old relationship. This is analogous to what happens after marriage when one partner falls in love with a new person while the other feels emotionally dependent and abandoned. In such cases of unilateral continuing involvement, termination is not easy because it disrupts old patterns. Bolton (1961) suggested that couples may be just as addicted to one another as a drug addict is to heroin: "The individual seeks to perpetuate a relationship in order to avoid the psychological withdrawal symptoms accompanying cessation of sexual, affectional, or prestigeful relations".

Ambivalence about Ending a Relationship

It's difficult to give up the known for the unknown. Those who are reticent in taking dating initiatives cling to the existing partner:

> *I know this can't go on but right now he's all I've got and he's better than nobody. And so until somebody else comes along I'll string along.*

Starting all over again is understandably difficult:

> *He's so familiar and comfortable. I hate the game of idle chit-chat you have to carry on with a new date.*

New prospects may look singularly unattractive by comparison to the empathic responsiveness of a partner dated for a long time:

> *I still have a strong feeling for Andy in spite of his faults. I've never met anyone so warm and understanding. Other people never seem to be able to appreciate my moods and bolster my ego the way he does.*

Maybe Andy is special. More likely others would yield as much rapport as soon as they were dated as long. Often the seemingly unique virtues in a partner instead reflect unique familiarity.

Sexual involvement may make breaking up difficult because of one's reluctance to lose a source of sexual gratification or because of guilt feelings about "loving her and leaving her":

> *I realize that Laura and I can't go on but right now I just can't resist her. As long as she has her door open I make a beeline for her apartment every Saturday night. On Sunday I don't feel so good about it.*

Reluctance to break up stems from altruistic as well as egocentric motives. When breaking up would hurt my partner as much as it would hurt me, my hesitation increases. No one likes to inflict pain on another:

> *We've gone together so long that I know Keith would be awfully hurt if I returned his ring. He's just gotten used to my being around. In fact the way he takes me for granted is one thing that gripes me about him. I'm afraid leaving him now would demoralize him completely.*

When emotional dependence is one-sided, the more mature person tires of the relationship first. Yet, knowing how much the partner gains emotional support from the relationship, s/he may hesitate to pull the props out from under him/her:

> *How do I explain to Jill that I want to do more dating with others before I say she's the right one (especially since I've been dating her for three years and still am not happy)? She's happy no matter what I do, as long as I decide on her in the end. I don't think I will, but she looks so sad when I mention any doubt, it breaks my heart.*

When the partner is emotionally unstable, continuing the relationship may seem the only way to prevent a nervous breakdown or even suicide. Though the risks may be great under such circumstances, the responsibility for preserving another's mental health should be transferred from romantic to psychiatric facilities.

When two persons have been deeply involved and their friends have begun to treat them as a couple, breaking up may be more easily said than done:

> *I lived just a block away from Gretchen and our families were close friends. We went together all through high school and junior college. Then I went away to the university and fell in love with the woman who is now my wife. When they heard about it, my family and Gretchen's were both shocked, and Gretchen came close to having a nervous breakdown. The whole gang at home accused me of being inconsiderate in letting her down this way.*

There are often good reasons on both sides, and deep ambivalence is painful—but must be resolved within each person before deescalation or termination can be dealt with decisively.

Aids to Terminating a Relationship

When terminating a relationship proves difficult, several means are available for making the break more easily.

Deescalation. One way out may be through deescalating the time and energy commitment, a gradual withdrawal that is less painful. Letting go of the reins may be exactly what is needed to allow each person to feel less crowded. In some cases, this change of pace gives the couple a chance to see how it feels and begin to test out other relationships. But for one partner to suggest deescalation may be as difficult emotionally as terminating completely.

A Clean Break.   Those who can't face a partner's disappointment may employ the U.S. mails to carry the fateful message. When a relationship is dead, it's best to bury it:

> *The relationship we've had is far from healthy. It is sick. I'm beginning to see that by hanging on I'm just wasting time, and losing out on possible better relationships out there. A friend helped me to see it's easier to open the door on the next experience when I've shut the door behind me on this one.*

The Example of Others.   Knowing that others change partners takes the onus off abandoning one's own. Repeated involvements are characteristic of modern dating, which means that experience in dissolving relationships is widespread. We have already reported that Michigan undergraduates typically had gone steady with two partners, and the Minnesota undergraduates studied by Kirkpatrick and Caplow similarly had at least two "important love affairs." Broken engagements, though less common than discontinued uncommitted loves, are by no means rare. Among the Burgess and Wallin engaged couples, 24 percent of the men and 36 percent of the women had broken at least one previous engagement, and 15 percent of the current engagements subsequently ended.

Support from Others.   It is not necessary to go through crises alone. Telling friends of the decision is one way of burning one's bridges to prevent retreat:

> *The first few times I refused more dates with Shep were the hardest. After that it wasn't so bad. My friends were skeptical at first because I had sworn off him so many times before. I finally convinced them that I really meant business this time and needed their help. They were grand too. They fixed me up with dates to help me get my mind off him. That really made the break a lot easier.*

A sympathetic counselor or therapy group can provide similar encouragement and help in working through ambivalent feelings as well as practice in role-playing how to carry out the decision.

Since a good future relationship can be delayed by getting stuck in a bad present one, we give people practice in ending an involvement at the end of our Singles workshop. This exercise starts with recalling the good things about the friendship and ends with dealing directly with specific details of termination.

Table 2–4   Feeling after Termination of an Affectional Involvement, for Men and Women

Feeling	Men	Women
Crushed, hurt	12%	19%
Angry, bitter	9	8
Remorseful	7	7
Mixed regret and relief	22	21
Indifferent	19	16
Satisfied	12	8
Relieved	15	17
Happy	4	4
Total	100%	100%
Number of respondents	230	414

Adapted from Kirkpatrick and Caplow, 1945: 124.

Recuperating from "Bereavement"

Knowing how often dissolution reflects mutual disinterest or growing interest in an alternative partner, we should not expect many individuals to feel shattered. Only those who are dropped when they still wish to continue a relationship are likely to be hurt

Table 2–4 shows that negative reactions were far from universal. Almost as many were pleased the affair had ended as were not. Most typical, however, were those who were indifferent or ambivalent.

Further confirmation of the untraumatic nature of most breakups is found in the report that half the Minnesota students required no recuperation period while less than a fourth took more than a few weeks. Rarely is breaking up as awful in practice as it sometimes appears beforehand.

③ Sexual Involvement

We have already identified sexual attraction as one of the major elements in affectional involvement. In this chapter we will focus on sexual involvement itself, with or without affection.

In Chapter 1, we saw that making love is one of the major motives for dating and one of the major activities when men and women get together. Physical contact in one form or another is a ubiquitous feature of being together. The only questions are how deeply we will become involved and how fast, not whether we will touch at all. And if you and I differ in our feelings about getting sexually involved, how will we resolve those differences?

To answer these questions, we need to look at what couples actually do and to assess the consequences of alternative patterns of sexual involvement. Then we will be in a better position to explore the problems involved in sexual decision making before marriage.

THE COURSE OF SEXUAL INVOLVEMENT

For contemporary Americans, what are the patterns of sexual involvement prior to marriage? What are the circumstances under which couples get involved? How well do they know each other before they become physically intimate? How long have they gone together? How committed are they to each other? And where do those who are not living together find the privacy for intimate behavior?

Readiness for Involvement

The sexual side of dating usually develops spontaneously. Anyone from an affectionate family finds it natural to be affectionate. But if one's parents are undemonstrative, one function of going together may be to get used to being affectionate. Gradually the individual can become more comfortable with his/her own sexuality:

> My girlish ideas about love and sex changed a lot in the last few years. I used to abhor any demonstration of affection. In high school I seldom kissed a date and always felt awkward when I did. As far as sex went, I was really mixed up. About the time I was seven or eight I decided I never wanted to hear anything about sex. When my brother asked my parents about it I would plug my ears and sing songs so I couldn't hear anything. Later in my teens I got in on hen-sessions so I wasn't entirely naive.
>
> Fortunately, I met a man in college who was able to help me overcome these attitudes. It wasn't an easy or sudden change, and Dick has admitted to me that he almost gave up in his attempts to convert me into being able to express myself more completely in a love relationship. However, I progressed slowly as he subtly laid the groundwork until I was gradually able to take the next step.

Self-disclosure and Sexual Involvement.   Sex has often been described as a self-revealing experience, not only in the physical sense but also emotionally. For those who feel unready to open themselves verbally, sexual intercourse may seem an invasion of privacy.

In a study of senior men at Princeton University, Komarovsky (1974) found that men who chose a woman as their chief confidante revealed more of themselves to her than did men who chose a man friend, a parent, or a sibling. Within the sample, there was a significant relationship between having had intercourse and the amount of information about their own personalities that the men had revealed—to anyone. This could be seen in several ways: (1) all ten men in the sample who had revealed most about themselves were sexually experienced, whereas half of the men who had revealed least about themselves were sexually inexperienced; (2) among men who chose male friends as their confidants, sexually inexperienced men were overrepresented (72 percent of those preferring male confidants had never had intercourse with a woman compared with 26 percent of the senior men generally); (3) within that same group, sexually inexperienced men disclosed less of themselves to their male friends than did men who had had sexual experience. The main impression this study leaves is that sexually inexperienced seniors were generally more uptight and reserved about revealing themselves to others. So sexual involvement seems to be related to a willingness to disclose oneself to other people, especially to members of the opposite sex.

Self-esteem and Involvement.   The relationship between how one feels about oneself and one's readiness for sexual involvement depends on whether one's reference group believes in premarital involvement or in abstinence. In conservative circles, those who think highly of themselves tend to refrain from intimacies that violate their convictions; conservative women who engage in sexual relations tend to be those whose self-esteem is so low that they are desperate for anything remotely resembling affection and acceptance from men. Conversely, in liberal circles where sexual involvement is viewed positively, those who are high in self-esteem most self-confidently achieve the desired involvement, whereas those low in self-esteem less often achieve what they desire.

Table 3–1 is drawn from students at Bard College (New York), which has long been noted for the liberal sexual beliefs of its students. Perlman (1974) found that more than 90 percent of the student body approved of premarital intercourse with affection and two-thirds approved of sexual intercourse between partners who are not particularly affectionate. The table shows that in this environment, students with high self-esteem had engaged in sexual intercourse with a larger number of partners than those with low self-esteem. By contrast, at the University of Manitoba, Canada, which Perlman described as "moderate" in its sexual attitudes, high–self-esteem students had slightly fewer sexual partners than low–self-esteem students. Thus, Bard College illustrates the way in which sexual involvement is related to high self-esteem in a permissive environment whereas Manitoba shows the ambiguous relationship between sexuality and self-esteem in a more conservative environment. Presumably, the Bard pattern will become more common in the future as the sexual revolution continues.

Readiness for sexual involvement is not only psychological but biological. Since sexual behavior is influenced by the chemistry of the body, sexual activity increases at certain stages in the menstrual cycle. Ivey and Bardwick (1968) found that women were most likely to engage in sexual activity just prior to menstruation, when they felt depressed and

Table 3–1   **Number of Partners in Premarital Intercourse by Self-esteem, for Men and Women**

	SELF-ESTEEM	
	Low	*High*
Men	4.4	4.8
Women	3.0	4.4

Adapted from Perlman, 1974: 472. *Source:* 113 men and 129 women at Bard College, a small liberal arts college in New York State. Figures give the average number of partners in premarital intercourse for students who were consistently high or consistently low on two different measures of self-esteem.

anxious. They also reported that their motivation for this sexual activity was to make the man happy and to increase their own sense of security in the relationship at a time when they felt submissive, dependent, and low in self-esteem.

Carol and Ray Blatt (1970) suggested that sexual activity under conditions of high self-esteem (typically, at ovulation in the middle of the menstrual cycle) is more apt to have a flirtatious character and to be more of a "peak experience":

> This experience, like the dominance interaction which preceded it, will further contribute to the female's self-esteem, in contrast to the experience of submission typical of premenstrual copulation, which necessarily lowers her self-esteem while adding to her sense of security.

The Blatts also suggested that security-motivated sexual behavior reduces the level of sexual excitement for the man and is less fulfilling for the woman. However, when partners relate to one another at equally high levels of self-confidence, the experience will be highly exciting for both of them.

Depth of Involvement

Couples differ in how physically involved they become with each other. Many go all the way to intercourse at some point prior to marriage. But others stop short, perhaps refraining simply from intromission itself, perhaps avoiding genital contact of any kind, perhaps always keeping their clothes on when they are together.

Data about sexual intimacy have a way of becoming obsolete. We live in a time of sexual revolution, with increasing numbers of Americans experiencing greater intimacy before marriage. In examining data with respect to sexual involvement, it is important to note when the facts were gathered to assess the stage in the revolution that they record.

In reporting these data, we are not trying to prove either that people should do something because the majority do it, or that they should refrain from something because the majority don't do it. We present this information in the belief that knowledge is power—if I am aware of something, I can deal with it more intelligently than if I am unaware. What, then, are the facts about premarital sexual involvement in America?

Table 3–2 shows that a large proportion of juniors and seniors at American colleges in 1969 had experienced sexual intimacy, although the proportions were somewhat lower for the greater degrees of involvement. There are few sharp breaks in the table from one level of involvement to another. This contrasts with data from earlier generations, when many students drew the line at petting, with substantially fewer experiencing intercourse.

Table 3–2 Sexual Involvement of Upper-class Men and Women

Specified Sexual Involvement Ever Experienced	Men	Women
Deep kissing	96%	97%
Stroking woman's clothed breasts	90%	78%
Stroking woman's naked breasts	83%	68%
Stroking woman below waist	81%	61%
Stroking both man and woman below waist	63%	58%
Nude embrace	66%	50%
Sexual intercourse	58%	43%
One-night date involving intercourse; never dated person again	30%	7%
Number of cases	644	688

Adapted from Luckey and Nass, 1969: 374–75. *Source:* Single juniors and seniors from 21 public, private, and church-controlled colleges and universities in all regions of the United States. Reciprocal percentages had never experienced the particular degree of sexual involvement.

The picture in Table 3–2 of progressive involvement in greater intimacy matches Hunt's report (1974) for Americans who had completed their dating careers and moved on into marriage. Hunt discovered that for most Americans, especially in recent years, petting was merely a stage in progressive involvement. Persons born after 1937 were less likely than their elders to have petted short of intercourse and more likely to have gone all the way. Hunt also had the impression that the typical woman engaged in petting without intercourse for only three or four years before moving on to intercourse, either in or outside of marriage; this was roughly half the time Kinsey had reported earlier.

Table 3–2 shows that a majority of upper-class male students at a cross-section of American colleges had already experienced sexual intercourse and that their women counterparts were not far behind. The chief difference between the sexes was that four times as many men as women had experienced one-night affairs that included sexual intercourse. This discrepancy suggests that many men found partners for these episodes off campus, among noncollege women. The woman was seldom a prostitute, however; only 4 percent of the men had ever paid for the privilege of having intercourse with a woman.

Taking only those students who had already engaged in intercourse, the average age of the first experience was 17.9 for the men and 18.7 for the women. Since most of the students were between 20 and 22 years of age when they were interviewed, they had already had several years' experience in intercourse. Luckey and Nass found that these respondents had usually had more than one sexual partner by the time of the study.

Presumably, by the time these men and women married, the proportions experiencing each level of premarital intimacy would have risen still further. The average number of partners in intercourse might fall as more men and women experienced their first intercourse with the person they eventually married (although, conversely, the number would tend to rise still further for those who started intercourse early). The average age of first intercourse would rise as the total group moved toward marriage.

In a study of adults in 24 cities across the United States, Hunt (1974) found that 95 percent of the young (under age 25) married men and 81 percent of the young married women had engaged in sexual intercourse prior to marriage. These figures show that for urban Americans born after 1948, premarital intercourse had become widespread by the time of marriage, although less common during college.

Some of the apparent gap between the college study and Hunt's national data diminishes when we look at comparisons between cross-sectional samples of students at the same institutions. At the University of North Carolina at Chapel Hill, Bauman and Wilson (1974) found that in 1968 the percentage of students who had ever had intercourse was roughly comparable to Luckey and Nass's college students: namely, 56 percent of the men and 46 percent of the women. Just four years later, however, the percentages had jumped to 73 percent for both sexes—an amazing increase in so brief a period. At conservative Illinois State University (a former teachers' college in Normal, Illinois), Walsh and his colleagues (1976) found that the proportion of unmarried students who ever had intercourse during their four years of college jumped from 36 percent for the class of 1971 to 69 percent for the class of 1974. These comparisons suggest that a major sexual revolution occurred among American young people in the late 1960s and early 1970s, during which premarital coitus ceased to be optional and became normative in many circles.

Hunt's data from his already married respondents shows that men and women differed sharply in the number of their sexual partners, even among the youngest age group. Men who had ever participated in premarital intercourse typically had six different partners, whereas a slight majority of the experienced women had only one partner. This difference partly reflects the fact that women tend to marry soon after graduation whereas men are likely to remain single a few more years. Hunt found that the longer a man or woman remained single, the broader the range of sex partners. By the time they were in their late twenties and early thirties his single men were having sex with four different women per year and his single women with three different men. But, since most people marry before age 25, these were exceptional cases. Generally speaking, the earlier people marry, the fewer the number of sexual partners they have, and, in the case of women especially, the greater the likelihood that the partner will be the person they marry.

Casual versus Serious Liaisons. Men and women differ also in the extent to which they require a serious emotional relationship before they are prepared to become sexually involved. For women, generally, the greater their affectional involvement, the more intimate they become. Men, however, are less apt to restrict their sexual behavior to serious affairs.

Table 3–3 shows that roughly 45 percent of the Burgess and Wallin engaged couples had premarital intercourse with each other. The men and women differed chiefly in their previous sexual experience. Half the men but only one eighth of the women had intercourse with anyone else. If the women had intercourse at all before marriage, it was usually confined to the fiancé. The men, however, were more apt to be sexually polygamous.

Hunt (1974) failed to report precise figures on his male respondents except that the median total of six premarital partners for his youngest husbands who had sex with anyone prior to marriage suggests that an extraordinarily small proportion must have had sex only with the fiancé. For the women, however, having sex only with the fiancé was still the modal pattern when Hunt's data were gathered. Between the 1940s and tbe 1970s, a major new development was the increased number of women who had premarital intercourse not only with the man they married but with other men as well. Presumably, by the 1970s that had become the dominant pattern for men. So, if men and women ever have sex before marriage, they are especially likely to do so with the eventual marriage partner, although they may also have sex with others as well.

In the decades following the Burgess and Wallin study, American women became less insistent on engagement as a precondition of intimacy and began making their sexual decisions more on the basis of particular circumstances than on the formality of the relationship.

Table 3–4 shows that in the decade between 1958 and 1968 women students at Temple University in Philadelphia became more involved in sexual intercourse at every level of commitment, but the greatest change

Table 3–3   Premarital Intercourse with Fiancé(e) and Others, for Men and Women in Two Generations

	BURGESS AND WALLIN		HUNT
Partner in Premarital Intercourse	*Men*	*Women*	*Women*
None	32%	53%	19%
Fiancé(e) only	17	36	43
Fiancé(e) and others	28	10	35
Others only	22	2	2
Total	99%	101%	99%
Number of cases	580	604	Unspecified

Adapted from Burgess and Wallin, 1953: 330. *Source:* College-educated couples in Chicago, 1940–43. Adapted from Hunt, 1974: 153. *Source:* Married women under age 25 interviewed in 1972.

Table 3–4   Premarital Intercourse by Degree of Commitment, for Women in 1958 and 1968

	DEGREE OF COMMITMENT		
Year	Casual Dating	Going Steady	Engagement
1958	10%	15%	31%
1968	23%	28%	39%

Adapted from Bell and Chaskes, 1970: 83. *Source:* 250 women at Temple University (Philadelphia) in 1958 and a comparable sample of 205 students in 1968. Reciprocal percentages had not had sexual intercourse at the time of the study.

was the increased willingness of women who were dating casually to go to bed with their partners.

When Bell and Chaskes analyzed the sexually experienced women in their later sample, they found that 75 percent had had their first intercourse on a casual date, 6 percent while going steady, and 19 percent while engaged. The proportion having first intercourse during engagement would be higher if this study were repeated after the entire sample had an opportunity to experience an engagement ending in marriage. Nevertheless, they reveal strikingly how early in their dating most sexually active college students become sexually involved.

Speed of Involvement

For persons whose first intercourse comes on a casual date, the speed of sexual involvement is naturally faster than for persons who do not become that intimate until they are engaged. At one extreme, most prostitutes are eager to get the sex act over with so that they can get on to another customer. At the other extreme, those who do not become sexually involved until after they get engaged usually have months or years of association behind them.

Table 3–5 shows how sharply men students at Oregon State University differed in the speed of becoming sexually involved depending on the nature of the relationship. The largest category involved exploitive dates that were engaged in purely in the hope that they would result in intercourse (the man reporting no feeling for the woman as a person). In friendly dates, the possibility of intercourse arose after dating had already begun for broader purposes.

Kirkendall's research suggests a qualitative hierarchy of premarital intercourse. In terms of the time allowed to develop a personal relationship as well as the amount of communication, responsibility, mutuality, and the like, prostitution falls at the bottom and engagement at the top.

Table 3–5   Time between First Meeting Partner and First Intercourse, by Nature of Relationship

	NATURE OF RELATIONSHIP					
Time prior to Intercourse	Prostitute	Pickup	Exploitive Date	Friendly Date	Serious Date	Fiancée
Less than one week	100%	96%	32%	7%	0%	0%
One week to two months	0	3	43	17	2	0
Two to twelve months	0	1	18	56	36	20
Over one year	0	0	7	20	62	80
Total	100%	100%	100%	100%	100%	100%
Number of partners	91	116	219	112	93	25

Adapted from Kirkendall, 1961: 258. *Source:* 200 men students at Oregon State University, reporting on all the persons with whom they had ever had intercourse.

The higher the threshold at which premarital intercourse occurs, the richer the circumstances.

Closely correlated with the casualness of most men's experience is their lack of communication about marriage, possible pregnancy, or even whether to have intercourse itself. The man's approach is frequently indirect, and both partners rely heavily on nonverbal gestures and symbols:

> *I remember many first dates when I would try constantly to figure out what the woman was thinking of me. What did different signs mean? If she didn't wear a bra or left her blouse partly unbuttoned, I assumed she was more available. These assumptions weren't always correct, but they encouraged me to see how far I could go.*

One "advantage" of nonverbal communication is that it is more ambiguous. One partner can seduce the other by easy stages, sometimes without his/her realizing what is happening. To speak of sex would seem too blatant and invite a rebuff. Subtlety allows progressive intimacy without an explicit decision. Kirkendall concluded that "communication about sex is very difficult. Generally speaking, it seems easier to engage in actual intercourse than it is to refer openly to it."

There are exceptions, however, particularly after engagement. In Kirkendall's sample, nearly half the sexually experienced engaged couples communicated extensively before initiating intercourse. Most of their talk was understanding in nature rather than argumentative or persuasive. The more serious the relationship, the higher the quality of interaction between the partners, as measured by the amount and kind of communication and by the willingness to assume responsibility for potential consequences (such as pregnancy).

Duration of the Relationship.   Any given relationship tends to become more intimate the longer it exists. This is especially true within engagement. For example, only 39 percent of the Burgess and Wallin couples with short engagements (under nine months) went all the way versus 50 percent of those who were engaged more than 15 months. Intimacy tends to be progressive, so the longer a couple are engaged, the greater the likelihood of sexual intimacy.

Just as the likelihood of having intercourse increases the longer a couple go together, the more dating partners a given individual has, the greater the chances of becoming sexually intimate with at least one of them. This is partly due to the increased number of opportunities for sex. In addition, however, the wider the variety of dating partners, the greater the probability that one of those partners will be sexually experienced or persuasive enough to initiate more intimacy.

Bell and Chaskes (1970) found that the younger women were when they began dating (and therefore the longer their dating careers up to the time of being interviewed), the larger the proportion who had engaged in premarital intercourse (31 percent of those who began dating before age 15 versus 12 percent of those who began later). They also found that the larger the number of men they had dated, the more likely they were to have gone all the way with at least one of them (36 percent of those who had dated more than 20 men versus 14 percent of those who had dated fewer than 20). Similarly, intercourse was more widespread among women who had gone steady with three or more partners (46 percent versus 22 percent for those who had had two or fewer steadies). These statistics show that the greater the exposure to the possibility of intercourse, the greater the likelihood that people will actually experience it.

We saw earlier that in conservative circles, persons low in self-confidence are more apt to become sexually involved. In earlier generations, when our society frowned on sexual experience for women, the least attractive women physically were generally the most willing to have sex. As the climate of opinion has become more liberal, that situation has changed. Kaats and Davis (1970) found that the most attractive women at the University of Colorado were more apt to have had sexual intercourse than their less attractive classmates (for sophomores, these figures were 56 percent of the more attractive women versus 34 percent of the less attractive ones). Attractive women also had intercourse with a larger number of partners than their less attractive counterparts.

First versus Subsequent Intercourse.   The first experience is the most difficult—for an individual or for a couple. Fear of inadequacy, fear of being hurt, and anxiety about the unknown are most acute then. Uncertainty about the partner's response and the need to persuade him/her to cooperate or to involve him/her nonverbally make the first experience of complete intimacy a major event. Once the barrier is broken, restraint tends to diminish.

For couples who have intercourse often, it becomes more routine, hardly needing persuasion any more. Even so, it seldom becomes as routine outside of marriage as within it. Hunt (1974) found that young single men and women in his sample were conspicuously leisurely in their lovemaking, typically spending a half hour about equally divided between sexual play and a sustained period of intromission.

THE CONSEQUENCES OF SEXUAL INVOLVEMENT

We have seen that premarital intimacy varies enormously in degree and quality. Its consequences are equally diverse. Even when discussion is limited to a single type of intimacy, the consequences are affected by many situational variables. For simplicity, we will concentrate on complete intimacy.

Physical Consequences

The physical consequences of sexual intercourse are relatively unique in comparison with lesser degrees of intimacy. Short of genital apposition, conception is impossible and venereal infection is unlikely.

Venereal Disease.   Despite the discovery of better methods for curing venereal disease, the risk of infection has not disappeared. Indeed, the sexual revolution, by increasing the number of persons who engage in sexual intercourse with multiple partners, has made venereal infection an increasing hazard. As of the mid-1970s, a public health official described that risk as "moderate" and pointed out that it was greatest in college towns and in cities where large numbers of single people congregate. The risk was also greatest among people under age 30, presumably because they were the most sexually active. The Public Health Service reported that in 1974 there were 38 cases of syphilis and 469 cases of gonorrhea per 100,000 in the total U.S. population.

The following information on venereal disease is drawn principally from the *Birth Control Handbook* of the Students' Society of McGill University (1969).

Syphilis is the most dangerous venereal disease. It is acutely infectious and invades every system of the body if it is not treated. With treatment by an injection of penicillin, the early stages of syphilis can be completely cured. Syphilis is transmitted only through intimate sexual or physical contact.

The primary stage of syphilis usually shows itself about three weeks after exposure to infection, though a range of up to ninety days is possible. The symptom is a chancre, or sore, on the genital organs, the anus, or, in some women, on the cervix. Chancres may appear in the mouth after kissing a person with secondary sores. The sore may be neither painful nor itchy and may go unnoticed, possibly even disappearing after several days. Thus, many persons do not realize the serious nature of their condition and the fact that they remain highly infectious to other people even though the symptoms have disappeared.

If untreated, syphilis progresses to a second stage, the symptoms of which are sore throat, skin rash, enlarged glands (particularly about the genitals), swollen joints, fever, headache, pain in bones and joints, and patchy balding. These symptoms may come and go for about four years, during which time the individual continues to be highly infectious. The untreated disease then enters a latent (hidden) state, giving no visible symptoms of its presence, which may last from five to fifty years.

The final stage may manifest itself in any body system, the cardiovascular and nervous systems being the most common. Symptoms may develop slowly or suddenly and may lead to extreme mental and physical deterioration and death. Since diagnosis is difficult, more than one blood test is necessary.

Gonorrhea is a disease of the linings of the genitourinary organs that is also transmitted through sexual contact. The incubation period is from two days to three weeks. In women, the urethra and cervical canal are infected first, but, because these are internal organs, the infection may be undetected. Untreated, various complications may arise. The glands in the genital area may become swollen and painful and the rectum and Fallopian tubes may become inflamed, possibly causing sterility, if not treated. On infection, males experience a burning sensation when urinating and a discharge of yellow pus from the urethra. This discharge is highly infectious, and the bacteria may be transferred to the eyes. Untreated, the bacteria spread to the bladder, causing cystitis, to the seminal vesicles or to the epididymis, causing a hard, tender swelling in the scrotum. Sterility can result. In both male and female, the gonococci may enter the bloodstream and cause arthritis or inflammation of the joints.

Syphilis and gonorrhea may be passed on to newborn babies unless the mother is treated successfully early in pregnancy. The baby of a diseased mother may be born dead or be itself diseased. The eyes of all newborn babies are treated with silver-nitrate solution or penicillin drops as a preventive measure against gonorrheal infections that can cause blindness.

Penicillin is the standard treatment for gonorrhea, though it is not totally effective because the bacteria have developed resistance to this treatment. Though penicillin continued to be the most effective drug at this writing, sixteen times the original amount had to be used to be effective. In 1976 some strains of gonorrhea not responsive to the usual penicillin dosage appeared in the United States. A new drug, spectinomycin, was being saved for later use as some gonorrhea germs develop greater immunity. There were oral medications available, tetracycline and erythromycin, but these were less desirable since they may produce diarrehea and other gastrointestinal side effects.

Most county health departments have venereal disease clinics, offering treatment that is either free or billable to Medicaid. Infected persons are expected to provide medical personnel with the names of their sexual partners in order that the latter may be reached for treatment.

Anyone engaging in sexual intercourse is on safer ground if s/he knows the partner well to be sure that each will be notified in case of infection. If communication does not exist, it is wise to have a checkup two weeks after intercourse with a new lover. Persons engaging in sexual activity with diverse partners would do well to have monthly checkups.

Pregnancy. Premarital conception is an even more common consequence. Almost one-fifth of the sexually experienced women in Kinsey's sample had had at least one premarital pregnancy. The invention of improved contraceptives did not automatically solve the problem of preventing premarital conceptions. Many of the most effective methods of contraception require a prescription that some young single women are reluctant to request. Moreover, the unpredictable and uncommunicative character of most premarital intercourse is not conducive to the regular practice of contraception. Many couples take chances; and the more chances they take, the more apt they are to "get caught" with an unwanted pregnancy.

As recently as 1972, Hunt (1974) found that one-sixth of the sexually active single women under age 25 were not using any method of birth control. Although a majority were on the pill, a considerable minority were using unreliable methods such as rhythm or withdrawal or were using reliable methods irregularly rather than consistently. Hunt did not report how many of these women had actually become pregnant, but he did report that fear of pregnancy was the greatest source of regret after the first experience of intercourse (when contraceptive precautions were least likely to have been taken).

In a study of 16- and 17-year-olds in West Germany, Sigusch and Schmidt (1973) found that the proportion of women using no contraception decreased from 29 percent at first intercourse to 12 percent subsequently, and those relying on withdrawal decreased from 27 percent to 16 percent, whereas reliance on the pill increased from 16 percent to 37 percent (with other methods remaining about the same). Thus the risks of pregnancy, especially high in first intercourse, remained appreciable subsequently through continued reliance by a minority on undependable methods or no method at all.

Even for college students who are living together (who presumably are less likely to take chances with birth control), pregnancy remains a hazard. As recently as 1975, Bower found that one-fourth of a largely student sample of women, who were currently living with a man and who had typically had about seven other sexual partners previously, had already had at least one accidental pregnancy. This shows that long after the development of the pill, unintended conception was still a substantial risk for sexually active unmarried couples.

When a pregnancy occurs, the usual alternatives are to have an abortion or to get married. Even before abortions became legalized, they were the preferred alternative. Some three-fourths of the premarital pregnancies of the women interviewed by Kinsey and his staff were aborted (Gebhard, 1958). Since abortions have become more accessible, this percentage has presumably increased.

A small proportion of single women choose to bear their child and then place it for adoption or (in an even smaller number of cases) keep the child and raise it singlehanded.

Nineteen percent of Kinsey's premaritally pregnant couples got married. A few of them also obtained abortions, but most had live births. Many of these couples had planned to marry eventually. However, an unwanted pregnancy raises problems. Early marriage disrupts the compatibility testing process, so that couples of doubtful compatibility get married who otherwise might have broken up.

Substantially more interfaith than homogamous marriages in Detroit involved premarital pregnancies (32 percent of mixed couples versus 17 percent for Protestants and 20 percent for Catholics). Pratt (1965) suggests, "A plausible interpretation here is that interfaith marriages are quite frequently brought about by the fact of pregnancy where a marriage might not otherwise have occurred."

Doubt about whether her husband married her because he loved her rather than just because she was pregnant may plague a wife the rest of her life. For him, it may be an excuse to shirk his marital responsibilities or abandon them altogether. Forced marriages are often so rushed and so embarrassing that they bypass religious ceremonies in favor of civil weddings. In Detroit, almost half of all civil ceremonies versus less than one-sixth of religious weddings involved couples who were already pregnant (Pratt, 1965).

When students become pregnant, premature parenthood frequently terminates their education. (Pratt found that 13 percent of all Detroit marriages in which both partners were college dropouts were premaritally pregnant compared to only 4 percent of marriages in which both partners finished college.)

The husband-wife relationship is strained when the complications of pregnancy and parenthood are added to the crucial first year of marriage. Christensen and Meissner (1953) found that these problems almost doubled the divorce rate for premaritally pregnant couples. Moreover, their divorces were obtained unusually fast. The more immature the couple and the less compatible they are, the greater the likelihood of divorce. To us, this suggests that having an abortion or relinquishing an illegitimate child for adoption may have fewer negative repercussions for everyone concerned than marrying prematurely.

An increasingly permissive peer-group atmosphere accompanied by a decrease in the institutional and parental controls surrounding young adults puts the responsibility upon individuals to know the "facts of life" and to take the precautions that are necessary to avoid an unwanted pregnancy. Couples who choose to become physically intimate need to discuss the risk of pregnancy (since no contraception is foolproof), the method of preventing pregnancy (see Chapter 15, on Family Planning), and the alternative they prefer to follow in case a pregnancy occurs.

Heightened Sexuality.   Women gradually become more sexually responsive with increased sexual experience. This is one of the physical consequences of premarital intimacy:

> When we first started going together, Sarah was rather cold and I could tell that she was a virgin. I told her the "facts of life" which were all pretty new to her. At first she was against sex, but I gradually worked around to it. After a while she discovered that she enjoyed it too, and now she's even more eager than I am.

Table 3–6 shows that almost a third of cohabiting students polled at two Florida state universities found their first experience of sexual intercourse unsatisfactory (typically while they were still in high school). In the intervening five to seven years, these relatively liberal students had generally had intercourse with at least two other persons besides the initial one and the person with whom they were currently living. Taking all their later intercourse together, their satisfaction usually increased. So, sexual experience not only intensifies awareness of the sexual dimension of life, but the greater the amount of that experience, the more satisfying it tends to become. The capacity for sexual responsiveness and the art of sexual interaction are both learned behaviors, and learning comes with experience.

When sexual feelings are aroused, the physiological tendency is toward release through climax. Most petting, however, stops short of this point. Only a third of Kinsey's men and women who engaged in petting

Table 3–6   Satisfaction with First and Subsequent Intercourse, for Men and Women

	MEN		WOMEN	
Satisfaction	*First*	*Subsequent*	*First*	*Subsequent*
Very satisfactory	11%	27%	15%	36%
Satisfactory	58	68	53	46
Unsatisfactory	31	5	32	18
Total	100%	100%	100%	100%
Number of cases	79	78	79	76

Adapted from Kieffer, 1972: 64–65. *Source:* Cohabiting students at Florida State University and University of South Florida reporting on first intercourse (typically at age 16) and subsequent intercourse generally (typically with four or more partners including the one with whom they were now living).

ever experienced orgasm as a result (1953). Hence premarital petting usually means stimulation without release. Some individuals are impelled by this heightened tension to sexual intercourse. Others find release through masturbation. For the rest there remains the problem of living with tension. A few of Kinsey's men and women experienced localized pain in the genital region. How much pain is experienced may depend on the intensity of the petting. Shipman (1968) found that 44 percent of men who petted "heavily" at Wisconsin State University suffered testicular pain. Note, however, that this pain was apparently not acute enough to prevent them from continuing to engage in this activity. More common are simple frustration and preoccupation with this frustration. When one is sexually aroused, it's difficult to think of anything else. After enough time elapses (perhaps in such traditional distractions as cold showers or vigorous exercise), passions may cool. The physical effects of petting are keynoted, however, in the word "frustration":

> We've done so much petting that it's becoming a natural part of our life. But it's been quite frustrating for both of us. Petting gets you all worked up but then you have to stop. I don't like it but I do.

Along with negative feelings of frustration go positive sensations—the pleasures of sensual stimulation. Frustration implies not simply a negative, but an ambivalent, situation. In tantric yoga, frustration is deliberately cultivated as a means of heightening sexual tension and raising the energy level of the partners. In giving and receiving massage, similarly, a couple may experience a heightened sensitivity to one another's bodies. Sensual experiences of touch are one way of getting high without drugs, a way of expressing affection nonverbally.

The frustration of sexual arousal short of climax may be a positive experience despite, or perhaps because of, the tension involved. For many couples, such tension is resolved sooner or later by individual or mutual masturbation, by achieving climax through sexual intercourse, or for the man by nocturnal emissions. This release of sexual tension is another source of pleasure. Regardless of whether couples experience the prolonged tension of sexual play without release or the sequence of arousal followed by release, the sexual side of their lives takes on increased importance.

Psychological Consequences

In comparison to such tangible effects as pregnancy, abortion, and disease, the emotional consequences of intimacy are more difficult to measure. Feelings aren't always clear cut, and research results must be treated cautiously. Verbal responses depend on the wording of questions and the context in which they are asked.

How many of those who become sexually involved regret it later? When Kinsey asked adult women how they felt about the premarital intercourse they had had years before, few reported regrets. However, when college students were asked about their current behavior, more qualms were revealed.

Table 3–7 shows that the greater the degree of intimacy, the greater the proportion who felt guilty. (More than twice as many women as men reported guilt feelings, but patterns were similar for the two sexes.) More important than degree of intimacy, however, was the individual's own sexual standard. Guilt was experienced universally by those whose behavior violated their own standard. It was rarest among those who stopped short of going as far as their standard would allow. Curiously, guilt was relatively widespread among those who were moderately to extremely intimate and yet said they believed their behavior was all right. Apparently, liberal philosophies sometimes masked latent inhibitions that rose up to plague those who engaged in petting or intercourse. Perhaps if one violates such scruples often enough they eventually disappear, but "believing" in the rightness of sexual intimacy is no guarantee against feeling guilty afterward. Religious devoutness and the strict moral teaching of certain churches predispose people to feelings of guilt. Although few of Kinsey's devout Catholic women violated their taboo on premarital intercourse, fully half of those who did subsequently regretted it. Similarly, Christensen and Carpenter found sharp differences among Mormon, midwestern, and Danish students in the pleasantness or unpleasantness of feelings the day after first intercourse (see Table 3–8). The Mormon faith is similar to Catholicism in its stringent opposition to premarital intimacy. Scandinavia, on the other hand, is secular and permissive. The stronger the cultural support for premarital intercourse, the more positive the personal reactions.

Table 3–8 also shows that the less common the behavior was in a particular group, the more likely the individual member was to have

Table 3–7   Guilt Feelings about Current Sexual Involvement, by Sexual Philosophy

Current Degree of Sexual Involvement	SEXUAL PHILOSOPHY *Maximum Permissible Intimacy*		
	Necking	*Petting*	*Intercourse*
Necking	25%	5%	0%
Petting	100%	63%	42%
Intercourse	100%	100%	56%

Adapted from Reiss, 1967: 116. *Source:* Men and women students in certain classes at the State University of Iowa. Reciprocal percentages of students reported no guilt feelings about their sexual behavior.

Table 3–8   Feelings after First Intercourse, for Men and Women at Three Universities

Feelings	UNIDENTIFIED MORMON UNIVERSITY		PURDUE UNIVERSITY		UNIVERSITY OF COPENHAGEN	
	Men	Women	Men	Women	Men	Women
Pleasant	33%	14%	45%	35%	71%	73%
Unpleasant	67	86	55	65	29	27
Total	100%	100%	100%	100%	100%	100%
Number of experienced students	37	7	107	29	93	49
Percent of total students who had ever had intercourse	39%	10%	51%	21%	64%	60%

Adapted from Christensen and Carpenter, 1962: 68–69. Pleasant feelings involved happiness, relaxation, or sense of conquest. Unpleasant feelings involved tenseness, remorse, guilt, disgust, fear of others' knowing, fear of religious punishment, fear of pregnancy, or fear of venereal disease.

unpleasant reactions. For both men and women, the smaller the proportion of students who ever had premarital intercourse, the larger the proportion with negative reactions. This suggests the profound influence of group norms on the meaning of sexual experience. Similarly, Bell and Chaskes (1970) found that the lower the rate of premarital intercourse in a religious group, the greater feelings of guilt among those people who did have intercourse. So, the probability of experiencing negative feelings afterward can be predicted not only by examining one's own convictions, but also by referring to the views held by the groups to which one belongs.

Qualms about intimacy depend on three factors: the strength of one's scruples, the degree of intimacy, and the crudity or sensitivity with which intimacy occurs. If the relationship is exploitive or merely casual, regrets are more likely than when the participants love each other.

Table 3–9 shows regret was felt more often when intimacy occurred

Table 3–9   Feeling of Going Too Far in Having Intercourse, by Degree of Commitment, in 1958 and 1968

	DEGREE OF COMMITMENT		
Year	Casual Dating	Going Steady	Engagement
1958	65%	61%	41%
1968	36%	30%	20%

Adapted from Bell and Chaskes, 1970: 83. *Source:* 250 women students at Temple University (Philadelphia) in 1958 and a matched sample of 205 students in 1968. Reciprocal percentages felt they had not gone too far when they had had intercourse.

prematurely. The less committed the couple, the more regrettable intercourse seemed. When intimacy occurs within a context of love and commitment, regret is less likely.

Although guilt feelings continued to be less in 1968 among those who were the most committed to their partners, a major change from 1958 occurred in the decreased guilt over casual sex. Premarital sex was becoming not only more widespread but less guilt-ridden as well. If this sexual revolution proceeds, guilt feelings and other unpleasant emotional reactions may become as rare in the United States as they were in Scandinavia. In the meantime, differential reactions to sexual experience depend on the personal convictions, the peer group, and the cultural norms of the participants. Sex before marriage can be a positive or a negative experience, depending on such forces within and around the persons involved.

Interpersonal Consequences

Crucial to a book on marriage is the effect of intimate behavior on the relationship between partners. The short-range question is whether intimacy strengthens or weakens the relationship; does it increase or decrease the likelihood that couples will marry? In the long run, how is premarital intimacy related to marital sexual adjustment and to marital satisfaction?

We have already seen that premarital intercourse (1) sometimes results in pregnancies that (2) sometimes result in marriages that (3) sometimes would not otherwise have occurred. Indeed, Kirkendall (1961) reported that some women tried to become pregnant in the hope that this would persuade the partner to marry them.

Premarital Consequences.   Except for occasional forced marriages, in the past intimacy produced more broken relationships than strengthened ones. More engagements were broken by the Burgess and Wallin couples who had intercourse than by those who did not (18 percent versus 11 percent), and the more frequent the intercourse, the larger the proportion broken (1953). However, this study was made at a time when sexual involvement was associated with low self-esteem. Quite possibly the correlation between intercourse and broken relationships has diminished or even reversed as premarital sexual intimacy has become more socially accepted.

Kanin and Davidson (1972) examined the effect of intercourse on Purdue University couples and found that about half the group felt it had "somewhat intensified" their love for one another, about 30 percent felt their love had been "greatly intensified," and only about 5 percent thought there had been any decrease. Table 3–10 shows that a disproportionately large number of the students who reported that their love either stayed the same or lessened were only mildly in love at the time they went

Table 3–10 Effect of First Intercourse on Feeling toward the Partner, by Love for the Partner

Effect of First Intercourse on Love for Partner	DEGREE OF LOVE FOR PARTNER	
	Strong	Mild
Intensified	86%	62%
Same or decreased	14	38
Total	100%	100%
Number of cases	140	40

Adapted from Kanin and Davidson, 1972: 213. *Source:* Sexually experienced men and women at Purdue University reporting on their current or most recent love relationship (most of which were steady or engaged relationships).

all the way. Apparently, the effect of premarital intercourse on the relationship between the partners depends on the quality of the relationship. The more loving the relationship, the greater the chance that sexual intimacy will be beneficial instead of detrimental. We cannot be sure that intercourse actually strengthened these relationships, since Ard (1974) found that couples who abstained from intercourse were even more likely to feel that their abstinence had benefited their marriage. Perhaps the crucial question is not whether two people become sexually intimate, but whether they are able to negotiate successfully about how intimate they wish to become. Teamwork in making and implementing the sexual decision probably matters more than the nature of the decision. Here is a case characterized by unusual mutuality of understanding:

> Until we got engaged, the limit of our physical intimacy was a deep kiss. From that point forward, we progressed gradually through light petting to heavy petting and, finally, to intercourse. Neither of us had had prior sexual experience other than kissing, and in retrospect, we have enjoyed learning together.
>
> Generally, I took the lead, but we had a tacit agreement that we would make progress slowly, mixing discussion with discovery. Before and after progressing to the next level, we both freely gave our views concerning the implications of the act and our attitudes toward what we were doing. This process of mutual learning and mutual understanding was and is a valuable and cherished experience to us.

When premarital intercourse is based on a foundation of acquaintance, love, and commitment to marriage, it is likely to increase the couple's feeling of closeness. Kirkendall (1956) found, however, that very few of his couples prepared the way for intercourse by full and free discussion, placed the importance of their total relationship ahead of sex, or were motivated primarily by love for each other. Only under those circumstances, he believed, did couples "have a chance to engage in premarital intercourse without damaging results to their interrelationships."

What happens when one partner pushes toward intimacy before the other is ready? Such premature initiatives are almost exclusively masculine (not that women never initiate sexual activity, but their partners are seldom reluctant). Kirkpatrick and Kanin (1957) found that Indiana University women who had been offended by an aggressive partner most often were angry. They frequently felt disgusted or disillusioned with the man, afraid of further aggressiveness, or guilty about their own involvement. After being offended once, they often refused to date the aggressor again and warned their friends about him. If a couple were already going steady or were engaged before the sexual offense, they were less likely to break up. But even engagements sometimes collapsed when men pushed their sexual desires to the point of violence.

This study dramatizes the difference between intimacy that expresses mutual love and that which pushes a woman further and faster than she is prepared to go. Loving intimacy may strengthen a relationship, but the same intimacy forced on a reluctant partner can ruin it.

Marital Consequences.   Locke (1951) found that more divorced than happily married persons had had premarital intercourse with several people, not just the future spouse. Similarly, Terman (1938) found the greatest marital happiness among couples who postponed intercourse until marriage, next where it was restricted to engagement, and least where multiple partners were involved. Burgess and Wallin (1953) found that the more frequently a couple had had premarital relations with each other, the lower their marital happiness, mutual satisfaction, love for one another, and confidence in the permanence of their marriage.

All of the studies cited in the previous paragraph are rather dated. It is possible that the increased liberalization of attitudes toward premarital sex in our society has decreased the negative consequences for marital happiness. Indeed, Edmonds, Withers, and Dibatista (1972) found among married couples in Winchester, Virginia, that although premarital sexual abstinence was still positively correlated with marital adjustment, the size of the correlation was so small as to be practically meaningless. As of this writing, there is no firm evidence that becoming involved sexually before marriage generally benefits the marriage, but on the other hand, most of the negative effects seem to have disappeared.

The specifically *sexual* satisfaction of sexually experienced wives excels that of novices. Kanin and Howard (1958) found that experienced women were more satisfied with intercourse during the first two weeks of marriage. In fact, the greater their prior intimacy, the greater their sexual satisfaction on the honeymoon. Although Chesser's experienced women

(1957) reported the same sexual advantage on the honeymoon, their superiority diminished within the first few months of marriage and disappeared altogether after that.

These findings reflect the fact that heightened sexuality is a consequence of intimacy. The sooner a woman begins to be sexually active, the sooner she becomes sexually responsive. This does not mean that the sooner one begins, the more satisfactory the initial experiences, even from a purely sexual point of view. If there is any difference at all between initial intercourse before marriage and initial intercourse after marriage, we would expect the latter to benefit from the security and legitimacy of marriage. Given the same *amount* of sexual experience, women who wait until they are married may be more responsive than those who rush into sexual intimacy. We will see later that the happiest married couples and the warmest mothers are those who delay getting married or having children until they are fully ready. Probably the quality of sexual experience also rises with increased readiness.

Premarital intercourse blurs the distinction between being single and being married. Couples who have already had intercourse are less apt to take a honeymoon. (Only 47 percent of Kanin and Howard's sexually experienced student couples took a honeymoon, compared to 87 percent of the restrained couples.)

Premarital intercourse also weakens the boundary line between marital and extramarital sexual behavior. In Kinsey's female sample, those with premarital intercourse were more than twice as apt to engage in extramarital intercourse (29 percent versus 13 percent for the premaritally restrained). Athanasiou et al. (1970) found that the earlier in advance of marriage premarital intercourse began, the lower the commitment to the first sexual partner, and the larger the number of premarital partners, the greater the likelihood of engaging in extramarital intercourse. Those who do not consider wedding vows necessary to intercourse before marriage are less likely to adopt this position after marriage.

THE NEGOTIATION OF SEXUAL INVOLVEMENT

So far our discussion of premarital intimacy has focused on what people do and what the consequences are. We come now to the question of how particular couples can resolve their differences and maximize their satisfaction with their sexual behavior.

Karen (1959) found widespread inconsistency between ideals and practices among students at San Diego Junior College. Violations of their own ideals occurred most often in casual dating when many men's "predatory-recreational orientation" was not yet balanced by interest in the partner's welfare. Though women less often take the initiative in violating their own standards, they are not immune to the temptation, especially when faced with what Burgess and Wallin described as the "frequent and intensive erotic stimulation" that usually precedes final breakthroughs in intimacy.

Communication Problems

An ambiguous norm invites infractions. A vague situation invites an eager partner to test the limits. Failure to communicate one's convictions exposes the person to the possibility that those hidden convictions will be unknowingly violated by an eager partner. Kanin (1957) concluded from a study of episodes in which dating partners attempted to force intimacies which women found offensive or displeasing that such offenses were "a consequence largely of poor communication."

In a later article, Kanin (1969) pointed out that a large proportion of these offensive sexual episodes occurred between partners who had not talked at all about their sexual wishes. Most of the men who attempted forceful intercourse bordering on rape had misinterpreted the woman's willingness to engage in genital sex play as indicative of her willingness to go all the way. Sometimes they made assumptions about the woman's accessibility based on the kinds of clothes she wore or on such gestures as removing some or all of her clothing. Some men jumped to the conclusion that the partner was sexually available simply because she had accepted a date and had been wined and dined at considerable expense. These cases illustrate how easily nonverbal behavior can be misunderstood and how frequently assumptions about another person can be wrong.

Repeated offenses by the same man were rare because the victims successfully communicated their displeasure. Most women either broke off the relationship or revealed their convictions forcefully once they had been violated. Common reactions to sexual aggression on first dates were screaming and fighting, on intermediate dates quarreling and turning cold, and on later dates crying and pleading with the man to stop. None of these outcomes is very pleasant to experience—neither the aggression for the woman nor being criticized and then perhaps suddenly dropped for the man. Yet these are the risks of inadequate communication for couples where either partner has reservations about getting sexually involved.

The chief responsibility falls on the conservative partner to express his/her convictions when pressed to go farther than s/he wants. Instead of simply saying no, s/he can contribute to the emotional growth of the relationship by discussing the issue fully. Once a standard is clarified, it is more easily respected. Whenever discussion reveals conflicting norms, sexual intimacy must be limited to the least common denominator if the conservative partner is not to be offended. People sometimes wonder whether they should ignore their own convictions in order to express their love. Affirmative answers to this question cause trouble. In the long run, the only way to preserve one's self-respect and personal integrity is by sticking to one's beliefs.

Negotiation of Differences

Although we have emphasized the control function of the conservative partner, this does not mean that there is no place for exploring the views and wishes of both partners. It may be difficult for the liberal partner to put his/her sexual wishes into words in the face of known reluctance by the other, but both persons are likely to experience a feeling of relief when the eager partner's sexual fantasies are out in the open. Tension usually falls when secret desires are expressed, releasing the energy that has been required to keep them hidden. The conservative partner, in turn, usually appreciates having been trusted to hear about those sexual wishes, even if s/he does not feel ready to act on them. After sexual wishes have been verbalized, they can be dealt with more effectively than when they are only inferred on the basis of nonverbal gestures.

Nonverbal maneuvering frequently takes on a seesaw character in which the eager partner pushes for intimacy until encountering resistance, after which s/he backs off uncertainly. Open discussion offers the opportunity of ascertaining the partner's feelings ahead of time so there is less chance of offending him/her in the first place. If couples still run into trouble, follow-up discussion provides a chance to find out just what was offensive and just how far short of that point the partner is willing to go.

The course of sexual involvement is frequently uneven enough to require repeated verbal sharing in order to be most satisfactory. Because feelings may change, the eager partner may need to inquire from time to time whether the other's previous reluctance has given way to readiness for a new level of intimacy. Nor is desire always one-sided. When physically fatigued, ill, unhappy, or angry, the partner who is usually more interested in sexual involvement may not feel like touching or being touched. So negotiating about sexual involvement is at best an ongoing process, not something to be settled once and for all in a single discussion.

Negotiation can be successful only when both partners are acting in good faith. Unfortunately, this cannot be taken for granted. Kanin (1967) found that 27 percent of the college men in his sample who had never sexually offended a woman and 80 percent of those who had forced a woman to the point where she felt outraged had engaged in at least one of the following tactics in their eagerness for intercourse—attempting to get a woman intoxicated, falsely professing love, falsely promising marriage, or threatening to terminate the relationship. Kanin also reported that many of the men who were sexually aggressive did not "take no for an answer," believing that women who expressed reluctance to have intercourse did not mean it and were only feigning disinterest. Telling lies or discounting the partner's statements sabotages the communication/ negotiation process and requires both skepticism and vigorous inquiry to be sure where the situation really stands. If one's partner is constitutionally disposed to aggression and exploitation, successful communication and negotiation may be impossible. Terminating the relationship may be the only solution. In other cases, patient and persistent attempts to break through misunderstandings may succeed in creating agreement on a mutually acceptable pattern of sexual involvement.

4 Living Together Unmarried

When we started writing this book, we planned to entitle this chapter "Living Together before Marriage," but it soon became apparent that living together does not necessarily lead to marriage or involve any intention to marry. Indeed, a study in Boulder, Colorado by Lyness, Lipetz, and Davis (1972), showed that couples who were going together were more marriage oriented than couples who were living together unmarried. Just as dating used to be the equivalent of "courting" but has long since lost that serious connotation, and just as sexual involvement used to create heavy pressure to get married but now is less apt to be seen that way, living together has lost any necessary link to marriage.

Writing this chapter was difficult, for living together unmarried is a relatively new phenomenon and has not been fully researched. The existing studies seldom trace the consequences of living together for the subsequent marriages of the participants, either to each other or to third parties. So the long-range consequences of this behavior are not yet known.

Those who were living together unmarried in the early 1970s were a deviant minority. Hence, some of the seeming effects of this living arrangement were due not so much to the living together as to the fact that persons radical enough to violate social convention were not a cross-section of the general population. For example, the cohabiting couples in Boulder had been less happy as adolescents than couples who were simply going together. Negative selective factors may motivate some people to live together to get away from their parents or may free them to engage in behavior that they know their parents disapprove of.

At Penn State, Anderson (1974) found that students in the social sciences were more apt to be living together than those in the physical sciences, which correlates with the tendency of social science students to be more liberal politically. At the University of Georgia, Guittar and Lewis (1974) found few differences in personality between students who were living together and ones who were not but the cohabiting men were unusually warm and affectionate while the women were unusually emancipated, aggressive, and competitive. This suggests that the men were unusually open to intimate relationships and that the women were unusually free of conventional restraints to such unconventional living.

As early as 1971, however, Arafat and Yorburg (1973) found that students at the City College of New York who were living together unmarried were no more radical in their social origins and general social orientations than the student body in general. They majored in the same fields of study and came from the same social-class backgrounds. Only in religious attitudes were the cohabiting students more radical. It may be no accident that this similarity in social backgrounds between those who were living together and those who were not was found in the extraordinarily liberal environment of the nation's largest city. As cohabitation becomes more widespread and socially accepted, it will by definition be less and less limited to the radical few.

Just how many Americans ever live together without being married depends on the definition one uses. Cohabitation, like marriage, is an experience of varying duration, but unlike marriage it has no formal beginning. It may vary all the way from a brief visit to a friend's house or a joint vacation trip to living together over many years (which used to be called common-law marriage)—and still is in some states.

Differences in definition make it difficult to compare one study with another. At Penn State, almost half of the senior class of 1972 reported that they had at some time lived with someone of the opposite sex (Peterman, Ridley, and Anderson, 1974). The rapid increase in the proportion of college students engaging in premarital intercourse that we saw in Chapter 3 is paralleled by a similar increase in the proportion of students who ever live together. The Penn State study reported that whereas only 4 percent of the class of 1972 had cohabited at some time during their freshman year, five times as many of the class of 1975 (19 percent of the men and 25 percent of the women) had had that experience during the fall or winter term of their freshman year. If we extrapolate from this finding, it seems likely that a majority of the latter class would cohabit with at least one partner by the time they graduated. Thus, living together unmarried seemed well on the way to becoming transformed from a deviant minority experience to a majority experience for American college students by the middle 1970s. Even so, for most of these students it was still an occasional, short-term experience that only a minority engaged in at any one time. But to have experienced what it is like to live with someone else however briefly broadens the range of heterosexual experience prior to marriage from the traditional narrow base where couples entered marriage without ever having lived with anyone except their family and perhaps a roommate of the same sex.

MOVING IN: THE PROCESS OF RESIDENTIAL INVOLVEMENT

In the preceding chapters, we have described the gradual way in which couples become involved affectionally and sexually. People seldom fall in love at first sight and seldom go all the way sexually on first contact. Similarly, they seldom begin living together at one definitive moment. If living together is defined as a combination of sleeping together, eating together, and moving one's belongings to the same location, it frequently occurs in piecemeal fashion. Usually it results from a gradual process of becoming residentially involved.

Prerequisites for Living Together

How well do people know each other when they begin sharing the same space? How long have they known each other? How long have they been going together? How do they feel about each other? And how involved are they sexually?

Length of Going Together. No information is available on the length of time the average couple have known each other before they start living together. However, a number of studies report how long couples have dated each other before they establish a common habitation. Kieffer (1972) found that students at two Florida state universities had typically gone together two or three months before they started living together. Danziger and Greenwald (1973) studied a broader group of students and college graduates, ranging in age from 18 to 27, and found that the average length of time couples had gone together before they started living together "on a permanent basis" was about eight months.

Both of these figures are strikingly lower than the 18 months that Hollingshead (1952) found was the average time from beginning dating to getting engaged. This suggests that for many couples the decision to start living together is less momentous than the decision to get engaged. Engagement involves a promise to get married, a lifetime (or at least a long-term) commitment. Moving in together is seldom as future oriented as that. Couples begin living together because that is what they want to do now. The future for them is open-ended. Thus, the time required to feel ready to live together is typically less than to get engaged.

Presumably, the longer couples go together before they start living together, the better prepared they will be to cope with the stresses of establishing a common household. So far, however, no one seems to have studied the relationship between length of going together and success in living together.

Affectional Involvement.   In view of the speed with which most couples start living together, we would not expect them to be very marriage oriented. Rather, couples should typically be dating, but not yet engaged.

Table 4–1 shows what extraordinarily small proportions of students were engaged when they started living together. At both Cornell and Texas, the typical couple were involved enough to have stopped dating other persons. Substantial minorities, however, were either not yet that committed to each other or didn't believe in confining their dating to just one relationship. To use the traditional terminology, most couples were going steady in an exclusive dating relationship that they did not see as necessarily leading to marriage.

Sexual Involvement.   Since one definition of living together is sharing the same bedroom, the question of sexual involvement seems redundant. Can't it be taken for granted that couples are sexually involved before they start living together and, even more, that couples who live together always "sleep together"?

Studies show that the relationship between sexual and residential involvement is close, but not that simple. To be sure, persons rarely start living with someone prior to their first sexual experience. Nevertheless, Montgomery (1973) found one person in his sample at the University of Massachusetts whose first sexual experience came after moving in with

Table 4–1   Affectional Involvement When Couples First Started Living Together on Two University Campuses

	UNIVERSITY	
Affectional Involvement	*Cornell*	*Texas*
Formally engaged	2%	6%
Tentatively engaged (contemplating marriage)	10	14
Strong affectionate relationship; not dating others	58	50
Strong affectionate relationship; also dating others	25	16
Friends	4	*
Other	1	*
Total	100%	*
Number of cases	92	173

Adapted from Macklin, 1974: 28, and Shuttlesworth and Thorman, 1973: 4. *Sources:* Sophomores and seniors at Cornell who had lived with a person of the opposite sex at least four nights a week for at least three consecutive months. At the University of Texas, students enrolled in eight undergraduate courses.
*Data not reported.

his/her partner. But this is no different from persons who get married without having engaged in premarital intercourse.

In Montgomery's sample, a considerable number of couples had not had intercourse with each other (even though they had experienced it with other partners) prior to the time they started living together. Some of these did not become involved with each other sexually until days or weeks after they started living together. At Cornell, 8 percent of couples had their first intercourse with each other after they had lived together for at least three months. Another Massachusetts couple and three more Cornell couples had not yet had intercourse with each other at the time they were interviewed. They were simply roommates rather than sexual bedmates.

Some arrangements start from a single person looking for a compatible housemate. Friendship, affection, and sexual involvement may or may not grow out of living together: sharing a roof, rent, and board. Most of these persons begin with separate bedrooms. Valuing privacy, each partner may keep his/her own bedroom even after becoming intimately involved, which means that they do not take sex for granted and want to choose whether they will have sex or not:

> I needed a place to live and certainly didn't want to live alone. On the student union board I found three grad students who needed one more for their house. We liked each other and were a congenial group. Gradually, Steve and I became more and more intimate. In some ways we all still enjoy the others' presence and in other ways they feel left out by our closeness and we feel hampered by their constant advice to us. At the end of the semester, Steve and I are thinking of moving out to have a place of our own.

To share the same bedroom and especially to share the same bed usually, but not necessarily, entails a complete sexual relationship. Usually the sexual involvement comes first and the residential involvement later. But Montgomery concluded his study of the relationship between the initial coital experience and the initiation of living together with the statement that "such a wide variation existed that no pattern was ascertainable." Our own conclusion is that residential involvement is normally, but not necessarily, preceded by complete sexual involvement, but the timing of the two forms of involvement is highly variable and not necessarily close.

To summarize, most couples who start living together on American college campuses have gone together for several months and have become affectionally involved enough to feel that they are in love with each other and are prepared to cease dating others, even though they are not sure they want to get married. Normally, they have already made love to each other (and are apt to have had other sexual partners previously). Against this background of affectional and sexual involvement, residential involvement frequently seems a natural step in the evolution of their relationship.

Moving In—Event or Process?

We have already seen that "sleeping together" normally begins considerably earlier than living together. And if living together is defined as sleeping in the same bedroom at least four nights a week, cohabitation becomes not an all-or-none phenomenon but a matter of degree. Many couples do not begin living together full-time all at once, but by stages. Moving in is sometimes a gradual process rather than a single event.

Dual Residences.   On college campuses, couples may spend more time together than separately (that is, sleep together at least four nights out of seven) and continue to maintain separate residences. This coexistence of separate residences provides an ecological base for gradual rather than decisive moving in.

At Cornell, Macklin (1974) found that three-quarters of the cohabiting students maintained two "official" residences. At Penn State, a similar proportion listed separate mailing addresses (Peterman et al., 1974). The Cornell students said the major advantages of keeping separate residences were to prevent their parents from knowing what they were doing, to maintain their relationship with friends of the same sex, and to have a place to retreat to from the congestion of overcrowded living quarters and from the tensions of living together. Two-thirds of the Cornell students living away from their official residences returned there every day to pick up their mail, visit their old roommates, and get some of their belongings.

As long as separate residences are maintained, living together is less than full-fledged. Perhaps it would be better to call such an arrangement "visiting" rather than true cohabiting. A visitor may stay for a considerable length of time but always has the option of returning home. Perhaps this visiting quality explains why one-sixth of the Cornell students lacked a feeling of "belonging" or of being "at home" where they were spending most of their nights. Such a visitor's sense of belonging is impaired by the fact that s/he is literally an intruder in the place the partner shares with his/her old roommates.

Visiting, then, is a first step in the process of moving in.

Gradual Involvement.   At Cornell the typical pattern was for the woman to move in with the man without giving up her old residence. She did not move all her clothes and other belongings en masse, but divided them between the two locations. Presumably, the longer she lived with the man, the larger the proportion of things she moved. However, since the man generally shared his apartment with other men, the woman was moving into space that was not originally intended to accommodate her. So the amount of storage space was limited, creating a barrier to moving in all of her stuff.

The early stages of residential involvement frequently grow out of the desire of couples who have spent the evening together to spend the night together. After making love, getting up out of bed and going home late is a drag. So couples who see one another several evenings a week begin spending the night together and then gradually bridge the gap between nights by spending whole weekends together. At Cornell three-quarters of the students had simply drifted into sleeping together more than half the time rather than ever discussing whether or not they wanted to live together.

Presumably, it is chiefly when deciding to give up their separate residences that real decision making occurs for most couples. That final decision is most apt to occur only after the process of beginning to live together has progressed considerably toward full-time cohabitation.

Insofar as living together is not a deliberate decision and not a full-time affair, it involves relatively little commitment. Only when couples have burned their bridges by giving up their separate residences does their commitment become very explicit. At that point, they begin receiving their mail at the same address, they may sign a joint lease, their parents are more likely to be aware of their relationship, and they pass over the boundary line from being separate individuals who choose to spend part of their time together to being a couple buttressed with a common residence and a public identity.

At the University of Iowa, Johnson (1975) found that the motivation for moving in together was frequently accidental. A majority of his respondents had made no real decision to live together but "sort of drifted into it." And even for couples who supposedly made a decision, the reason was more apt to be an outside event than anything intrinsic in the relationship. The precipitating event most often was that one partner lost a same–sex roommate who had been paying half the rent for an off-campus apartment or that one person's lease expired so s/he needed a place to live. Thus economic convenience was the major factor triggering off beginning to live together. This suggests that moving in together may not prove very much about the nature of a relationship, although it may have considerable consequences for that relationship.

THE CONSEQUENCES OF LIVING TOGETHER RATHER THAN GOING TOGETHER

What difference does it make whether people ever live together unmarried? This can be assessed from two perspectives: What are the effects of living together rather than separately? And what are the effects of living together unmarried rather than married?

The first question is easier to deal with. As soon as people start living together, they begin to experience changes in structural convenience, togetherness, and personal growth.

Structural Convenience

We have already seen that one reason couples begin living together is that it is inconvenient to live separately.

Propinquity.   Living under the same roof saves the trouble of commuting to see each other. So much time is spent going back and forth between the partner's residences—time that could be saved if they were living in the same place. Propinquity saves on transportation, time, and trouble.

Similarly, communication is difficult when people live out of earshot of each other. Dormitory phones are notoriously busy, and even apartment phones are apt to be tied up by roommates. The unrestricted flow of conversation at any hour of the day or night for persons living together outstrips the convenience of even unshared private lines. Besides, so much of human communication is nonverbal that face-to-face, body-to-body communication cannot be duplicated over a wire.

Economy.   People can live together more cheaply than apart—provided that they are prepared to give up their separate residences. To move in with one partner and still pay rent on the other's domicile is hardly economical. But when couples maintain only one household instead of two, they can live more cheaply.

In addition to saving on rent, they may save on food and other costs. Cooking for two seldom costs twice as much as for one and certainly saves time. Two may be able to manage with one car instead of two, one television set instead of two, and so on. One obstacle is that few couples who begin living together unmarried have made enough of a commitment to each other to feel safe in discarding their separate appliances. After all, in another month or two they may be living separately again and will need them back. So the primary economies of moving in together are likely to be in food and rent rather than in the equipment it takes to keep house.

Togetherness

Living together rather than separately by its very nature gives couples a larger share of their time together. This makes possible not only easier communication but easier participation in all sorts of activities, not the least of which is sex.

Sexual Companionship.   We have already seen that most couples who have been going together become sexually involved with one another. But it is one thing to engage in occasional sex when the opportunity presents itself and quite another to be able to make love spontaneously whenever they feel so inclined. Relatively few couples decide to live together in order to be able to have sex. But for couples in love, the opportunity to express that love sexually with each other on any day of the week—not just on dating evenings—is one of the major attractions of living together. Lyness et al. (1972) found that couples who were living together in Boulder were more satisfied with their sexual companionship than couples who were merely going together, the difference being especially great for men.

Commitment.   Living together unmarried involves less commitment than being married. Nevertheless, compared to simply going together, moving into the same residence demonstrates a kind of commitment to the relationship, at least for the time being. In the words of Thorman (1973):

> A cohabitant's continued presence ... is an omnipresent proof of commitment and, because it is pervasive, it is a constant reinforcement to the relationship. When the association is grim, continued presence is a very real piece of commitment evidence. Commitment is obvious if a person continues to live with another when he or she is free to leave. This is especially the case when the compromises that are a part of the relationship are ones of great moment and sacrifice.

Structurally speaking, moving in together involves a step upward in the involvement and interdependence of the two partners. It may or may not involve increased emotional commitment as well. Some studies found that going-together couples were more committed than living-together couples to the continuation of their relationship. Nevertheless, for the time being, couples who live together have committed more of their resources of time and energy and money to their togetherness than couples whose chief commitment is to a future life together after marriage.

Brown and her colleagues (1975) reported that students at San Diego State University who were living together were "very committed" to their relationship and that the great majority (82 percent) were satisfied with the way their relationship was going.

Overinvolvement.   It would belabor the obvious if we were to spell out the myriad other ways in which living together creates more togetherness. What may not be so obvious is that sometimes it brings too much togetherness.

Table 4–2 lists the problems that were experienced by cohabiting women at Cornell. Overinvolvement tops the list in terms of severity. These women felt that they spent too much of their time with the partner,

Table 4-2   Severity and Incidence of Problems Experienced by Women Students During Cohabitation

Problem	Severity	Incidence
Overinvolvement (loss of identity, lack of opportunity to participate in other activities)	1.3	60%
Differing degrees or periods of sexual interest	1.1	70%
Jealousy of partner's involvement in other activities or relationships	1.0	52%
Feeling of being trapped	1.0	46%
Feeling of being used	1.0	41%
Lack of orgasm	0.9	66%
Fear of pregnancy	0.9	50%
Lack of privacy	0.8	53%
Vaginal irritation or discharge after intercourse	0.8	47%
Lack of adequate living space	0.8	41%
Conflict with apartment mates or housemates	0.6	23%
Man's discomfort during intercourse	0.5	36%
Feeling of not "belonging," not being "at home"	0.5	29%
Guilt at beginning of relationship	0.4	31%
Man's impotence	0.4	21%
Lack of money	0.3	19%
Guilt during relationship	0.2	17%
Disagreement over use of money	0.2	13%
Guilt at end of relationship	0.1	12%

Adapted from Macklin, 1972: 469. *Source:* 29 upper-class women students at Cornell University reporting on their experiences in sharing the same bedroom with a man at least four nights a week for at least three months. Severity ranged from 0 = no problem to 4 = a great problem. Reciprocal percentages experienced no problem in the relationship.

leaving too little for other friends and activities. Some women invested so much of themselves in the relationship that they lost their sense of having a separate identity. Some felt that their partners were not investing as much of themselves in the relationship as they were, and felt jealous of outside relationships and activities. Persons who are merely going together are less likely to be confronted with such outside interests since they may engage in them less obviously than if they were under the nose of a cohabiting partner. Feelings of being trapped or being used were also widespread among the Cornell women and presumably are also less common for dating students.

To seek the satisfactions of togetherness by living together is to risk getting too much of a good thing. All relationships require balancing intimacy with independence. For couples who don't live together, the problem is achieving enough intimacy. For couples who do, the problem is holding on to enough independence.

For most couples the costs in overdependency are outweighed by the gains in intimacy. At Cornell, 93 percent of the cohabiting men and women (Macklin, 1974) found their overall experience pleasurable or very pleasurable, whereas only one person in 92 rated it unpleasant. A somewhat larger proportion confessed that cohabiting had its painful side when given a choice of a combination of pleasure-pain and maturing–not maturing ratings. Thus 18 percent called it "maturing but painful," compared to 74 percent for whom it was both maturing and pleasant.

Unfortunately, we do not have comparable ratings from dating students at Cornell. At Colorado, Lyness et al. (1972) found that persons who were living together rated their relationships no more happy than those who were just going together, despite the fact that the latter were less satisfied sexually. Apparently, the greater commitment to marriage and greater trust and respect between partners who were going together more than offset the frustration that they experienced in the sexual area. If we were to hold constant differences in marriage intentions, trust, and respect and look simply at the effects of living together, presumably moving in would bring most couples a net increase in their overall satisfaction.

Personal Growth

Regardless of whether a particular experience of living together succeeds or fails, people rarely regret having tried it and almost always say they would do it again if they had their lives to live over again. This enthusiasm reflects the conviction of the participants that they have learned from the experience. Problems may be painful but they also are a source of growth. Many persons who have lived together without being married recommend this experience to their friends.

At Cornell, 91 percent rated their experience as either maturing or very maturing, and no one described it as "not at all maturing" (Macklin, 1974). No one, similarly, found it a detrimental experience, no matter how painful it may have been.

Macklin asked her respondents to specify how they had grown. Ninety-six percent felt they had learned more about what is involved in a one-to-one relationship. Almost as many (94 percent) felt they had learned more about themselves individually through the feedback that came from living with someone else. Eighty percent or more felt they had gained in self-confidence, emotional maturity, ability to understand and relate to others, and insight into the opposite sex.

For most participants, living together stretches them personally and increases their ability to interact with others in intimate situations.

A Test of Marital Compatibility

Even though most students who live together are not very marriage oriented, one byproduct of living together is the discovery that they would (or would not) like to marry the partner. Living together is a quasi-marital experience, a preview of what marriage would be like.

Persons who have never lived together unmarried may question whether this is a necessary prelude to marriage, but most of those who have lived together would never risk marrying anyone without pretesting the relationship in this way. More than half the Texas cohabitants (Shuttlesworth and Thorman, 1973) and more than three-fourths of the Cornell cohabitants (Macklin, 1974) say that they would never marry anyone without living with the person first.

For couples whose love is intense enough, living together may not be indispensable. For those in doubt, it may resolve those doubts one way or the other. Presumably, living together unmarried weeds out incompatible combinations that would otherwise end in divorce. And since getting a divorce entails more grief and expense than ending a cohabiting relationship, that is a net gain. But if this testing is to be effective, couples must have both the personal toughness and the social freedom to terminate relationships that don't pass the test. As Macklin says (1975):

> If cohabitation is to serve as an important screening device in the courtship process, it will be essential that external social forces not press the couple into a premature decision to marry, and that continuation of the relationship not be seen as a major criterion of its success or value.

THE CONSEQUENCES OF BEING UNMARRIED RATHER THAN MARRIED

If two people are living together, what difference does it make whether they are married or not? This is not an easy question to answer, but it is one with which we must struggle.

Reasons for Not Marrying (Yet)

One way of looking at this question is to ask cohabiting persons why they didn't get married. For most students who are living together, the answer reflects their conviction that getting married is a more serious undertaking than simply living together.

At Cornell more than three-quarters of the students who were living together hadn't even considered the possibility of getting married (Macklin, 1974). This was chiefly because they didn't feel ready to commit themselves to a long-term, full-fledged marital relationship. Living together is a here-and-now affair that can be entered into without calculating its long-term implications. Getting married is a bigger step that involves merging one's life more fully with another's, and thinking about the possibility of having children. Persons who drift into living together without clear-cut goals are not ready for such momentous decisions.

A second major reason for not getting married is uncertainty about the particular partner. Most participants in campus cohabitation have not gone together long enough or lived together long enough to be sure they want to marry. Consciously or unconsciously, they are still engaged in the process of finding out whether their relationship is worth cementing in marriage. They enjoy living together for the present but are not sure whether they want to live together "for always." So it would be premature to marry the person this early in the development of their relationship.

Many nonstudents feel the same way. They are more or less monogamous, committed to a primary relationship, and feel more permanence and security than if they were not living together. But they are not sure they want to commit themselves to a long-term relationship and are not ready to take on the responsibility of having children.

The Presumed Costs of Marrying.   Some people believe that getting married might be detrimental to their relationship. This belief is especially common for persons whose own parents were unhappily married, who believe that getting married might somehow propel them into the same unhappiness. At the University of Texas, a majority of Shuttlesworth and Thorman's respondents (1973: 13–14) felt were better off living together unmarried than married:

> Although marriage might in some instances be agreed upon for practical reasons (such as parental approval), the majority of the couples in our sample believed that the voluntary, spontaneous aspects of their relationships would suffer greatly once they entered into a legal marriage. Students who are living together unmarried not only question the need for a legalized relationship. They also look upon marriage as a rather poor substitute for cohabitation.

Hennon (1975) found that cohabiting couples felt their relationship was "freer" than if they had been married. They worked harder at keeping their relationship viable because they could not take as much for granted. He noted, however, that if such couples were to live together for a long time, their relationship might suffer some of the same taken-for-grantedness that couples who have been married equally long experience. But as long as a relationship lacks security, it correspondingly needs and benefits from constant attention.

Johnson (1969) found that cohabiting couples in Iowa City were more equalitarian both in their decision making and in their division of labor than were married couples. He attributed this to the lack of commitment in the nonmarried relationship. Couples who got married began to specialize in their division of labor and, to a lesser extent, turned decision making over to the person most concerned about the issue. For persons who prize equalitarianism, such changes are feared and seem reason enough not to get married.

Antimarriage attitudes are held by many persons in the women's movement. They believe that getting married inevitably means surrendering to male dominance and oppression. Thorman (1973) quotes a graduate student at Texas:

> I just can't imagine myself in the role of a wife, and that is one reason I am much happier just living with Al without any thought of getting married. This image of myself is part of my idea of what I think of as equality of the sexes. As long as I am not anybody's wife, and don't have to be identified as anybody's possession, I can feel that I am an equal partner in a relationship with men. If I am identified as someone's wife, I lose that sense of independence and equality which is so important to me.

Many cohabiting couples fear that marriage would result in a loss of personal identity. Keaough (1975) interviewed a couple who had decided not to get married because, "We'd no longer be separate people. We'd be 'The Danforths.'" A second woman in her sample had been married and found it unsatisfactory so she divorced her husband and lived happily with him unmarried:

> I feel concern for him but I don't feel obligated to him. I don't want anyone to be responsible for my life and I don't want to be responsible for anyone else's.... In marriage I ceased to be me and became his wife. Our marriage died but the relationship lived—that's the best thing that came out of the divorce.

This case shows that in a particular case getting married can alter a relationship for the worse. But that doesn't happen automatically. It happens only when couples believe it is inevitable and fail to take responsibility for making their marriage the way they wish it to be. Those couples who know what they want can make their marriage just as equalitarian as they like and can share their household tasks as much as they like. No matter how much the average marriage may become taken for granted or specialized, such tendencies can be counteracted by couples who are prepared to work at making their marriages grow year in and year out.

Social Repercussions of Living Together Unmarried

Pioneers in any deviant behavior are likely to experience some harassment from the establishment. But as that behavior becomes more widespread, discrimination and persecution will gradually disappear.

In the early days of cohabitation, students were expelled from college, thrown out of apartments, and otherwise harassed. But as the general public became more used to the idea of people living together without being married, they ceased such punitive behavior. At Cornell, Macklin

(1974) found that only 6 percent of cohabiting students had ever experienced any negative reactions from landlords, employers, or other functionaries. A slightly larger number (8 percent) had experienced disapproval from other students, but these negative reactions were almost always to the partner chosen rather than to cohabitation as a life-style.

Despite the fact that negative social repercussions are rare, the fact that they occur at all contrasts with the positive attitude of society toward marriage. Some people are criticized for marrying too young, for marrying in haste, or for marrying the wrong person, but marriage as such is highly esteemed whereas living together unmarried is seldom praised and at best tolerated. In that sense, cohabitation lacks the social support that marriage receives.

Parents.   Toleration by outsiders is based on the belief that what couples do with their "private lives" is none of the outsiders' business. Parents, however, are another matter.

Parents have traditionally felt responsible for seeing that their children get off to a good start in life educationally, vocationally, and maritally. The liberation movement has diminished parental control as some young people have dropped out of college, adopted counterculture lifestyles, and joined the sexual revolution. Nevertheless, both generations continue to feel more sensitive to one another's behavior in the affectional-sexual-marital area than in any other, partly because this is the area where the parents' own relationship provides a model—good or bad— for their children. For children to experiment with new ways of relating that their parents never experienced creates problems for many parents:

> I know my parents are threatened by our living this way. If we are right, then they must be wrong, they seem to say, Why can't they relate their way and we ours without getting all entangled in who is right? Their identity as good parents in the eyes of relatives and friends seems to be threatened by our failure to meet their expectations. They "failed" and we are to blame! I feel their enormous resentment and wonder if our sticking it out is worth it.

Some couples eventually yield to parental pressure to marry, caring more for the continuation of family ties than for preserving the nonform of their quasi-marriage.

Some of the resistance from parents comes from having no adequate or socially acceptable names for the partner of their son or daughter:

> After three years of their living together and our increasing love for her, I began calling Jean my "daughter-in-love." It seemed good because it carried with it the connotation of my love and acceptance of their relationship. But some of my family and friends were horrified and made

> *it hard, telling me that we have been too permissive. My term lost its magic. Now I refer to her as my son's "woman" and that sounds awful. I refuse to call her my son's "lover."*

A large proportion of persons who live together unmarried react to this problem by concealing their behavior from their parents. Four-fifths of the Cornell students (Macklin, 1974) had engaged in such deception, and many of them had felt sorry or guilty about it.

A small minority of cohabitants deliberately tell their parents about their partnerships (presumably, those who feel most confident that their parents will accept or at least respect their behavior). Other parents accidentally discover the truth that their children have attempted to hide from them. What are the reactions of parents who learn of their children's cohabitation?

At the City University of New York (Arafat and Yorburg, 1973), over half of the parents disapproved of the cohabitation although a sizable minority (36 percent) were tolerantly neutral. At Cornell, parents who knew about the cohabitation were more often tolerant (about half), but 30 percent of those who knew not only strongly disapproved but tried to terminate the arrangement. Thus, the parents of these students caused their children considerable stress, and we may conclude that most of the students who attempted to hide their relationship from their parents were correct in predicting that their parents would view the unorthodox living arrangement with disfavor. However, there are exceptions, and we are among them:

> *Though it took some time to adjust, I [Margaret] can say now from middle-age viewing that I am glad my sons choose to live with their women friends as they test the goodness of the relationship. I keep saying to [Bob] their father: "How did we dare take the step of life-long commitment to each other based on such slim knowledge of each other?" Because we were unaware of any other way. We didn't know we didn't know each other. I like the testing now in everyday living—the sharing economically, the having to live with the everyday irritations, the ups and downs of life—that my children are doing before they decide to get married.*

If pregnancy occurs, parental support and advice are needed, but some couples feel that even this is their own private matter. They may decide to have the baby without marriage and without advice. Since most couples have abortions, parental dismay may be even more fierce when grandchildren are born than for the more familiar living together:

> *Few of my friends have been spared the ordeal we went through when our children began to live with their special partners, preferring not to marry, so I don't feel that different from other parents in my generation.*

I learned to grin and bear it. But the coming of a baby has been something else!

Keiser (1974) found that cohabiting couples at Southern Illinois University seldom had any clear-cut agreement as to what would happen if the woman were to get pregnant. Despite our general sympathy with the idea of cohabitation, we as parents and grandparents are dismayed at the way so many members of our children's generation have failed to face the pregnancy issue until after they have been forcefully confronted by an actual conception.

Friends. Although parents seldom provide emotional support for children who live with someone of the opposite sex, friends are more supportive. Partly this is a selective matter. Persons who live together unmarried are apt to know others who have done the same.

Despite the fact that friends provide some support for cohabiting students, Table 4–3 shows that such support is less extensive than that which comes with marriage. This is partly because living together unmarried is less visible, so fewer people know about it, and partly because unmarried couples conceal their cohabitation from parents. It also reflects the fact that our society puts its full weight on the side of the lifelong continuation of marriage, whereas there is no corresponding norm predisposing onlookers to disapprove of the ending of a cohabitation. In any case, one difference between living together unmarried and getting married is that marriages receive widespread external support to buttress the relationship when the going gets tough and to applaud it when the relationship goes well. On the whole, then, living together unmarried gets a mixture of support from friends and hostility from parents, whereas staying married gets support from all quarters.

Table 4–3 Personal Support for Cohabitation and for Marriage, for Men and Women

Number of Significant Others Who Would Dis- approve Termination	MEN		WOMEN	
	Cohabiting	Married	Cohabiting	Married
Under five persons	89%	26%	100%	42%
Five or more persons	10	74	0	58
Total	99%	100%	100%	100%
Number of cases	19	19	19	19

Adapted from Johnson, 1973: 402. *Source:* Matched samples of cohabiting and married student couples at the University of Iowa. Percentages refer to the number of persons "whose opinions were important to the respondent, knew about the relationship, and would disapprove of its termination."

The Adequacy of Improvised Residences

Some of the differences between living together and being married reflect the fact that married couples normally establish their own home (apart from other people) and equip it for comfortable living. Many couples who drift into living together unmarried have neither the privacy nor the equipment for living comfortably.

Privacy.   We have already seen in Table 4–2 that a majority of the Cornell women students complained of a lack of privacy and that 23 percent reported that they had been in conflict with persons living in their apartment. Usually those persons were the man's old apartment mates. While the man may have chosen friends to share his apartment, the woman usually came in later and had no voice in selecting her extra living companions.

At Penn State, 60 percent of the cohabiting students lived with third parties (Peterman et al., 1974). Some of these "outsiders" shared not only the same apartment but the same room. No wonder privacy is a problem!

Macklin (1974) gives more detailed statistics from Cornell about living arrangements: 60 percent shared an apartment with outsiders. Another 20 percent lived together in a dormitory room that must have been either a single, too small for two people, or a larger room shared with a third party. Another 10 percent lived together in a fraternity house, where they may have had a bedroom of their own but shared their meals with a large group of men. Only 15 percent of Macklin's respondents had the good fortune to live alone as a couple in an off-campus setting. Whereas living alone is the normal housing arrangement for married couples, these unmarried couples were cohabiting under inauspicious circumstances. This is another sense in which many unmarried student couples lack the institutional support from which married couples benefit.

Equipment.   We know less about the facilities that these couples have for living together, although we can infer their inadequacy from their makeshift character.

Whereas married couples normally establish a household in which they expect to stay for some time, unmarried couples frequently don't know how long they will be together and whether it would be worthwhile to invest in the equipment for joint living. When married couples move to another location, they take their equipment with them, whereas unmarried couples often break up at the end of a school year or when one partner takes a job elsewhere.

Married couples usually pool their finances and seldom worry about who owns what (until they get a divorce). Unmarried couples frequently keep their finances separate (Macklin, 1974), and therefore are not comfortable with combining their financial resources to purchase major furnishings and equipment that would have to be parceled out if and when they come to a parting of the ways.

For such reasons, unmarried couples tend to make do as best they can with equipment that was frequently intended to serve an individual rather than a couple or to serve the original apartment mates minus the interloper. Many couples find their housekeeping activities handicapped by inadequate equipment, their sleeping by too narrow a bed, and their personal belongings cluttered as a result of inadequate storage space. These deficiencies make life more difficult for the couple themselves and intensify the conflict with any extra persons with whom they may be living.

The Adequacy of Improvised Relationships

To live in crowded, ill-furnished quarters is bad enough, but living together often suffers from intrinsic deficiencies in the relationship itself. These deficiencies have to do with the very fact that the couple are unmarried and ipso facto less committed to each other than married couples. This lack of commitment has two facets: the partners hold back on merging their lives together, and they hold themselves open to the possibility of terminating their relationship.

Partial Commitment.   We have already seen that unmarried couples frequently hold back from pooling their finances and from equipping themselves with adequate living quarters. Such practical deficiencies are symptoms of a lack of commitment to their relationship.

Table 4–4 shows how much less committed the unmarried couples at the University of Iowa were than a matched group of married couples. The difference was especially marked between the two sets of men. This means not only that the cohabiting couples were less committed to each other than the married couples were, but that the former faced the added problem of differential commitment. The strain on a relationship would be less if both partners were equally uncommitted to it. But when the woman strongly desires to stay with the man and the man is less sure, she is likely to put pressure on her resistant partner and/or to feel unhappily insecure.

Another expression of partial commitment is that more cohabiting than married persons in the Iowa sample sometimes wished they had not become so involved (Johnson, 1969). This comes as no surprise in view of the casualness with which many unmarried couples drift into living together. Wishing they hadn't moved in together is reminiscent of the feelings of being trapped that we saw in Table 4–2. These feelings reflect an uncertainty about the relationship that reflect its half-grown, not yet matured, quality in contrast with the ripeness of most marriages.

Table 4–4   Commitment to Cohabitation and to Marriage, for Men and Women

Strength of Desire to Stay Together at Least Five Years	MEN		WOMEN	
	Cohabiting	Married	Cohabiting	Married
Very strong	32%	78%	63%	89%
Intermediate	16	22	0	5
Fairly strong	16	0	5	5
Intermediate	0	0	0	0
Not at all strong (wish to stay together less than five years)	37	0	32	0
Total	101%	100%	100%	99%
Number of cases	19	18	19	19

Adapted from Johnson, 1973: 401. *Source:* Matched samples of cohabiting and married student couples at the University of Iowa.

For some unmarried couples, lack of commitment feels like an advantage:

> *We like the independence we feel in living together which is the opposite of "settling down." Physically, too, we are less settled and for us that's an advantage because it means keeping our lives free of material clutter. There are fewer conveniences and less space for privacy but for right now we can live with that. We take breaks from each other but with the intent of coming back. These breaks are tests of how much we want to come back.*

Freedom to Leave.   Paradoxically, cohabiting couples not only are more apt to feel trapped in their relationship, but are also more likely to emphasize their freedom to terminate that relationship. This doesn't mean that breaking up is necessarily easy. It may be easier to move out of an unmarried relationship than it is to get a divorce. But some couples who have lived together for quite a while still find it hard to disentangle their lives when they wish to do so. It is more difficult to break up housekeeping than to stop going together. All the latter takes is not initiating the next date. Ending cohabitation requires the more drastic step of moving out. For indecisive persons whose cohabitation grew by an accretion of tiny steps, moving out may seem starkly abrupt. Fortunately for college students caught in unwanted arrangements, there is always the end of the school year or the end of college itself, when breaking up can happen relatively easily.

The end of cohabitation is easier than ending a marriage because

cohabitation involves less complex interdependencies and fewer for-
malities. The less two people have merged their lives together, the more
easily they may separate. The less they have informed their friends and
relatives of their commitment, the less embarrassment in breaking up. The
less they expected to be together on a long-term basis, the less disappointment when the relationship ends. And the informality of living together
unmarried saves the cost in time and money of employing lawyers and going
to court to certify that they don't want to live together any longer.

To be free to leave relatively painlessly feels good when one wishes
to leave. But to a partner who wants to stay, the other person's freedom to
leave causes insecurity. Every freedom has its cost, and the price tag on
freedom to leave is insecurity in the relationship. Keiser (1974) found that
while some couples found the freedom to terminate advantageous, others
found that it made it "too easy to walk out."

One cohabitant found both advantages and disadvantages in this
looseness of commitment:

> With no long-term commitment we focus on the here and now. We
> are forced to deal with our problems regularly. And yet if you ask me if I
> feel secure, the answer is "no."

One couple who lived together for eight months before marriage recalled
the period as "too intense, too wearing" and found it a relief not to be so
constantly conscious of how they were feeling and whether they should
or should not stay together. The husband said, "I found tremendous security in the decisiveness of being married."

Sexual Exclusivity.   The very insecurity of living together unmarried may
account for the fact that most unmarried couples are sexually exclusive
despite the fact that their ideology tends to advocate sexual freedom.

Montgomery (1973) found that "a large percentage of cohabitants . . .
believed that extra-cohabitant sexual activity should be allowed." Similarly, Thorman (1973) found that cohabiting students openly advocated
freedom to "pursue outside sexual interests." Theoretically, sexual freedom is consonant with the radicalism of living together without being
married. Yet, in practice, few unmarried couples have outside sexual
relationships. At the University of Massachusetts, Montgomery found
only 5 out of 62 persons who had had outside sexual experiences while
they were living together. At the University of Iowa, 39 percent of the men
and 27 percent of the women in Johnson's sample (1975) had been sexually involved with outside partners, but a majority of both sexes were
committed to a personal policy of sexual exclusiveness, and a sizable
minority expected their partners to be similarly exclusive. The strength of
this dedication to exclusivity was evidenced by the fact that 25 percent of
the men and 51 percent of the women had had opportunities for outside
sexual involvements that they had refused. These data show that sexual

exclusivity rather than sexual freedom is what cohabiting couples generally practice. Presumably, their relationship is so new and fragile that external involvements would be threatening. Thorman (1973) quotes a woman cohabitant:

> I think that intellectually I'm very broadminded and accept Tom's statement that we are free to have sex with someone if that is what we want. I don't know if I would be really able to accept that emotionally. I think it would really shake me up pretty much. And I think Tom would really care if I had a strong personal or sexual interest or relationship with another man. We both have our friends—he has girlfriends and I have boyfriends—but it ends there. No real involvement with dating or sexual relationships. When we started living together we just sort of automatically came to the point where sex is just between the two of us.

Note that this couple did not make a decision in favor of sexual exclusivity. Indeed, their supposed policy was sexual openness. Yet, in practice, they limited their sexual activity to one another. Their relationship was too new and their energies too absorbed in building that relationship to be able to cope with the complexities of relating to others at the same time.

This concentration of sexual energy within a new relationship is not unique to unmarried couples, but characterizes newly married couples as well. Jessie Bernard (1972) noted that newlyweds unsure of the permanence of their relationship tended to hold one another to sexual exclusivity. So it matters little whether couples are living together married or unmarried—as long as their relationship is relatively new, they concentrate their energies on building that relationship. The diversions of energy and the strains of jealousy created by outside relationships would be too threatening to core relationships that have not yet become firmly established. The difference between married couples and unmarried ones is that the latter are generally even less well established and therefore would probably be even more damaged by outside involvements.

Living together unmarried, then, tends to be less secure than being married—both because the partners have committed themselves less fully to each other and because they have kept their options open in terms of greater freedom to leave. Were they to widen those options even further by experimenting with alternative partners while living in such a fragile structure, the relationship would risk collapse. Few couples choose to take that risk.

Shared Housework?   One reason some couples choose to live together instead of getting married is in the hope that they can avoid falling into traditional gender roles in the division of labor. Stafford (1975) compared married and cohabiting couples at the University of Nevada and found that women did most of the housework regardless of whether they were married or not. But some marginal differences appeared between the two sets of couples. Men and women who were living together unmarried more often performed chores that have been traditionally linked to the opposite sex than did those who were married. And only a minority of either group shared particular tasks equally, although the size of that minority was larger among the cohabiting students. Out of eighteen household tasks, Stafford found that roughly three-quarters were shared equally by more cohabiting than married students. This does not prove that the lack of being married was the cause. The married couples had been married four years on the average, whereas the cohabiting students had been living together only one year. We will see in Chapter 12 that the division of labor tends to become more traditional and more specialized the longer a couple live together. So, living together without being married may be fragile protection against falling into a sexist division of household tasks.

THE OUTCOME OF LIVING TOGETHER UNMARRIED

Few couples go on living together indefinitely. Either they get married or they break up before too many months go by.

Getting Married

What proportion of couples who start living together eventually get married? How long do they live together before they formalize their relationship? And are their marriages any different in quality because they lived together beforehand?

These are the crucial questions about the consequences of living together unmarried. Unfortunately, we have very few answers. Living together unmarried is too new for us to have been able to discover the long-range consequences. And longitudinal research is too difficult for most researchers. Someday we will have definite answers. In the meantime, we can do little more than speculate.

The Incidence of Marriage.   We already know that most college students who live together have not decided whether they want to marry each other. Living together is an opportunity to try out the relationship and discover whether the problems are so severe that marriage would be inadvisable. From this point of view, living together reduces the probability that incompatible couples will marry.

On the other hand, persons who are afraid to marry sometimes find their readiness for marriage increased by living together successfully. This is particularly useful for persons who have already failed in marriage. Berger (1974) studied couples who began living together after graduation from college. She found that persons who had previously been through a divorce or who worried about marriage in general felt reassured by their success in living together and became more willing to get married than they would have been otherwise.

We do not know what proportion of all the persons who ever start living together end up marrying each other. We know that the vast majority of couples who ever go together do not marry. We will see in a later chapter that a substantial minority of all couples who get engaged do not marry. Living together falls in between. In terms of commitment, it is similar to going steady. And, since most steady couples do not marry, it seems safe to assume that most couples who start living together won't marry either. However, for any particular couple, the chances of getting married may be better than fifty-fifty—the greater their commitment to one another, the more marriagelike their living pattern, the older they are, and so on.

The Interval to Marriage.   Both Berger (1974) and Rosenblatt and Stevenson (1973) found that married couples who lived together prior to marriage had generally done so for about a year. That is roughly the length of the average American engagement. Presumably, a year is long enough to find out whether two people are compatible. If they live together much longer than that and fail to get married, it may mean either that they are too turned off to the marriage system ever to want to marry anyone or that they are too turned off to each other. For such reasons, the proportion of couples ever marrying probably declines for those who live together for more than one year. At the other end of the time span, we know that many couples break up soon after moving in together (just as more marriages break up in the first year than in any later year). Perhaps somewhere around a year is an optimal period for couples to live together and then move on into marriage. But the reader will recognize that this is almost pure speculation at this early stage in the research game.

The Quality of Marriage.   We know very little about how the marriages of cohabiting couples compare with those of persons who do not live together until after they get married. The safest assumption is that patterns worked out during cohabitation tend to persist after marriage (Berger, 1974). Insofar as cohabiting couples are equalitarian in their decision making and financially independent of one another, these patterns may persist after marriage. Since women living with a man outside of marriage do not adopt his surname, they may be less apt to surrender their maiden name when they do get married. In such respects, postcohabitation married couples may be more "liberated" than others.

Whether there are lingering effects of the insecurity of improvised relationships and whether that insecurity results in more dynamic, aware marriages or more brittle marriages we don't know. The experiment of living together and then marrying is still being carried on in the laboratory of American society, and the results of that experiment are just beginning to come in. So far, the results are inconclusive. Olday (1976) compared married students at Washington State University who had lived together before marriage with those who had not and found no difference in marital satisfaction, husband-wife conflict, or equalitarianism. The only difference was that couples who had lived together married about seven months later (in terms of age at marriage) than those who had not. This suggests that it made no difference for these student couples whether they were married or not—the only difference lay in being labeled married or in living together without the label. Similarly, Gross (1976) concluded from interviewing couples in San Francisco: "In general, I've learned that all couples living together in an intimate relationship, whether married or not, share many of the same day-to-day experiences."

Nevertheless, insofar as couples have delayed marriage and lived together unmarried because they wish to forge a different type of relationship, that experimentation seems likely to accelerate the trend from traditional marriage to the marriage of the future—more open, more equalitarian, more shared, more independent.

Getting "Divorced"

If it is true that most experiments in cohabitation end in terminating the relationship, do the participants view those experiments as failures? Most divorced persons think of their marriages as having failed. Yet most of them are eager to marry again and actually do. So even though the particular marriage failed, the system of marriage is not rejected.

For ex-cohabitants, similarly, the experience may have been painful, and yet few persons who try living together wish they hadn't. Macklin (1972) found that more than 60 percent of her Cornell women would live with the same person again if they had their life to live over, even in the case of relationships that had already broken up.

We have seen the benefits that the participants felt they had gained from living together. These benefits are not limited to relationships that result in marriage or even to relationships that last a long time. Even when living together ends in an early "divorce," there is much to be learned in the process.

"Remarriage" with a New Partner

Just as most divorced men and women seek and find a new partner so that they can try again to have a successful marriage, most unmarried persons who split up go on to live with a new partner. We have seen that most people who have cohabited outside of marriage feel that they would not want to marry anyone without pretesting that relationship. Since most ex-cohabitants marry someone eventually, this requires them to have at least one more experience of living together prior to marriage.

For college students not yet ready to marry anyone, repetitive experiences are common, especially when the definition of cohabiting is loose enough to cover short-term experiences. At Penn State, where Peterman et al., (1974) asked simply "Have you ever lived with (eating, sleeping, socializing at the same residence) someone of the opposite sex?", half the students who had ever lived with at least one person had already had that experience with more than one partner. For half the men and almost a third of the women, these experiences lasted less than a month. Two-thirds of the repeaters had not stayed with any of their partners for more than three months. College campuses lend themselves to brief trial-and-error experiences of cohabitation. As living together unmarried becomes more common, the typical American may live with several different persons before finally settling down to marriage with one. By that time marriages too may typically come in series. If so, we can be sure that the interval between marriages will be devoted to further cohabitation to test each subsequent marriage.

As of this writing, we are a long way from a general pattern of premarital living together, but the trend of our society is in that direction. Presumably, the consequences of that trend depend more on how humane those experiences are rather than on the fact that people do or do not cohabit in and of itself.

5 Choosing a Marriage Partner

Marriage is one of the three great events in life—along with birth and death. Birth just happens, and death is largely beyond our control. Marriage, however, can be influenced more actively. We can decide whom to marry and when to marry. The crucial decision is the first.

In a society where so many marriages fail, marriage counselors often see troubled couples too late to help them. If they had never married in the first place, they would have been spared much grief. If they had been better matched, they would have experienced a richer life together. The marriage die is cast largely in the process of mate selection.

THE NATURE OF COMPATIBILITY

Compatibility is the extent to which a couple's intrinsic characteristics fit together. Countless dimensions of compatibility could be discussed. In this chapter we have selected *personal* compatibility in temperament, needs, and values. Questions of *social* compatibility are reserved for Chapter 6.

Temperamental Compatibility

By temperament we mean the individual's physiological activity level and response pattern. Little research has been done on constitutional factors in mate selection and marital success. However, Wallace (1960) has pointed out that the behavior-controlling glands of one normal individual may be five to ten times more active than those of another. He believes that:

> such biological differences help to explain many of the common prob-
> lems and conflicts in mating and marriage: why one spouse is always
> active—bubbling with excess energy—and the other is inactive, quiet,
> and phlegmatic; why one spouse can't get going until late afternoon
> and doesn't want to go to bed before midnight, and the other works
> best in the morning and likes to go to bed early; why one partner wants
> sexual intercourse daily, or twice daily, and the other finds weekly or
> even monthly intercourse adequate.

Differences in energy level are predictable in marriages between partners of different ages. The older partner is likely to have less energy—to be less interested than the younger one in mountain climbing, tennis, or having children. Individuals of the same age may also differ in their responsiveness to stimulation. Some people are nervous and excita-ble, irritated by the slightest discomfort or distraction. Others are calm and even-tempered under provocation. Some lash out angrily at their environment while others retreat into silence that lasts for days.

Temperamental differences create rifts, test the individual's ability to empathize, and are bridged only by substantial effort. If he is forever cool, objective, and rational and she forever emotional, he may become increasingly irritated by her outbursts and she may hoard up increasing resentment because he never shares his feelings.

Compatibility of Needs

All animals have physical needs, especially for food and sex. The under-lying goal of both needs is tension reduction, to assuage hunger pangs or release sexual tension. But psychological conditioning endows these physical drives with secondary emotional pleasures and anticipations. In growing up, human beings acquire other needs that have nothing to do with biological requirements. Through reward and punishment they come to value persons and activities as sources of psychological pleasure and anxiety reduction. Because parents are the chief agents of reward and punishment, they are the primary sources of social needs.

Much learning occurs so early in childhood that needs are largely unconscious. They can be raised to consciousness by developing insight. The more aware an individual is of his/her needs, the more intelligently s/he can choose a marriage partner. Hidden needs are difficult to recog-nize when masked by reaction formations. The son of an overprotective mother may need to be submissive. Men, however, are not supposed to be submissive, so he may react in the opposite direction with strenuous attempts to dominate. Similarly, a woman with an underlying need to dominate may react with studied submissiveness.

When conscious needs camouflage unconscious ones, successful mate selection is difficult. For example, a reactively domineering man is likely to choose a submissive wife who will fail to meet his hidden dependency needs.

Having noted the complexities caused by unconscious needs and reaction formations, we will henceforth ignore them.

For the sake of simplicity, we will deal with needs as if they were always conscious and direct.

Complementary Needs.   In complementary areas, opposites attract. The most important complementary needs involve *dominance* and *submissiveness* (Winch, 1958). If I need to dominate, I will tend to marry someone who needs to be submissive. The more dominant I am, the more submissive my partner should be:

> *I need someone to check my impulsiveness. I can never say no or refuse a favor. Besides, I overestimate my physical capacities. Consequently, I am always trying to do too many things at one time, and I end up running around in circles, not knowing which way to turn. Les is always able to straighten me out and help me find the right direction. I depend on his ability to extricate me from my own maneuverings. I wouldn't be surprised if he gets a kick out of straightening me out too.*

This wife's submissiveness got her into outside-the-family troubles that her husband resolved through his own forcefulness. He derived a sense of accomplishment from her dependence on him. This combination of dominant husband and submissive wife was once the prescribed pattern.

What about a man who needs to be submissive? An an individual, he needs a domineering wife. Yet if he marries such a woman he will be called "henpecked." When personal needs and social pressures conflict, marriages are less happy than when personal needs fit social expectations (Blood and Wolfe, 1960). Nevertheless, compatible needs may be more important than social pressure for those who are forced to choose between them.

If both marriage partners need to dominate, the result is explosive. As each seeks to dominate, competition breaks into open conflict. Instead of meeting each other's needs, the partners vie for top position. Perennial conflict results:

> *I wish my wife would leave the store alone. She keeps coming over and acting like she owns the place. Unfortunately right now the business is incorporated in both our names which she uses as an excuse to meddle in it. When I suggested that it be put in my name only, she accused me of trying to put something over on her. I've tried to get her to sign an*

agreement that she won't come over the the store any more, but she won't do that either.

When both partners need to be submissive, the relationship may be equally frustrating, though less dramatic. If neither partner is able to make decisions or to provide warmth and reassurance, the marriage will be hollow and disquieting.

When both partners are dominant or both submissive, each partner seeks what the other cannot give. Competitive marriages frustrate both participants.

One clue to dominance and submissiveness is the partners' birth order in relation to their siblings. First-born children tend to be dominant and last-born children to be submissive. For this reason, first-born children are most apt to be compatible with last-born children, whereas if they marry other first-born children they are likely to be involved in competition for dominance.

Kemper (1966) found that business executives with the happiest marriages had chosen wives who duplicated their childhood sibling structure: oldest sons married to youngest daughters or youngest sons married to oldest daughters. Contrastingly, oldest sons married to oldest daughters apparently fought for top position while youngest sons paired with youngest daughters were reciprocally disappointed by the other's spinelessness.

Table 5–1 reveals a similar finding: married women in Israel reported reactions to their husbands that reflected their comparative birth order. Complementary marriages between first-born husbands and last-born wives or vice versa were the happiest. Conversely, competitive marriages between two oldest, youngest, or only children were unsatisfactory. The authors commented that middle children seemed to be remarkably adjustable and hence had satisfactory marriages no matter whom they married. But for first-born, last-born, or only children, the person they married mattered a great deal.

Table 5–1   Marital Adjustment, by Birth Order of Spouse

	BIRTH ORDER					
	Oldest and Youngest	Middle and Any	Oldest and Only	Oldest and Oldest	Youngest and Youngest	Only and Only
Marital adjustment	32.7	31.3	25.3	17.0	16.7	16.4
Number of cases	67	29	32	42	29	37

Adapted from Weller, Natan, and Hazi, 1974: 796. *Source:* Married women attending cooking, sewing, home economics, and cosmetics classes in Tel Aviv, Israel.

So far we have assumed that people are either dominant or submissive. But most people are neither. They fall somewhere in the middle. Rather than wishing to dominate or be dominated, they prefer to give and take in a fifty-fifty relationship. Hence they need similarly equalitarian spouses.

Complementarity applies to several other needs: for instance, *nurturance* and *succorance*. Some individuals need to nurture others: "to give sympathy and aid to a weak, helpless, ill, or dejected person" (Winch, 1958). Others have the complementary need for succorance: "to be helped by a sympathetic person; to be nursed, loved, protected, indulged." A man with a strong need to nurture would be compatible with a wife with a corresponding need to receive succorance. However, the average man and woman are capable of both nurturing and being nurtured.

A third pair of complementary needs is *deference* and *recognition*. An individual who needs to admire and praise others would enjoy being married to someone with a corresponding need to "excite the admiration and approval of others" (Winch, 1958). Perhaps because of the masking effect of conventional roles in early dating, Kerckhoff and Davis (1962) found that complementary needs did not affect couples in their first 18 months of dating. However, couples subsequently moved closer to marriage who were complementary in their needs (1) to control versus to be controlled, (2) to include others versus to be included in activities, and (3) to give affection versus to receive affection.

Opposite traits and needs may serve as a model for the partner to emulate. As each respects the other's contribution, opposites may flow into a satisfying mesh. So, in a sense, appreciation for the other is the primary compatibility. In our own marriage, Bob loved and needed my (Margaret's) warmth and enthusiasm. In time he overcame his cool, "unfeeling" detachment. I loved his calm, unruffled sureness and needed that in my life. He checked my impulsiveness, and in time I became more rational and objective, like him. We helped the underside of each other to develop.

Complementarity must be distinguished from contradiction. Some couples seize the label of complementarity and pin it on any difference between them. But if she is sociable and I am solitary, our needs are not complementary but conflicting. If she is obsessively thrifty and I am extravagantly generous, we will clash. If she is naively idealistic and I am prudishly practical, we may manage to compromise on some middle ground, but it won't be a *happy* medium. Such differences may be resolvable, but only by spending energy on them. In contrast, complementary needs fit so beautifully that they require no compromising. They are reciprocally and simultaneously satisfied.

Parallel Needs.　Complementary needs determine how partners treat each other. If marriage were the whole of life, these needs might be the only kind. But husbands and wives also participate in the outside world. Activities outside the family provide alternative sources of gratification. Needs that are not gratified by the partner can be met elsewhere. Indeed, some needs are more easily gratified outside the family than inside. For example, the need for achievement is measured in money, power, and prestige that can be gained only outside the home.

To be successful in his/her occupation, a person must invest time and energy there. As a result, family members may be neglected. What kind of partner would be ideal for an ambitious person? Are there individuals who would welcome a partner's success rather than feel neglected? Are there persons who would prefer an ambitious spouse to one who spent his/her spare time relaxing around the house? The spouse of an ambitious person needs to be success oriented him/herself. S/he doesn't have to engage in public affairs, but must get vicarious satisfaction from the partner's triumphs.

Opposite to the need for achievement is the need for affiliation (to be close to other persons). Sexual and affectional activities are valued by affiliative persons. They would rather invest their energies in making love than in making money. Compatibility for them consists primarily in their orientation toward interaction with the partner rather than with outsiders. But compatibility also consists in preferring a similar frequency of sexual activity. A couple may be equally internally oriented but incompatible because one partner wishes to have sex almost every night while the other would rather play pinochle. So compatibility requires not only a common inward/outward orientation but a common preference for a particular activity.

Normally we assume that a person with a strong need for affiliation will prize the partner's company and would feel neglected by an externally oriented spouse. But sometimes the desire for affiliation extends to others besides the spouse. Some persons wish to "affiliate" not only with the spouse but with others, in opposition to the traditional view that marriage is an exclusive relationship. For individuals who believe in an affectionally and/or sexually open marriage, finding a compatible partner who shares these views is especially important. Many persons can tolerate a vocationally ambitious spouse on the ground that the whole family benefits from his/her occupational success, but being married to someone who wants outside intimate relationships is difficult to cope with if one wishes to have that affection and/or sexuality all to oneself.

Multiple Needs.   So far we have discussed only one need at a time. But people have a variety of needs, and this variety complicates matchmaking. For example, a woman who needs to dominate and also desires upward mobility faces a quandary. Any man dependent enough to satisfy her need to dominate is not likely to be a successful breadwinner. So she must choose between her needs or compromise both of them.

Such choices are affected by the intensity of the various needs. The stronger the need, the more emphasis it deserves. On the other hand, marital compatibility may be less crucial for people with externally oriented needs than for those with marriage-oriented ones. The chief problem for an ambitious person is to choose the right corporation, not the right spouse. So the stronger and the more marriage oriented the need, the greater the importance of marital compatibility.

Since marriage is a reciprocal affair, compatibility has dual advantages. If my partner's needs are compatible with mine, not only will s/he be able to satisfy more of my needs, but I will be able to satisfy more of his/hers. If our marriage is to succeed, each of us must be able to meet the other's needs. The more compatible our needs, the more rewarding our relationship will be.

Early in our own marriage, our personality characteristics looked like this:

Bob:	**Margaret:**
Rational	Emotional
Objective, cool, feelings more hidden	Warm, impulsive
Not so intense	Intense
High energy, compulsive drive	Lower energy Needs more sleep Tires more quickly
Sharp, fast	Slower to react to mental tasks
Productive Efficient planner and programer Good at forethought	Ambivalent, indecisive Good at hindsight Good evaluator
Confident, dominant Oldest sibling	Agreeable, submissive Youngest sibling

Each of us was attracted to the other's characteristics as a balance to his/her own. Even though we occasionally rub each other the wrong way, on the whole we find these differences attractive and have gradually incorporated the other's good points in our own lives and mellowed in our initial characteristics.

Compatibility of Values

A value is a preference that affects choices among alternatives. Values come into play especially in allocating scarce resources. If my wife's values are the same as mine, we can easily decide how to spend our money and leisure time. But if she likes mink stoles and sports cars while I like rare books and stereo records, we will have a difficult time stretching our resources to satisfy both of us unless those resources are extraordinarily large. On the other hand, with modest tastes and reasonable funds, perhaps each of us can fulfill some of our preferences even if we don't like the same things.

Consensus in values is rewarding because each of us feels accepted by the other. Conversation flows more easily when values are similar. Encounter across divergences is stimulating and challenging, but perpetual debate may be too strenuous to be sustained for long and too dissonant with the solidarity expected of marriage.

For example, people differ in the importance they attach to conformity. For some individuals, the only way to feel right is to be impeccably dressed and to mirror the opinions of the establishment. For others, it is equally important to stand out from the crowd, to be proud of independence and nonconformity. Such diametrically opposite values clash so violently that the "man in the gray flannel suit" and the "hippie" are unlikely to date, much less marry:

> *If I want to do something and feel okay about it, I don't care what anybody else thinks. Peg is always thinking of our image, especially my image. I tell her she'd rather please all those others than please me!*

The values of "middle Americans" differ wholesale from those of persons who choose alternative life-styles. People who believe in the simple life may eschew modern conveniences and limit their earnings so drastically that they do not have to pay any income taxes for military purposes. Those people who live communally limit their devotion to their partner by their loyalty to an intentional community. For participants in the drug culture, psychedelic experience may be a primary use to which money and time are allocated. In such cases, compatibility of life-style becomes overwhelmingly important because it has such drastic ramifications. To marry across major differences in life-style would entail at least as much strain as any of the mixed marriages described in the next chapter.

Value consensus makes relationships more enjoyable from the very first date. After the computer-arranged dance at Iowa State, couples who saw eye to eye on the importance (or lack of importance) of dancing ability, campus popularity, fraternity membership, stylish clothes, and good looks (1) were most satisfied with each other and (2) found it easiest to talk to each other (Coombs, 1966).

Similarly, during the first eighteen months of dating, Duke University students moved closer to marriage if they held the same standard of family success—a respected place in the community, husband-wife companionship, healthy and happy children, or economic security (Kerckhoff and Davis, 1962).

Newcomb (1961) found that men students developed the closest friendships with peers who held the same opinions about sex, politics, religion, race, and other controversial issues. The greater the agreement on values, the more students were attracted to one another as they got better acquainted.

Husbands and wives do not need to agree on everything. No two people ever hold identical values or have identical interests. In their leisure time, husband and wife can go their separate ways in pursuit of divergent interests, provided that the values involved are not antithetical.

Incompatible Values.   The most severe incompatibility involves areas where differences are not allowable. For example, a church that defines itself as the only true religion creates value conflicts for members who enter mixed marriages (see Chapter 6). In contrast, religious differences between groups that tolerate each other cause less difficulty. Philosophies of life may be antithetical:

> *I am an optimist, a romanticist, and an idealist. I'm always willing to give people the benefit of the doubt. Thus I would be completely incompatible with a cynic or someone who is embittered and disillusioned with life. That's why I broke up with Frank. In the beginning I accepted his cynicism with a grain of salt. I felt it was probably a result of some disillusioning experience and that through example I could change his views. However, I came to realize that this wouldn't work because his cynicism touched on areas where I could exert no influence (for example, his business dealings). At first his attitude angered me (How could he be so jaded?). But gradually I began to feel sorry for him, in that I was in love with life and he wasn't. Pity, I came to realize, is no basis for love or marriage.*

Marital strain may arise not only from irreconcilable beliefs but also from preferences for different pair-structured activities. Mixed marriages, for example, involve not only different beliefs but different institutional memberships as well. My wife and I might have identical beliefs, but if she went to the First Church and I to the Second Church of the same denomination, we would both be frustrated.

How can a man entertain at home if his wife abhors the idea, or a woman dance with a husband who has no sense of rhythm? In the latter case, the husband can try to learn, but it would be naive to pretend that effort alone can produce compatibility in all areas. Couples whose interests and values coincide are fortunate.

TESTING FOR COMPATIBILITY

How can a couple find out how compatible they are? For those who grew up together from childhood the answer is easy:

> *Shirley's and my parents lived within three blocks of each other and our mothers wheeled their baby carriages together. (There is just one month's difference in our ages.) Both families attended the same church so that the two of us came up through Sunday school, catechism, and Luther League together. We also went to the same schools. Our families and friends took our courtship very much for granted and I guess maybe we did, too.*

Childhood friends know each other so well that no special testing is needed. Strangers, however, may fantasize compatibility where none really exists.

Self-deception

Finding the right person is complicated by the human penchant for wishful thinking. If a date seems attractive at first glance, imagination tends to fill in the missing details. Perhaps this is "the one." The less I know him/her, the easier it is to believe s/he is.

The more insecure the individual, the greater the need for idealizing the partner. An insecure person may crave security so much that s/he "finds" it in every date. While this illusion normally disappears with acquaintance, it sometimes persists for a remarkably long time. One woman talked herself into believing that her fiancé was about to set the wedding date, when in fact he was on the verge of breaking the engagement:

> *I know I'm constantly engaging in wishful thinking. I keep thinking things are going to be rosy again. Maybe the reason is because I was so much happier last year when we first fell in love than I am now. It felt real good to have someone who loved me and whom I loved.*

Newcomb (1961) found that some male students living in an off-campus house at the University of Michigan were more realistic than others. Those men with nonauthoritarian personalities were able to recognize value discrepancies when they encountered them and changed friends accordingly. But authoritarian students clung desperately to their first friends even after discovering that they were incompatible. They resolved the discrepancy by self-deception, overestimating their value consensus in order to salvage their relationships. The problem for marital compatibility testers is to decide whether to commit themselves to a permanent relationship. To resolve cognitive dissonance by self-deception is to beg the question.

Chamblis (1965) reported that friendship normally grows between people whose encounters are self-validating. Congruence between partners requires each to see the other in the way the other sees him/herself. To be overrated by the partner is uncomfortable. To have to live up to exaggerated expectations may be good for one's character, but it is too strenuous for friendship. The proverbial rose-colored glasses may create an illusion of love in the wearer, but they are likely to scare off the partner. How can self-deception be prevented and cured? That is the task of compatibility testing.

The Elements of Compatibility Testing

The more varied a couple's activities, the more thorough their discussions, and the more intimate their acquaintance with each other's families and friends, the better they can foresee what marriage to one another would be like.

Varied Activities. Variety can be found in participant as well as spectator activities. Some couples rely on films, concerts, and sports events where entertainment is provided by the management. But this is too easy. Marriage requires people to be able to enjoy themselves when they have only their own resources on which to depend. Although television provides potential entertainment after marriage, it takes more than that to hold a marriage together. Only by doing things that require no admission ticket can people discover how much they enjoy each other.

Dates also vary in physical setting. Traditionally, dating is catalyzed by starlight, perfume, and alcohol. Does the relationship fall flat when these props are removed? Or does companionship survive cold cream, diapers, and garbage?

Group activities and pair-dating yield different perspectives. In double-dating and partying, one discovers new dimensions of the other's personality as well as skills or lacks in socializing:

> *Every time we share with friends I [Margaret] learn something new about Bob. I used to say afterward, "Well, I never knew you thought that!" as if he had intentionally hidden that part of himself from me. I've come to realize that different people and conversations stimulate new awarenesses. Social situations provide a kind of consciousness raising which supplements what we learn about each other in private.*

Dating is also an opportunity to try out each other's hobbies—the unshared ones—to see whether they offer potential common interests:

> *Dan is a bird watcher. When he first told me I thought it was silly. And when spring came I began to resent the time he put in on it that he could have spent with me. Finally one day he persuaded me to go along with him. I was surprised how much fun it was! He started telling me*

*about how the birds migrate and a lot of other stuff I never knew before
and I got quite fascinated. Before I know it I'll turn into a bird watcher too.*

Acquaintance with idiosyncratic interests doesn't always produce conversion. But if the effect is short of toleration, trouble lies ahead. When the
result of trying out his interest in boxing matches or hers in church services is disgust that anyone could spend his/her time so foolishly, friction
can be predicted. Avoiding group activities to prevent being embarrassed
by the partner is a bad omen:

> *I hate the superficial chit-chat and teasing and joking at parties but
> Bud loves it. He usually becomes the life of the party, and I tell him he's
> an egomaniac. I melt into a dark corner, feel lonely, and blame him later
> for not paying attention to me all evening.*

There is no reason why every couple must try all the activities discussed here. The crucial task is to experience those activities that are most
salient to the particular individuals. Since interests differ from couple to
couple, relevant activities will differ accordingly.

Discussion.   Simple as it may seem, talk is also a step toward better
understanding. Of course people talk, but what do they talk about? The
weather, the news, the music, how you look tonight—or do they talk
about themselves, about what makes them tick: their feelings, aspirations,
troubles? When dates begin to share intimate thoughts as they would with
their closest friends, mutual understanding results. In our own case:

> *Margaret and I [Bob] went together for a long time before we got to
> know each other. We went places and did things—had a lot of fun. But
> one evening in front of an open fire we let our hair down. Talking about
> the things that meant the most to us, what we wanted to get out of life,
> and a lot of other things we'd never mentioned before, we began to feel
> we were meant for each other. After that I had a different feeling toward
> her.*

Whereas activities provide opportunities to explore contemporary
pleasures and problems, conversations can probe the past and the future.
Knowing each other's past makes it easier to understand the other's reactions and to foresee the future. If I know how my partner got to be the way
s/he is, my empathy for him/her should increase.

Occasionally, the question whether to confess past troubles arises.
Do individuals have an obligation to talk about their past? This is not
information one shares with casual friends. On the other hand, if it is to be
shared at all, it deserves to be part of compatibility testing rather than be
delayed until the proverbial "final confession" before marriage.

Whether to confess a delinquency depends on whether it is likely to affect the partner. If s/he is likely to hear about it from others, better to hear it from me. If suspicion is already in the air, better to present the facts than to allow uncertainty to threaten the relationship. On the other hand, if a brush with the law or with a prostitute was a transitory episode, not likely to be repeated, there is less urgency about sharing, even though self-disclosure may be beneficial.

When relationships are just forming, information about previous involvements may be emotionally threatening. To confront the partner with details about past intimacies is unpleasant for the partner to hear. Burgess and Wallin (1953) found that talk about former friends of the opposite sex provoked more "reticence, tension, or emotion" during engagement than any other topic of conversation. When men confessed some or all of their previous sexual involvements to their fiancées, the latter's reactions were more often unfavorable than favorable (39 percent versus 12 percent, the remainder being neutral).

There is a time and a place for self-revelation. The time to share is when one feels like it—when it is safe to do so. There is no right or wrong way to do it. But the more two people share, the more they get to know about what marriage to one another might be like.

Many aspects of marriage *can't* be tested ahead of time but *can* be discussed. Ideas about preferred family size or ways of raising children can be explored.

Table 5–2 shows how many more topics were discussed by modern couples than by couples a generation or two earlier. One-fourth of the grandmothers never discussed any of these topics before marriage, but reticence dwindled to 11 percent among the mothers and almost disappeared (1.5 percent) among the daughters.

Such conversations involve a search for areas of agreement. It's fun to find that you have the same ideas I do. Yet if talking is to do more than

Table 5–2 Premarital Discussion of Aspects of Marriages, in Three Successive Generations

	GENERATION		
Topic Discussed	*Grandmothers*	*Mothers*	*College Alumnae*
Having children	19%	55%	85%
Place to live	60%	73%	80%
Man's occupation	29%	45%	76%
Woman's occupation	8%	30%	74%
Religion	33%	46%	73%
Handling money in marriage	19%	39%	63%
Average number discussed	1.7	2.9	4.5
Number of cases	200	200	200

Adapted from Koller, 1951: 369. *Source:* Alumnae of Ohio State University, their mothers, and grandmothers. Their modal ages were 23, 48, and 78, respectively. Reciprocal percentages did not discuss the particular topic before marriage.

contribute to an illusion of bliss, there must be a willingness to differ too. Being frank requires the expression of unique views as well as hugging common ground.

Solving Problems. The ability to arrive at mutually satisfactory decisions is vital to marriage. Dating couples inevitably have decisions to make—about where to go and what to do. Sometimes decisions are passed over too lightly. A woman may allow a man to make decisions on dates that she would be unwilling to let him make after marriage. Before engagement is the time to test one's problem-solving ability:

> *Al always wants to get his own way. I used to let him get away with it, but I don't any more. Then I thought maybe I'd lose him if I disagreed with him because I wasn't sure he was in love with me. Now that I know he is, I stand up more for my own rights, and he respects me more.*

In addition to capitalizing on current decision-making opportunities, couples can work toward tentative solutions to problems they anticipate in marriage. Agreement in principle about what church to attend or how they feel about an open marriage may affect whether a couple will want to commit themselves to one another.

Meeting Friends. A person can be understood better by looking at his/her friends. Guilt by association may be poor politics but good psychology. The company one keeps is seldom accidental since common interests and backgrounds draw cliques together. If a date looks attractive but his/her friends seem odd, they suggest other aspects of his/her personality:

> *We got pinned last summer but somehow things haven't been going the way they should. We have very compatible personalities, but I think her friends have a bad influence on her. She's a music major and she hangs around with a bunch of long hairs who I think are nuts. She even admits herself that she lives a dual life—one where she's always acting, trying to impress people; the other when she's around me which is more settled, more domestic. The trouble is I can't get her to quit playing around with her arty friends.*

This student overestimated his compatibility with his friend. If he had taken a closer look he might have discovered that her "nutty" friends met needs in her personality that he didn't. His revulsion to her friends was a warning that they might be a poor match for each other.

Visiting Each Other's Homes. Getting acquainted with the partner's family produces some of the same advantages as getting to know his/her friends. People usually resemble their parents. Her mother previews what a woman may look like twenty-five years and twenty-five pounds later. The mother's behavior previews the mother the partner is likely to become—indeed, the person she is likely to be—in middle age. People grow up in families. They watch their fathers and mothers play the roles of husband and wife. Unconsciously, they learn their parents' ways.

Usually children take their parents as models. At three their favorite game is playing "Daddy and Mommy." By the time they are ready for marriage, they have absorbed their parents' patterns and learned the repertoire of behavior that was played before their eyes.

If parents are unhappy or the child dislikes the way s/he is treated, s/he may reject their example and choose a different role. A rebel's ideas about marriage may be more explicit because they have been chosen out of conflicting possibilities:

> My dad never had any time to do things with mother. Even on weekends he was always thinking up new schemes for his business. Mother used to gripe about how dad never took her out and hardly had any time to talk to her. I decided that when I married I was going to treat my wife better than he did.

Children from happy families not only take their same-sex parent as the model for themselves, but take their opposite-sex parent as the model for their marriage partner. Luckey (1961) found in University of Minnesota alumni a close resemblance between the personality characteristics happily married women saw in their fathers and those they saw in their husbands. Similarly, men with the best marriages more often saw their mothers reflected in their wives. Conversely, the poorer marriages less often continued the patterns learned in childhood.

If we could have verbalized why we felt attracted, we might have said:

> I [Bob] saw in you things that made me feel close to my mother: religious, musical, natureloving, and serious. Likewise, I [Margaret] sensed in you those qualities I respected in my father: religious, dedicated to important values and causes, a fine mind, dependability, and devotion to wife and family. This serious part of ourselves made us feel comfortable with each other. Conversely, when humor seems directed at us we are uneasy. I'm sure it recalls the teasing he got from his father, and for me the fear of being the butt of family jokes because I was the baby in the family.

Persons may reject their families. They may disagree on political and social issues, adopt new values, and make their own way in the world. Yet the very fact of rebelling, instead of growing up with parental support and encouragement, makes a difference:

> I don't think I really understood John until I met his father. His dad rules his family with a heavy hand. When he opens his mouth, everyone

is supposed to jump. John's mother has put up with it all these years, but I never would. And John didn't either. He used to argue with his father about ethnic problems and tried to puncture his father's stereotypes. But it didn't do any good. Now I can appreciate better why John is so touchy about some things and why he's so enthusiastic about "the group process."

When persons react against their parents they are extrasensitive. Understanding the family background permits us to make allowances for the other's bizarre reactions to seemingly innocuous situations. By visiting the family it is possible to anticipate overreactions.

More important, however, than just meeting the partner's parents is seeing how s/he gets along with them. This adds depth to compatibility testing since it reflects the parents' influence during his/her formative years. A student may have learned to control childish reactions since she left home, but they tend to reappear on visits to parents. Sometimes the picture isn't very pretty.

I'd never seen Irv so down in the dumps as the week we spent at his home during spring vacation. Everything his folks said seemed to rub him the wrong way. When his mother asked him to do something he would do it, but grudgingly and with the least possible effort. I had never seen him so irritable either. To see my beloved partner acting like a child was quite a shock.

Why can a visit home bring out the worst in a person? Because growing up is seldom smooth. Childhood is often a time of tension, anxiety, and conflict and going home reactivates old feelings of resentment, jealousy, and rebelliousness. Until a person can relate as an adult to his parents, visits are apt to revive old parent-child behavior.

Child-parent behavior patterns are not necessarily transferred into marriage. However, a look at family relations shows what repertoire of behavior is potentially available. If the look is too frightening, the relationship may end. If it is inviting, it enhances the attractions of marriage.

Other ends are served by visiting the family. Prospective in-laws provide a preview of in-law relationships. Moreover, the home setting enables couples who have never lived together to participate in domestic activities. They can see what it's like to take care of a baby sister or rake the lawn. If prosaic chores are fun when performed together, marriage becomes more attractive. Visiting families is, therefore, a multiple means of compatibility testing.

Taking Time. With so many time-consuming activities already proposed, it is hardly necessary to suggest taking time for its own sake. Nevertheless, time serves a useful purpose. If it were magically possible to complete the other tests instantaneously, length of relationship would become important in its own right. Time tests the wearing qualities of a relationship. As the months go by, do we still get along, or do we get on each other's nerves?

> I need a man who is dominant, and at first Carl seemed just right for me. But as time progressed I began to notice aspects of our relationship that didn't bode well for the future. He had such a domineering personality that at times I felt my individuality was being stifled. In a discussion of some controversial matter he would assert his views but never give mine a fair trial. Often the only retort he could think of was to say that my ideas were naive—what could I say except that his were cynical? After a while we began to reach so many stalemates that rather than go through the frustration all over again we started to avoid certain topics—religion, child-raising, fidelity. Because of his domineering attitude, many of our attempts to solve problems were unsuccessful, too. He would listen to my ideas, but then go right ahead and do what he originally intended. I finally realized that the kind of dominance I wanted was not that extreme. I'm glad now I didn't rush into a quick engagement the way he wanted to.

Some couples lose interest as the relationship becomes "old hat." Half the excitement may have been due to novelty. Marriage is designed to last a long time. When the wedding vows promise "till death," it is fitting that time be spent in pretesting the relationship. How much time is enough? Hollingshead (1952) found that the average New Haven couple dated for a year and a half before getting engaged.

Table 5–3 shows that the longer the prior acquaintance, the greater the proportion of engagements that lasted into marriage. Conversely, the shorter the dating span, the more likely an engagement was to be broken. In a study of working-class British couples, Slater and Woodside (1951) found a parallel increase in the proportion of couples who were happily married according to the length of acquaintance. The proportion who were happily married was only 50 percent for those who married less than

Table 5–3 Outcome of Engagement, by Length of Acquaintance

Outcome of Engagement	LENGTH OF ACQUAINTANCE BEFORE ENGAGEMENT		
	Less than 18 Months	18–35 Months	36 Months or More
Broken	18%	12%	9%
Unbroken	82	88	91
Total	100%	100%	100%
Number of couples	356	290	354

Adapted from Burgess and Wallin, 1953: 286. *Source:* 1,000 college-educated engaged couples in Chicago.

a year after they met, 59 percent for those who waited at least one year, and 63 percent for those who married two to three years after meeting. However, those who did not marry for more than three years after meeting were less happy (42 percent), perhaps because their marriages had been delayed by doubts, parental opposition, or other obstacles. Other things being equal, the longer people know each other prior to committing themselves, the more likely they are to have a lasting and happy relationship. Given time to discover their incompatibility, those without such happy prospects are more likely to opt out of the relationship.

The number of months needed for compatibility testing depends on several factors. The older and more mature the couple, the sounder their judgments will be. The more intensive and diversified their dating with each other, the greater the value of the passing months. Conversely, young and inexperienced couples who see each other only seldom need extra months to be sure.

Is separation a good test? Short separations are not likely to dissolve well-established relationships. But for immature couples clinging together or incompatible couples blinded by emotional involvement, being apart may bring detachment, an opportunity for reflection, and better perspective. When forced by parents, separations often boomerang, leading to the rebellious resolve to preserve a doubtful relationship or a defiant elopement. Voluntarily undertaken, however, separation may benefit couples too deeply involved to be objective.

Long separations, on the other hand, can destroy even *sound* relationships. Just as friendships wane when friends move away, love tends to fade when unreplenished by contact. Long separations allow old ties to be replaced by new ones. Separating does test relationships, but the longer the separation, the harder the test. Even the best partner may be lost if tested too severely.

Sexual Experience. Is sexual intercourse a useful means of discovering whether people are right for each other? If sexual compatibility were a question of physique, this evidence would be crucial. However this is not the case. Human beings of almost any shape and size can relate sexually. For this reason, it is not necessary to "try each other out for size."

The main factors in sexual compatibility are psychological, not anatomical. But the psychologies of premarital and marital intercourse are not the same. Premarital intercourse suffers from the handicaps of a less secure relationship devoid of social and religious sanctions. Couples who are satisfied with their sexual experience before marriage can assume that they will continue to enjoy sex after marriage. On the other hand, if sexual experience is unsatisfactory before marriage, this does not necessarily prove that they might not be able to work out a satisfactory adjustment after marriage, given more time and the security and social acceptability of sex within marriage. Couples who feel guilty or anxious in intercourse before marriage might function satisfactorily after marriage.

Couples who choose not to engage in sexual intercourse before marriage can assume that, with time and patience, they will be able to cultivate a satisfactory sexual relationship after marriage.

Living Together.   We saw in the previous chapter that living together is in many respects the ultimate test of compatibility. If the conditions for living together are inadequate, it may be an unduly severe test. Some couples who break up because their privacy is impaired or their insecurity is too demoralizing might have made it if they had gone the orthodox route of living together within the security of marriage and a home. But the more severe the test, the greater the guarantee that those who pass it have what it takes to survive in marriage.

Parental Guidance

Parents typically comment on their children's dating partners and marriage plans. If they are wise, they will emphasize sharing and guidance, not pressure and directives. As parents express their feelings about dating partners, children may benefit from their perspective:

> *My parents have never forbidden me to go out with anyone, but they always let me know if they don't like my date, either by teasing me or by not saying anything. If they do like someone I go out with, they tell me so and what they like about him, and I find that I always have a much better time when I am out with someone I know my parents like.*

When parents and child disagree, the child tends to discount their opinions. Parents belong to another generation with different ideas and different experiences. Their acquaintance with the child's partner is superficial. No matter how much the parents go out of their way to talk to the partner, their contact is slight compared to the time the couple spend together. Besides, parents typically stress values other than the tenderness, companionship, and love that most couples emphasize. Men students at the University of Wisconsin's Milwaukee campus were advised by their parents to find a woman (1) of the same religious faith, (2) who would be a good wife and homemaker, (3) from a good family background, and—only last—(4) with a pleasing disposition and personality (Prince, 1961). Their advice for women was similar except that the man's financial prospects were deemed even more important than his religion. Commented one coed:

> *My mother has told me to be sure to select a mate of the same religion, one who has a good job, and who is dependable. However, I feel that she is too interested in having me marry someone with money*

rather than someone I love. In this way, I don't feel she is regarding me. She wants prestige for herself.

Despite such limitations, parental response is usually helpful. Because parents are less involved, they may see aspects of the relationship that the participants have overlooked:

> *Six months before I finally came to my senses and broke our engagement, my family was up in arms about it. My brother told me I was getting a raw deal and my folks were dead set against the marriage because of the way Don was treating me. They thought it was rude and inconsiderate of him to keep breaking dates at the last minute the way he did. But I kept hoping for the best.*

Parents have a useful time perspective, too. As members of an older generation, they can see farther ahead than young daters care to look. The latter focus on the present and near future. But parents' long-range views throw a different light on the seriousness of present incompatibilities.

Parents are also apt to have a keen appreciation of their child's needs. Having lived with the child so many years, they may know him/her even better than s/he knows him/herself:

> *Dad said I'd never be happy with Ray because he was selfish. At the time I couldn't understand what he meant. Ray spent money so lavishly on me that he seemed the most generous person I had ever known. In fact, I thought some of Dad's relatives were the stingy ones because they were so tight with their money. . . . But now that I've been married to Ray a few months I've discovered that the only person he's really interested in is himself. He never gives either his time or his love to anyone else. I guess Dad knew better than I that Ray wasn't right for me.*

Parents have so many bases for judgment that their opposition is often a harbinger of doom. Table 5–4 shows that twice as many engagements terminated short of marriage or early in marriage when both parents were opposed as when both approved. Nevertheless, a majority of the parent-opposed marriages did survive at least three years. Parents are sometimes wrong and the couple right. The problem is how to tell the difference.

Irrelevant Opposition. Some parents are irrational, jealous, and more concerned with their own emotional needs than with the child's welfare. A widowed, divorced, or unhappily married woman may be so emotionally dependent on her son that she cannot let go. A mother may hang on to her last child. Such a parent may criticize any prospective partner, no matter how suitable.

Table 5–4 Duration of Relationship, by Attitude of Woman's Parents

	ATTITUDE OF WOMAN'S PARENTS		
Duration of Relationship	Both Approved	One Disapproved	Both Disapproved
Broken before marriage	13%	16%	32%
Broken after marriage (separation or divorce)	4	7	4
Married three years or more	83	78	64
Total	100%	101%	100%
Number of couples	660	45	91

Adapted from Burgess and Wallin, 1953: 561.

Other parents may use criteria rejected by the child. A Baptist mother may wish for a daughter-in-law who belongs to the same church, but if her son is an agnostic, that is meaningless. Similarly, a businessman's objections to his daughter's "impractical" fiancé are not likely to override their shared interest in theatrical careers. Parental advice is inappropriate when the child has been upwardly mobile. A higher social status involves new tastes and values difficult for parents to understand. Bell and Buerkle (1962) found that, on the average, mothers of women students at Temple University in Philadelphia had only 11.7 years of education. Faced with upward educational mobility, a majority of the mothers and even more of the daughters (55 percent and 77 percent, respectively) felt that a girl should marry the man she loves even if her mother "strongly objects" to him.

A third criterion is the structure of the family. If parent-child ties are close, opposition is more serious. In an aristocratic or wealthy family, the older generation carries more weight. Especially if the son is to join his father's business, parents are more apt to veto an unsuitable daughter-in-law. Conversely, if parent-child relationships are remote, opposition matters less.

Although marrying in the face of parental opposition strains parent-child relationships, anguish can be mnimized by mutual consideration. Secret marriages or living together in secret bypass hostile parents, but alienate them even more when discovered. Most parents want to attend the wedding even if they aren't enthusiastic about the match. They appreciate being kept informed of their child's plans, even when they disagree with them. Sensitive handling of parental opposition may not dissolve it immediately, but can pave the way for better relationships in the long run.

Friends play similar roles in mate selection. They are more likely to share the individual's values than are parents. Through double-dating they may get to know the partner well. However, they express their doubts less often because they lack the legitimacy of parents (Mayer, 1957). If friends fail to express disapproval, this doesn't necessarily mean that they approve. Reticence can usually be interpreted as disapproval. Burgess and Wallin found (1953) that in those rare cases where disapproval was actually expressed by friends, their doubts spelled future trouble.

Professional Testing

Up to this point we have described activities that couples and parents undertake as amateurs. Although such testing is usually sufficient, professional assistance may be needed in special cases.

Computer Selection.   Like computer dating, computer matchmaking has all the virtues and all the limitations of the scientific and human resources invested in the computer's memory bank. If the information fed into the computer is relevant to marriage and if the applicants are a cross-section of the eligible market, the machine will recommend matches that are worth considering. The joker is the second *if.* While a computer dance on a college campus may attract applicants by the hundreds, professional introduction services tend to attract particular segments of the marriage market: (1) women culturally handicapped in finding marriage partners, and (2) individuals past the normal age of marrying. The result is that men who seek computer assistance have a wide range to choose from, but the older a woman gets, the less likely she is to find it useful. On the other hand, the older she gets, the less her competitive strength on the "outside," too, so that even a badly skewed computer pool may be worth trying if she seriously wants to marry.

Premarital Counseling.   A skillful premarital counselor can help couples of doubtful compatibility. Any man and woman who find themselves in conflict within themselves, between partners, or between themselves and their parents would do well to seek professional counsel. Parents can usually be counted on for feedback, but a professional person is more dependable. Parents have little knowledge to draw on save their own marriage experience and the marriages of their immediate circle. Counselors have the double advantage of scientific knowledge about marriage and experience in counseling other couples, so their perspective is broad. For the couple themselves, discussing their situation with a neutral party is likely to yield new insights and objectivity.

Increasing Compatibility

Compatibility testing reveals whether couples are compatible or incompatible. When incompatibility is discovered, couples usually break up.

But sometimes people feel that compatibility could be increased by changing the partner's personality. Is this possible?

Human personality is not static. No matter how old they are, people keep changing their interests, attitudes, and reactions. Moreover, one's behavior depends to a large extent on how one is treated. With proper handling, could the partner behave better? The possibility of change is often dismissed with a sneer—"You can't change a leopard's spots." Personalities seldom change very much, to be sure, but that doesn't mean they don't change at all. The easiest change is to develop latent potentialities. Before going together, one partner may never have been exposed to the other's church, sport, or hobby. Common interests could develop spontaneously once the novice is introduced to them.

More difficult are changes in old ways of doing things, especially in temperament and need-feeding habits. Even these attempts don't always fail, however:

> *I think Esther's pressures have been good for me. I used to put off studying until the last minute, but now I'd rather study first and play afterward so I can enjoy the playing more. Esther's changed, too, since we started going together. She has a pretty sharp temper and she used to jump on me and not care. But now she and I sit down and talk things over before she erupts.*

Several aspects of this couple's approach contributed to their success:

1. The reform program was not one-sided, but recognized that both partners had deficiencies.

2. Changes were pursued openly with no attempt to "put something over" on anyone.

3. As a result of this process of persuasion, each partner accepted the other's desires as a goal for the self and felt supported by the other's love. The critical partner did not put pressure on a reluctant person but helped in attaining shared goals.

4. Dissatisfactions were dealt with. The changes wanted in the present were pursued early in the relationship rather than merely hoped for in the future. If improvement in compatibility is necessary to marital satisfaction, it should begin well before getting engaged.

Before Engagement.   An old proverb says: "Don't marry a man to change him." There are two reasons why desired changes should be tried out before deciding whether to get married. The main one is that personal effort or even professional therapy may not succeed. It is seldom possible to predict how much a person will change. Marriage is too serious to enter on faith that the partner will "come around" eventually. It can be undertaken safely only when each partner can stand the other as s/he is.

Another advantage in pursuing change early is that courtship is one of the most flexible periods in life. When there is hope of winning someone's affection, the incentive to change is strong. This may provide the impetus without which therapy is useless and reform impossible. In our own case:

> I [Margaret] had tried for years to give up smoking for the sake of my health and never succeeded. When I decided Bob was the man for me, I was surprised how easy it was to stop. I knew he'd never marry a smoker. And I knew he was more important than smoking. It was a neat time to break the habit when I was getting so much satisfaction out of our relationship.

There is always a risk that changes will be only temporary. After marriage old patterns may reassert themselves. But pessimism is not necessarily realistic. The new relationship reinforces changes, reducing the danger of backsliding.

To assume that change will occur automatically after marriage is foolhardy. To marry the proverbial drunkard in order to reform him/her is likely to result only in martyrdom. Some people will change over the years, but you can't count on change. Love and effort can perform miracles, but reform can never be guaranteed. Change is not predictable.

THE FINAL DECISION

The time comes when the results of compatibility testing must be assessed and acted upon. A couple must get engaged, break up, or postpone the decision still longer. Eventually, however, the decision will be made by default if in no other way.

Standards of Compatibility

Some couples worry about too much compatibility. They fear that similarity of interests may lead to boredom. But changes in family life, vocation, and community guarantee that no couple need ever stagnate. The problem is never "too much" compatibility, but too little.

How much compatibility does it take for a good marriage? The answer lies in the balance between the costs and rewards of the relationship. For couples who quarrel often or feel chronically insecure and dissatisfied, marriage would drain their emotional resources. Marriage can never be all reward and no cost, but the effort expended should result in meeting the other's needs. A couple's own doubts are a sign of incompatibility. Doubts were relatively rare among Burgess and Wallin's engaged men.

Their fiancées, however, tended to be less confident. Uncertainty often foretold a broken engagement or divorce (see Table 5–5).

Basic uncertainty frequently means that something is wrong with the relationship, or at least with the readiness of the partners to get married. Therefore, it is unwise to marry as long as either partner is unsure.

The Necessity of Risking

Choosing a marriage partner requires taking two kinds of risks: (1) At some point in life I must decide I want to marry a particular person in spite of the fact that other persons whom I have not yet met may turn out to be more desirable than this one; (2) My decision must be based on this person as s/he is now, without knowing how s/he will change during the course of our marriage.

If mate selection involved choosing the best of all eligible partners, it would be simpler. A choice among visible alternatives is relatively easy. Unfortunately, the choice must be made between a visible prospect and invisible alternatives. If the current prospect meets minimum standards, marrying him/her might be better than marrying no one. What a pity, however, to marry him/her today and discover someone better tomorrow!

Whether to wait for somebody better depends on how good the chances are. Do more compatible people exist, or is this just daydreaming? How eligible am I? If better partners exist, what are the chances that they will be interested in me? This is partly a question of time. For teenagers the chances of encountering more compatible partners in the future are excellent. Past the age of 30, the chances that a single woman will marry *anybody* dwindle to less than fifty-fifty. Somewhere in their late twenties, most people quit waiting for someone better and marry whoever

Table 5–5 Duration of Relationship, by Woman's Confidence during Engagement

Duration of Relationship	ENGAGED WOMAN'S CONFIDENCE OF SUCCESS IN MARRIAGE		
	Very Confident	Confident	Uncertain
Broken before marriage	13%	20%	31%
Broken after marriage (separation or divorce)	3	4	15
Married three years or more	84	76	54
Total	100%	100%	100%
Number of couples	571	209	48

Adapted from Burgess and Wallin, 1953: 565.

meets their minimal standards, if they want to marry at all. Up to that age, waiting often pays off:

> When I was a senior, I fell in love with a man who wanted a wife to cook, to entertain, and to make babies—nothing else. I was tempted to marry him, but after a struggle I came to the conclusion that I couldn't surrender my intellectual interests. I gradually became more sure that there would be other loves—that life could go on without him!
>
> I met my husband a year later. I had never met anyone so interesting to talk to or with so bright a mind. I was drawn to someone with so wide a range of interests, someone gentle and considerate, yet who knew who and what he was, and someone with a wonderful sense of perspective.

The second risk I must take is in marrying this person as s/he is now with no way of knowing what either of us is going to be like in the future. Both of us will change. The chances of our growing apart are just as good as our chances of growing together (Kelly, 1955). Nor can I assume that if we do change in different directions that this will be all my partner's fault. It will be the joint product of our failure either to stay as we are now or to grow in the same direction. All I can do is choose on the basis of our present compatibility, with no guarantee that anything will stay the same in the long run. The best guarantee of a good future together is to do everything possible to make a good present.

> I want to keep being aware of who I am and what my needs are right now and I want to be aware of who you [Bob] are and what you need right now.
>
> If we can live well in this present together and feel easy and comfortable with who we are and how we are relating now I believe we can do the same in all the future presents.

Regardless of whether one marries enthusiastically or settles for a satisfactory minimum, marriage always involves commitment. It means committing oneself to this person even if a more intriguing one turns up later, and without knowing whether our needs and values will diverge in later years. It also means creating a long-term relationship by applying skill and effort. Choosing a partner is only the beginning of marriage.

6 Mixed Marriages

Preceding chapters have focused on the personal characteristics of potential marriage partners. This chapter considers their social roots and involvements. Most people "marry in" (that is, homogamously). The exceptional heterogamous cases encounter extra problems that require compatibility testing.

Homogamy promotes compatibility of interests and values. In addition, it provides a supporting framework of social relationships. Membership in the same organization and social circle buttresses the relationship between the partners. The social pressures and personal preferences that cause homogamy in the first place help to cement homogamous marriages. Parents and friends provide encouragement. Church, clubs, and ethnic organizations offer opportunities for joint leisure-time activities. The identification of husband and wife with the same groups gives them a secure feeling.

TYPES OF MIXED MARRIAGES

Despite the pressures for homogamy, mixed marriages do occur. Marriages may be mixed along only one dimension or along several. Most mixtures are unidimensional. For example, American soldiers who married Filipino women after World War II usually chose mates with education and social status similar to their own (Hunt and Coller, 1957). Since unidimensional mixtures are most common, they will be the focus of the remainder of this chapter. Where mixtures are multidimensional, problems are correspondingly multiplied.

The degree of mixture depends on the degree of identification of the partners with their own groups. In some cases the tie is so residual that the marriage is mixed only externally, not internally; that is, the social involvements of the partners may conflict, while their values and interests do not.

Residual Mixtures

The chief external complication in residual mixtures is that parents feel rejected by their children. The latter may either abandon all ties with the parents' group or, worse yet, shift their identification to the partner's group.

Loss of Identification.   Second-generation Americans are a classic example of lost identity. Whereas first-generation immigrants cling to the language and customs of the old country, subsequent generations are increasingly identified with American culture. As a result, the rate of intermarriage between ethnic groups rises from generation to generation.

The United States is such a mobile country that people desert all sorts of groups, not just old-fashioned ones:

> *I was brought up Catholic and my mother is pretty religious now. But since I came to college I've gotten away from the church. I still go occasionally when I'm home, more out of respect for my mother than anything else. But I don't accept the official beliefs anymore. I'm beginning to wonder whether I should list myself as Catholic at registration time.*

To call this student Catholic would be misleading. When group identification is so attenuated, it loses most of its meaning. Were he to marry a Protestant it could hardly be called a Catholic-Protestant marriage. Yet even in such cases there are potential problems. A devout Catholic mother is likely to want her grandchildren baptized and raised in that church. And even the son may discover he wants his children baptized and confirmed as he was. Nevertheless, his marriage would be considerably less mixed than if he were a "good" Catholic.

Children of mixed marriages are more apt to enter mixed marriages themselves. In Detroit, children of interfaith marriages were twice as likely to marry out as children of homogamously Protestant or homogamously Catholic parents (Besanceney, 1962). Children of mixed marriages are likely to have identity problems, and their parents before them may have contracted their own mixed marriages as a result of initially weak religious identification.

Transfer of Identification. A second residual mixture involves persons who have actively joined another group. Religious converts and social climbers are good examples. Rabbi Richard Rubenstein (1963) concluded that many Gentiles marrying Jews were also "marrying" the Jewish community (that is, converting to Judaism). He felt they wanted to "join the community of the alienated," or were attracted to an intellectual or artistically sensitive way of life they had encountered among Jewish friends.

In one Nebraska city, Babchuk (1967) found that a large proportion of interfaith mixtures became residual as one partner changed religions at marriage, resolving the background difference and bringing the couple into religious homogamy. Typically, this change was made at some point after the couple decided to get married but before they had children. Otherwise, it was made before the first child was old enough to know the difference. These converts attended church even more often than ordinary members of the faith but became church leaders less often. Presumably, religious mobility minimized strain in these marriages.

Social climbing requires learning the behavior patterns of the new group and unlearning the patterns of the old. A working-class boy must avoid swearing, "dirty" jokes, and sexual promiscuity to enter the middle class. He must learn to study hard, save money, and dress neatly. Then he may become sufficiently identified with the middle class to be able to marry a schoolteacher with only mild "mixing." She might notice occasional slips in grammar and etiquette, but otherwise might encounter few internal problems. His parents' reaction would depend on whether they felt bereft or proud of their son. In either case, they are likely to feel uncomfortable with a high-status daughter-in-law. Her parents, on the other hand, are apt to doubt that he is good enough for their daughter. So in-law relationships are not likely to be easy in either direction.

The greater the difference between groups, the greater the difficulties with in-laws. For parents, it may be a tossup whether it is worse for their child to lose interest in their values or to join the "enemy camp." For parents who take their religion seriously, a switch to an alien faith may be less disappointing than a total abandonment of religion. Conversion from one loyalty to another may be consciously wholehearted without wiping out unconscious traces of childhood socialization. In times of emotional stress—whether negative or positive—an individual is liable to "forget himself" and slip back into old patterns, to the dismay of both partners. For example, foreign partners may find their native language more available than English when they lose their tempers.

When loss of identification persists for generations, "pseudomixture" might be a better term than "residual mixture." In Manhattan, Heiss (1960) found that intermarried "Catholics" often came from homes where religion was unimportant, and intermarried "Jews" had parents who never attended religious services. Under these circumstances even the residual consequences of intermarriage are less likely to occur.

Residual mixtures are halfway between homogamous marriages and the genuine mixtures in which we are mainly interested. Genuine mixed marriages may be defined as ones in which each partner retains identification with a separate group, holds differing beliefs and values, and follows a different way of life.

PROBLEMS OF MIXED MARRIAGES

Contrasting backgrounds create potential problems. Not all of these materialize in every mixed marriage, but possible trouble spots should be explored in contemplating such a marriage. Some problems are characteristic of all mixed marriages, while others occur only in specific mixtures.

Between Husband and Wife

At the very beginning, interreligious couples face the problem of choosing one partner's wedding ceremony over the other's or improvising some other solution to minimize conflict.

Mixed couples bring conflicting cultures into their marriages. Domestic rituals may differ. Dietary differences complicate menus for the cook and flood the house with "strange odors." The church calendar differs for Christians and Jews, with Christmas and Easter as unfamiliar to the Jew as Hanukkah and Yom Kippur are to the Christian. Decisions about whether to put up a Christmas tree can be difficult.

Marriage patterns may differ between cultures. A second-generation Syrian American reported that when men of his nationality background married "old" Americans, trouble ensued because the wife's "aggressiveness and independence" clashed with the husband's expectations. By contrast, wives from "back home" were properly submissive.

Differential Identification. Quite apart from conflicting values and cultures, a mixed marriage is "a house divided against itself." Husband and wife have roots in contrasting traditions that create a sense of estrangement. A Protestant wife writing in a Catholic magazine concluded thus:

> I have never had occasion to alter my original opinion that my husband is the finest man I have ever met. . . . But even so, there is still that intangible consciousness of effort that is always with us, always standing as a barrier. We must live with this as with a stranger in the house. And no one relaxes when there are strangers in the house.

People from contrasting backgrounds can take less for granted—fewer assumptions, values, habits. Hence they have to work harder at communicating with each other. When trouble arises, the difference is magnified. Most men and women unconsciously share the prejudices that exist between groups—prejudices held by minorities as well as majorities. Traditional stereotypes become painful epithets when invoked in domestic quarrels.

Differential Participation. Insofar as mixed partners participate separately in their own groups, their solidarity is weakened. Finding common friends is difficult since cliques tend to be segregated the same way marriages are. Sometimes other mixed couples are available. World War II veterans with Japanese wives associated almost exclusively with similar couples in Chicago (Strauss, 1954). Small communities rarely offer a mixed clique, so separate friends or few friends become the only choices available in the face of social ostracism.

If each partner participates in their own group, the couple are deprived of what could otherwise be a binding element. At worst, this produces conflict. Where other couples go to church together, interfaith couples go separately.

Between Parents and Children

When children come, which group will they be reared in, participate in, identify with? This is a difficult problem in interfaith marriages:

> *There was only one major conflict in our family. Owing to the religious faction (my mother is a Quaker and my father Jewish Reform) neither parent had fully conceded to the other. The problem was not one of conflicting theologies, because these two religions are about as similar as any two but, rather, one of frame of reference. This is exemplified by the fact that before marriage my parents decided any boys would be trained in the synagogue and any girls would go to the Friends Meeting. Luckily there are no boys, because that would have emphasized the already existing conflict. Although there were no arguments or even discussions about this topic, the conflict was conveyed subliminally to me, making my parental attachments, identifications, and so forth, unusually difficult by creating a sense of conflicting loyalties. This problem has existed for me as far back as I can remember, even in grammar school where I was first exposed to anti-Semitism in the form of ridicule from playmates. My identification and ultimate participation in Jewish or non-Jewish groups is still unresolved and probably will remain so until I marry. This remains a problem because I have long since discovered that in realistic adult situations (as contrasted with university life) participation in and vacillation between both groups is practically impossible from the standpoint of acceptance and the resulting rewards of group identity. I*

think I prefer to marry a Jewish man mainly because I perceive that there would be greater security derived from functioning entirely in the more clearly defined and highly integrated Jewish group.

If one partner's group identity is more meaningful than the other's, the latter will usually yield over this issue. (This concession resolves much of the conflict between the parents, though it does not prevent the children from being exposed to the split identity of their parents.) Among twenty Jewish-Gentile couples in New York City, where one partner hesitated to marry out but the other didn't care, four couples were unable to agree how to raise the children, but the other sixteen raised them in the faith of the reluctant partner (Mayer, 1961). Where both partners are equally committed, the question is less easily resolved.

Conflict between mixed-marriage husbands and wives over how to raise their children affects the children most directly. But children are remarkably sensitive to *any* problems that disturb their parents. Any husband-wife or kinship conflict in a mixed marriage is likely to be felt by them. Some children "act out" their inner disturbances in delinquent behavior. The study summarized in Table 6–1 found that juvenile delinquency was two to eight times as common in mixed marriages as in unmixed ones.

One consequence of the difficulty of raising children in a split household is a tendency to have fewer children. Among white families in Manhattan, the interreligious birthrate decreased the most for Catholic individuals compared to homogamously Catholic couples matched in other respects. For Jewish and Protestant individuals who married out, the number of children also decreased, though not as much. Specifically, the birthrate fell .34 child for intermarried Catholics, .25 for Jews, and .19 for Protestants (Heiss, 1961). Even when religion is held constant, international couples have fewer children. For example, Catholics married to Catholics had fewer children when one parent was foreign-born than

Table 6–1 **Arrests for Juvenile Delinquency in Children of Religiously Mixed and Unmixed Marriages**

Religious Identity of Father	PERCENTAGE OF CHILDREN EVER ARRESTED BY RELIGIOUS HOMOGAMY OF PARENTS		
	Unmixed Marriage	Mixed Marriage	Ratio
Protestant	5.8%	11.1%	1.9X
Catholic	4.0%	9.8%	2.5X
Jewish	5.1%	41.1%	8.0X

Adapted from Zimmerman and Cervantes, 1960: 158–59. *Source:* Families of St. Louis high-school seniors.

when both were Americans. Similarly, in Protestant marriages, fertility was lower in international marriages than in domestic marriages (see Table 6–2).

External Problems

No matter how cohesive a couple may be internally, mixed marriages encounter external stress. Pressure is greatest when group ties are visible to outsiders (as in interracial marriages) and when the groups are hostile toward each other.

Alienation from Families. Family opposition to mixed marriages is most acute before the wedding. If opposition is strong enough, it leads some couples to get married "behind their parents' backs." Though not all out-of-state weddings are elopements, mixed marriages ceremonialized away from home symbolize estrangement from parents. In Iowa in the mid-1950s, for example, only 12 percent of intrafaith weddings involved brides from other states compared to 28 percent of interfaith weddings (Chancellor and Burchinal, 1962).

Most mixtures produce in-law difficulties. To mixed couples, in-laws appeared aloof (Duvall, 1954). A foreign husband described his relationship with his American in-laws thus:

> I often thought of my in-laws as being distant toward me, especially when I remember that they objected to our marriage at first. But as I got to know them better, I gradually changed this impression about them. Nevertheless, I still feel tense and uneasy whenever they visit us or when we visit them.

Whereas in-law problems are relatively rare in unmixed marriages, they are almost universal in mixed marriages (see Table 6–3).

Mixed marriages not only have more difficulties but fewer intergenerational activities such as financial help, visiting, and joint vacations

Table 6–2 Number of Living Children in Unmixed and Mixed Nationality Marriages, by Religion

Religion of Parents	AVERAGE NUMBER OF LIVING CHILDREN BY NATIONALITY OF PARENTS	
	Unmixed Nationality (Both Americans)	Mixed Nationalities (One American, One Foreign)
Both Protestant	2.49	2.38
Both Catholic	2.76	2.42

Adapted from Bresler, 1961: 17. *Source:* Parents of students at Brown University.

Table 6–3 Intergenerational Difficulties in Religiously Unmixed and Mixed Marriages

Intergenerational Difficulties	RELIGIOUS HOMOGAMY	
	Unmixed	Mixed
Yes	18%	90%
No	82	10
Total	100%	100%
Number of cases	156	39

Adapted from Sussman, 1953. *Source:* Interviews with middle-class New Haven parents of married children.

(Sussman, 1953). Though aloof from the son-in-law or daughter-in-law, older couples put pressure on their children to keep them in line with family traditions. Such pressure focuses on the grandchildren. Interfaith marriages occasionally provoke a tug-of-war between the two sets of grandparents. At the very least, in-law pressures make the losing parent feel worse:

> I come from a devout Catholic family and my wife from a very strong Protestant one. She raised all the children Protestant. My family still condemns me for it, but Martha put her foot down on this before we were married. I still feel guilty about the whole situation even though I'm not a practicing Catholic and don't believe in much Catholic dogma myself. Needless to say, Martha and I have never been very close to the relatives on either side.

Mixed couples seldom lose all kin ties, however. Firth and his associates (1970) found that most parents and siblings eventually accepted interreligious marriages. Rather, it was more distant relatives who typically severed their ties with mixed couples. Apparently the immediate family's love is strong enough to override their dismay at an unorthodox partner, but more remote kin do not have the advantage of close affectional bonds nor as much opportunity to get to know the stranger. So aunts, uncles, cousins, and so on are apt to shun both the stranger and the out-marrying member of the family. The chief pain over this shunning may be felt not by the young couple, but by parents who are acutely aware that their siblings disapprove of the marriage that their child has contracted.

Friendship Problems.   In Manhattan, Heiss (1961) found that intermarried couples had fewer close friends than homogamous couples. Protestant partners were not bothered by this, but the loss was strongly felt by Jewish out-marriers. Catholics in mixed marriages were also more apt than their unmixed confreres to say they wanted more friends. Apparently friendship problems are created generally for Catholic/Protestant or Jewish/Gentile couples, but the stress caused by social isolation varies with one's sensitivity to social discrimination.

Institutional Alienation.   Persons who marry out tend to have initial ties with their group that are already weak. Because their institutional affiliation is weak, they have more contact with outgroup members during the dating years. When they meet someone of a different background, the fact of that difference is less of an obstacle to falling in love and getting married. So mixed marriages typically involve persons who are already somewhat alienated from their institutional memberships.

Once they enter such a marriage, the partners presumably are further alienated from their organizations since active participation would strain the solidarity of the marriage. Institutional alienation, therefore, tends to be both cause and effect of intermarriage.

Table 6–4 shows that out-marrying persons in Indiana tended to be less active in their churches at the very beginning of their marriage, namely, in their wedding ceremony. Roughly two to three times as many couples marrying across religious lines were married in a civil ceremony rather than by the priest, minister, or rabbi of either partner. When a couple are divided in their religious ties, compromising on a civil ceremony may be less divisive than choosing one partner's ceremony and rejecting the other's. The institutional alienation that characterizes mixed marriages may protect couples from potential trouble. Better perhaps to participate in neither church than to leave one partner feeling affirmed and the other alienated by choosing just one. For persons who marry across group lines, the best way to preserve the solidarity of their partnership may be to weaken their ties with the diverse groups from which they come.

Table 6–4   **Nonreligious Wedding Ceremonies in Religiously Unmixed and Mixed Marriages, by Faith of Wife**

	PERCENTAGE OF NONRELIGIOUS CEREMONIES, BY RELIGIOUS HOMOGAMY		
Faith of Wife	*Unmixed*	*Mixed*	*Ratio*
Catholic	20%	32%	1.6X
Protestant	19%	43%	2.3X
Jewish	17%	61%	3.6X

Recomputed from Monahan, 1973: 198. *Source:* Sampling from state-wide marriages in Indiana, 1962–67. Reciprocal percentages were married in religous ceremonies.

Decreasing Problems

Most kinds of intermarriage are becoming more common in the United States—especially Catholic-Protestant, Jewish-Gentile, and black-white marriages. The gradual integration of Catholics, Jews, and blacks into American society has increased contact between groups and decreased the social and economic barriers that previously separated them. The ecumenical movement has stimulated dialogue between Catholics and Protestants. Anti-Semitism is on the wane and race prejudice has become socially taboo.

Increased acceptance between groups has triple effects. Not only does it (1) increase the rate of mixed marriages but it (2) increases the likelihood of conversion and (3) decreases the problems created.

One illustration of decreasing problems comes from Providence, Rhode Island. Whereas in an earlier generation Gentile wives of actively Jewish husbands retained their separate identity, more recently they were apt to convert to Judaism. Before, Gentile wives of Jewish men bore 30 percent fewer children than Jewish wives. In a later generation, the gap narrowed to 10 percent. And whereas earlier mixed marriages were delayed by the obstacles involved ("mixed" husbands and wives were older than usual), the age lag subsequently disappeared (Goldstein and Goldscheider, 1966). Internal and external strains are not likely to disappear altogether, but our shrinking planet promises to become a more viable home for mixed marriages.

Difference as Opportunity

The statistics cited in this chapter suggest that the average mixed couple react negatively to their differences. But exceptional cases can be found. The extraordinary people whom Maslow (1954) called "self-actualizing" were less afraid of differences, better able to tolerate them, even able to appreciate them. For broad-minded people, mixed marriages are another opportunity for mind stretching. The adventure of sharing another culture and discovering firsthand how "the other half" lives, enlarges their capacity for empathy and their understanding of humanity:

> You ask me if I would marry Joan again if I had my life to live over again, and my answer is yes. It isn't easy for a rabbi to have a Gentile wife. Some people raise their eyebrows, you know. But since much of my counseling is with students considering intermarriage, my own experience helps me to understand the situation they're in. Raising our own children has been hard work but rewarding as we've tried to introduce them to the best of both our religious traditions. But the main reason I'm

glad I married Joan is because we still love each other so deeply after all these years.

We assume that extraordinary people rarely intermarry just for the sake of broadening themselves. Probably their primary motive is general similarity and love. But once they find themselves in a mixed relationship, they transform it into an opportunity for mutual enrichment. In this sense mixed marriages are risky. But high-risk games have high payoffs—for those who win. For extraordinary people, mixed marriages may yield extraordinary excitement and creativity. For ordinary people, the low-risk sureness of modest returns from a homogamous marriage is a safer bet.

CATHOLIC-PROTESTANT MARRIAGES

Religious differences present obstacles to personal relationships, especially for persons who believe theirs is the only true faith. Such couples lack not only spiritual unity but also the respect for each other's convictions that makes it possible to live and let live. Marriages between "good" Catholics and "good" Protestants tend to experience tensions. If couples do not feel them spontaneously, relatives and clergymen often create them.

Interfaith marriages are vulnerable to the usual in-law problems. Religious training of children is extra difficult if their church affiliation is considered a matter of eternal concern. Differences in values are most acute over birth control, though they may also occur over politics, civil liberties, parochial schooling, and the like. If both partners attend their own churches, they are separated at times that are normally family oriented.

McLean (1953) found that well-educated Protestant-Catholic couples resolved many of their problems before getting married. A third of his couples discussed their religious differences extensively before marriage and nearly all did to some degree. Most couples planned what church they would attend and agreed on the religious training of children. However, only a minority decided in advance about birth control.

The Catholic Church imposes special regulations on marriages between Catholics and other Christians. The Catholic partner must promise in writing to raise the children Catholic. For the marriage to be valid in the eyes of the church, the wedding must be performed by a priest or the non-Catholic ceremony must be sanctioned in advance by the Catholic partner's bishop.

These regulations reflect the influence of the ecumenical movement and are sometimes symbolized by designating mixed marriages as "ecumenical marriages." Mixed couples are encouraged to receive instruction in both partners' faiths before marriage and to attend both partners' churches every Sunday. However, the requirement that the Catholic partner wholeheartedly practice his/her own faith implies a moral obligation to practice Catholic teaching about birth control.

Just because the Catholic Church lays down these regulations does not mean they are always followed. The rules about wedding ceremonies are violated by American Catholics almost as often as they are observed. The violators frequently are nominal Catholics whose church affiliation is relatively meaningless. In other cases they are persons whose non-Catholic partners are unwilling to accept the Catholic conditions.

Consequences of Interfaith Marriages

Anticipating negative consequences, a considerable proportion of interfaith couples break up before marriage. In Burgess and Wallin's sample (1953), 19 percent of engaged couples of differing faiths broke their engagements compared to 11 percent of couples of the same faith. Because of this higher dropout rate before marriage, mixed couples who do marry represent a select group with somewhat better prospects. Despite this selectivity, they have more than their share of marital troubles.

Marital Failure. We have already seen that interfaith couples bear fewer children than homogamous couples. The strains that depress the fertility of mixed marriages sometimes destroy those marriages altogether.

Table 6–5 shows that for both Catholic and Protestant women, the divorce rate in interfaith marriages was several times the rate for intrafaith marriages. This Iowa study found that denominational affiliation made little difference when one Protestant married another. When Catholics married Protestants, the more alike the two churches, the less the strain. For Catholics married to members of "high" churches (Lutherans and Presbyterians), the divorce rate was only two and a half times the Catholic norm. In marriages with members of "low" churches (Methodists and Baptists), it was four and a half times as high. The highest rate of all occurred in marriages with "unspecified Protestants" belonging to no church at all (almost 20 times the normal Catholic divorce rate). It is more

Table 6–5   Divorces in Religously Unmixed and Mixed Marriages, by Faith of Wife

	PERCENTAGE DIVORCED BY RELIGIOUS HOMOGAMY		
Faith of Wife	Unmixed	Mixed	Ratio
Catholic	1.4%	10.6%	7.6X
Protestant	5.1%	12.1%	2.4X

Adapted from Burchinal and Chancellor, 1963: 357. *Source:* Professional and managerial men married in the state of Iowa between 1953 and 1959 who were divorced by the end of 1959. Reciprocal percentages were still married.

difficult for a person who holds religious values to get along with someone who rejects that whole orientation toward life than to marry someone with a *different* religious orientation. To be equally serious about religion gives an interfaith couple a common value, whereas a devout believer is doubly estranged from a nonbeliever of different background.

Religious Dilution.   Partners in mixed marriages attend church less often than unmixed couples. We have suggested before that some of this lesser church attendance begins prior to marriage, but some of it may result from the mixed marriage. To disentangle the selective effect from the effect of the marriage itself would require comparing the church attendance of persons prior to meeting one another with their attendance after marriage. In the absence of such a comparison, we present in Table 6–6 a comparison of the frequency of attending church during engagement with the frequency after marriage.

Table 6–6 shows that a substantial proportion of Burgess and Wallin's Catholic respondents who entered mixed marriages were already infrequent church attenders before marriage and stayed that way after marriage. For the Catholic men entering mixed marriages, these consistently infrequent churchgoers were matched by an equal number who went less often after marrying out than they had before. For the women, the selective effect was greater than the marriage effect. Indeed, there were just as many Catholic women in unmixed marriages as in mixed ones who decreased their attendance after they got married.

Another way of looking at Table 6–6 is to ask what happened to actively religious Catholics when they got married. We can do this by comparing the percentage who decreased their attendance with those who maintained a high frequency of attending church. Of active Catholic men entering homogamous marriages, only one-tenth decreased their church attendance after marriage, whereas half of the active men in mixed

Table 6–6   Frequency of Church Attendance before and after Marriage in Religiously Unmixed and Mixed Marriages, for Catholic Men and Women

	CATHOLIC MEN		CATHOLIC WOMEN	
Church Attendance	*Unmixed*	*Mixed*	*Unmixed*	*Mixed*
Consistently frequent	69%	32%	74%	42%
Increased	12	4	2	0
Decreased	8	32	15	12
Consistently	10	32	8	46
Total	99%	100%	99%	100%
Number of cases	49	28	47	24

Adapted from Haerle, 1969: 210, 212, 213. *Source:* Catholic participants in Burgess and Wallin's longitudinal study (1953) who were interviewed during engagement and again in the early years of marriage. Church attendance was defined as consistently frequent if the same person attended church three or more times a month both during engagement and after marriage.

marriages quit going to church as often. For women, the differences were small, but in the same direction. Seventeen percent of the active women decreased their church attendance in unmixed marriages and 21 percent in mixed marriages. Thus even for individuals to whom religion mattered most before marriage, mixed marriages had a diluting effect.

We conclude, then, that on the whole religious dilution in mixed marriages seems to be more a cause of willingness to enter those marriages in the first place than a result of entering the marriage. The fact that Catholic men surrender their premarital attendance more often than Catholic women may reflect the fact that women generally tend to take their religion more seriously and are the primary child-rearers with respect to their children's religious education. Thus, a Catholic man's decreased church attendance may reflect the fact that he is outnumbered in a predominantly non-Catholic family when he marries out.

If parents in mixed marriages are initially and/or subsequently irreligious, it follows that their children will also be irreligious. Some receive little or no religious education and identify with neither parent's church. The remainder tend to adopt the faith of the mother, especially in the case of daughters. In Landis's 1960 study, 75 percent of the daughters and 65 percent of the sons followed the mother's faith, regardless of whether she was Catholic or Protestant. Croog and Teele (1967) found that college-educated Catholic sons of interreligious marriages went to Mass just as often as those from all-Catholic homes, but college-educated Protestants from mixed homes went to church significantly less often than those from all-Protestant families. Whereas 30 percent of the latter went to church every week, only 3 percent of the sons from mixed marriages went that often.

We have seen that interreligious marriages fail more often and interfere with the faith of both parents and children. Chapter 15 will show that they also involve compromises in contraceptive practice for both the Catholic and the non-Catholic partner.

JEWISH-GENTILE MARRIAGES

Despite the fact that there are fewer Jews than Catholics in America, they marry out less often. Residential and social segregation reduce opportunities for Jews and Gentiles to fall in love. Centuries of persecution have produced strong Jewish in-group preferences, particularly for those who identify with Judaism or Zionism as religious and ethnic faiths. Nevertheless, the assimilation of Jews into American life is producing more intermarriages.

Reform Jews marry out more often than Conservative or Orthodox Jews whose culture patterns are more distinctive and whose lives are more segregated (Bigman, 1957). For Orthodox Jews, a child who married a Gentile was traditionally considered dead. His name was no longer mentioned. He was shunned personally and stricken from the parents' will. More recently, said Gordon (1964), family reactions were seldom this severe.

Jewish attitudes toward intermarriage depend on how available Jewish partners are in the local community. In New York City, Mayer (1961) reported that Gentile partners were often surprised to discover "how strongly Jews (felt) about intermarriage." But in southern Illinois small towns, where almost 40 percent of all Jews married outside their ethnic group, Schoenfeld (1969) found attitudes far more tolerant. There the typical attitude of parents was "I would prefer that my son marry a Jewish girl, but it is his choice, and as long as she is a good girl it will be all right." Paradoxically, then it is not the more cosmopolitan large cities of the United States that are most tolerant of interethnic marriages but rather those areas where the Jewish population is so small that intermarriage becomes a necessity for a large proportion of sons and daughters.

Negative reactions to prospective mixed marriages may not be expressed directly by parents afraid of seeming prejudiced. Almost one-third of Mayer's Jewish-Gentile couples (1961) suspected that their parents were more unhappy than they let on. Many parents translated their opposition to the prospect's ethnicity into criticism of his/her personality, appearance, occupation—"everything except the fact that she was Gentile." Contacts with the prospective child-in-law tended to be cold, reserved, and distant more often than explicitly hostile.

Mayer also found that many mixed couples had been brought together initially by a common friend. Mutual friends bridged the gap created by conflicting group identities. They provided a social base on which the new love could be erected. Peers were more apt than parents to share the individual's values and therefore to be less hostile to the prospective partner. However, friends who did have negative reactions rarely expressed them because they did not feel they had the right to volunteer their opinions unless they were asked. This means that no news cannot be assumed to be good news.

Once the decision to marry is made, Jewish-Gentile couples must decide whose wedding ritual to use. Mayer (1961) found among sixteen couples in New York City where one partner was reluctant to marry out of his/her faith, fourteen couples married in the reluctant partner's ritual. This seems like an appropriate solution where the other partner doesn't care. The remaining two couples chose to marry in a civil ceremony. This has the virtue of leaving neither partner with the feeling of having lost out to the other, but the corresponding disadvantage that neither "wins" the chance to use his/her traditional ceremonies.

Marital Failure. Table 6–7 shows five or six times as many failures for Jewish-Gentile marriages as for unmixed Jewish marriages. The same study by Zimmerman and Cervantes also found that for Catholic men marrying out

Table 6–7   Desertions and Divorces of Jewish Men in
Communally Unmixed and Mixed Marriages

| City | PERCENTAGE OF DESERTIONS AND DIVORCES BY COMMUNAL HOMOGAMY | | |
	Communally Unmixed	Communally Mixed	Ratio
Omaha	13%	62%	4.8X
St. Louis	9%	44%	4.9X
Boston	5%	25%	5.0X
Denver	8%	48%	6.0X

Adapted from Zimmerman and Cervantes, 1960: 153–54.

the ratio of divorces and desertions tripled, and for Protestants marrying out it doubled, in comparison to unmixed marriages. This suggests that Jews lose more in marital stability when they marry out than do Catholics or Protestants.

Ethnic Dilution.   In most American homes, the mother is primarily responsible for religious rituals. Jewish-Gentile marriages are no excpetion. In Washington, D.C., 59 percent of intermarried Jewish mothers had conducted Passover services in their homes at least once, but only 19 percent of intermarried Jewish fathers had ever done so (Bigman, 1957). The children of these marriages generally indentified with the mother's faith and chose a marriage partner from her faith.

Illustrative of the mother's influence is the experience of Gentile mothers in mixed families within the 20,000-member Jewish community in Providence, Rhode Island. Children in these families were subjected to many forces influencing them toward a Jewish identity—fathers, neighbors, friends, and community institutions. If the mother converted to Judaism, all of the children considered themselves Jewish. But if the mother did not convert, only 58 percent of the children became Jewish despite the family's public identification with the Jewish community (Goldstein and Goldscheider, 1966). We can easily imagine how many more children would identify with a Gentile mother if the family were not embedded in a large ethnic community.

We can generalize, for both Catholic-Protestant and Jewish-Gentile marriages, that children tend to follow in their mother's footsteps. In most families, child-rearing is primarily the mother's responsibility and religious and cultural training are her special province; as a result, her values are transmitted to the children more often than her husband's.

In the Washington D.C. study, most families reared all their children either as Gentiles or as Jews. Less than one-tenth raised some children one way and some the other. Gordon (1964) commented that in the latter families "the likelihood of marginality and personal insecurity for the children is further increased." It is difficult enough to have parents with different identities, but it is an even greater strain to split siblings. The fact that persecution has so often been the Jewish fate gives the question of group identification strong emotional overtones. Gentiles marrying Jewish partners may encounter prejudice and discrimination. How much the Gentile partner and the couple's children feel the brunt of such practices depends on where they live and on the extent to which the family is identified as Jewish. The very existence of such unpredictability adds to the tension.

INTERNATIONAL MARRIAGES

International marriages require a drastic change of residence for one partner, usually the woman. It is often said that women make most of the adjustments in marriage, but this is especially true when they move to another country. The partner who moves geographically must change personally as well. The problems of any immigrant confront the foreign spouse—learning to speak and write a new language, to like new foods and sports, to understand new customs and values.

The toughest problems that confront an international marriage are not the ones that reflect the difference between the immigrant and the foreign culture but those which obtrude within the marriage itself. When the immigrant is already familiar with the foreign country and the marriage is contracted there in the first place, those differences are more easily anticipated. But for international couples who marry within one partner's country and then migrate to the other's homeland, the belated emigrant may experience drastic changes in the partner.

Atkeson (1970) reported that an American nurse who married a Filipino doctor during his training in the United States found that he seemed quite Americanized as long as they lived in this country. But as soon as they moved to the Philippines, the husband "readapted himself to Filipino culture, seemed a different person to his wife from the husband she had known in the United States." He became more submissive, less emotionally expressive, and less affectionate in his home culture than he had been when she was making the decision to marry him.

Adapting to a new homeland is aided by the spouse and his/her family. Strauss (1954) found that the American husband's parents "generally greeted their Japanese daughters-in-law warmly ... and played an important part in the acculturation of the bride, teaching her about shopping, about kitchen equipment, and the like."

Facilities and equipment are mastered more easily than the subtleties of language. For Japanese war brides, language was the toughest problem. "The difficulty was greatest in times of crisis or emotional excitement and in such situations as the discussion of technical matters or joking" (Schnepp and Yui, 1955). The strain of having to speak a foreign language creates a longing to mingle socially with compatriots so that the native tongue can be enjoyed again.

Table 6–8 shows that a large proportion of persons entering Indian-Western marriages in India had already had extensive international experience prior to meeting the marriage partner. Many of these persons had already established an international life-style and were members of religious, scientific, or organizational communities that transcended national boundaries. Cottrell quoted one Indian as saying it would be far more difficult to marry a "parochial Indian" than to marry a Westerner with an international orientation. Most of the Western men and Indian women entering these marriages already identified with more than one culture before they met. In this sense, the process of adapting to their international marriage began long before. Indeed, 70 percent of the Indian wives entering these marriages grew up in families that lived abroad during their childhood.

Despite their prior exposure to foreign cultures, the Western women living in India with their Indian husbands found that experience especially difficult whenever they lived with or visited the husband's family. One-third of the wives in Cottrell's sample had had this experience and most of them found themselves overwhelmed by the size and complexity of that family, with their privacy invaded and their access to their husband displaced by his involvement with his mother and elder siblings. Cottrell (1975) quoted one of the wives:

> When living with his family all of us, neighbors and family, lived on the roof. We had no room of our own. In three months I could never talk to my husband. There is no comprehension of privacy. By the end of three months I had no courage left to fight. Rooms were always crowded. Everyone gazed at me to see how I drink tea, etc. When all were asleep at night I used to go down and sit in the room and say "thank God I don't have to look at anyone."

Wives resented the fact that their husbands adhered to the customary prohibition on touching them in the presence of other family members

Table 6–8 Cross-National Experience Prior to Meeting Foreign Marriage Partner

Prior Cross-National Experience	Indian Husbands	Western Wives	Western Husbands	Indian Wives
Highly international	60%	10%	19%	42%
Internationally experienced	22	38	75	21
Superficial experience	12	39	6	37
None	0	12	0	0
Total	100%	99%	100%	100%
Number of cases	72	89	16	19

Adapted from Cottrell, 1973: 739–41. *Source:* Indian-Western couples living in India.

and allowed their mothers or elder siblings to make decisions about which the wives were not even consulted. Not only did these women find themselves powerless in relation to the authority figures in the larger family, but their own authority was undermined with respect to their children. Living in a joint family made it impossible to teach their children Western manners. In the words of another wife from Cottrell's sample:

> [Indians] eat with their hands which I dislike very much. The kids see others do it and they do it. It is not proper and it revolts me. They say their cousins do it and ask if it is bad. How can I say it is impolite; when the kids tell their cousins they say you criticize them.

These problems arise partly from living in someone else's house instead of one's own. To some extent they are echoed when any couple lives with their in-laws. But in cross-national marriages, these problems are exacerbated by the cultural differences.

In marriages between American men and Filipino women, the sharpest conflicts involved child-care, keeping house, and sexual attitudes and practices (Hunt and Coller, 1957). The first two were moderated by the husband's tendency to think of them as the wife's domain, even if he disapproved of the way she handled them. The wives were sexually modest and passive by American standards, which disappointed and frustrated the husbands.

To change lifelong habits may seem worthwhile for a foreign spouse rewarded with the high American standard of living. But an American woman who emigrates finds fewer compensating advantages and is apt to be viewed with suspicion in the new country:

> *Coming from a subsistence economy, I gave first consideration to the question of differences in our level of living. I tried my best to inform Diane as accurately as I could about living conditions in Chile—discussed them in detail, gave her materials to read, and cautioned her against forming impressions from tourist advertisements. In addition, I suggested that she should talk to other people—Americans as well as Chileans—who could give her a more detached evaluation of my country. One of these was a missionary who spent five years in my country, and he had a lot to tell Diane.*
>
> *Second was the question of the trustworthiness of an American wife. This question kept coming to my mind because of the stereotype (probably gained from the movies) that the people at home have about American wives, especially those married to racial minorities, which is not very complimentary. I also informed Diane about this. In my effort to resolve this question, I took into consideration the following items: (1) Diane's family background that was furnished to me by a townmate of hers; (2) the judgment of a friend of mine with whom I arranged a double date so*

that he could see Diane for himself; (3) my own evaluation compared to the comments of other people whose judgment I respected.

Some international couples disagree about which country to settle in. One American veteran of World War II wanted to go back to Japan, whereas his Japanese wife wanted to stay here. How much cultural retraining is required depends on the culture. Mates from English-speaking countries have fewer problems than those who must learn a new language. Western Europeans are more like Americans than Orientals or Arabs.

We cannot assume, however, that the best international marriages always involve the greatest cultural similarity. If that were the case, the best marriage for a Japanese war bride would be to a Japanese-American man. Yet Kimura (1957) found that fewer women in Hawaii were satisfied with such a husband than with one of a different nationality background (39 percent versus 75 percent). The trouble with the Japanese/Japanese-American marriages was that the Japanese wife thought she was marrying an emancipated American man, whereas the husband's family advocated traditionally authoritarian Japanese ways that she hoped to escape. The Japanese-American culture was not different enough from what she left behind to give her the new values she sought. In this case ethnic homogamy created value incompatibility, making matters worse rather than better. Conversely, wives of non–Japanese-American men were treated with more respect by the husbands' families and were allowed to work out their desired marriage patterns with less interference.

International marriages occur more often between American men and foreign women than between American women and foreign men. Which partner is American and which country the couple settle in are crucial determinants of the problems involved.

Fujisaki (1970) interviewed Japanese war brides in Los Angeles and reported that a large number of their marriages ended either in divorce or in serious conflicts. DeVos (1959) found that San Francisco Bay area brides had hoped that their American husbands would be kind and helpful, while the men hoped their Japanese wives would be passive and dependent. In actual practice, the men fluctuated between passivity and violence to which the women responded by challenging, castigating, and attempting to control them. Both sexes were disappointed with the way their marriages turned out. The relationships sank into apathy and noncommunication, occasionally marred by quarrels that provoked the husbands to violent outbursts.

At the time DeVos studied these couples, many of the marriages were relatively new. Presumably, many of them subsequently collapsed. After the most unhappy marriages had disintegrated, the surviving ones were not necessarily regretted. Strauss (1954) found in the Chicago area that Japanese war brides and their husbands who were still living together were coping to their own satisfaction with the difficulties that they encountered.

INTERETHNIC MARRIAGES

Combining some features of international marriages, interclass marriages, and interracial marriages are marriages between persons whose families immigrated recently from different foreign countries. Hawaii is an excellent place to study the effects of ethnic intermarriages because so many national backgrounds are represented there. By comparing divorces granted with marriages contracted, Lind (1964) was able to compute divorce rates for various ethnic groups. For homogamous marriages, these fell into three main categories:

1. Stable groups (Japanese or Chinese—15 to 18 percent divorced)
2. Intermediate groups (Caucasians—35 percent divorced)
3. Unstable groups (Filipino or Puerto Rican—46 percent divorced)

Unlike Catholic-Protestant marriages (whose divorce rates are higher than either group taken alone), most interethnic marriages produced divorce rates between the rates for the two groups involved. (For nineteen out of twenty-nine interethnic combinations, the divorce rate fell between the rates for the separate ethnic backgrounds.) This suggests that for most couples, interethnicity is no more of a problem than is inter-denominationalism for American Protestants. However, the remaining ten ethnic combinations were exceptions to this rule: four had divorce rates higher than either partner's group, and six had fewer divorces than would be expected. Caucasian women were involved in the two "worst" combinations, and Caucasian men in two of the three "best" mixtures (see Table 6–9).

The most detrimental combinations involved Caucasian women married to Japanese or Chinese men whose ethnic groups normally have the lowest divorce rates in the entire islands. Perhaps the very stability of those groups was the source of trouble. We have already seen that Japanese war brides married to Japanese-American men had conspicuously unhappy marriages. Apparently, the same solidarity of family structure that oppressed those liberation-seeking women also annoyed already liberated Caucasian women. We assume that Japanese and Chinese husbands and their extended families sought to assert their authority over these wives—without success. A Caucasian-American wife is too assertive to submit to patriarchy. She would rather get a divorce. Caught in a power struggle with a domineering husband and family, a wife accustomed to equality opts out.

At the opposite extreme, the most beneficial marriages paired Caucasian men with Puerto Rican or Filipina women. Here the converse situation existed. Caucasian men are accustomed to equality but women from Spanish cultures expect to be submissive. The relatively low status of their native economies made the wife look up to her "American" husband and feel grateful to him. For her this was an unusually "good"

Table 6–9 Detrimental and Beneficial Ethnic Mixtures, by Ratio of Divorce Rates in Ethnically Unmixed and Mixed Marriages

	DIVORCE RATE BY ETHNIC HOMOGAMY		
Detrimental Mixtures	*Unmixed*	*Mixed*	*Ratio*
Japanese man	15%		3.9X
Caucasian woman	35%	58%	1.7X
Chinese man	18%		2.4X
Caucasian woman	35%	43%	1.2X
Beneficial Mixtures			
Filipino man	46%		0.7X
Puerto Rican woman	46%	32%	0.7X
Caucasian man	35%		0.7X
Filipina woman	46%	24%	0.5X
Caucasian man	35%		0.6X
Puerto Rican woman	46%	20%	0.4X

Adapted from Lind, 1964: 22. *Source:* Divorces granted 1958–62 per 100 marriages contracted 1956–60 for the entire State of Hawaii.

marriage that she would be reluctant to leave. Such marriages are not the most satisfying from the standpoint of the interpersonal criteria used in this book. They may be deficient in companionship and empathy. But they are extraordinarily stable.

Prospects for a successful marriage in the following case are not clear. However, an Anglo-Saxon woman marrying an Italian-American man seems likely to encounter sharp challenges after marriage:

> During the early stages of our relationship, Angelo purposely over-emphasized the things that were closest to his heart in order to elicit my most violent reactions. The men in his family are engaged in a series of entrepreneurial activities that have been extremely lucrative. Angelo's choice of an occupation is almost entirely dependent upon his prospects for making money—in large quantity. This attitude was distasteful to me. I have lived modestly all my life, and have never been inclined to regard money as an index of status or prestige. I was rather amazed when he interrogated me about the material arrangements I would require of a prospective husband—that is, the kind of house, the type of vacation, and so on. It seemed almost as though he was offering me a dowry, and I was taken aback by the businesslike quality of the transaction. However, I slowly came to reconcile myself to these and other aspects of his thinking as I saw them more within the context of his family's expectations.
>
> When we had been seeing one another steadily for about six months, Angelo introduced me to a good friend of his—a middle-aged contractor who drove a white Cadillac. I had very little in common with this man, but I recognized the event as a challenge to my sociability and attempted to make the most of it. A week later the friend appeared again

and I was obliged to invite him to join us at a large party given by a classmate of mine. This time the three of us were together for a whole evening, drinking, dancing, learning how to shoot pool, and so on. Several weeks elapsed before I learned the true identity of this mysterious friend—he was Angelo's brother (an emissary from the other camp) scrutinizing my behavior under "normal conditions."

I was being groomed—in numerous subtle ways—for marriage into a style of life essentially foreign to my own, and, in a sense, the older brother was performing as the first (and probably most sympathetic) judge of my progress. The experience made me more consciously aware of what might be my major difficulty in adjusting: I had become accustomed to a kinship system that was based upon limited communication and tacit understanding very much in contrast to the active mutuality and interdependence that marked many facets of Angelo's familial responsibility.

BLACK-WHITE MARRIAGES

American anxiety about black-white marriages is illustrated by nearly unanimous hesitation in opinion polls. For example, 80 percent of the students questioned in 40 American colleges and universities labeled interracial marriage the most difficult type of mixed marriage (compared to 9 percent for interreligious or intereducational marriage, 4 percent for international marriage, and 3 percent for interclass marriage as measured by economic background—Gordon, 1964).

Trouble for interracial marriages comes chiefly from without. The segregation, discrimination, and prejudice of American society can hardly fail to affect individuals who defy the "rules." If the minority partner is recognizably black, the couple will be the frequent target of curiosity, if not of ostracism and abuse. In a study of middle-class couples in New York City, Smith (1966) found that white partners experienced the discrimination and segregation to which blacks are usually subjected. Both partners were stared at by strangers, interrogated by new friends, and occasionally beaten by new enemies. Forceful intervention by unofficial strangers was rare, however, compared to their "rather common" experience of being stopped by police on highways. Policemen could hardly imagine that a black-and-white couple might be married. The woman was assumed to be either a prostitute or a maid, the man either a rapist or a chauffeur. To minimize hostile reactions from the community, interracial couples often hid their relationship from public view. (Smith's couples rarely announced their engagements publicly, rationalizing that "society would do a rather thorough job of 'publicizing' their marriage anyway.")

In most communities, a mixed family becomes socially black—except in those rare metropolises where interracial couples form their own subcommunity. Rejection by relatives is more severe from the white side. For black relatives, a mixed marriage may tap the sympathy acquired through generations of persecution. Smith found that alienation from parents was the most difficult emotional problem encountered by white partners.

The main question for the white partner is whether he or she is prepared to become black. If so, Smith reported that external persecution sometimes drew husband and wife closer together. However, outside pressures had at least occasional inside repercussions. The black partner tended to be supersensitive. The establishment of the relationship usually depended on overtures from the white partner, since most blacks were afraid of being rejected if they made any advances. After marriage, the black partner tended to be touchy about racial slurs and to insist on the white partner's need to learn to "understand" blacks. Interracial marriage is never easy in contemporary America—even in cosmopolitan New York City.

For the United States as a whole, interracial marriages fare no better than other kinds of mixed marriages. Table 6–10 shows that marriages between blacks and whites that were contracted during the 1950s were far more apt to have ended by 1970 than were either homogamously black or homogamously white marriages. Disintegration rates for mixed marriages ranged from 1.7 times greater for black men married to white women instead of black women to 5.3 times greater for white men who married out instead of marrying in.

INTERCLASS MARRIAGES

Interclass marriages involve couples who differ markedly in education or whose fathers differ significantly in social status as measured by occupation, income, and/or education. We will exclude residual mixtures where

Table 6–10 Survival/Disintegration Experience of Black and White Unmixed and Mixed Marriages

Marital Status in 1970	Husband: Wife:	UNMIXED MARRIAGES		MIXED MARRIAGES	
		White White	Black Black	Black White	White Black
Still married		90%	78%	63%	47%
No longer married		10	22	37	53
Total		100%	100%	100%	100%
Number of cases		8,430,979	780,239	7,534	6,082

Adapted from Heer, 1974: 250. *Source:* All couples married in the United States between 1950 and 1960. Data gathered by the U.S. Bureau of the Census in 1970.

one partner has been upwardly mobile to the other partner's level and will concentrate on genuine mixed marriages where the partners' social position differs when they marry.

Husband-High Marriages

Just as international and interethnic marriages differ according to the relative position of the partners, so do interclass marriages. Usually it is the woman who marries up. From her point of view, this makes a "good marriage" since she can hope to share her husband's prestige as well as his standard of living. Feldman (1966) found that some men preferred a low-status woman's old-fashioned interest in children, religion, and sociability to a college-educated woman's interest in career and community affairs. A man may find a low-status girl physically attractive and not be bothered by her lack of social niceties.

Scott (1965) pointed out that low-status women expected less and were therefore less expensive to date. High-status men discovered that "the favors, including the prospect of marriage, of low-status women can be had for a smaller investment of their own scarce time, money, and emotion." Time-short medical students were especially apt to find low-status women attractive for this reason. This is hardly the path to a productive relationship, but it is certainly the path to an inexpensive one for men more interested in their careers than in their marriages.

Elder (1969) found that middle-class men who married women of working-class origins chose those who were outstanding in their sex appeal, physique, grooming, and general appearance as rated by outside observers. These appearance factors led the men to overlook the difference in family backgrounds and may have left both partners with a feeling that they had made a fair exchange in the mate-selection marketplace.

Yet research on the outcome of such marriages suggests that male prestige cannot be exchanged for female beauty without producing a less satisfactory marriage than a socially unmixed one. Table 6–11 shows that husband-high marriages were generally less successful than homogamous ones. Such couples are likely to find their conversations less productive than persons with similar backgrounds. Feldman (1966) found that differentially educated marriage partners felt less close after conversing with each other—apparently because talking exposed their differentness.

> In the early months of our relationship I felt loved for myself but soon thereafter I realized that Don was embarrassed when my dress and my conversation didn't measure up to his expectations of a good executive's wife. He frankly felt I didn't promote his best interests with his business colleagues and urged me to improve myself. Fortunately, this expectation of his became apparent before we got caught in a bad marriage.

Wife-High Marriages

The problems of husband-high marriages are mild compared to those of wife-high marriages (see Table 6–11). The latter are difficult for the wife if the husband's income provides less than her accustomed standard of living. To be sure, most couples start with less than their parents have attained, but husband and wife are usually "in the same boat." What bothers a high-status wife is that her comedown is greater than her husband's. What hurts even more is seeing her children deprived of luxuries she enjoyed in childhood. The fiancée of a modestly paid high-school teacher expressed her anxiety thus:

> *Bruce will probably earn less than half what my father pays in income tax. This won't bother me too much because my family has never lived on a showy plane. But I'm afraid that when my children are old enough to demand things, I won't be able to give them all the money they want. I don't want them to have to pinch pennies when they get to college but to be able to splurge and eat out whenever they want to. I don't want them to have to worry about money or even think about it.*

A man who marries up has problems, too. He is touchy about finances. Gifts from his wife's family are reminders of his lower income. His wife pressures him to get ahead. Such sensitivities do not make for easy marital or kinship relations. The problems of wife-high marriages are not only financial. The husband's lower status tends to pull the wife down to his level of reputation and participation in the community. Moreover, the man's self-confidence is undermined by the wife's disappointment over his occupational "inadequacy."

Table 6–12 shows that men with less education than their wives were more likely than others with equal or greater education to resort to violence within the family. Most of their violence was directed against their wives, although some was directed against their children. Men who

Table 6–11   Marriage Adjustment, by Comparative Class Status of Husband and Wife

	COMPARATIVE CLASS STATUS		
Marriage Adjustment	*Same*	*Husband Higher*	*Wife Higher*
Good	53%	35%	28%
Fair	26	33	31
Poor	21	32	41
Total	100%	100%	100%
Number of cases	215	116	65

Adapted from Roth and Peck, 1951. *Source:* Burgess and Cottrell's married couples in Chicago, 1931–33. Social class was measured by a composite index of status characteristics.

Table 6–12 Family Violence, by Comparative Education of Husband and Wife

	COMPARATIVE EDUCATION	
Husband Violent	*Wife Higher*	*Equal or Husband Higher*
Yes	45%	9%
No	55	91
Total	100%	100%
Number of cases	31	119

Adapted from O'Brien, 1971: 695. *Source:* Couples filing suit for divorce in a midwestern city.

suffer from a sense of inferiority in relation to their wives are particularly apt to react violently when the marriage goes sour.

While wife-high marriages generally experience psychological strains, Roth and Peck (1951) found that the most disastrous marriages involved women who had been upwardly mobile past their husbands' position. Women who start out lower and end up higher are superconscious of their social status and supersensitive about their husbands' inadequacies. The men in turn feel inferior because of the wife's success.

Marriages that start off handicapped by educational differences need not be trapped in that discrepancy. Expanding facilities for adult education for both sexes and the new emphasis on continuing education for women offer opportunities for removing educational deficiencies. Even in middle age, mothers and fathers of growing children may restore their self-confidence and revitalize their marriages by going (back) to college.

INTERGENERATIONAL MARRIAGES

Marriages between persons widely enough separated in age to be the equivalent of parent-child marriages are rare. They are frequently remarriages for one or both partners and therefore divorce-prone.

Figure 6–1 shows not only that divorce rates tend to be high for persons who are widely separated in age, but also that smaller differences in age also raise the divorce rate to a lesser extent. Presumably, in these days of rapidly changing attitudes toward the relationship between men and women, persons whose ages differ by only a handful of years have grown up in a distinctively different culture. We saw in Chapter 3 that students in succeeding college generations (only four years apart) experienced quite different environments with respect to premarital sexuality. So spouses of different ages may have different attitudes with respect to such controversial issues as open marriage or women's liberation or exotic sexual practices. Conversely, Figure 6–1 suggests, couples of the same age are likely to be the most compatible.

Sizable age differences affect the balance of power in marriage. Since

Figure 6-1 Divorce Rates by Comparative Age of Husband and Wife

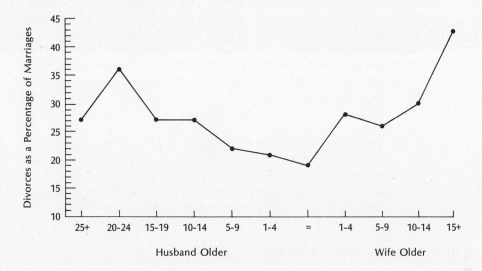

Adapted from Schmitt 1969: 49. *Source:* All divorces granted in Hawaii 1964-1966 compared to all marriages 1961-1963, exclusive of those involving persons of difference ethnic groups.

the average husband is several years older, influential age differences are correspondingly skewed. Blood and Wolfe (1960) found that husbands who were eleven or more years older and wives who were four or more years older had significantly more power than the ones in between. In extreme cases, older husbands had a father-daughter relationship with their wives. Having lived longer, they had more savoir-faire and sophistication, so their wives looked up to them and depended on them. Conversely, older wives tended to mother young husbands, taking care of them and supplying the main strength in the marriage.

Although the greater the age difference in either direction, the higher the divorce rate, the problems in intergenerational marriages are more severe in wife-older marriages, just as they are in wife-high interclass marriages. "Mother-son" marriages had significantly higher divorce rates than "father-daughter" marriages with the same age difference. Presumably, this reflects the bias of our culture that dictates that men "should" be either the same age or older than their wives, but not younger.

Theoretically, we would expect age differences to be felt most acutely in the beginning years of marriage and toward the end of life. The divorce statistics from Hawaii reflect mostly the earlier years since most marriages fall apart, if they are ever going to, in the first few years. When people are in their teens or early twenties, a difference in age of a few years implies a major difference in experiences and maturity. At the end of life, whichever partner is older may go downhill into fatigue and senility while the younger partner is still in the prime of life, creating difficulties in leisure-time preferences, and so on. At that stage, the older partner may be glad to have a younger spouse to take care of him/her, but the caretaker is likely to find this more burdensome than if they were facing their declining years together. So generational homogamy predisposes couples to marital harmony and mutual understanding, whereas intergenerational marriages must cope with personal and cultural strains.

To every generalization there are exceptions. Some marriages not only survive in the face of age differences but thrive on them:

> *I came to know him first as my teacher and he continued to teach me all our married days. I had the highest respect for his ideas and looked up to him as a model. Being younger, I was able to care for him in his last years. Our companionship was very precious. Even though I am lonely now, I wouldn't change those years for anything.*

EVALUATING THE PROSPECTS FOR A MIXED MARRIAGE

The hazards of mixed marriages are clear from the preceding pages. Nevertheless, *some* mixed marriages turn out well. What makes the difference between the ones that succeed and those that fail? The answer depends on each couple's ingredients for marriage.

Prerequisites for Success

For mixed marriages the prerequisites are the same as for other marriages—compatibility, skill, effort, commitment, and support—but they are more crucial than usual.

Compatibility. Greater compatibility in other respects is needed to offset the mixture. The amount of incompatibility involved in the "mix" differs. There is less to fear from a residual mixture than from a genuine one. Even genuine mixtures vary in their strain potential. A "high-church" Episcopalian or Lutheran feels more kinship for Catholic liturgy, a Unitarian for Reform Judaism, an expert on Asia for a Chinese wife.

In interclass marriages, Roth and Peck found that the wider the class difference, the more the marriage suffered. This can be extended to all mixed marriages—the greater the difference between groups, the greater the problems that must be offset by compatibility in other respects if the marriage is to succeed.

Skill. The wisdom of marrying out depends partly on the couple's coping ability. The more skillful they are, the better they can resolve their differences. A genuinely mixed marriage will test their problem-solving skills to the utmost. Maslow's "self-actualizing people" were unusually skillful. They were more confident of their ability to cope with the stresses of mixed marriages and even found them stimulating. Maslow (1954: 259) stated:

> In the more external and superficial characteristics, e.g., income, class status, education, religion, national background, appearance, the extent of homogamy seems to be significantly less than in average people. Self-actualizing people are not threatened by differences nor by strangeness. Indeed, they are rather intrigued than otherwise. They need familiar accents, clothes, food, customs, and ceremonies much less than do average people.

If a couple find it difficult to deal rationally with problems, if they are easily provoked to rage or moodiness, if they are short on patience and sympathy, one prerequisite for successful mixing is missing.

Effort.   Mixed marriages require more effort than unmixed ones. For mixed couples unwilling to make the extra effort, the relationship may fall of the weight of the mixture. With effort, couples can "make the best of a bad situation."

The stress of mixed backgrounds requires an extra measure of love, willingness to sacrifice, and concern for the partner's welfare.

Commitment.   The very anxiety created by the prospect of a mixed marriage, the warnings of others, and the soul-searching deliberations mean that when the decision to marry is finally made, it is likely to be firm. To marry in the face of social pressure is to take a stand that is humiliating to break. Not only to outsiders, but to oneself and to each other, the resolve to make a go of it is unusually explicit—and unusually necessary. Firm commitment does not guarantee success, but it helps mixed couples get through many of the troubles they are bound to encounter.

Support.   Even hostile parents or friends are likely to switch from opposition to support once they lose the battle to prevent a mixed marriage and are faced with a fait accompli (see Table 6–13). In exceptional cases where parental hostility persists, it may be advisable to move away. Couples faced with strong community opposition may also flee to safer ground. Flight may be cowardly, but a safe haven can make the difference between support and disruption. Mixed marriages can seldom afford less than the best social environment.

Table 6–13 shows how strongly parents reacted when first confronted with a Jewish-Gentile involvement. But the same parents moderated their opposition considerably by the time of the wedding. In assessing this table, we need to remember that it does not tell us how many other couples broke off their relationship because their parents remained adamantly opposed.

Table 6-13 Parental Opposition to Jewish-Gentile Marriages, before and at Marriage

Degree of Parental Opposition	On Learning Relationship Was Serious	At Time of Marriage
Strong	70%	27%
Moderate	20	17
Mild	10	41
None	0	15
Total	100%	100%
Number of cases	29	29

Adapted from Mayer, 1961: 170. *Source:* Jewish-Gentile couples in New York City who initially resisted intermarriage but who eventually married across communal lines.

Procedures for Deciding

To determine whether they meet the prerequisites for success, mixed couples need all the usual compatibility testing, and then some. A distinctive step for mixed couples is participating in the activities of both groups in order to understand each other's backgrounds. Most interfaith couples attend services at both churches. One white woman went to live in Harlem to help decide whether to marry a black man. Immersing herself in an impersonal mass of strangers of her friend's race gave her fresh insight into the social complications of an interracial marriage (Karpf, 1951).

Other mixed couples are usually glad to share their own experience. Caution is needed, however, in interpreting the experience of any particular couple. Some couples are miserable and others are blissful. Couples already divorced have disappeared from public view. Nobody else's experience guarantees what will happen in one's own case. Nevertheless, such conversations reveal potential problems and potential solutions.

Making the Final Decision

The final decision whether to marry out depends on the attractiveness of the particular prospect and of the alternatives. A mixed marriage may seem advisable if there is little chance of a homogamous one, either because homogamous partners are scarce or because one's bargaining power is low. Overall compatibility with a mixed partner may be greater than with the best homogamous partner met so far or likely to appear in the future.

Because they involve special problems, mixed marriages require extra testing in advance. If the tests are passed with flying colors, there is little reason to fear heterogamy. Although mixed couples have a higher casualty rate than unmixed ones (both in broken engagements and broken marriages), most mixed marriages that last are good ones. The risks may be greater, but they aren't necessarily overwhelming. Some mixed marriages aren't much different from unmixed ones. And some mixed couples find in diversity a breadth of experience that they prize. In the last analysis, each couple must decide for themselves.

Once the decision has been made, it is easy for mixed couples to blame the background difference as a "cause" of all their troubles. To do so, however, is to block the possibility of negotiation—since backgrounds can't be changed. The reality of the past need not totally determine the present. If a couple want good things in the present and are willing to put energy into what they want, they can find ways to live with most differences.

We are impressed with the extent to which mixed marriages have become less hazardous in our own lifetime than they used to be. As barriers of segregation and discrimination have been reduced, empathy and understanding have increased. So, many of the mixtures that proved troublesome in earlier generations seem likely to cause less trouble in the future.

7 Readiness for Marriage

Becoming involved and making a wise choice of partner are the first steps toward marriage. But a couple may seem compatible, very much in love, and still not be ready for marriage—yet. Are they personally mature enough to take on the responsibilities of marriage? This is primarily a question of age and experience, though in special cases other problems block the way. Some problems are internal residues of unhappy family backgrounds. Some are external obstacles that delay engagement and marriage.

PERSONAL READINESS FOR MARRIAGE

Couples who get along well on dates may nevertheless lack the prerequisite for married living. Marriage embraces more aspects of life and requires taking more responsibility. To be successful, it requires special skills and resources.

Emotional Maturity

The most important ingredient in readiness for marriage is awareness of the self, that is, the ability to identify my own feelings and intentions. I am emotionally mature when I have arrived at adulthood and am no longer a helpless infant, a naïve child, or a rebellious adolescent.

Emotional maturity comes from having experienced enough changes and crises to become aware of my particular ways of feeling and responding. To know my own identity is to identify the many parts of myself and to dare to express the part that is real at the moment as opposed to being out of touch with my feelings, or behaving as someone else thinks I should.

Sometimes maturity is best understood in its absence:

> *I really love Roy and would marry him today if he asked me but he doesn't want to commit himself. He likes me but he also likes other women as well. He really treats me terribly. He frequently won't negotiate anything and if he does agree to something I want he breaks the agreement whenever it doesn't suit his need.*

A mature person has the ability to establish and maintain personal relationships. Infants lack this ability. They depend on those who gratify their needs without being able to give in return. Adolescents, on the other hand, are too eager to demonstrate their independence to be secure in their relations with others. Maturity involves both the ability to give (which infants lack) and the ability to receive (which adolescents distrust). In other words, a mature person has the ability to love.

Empathy is the ability to perceive the feelings of others. Immature individuals are so wrapped up in their own needs that they can't understand how others feel. Small children are egocentric and take years to learn to recognize the feelings of others. This does not mean they surrender their own identity in the process, but they learn to respect the identity of others.

Beyond recognizing others' needs is willingness to assume responsibility for meeting them. Immature persons may have moments of altruism, but they shy away from long-term commitments that might interfere with their shifting interests. Getting married means taking on a long-term responsibility, entering into a contract to respond to my partner's needs to the best of my ability. Having children is an even greater responsibility because of their utter dependence. To the immature, such responsibilities are disconcerting. To the mature, they are a challenge:

> *There is a lot more to being ready for marriage than just being able to handle my own problems. Part of mature love is being able to support and help my wife when she has problems and not depend on her to always be my emotional support. It is being able to stand on my own and being able to help her even when I am already carrying a load of my own.*

To say one should be able to establish and maintain a personal relationship, be empathetic and assume responsibility before marriage is not helpful for the reader who doubts whether s/he is or ever will be ready. The old saying "You'll know when it's the right person and the right time" isn't good enough for these days, when many have doubts about whether they are marriage material or whether marriage is right for them.

Maturity is relative. I am emotionally mature at moments and at other times I fail miserably to meet my own and others' expectations. Emotional readiness is that state that comes again and again in life as I accept that I am never "grown up" and "ready to be happily married for the rest of my life." Realistic expectations allow me to accept myself as I am and you as you are. Maturity brings an awareness of the inevitable flow between stability and change. With maturity comes a trust in the meaning of all the changing.

But I am what I am must be coupled with I will be what I will be: acceptance of my reality in the now coupled with reaching out seriously toward what I want to be. I can change and grow. Acceptance without goals is static. Growth is a never-ending process. Maturity is another way of defining integration of the many differing parts of the self that must occur again and again as I go wider and deeper into knowledge of myself and the world.

Many treatises on divorce list unrealistic expectations of marriage as a prime cause. What kind of expectations allow me to be myself and allow you to be yourself now and through the changes that we will encounter in our individual and collective lives?

Before making a contract with you I need to discover what I want for myself. I can be truly committed to you only as I am true to myself.

The questions below may increase self-awareness at a time when there is a danger of losing oneself in the other. Our own marriage would have benefited if we had consciously faced some of these questions earlier. Actually such questions are very real to us even now, in our thirty-third year of marriage. Perhaps they will enable others to test their own readiness for marriage.

Identifying Myself

Who am I? What do I expect of myself? Do I dare to be myself? Am I more eager to please others than to please myself? Am I trapped in roles that do not fit or satisfy me?

How do I conform? Am I afraid of nonconformity? How would I feel about you if you behaved in a way that I disapproved of? that my parents disapproved of? that "society" disapproved of? How important is it to me that everybody like you?

Fears of Failure.   How do I feel about failing? About not living up to my goals and intentions? About my limitations? How do I face my failures? Do I beat myself and feel ashamed? Can I admit to myself and to you that I have limitations? Can I use my "failures" to teach me how I need to change? Can I accept that I am not perfect? Can I accept my own humanness and share that with you or must I forever be defending my good image against your disillusionment? Can I relax and just be me? Can I be honest with you? Can I speak to you directly without subterfuge?

Fears of Involvement.   Am I able to reach out to meet you? How often do I ask for what I want: for affection, for listening to me, for sharing your feelings with me? Am I willing to ask you for time? Do I dare admit that I love you? Can I admit that I have needs without feeling guilty, blaming myself for not being independent? How much am I willing to reveal myself to you?

Fears of Rejection.   What if you do not hear me or respond to me or if you criticize me for being who I am? Can I understand that this is your perspective—the way you see things right now; that your perspective may differ from mine, but may still be useful to me? Do I take your difference from me as criticism? as rejection?

How do I deal with my fear of rejection? Do I assume you will reject me if I do not please you? Do I take your anger or frustration or expression of your own emotions as a rejection of me? Do I interpret your enjoyment of others as a rejection of me? Does my acceptance of myself depend on your acceptance of me?

Fears of Commitment.   Am I ready for commitment? What does it mean to me to commit myself to you? What is my experience with making time and energy commitments? For how long am I able to commit myself? How do I feel about committing myself exclusively to you? How primary do I wish my marriage to be in my total life? How important to me is an intimate long-term relationship?

Am I afraid of getting caught and unable to get out? Do I fear committing myself and changing my mind later? Am I afraid of losing my freedom to do and say what I wish? Am I afraid of your reasoning? Am I afraid to let you know what my limits are?

How do I relate change and commitment? Suppose I change? Suppose you change? How can we be true to each other and not be caught in promises we can't keep and guarantees that can't be fulfilled?

Am I clear about what I want in marriage? In a relationship? How do I work on my lack of clarity? Is it all right to be ambivalent? How do I feel about consistency? How do I deal with my own change of mind and feeling? How do I view my own changeableness?

Fears of Encounter.   How strong am I? Would I be demolished if we disagreed? Would I be demolished if you went away? Can I get along without you? Are you essential to my well-being? How do I defend my rights? Do I believe that I have rights? What does it mean for me to be assertive? Can I be assertive without being hostile toward you?

What do I do with my frustration? How do I cope with anger? Do I have a right to express my anger? Am I afraid of my anger? How can I accept my anger and express it without getting into trouble? How do I cope with your anger? Does it panic me? Do I believe that my anger can tell me about my need? Can I use my anger as a signal of a need for change?

How flexible am I? How easy is it for me to change my mind, my attitude, my feeling, my behavior? How difficult is it for me to let go of a hurt? How important is it that we agree on everything? How do I behave when we disagree? Can I stand up for myself without putting you down? Can I be right without you being wrong? How important is it for me to win? What happens when I lose? Is it really possible for us to find a way where no one loses? How do I give criticism? How do I take criticism?

How much am I willing to dialogue with you? What does it mean, to dialogue? to negotiate? What does it mean to respect myself? What does it mean to respect you? How able am I to listen to you and hear you? How important is it to me that I be heard?

Do I let you push me around? When you oppose me do I withdraw? Is being direct different from being agressive when I feel strongly about my own beliefs? How good a fighter am I? Am I a "fair fighter"? Am I willing to stay with a fight? Under what circumstances? What does sensitivity mean? How does this differ from "supersensitivity"?

What do I do with my hurt? What do I do with your hurt? Do I overprotect myself or you against hurt? Is pain inevitable, or is there a way to avoid it?

Fears about Caring.   What is caring? What is loving? What does it mean to be supportive? Do I need to be cared for? Do I want you to support me? Am I willing to ask for it when I need it?

How important is it that you show affection for me? How important is sexual expression to me? Am I willing to initiate intimacy as well as to receive it? Am I able to say no when I don't wish to give or receive? How do I say no?

Do I care for myself? Will I allow you to punish me? Will I protect my own space? What does privacy mean to me? How much privacy do I need? Will I seek outside support when I need it?

Will you keep me from being lonely? Am I afraid of solitude? Do I value my aloneness? Do I need you to fill up my spaces? Do I take time for myself?

Readiness for marriage is based on how I feel about myself as much as on how I feel about you, on what I know about myself even more than what I know about you. It is to be able to identify my state of being, my varying emotions, my wants, and to monitor my own behavior in relation to these.

I will never be perfect nor will you. But if I feel ready to meet you, to engage with you, that is most important.

Old Enough to Get Married

Becoming emotionally mature takes time, so age is a crude index of maturity. How old must a person be to be ready for marriage?

Figure 7–1 shows how sharply divorce rates are affected by marital unreadiness in terms of age at marriage. For both men and women, the younger the age at marriage, the higher the divorce rate. Indeed, for the Californians included in this study, the chances of a marriage ending up in divorce exceeded fifty–fifty until age 19 for women and age 22 for men.

Some of the declining divorce rate for persons marrying in their later twenties reflects the fact that the latter are more apt to be better equipped for marriage educationally and in other ways. Glick and Carter (1958) found that women who graduated from college were almost 24 when they married and male graduates were typically 26. Nevertheless, we assume that even when other things are equal, the chances of marital stability are undermined when people get married much before their middle twenties.

Although younger-than-average marriages do not automatically fail, they face extra hazards that make extra maturity imperative. Couples marrying earlier than usual need to be precociously mature if their marriages are to survive.

Social Maturity

A person may be emotionally mature and yet not have experienced enough social life to be ready for marriage.

Figure 7-1 Percent Divorced by Age at First Marriage for Men and Women

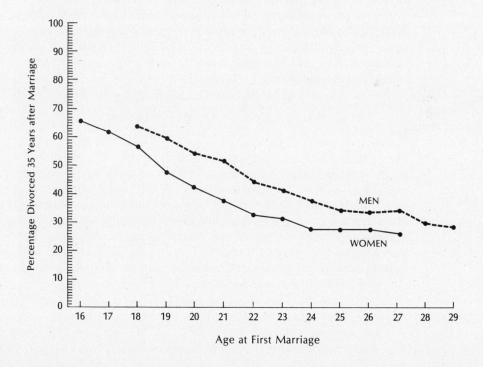

Computed from Schoen, 1975: 553-554. *Source:* State of California, 1969. Cumulative divorce rates by 35th year after marriage.

Enough Dating. Getting acquainted with new persons is a fascinating experience. New partners may automatically look more interesting than existing ones. Individuals who date only a handful of persons may feel later that they missed something and wonder what others are like.

Sooner or later, most people discover that new pastures are not likely to be any greener than those they have already visited. Instead of exploring further, they want to settle down. How many partners it takes to satisfy a given person cannot be predicted—maybe a dozen, maybe 50 members of the opposite sex. In any case, one characteristic of social maturity is a willingness to disregard unknown potential marriage partners and commit oneself to building a primary relationship with a particular person.

When people tire of the insecurity of dating, they are socially ready for marriage. Having dated widely enough for new partners to lose their fascination, they can concentrate henceforth on the one who interests him/her the most.

Enough Single Life. Besides dating enough, it is important to be independent for a while. Just after becoming emancipated from parents is too soon to take on the responsibilities of marriage. Single life has advantages. Spare time can be used as one sees fit. Jobs can be changed. Travel is limited only by the time and money available. The single person does not have to consult anybody's wishes or cater to anybody's moods.

Women especially need to prove to themselves, their parents, and the opposite sex that they are capable of supporting themselves and managing their own destinies. Supervised more closely than their brothers in childhood, they need to achieve a full sense of personal identity before being ready to get married.

Emotional Health

The dividing line between emotional immaturity and emotional disturbance is a fine one. When maturity fails to develop in due time, the individual may be permanently disqualified from marriage unless s/he gets help. Human personality is so complex that emotional problems take many forms. Among the signs are moodiness, anxiety, insecurity, and suspiciousness. Every person has such feelings occasionally. But when they are constant, they ruin interpersonal relations. They may plague the individual with imaginary difficulties. A jealous man whose friend actually was devoted to him is an example:

> *Clyde has done a funny thing this winter. He's a good dancer and we used to go to parties a lot. But lately I can't get him to take me anymore. He mentions something about being afraid the other fellows will steal me away from him and suggests we go to the movies instead.*

Marriage to such a person would be a nightmare of harassment: Who came to the door today? Who was that on the phone? Why did you talk to that person at the party?

Emotional problems usually bear the trademarks of immaturity: possessiveness, irresponsibility, and unpredictability. Occasionally, however, they take the opposite form—"overmaturity" or excessive rigidity. An oversocialized person may be unable to tolerate the frailties of others:

> *I don't think Janie realizes how often she criticizes me. She couldn't understand why I ran out of money last semester and accused me of being irresponsible and lacking in foresight. She tells me I don't study hard enough and could get better grades if I only wanted to. After we've been to a party she tells me all the things I did wrong.*

Perfectionism may be applied not only to the partner but to oneself, producing masochistic overaltruism. Though an excellent giver, such a person may be unable to accept love in his/her anxiety to avoid any hint of selfishness.

Emotional problems can usually be traced to the parent-child relationship. Where that relationship was twisted and tense, the grown child's negative reactions are often transferred to the spouse:

> *When I go home I get a tight feeling in my abdomen because of the way my mother harangues me. She infuriates me so much that I just have to get up and leave the table. I'm afraid that when I get married I'll be oversensitive to my wife and react the same way if she ever is the least bit critical of me.*

Desensitization. Because emotional maladjustment can wreck a marriage, such persons are not ready for marriage. Are they therefore permanently "unmarriageable"? Some people's problems are so difficult that no help is enough. For many, however, change is possible. Emotional disturbance is not likely to diminish simply with the passage of time. Nor do problems often yield to self-help through self-analysis. If one's emotional response system is out of kilter, going to a skillful counselor is required as preparation for marriage.

Illustrative of the unhappy consequences of failure to get help with personal problems is Springer et al.'s finding (1974) that persons who had suffered one or more broken engagements had less happy marriages. Presumably, if these persons had seen their broken engagements as signs of personal unreadiness for marriage and had taken advantage of the opportunity to get professional help, their marriages would have benefited. Unfortunately, many people faced with interpersonal troubles tend to blame the partner rather than to look within themselves to see what the failure of an intimate relationship shows about their need for therapy before entering another relationship.

Marriage Models

Most people learn how to be marriage partners in the process of growing up. They learn what it means to be a husband and a wife by observing their father and mother. When parents set a good example, this readiness can be taken for granted. When they do not, children may not be prepared for marriage. The parents' faults tend to haunt the next generation. Old patterns are either blindly repeated or desperately rejected, leaving a strained clumsiness:

> *Tony's father is from the old country and he still has a lot of old-country ideas about husband-wife relations. He has pretty bad temper tantrums every once in a while during which he beats his wife and once he even threatened her with a gun. I never realized it before but Tony really treats me pretty much the same way. When he shoves me around and gets mad at me for having my own ideas it's just like his father and mother all over again.*

This son unconsciously imitated his father. Others reject the unhappy example of their parents. Because they lack a better model, they are apt to lean over backward in their anxiety to avoid their parents' mistakes. They try too hard—feeling so anxious about parental trouble spots that they overreact to problems. Events that would cause only minor irritation in an ordinary marriage plunge others into terror and despair:

> *All I did was take a little nip at the office party, but she really told me off when we got home. She said I was so tipsy I made a fool of myself with the stenographers. Well, it just wasn't so. I was only enjoying the spirit of the occasion. Just because her old man was a drunkard and a philanderer doesn't mean I'm going to turn into one!*

Those whose parents were unhappy become oversensitive. Their eagerness to avoid their parents' difficulties boomerangs. Their very attempts to prevent trouble cause trouble:

> *My mother-in-law had an affair and my husband has never been able to forget it. He seems to have lost faith in women as a result and is afraid I'll go off and leave him for someone else. To prevent that he keeps me home all the time except when he can go out with me. It's begun to get on my nerves so much that if he keeps on chaperoning me he'll drive me away himself.*

These cases suggest one reason why children from unhappy homes are poor marriage risks. Conflict and divorce churn on from generation to generation.

Remodeling for Marriage.   Should children from unhappy homes never get married? No more than emotionally immature or maladjusted individuals. Initial unreadiness doesn't necessarily disqualify people permanently. Some things can be done to break the spell of the parental model and provide a better model.

People who react against their parental example are apt to think they have broken away from their influence. However, rebellion is itself a sign of continuing susceptibility. To replace either apprehensive rejection of the parents' behavior or unconscious identification with it, insight and awareness are needed. If I understand how my parents' actions influenced me, I will be able to marry more confidently. Insight makes it easier to tolerate residual sensitivity. It may even produce a sense of humor about inherited trouble spots. Premarital counseling provides a setting for talking out bitter memories and fearful anticipations.

To break the spell of the past, however, creates a vacuum. A new marriage model is needed. Reading and study may help. Better yet is the opportunity to learn from a smooth-running family:

> My folks had so much trouble getting along that it was no fun going home to hear them quarrel. Ever since Lesley and I have been going together I've spent most of my vacations at her house and it's been a real eye-opener for me. Her mother and dad are friendly, easygoing— everything my parents aren't. It's been good for me to be able to live for a while in a house where the air isn't blue all the time.

For other people, married friends may provide the desired example. Alternative models help erase the memory of trouble at home.

CIRCUMSTANTIAL READINESS

External circumstances are less important than personal readiness. Couples can undergo almost any physical hardship and come out stronger, *provided* they don't blame each other. Geiger (1955) found in the U.S.S.R. that family solidarity was increased by political persecution blamed on the government but was decreased by financial problems blamed on the husband.

The unforeseeable tragedies of marriage cannot, by definition, affect the decision about when to marry. The relevant question is whether people are prepared to cope with foreseeable problems. If hardships clearly lie ahead, are both partners ready to tackle them as challenges to be surmounted rather than as grudges to be borne against each other? When handicaps are assumed voluntarily, they are less likely to threaten a relationship. Nevertheless, circumstances are sometimes so inauspicious that they augur for delaying the wedding.

Financial Resources

How much money does it take to get married? The answer depends in part on the values of the couple. But Cutright (1970) found that the higher a man's income, the greater the likelihood that he would get married. So the higher a couple's joint income, the greater the chances that they will feel they can afford to get married.

Few couples begin marriage at the level their parents have reached. Except when upward mobility is unusually fast, the couple's first paychecks are lower than either his parents' or hers. Consequently, the new marriage begins on a more meager footing than either partner experienced at home.

The fact that both suffer similarly is a saving grace. If eating hamburger and making do with secondhand furniture in a one-room apartment is an equal comedown for both, neither is likely to feel bitter. Stretching dollars can be challenging.

What if the couple's own resources are not adequate? Does this mean they must not get married, or may parents legitimately help?

Parental Subsidy.   To some people, help from parents would be unthinkable. It would sacrifice bitterly won adulthood. Financial dependence, after all, is still dependence, and supportive relatives are likely to be influential relatives. Nevertheless, for people sure of themselves, aid from others need not create anxiety:

> In our family there is a regular tradition of helping each new generation get started in marriage. The old folks are glad to do it because they don't need the money themselves. The young couple aren't supposed to repay the parents but are expected to pass the money on to their own children when they get ready to be married. This way each generation gets help when they need it most.

From a financial point of view this policy makes sense. When a couple are in their twenties and thirties, their income is low but their child-rearing and house-buying expenses are high. The result is heavy pressure on the budget. At the same time their parents' earning power has reached its peak while their expenses have dropped with the launching of their children (and perhaps with completion of their mortgage payments). The senior family has a financial surplus precisely when the junior family has a shortage.

Many middle-class parents help their children financially. Sussman (1953a) found that more than three fourths of his New Haven families gave regular financial help to their married children. The following is a typical parent's attitude:

> *At today's prices and costs of housing you can't expect children who have just finished school to be able to build or buy a house or even to live decently in an apartment without help from the family. It might have been all right in my day to say, "You are 21, you are on your own." Today it is different. Our feeling is that we have enough money now that we really don't need, and after all, our desires are very few at our age. So why not help the children?*

Parents can proffer their help diplomatically. Wedding gifts like a home, an automobile, or a substantial check are more acceptable than a regular stipend. Christmas and birthdays provide customary occasions for presents. Sussman found that help that met genuine needs did not create friction between generations. Only where the parent-child relationship has been chronically tense is trouble likely. Normally, parental aid provides a workable alternative to postponing an otherwise impecunious marriage.

Resources of Time

The next chapter describes the planning necessary for the wedding, honeymoon, and first year of marriage. To rush through this planning means going into marriage ill prepared, risking miscalculations that get things off to a bad start, and causing worry during an otherwise delightful period of anticipation. A generous interval is needed to pave the way for the wedding day.

Here we wish to discuss time for living together during the first year of marriage. If a couple know they will be separated after the wedding, should they wait for a more auspicious time? The answer depends both on the length of the separation and the length of the interval between the wedding and the date of departure.

Differential Socialization during Separation. Both partners will change while they are apart. This is not due to separation alone, for personalities change constantly. When people are together, however, changes can be adjusted to as they occur. New interests and behavior patterns develop so gradually that people hardly realize what is happening. But if people are apart, the cumulative effect of the same changes becomes more conspicuous.

Personality changes not only pile up during separation but are accentuated by it. When couples are together, they are exposed to similar influences. Separation introduces differential influences. In military separation this change of environment is especially marked:

> *When I was drafted into the army, I began an entirely new phase of my relationships and views of the opposite sex. Broad-mindedness was*

the only asset I acquired in regard to women due to the service. I found that the average serviceman was interested in one main object in women—sex. After getting out of basic training, I was transformed by my environment from a "good little boy" to one of their kind, which consisted of wine, women, and sex. In the service I learned through actual experience about "good" women and "bad" women. To the common serviceman the latter were preferred. In my wandering from Chicago to Germany, Hawaii, and Vietnam, I acquired a knowledge of "worldly" women. I met many women in the service, but maybe because I was a soldier I didn't meet many "nice" ones. By the time I returned to America I had obtained a disgust for womanhood.

Personality changes result from the contrasting experience of separated partners. The greater the contrast, the more they are liable to grow apart. The shock effect of these changes can be reduced and the nature of pending readjustments anticipated by adequate communication. The principal vehicle for this must be correspondence:

> *When I was on the other side of the world, it was really difficult for us to communicate with each other. It took so many days to get an answer back and by the time I did, my mood had changed and I had forgotten what I said before. I begged him to tell me what was going on in his mind, to discuss his problems with me, but all he could manage was to write me after he had already made up his mind to change careers. It made me feel terribly left out to discover that he had been agonizing over such a big decision without my being able to be involved in it. But I know that both his letters and my letters had degenerated into mere travelogues because meaningful communication by mail was so difficult.*

Letters are a poor substitute for face-to-face conversations, yet they can convey emerging aspirations and interests, disillusionments and problems. People are often reluctant to communicate these changes for fear that they will be misunderstood because their meaning will not be adequately conveyed. But misunderstandings can be clarified in later letters. The long-run interests of any couple are best served by frankness.

Maintaining a Separate Relationship. Separation weakens love by preventing interaction. The longer the separation, the more the relationship atrophies. The weaker the relationship in the first place, the less strain it can survive.

Burgess and Wallin (1953) found that separation was a major cause of severed engagements. Even couples who avoid new involvements find that rapport dwindles and divergences grow. However, new involvements are the greatest threat. The greater the interaction with new partners, the greater the likelihood a new love will supersede the old. A commitment in engagement or marriage may be revoked if a new relationship over-shadows it. Only the timely interruption of a college separation salvaged the following relationship:

> *When I saw Sunny again during vacation, I realized that my doubts about her had been due to the fact that she wasn't with me at college. Last fall I had a strong need for feminine companionship and felt a considerable tug in the direction of a woman in my Poli. Sci. class. Although I was attracted to her, I felt guilty when I dated her because I was engaged. I'm glad now to discover that Sunny really is the one for me after all.*

Separation after marriage is less apt to terminate the entire relationship. But if it comes during the early months, it disrupts a crucial period of adjustment. If the process of learning to live together is interrupted before minimal satisfaction has been achieved, each partner may worry about the durability of a half-built marriage:

> *Max and I had only two weeks together before he was shipped out. In general we had a grand time, but not sexually. I was sexually inexperienced and our sexual relations weren't satisfactory for either of us. I feel very guilty about not having been a better partner to Max in this way, and I'm afraid that he resents it.*

Marriages are best timed when they allow both advance preparation and a solid year of post-wedding interaction before an extensive separation. If this much time is not available, perhaps the marriage would be better deferred.

Adjustment to Reunion. Change during separation necessitates readjustment on return. Although few people think of reunion as a crisis, Hill (1949) found it frequently is. If couples recognize that growing apart is normal, they will be less disturbed. If they approach reunion determined to work out a new relationship with this partial stranger, they are more apt to succeed. For married couples, a second honeymoon provides an opportunity for getting reacquainted and dramatizes the fact that they are not resuming an old marriage but making a new one.

Even if no observable divergences arise, a dyad is inevitably weakened by the dearth of interaction. Married or not, the relationship must be rebuilt. Even though the process is likely to be telescoped this time, a feeling of intimacy must be reestablished. Since the time necessary for rekindling love cannot be predicted in advance, separated couples may more safely leave their relationships open-ended than predetermine a post-separation wedding date. Better to leave the date-setting for a time when they feel psychologically ready than to shortchange their recuperation time after a long separation.

Student Marriages

Student marriages present few new problems beyond those already discussed. Studying is an unpaid occupation; hence most students lack financial resources. Heavy schedules may limit the time a couple can devote to one another. New, however, is the threat to educational plans presented by marriage.

Financing Student Marriages. Lansing (1960) studied a national sample and found that 61 percent of the average student's college funds came from parents, 23 percent from personal earnings, 8 percent from scholarships, and 8 percent from other sources. How are these resources altered when students marry?

Since two can live together as cheaply as two alone, marriage affects total expenses relatively little (as long as there are no children). However, the allocation of expenses changes. At Michigan State University, Shaffer (1963) found that married students spent less on clothes, perhaps because they no longer dressed up to impress the opposite sex.

As for income, the chief question is whether parents will continue to subsidize their children after marriage. We have already described the practice of subsidizing young families generally. Some parents especially want to assist children who marry while they are still in college in order to enable them to complete their education. College savings are thought of as "belonging" to the children, regardless of whether they are married or not. Parents are especially apt to continue paying tuition after marriage.

Table 7–1 shows that married students received far less parental

Table 7–1 Financial Support of Married Students, by Roles of Wife

| | ROLES OF WIFE | | | |
| | Nonstudent | | Student | |
Source of Income	Childless	Mother	Childless	Mother
Husband's current earnings	11%	35%	27%	29%
Wife's current earnings	62	15	19	7
Couple's savings	4	13	8	15
Parental subsidy	3	7	24	28
Scholarships	17	20	13	19
Miscellaneous	2	12	8	0
Total income	99%	102%	99%	98%
Number of couples	84	66	35	11

Source: Unpublished study by Rex Richards and Barry Stulberg of married students at the University of Michigan, 1955–56. Two thirds of the husbands were graduate students. Percentages are the proportion of total income derived from the particular source. Most couples relied on more than one source.

subsidy than the single students reported above. Much of the difference results from the fact that married students are not a typical cross-section of the student body. Many of them are older and more advanced in their studies. Hence they are more self-sufficient than most undergraduates. Even when both partners were in school, parents provided less than half as much support as usual.

The gap is filled primarily by the couple's own earnings. Frequently the wife works to finance her husband's education. Under such circumstances marriage may be a financial gain to the husband, enabling him to complete his education faster than if he were self-supporting. The danger is that the man's gain may be the woman's loss:

> *For six years I slaved to put Bill through college and two years of graduate school. Then it was my turn. Bill agrees, but he hasn't found a job and there just isn't any money for me. I really resent the situation, and I resent him for not being more appreciative and for not working harder to get a job that will pay my way.*

> *I'm tired of makeshift living arrangements and unsatisfying temporary bread jobs. I'm tired of working to support a guy who has lost his motivation in grad school. I'm losing hope of ever getting out of this place and losing faith in our marriage.*

If both partners are students and especially if children are born, making ends meet is likely to be difficult:

> *At first I worked to finance the family while he went to school. When the children came he worked part time, which slowed down his study program. I couldn't wait so I've gone back to school. We both work part time and go to school part time, and both try to be good parents on the side. Between it all, the marriage is going down the drain. We've no energy or love left for each other.*

Financing a student marriage is difficult unless the wife has already completed her education and the couple postpone having children. The other exception is when parents continue to support their children after marriage—but this is not the general practice.

Scheduling Multiple Responsibilities.   If neither partner works full time, marriage may be no more time-consuming than single life. Extra time spent cooking and keeping house may be offset by reduced "dating."

But if either partner combines work and study, his/her time is hard pressed. Something has to give. At Michigan State University it was recreation, not studying, that suffered (Thorpe, 1951). For mature individuals, this may be no great shock. For the immature, or for the stay-at-home wife of a hard-working student, a slash in recreation can be painful:

> *My wife isn't romantically involved with anyone else but she keeps wanting to go out with anyone she can find because she says it's too boring here at home. She seems to have decided she just doesn't want to be tied down any more. She likes to dance and I don't, but anyway I just have to stay home nights and study.*

The shortage of time requires flexibility with housework. If the wife is going to school, the husband is pressed to help out with housekeeping and babysitting. Nevertheless, in most student marriages, wives carry the major burden. At Syracuse, student husbands spent one hour a day in housework, student wives three hours a day (Chilman and Meyer, 1963). Perhaps that explains why wives studied less than unmarried women. Where only the husband was a student, the average wife tried to protect his study time from household burdens (Christopherson et al., 1960).

Given the multiple demands of studying plus working plus keeping house, time must be carefully rationed. A schedule of daily and weekly routines guarantees that time is allocated to crucial activities:

> *We have a very strict schedule in which every minute of our day is utilized to the utmost. We have a full schedule of classes from eight to noon and work from one until about six. Then we hurry home, hurry through dinner and dishes, and go straight to studying until about eleven every night. Saturday is spent doing housework and washing and ironing. We work together on everything. About every other Saturday night we take off from our studies if we see we can both afford to, and we relax. Sunday mornings are spent at church. Sunday afternoon we try to spend about an hour visiting one of our families, and the remaining time we study. Our matched schedule leaves a lot of time when we are both working together and can talk. Even though we probably work harder than any couple on this campus, we believe our marriage is the happiest one there has ever been.*

The Burden of Children

If, to all these responsibilities, children are added, full-time study may become impossible. The woman's college career is usually impeded, if not terminated altogether. Her difficulty in continuing work once she has a child increases the husband's financial responsibilities. Hence, young fathers are less apt than childless married men to go to school full time. (In the Michigan study, only 52 percent of graduate student fathers were going to school full time compared to 79 percent of those without children.)

Children interfere with studying at home. Eshleman and Hunt (1967) found that twice as many fathers as childless married men did all their studying away from home.

Students who attempt to combine going to school with having children often find not only their education but their marriage impaired. Hurley and Palonen (1967) found that student couples burdened with children had less satisfactory marriages than childless couples. The larger the number of children, the more the marriage suffered.

Foreseeing such complexities, many married students attempt to postpone childbearing until after graduation, or until the latter part of graduate study. Conversely, students who do not believe in contraception tend to shy away from marrying. However, contraception is not universally practiced by college students. Eshleman and Hunt (1967) found among married students at Western Michigan University—most of whom were juniors and seniors—that half of the Catholic students and 13 percent of the Protestants were using no method of birth control.

Nor is practicing contraception a guarantee of success. In the late 1960s, Price-Bonham (1973) found at a midwestern university that 58 percent of the married students had children, a large proportion of whom resulted from unplanned pregnancies. Many of the marriages were apparently precipitated by premarital pregnancies (almost one third of the women were pregnant at the time they got married). Almost a third of the total group had had an unplanned pregnancy after marriage. So, unintended conceptions were a major factor in the lives of those married students.

Protecting Educational Goals

We have already described children as a threat to the college career of both husband and wife. For students who avoid having children, how does getting married affect their education?

Table 7–2 is not restricted to childless couples but shows what happened to the college careers of men and women generally who entered

Table 7–2   Dropping Out of College, by Marital Status of Men and Women

	MEN		WOMEN	
	Unmarried	*Married*	*Unmarried*	*Married*
Dropped out by senior year	9%	20%	8%	49%
Still enrolled	91	80	92	51
Total	100%	100%	100%	100%
Number of cases	851	857	1,273	1,234

Adapted from Bayer, 1972: 607. *Source:* Members of the class of 1969 by enrollment status in the fall term of their senior year. These students were a subsample of a study by the American Council on Education of students enrolled in more than 250 American colleges and universities.

college directly from high school. Whereas less than 10 percent of the single students dropped out by their senior year, 20 percent of the men and almost half of the women who got married dropped out before the beginning of their senior year. This suggests that getting married endangers the completion of a college education for both sexes, but especially for women.

In addition to inducing students to drop out completely, marriage also forces students to drop out partially—that is, to go to school less than full time. In a national sample of graduate students, Feldman (1973) found that approximately twice as many married as single students were enrolled part time. (Part-time enrollment jumped from 24 percent for single men to 40 percent for married men; for women, the comparable figure increased from 38 percent to 71 percent.) Thus marriage tends to be an impediment not only to staying in college at all, but especially to staying in full time.

Whether women stay in school or drop out depends on how academically ambitious they are. At Syracuse University, achievement-oriented wives stayed in school whereas those who lacked educational goals and were interested in creating a warm, sociable home dropped out (Chilman and Meyer, 1960). Presumably, dropout wives get what they want in the short run. But two questions arise. (1) What will happen to their marriages as their husbands outstrip them educationally? (2) What jobs will they be prepared to assume if and when they want to go to work? In the short run, these women don't care about educational goals. In the long run, they may regret it:

> We got married at 18. Since I preferred marriage to a career, I really enjoyed working to help him through college and grad school. Ten years later I've waked up to my desire to go to art school, but he says we just can't afford the cost of the tuition or the cost of constant babysitters.

Because marriage has a selective effect on college students, weeding out those who are least academically oriented, it should not surprise us to discover that those who stay in college do about as well as students who remain single.

At Florida State University, married students earned better grades the term after marriage than the term before, but so did comparable non-marrying students (Cohen et al., 1963). Some studies show greater gains for married students than for single students. At Stanford and San Jose City College, married men majoring in political science, economics, and education gained significantly more than single men; physics and English majors improved at the same rate, regardless of marriage; but chemistry majors who married fell behind those who stayed single (Schroder, 1963). These findings suggest that marriage may increase the academic efforts of students who are not already working up to their capacity.

The fact that married students who manage to stay in college do all right in their studies shows that college and marriage are not inevitably incompatible. However, educational goals can best be achieved under the following conditions: (1) parental or institutional financial assistance; (2) postponement of childbearing; and (3) postponement of marriage itself until one partner has finished his/her education.

Living with Education-induced Tensions. Like salesmen on commission, athletes in competition, and entertainers before the public, life for students is full of tension. Grades for a whole term may hinge on a final examination. Term paper deadlines must be met. Graduate students face comprehensive examinations covering vast fields of knowledge and the agonies of grinding out a doctoral dissertation. Even for those who surmount every hurdle without stumbling, there is anxiety enough to cause tension in marriage. Irritability and critical reactions make university counselors talk about a "graduate school syndrome" of marital difficulty.

For those who fail academically, there are tougher problems. Some lash out at their partner in displaced retaliation. Others sink into depression. Spouses in academic difficulty are hard to live with. Few of these feelings are unique to student marriages. But they are predictable enough to test the maturity, patience, and compatibility of those who marry on campus.

8 Getting Married: Engagement, Wedding, and Honeymoon

This chapter may seem out of style to couples who are deeply involved affectionally, sexually, and residentially and who through living together have come to experience the same love, loyalty, and desire for continuity as others who decide to get married. For some, the choice not to get married is a political statement resisting the right of the state to intervene in their personal lives. Others fear that to be married would mean taking on roles and stereotyped behavior that they see trapping their friends and parents. They believe their relationship needs to steer clear of the "forms" of marriage.

We personally believe that when traditional rituals, vows, and ceremonies fail to express the meaning that a couple want, new forms can be created to fit the participants' needs and desires. The main purpose of a ritual is not to satisfy tradition but to clarify the significance of a special relationship. For a couple to ceremonialize their relationship is to proclaim publicly that which they already know privately: to share with family and friends in order that these others may understand and be with them in their joy. For those who are religious, the ritual goes beyond its social significance in consecrating their relationship to God. Ideally, those who attend the ceremony by their very presence express their commitment to care for and support this couple.

Writing this chapter when our own children have chosen not to be married, it becomes clearer to us than at the time of our own engagement and wedding that these ceremonial times can serve the needs of couples at this stage of their journey. To decide to get married now is to choose to formalize a relationship, to make it more definite and to project it farther into the future rather than to live only in the present. A wedding is the central occasion when this public commitment takes place. But an engagement is a first step in this process and a honeymoon the culminating private celebration of the transition from just going/living together to being married.

THE ENGAGEMENT

The gift of a diamond ring and some kind of gathering where an engagement is announced are familiar ways of celebrating the engagement.

Engagement is a time of sharing with families and friends the joy of deciding to formalize a relationship in a more serious commitment. In our case:

> Since our coming together was aided and abetted by many graduate school friends we wanted to announce to them our decision to get married. My [Margaret's] mother was visiting at the time. With her and our friends we shared silence and out of this silence spoke of our decision and our mutual hopes, followed by feasting and dancing. It was like a wedding but was actually our engagement ceremony.

Getting engaged serves notice that the relationship with the partner preempts all others, including parents. It is a time of separating from parents, of cutting the cord.

The engagement period offers an opportunity for each partner to become better acquainted with relatives and friends. In my case (Margaret):

> We were a close family—sister, borthers, parents and grandparents, cousins, aunts and uncles. It was exciting to return home with a ring on my finger and be able to share with confidence about this important person and coming event in my life. I felt very adult and very sure of myself. All my relatives felt it too and treated me with a new respect. Each time I told them what Bob was like and what I believed we had in common I felt more sure. By the time he arrived to visit, their hearts were ready to receive the stranger. It was a good time.

Timing the Engagement

Couples rarely get engaged until they know when the wedding will be (what month, or at least what season). To be engaged with no end in sight is too stagnant. Engagement is not an end in itself but a commitment to get married. Its meaning is distorted unless the goal is calendared.

Conceivably, a couple could plan to marry in June two years hence. In practice, most engagements run less than a year. In New Haven the average for the whole city was ten months (Hollingshead, 1952). Among Ohio State University graduates, the median was only six months, and growing shorter from generation to generation (Koller, 1951).

Engagements of more than a year tend to lose their momentum. Although a year seems a workable maximum, the minimum is less easily determined. Suffice it to say that several months are needed if the functions of engagement are to be carried out fully, even if the couple are completely ready for marriage.

The Functions of Engagement

Implicit in our comments on the meaning of engagement have been the functions it is designed to serve: public notice of serious intent, the last chance for compatibility testing, and time to plan for getting married.

Public Announcement.   Engagement notifies families and friends that the couple intend to marry. Parents who had misgivings from the start but hadn't taken the affair seriously may belatedly intervene, hoping to head off a marriage. On the other hand, parents who wished their child had found a better mate may now resign themselves to the inevitable. More positively, they may try to establish a better relationship with their prospective son- or daughter-in-law.

A secret engagement is a contradiction in terms. Publicity gives the couple a chance to discover how it feels to be officially committed.

Residual Compatibility Testing.   No matter how long a couple have gone together, engagement introduces a new twist. They may have seen a great deal of each other, but were not yet committed to spending their lives together. Engagement brings a sobering realization of the imminence of marriage. In unexpected ways, it alters the tone of the relationship:

> *Before I got engaged, I was very romantic about Dick. We were both trying to impress each other with our best behavior. After we got engaged and began to plan for a future together, I was shocked at my practicality. Where I used to be impressed at his extravagant gifts and flowers, I now began to worry. I suddenly became analytical. Before we were engaged, if we would argue neither one of us was too upset, but now we take our disagreements very seriously and try to understand the cause. We feel very secure in our love for each other, but we realize that we have many problems to solve. Both of us have spent two years playing games—now that we are facing reality, we run into many conflicts. We probably would*

have been better off if we had been more objective two years ago. However, I suppose neither one of us was interested in marriage at the time.

In this case, engagement improved the relationship. Sometimes the opposite effect occurs. Sometimes the fact that the chase is over and the partner won takes the momentum out of love. If attraction depended on uncertainty about the partner, the security of engagement may be too dull. Or perhaps the fiancé(e) becomes possessive and inconsiderate after the pact is sealed.

The prospective mate may now be seen in a new light as the wedding draws near. Some engagements are bound to be broken. They embarrass all concerned because engagement is so public. Yet the complications are mild compared to divorce. One virtue of engagement is that it is a revokable commitment. It is an opportunity to see what it feels like to be almost married, but not quite—partly committed but not completely. It's the last chance to pretest the marriage.

Most couples do their major compatibility testing before they get engaged. Hicks (1970) found that married graduate students at Penn State felt that the main testing and exploration had occurred before engagement, rather than during it. So compatibility testing is only a residual function of engagement, to be accomplished this late only insofar as it has been slighted previously or insofar as unexpected incompatibilities emerge.

Planning the Wedding.   The wedding requires many decisions. Setting the date involves balancing many factors. An ideal date allows ample preparation time and honeymoon time. It enables relatives and friends to attend. And it utilizes the desired clergyman and facilities for the wedding and reception (often committed months in advance for the crowded June calendar). Booking the honeymoon may take less notice but still must be arranged.

Professional Preparation for Marriage.   Most states require a blood test for syphilis before issuing a marriage license. More comprehensive preparation for marriage may include physical examinations to detect conditions that could be remedied by medical or surgical treatment. Anatomical and physiological irregularities in the reproductive system may be discovered. Most defects can be corrected. In cases where the doctor discovers that a couple could never have children, stock-taking is inevitable. A woman who has anticipated the day when she would bear children may abandon a sterile man. Either partner may want children who are "flesh of my flesh and bone of my bone." In any case, having the information before marriage helps couples know what to expect.

For inexperienced women, preparation for sexual intercourse includes dilating the vaginal opening (by the doctor or by the woman herself following the doctor's instructions). Contraceptive instructions and materials may be secured from a physician or a Planned Parenthood Clinic. Some doctors offer sexual counseling.

Most clergymen provide premarital counseling. Some refuse to marry anyone who has not been instructed in marriage. Couples may consult their pastor about marriage generally, and not just about the wedding.

Planning for Married Living. As soon as the honeymoon is over, the newlyweds will settle into a new way of life. In earlier generations this was left to chance or entered on faith, but the trend has been to plan more carefully ahead of time. We saw in Table 5–2 that typical topics of engagement conversation are handling money, having children, where to live, religion, the wife working, and the husband's occupation. Over three generations the number of Koller's engaged couples who never discussed any of these issues dropped from one fourth practically to zero, whereas the number discussing all of them rose from 5 percent to 50 percent.

Not only may discussing how to handle money be useful, but also preparing a budget for the first year of marriage. Agreement is needed on whether to practice birth control. Setting up housekeeping involves finding a place to live and choosing furniture and equipment. Planning may be not only valuable but enjoyable. As with a trip abroad, half the fun of being engaged is anticipating the experiences ahead.

Table 8–1 suggests that planning builds a more solid foundation for the marriage to come. Although planning both the wedding and the marriage are essential functions of engagement, the latter was the more valuable of the two among these graduate student couples at Penn State. Those who emphasized marital planning had especially good marriages several years later.

During engagement, then, there are multiple functions to be accomplished, but the most important function is to make decisions about life after the wedding ceremony is over.

The Consequences of Engagement

The decision to get engaged changes the way partners view each other and the way they are viewed by outsiders.

The married graduate students at Penn State told Hicks (1970) that after they got engaged they began thinking more about the future of their relationship and felt more secure in that relationship. More of their energies were absorbed in each other and they spent more time alone together than they had before. They understood one another more easily than before, perhaps because they had been going together longer and felt secure in their commitment to one another. They became more intimate emotionally and physically and exchanged more personal gifts. In short, they felt closer and enjoyed anticipating their future together.

Table 8–1 Marital Adjustment, by Major Purpose of Engagement

	MAJOR PURPOSE OF ENGAGEMENT	
Marital Adjustment	Planning the Wedding	Planning the Marriage
Highest quartile (good)	15%	26%
Second quartile	15	26
Third quartile	28	26
Lowest quartile (poor)	42	22
Total	100%	100%
Number of cases	53	125

Recomputed from Hicks, 1970: 61. *Source:* Graduate students at Pennsylvania State University, typically married about four years.

At the same time, these couples found that getting engaged resulted in being treated differently by others. Their families treated the prospective son- or daughter-in-law more like a member of the family. Both relatives and friends treated the couple more as a pair. The engagement cemented the relationship in the eyes of outsiders, giving the couple more freedom from control by their parents but integrating the outsider with their prospective in-laws. All these processes resemble what happens even more intensively when couples move on into marriage.

Conflicts.   Couples who can't get along with each other tend to break up early on, but those who get engaged are not immune to conflict. Burgess and Wallin's couples (1953) typically disagreed in several areas. Their biggest problems were how they dealt with their families, how they dressed and acted in public, and their separate friendships. Kirkpatrick and Hobart's Indiana University couples (1954) quarreled most about neatness, in-laws, and economic roles.

These conflicts reflect the engagement situation. Couples close to marriage seldom quarrel about such accustomed matters as dating (the rarest source of conflict in the Burgess-Wallin study). Rather, they have trouble over their external relations with family and friends, their public appearance, and the economic roles that will support them after marriage.

An engagement is not easy to break off—it entails a public acknowledgment of failure, a ring to return, and so forth. It is more difficult yet for couples who don't change their minds until after the wedding date is set, invitations are sent, travel reservations made, and gifts begin to arrive. If family and friends thought it was a good match, disengagement is all the more difficult.

No matter how painful breaking an engagement may be, terminating a marriage or living in an incompatible marriage is worse. Many people come to regret their marriages, but few who break up in advance regret it.

THE WEDDING

Couples who are sure of their relationship and the nature of their commitment are ready to share that commitment with their family and friends. Such sharing is usually called a celebration, and some are still willing to call it a wedding! But some are not:

> *Bert and Jean feel that marriage is not for them. By avoiding marriage they hope to avoid "roles" and all those inhumane ways of relating that either continue in the "usual" marriage or end in divorce. But an unplanned pregnancy left the older generations in the family amazed, bewildered, and concerned. They feel uncomfortable and don't know how to relate, not sure whether Bert and Jean intend an ongoing commitment. Many in the family feel cut off when they'd like to be supportive.*

A public celebration resolves such discomfort by including parents and relatives in an affirmation of commitment.

What does it mean to share a decision with others? When I make an explicit agreement with another person and shake on it, I take the agreement more seriously than if it exists only in my mind as a good intention. Without formal verbalization it is easier to change my mind. When I share within a group my hope for the future, I feel more committed to that hope and more able to carry it out because these friends are with me and will help me bring it to fruition. When two of us speak our intentions in the presence of a group of people we care about, we take more thought for the meaning of these "vows," trying to express them in ways that speak especially for us, but also in ways that can be heard by them. Having to verbalize and put into some form our intentions is a way of clarifying them for ourselves and for our community. The form we use to make our commitment need not be empty. It can be as meaningful to everyone concerned as we want to make it.

The Wedding Ceremony

Seligson (1973) found that the great majority of first marriages were held in traditional places and ways. Seven-eighths of the weddings were held in a church or synagogue and four-fifths of the couples were formally attired.

But even in traditional places and traditional clothes, the content of the ceremony is not necessarily traditional. To be sure, most churches have customary ceremonies and some allow no leeway, but the "free churches" permit couples to modify the ceremony. Some couples prefer to speak their own vows. Some alter the vows: for example, omitting the bride's promise to obey. Alterations are more apt to be improvements than mere deletions. Here is the ceremony used by our friend Mary Stuart on a Virginia mountaintop in 1971:

1. Silence—5–10 minutes
2. Reading of I Corinthians 13
3. Reading of "On Marriage" from *The Prophet*, Gibran
4. Marriage Commitment Service (done responsively) (and in unison at certain places)

> Having lived together for better than two years, we have no illusions about marriage. Instead we have an understanding of the needs each of us have, the peculiarities of each other, and the stumbling joy of our intimacy. We now feel comfortable taking a leap of faith, making a commitment of greater permanence.
>
> We are not here to proclaim vows but to express to all the promises we have grown to feel between us—love, protection, guidance, companionship, sharing, joy and warmth, and sensitivity to the deep personal needs each of us have. We wish to say before all that we are bound together by these promises.
>
> But we are not prophets; we cannot say "till death do us part." The years before us may conceal changes in our lives and in ourselves that may call for changes in our relationship. We are the product of changing times. We are the captives of changing times. It is only realistic to recognize this. And yet we already understand and know each other and have found ourselves to be capable of dealing with life together.
>
> The question of marriage has provided for us a stopping point—a chance to examine where we have been and whether we can or should continue together. From this time we are no more husband and wife than we have already grown to be. We are two human beings searching, experimenting, hoping, and loving together.
>
> *It is our hope that*
> *As I become I and you become you*
> *May I reflect you and you reflect me separate in unity, one and yet two—*
> *Growing together and moving alone.*
> *Like the music in sunlight, the rainbow of laughter,*
> *May life's pain be more joyous with my hand in yours*
> *Like the silence in thunder, the shout never spoken,*
> *May the aura of love surround both our lives.*

5. Song
6. Celebration Feast

This wedding illustrates the Reverend William Glenesk's description of what he called "the new wedding":

The new wedding is a ceremony to confirm what a couple has found by living together, not to make promises about what they hope will happen. It is a celebration of what is already there, a public reaffirmation of the commitment and continuity, rather than a beginning (Seligson, 1973).

Weddings are for celebrating with family and friends a love that has been confirmed through experience and a desire to be committed to a long-term relationship. It is a way of affirming community in the midst of community.

But what if the two families belong to different cultural traditions? Or what if the young couple have chosen still a third approach? Some couples go along with traditional ceremonies to please their parents. Yet, with imagination, ways can be found to satisfy all parties rather than to alienate some. The challenge is to include the best elements of both or all traditions in planning a celebration that will cross over the separate traditions. In our own case:

> How could we combine our new-found Quaker way of getting married with Bob's parents' Congregationalism in Margaret's home Presbyterian Church? We were determined to say our own vows without a minister. In addition we chose hymns, scripture, and readings that expressed things we all believed. In between there was time for Quaker silence and a chance for family and friends to speak out the love that we all shared together. And everyone approved—afterward!

When Carolyn Hamm married David Arond, the ceremony drew elements from the Quaker and Jewish traditions of the two families:

> Singing "Kum Bah Yah," Carolyn and David entered from opposite directions and met under a gold canopy with a potted fig tree at its side. David's grandfather gave the traditional blessings, first in Hebrew, then in English. David and Carolyn drank wine from the one cup, sang an Israeli love song, and read together their covenant of joy with the traditional Jewish shawl around their shoulders. Out of the Quaker silence that followed, almost every member of both families and many friends shared their thoughts. Carolyn's youngest brother quoted from The Prophet. At the end, we all made a big circle, holding hands and singing "Every man 'neath his vine and fig tree shall live in peace and unafraid," an Old Testament quotation that captures the Quaker emphasis on peace and harmony.

Some brides and grooms depart from the traditional organ music by asking friends to play the guitar, recorder, or flute. Their favorite passages may be read from the Bible or from poetry. The rewards are rich for those who create a ceremony that expresses their ideals for their new life together. What matters is that the ceremony fit the couple's values, affirming their aspirations and pledging their commitment in terms that are meaningful to them.

Presumably, the more elaborate the ritual, the greater the awareness in both the couple and their relatives and friends that the wedding signifies a major change in relationships. One characteristic of cohesive social organizations is clear-cut boundary lines. One way of sharpening the boundary between not being married and being married is to elaborate the ceremonies that mark the time of crossing the line.

The Reception

The reception allows each member of the wedding to congratulate the bride and groom individually by handshake, kiss, or hug. It is also a party celebrating the wedding. The wedding breakfast or wedding cake represents symbolically the first meal together of the couple as husband and wife.

The reception is the most expensive part of most weddings. The party may be a gala affair with dancing until the early hours. Liquid refreshments may be costly. Families with limited means may have to choose between limiting the guests at the reception or limiting the cost per person. Etiquette allows the former discrimination to be made between those invited to the wedding alone or to the reception also. However, guests don't like to be discriminated against, so it may be preferable to stretch the budget to fit the people. If people are more important than refreshments, champagne can be dispensed with. True friends are not offended by simplicity, and merriment does not have to be stimulated.

In New Haven most families invited all the wedding guests to the reception. (The median attrition from wedding to reception was a mere 18 from the typical 177 guests at the church, according to special computations Hollingshead made for us.)

Members of the Wedding

Who is the wedding for—the bride and groom, the parents, or the spectators? When there are conflicts between parties, how can they be reconciled?

The Couple.   The central participants are the bride and groom. To say this seems trite, yet some couples' wishes are ignored in the complexities of organizing the ceremony. Sometimes a bride stands by while her parents run away with the wedding. This reflects dominating personalities or social ambitions of the parents. Exploiting the wedding to serve their own needs may be defended because the bride's parents pay the wedding expenses:

> *I'm very much afraid my father is going to dominate the wedding plans. He seems to think that since he's going to pay for the wedding he can buy just the kind he wants. Sometimes I feel so disappointed I'd rather junk the whole church wedding, but I'll probably make the best of the situation when the time comes.*

Such a situation is out of balance, the couple getting married overshadowed by their elders.

The Parents.   The wedding marks a turning point for parents as well as for their children. With the launching of each successive child, the nest becomes emptier, the parents' responsibilities diminish, and their freedom increases.

A son's or daughter's marriage is a bereavement. There is joy in the child's happiness. But when children leave home forever, a void is left behind. Going away to college or work paves the way for this bereavement, but family ties are still unbroken. Home is still the place to go when in trouble and during vacations. At marriage, however, the children transfer their loyalty, their dependence, and their home base. As a result, family life is never again quite the same for their parents.

The impact of the wedding depends on the parents' personalities. For a mother whose life for a quarter century has been wrapped up in her children, the effect is drastic (as her tears bear witness). Parents feel deeply involved with children they've nourished, enjoyed, and worried about for 20 years or more.

The Clans.   Weddings are occasions for the gathering of the clan, matched in importance only by funerals. They may be a family reunion for aunts, uncles, and cousins who otherwise seldom see each other. They are an excuse to abandon everyday cares and fly halfway across the country. For a few hours the bride and groom may hold the center of the stage, but for the rest of the weekend the kin group dominates the scene as it celebrates the marriage of one of its offspring. Tears flow, stories are told, and for a while the hands of the clock are pushed back.

For such a clan, a wedding is not so much planned by the couple for their guests as staged by the clan for their protégé. For a clan member not to be invited would be unthinkable. Even members who are not ordinarily on speaking terms are dutybound to be invited and to attend. One of the miracles of wedding feasts is the transformation of disunity into reunion.

For young people who have always belonged to such a kin group, a clan wedding is taken for granted. For those who marry into one, the prospect may seem overwhelming. But if one is to become a clan member, the time to join is on one's wedding day.

Friends.   Less involved but still interested are friends of both families. Numerous, sometimes innumerable, they pile up on invitation lists at an astonishing rate. If both partners come from the same community, the pressure of this "cloud of witnesses" on the wedding budget becomes insistent.

The friends of the bride and groom—classmates and favorite teachers—are obvious participants. From among them are recruited the bridal party, the best man, and the ushers. They bring joy to the couple.

But what about the parents' friends and business associates? They are interested in the couple, even if that interest isn't reciprocated. When the child of an employee or bridge partner gets married, they want to see how the bride and groom look and share both their happiness and the happiness of the parents.

Conflict of Interests.   With so many different people involved, it would be miraculous if everyone had the same ideas. But two parties are apt to clash—the couple and the woman's parents.

The commonest conflict is over the size and cost of the wedding. The younger generation often want to restrict invitations to their personal acquaintances, whereas the older generation want a wider circle of guests. Paradoxically, parents often want to spend more, while the bride wants them to save their money or give her a bigger wedding present instead.

As a general rule, the parties most concerned with the particular issue should have the most influence. If the details of the wedding ceremony or the members of the bridal party are at issue, these affect primarily the bride and groom. But adding relatives and family friends to the invitation list is the parents' concern. Hence, conflicts over wedding size should normally be resolved on the large side. If parents want to spend their own money, why shouldn't they? Young people who worry lest a large congregation spoil their sense of intimacy can take comfort in realizing that they will be so absorbed in the ceremony that they will be oblivious to extra faces. In our own case:

> There's only one thing we would do differently if we were doing it over again. We felt that we wanted to limit the invitations to the very closest friends and relatives. So we ruthlessly crossed off the list an awful lot of people who would have liked to be there. We realize now that it really wouldn't have made any difference at the time to us and we've regretted ever since that we were so exclusive.

In recommending that conflicts be settled on the large side, we do not mean to advocate a particular number. Bowman (1960: 255) suggested, "A wedding, like a garment, should fit. . . . As is true of a garment, there is no point in having the largest one possible." A fitting size reflects the number of relatives of both families and friends of both generations who are geographically accessible and personally important.

In actual practice, the typical wedding of middle-class Londoners (Firth et al., 1970) attracted 50 guests, of whom 40 were friends and 10 were relatives. In general, the smaller the wedding, the larger the proportion of relatives. Almost three quarters of all available parents attended, but less than half the living siblings, one fifth of the parents' siblings (that is, the couple's aunts and uncles) and very few more remote relatives. Where parents were absent, this was chiefly due to factors beyond their control, such as illness or distance. But about 10 percent of the parents deliberately were not invited or refused to attend because of bad feeling about the marriage, most often because the son or daughter was marrying out of the family religion or, worse yet, was converting to an alien faith. On the other hand, Firth and his colleagues found that some parents came to the wedding despite the fact that they had opposed the marriage— including one man's mother who had tried to break up the couple but came to the wedding under sedation to calm her nerves!

The researchers summarized their findings about wedding guests by saying that "the parents of bride and groom invite their kin, whereas the bride and groom invite their friends."

Where children have radically different ideas about weddings from their parents and especially where mixed marriages are involved, conflicts between the generations are often severe. At worst, the views of the two generations may be mutually irreconcilable:

> *Jane and I worked out our own ceremony and said our own vows without a priest. My mother, being a devout Catholic, was so upset that she wouldn't come to our wedding. The hurt is still there between us and at times clouds our marriage.*

If the decision is to go against strong parental desires about the wedding, the couple may feel good in their independence. But if parental relations are important, extra energy will have to be channeled in to heal the rift. An unresolved conflict with parents can be a thorn in the side of a marriage. If a couple can work out a wedding ceremony and celebration that fits their needs and at the same time take into account their parents' needs and desires, it bodes well for the couple's ability to negotiate with each other and their in-laws in the future.

Commitment. Getting married is a time of making public commitments to one another. Those commitments will grow and change with the passing years and new experiences. Thinking through their initial meaning is a fruitful activity during the transition from engagement to marriage.

Commitment has many levels and meanings for different people. Every couple desiring a continuing relationship needs to define for themselves what the concept means for them. The vows stated publicly can reflect this understanding of their commitment.

When the authors got engaged, we assumed that our feeling of deep affection bespoke our commitment. Decades later, after some particularly rough years, I (Margaret) formulated more explicitly the meaning of commitment for me:

> *My commitment to you is not based primarily on past intentions or promises, or holding fast to traditional expectations about how a wife ought to behave. My commitment is not so much to a marriage as to a person, to you very specifically.*
>
> *My commitment is to respect you as a person, the real you, not the one that I concoct in my imagination, or the one I crave at a particular time. It's a commitment to strive to hear your reality in this present time. It's a commitment to help you to be true to your reality, to be with you, not against you.*
>
> *My commitment is to growth, desiring that each of us act toward the other in ways that allow us to change, to explore and find new territories alone and together.*
>
> *My commitment to you is an expressed intention to relate, to reach out to you, to struggle to find that mutual ground that nurtures us both. Insofar as I act on this intent to love and care and be aware, the areas of our mutuality increase. The bridge between us is not a happenstance. This is a commitment to responsibility. I am not responsible for you but I take responsibility for reaching out toward you rather than waiting for you to come and meet me. I take responsibility for asking you when I need you rather than blaming you for being insensitive to my needs.*
>
> *Commitment is another word for focusing. I intend to commit my main energy and time to you since you are so important to me. I want to focus on the good that holds us together and not on the grievances that separate us.*
>
> *This commitment is not the same as my feeling of love and affection and is beyond how either of us feels at any particular time. It is rooted in trust that grows out of our experience of having loved and struggled and found better places. Holding fast to this memory of having made it before, I trust that we can continue to manage our continuing conflicts. I accept the coming and the going, the ins and the outs, the ups and the downs, and have faith in our ability to return to home base.*
>
> *Commitment is grounded in my will, the will to hang on when it would be easier sometimes to run away, the will to keep wrestling when I want to avoid, to blame, or to cop out.*

Vows that are self-written these days rarely promise to live together "until death do us part." Yet most vows are taken with the hope of permanence, with the intention of continuing the caring and struggle in which we are now engaged. But the most meaningful commitment may be to the present and to the immediate future. For me (Bob):

*I still hope that my relationship to you will last "as long as we both
shall live." But the longer I live, the more I realize that it is pretentious to
think of that as a promise rather than as a statement of hope. I now realize
how very changeable life is—how much I change and how much you
change. Hopefully, we will be able to respond to those changes in each of
us in ways that will enable us to go on living together creatively. But my
main commitment to you is not a lifetime contract signed on a dotted line
but a commitment to struggle with you in the here and now across the
gaps that arise between us. I have faith that if we do our best to grapple
with each crisis as it comes along, we will maximize the chances of being
able to grow old together. Each year when our wedding anniversary rolls
around, we'll want to reevaluate and hopefully renew this commitment. I
feel that the farthest ahead I can see with any certainty is to say I want to
go on living with you for another year. And then next year I trust I'll want
to renew that commitment for still another year. But meantime, year in
and year out, my main commitment to you is not to the future (and
especially not to the dimly perceivable long future) but, rather, to be
present to you today.*

Contracts   Most couples take their contract largely for granted. They expect their marriage to resemble their parents' and/or their peers' marriages. They accept the cultural patterns in which they have been steeped.

For couples who wish to depart from traditional norms, working out
new patterns takes conscious effort and may be most explicitly achieved
by writing their ideas down. Sometimes this contract is simply a private
affair between the two partners. Sometimes it is incorporated in the wedding ceremony itself as a more explicit statement of the relationship to
which they commit themselves:

> Seeking the guidance of the Holy Spirit, and the wisdom of our fellow
> human beings, we, Mary Ellen DesRosiers and Richard Beaty Klein-
> schmidt, take each other as partners in marriage. We do this as a
> result of our growing commitment to one another, and see this as an
> obligation to treat each other with tenderness and responsibility. We
> will make every effort to insure that our relationship will be a nurtur-
> ing and long-lasting one.
>
> We seek to base our marriage on equality, and therefore see the
> following points essential:
>
> Any decision to have children will be mutually agreed upon,
> and, should we become parents, we will strive to share equally the
> obligations of parenthood and child care.
>
> We will share responsibility for providing income, making major
> financial decisions, and repaying our debts.
>
> We each may retain and use our own surnames.
>
> We will share responsibility for the chores of housekeeping.
>
> As part of our commitment to making this a growing and con-
> tinuing relationship, we agree to seek the help of others when prob-

lems arise that at least one of us feels we are not solving ourselves. We furthermore agree that neither of us shall abandon this relationship without first seeking guidance from a committee for clearness appointed by the Society of Friends, or from some other mutually agreed upon group or individual.

This agreement may be amended, provided we both agree upon the changes.

Ultimately, we see the strength and fate of our relationship as determined not by this paper, but by our openness to the Divine Light, a power greater than ourselves (DesRosiers and Kleinschmidt, 1973).

The previous contract is typical in emphasizing shared responsibility and decision making. Sussman (1975) pointed out that the self-examination, communication, and negotiation that are involved in developing a contract affect the marriage. When a couple sit down to work out a contract, they engage in a process of mutual decision making that is likely to make their marriage more equalitarian. Contracts frequently include provisions governing dual career opportunities, choice of residence, family planning, child care, housekeeping, extramarital involvements, and relations with relatives. Contracts also usually include provisions for change by mutual consent as conditions and the couple themselves change. They may be intended to last for a specific period (as for a year, subject to renewal) or for a stage in the relationship (for example, until a child is born). In any case, contracts help couples clarify their preferences and create the relationship they want.

THE HONEYMOON

During the engagement and wedding the growth and testing of the dyadic relation was meshed with growth and testing of family ties.

But on the honeymoon the couple turn back toward each other away from the social milieu out of which they came and to which they must later return. This is a time for them to be alone, to center down on the essence of their relationship. The time before and during the wedding is often strenuous and filled with people. Now the couple can retire to the "wilderness," as many actually do, to enjoy the pure one-to-one.

The word "honeymoon" suggests taking time for the expression of affection, for the physical expression of intimacy in an atmosphere where nature offers quiet and serenity, taking time to slow down after the excitement of clan sharing.

Unlike the preceding ceremonies, which were distinctively public, the honeymoon is private. The new dyad needs celebrating as a separate unit. The honeymoon provides the first chance to be alone as a married couple. With nothing to divert their attention, they become aware that they are really married at last.

Discovering what it means to be married involves new revelations.

After all the compatibility testing that has been advocated, it may seem doubtful that people could get any better acquainted. Yet being married feels different from even the most intimate going together.

Central to the intimacy function of the honeymoon is sexual intimacy. Those who have already been sexually involved often dispense with a honeymoon (Kanin, 1958). But for the uninitiated, the first intercourse represents the consummation of the marriage. It completes the "joining together" proclaimed in the wedding ceremony.

For some, intimacy is so frightening that they cut their honeymoon short and hurry back home:

> The desire to return early seemed related to anxiety about the intimacy situation. If there is a lot of anxiety about being involved in an intimate two-person situation, one may expect a corresponding sense of relief or even eagerness at the prospect of returning to a more diffuse pattern of relationships (Rapoport and Rapoport, 1964).

Criteria for the Honeymoon

If the marriage is to be celebrated most satisfyingly, what conditions must be present?

Privacy. Achieving a sense of identity as a married couple requires leaving the reception behind. However, newlyweds are seldom allowed to escape unnoticed. Ambivalence about letting them go is expressed toward the departing couple in the customary jokes, which

> have the covert purpose of hindering the couple's departure. These include tampering with the couple's automobile, hiding their luggage, etc. Furthermore, a number of devices, such as signs, streamers, or tin cans fastened to the automobile, stones placed in the hubcaps, and, again, the confetti, serve to make the couple conspicuous, and thus have the sense of minimizing or negating the sense of privacy which has been granted to them (Slater, 1963).

Most couples hope to escape the watchful eyes of others. However, newlyweds are conspicuously happy and self-conscious. Try as they may to disguise their honeymooning, they are apt to give themselves away. In our own case:

> When we drove up to the Inn, we were determined to act calmly and naturally so that no one would know we'd just got married. Margaret went in first to pick up the reservations and I [Bob] followed with the suitcases. Despite my efforts to appear blasé the guests in the lobby seemed to be looking at me and nodding their heads knowingly. While I was disconcertedly trying to figure out how they guessed our secret,

Margaret turned around and burst out laughing. I had perched her hat on my head while unloading the trunk and it was still there!

Unself-conscious enjoyment of sexual intimacy requires being able to withdraw behind closed doors, undisturbed by visitors or phone calls. Guaranteeing privacy is one reason for traveling away from friends and relatives. Privacy doesn't require fleeing to the woods, but simply to an anonymous environment. A peculiarly American custom is the honeymoon hotel at Niagara Falls or Miami Beach where couples are seated together at long tables (men on one side, women on the other) or paired off at tables for four. The Rapoports (1964) commented that "Europeans tend to be astonished by this custom, noting that they would wish to get away from other people at such a time, certainly from others in the same situation." Yet organized sociability may be as reassuring for newlyweds unsure of their ability to sustain a dyadic relationship as is double-dating for shy teenagers. A *Newsweek* article (1969) reported that the average age of honeymooners at a Poconos resort was 19, suggesting that such resorts appeal particularly to young couples who feel too insecure to go off on their own. For those who are insecure, a specialized resort may offer some of the benefits of group therapy (Gersuny, 1970).

Novelty. The honeymoon accentuates the discontinuity between the premarital and the married state. In order to emphasize this discontinuity, it must differ from simply beginning the marriage. Some couples hide away in their new apartment, but this waters down the distinction from the rest of marriage. A honeymoon ideally involves a wedding "trip"— not that the couple must go far away but, rather, choosing a distinctive location (away from their parents and from their own new home), accentuates their transition.

Leisure. Leaving home is necessary to get away not only from social obligations but from occupational ones. Even without going back to work, moving immediately into a new apartment would be too practical to make it possible to concentrate on each other as persons. A honeymoon is a type of vacation. Like all vacations, honeymoons take time. Some people call a weekend a honeymoon, but they would hardly call it a vacation. Most people, fortunately, manage the week or two that celebrating deserves. (Hollingshead found the New Haven average was nine days.)

But a honeymoon is not an ordinary vacation. The only one of its kind, it deserves to be extraordinary. Whatever the couple deem most enjoyable should be the criterion for choosing the proper locale.

Economy. The enjoyment of leisure is affected by the cost. If the honeymoon costs so much that the first year of marriage is financially undermined, its attractiveness diminishes. Only if the cost is borne by the parents is it irrelevant to honeymoon enjoyment. We were fortunate in having the use of some friends' cottage free of charge. For most couples, the uniqueness of the honeymoon makes it worth more than the usual vacation budget.

Immediacy. The most nearly absolute criterion for the honeymoon is that it follow the wedding immediately. This is one of the few now-or-never situations. It is not absolutely necessary to take a honeymoon, but to postpone it is to turn it into a mere vacation. To celebrate a marriage, the honeymoon must be taken at once.

Usually it is (honeymoons were skipped by only 6 percent of Hollingshead's New Haven couples). For married students, however, limited money and time more often bar the way. Thirty percent of Kanin's married students failed to take a honeymoon. This was one of the sacrifices exacted by marrying before the husband was occupationally launched. Similarly, Hollingshead's individuals who had been married before felt less need to repeat with a new partner what they had been through before.

Ideally, every couple making the transition into marriage should take a honeymoon trip of at least a week's duration if they can afford the time and money:

> There is a very dismal aura to the thought of getting married on Wednesday and going to work on Thursday. It is almost as if someone could ask you, "What did you do yesterday?" and you could answer, "Oh, nothing much. I just got married!"

2

MARRIAGE

Once a couple return from their honeymoon, they begin to experience what they have promised one another in their wedding ceremony. Loving and cherishing are experienced especially powerfully in their sexual life (Chapter 9). But togetherness in bed is only one of the ways couples spend their leisure time. Chapter 10 wrestles with the balance between separateness and togetherness in spending that "spare" time. Chapter 11 brings the sexual, togetherness, and separateness issues together in the tough questions involved in the relationship between being married and being emotionally and/or sexually involved with other persons.

Involvement outside the marriage links individuals not only with other sexual and affectional partners, but with employers (Chapter 12) and with relatives who have become the spouse's in-laws (Chapter 13). All these issues and more are potential sources of conflict that benefit from increased skill in communication and problem solving (Chapter 14).

9 Sex in Marriage

The theme of this book is the achievement of intimacy between men and women. Sexual intercourse can provide the ultimate intimacy—but it doesn't necessarily. Physically, to be sure, intercourse involves the greatest intimacy, the greatest revelation of the self, the maximum interaction of body with body. But sex does not necessarily express psychological intimacy. When mental blocks exist between husband and wife, when one forces him/herself upon the other, when one begrudges being "used," physical intimacy is shorn of emotional unity.

The challenge of marriage is to integrate the sexual and nonsexual aspects of life to produce a communion that is fully personal, relating the whole man and the whole woman.

SEX AND THE REST OF MARRIAGE

Traditionally, sex and marriage go together like a horse and carriage, but successful "hitching" depends on more than good sex. For some, sex is the only tie that binds people in an otherwise disinterested relationship. Some couples stay together when there is little congeniality left except the fun they have in bed. Eventually, this part of their marriage is likely to join the rest and phase out.

Women's liberation and the sexual revolution have enormously increased men's and women's desire for satisfaction in marriage. Women and men are less willing to settle for either physical or emotional deficits in their relationships. These are days of great expectations.

Trouble in one area of marriage spreads quickly to others. Sexual inadequacy leaves couples tense and irritable, liable to flare up when other frustrations arise. Conversely, nonsexual problems disrupt sexual satisfaction. Partners with grievances take their defenses to bed. If they give in to the other's sexual demands despite their resentment, the image of tyrant/slave looms up.

Because of this reciprocal influence between sex and the rest of marriage, most couples are either satisfied or dissatisfied with both the sexual and nonsexual aspects of their relationship. Chesser (1957) found a close correlation between the wife's sexual satisfaction and her love for her husband. Terman (1938) found positive correlations between both partners' marital happiness and their frequency of intercourse, their degree of physical release from intercourse, and the wife's frequency of orgasm.

The crucial test comes in exceptional cases where the sexual and nonsexual aspects of marriage are out of phase. If sexual adjustment is high and marital adjustment is low, will the marriage get better or will sex deteriorate? For husbands in one followup study, the answer was fifty-fifty, regardless of whether it was the sexual adjustment or the nonsexual that was initially poor. Half the marriages wound up consistently high, the others consistently low (Dentler and Pineo, 1960). So sex and the rest of marriage seem to influence each other equally.

Table 9–1 shows how close the relationship was between marital closeness and sexual pleasure among Hunt's married men and women. At the extremes, almost nobody found sex unpleasant when their marriage was good and hardly anybody found sex very pleasurable when their marriage wasn't good. The chief irregularity in the data is the 47 percent of men in nonclose marriages who still found sex mostly pleasurable, which is balanced to some extent by the fact that more men than women found sex unpleasant when their relationship was distant.

Table 9–1   Sexual Pleasure by Marital Closeness, for Men and Women

Sexual Experience during Past Year	MARRIED MEN Closeness to Wife			MARRIED WOMEN Closeness to Husband		
	Very Close	Fairly Close	Not Close	Very Close	Fairly Close	Not Close
Very pleasurable	79%	45%	12%	70%	30%	10%
Mostly pleasurable	20	50	47	26	58	28
Neutral	1	2	17	1	8	45
Mostly or very non-pleasurable	0	3	24	3	4	17
Total	100%	100%	100%	100%	100%	100%

Adapted from Hunt, 1974: 231. *Source:* Approximately 1,440 married men and women in 24 cities across the country.

A Question of Values

How strongly sexual problems affect the rest of marriage depends on the importance given to sex. If sex is unimportant, sexual inadequacy is less disappointing.

When women were divided into those with strong and weak sexual desires, sexual deprivation depressed marital happiness most for those whose desires were strongest (Wallin, 1957). This suggests that deprivation is relative, depending not so much on amount of sexual experience as on the relationship between actual and desired experience.

SEXUAL EQUIPMENT

Differences between the sexes in anatomy, physiology, and psychology affect sexual experience. These are the ingredients with which couples face the task of fashioning a satisfying sexual relationship.

Sexual Anatomy

Couples don't have to know as much anatomy and physiology as a physician in order to achieve satisfaction. Nevertheless, some facts have practi-

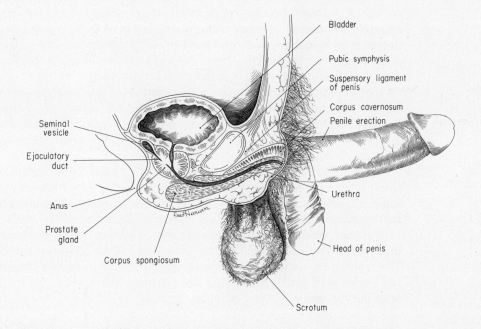

Figure 9-1 Male genital organs.

cal implications for marital sexual behavior, and a basic vocabulary aids communication. In both sexes, clusters of nerve endings sensitive to touch provide the major sensations of sexual experience.

The Genital Area. In men these nerves center chiefly in the penis, especially in the head of the penis. In sexual excitement, spongy tissues become so engorged with blood that the penis almost doubles in length to an average of six and one-quarter inches (Masters and Johnson, 1966).* The length of the erect penis is not proportional to its flaccid size. Rather, a short penis tends to lengthen more than a long one. The erect penis stands out stiffly from the body, enabling penetration of the vagina. Erection stretches the skin covering the head of the penis, increasing its sensitivity to tactile stimulation (see Figure 9–1).

The female analogue of the penis is the clitoris (see Figure 9–2). Much smaller than the penis, the clitoris is embedded in fleshy tissues so that some women are unaware of it. Nevertheless, like the penis, it enlarges when its spongy blood vessels expand in sexual arousal. With further arousal, it retracts to become even less accessible than usual. The head of the clitoris is so sensitive that it is liable to become irritated if manipulated directly. Many women prefer indirect stimulation of the clitoris via manipulation of the pubic mound, the inner lips, or other adjacent areas.

After the clitoris retracts, direct stimulation by manual manipulation or penile contact becomes practically impossible. However, indirect stimulation occurs "in every coital position where there is a full penetration of the vaginal barrel by the erect penis" (M/J). Some women achieve more rapid and intensive clitoral response in the female-superior position, which allows them to control coital movement.

Most women enjoy indirect stimulation of the clitoris during orgasm. This may or may not come with continued thrusting by the man. Because most men prefer to cease thrusting on reaching climax, the woman's climax ideally precedes the man's. If not, the man may manually stimulate her to orgasm.

The interior of the vagina has very few tactile nerve endings, but some of the tissues surrounding the vaginal entrance are highly sensitive, especially the small inner lips. These are pleasurably stimulated by the rhythmic movements of the penis during intercourse.

If the hymen is large enough to prevent easy entrance of the penis, it interferes with first intercourse, often tearing and bleeding in the process. The woman needs to prepare ahead of time by inserting her fingers into her vagina and gently stretching the opening. Occasionally, a thick and resistant hymen may need surgical cutting.

*This chapter draws heavily on Masters and Johnson's laboratory investigation of human sexual response. For simplicity, we will henceforth omit the date in referring to Masters and Johnson's 1966 book or use the abbreviation M/J.

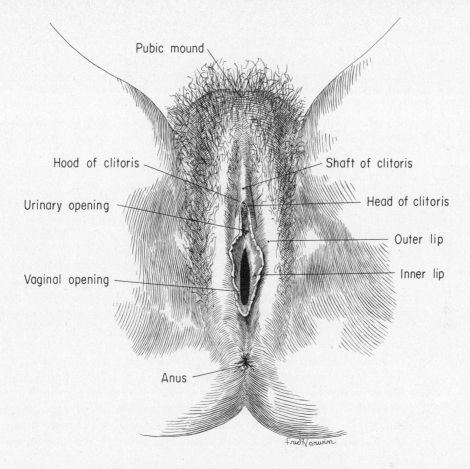

Figure 9-2 Female genital organs.

The vagina is elastic in length and diameter and is equipped at the entrance with engorgable spongy tissues and a sphincter muscle that enable it to adapt to the penis. Even though individuals of both sexes differ considerably in the size of their genital organs, vaginal adaptability makes anatomical incompatibility rare. Among Masters and Johnson's 400 women subjects, only two had vaginas small enough to feel pain if intromission occurred before they became aroused enough to be fully dilated. When stimulated, even these women could receive a penis of any size. One has only to realize how much the vagina stretches during childbirth to appreciate its extraordinary flexibility.

Muscles torn in childbirth may require surgical repair to prevent pain during intercourse. Loss of muscular tone may create a problem of vaginal enlargement. Fortunately, the vaginal sphincter muscles are subject to voluntary control and can be strengthened by deliberately tightening them.

Sexual Physiology

In both sexes, sexual stimulation produces two major responses: (1) vasocongestion (concentration of blood in particular locations) and (2) muscular tension.

Sexual Arousal.   The initial physiological response of the male is erection of the penis due to vasocongestion of the spongy tissues. Its analogue in the female is lubrication of the vaginal walls by a process similar to sweating. Masters and Johnson found that both responses occur with equal ease under either physical or psychic stimulation.

During sexual arousal, muscular tension produces an erection of the nipples in three fifths of all men and women (M/J). Blood flowing to the breasts enlarges them most extensively in women whose breasts have not yet been stretched by milk produced after childbirth.

Blood flowing to the skin produces a measles-like rash known as a "sex flush" in a minority of males and a majority of females. This reaction is irregular but increases with extensive sexual experience. A minority of men and women feel a cold sweat after the sex flush disappears at orgasm.

The Nature of Orgasm.   Although preadolescent boys achieve climax without ejaculation, after puberty the two are essentially synonymous. Involuntary contractions of various muscles force the seminal fluid from the penis under such pressure that it may be projected as much as one or two feet. (In intercourse this deposits sperm deep in the vagina adjacent to the cervix.) The larger the volume of fluid ejected, the more pleasurable the sensation. Volume generally increases the longer the interval since the last ejaculation.

The focus of female orgasm is the outer third of the vagina. This segment of the vaginal wall becomes congested with blood and reacts in orgasm with a series of strong, rhythmic contractions approximately one second apart (the same interval as in male ejaculation). The larger the number of contractions, the more intense the orgasm. Masters and Johnson labeled three to five contractions "mild," six to eight "normal," and eight to 15 "intense." They described the sensations of orgasm as follows (1966: 135–36):

1.   Orgasm has its onset with a sensation of suspension or stoppage. Lasting only an instant, the sensation is accompanied or followed immediately by an isolated thrust of intense sensual awareness, clitorally oriented, but radiating upward into the pelvis.

2.   A simultaneous loss of overall sensory acuity....

3.   ...a sensation of "suffusion of warmth" specifically pervading the pelvic area first and then spreading progressively throughout the body....

4. ... a feeling of involuntary contraction with a specific focus in the vagina or lower pelvis.... [The] sensation ... of "pelvic throbbing" ... though initially concentrated in the pelvis, was felt throughout the body ... often ... continuing until it became one with ... the pulse or heartbeat.

Although the penis and vagina are the focus of orgasm, many other parts of the body are involved. Contractions of the vaginal ring are paralleled by contractions of the uterus, especially in women whose uterine muscles have previously contracted in childbirth. Both sexes breathe faster and more deeply, the heart beats faster, and the arms, legs, and neck may jerk in muscular spasms.

After orgasm, the blood that has engorged the penis, vaginal wall, clitoris, and breasts disperses more rapidly for men than for women. Consequently, men relax and fall asleep faster.

Orgasm Capacity.   Both sexes attain orgasm more easily in masturbation than in intercourse. Masturbation enables individuals to stimulate themselves more effectively and to focus on their own sensations.

In Kinsey's research, men and women differed in their speed of attaining orgasm through masturbation. Although there was great variation among individuals of the same sex, the average woman required twice as long as the average man. Unfortunately, no comparable data are available for intercourse. However, the fact that climax in intercourse is less regular for women than for men suggests that women may be slower there too.

For most men, most of the time, ejaculation follows erection. If a man is capable of being sexually aroused, he can usually go all the way to climax. But among Hunt's husbands under age 25, 15 percent failed to ejaculate at least one fourth of the times they had intercourse. So orgasm cannot be taken for granted even by men.

Women are even more variable. Only 53 percent of Hunt's married women (1974) always or almost always had an orgasm in intercourse. For 21 percent, orgasm came about three quarters of the time; for 11 percent, about half the time; for 8 percent, only one in four times; and for the remaining 7 percent, seldom or never.

This lesser dependability of the female for experiencing orgasm is offset by an ability in many women (but few men) to achieve repeated orgasms within a few minutes. Moreover, successive orgasms are increasingly pleasurable for the female, but decreasingly so for males as the volume of their ejaculate decreases (M/J).

Orgasms are physiologically necessary for men. Accumulated semen must eventually be released through involuntary nocturnal emissions ("wet dreams") if in no other way. Women have no comparable inevitability.

Sexual Psychology

Sexual activity results not only from physiological forces but from psychological suggestion and attraction.

Erotic Arousal.   In Kinsey's day, erotic materials were more apt to arouse men, whereas women were more responsive to materials dealing with love and romance. With the sexual revolution and the liberation of women, these differences between the sexes have diminished. Hunt (1974) found that American women had become more responsive to sexual stimuli than they had been a generation earlier, narrowing the gap between the sexes.

Table 9-2 portrays the sexual responsiveness of sexually liberal German students. Large proportions of both sexes were sexually aroused by erotic movies and slides. The day after seeing the films, women were just as likely as men to feel more turned on than they had the day before. On the whole the men and women were rather similarly aroused by these visual stimuli.

Sex and Love.   The more mature people become, the more they tend to integrate sex and love. In his study of mentally healthy people, Maslow (1953) found that "sex and love can be and most often are very perfectly fused with each other in healthy people.... Self-actualizing men and women tend on the whole not to seek sex for its own sake, or to be satisfied with it alone when it comes."

One woman related:

> There is a direct connection between my ability to move easily to orgasm and my emotional state. When I feel good about myself because I have recently shared myself authentically with another person and ex-

Table 9-2   Sexual Arousal in Response to Erotic Films, by Men and Women

Sexual Arousal while Viewing Films	Men	Women
Experienced an erection	86%	——
Experienced genital sensations (feelings of warmth, pulsations, etc.)	——	65%
Day After versus Day Before		
Experienced more sexual fantasies	33%	35%
Experienced greater sexual tension	32%	35%
Experienced greater desire for sexual activity	41%	46%
Number of cases	128	128

Adapted from Schmidt and Sigusch, 1970: 277, 279. *Source:* Students at Hamburg University, three quarters of whom had already engaged in sexual intercourse. Reciprocal percentages did not experience the specified sexual arousal.

perienced their sharing with me, my body is more open. If I am not feeling emotionally "together" with another person, I usually can't be led to orgasm.

Sexual satisfaction is broader than orgasm. As there are infinite ways of defining and expressing love verbally, so there are infinite ways of giving and receiving physically. Those who are comfortable with their sexuality and with one another can respond lovingly, whether or not they are in the mood for intercourse. To expect a mutual high interferes with the down-to-earth goodness and everydayness of sex, which is as necessary and natural as eating and sleeping. More often than not, one partner will feel the desire to make love, and the other will respond, not always passionately.

The strain of child-rearing or job pressures may be released through sexual pleasure. Discouragement and depression may be healed by being touched and caressed. If one partner wants sex and the other doesn't, the latter's love and caring may enable him/her to give and receive because the other asked:

> *In general, I know that Bruce has greater sexual needs than I, but our lack of equality in our needs doesn't make me feel exploited or used—far from it. It is always good to be wanted and I can truthfully say, always good to satisfy him. This doesn't mean I don't feel free to say no if I'm fatigued. But he doesn't take that as a rejection. It's just my particular reality at that moment.*

Giving and taking need not always be equal. Men and women can bridge their differences when sex is synthesized with love and the rest of marriage.

In Rainwater's 1965 study of middle-class marriages most wives (59 percent) enjoyed sex as much as their husbands. Even where husbands enjoyed it more than wives, both partners had essentially positive feelings. Differing degrees of enthusiasm for sex in general or at particular times need not be measured any more than differing appreciations of ice cream flavors, sunsets, or flowers.

DEVELOPMENT OF THE SEXUAL RELATIONSHIP

At least as much as any other aspect of marriage, the sexual relationship changes over time.

The First Experience

Whether it comes after marriage or before, whether with financé(e) or stranger, like a first parachute jump or first childbirth, the first intercourse is an adventure long remembered. Since no art can be perfected without practice, initial doubts and anxieties are understandable. The more secure the relationship, the more easily qualms can be shared.

Many couples become sexually involved before they get married. Others follow the traditional pattern and wait to share sexual intimacy until after the legal or religious ceremony. Regardless of when sex begins, to be prepared before that first occasion is valuable. There are endless resources. Peers are sometimes knowledgeable. Fortunate the man and woman who have parents or older siblings with whom they can comfortably converse. In many communities there are clinics providing counseling and contraceptives. Courses and workshops in human sexuality are provided by schools, churches, and communities for persons of all ages. Finally, there are books and films—some cornier than others, but all reflecting the fact that sex is a form of human communication as natural as eating, as far as the hunger goes, but clumsy in the absence of knowledge.

For most people, early intercourse does not function as well as more practiced occasions. This does not mean it is necessarily unpleasant, but it is less satisfactory than it will become later. The mutual love and consideration that benefit sexual relations under any circumstances are especially needed at the initiation.

Intercourse reveals the body to the partner—perhaps for the first time. It also reveals the person in a new light. For the man, there are hazards in achieving or maintaining an erection or in reaching a climax soon enough but not too soon. For the woman, questions have to do with relaxing, becoming lubricated, and achieving an orgasm.

In the context of love, "failures" can be forgiven. The risk of clumsiness is the price paid by couples who choose to initiate sex together. Counterbalancing that risk is a sense of mutuality derived from adventuring together.

The Wedding Night.   For inexperienced couples, the wedding night is the traditional time for initiation. However, rules are made to be broken when they don't fit. All sorts of reasons cause postponement: menstruation, contraceptive inadequacy, lack of opportunity, fatigue, and reluctance. The first experience deserves auspicious circumstances. If circumstances aren't right the first night, they are worth waiting for. Just because a couple don't feel ready to go all the way is no reason not to touch each other. Sex, after all, is more than genitality. To rush into intercourse without exploring each other's bodies would be insensitive. So, couples who are exhausted on their wedding night may want simply to snuggle and caress one another. The thing that matters is that intercourse happen spontaneously and pleasurably as an outcome of loving each other.

The Honeymoon.   For the initiated and uninitiated alike, the honeymoon is a time of sexual enjoyment. Even couples who have had intercourse before find the circumstances changed. Usually the honeymoon provides more leisure than before.

With experimentation and practice, the inadequacies of the initial experience are soon left behind. Table 9-3 shows that both inexperienced and experienced brides found the whole two weeks after the wedding more satisfying sexually than the first marital attempt. Experienced wives had a head start, to be sure, but by the end of a fortnight, the novices caught up with where the experienced ones had been before. For both groups initial intercourse was less satisfactory, but couples soon learned how to make it more meaningful.

One problem is what doctors call "honeymoon cystitis." Although the cause is not entirely certain, frequent intercourse may produce a bacterial infection of the female bladder (perhaps as a result of penile irritation of the bladder through the vaginal wall). The first symptoms are increased frequency of urination and a burning sensation during urination. Couples need not refrain from intercourse for fear of causing this problem, but if it arises the woman should seek medical treatment. Even old married couples risk the same problem if they markedly increase their frequency of intercourse; so it may plague second honeymoons as well as the first.

Learning the Art of Sex

Sex manuals offer instruction in the skills of lovemaking. The most important lessons, however, are not found in books. Each individual must learn the meaning of sex for him/herself—and must learn from the partner how s/he wants to be treated.

Stimulation. The basic form of stimulation is touch. To focus prematurely on the erogenous zones of the body is to miss the opportunity not only to establish a foundation for sexual exchange but to experience

Table 9-3 Wedding Night and Honeymoon Sexual Satisfaction, of Sexually Inexperienced and Experienced Wives

Evaluation of Intercourse	SEXUALLY INEXPERIENCED WIVES		SEXUALLY EXPERIENCED WIVES	
	Wedding Night	Honeymoon Period	Wedding Night	Honeymoon Period
Very satisfying	18%	34%	33%	56%
Satisfying	29	42	39	36
Not satisfying	49	24	23	8
Very unsatisfactory	4	0	5	0
Total	100%	100%	100%	100%
Number of cases		100		77

Adapted from Kanin and Howard, 1958: 562. *Source:* Retrospective self-ratings of first marital experience and of first two weeks' experience by wives of married students at an Indiana university.

touching for its own sake, as enunciated by Masters and Johnson (1974: 238):

> Touch is an end in itself. It is a primary form of communication, a silent voice that avoids the pitfall of words while expressing the feelings of the moment. It bridges the physical separateness from which no human being is spared, literally establishing a sense of solidarity between two individuals. Touch is sensual pleasure, exploring the texture of skin, the suppleness of muscle, the contours of the body, with no further goal than enjoyment of tactile perceptions. And yet such is the nature of the sense of touch, which can simultaneously give and receive impressions, that the very pleasure a woman may experience in stroking her husband's face, for example, is relayed back through her fingertips to give him the pleasure of being aware of her pleasure in him.

To touch and be touched can be exquisitely beautiful when they are engaged in spontaneously without pushing for sexual arousal. The delightfulness of touching can be seen in the way adults respond to infants and pets. Indeed, the very name "pets" reflects the joy we derive in petting them. Conversely, the soothing warmth of being stroked can be seen with bedridden patients or crying children. Most people get too little of the touching for which their bodies hunger.

Masters and Johnson (1970) found that sexually troubled couples had typically bypassed touching and were preoccupied with genital arousal. In sex therapy, their patients were instructed to focus on touching the rest of the body, avoiding the genitals temporarily. This can be experienced by any couple when they give each other a massage.

For those who lack an adequate range of strokes, massage classes and workshops may increase the repertoire. But it is essential not to become technique-oriented. Once the techniques have been learned, the active partner can give most completely by turning off his/her conscious mind and allowing the massage to flow effortlessly and spontaneously from the fingertips. One's intuition is the best guide to what is needed by the partner. Once one has developed a capacity for intuitive massage, no two massages will ever be alike, and every massage can be a profoundly spiritual experience as the hands communicate a flow of energy between the partners.

This spiritual quality is enhanced by maintaining silence during the massage, save for the sighs of the recipient in response to particularly delightful strokes. By refraining from talking, both giver and receiver can focus their attention on the nonverbal transaction between them. This concentration may extend into a period of quiet before and after the massage. At night, the subdued light of candles or firelight heightens this meditative atmosphere. Some people like to stroke with the pulse of music. Alternatively, one may respond to the breathing of the receiver. Especially in massaging the back, if the giver can time his/her strokes to fit the exhalation of the partner, the massage becomes integrated into the partner's body rhythm.

Firm stroking can be facilitated by oiling the hands. Although special lotions are available at head shops, ordinary vegetable oils are effective and less expensive. One byproduct of using oil, Masters and Johnson found (1970), was that this helped couples overcome their squeamishness with respect to the body's sexual secretions—semen and vaginal lubrication.

Every couple must learn how to stimulate each other's bodies. The questions are both physiological and psychological: not only what parts of the body are most sensitive to touch, but what parts the partner wants touched. Eventually, all the erogenous zones are likely to be explored, but at first one may not be ready for some contacts. Caressing many parts of the body—the legs, the back, the neck, the ears—is likely to send shivers up and down the spine. As the giver experiments, the receiver is the only one who can report the results. Appreciative sounds and words give feedback, informing the partner what is good. Is firm stroking or a light, airy brushing desired? Perhaps a light touch pleases some parts of the body more than others. Learning depends on communicating reactions. In our case:

> *Sex got better for us when we both learned to slow down, became less production- and orgasm-oriented and freed ourselves from being embarrassed to take so much of each other's time. It was good when I [Margaret] finally realized that he wasn't stroking me just to be kind or because the books defined foreplay as necessary, but because he really enjoyed caressing me; my body was a joy in itself to him—not just a means to his or my satisfaction.*

Sex play is an enjoyable part of sexual experience. Loving words and touching turn on both partners, bringing the man to an erection and relaxing the ring of muscles surrounding the vaginal entrance and lubricating the interior of the vagina.

Although both partners may be stimulated by touching almost any part of the body, the peak is seldom reached by generalized stroking. For the woman, the area around the clitoris and the inner lips are the primary focus of stimulation. Slow stroking up and down between the vagina and the clitoris, alternating between light brushing and firm rubbing, or a gentle shaking of the clitoris will arouse her.

How much sex play is needed? As much as either wants. The man and woman may alternate, going as fast as one likes one time and as slow as the other desires another time.

Responsiveness.   A man hardly has to learn to be aroused. When moved affectionally, he is moved to touch. When he touches and is touched in return, his penis begins to harden. A man's penis knows how to reach out.

It doesn't have to be told. It seems to have a life of its own. Once aroused, it knows what it needs and wants. It knows where to go for satisfaction.

A word of caution for female initiators. Some men dislike having their penis stroked before they begin to get sexually excited because this seems like a sexual demand. In such circumstances, generalized caressing and intermingling of the two bodies may be more natural first steps.

Vaginal containment of the penis is different from masturbation and it may take time for the man to respond to the new sensations.

Arousal of the woman is stimulated both by the tender play of her lover and by her reaching out to him with her body. Because the woman's equipment is interior, she must learn how to be active as well as passive. Both tension and relaxation of muscles play a part in the physiology of arousal.

A woman initially must learn how to respond. The better prepared she is with knowledge of her body and how it can be stimulated, the better she will know what to ask for and how to respond in ways that will give her and her husband pleasure.

The woman new to sex can educate herself about her organs by examining her vulva with a mirror and exploring herself with her fingers so that she becomes familiar with how it feels to be touched. This can lead naturally to masturbation to enjoy those feelings to the fullest. The more she masturbates, the more her sexual feelings will develop. Even though there is no automatic transfer of responsiveness from masturbation to intercourse, masturbation provides a foundation on which a sexual relationship can be built.

Most women were not taught to explore and touch their own bodies. As children, they were made to feel guilty for engaging in such "self indulgence." Lacking experience with self-stimulation, they may find that penile thrusting does not stimulate the clitoral region effectively. Because they are unaware of the kinds of stimulation that can bring them pleasure, they cannot teach their husbands how to pleasure them manually. They may envy the husband's regular orgasms. Although they may blame their husbands, the key is in their own hands. They must take responsibility for communicating their own needs without assuming that the partner should know those needs or how to meet them.

It is nonsense for a woman to say, "If you really loved me, you would know how to give me pleasure." To expect that places too heavy a burden on the man. As in the rest of marriage, each partner is responsible for him/herself, for keeping his or her body in good shape (sex is strenuous and requires physical strength), for increasing awareness of his/her own sensitivities, and for taking the initiative when need and desire arise.

To increase the woman's sexual awareness and skill, Hamilton (1969) suggested that she practice lying on her back with her legs apart and knees bent, feet flat on the bed, imagining the man's body six inches above her. Continuing to keep her back flat on the bed, she can lift her pelvis to meet the imaginary body above it. Reaching to meet the man's thrusting increases tension in the thighs and in the muscles around the vaginal opening, which is essential if the woman is to move toward orgasm.

An exercise derived from bioenergetics involves lying on one's back, slowly raising and lowering the legs until a tremor point is reached, breathing heavily and allowing sounds to be vocalized, thereby learning to experience the vibrations and energizing associated with a "body orgasm."

Such preparation makes the woman readier for sexual involvement. From her masturbatory experience, she can teach her partner those ways of manual-genital stimulation that she enjoys the most. She can take over self-stimulation whenever her partner tires. In some positions in intercourse, she can touch herself while the man is thrusting inside her with his penis. His thrusting can also be matched by her pelvic movement. Mutual activity makes sexual intercourse most enjoyable for both partners.

Even if a couple take years to reach maximum responsiveness, the learning period need not be frustrating. This is a time of gradual progression from low-keyed sexuality to a higher pitch. There can be a sense of accomplishment even in minor gains:

> Although it was about two years after our marriage that I had my first orgasm from intercourse, I felt perfectly satisfied prior to that time. Perhaps a person doesn't miss what she hasn't had. Anyway, being together and learning about each other was pleasant in itself.

Our puritanical heritage makes some of us cringe at the thought of being sensual. But we can't have good sex without sensitizing our bodies and also being willing to help the other come alive. Sex that is mutual and vital occurs only with a woman's vigorous participation. She is more apt to reach an orgasm if she reaches out actively to the man. Muscular tension increases as she teasingly resists the man's opening of her thighs or reaches again and again with her pelvis. Rocking and rolling in rhythm with the man's thrusting promotes a further turn-on. Without tension there is no vasocongestion. As the congestion of blood in the tissues of the legs, pelvis, and genitals reaches a peak, suddenly the dam breaks and involuntary throbbing commences.

Alternating with this active tension is a passive quality. The woman may imagine as she exhales warm sensations streaming down the torso, flowing deep within her genitals and out the thighs, legs, and soles of her feet. Active reaching and receiving, tensing and relaxing, are both essential in sexual response.

Constricting the pubococcygeal muscle (the one used in urinating) builds tension and congestion in the vaginal walls and surrounding area.

This constriction is pleasing to the man as it makes for closer containment of the penis. By increasing the friction, it benefits both partners. Women may strengthen this muscle by consciously contracting it as an exercise.

Awareness of breathing is as essential in sex as in natural childbirth. Deep breathing increases the energy available in the blood. Exhaling fully (panting) empties the lungs and provides space for involuntarily sucking in more oxygen. Deep breathing and passion are not just literary correlates. As the body becomes excited and gives itself to the activity of sex, it must have breath to feed the fires of passion. The heart is stimulated and increases its pulsing, pushing more blood to the genital area. A few seconds before orgasm, the woman feels a strong pulsing of the heart. The whole body seems involved and at that moment she feels a spreading sensation of warmth like waves throughout the genital region.

Figure 9–3 illustrates the increased sexual responsiveness of women over time. Almost half the women in Kinsey's sample experienced their first orgasm from intercourse within the first month of marriage, and three fourths within the first year. From then on, some women each year learned to respond until by the fifteenth year of marriage only 10 percent had never been orgasmic in intercourse. By the time of Hunt's study (1974), the continuing sexual liberation of women had reduced the proportion of wives of all ages in his sample who "never or almost never" experienced orgasm in intercourse to 7 percent. This suggests that the number who never experience orgasm, even after many years of practice, must have dwindled almost to zero. Most women who are nonorgasmic can hope that eventually they will begin to respond more freely, either with increased experience or, failing that, with therapy.

Figure 9-3 Orgasm Experiences of Wives, by Length of Marriage

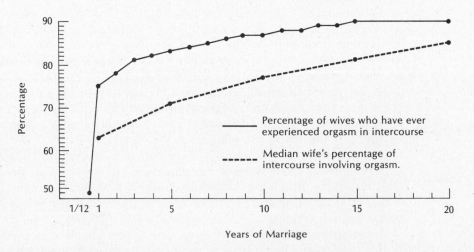

Adapted from Kinsey, 1953: 408.

Experience also makes orgasm more regular. The rising curve in the median wife's percentage of orgasm implies the gradually increased responsiveness an individual woman can expect. In contrast with other indices of marriage that decline over time, ability to respond sexually can be acquired only through experience.

The fact that some women never have an orgasm in intercourse does not mean that their sexual life is meaningless:

> *I enjoy sex very much with my husband, but I seem to be one of those women who is unable to have an orgasm during intercourse. It used to frustrate and worry me that I could not have that total experience with him. As I have learned to masturbate, I have discovered that the next day after we have made love I always feel a desire to masturbate and can easily have an orgasm alone. Though the masturbation is in private, the experience of emotional release seems to flow directly out of the love we shared the night before.*

Nonetheless, whenever a woman fails to experience orgasm, her physical pleasure is reduced. Moreover, Masters and Johnson reported that the vasocongestion of the pelvis in sexual arousal leaves many nonorgastic women feeling physically uncomfortable or even pained, restless, and irritable for some time afterward.

How frustrated a woman feels will depend on her expectations (and her partner's). If both partners recognize the unpredictability of feminine orgasm, they will be less disappointed. But disappointment is understandable. The choice for married couples lies between sympathetic and antagonistic handling of their disappointment:

> *In all the years we've been married, Debby has never had an orgasm and this disturbs both of us. She feels bitter about it and accuses me of using sex simply for self-gratification at an "animal" level. I feel frustrated too by my inability to make her have an orgasm.*

Frustration reduces the marital satisfaction of women who rarely have an orgasm. Gebhard (1966) found no variation in marital happiness in a broad middle range of orgasm capacities. But at the two extremes, women who seldom or never reached climax and those who almost always did found their marriages correspondingly less or more satisfactory.

Wives can live without orgasm, provided both partners accentuate the positive. If they concentrate on what both gain from the experience, they can get the most out of their limited circumstances.

Control. The converse problem for men is learning to control responsiveness in order to delay ejaculation. This is not a problem in most marriages. Hunt (1974) found that the typical man in his sample lasted ten minutes from intromission to ejaculation. But in the excitement of sex play men sometimes ejaculate before intromission. Since erection subsides rapidly, intercourse cannot be completed. More commonly, ejaculation soon after intromission leaves both partners disappointed with the brevity of contact. After ejaculation, the head of the penis is so sensitive that the man usually ceases thrusting. Indeed, Masters and Johnson reported that further thrusts are painful for most men.

Control may be achieved through both physical and psychological measures. Frequent intercourse reduces the physiological pressure for ejaculation by decreasing the accumulation of semen. A condom to sheathe the penis makes it less sensitive. By experimenting with the depth and rhythm of penetration, the man can learn what movements stimulate his wife without bringing himself to climax too soon. Certain coital positions may stimulate the wife more and the husband less.

Whereas concentrating on his own sensations and fantasies speeds a man's orgasm, concentrating on his wife's needs will delay it. By focusing on stimulating the wife, the husband will enhance his ability to sustain that stimulation:

> It used to be that he always came first and I got left. Finally, we learned to give each other turns. When we focus on my arousal he may lose his erection, but at least I had mine that time. Besides, if we start fooling around again, he will usually get aroused again.

Although the learning period is important for new lovers, once the fundamentals of sex have been mastered, it is important that both partners not take it all so seriously but allow themselves to let go and do what comes naturally. This means shifting attention away from pleasuring the partner onto experiencing for oneself the pleasure of touching the partner's body with one's own body and vice versa. In this way, sex avoids degenerating into "work" and becomes a sensual experience for both partners, as described by Hodge (1967: 165):

> Sexual intercourse reaches the peak of satisfaction and enjoyment for a couple when each person is free to be spontaneous. The man feels, says, and does what is most enjoyable to him. The woman feels, says, and does what is most enjoyable to her. In effect each person is saying to the other, "I am caressing you and speaking my feelings of love to you because it 'pleasures me' to do so, not because I am trying to please you or elicit some particular response from you." In such a satisfying sexual relationship the fact that each person's excitement and enjoyment is multiplied by the enjoyment of the partner is a happy by-product of the natural course of events rather than a contrived occurrence.

VARIETIES OF SEXUAL EXPERIENCE

It is important to liberate sex in marriage from routines or ruts. One way of doing this is to disrupt mechanical sequences. Some couples assume that just because they start something they must finish it, or just because they do one thing, something else must follow. Spontaneity and unpredictability go hand in hand. Sometimes sex play leads to intercourse, sometimes not. Sometimes intercourse follows prolonged sex play, but sometimes it occurs with little foreplay. Symbolic sexual experiences such as expressive massage or sexy dancing sometimes propel the couple into bed, sometimes not. Sexy movies or sexy fiction read aloud may heighten sexual desire, especially if they are not "used" merely to pave the way to intercourse but are elements added to the total life of the couple, providing a storehouse of memories to reverberate to subsequent sexual experiences.

Varied Techniques

The range of sexual experience in marriage has widened. The liberation of women, the equalitarianization of marriage, and increased education for both sexes have encouraged experimentation. Many couples approach marriage with the attitude that they will try anything once. They may not enjoy it, and may never repeat it. Nevertheless, the best way to find out is to try.

As a result of this willingness to experiment, oral-breast and manual-genital stimulation have become almost universal, especially for college-educated couples (Hunt, 1974). Oral-genital contact occurred for most of Hunt's couples, but by no means for all. Indeed, Kephart's 1954 study of Philadelphia divorces granted between 1937 and 1950 showed that wife-initiated divorce suits involving sexual complaints frequently blamed the husband's pressure for oral-genital contact. Presumably in any generation, being forced to engage in sexual acts that one dislikes is liable to ruin not only the sexual experience but the marriage itself.

Table 9–4 Married Women's Response to Oral and Anal Sex

Response to Actual or Imagined Experience	SEXUAL ACTIVITY		
	Cunnilingus	Fellatio	Anal Intercourse
Enjoy very much	39%	24%	2%
Enjoy sometimes	37	36	12
Indifferent	6	11	13
Dislike	10	16	42
Repulsed	9	13	30
Total	101%	100%	99%
Active incidence	80%	76%	24%

Adapted from Bell and Connolly, 1973: 6, 7, 8. *Source:* Nonrandom sample of 2,372 American married women biased toward high-educated working women. Women who had never had the particular experience were asked what they thought their reaction would be. Cunnilingus is oral stimulation of the female genitals. Fellatio is oral stimulation of the penis.

A more recent study (see Table 9–4) showed that relatively few married women disliked oral sex, although they were more apt to dislike performing fellatio on their husbands than being orally stimulated by their husbands. Anal intercourse, on the other hand, was a rare experience that was seldom enjoyed very much, suggesting that this might be a source of marital difficulty.

Along with varied techniques of sex play come varied positions in intercourse. Hunt (1974) found that having the woman above was the chief alternative to the man above, followed by the side-by-side, rear entrance, and sitting positions. Kinsey (1953) found that entering the vagina from the rear was used by many couples late in pregnancy. Unusual positions are often experimented with early in marriage, but abandoned in favor of customary ones as time goes on. Still, for couples who are bored, new positions provide a wealth of variety.

Varied Circumstances

Variety comes as much by changing circumstances as by changing techniques.

The way the husband and wife treat each other affects their sexual experience:

> Our sex life has improved a lot now that there is less tension between us. With my help around the house, Karen isn't so tired and so she's been able to enjoy intercourse more.

Few persons are able to enjoy sex when their marriage is in trouble. Love and sex must go together or sex turns bitter. Reconciliation must be achieved before sexual responsiveness will be released.

Freedom to enjoy sexual intercourse reflects the way the day's routine has gone as well as the state of the marriage:

> I enjoy sexual relations most when the day progresses favorably—if the children behave so my nerves don't get frayed. Similarly, George seems to be in a good mood after watching TV or after he's gotten a big job finished at the office.

In the happiest marriages, sex is fun. In the words of Maslow (1954: 251-52):

> It is quite characteristic of self-actualizing people that they can enjoy themselves in love and in sex. Sex very frequently becomes a kind of a game in which laughter is quite as common as panting. . . . The sex life of healthy people, in spite of the fact that it frequently reaches great peaks of ecstasy, is nevertheless also easily compared to the games of children and puppies. It is cheerful, humorous, and playful.

Marriage is not so monotonous as pessimists suppose. Nor is marital intercourse. Even when confined to a single position, it is never the same. Differences in mood color the experience. As partners go through life, establishing a home, raising children, and changing personally, intercourse mirrors the changing environment. The moon shining in the window one night and snow falling another create stage effects for the sexual drama. With changing moods and changing settings, intercourse is never completely routine. Even if it were always the same, it wouldn't be boring. Like a swim on a hot summer day, the tension and release of sexual exchange is refreshing:

> Some of the best times for us have been when we have made love in the middle of the day, lying in the sun on our livingroom floor or lying on the deck of our cabin with the blue sky above and a soft breeze blowing. It's fun having sex when we're on vacation and time stretches out endlessly before us and we're rested and full of energy. Then we forget about everything else and just play together.

Variations in Frequency

Couples differ enormously in frequency of intercourse, even those of similar age, length of marriage, number of children, and the like. Although Hunt's (1974) young married couples typically had sexual relations three or four times a week, some did only once a month or less while others averaged once a day or even more.

Happiness depends less on the absolute frequency of intercourse than on the relationship between actual and preferred frequencies. If both partners want intercourse often, happiness increases with frequent intercourse. But if sex comes more often than either partner prefers, it becomes a nuisance.

Figure 9–4 shows that wives were almost identically unhappy when they had intercourse more often than they wanted as when they had it less often than they wanted. Among the couples in Terman's sample, however, deficiencies were more common than excesses. Since intercourse requires the cooperation of two partners, either can deprive the other. Deficiencies result from the unwillingness of one partner to meet the other's wishes:

> John's appetite for sex and mine seem quite different. I seem to be impossible to appease while he seems disinterested very often. I have never reached a climax and feel destined to remain frustrated until this gap is breached. When I make overtures to him after three or four nights' waiting, he tells me to stop tickling him or pretends he is going to sleep. Several times I have told him the way I feel as openly as I can to which I get no response, no apology, and, even worse, no effort.

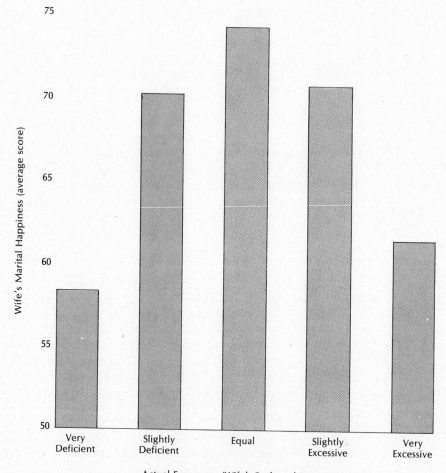

Figure 9-4 Wife's Marital Happiness by Relation of Actual Frequency to Her Preferred Frequency of Intercourse

Adapted from Terman, 1938: 282.

Terman (1938) found that the partners of dissatisfied individuals were almost as unhappy as they were. Hence, even when one partner gets his/her way, the other's reluctance reduces the eager one's satisfaction. Fortunate are couples who match frequency and preference (either by changing their frequency or adapting their preferences).

Obstacles to Intercourse. The prevalence of deficiencies reflects not only the tendency for intercourse to be confined to the least common denominator of preferences, but also practical problems.

Every month the woman's menstrual flow is apt to trigger a period of abstinence even though only one tenth of Masters and Johnson's female subjects felt that intercourse during menstruation was objectionable on either religious or aesthetic grounds. More than half expressed a desire for intercourse, especially during the latter half of the period. A substantial minority reported that masturbation to orgasm produced uterine contractions that expelled the menstrual fluid accumulated at the beginning of menstruation, relieving cramps and backaches. This suggests that intercourse during menstruation might be similarly beneficial. Nevertheless, most couples avoid it.

In the last six weeks of pregnancy and the first six after childbirth, many physicians prescribe abstinence. Masters and Johnson, however, believed the latter prohibition was unnecessarily rigid. They sympathized with couples who violate it, especially nursing wives whose lactation experiences arouse sexual feelings. They advocated resumption of intercourse as soon as the episiotomy and other vaginal traumas have healed. On the other hand, if the wife has a history of miscarriages, the ban may extend to the whole nine months of pregnancy, especially to the first three months when uterine contractions during orgasm are liable to provoke a spontaneous abortion.

Once children arrive, they interfere more with the timing than the frequency of intercourse. Couples who previously made love at odd hours of the morning or afternoon check their impulses until children are asleep. When children are ill or upset, undistracted time may never come. Children and work exhaust the parents. Illness in either partner diminishes enthusiasm for activity of any kind, sexual or otherwise.

Sometimes housing facilities are inadequate. Privacy for letting oneself go is disrupted by noise conveyed in either direction—into or out of the bedroom. Fears that children may hear (in the next room or worse yet, in the same room), that in-laws may hear (for families living doubled up), or that neighbors may hear (through apartment walls) inhibit natural expression. Intruding noises prevent the concentration needed to maintain sexual arousal. Masters and Johnson found that erection "may be impaired easily by the introduction of asexual stimuli" such as noise, talking about an extraneous subject, or a change in lighting or temperature.

The most serious obstacle to making love, however, is feeling unloving. Hunt (1974) found that couples who felt distant from one another were most apt to wish they had intercourse more often and to feel sexually deprived. Their frequency of intercourse fell off by a full third compared to couples who felt normally close.

Failure to get together in bed is both result and symptom of a lack of general togetherness. In such marriages, those occasions when the partner is willing to have intercourse or, better yet, makes a sexual overture acquire a particular poignancy as an indicator that things are better. Sexual relations acquire an extraordinary symbolic function. Far from being routine or taken for granted, they are prized as signs of forgiveness for past hurts and of hope for the future. Conversely, if the marriage gets bad enough, intercourse may eventually cease completely. At that point, one partner is likely to feel ready to move out of the house.

SEXUAL COOPERATION IN MARRIAGE

Partners whose interest in sex is similar have the fewest problems. Even for them, however, moods only occasionally coincide. When they have been to a movie, both may be eager. After an exhausting weekend with the kids or when the wife is bulgingly pregnant, neither may be interested. But since moods are individual, ups and downs often differ. When moods fail to coincide, then what?

The first step is communication. Subtly or openly, the interested partner and the reluctant partner express what they are feeling. From then on they must choose. Sometimes the reluctant partner cooperates for the sake of the other. On other occasions his/her reluctance is too great, and the eager partner backs down. In the long run, equalitarian couples strike a balance between decisions won by each spouse and between yeses and noes. Neither partner's wishes automatically prevail. The toughest problems face couples whose wishes differ consistently. For them, initiative and response are troublesome questions.

Initiative

When both partners are excited and rapport between them is high, a direct invitation to go to bed may be appropriate. But when one partner is excited and the other is not, then what?

One danger is that the horny partner will resort to pressure—either a macho quasi-raping of the woman or criticism of the partner's disinterest. Either tactic may procure some body contact, but the cost to the relationship is likely to be high. And high-pressure tactics are quite as likely to backfire in stiffened resistance.

The opposite danger is that the horny partner will simply jump to the conclusion that sex is unavailable because of the other's initial disinterest. S/he may give up too easily, assuming that the situation is hopeless. Although every would-be initiator must be prepared for the possibility of ultimate rejection, getting discouraged without half trying robs both partners of potential goodies. Many reluctant partners enjoy being pursued as evidence of how much they are loved, needed, wanted. And the initiator may be able to achieve the desired sexual pleasure by not giving up at the first sign of disinterest.

A wise initiator will use his/her knowledge of the partner's reluctance to figure out what kind of approach is most likely to stimulate a readiness for lovemaking. The traditional term for this was "the fine art of seduction." It is still something that husbands and wives practice on each other to their mutual satisfaction. To seduce one's partner means helping him/her to want to make love, even though that was not his/her original interest. Strategy will vary with the occasion and with the life-style of the couple. For some persons, food, wine, candlelight, and music create the right setting. For others, rapport-creating conversation is crucial. For still others, all that matters is being stroked, caressed, and loved. Persons in reasonably good health and not too tired are likely to be turned on, provided that the relationship between the two partners is sound.

When the initiative succeeds, the initiator can do something else to make seduction easier the next time—express appreciation for the good time s/he has had. The greater the initial reluctance, the more valuable such positive feedback becomes.

Response to Initiative

If one partner's sexual needs are stronger than the other's, going out of his/her way to meet them will express his/her love. Where needs are not symmetrical, the more each partner goes out of his/her way to serve the other, the more meaningful the marriage becomes. This is the opposite of the least-common denominator to which marriage so easily sinks. It goes beyond compromising halfway between the partners' desires. The ideal is for the less interested partner to please the more interested one. This is not to say that one must never rebuff one's partner. Some selectivity is inevitable. However, responding to sexual overtures as often as possible will increase the couple's enjoyment.

Table 9–5 shows that typically both sexes "usually" responded by going along with the spouse who raised the possibility of intercourse even

Table 9–5 Participation in Sexual Intercourse When Unilaterally Desired by the Spouse, for Husbands and Wives

Participate in Intercourse	Husbands	Wives
Always	37%	11%
Usually	51	57
Occasionally or never	12	32
Total	100%	100%

Recomputed from Nye, 1974: 243. *Source:* 210 sets of parents of third-grade schoolchildren in Yakima County, Washington. Percentages are limited to those persons who ever wanted to have intercourse when the spouse did not (6 percent of the husbands and 25 pecent of the wives reported that they never wanted to have intercourse at a time when the partner didn't want it, too).

if they didn't initially want it themselves. The sexes differed, however, in that husbands were more apt to respond to initiatives coming from the wife whereas wives were the chief refusers. Terman (1938) found that only unhappy husbands and wives refused intercourse very often. Refusal not only expresses sexual disinterest, but often punishes the partner for nonsexual grievances. The more sex means to the partner, the more potent a weapon the power to say no becomes. However, the weapon is liable to backfire. When sex sinks to bargaining and contentiousness, love is destroyed.

Fun

Although gentleness and sensitivity have an important place in sex (especially when sex is new), it is possible to have too much of a good thing. More experienced couples may find uninhibited roughness exhilarating:

> *I used to think that sex was beautiful, a gift that I could give my wife, a responsibility that I assumed to make her happy. I was a real gentleman in the literal sense of that term. So it was a real breakthrough to discover that being a gentleman was a burden that I resented carrying and that even Marian did not appreciate. When I said to her that I was tired of carrying the responsibility for her pleasure, it not only freed me of a burden but freed her to take responsibility for herself. We began to find that the more we reveled in the fierce, uninhibited passionateness of sex, the more we gave to one another. I realize now that my giving has to be the byproduct of being really engrossed in what I want to do. If I do what my body wants to do, what my intuition tells me to do, instead of programing a "thoughtful" and "considerate" approach to my wife, both of us will end up enjoying it more.*

PROBLEMS IN SEXUAL RELATIONSHIPS

Sexual problems frequently take physical shape—an insufficiently relaxed vagina, an excessively relaxed penis, or the disappearance of sexual activity altogether. The causes of these physical problems are often emotional and relational.

Disengagement

The longer most people stay married, the less often they have intercourse. This appears in declining frequencies by length of marriage, age of husband, or age of wife (see Figure 9–5).

Intercourse does not end abruptly when the man reaches 65—Hunt just ran out of cases. There is no age limit beyond which sex is universally

Figure 9-5 Frequency of Intercourse, by Age of Husband

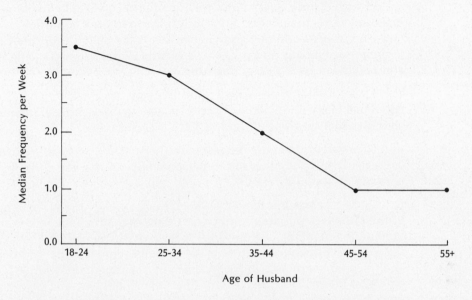

Adapted from Hunt, 1974: 190.

impossible. Menopause may bring increased enjoyment to women afraid of conception. However, both men and women generally avoid strenuous activity as they get older, not so much because they are incapable as because they are lazy.

Masters and Johnson reported that aging reduces the intensity of sexual responsiveness in both sexes. Vasocongestive and muscular tension reactions weaken or disappear, especially those involving parts of the body farthest removed from the genitals (for example, the sex flush and spasms of the hands and feet). Vaginal lubrication decreases after menopause so that a bit of saliva or a lubricating jelly may have to be used. Another geriatric problem is thinning of the vaginal walls so that thrusting movements of the penis irritate the adjacent bladder. This may be minimized by adequate lubrication and early ejaculation, but the woman may need a postcoital trip to the bathroom.

After menopause, the normal uterine contractions in orgasm become painful for some women. This may be treated with hormones. Masters and Johnson advocated endocrine replacement therapy for both sexes to reduce attrition of the sexual organs and maintain capacity for sexual functioning.

However, the main problem is not medical:

1.   For both sexes, the best way to maintain sexual capacity is by exercising it. Unused, responsiveness wanes. Exercised, that capacity remains alive.

2.   Sexual vitality requires physical vitality. Masters and Johnson observed with dismay that "rarely does the middle-aged male in our culture make any effort to maintain his physical being in good condition." Vigorous exercise for both men and women keeps the body fit for intercourse. Swimming, dancing, and yoga are especially useful for keeping the thighs and pelvis loose for sexual thrusting.

3.   A vital marriage provides a solid basis for sex. Masters and Johnson noted that many middle-class people became so preoccupied with outside activities that they had little time left for each other.

4.   To revive the flagging interest of the partner, Masters and Johnson encouraged continued attention to personal appearance and continued expression of sexual interest.

5.   The less frequent intercourse becomes, the greater the value of having it under the best possible conditions. Crises or distractions impair sexual functioning more than before since "sensitivity to mental fatigue is one of the greatest differences between the responsiveness of the middle-aged and the younger male" (M/J). Physical vigor is impaired by fatigue, overeating, or liquor. The tranquilizing effect of alcohol destroys the muscular tension necessary to erection. To put it positively, couples need to be emotionally and physically refreshed if intercourse is to be most successful.

6.   Last, older men must be willing to risk failing to achieve an erection or an ejaculation. Occasional failure is normal, even under the best of circumstances. The danger is that episodic failure will create fear of future failure. This makes anxious men discontinue intercourse with partners who remember their prior failures (even though they may be potent with a new partner). The crucial question is the couple's ability to tolerate occasional failure. The woman can support the man with understanding and empathy when he does not ejaculate.

Masters and Johnson concluded their chapter on "The Aging Male" with an optimistic forecast (1966: 270):

> There is every reason to believe that maintained regularity of sexual expression coupled with adequate physical well-being and healthy mental orientation to the aging process will combine to provide a sexually stimulative climate within a marriage. This climate will, in turn, improve sexual tension and provide a capacity for sexual performance that frequently may extend to and beyond the 80-year level.

Impotence

For a variety of reasons, impotence is an increasing problem as men grow older. Impotence was defined by Masters and Johnson (1966: 341) as disturbance of sexual function in the male that precludes satisfactory coitus. It varies from inability to attain or maintain full erection to total loss of erective powers.

Impotence is not directly concerned with ability to ejaculate, but only with the erection necessary to achieve intromission. It rises sharply in old age (see Figure 9–6).

Masters and Johnson found that impotence began more often when men had drunk too much than under any other circumstance. Prevention requires either avoiding intoxicated intercourse or recognizing that impotence under the influence of alcohol means not that one is too old for sex but too relaxed for it. Impotence induced by alcohol need not reoccur when sober—unless one is paralyzed by fear that it will. Fear is the greatest problem for men who have experienced difficulty in achieving or sustaining an erection, regardless of what the original cause of that failure may have been. Masters and Johnson (1970) noted that "fear of inadequacy is the greatest known deterrent to effective sexual functioning, simply because it so completely distracts the fearful individual from his or her natural responsivity by blocking reception of sexual stimuli created by or reflected from the sexual partner." In other words, the fearful partner becomes so preoccupied with watching his/her own reactions that it

Figure 9-6 Impotence, by Age of Man

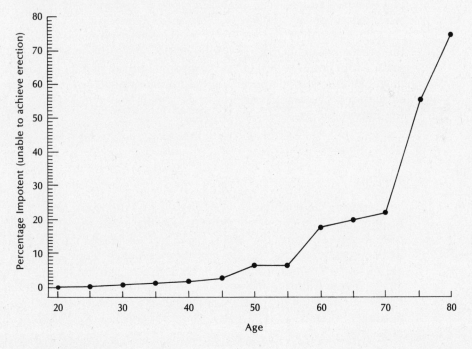

Source: Kinsey, 1948: 236.

becomes impossible to relax and respond naturally to sexual stimulation.

Conversely, a person who is able to accept occasional failure or even reasonably prolonged failure as part of the rhythm of life will keep the door open to the potential resumption of sexual responsiveness when the body is ready. One who can trust that the future will bring renewed sexual capacity is more likely to experience that renewal.

One way of relieving a man's preoccupation with his sexual performance is not only to shift both partners' attention away from accomplishment-oriented sex, but to transfer the basic responsibility for the man's sexual response away from himself to the wife. Masters and Johnson (1970) emphasized that the man's erection is not something that he can produce at will, but is basically an involuntary response to sexual stimulation. The wife is the one who is primarily responsible for providing that stimulation although the husband, too, may find himself sexually aroused as a byproduct of enjoying touching her body. One special responsibility recommended by Masters and Johnson was that the wife guide the penis to insertion in the vagina (thus relieving the man of the awkwardness of searching for the opening). They also recommended that the woman carry primary responsibility for teasing sex play, including mounting the penis as part of her stimulation. With the emphasis simply on the pleasure of each activity, erection tends to occur eventually and to be followed by ejaculation. By instructing their patients in such techniques, Masters and Johnson succeeded in helping almost three quarters of patients who had been previously potent and more than half of those who had never been potent in their entire lives.

At least half of all men suffer from inflammation and enlargement of the prostate gland as they get older. This frequently interferes with their sexual functioning. Following surgical removal of the prostate gland, most patients return to normal sexual functioning. However, more radical surgery to remove cancerous prostate glands may make sexual functioning impossible.

Frigidity

"Frigidity is the complete lack of sex desire with a resulting inability to respond to stimulation and arousal. On this level, frigidity is relatively infrequent" (Levine and Gilman, 1951). Such frigidity may mean inability to be sexually aroused or the negative response of vaginismus, an involuntary contraction of the vaginal muscles so tight that the penis cannot enter. Severe frigidity prevents sexual intimacy and strains the marriage severely. Often the difficulty can be traced to negative childhood conditioning:

> *Josie thinks sex is disgusting, though she spends her spare time reading love stories and movie magazines. In the ten years we've been*

married I've had to go without intercourse as long as three months at a time, when I'd prefer to have it every day. Her inhibitions are so strong that she feels sex should be gotten over with as soon as possible, without any talk. When she does relent, her attitude seems to be: "Let's pretend we didn't do it!"

Blazer's 1964 study of married virgins (married eight years on the average without ever having intercourse) showed the fears, disgusts, antipathies, and ignorance that trigger feminine frigidity. Fear that intercourse would cause pain, that the vagina was too small, or that the wife would get pregnant were common. (Medical examination showed that no vaginas were abnormally small.) More neurotic were fears of semen and of damaging the husband's penis. Most of these women, however, felt the penis was disgusting rather than fragile. Many thought sex generally nasty or wicked. For a few, contraceptives were the source of disgust and abstinence their way of avoiding both conception and contraception. Some women were basically hostile to men and in some cases preferred female partners. Some thought intercourse with a man implied surrender to male dominance and an admission of inferiority. Finally, a few preferred to "mother" their husbands rather than make love to them.

Masters and Johnson (1970) found that every one of their patients suffering from vaginismus was able to achieve dilation through the use of a graduated series of dilaters applied by the husband over a period of days or weeks. However, if the vaginal contraction had been caused by some kind of sexual trauma such as rape, this physical treatment needed to be paralleled by psychotherapy.

The Masters and Johnson technique for treating ordinary orgasmic inadequacy provides an opportunity for the husband to learn from his wife how to stimulate her body more effectively. This is done in a "non-demand" position in which the couple cannot move directly to intercourse—the man sitting up and his wife sitting between his legs with her back to him, leaning against his chest. In this position the man's hands are free to explore his wife's breasts, abdomen, thighs, and pelvic area, while the wife places her hand gently on top of his so that she can guide his direction and pressure in ways that please her. The man gradually learns the subtleties of stroking the clitoris and the inner lips, inserting his finger into the vagina and spreading the vaginal lubrication over the sensitive external area. After manual stimulation has been learned, Masters and Johnson recommend moving to the woman-above position in intercourse, which enables the wife to use the contained penis as a source of continuing stimulation. By repeatedly mounting and dismounting, the woman gradually increases her sexual arousal. Ultimately, a "lateral" position in intercourse provides freedom for both partners to engage in pelvic thrusting toward potential climax. This series of steps under Masters and Johnson's tutelage enabled more than 80 percent of women who had never had any orgasms at all or any orgasms in intercourse to become orgasmic in intercourse.

Recrimination

To have problems is a normal part of marriage, and a normal part of sex. Patience, understanding, and sympathy help solve problems or enable them to be endured less stressfully. To blame the partner or to blame the self is to make problems worse and to destroy the feeling of mutuality that is necessary.

> *You can't be totally responsible for my sexual fulfillment not I for yours. I can bring my need to you. I can initiate and bring my wanting to you. I can ask you to share this experience with me. But I cannot make you have a good experience. If you don't have a high I can't be held responsible. If I don't have an orgasm I can't blame you.*
>
> *It's bad stuff when I blame myself or feel guilty when you don't rave about how great it was.*

With attitudes such as these, even couples with relatively severe sexual problems should be able to resolve them.

10 Separateness and Togetherness in Leisure

As we grew up, marital jests were full of references to the wife as the man's "better half," depicting husbands and wives complementing one another, picturing each partner as incomplete without the other, and designating a dependency in which both had a right to be possessive. Such references were part of a traditional way of thinking about marriage claiming that love and loyalty require serving each other's needs.

The revolutions of the sixties questioned whether one half and one half can make a whole relationship. We suggest that one whole person plus another whole person equals two whole individuals who in their individual wholeness bring health to a marriage and sustenance to one another. We like to quote the motto: Each tub on its own bottom.

In the 1950s, the watchword of American marriage was togetherness. Ideally, couples spent all their leisure together. The more time couples spent together, the happier their marriages were assumed to be.

The movement for the liberation of women challenged that assumption. If married women were to be freed from domination by their husbands, they must develop their own individuality. This could be achieved partly through having a career outside the home. The traditional expectation that wives would devote their leisure to going places and doing things with their husbands was questioned as too narrow and confining.

A second challenge to the concept of togetherness came from the sexual freedom movement. The concept of a sexually and affectionally open marriage struck at traditional views of marriage as a sexually exclusive relationship. For both men and women. this movement proposed that sexual activities be added to the list of options for separate use of leisure time. Because this issue is so complex, we will reserve discussion of it for the next chapter, but note here that extramarital involvement poses the issue of separateness most acutely.

Separateness and togetherness are the yin and yang of marriage. They are not antithetical. Both are essential elements to be discovered and developed within the circle of a love that demands both. Too much separateness leads to alienation. Too much togetherness creates a smothering entanglement of personalities. Individuation and interdependence are both needed and both are desirable. Both intimacy and independence are scary and difficult but achievable. Fear signals that there is too little or too much of one aspect and we need to move toward its opposite. The task of marriage is to find a balance, integrating these elements.

COMPANIONSHIP IN LEISURE

Companionship is the central feature of modern marriages. Given a choice of five aspects of marriage, Detroit wives overwhelmingly said companionship was the most valuable (see Table 10–1). Indeed, in the 16 years from 1955 to 1971, Detroit wives substantially increased the importance they attached to companionship (and correspondingly decreased the importance of having children). The same studies, incidentally, showed that in 1971 wives were more dissatisfied with the companionship they experienced than with any other aspect of marriage, perhaps because they had the highest expectations in this area.

To be sure, the list of alternatives in Table 10–1 was not exhaustive.

Table 10–1 The Most Valuable Aspect of Marriage in 1955 and 1971

Most Valuable Aspect of Marriage	1955	1971
Companionship in doing things together with husband	48%	60%
Chance to have children	26	13
Husband's understanding of wife's problems and feelings	13	13
Husband's expression of love and affection	10	11
Standard of living—house, clothes, car, etc.	3	3
Total	100%	100%
Number of families	724	700

Adapted from Duncan, Schuman, and Duncan, 1973. *Source:* Representative samples of metropolitan Detroit wives.

Nor do we know whether husbands prize companionship as much. Nevertheless, companionship is so prominent in Table 10–1 that it is probably the most valued aspect of marriage for both sexes. This emphasis results from our system of marrying. Couples marry after months and years of going together. One might say they get the companionship habit.

Domesticated Companionship

When a couple begin living together (whether before or after marriage), they shift the structure of their relationship from one that requires making a date in order to see each other to one where being together is a natural accompaniment of such mundane activities as eating and sleeping. This means that a large proportion of their time together is devoted to practical concerns like cooking and reading the newspaper.

For couples who live together, some leisure-time activities are enjoyed at home (just as we saw in Chapter 1 that talking and making love were preferred activities of couples who are going together). Talking, reading aloud, playing double solitaire or Scrabble, dancing to the stereo, and watching television together are potential forms of companionship within the home.

Locke (1951) found the most popular marital activities were domestic—listening to the radio, music, and reading. In the years since his study, television replaced radio as the chief focus of entertainment inside the home, perhaps to the detriment of companionship. We often hear:

> All you do is sit there in front of the tube! We never do anything any more. We never talk. The tube talks for us, laughs for us, cries for us.

Television watching can become a barrier to intimacy at bedtime or a way to avoid making needed decisions. The path of least resistance is to push the button. On the other hand, discriminating use of television can stimulate, educate, and feed good conversation. After a strenuous day, watching television, listening to the stereo, or reading one's own thing in the same room may supply just the right combination of togetherness and separateness, but if "that's all there is" evening after evening the companionship can hardly be described as creative. In our home:

> I [Margaret] like it when we make music together, playing duets on the piano or with your cello and my piano or singing together some of the old musicals. We're always glad when we make the effort, even when we think we're too tired. And I like the way we've started reading aloud while one of us washes the dishes at night. As you read, I've become aware of your dramatic talents!

We have already indicated that sexual sharing is more apt to be vital if other domestic activities involve sharing energy, too.

Many wives complain about the lack of emotional togetherness in their marriages. More than anything else, they wish their husbands would talk about their feelings. The talking doesn't go deep enough:

> The first years we shared everything we felt but, as differences arose, so did the fear of displeasing the other, and we began to keep our feelings to ourselves.

To be afraid of being open about small irritations and disappointments leads to dulled feelings and a boring relationship. When couples become aware of this, they may decide to schedule a time each week (make a date!) when grievances and goodies can be shared. Such a structure may seem artificial but facilitates the directness that clears up misunderstandings and hurts before they accumulate:

> We have learned to set aside two hours after the kids are in bed on Wednesday that are just for us, for sharing where we are in our lives, for remembering the good things and for facing the hurtful and scary issues that are unresolved. This sharing may occur any other time in the week, but if it hasn't, our "date" helps it to happen. After we started doing this on a regular basis, it began happening naturally at other times as well.

Clearing the decks allows the togetherness time during the rest of the week to be freer and more real, not just a pretend togetherness.

Togetherness at home may also involve filling in for the partner on separate activities. It can be a time for discharging strains that cannot be vented in the outside world.

The test of real compatibility is to feel relaxed at home and not always have to be doing something. Home is where we can change into our old clothes and not feel pushed, where we can do what feels right at the moment. To take it easy together is the basic stuff of married companionship. Going out is the "frosting on the cake" that provides the change that gives a lift.

Going Out Together

Movies, parties, and sports events were mutual attractions for more than half of Locke's happily married couples. Couples who were subsequently divorced listed playing cards, drinking, and gambling as their preferred activities. Many couples manage to integrate card playing with successful marriage, but it presents hazards for incompatible couples. Games may pit husband and wife against each other or, worse yet, team them up so that blunders cause tension:

*I really enjoy playing bridge as long as I don't have to play with Art.
I'm not a bad player but our styles of bidding are different, and when I bid
too conservatively and miss those high scores he explodes. Then the
evening is ruined for me. We both love bridge, but if only he wouldn't
take it so seriously!*

Bad enough to lose points through the partner's "incompetence"—worse
yet if every point costs money. Scoring systems dramatize differential
competence in competitive games, confronting losing couples with un-
dodgeable evidence of their inadequacies. Cross-couple doubles pit husband and wife against each other so that each partner's gain is the other's
loss. Young (1964) found that for those whose recreation was deadly
serious, this bred hostility within the marriage and positive feeling within
the extramarital coalition.

Most gamblers lose more money than they win, and their families
suffer accordingly. In Locke's study, both gambling and drinking were
primarily masculine activities rather than mutual interests.

Drinking is closely related to marital dissatisfaction. Almost three
times as many of Locke's divorced as happily married couples reported
drinking together (19 percent versus 7 percent—a bigger difference than
for any other joint activity), but unilateral drinking was even more sharply
associated with divorce. Table 10–2 shows that marital satisfaction decreased among married couples the larger the amount of alcohol consumed:

*Early in our marriage, drinking together at the end of the day
seemed to help us let go of the day and its pressures, and share our
troubles more uninhibitedly. As long as our grievances were about our
jobs, drinking helped. But as unresolved irritations piled up between
Donna and me, it allowed deep hostilities to surface and we moved into
violent free-for-alls.*

Presumably, marital dissatisfaction both causes and results from
drinking. An unhappy marriage can drive a man or woman to drink. And

Table 10-2 Marital Satisfaction of Husbands and Wives, by Amount of Alcohol Consumed

	USUAL NUMBER OF ALCOHOLIC DRINKS/DAY			
Percent Satisfied with Marriage	*None*	*1–2*	*3–4*	*5+*
Husbands	93%	82%	82%	68%
Wives	82%	82%	77%	67%

Recomputed from Renne, 1970: 64. *Source:* Probability sample of households in Alameda County, California. The
statistics are for 1,115 male and 1,279 female white respondents under 45 years old. Reciprocal percentages were
dissatisfied with their marriages.

drinking lowers inhibitions against verbal and physical abuse of the spouse.

The depth of trust between partners determines how much they can share of their deeper selves. Persons who can never share bad feelings with their partner are candidates for addictions that can undermine their marriages. They may keep it inside and develop psychosomatic ailments. They may return to their parents for support, creating in-law tensions. They may find a friend who will accept the part of themselves and help them discharge their anger, frustration, or sadness, perhaps becoming a substitute source of affection:

> My husband is a good man and a good minister but the gospel of love that he preaches from the pulpit and practices toward the lonely single women of the church prevents him, on the one hand, from letting out his normal human frustration with me and, on the other, gets him into affectional involvements that he can't handle.

Compatibility of Interests. A striking feature of Locke's study was that the divorced couples reported more unilateral activities than the happily married couples. Some of this must be discounted because divorced people retrospectively exaggerate their differences. Nevertheless, the least we can say is that unilateral activities tended to become foci of marital conflict. Beyond this, while mutual interests in cards, drinking, or gambling were dangerous enough, unilateral interests were even more likely to lead to disaster.

Unilateral interest in other activities has fewer negative repercussions. Separate interests are tolerable, provided they are not considered immoral and do not provoke jealousy or squander the family's resources. Cards, drinking, and gambling suffer on all these counts. Conservative moralists consider them inherently sinful; hence if only the partner enjoys them, s/he is liable to condemnation. More tangibly, financial resources are jeopardized by the cost of liquor and by the threat of alcoholism to the husband's wage-earning capacity. Gambling, with or without cards, is a similar financial hazard.

Compatibility of leisure interests may be achieved by developing skills to match the partner's so that both may enjoy the same activity, rather than one feeling left out:

> I [Margaret] was jealous of Bob's sailing, so I learned to sail on my own and now we make a good nautical team. In a stiff wind, two are better than one.
>
> For years it hurt me that Bob spent time out with others playing chamber music. When I worked hard at improving my own piano playing, he began to play duets with me at home.

We find in our marriage counseling that couples who have lost the spark from their marriage find it rekindled as they brainstorm about what they would like to do together. By paying attention to high-priority interests, they may discover areas where they can develop skills mutually satisfying to both:

> *Because we spent so much time fighting about our incompatibility, we failed to see the many activities that we could enjoy together.*

Differential Needs.   The need to escape varies with the partners' activities. Husbands and wives who have exhausting vocational responsibilities enjoy being home for a change. If one partner has more outside activities than the other, the one who has been in the bustle of business all day is likely to want a quiet evening at home, while the partner who has seen too much of those four walls is eager to go places and do things:

> *After I've worked all day at home, I wish Floyd would take me to the symphony, ballet, or opera, but he never does. He says he likes to spend his evenings at home with me—at first I was flattered, but after four years I've had too much of a good thing!*

Differential external participation creates conflicting recreational needs. One partner's need for rest is as real as the other's need to escape. When needs conflict, what principle can be invoked? If the choice is between activity and passivity, between doing something and doing nothing, there is much to be said for doing something. Resolving conflicts in favor of activity produces a strenuous life but, in the original Latin, life is synonymous with vitality.

The Need for Change.   Before marriage, couples are often criticized for being too wrapped up in each other. After marriage, the chief danger is that other roles will prevent the husband and wife from paying enough attention to each other. Each partner feels taken for granted. Love fades with loss of enthusiasm for living.

When life gets humdrum, doing something special stimulates and re-creates both partners. As each is turned on to an event, they are more turned on to each other. For us:

> *Going out to a movie together revives that special feeling I [Bob] have for you. And theaters are conducive to cuddling, which makes me feel very loving there and when we get home!*

Stimulating outside people and interests nurture the life that flows between the two of us:

> *When work is hard and heavy we need quiet things like walking and canoeing and camping. When work is boring and depressing we need something to shake us up like folk dancing. When we are weary and cynical we need a silly play or movie.*

Rather than wait for the other to think of something and feel uncared for if s/he doesn't, we've both agreed to take responsibility for seeing that fun things get scheduled into our calendar. We've learned it's not good if only one of us plans all the outside activities.

Sociability

People who make the best marriage partners also make friends most easily. Before marriage, they have more friends of both sexes. After marriage, they maintain old friendships and make new ones. Marriage need not be exclusive in the sense that it terminates other friendships. Rather, it is the most comprehensive and durable of friendships. Marriage can link two sets of friends. Husbands and wives with the ability to establish good personal relations may get to know each other's friends so that they become common friends.

Babchuk (1965) found that half of his middle-class couples in Lincoln, Nebraska, shared all their closest friends, while the remainder had some separate close friends. Couples with the largest number of friends had both the most joint friends and the most separate friends, showing there is no necessary antagonism between the two. Similarly, Locke's happily married couples had more common friends than those who got divorced.

Because of both the personal sociability and the mutual companionship of happily married couples, they have more friends of both their own sex and of the opposite sex than unhappily married couples (see Table 10–3).

Where do joint friends come from? Table 10–4 shows that relatives and childhood friends comprise the original set that people bring to marriage. However, childhood friends are apt to be lost over time while relatives are not far behind in their mortality rate. New friends are met in

Table 10–3 Men Friends and Women Friends during Marriage, for Happily Married versus Divorced Men and Women

| Number of Friends during Marriage | MEN FRIENDS | | | | WOMEN FRIENDS | | | |
| | Husband's | | Wife's | | Husband's | | Wife's | |
	Married	Divorced	Married	Divorced	Married	Divorced	Married	Divorced
Many or several	87%	74%	56%	31%	64%	52%	86%	64%
A few or almost none	13	26	44	69	36	48	14	36
Total	100%	100%	100%	100%	100%	100%	100%	100%

Adapted from Locke, 1951: 232–34. *Source:* 200 happily married couples and 201 divorced couples.

Table 10-4   Sources of Joint Friends, by Age of Wife

	AGE OF WIFE			
Source	20s	30s	40s	Old/Young Ratio
Childhood	42%	29%	16%	0.4X
Relatives	13	8	6	0.5X
Neighbors	25	30	32	1.3X
Work	16	24	24	1.5X
Voluntary associations	5	8	22	4.4X
Total	101%	99%	100%	
Number of cases	74	136	28	

Recomputed from Lopata, 1971: 312, by omitting miscellaneous "Other" sources in order to highlight the changing importance of these particular groups. *Source:* Suburban Chicago area married women.

one's neighborhood and at work. For the older women in Lopata's suburban sample, another source of friends was clubs and organizations. Such voluntary associations provide the maximum freedom of choice in making new friends. The older couples become, the more they lose touch with their original friends and the more selective they become in making new ones based on congeniality of interests.

Friends as a Support Group.   Friends perform an important nurturing function. In six American cities, Zimmerman and Cervantes (1960) found most families surrounded by an enduring cluster of peers who shared their values. Individuals found support in the solidarity of the group and felt protected against outsiders with different values. The more homogeneous the group (in class, religion, kinship, and region of origin), the lower the divorce rate. The same compatibilities that promote marital stability reinforce that stability when extended to a larger group. When couples choose congenial friends, their leisure-time sociability supports their marriage. In our case:

> In the beginning, our commitment to one another was deeply enmeshed in our religious commitment. We left our parental religious backgrounds and found deep mutual satisfaction in the Quaker way of worship, group life, and social witness. In the Society of Friends we were married, and our children grew up with that religion and found an extended family that cared about their welfare. Visiting other Quaker families and sharing potluck together, our children played and stayed together when some of the adults were absent. We supported one another in our child-rearing ideas and those values became peer values for the children as they took conscientious stands during the Vietnam war. When we lived abroad, I [Margaret] often referred to our "beloved community" that we sorely missed. Some of our highest moments of togetherness,

*especially in the early and middle years, occurred through this associa-
tion.*

Table 10–5 shows that the larger the number of close friends and
relatives with whom Californians were in contact, the more satisfactory
were their marriages. Although we don't have detailed information about
the ways in which friends and relatives contribute to marital satisfaction,
we imagine that some of them serve as confidantes and sources of advice
when individuals have trouble with their marriages, and that they contribute ideas and suggestions that enrich the marriage. In addition to
informal counseling, they provide morale-building sociability that en-
riches the marriage. In any case, the evidence is clear that happy marriages are embedded in a framework of friends and relatives, and the
larger this circle is, the stronger the marriage is likely to be.

Couples learn from other couples when they share feelings:

> *Pam and Reg were like brother and sister to us. We could say
> whatever we felt. We learned new things about each other that hadn't
> been shared before because their ease in self-disclosure encouraged us to
> reciprocate.*
>
> *As Larry shared his feelings, I came to understand and appreciate
> him more. And we women made ourselves abundantly clearer to our
> husbands when we shared our united front on some issue!*

In our own case:

> *Sometimes I [Margaret] resented that Bob shared things with others
> that he had never revealed to me, but then I began to realize that it wasn't
> so much that he was withholding from me as that he was not in touch
> with a particular feeling until the group sharing brought it out. I found the
> same was true for me.*

Table 10–5   Marital Satisfaction for Husbands and Wives, by Number of Relatives and Close Friends Seen at Least Monthly

Percent Satisfied with Marriage	NUMBER OF RELATIVES AND CLOSE FRIENDS SEEN MONTHLY			
	0–2	*3–5*	*6–9*	*10+*
Husband	76%	85%	87%	92%
Wives	73%	81%	82%	84%

Adapted from Renne, 1970: 65. *Source:* Approximately 1,200 married men and married women in Alameda County, California. Reciprocal percentages were dissatisfied with their marriages.

On the other hand:

our level of sharing with other couples in the department was restricted. It was fun but we never went deep—joking, teasing, bragging, competing, professional bull, and children talk. I longed for the human touch—being able to share our disappointments and our weaknesses as well as our convictions and accomplishments.

Because it took so much energy to carry our separate job and family responsibilities in our early marriage, there was never time for us alone. I resented a lot of the couple obligations we kept getting caught in. Later we were smarter, and said yes only to those with whom we had a lot in common. We learned to find and create environments in which we were able to share at a level that was meaningful for all of us.

Most friendships are initially man to man or woman to woman, but for married couples they usually become couple-to-couple friendships. The closer a friendship is, the more likely it is eventually to include both partners in both couples. Despite this diffusion, many couples' friendships remain skewed along sex lines, the man interacting more with men, and the same for women.

Lopata (1971) found that the married women she studied in Chicago contacted their women friends so often during the day that couple-to-couple contact paled in comparison. One sixth visited friends at home on a typical day, another sixth met friends away from home, and 44 percent talked on the phone with at least one friend. Thus, daytime contact for women with their women friends was almost a daily occurrence, whereas evening contact happened only once a week and was confined largely to joint visits with the marriage partner. In our case:

During the years when Bob spent the day at the university, the neighborhood wives meant a lot to me [Margaret]. Sharing with them as we weeded or stopping to confide while borrowing an egg sometimes felt closer than what I was experiencing in our marriage at that time. Yet it basically supported our relationship since it provided personal caring and a place to discharge when Bob was not available. Without their friendship I would have been a more burdened mother and a bitchier wife.

SEPARATENESS IN LEISURE

Everyone agrees that married couples need to spend some time together. But the obverse question is more difficult: Should they spend *all* of it together?

In the flush of romance, couples dream of merging their lives. "The twain shall become one flesh" is extended to other activities besides sex.

Diverse interests and views are to be worked at until common ground is established. Separate friends and separate activities must be abandoned. Marriage should be a united front.

"Marriage prediction tests" imply that unification is desirable. To get the maximum score on Locke's test (1951), couples must engage in all conventional activities together.

Carried to its logical conclusion, however, the merging of personalities loses its attractiveness:

> *Before she got married, Charlotte had many, varied interests. She loved music and read widely. In short, she was an interesting person. Then she married. She was very much in love with Tim, so when at first she started acting and thinking like him, it was "cute." But then the situation reached a point where it became heartbreaking to her friends and relatives. She no longer talked from her own point of view. She now said "Tim thinks this" or "My husband says that," even in small matters. She even lost the power to get angry in her own right. She no longer said, "I was so mad," as she had many times before, but, "My husband was so mad." In short, she reached a point where she no longer had any individuality.*

To lose one's identity is to become a nonperson. At this extreme, togetherness is inconsistent with the growth of the personality, and without personal growth the relationship too deteriorates. Marriage requires enough separateness to enable each individual to be a real person.

Charlotte is unusual. In statistical studies, it is hard to locate marriages that suffer from too much togetherness. Most studies show that the larger the number of joint activities, the more successful is the marriage. They also show other benefits from joint use of leisure. Pratt (1972) found that the larger the number of activities that husband and wife engaged in together and the more companionship they enjoyed with the spouse, the better was their health. And Balswick (1970) studied couples where one partner was physically handicapped, finding that the more they attended sports events, fairs, and church services together, engaged in "relaxing activities" such as playing cards and watching television, and ate their meals together, the more successful the handicapped spouse was in securing full-time employment (presumably because of higher morale).

In short, while it is theoretically possible to have too much togetherness, most couples err on the side of too little rather than too much.

The ideal marriage balances unity and individuality. This ideal was expressed by Gibran:

> But let there be spaces in your togetherness,
> And let the winds of the heavens dance between you.
> Love one another, but make not a bond of love:

Let it rather be a moving sea between the shores of
    your souls.
Fill each other's cup but drink not from one cup.
Give one another of your bread but eat not from the
    same loaf.
Sing and dance together and be joyous, but let each
    one of you be alone,
Even as the strings of a lute are alone though they
    quiver with the same music.

Reprinted from *The Prophet* by Kahlil Gibran with permission of the publisher, Alfred A. Knopf, Inc. Copyright © 1923 by Kahlil Gibran; renewal copyright © 1951 by Administrators C.T.A. of Kahlil Gibran Estate and Mary G. Gibran.

Maslow (1953) found that his "self-actualizing" persons were extraordinarily intimate with their partners without becoming overdependent on them of losing their individuality. Togetherness and separateness are not necessarily incompatible, but both may flourish in persons with the most highly developed human capacities:

[Such persons] can be extremely close together and yet go apart quite easily. They do not cling to each other or have hooks or anchors of any kind. One has the definite feeling that they enjoy each other tremendously but would take philosophically a long separation or death. Throughout the most intense and ecstatic love affairs, these people remain themselves and remain ultimately masters of themselves as well, living by their own standards even though enjoying each other intensely (p. 86).

Individual Freedom.   Marriage need not end all individual activities and friendships. Husbands obligated to give up their good times with "the boys" find marriage stifling instead of invigorating:

I wanted to go to the office ball games on Wednesday nights, but my wife always manages to interfere so I never have any liberty. I'd like to go with the fellows to the fights, too, but she complains about that. You can't go out together all the time!

If Gibran is right about spaces in togetherness, they shouldn't. Separate activities threaten marriage chiefly when they engulf a person's leisure, leaving none for the spouse. Only when friends get in the way of all marital companionship is the partner justifiably resentful:

All summer long Mary has spent every Saturday afternoon playing golf with some of the other VPs and it annoys me. Not that I want to take her fun away from her. It's just that I like to play, too, and she never pays any attention to me. It makes me feel gypped and cheated. On our vaca-

tion last week, when she suggested a game to me, I nearly fell over. I think we both had a whale of a good time. I know I did.

This man didn't want to play golf with his wife all the time—only some of it. After she plays with him, he should be able to accept the next separation more easily.

The problem is not to choose between no freedom and complete freedom, but to balance freedom and togetherness. Moderation was consistent with marital happiness in Locke's research (1951): almost half of his happily married couples engaged in some, but not all, of their outside interests together. Moreover, we doubt the remaining couples' assertion of complete unity. Happy couples tend to overstate their togetherness. When checked more precisely, they confess to interests engaged in separately without offending the partner (Benson, 1955). In short, they share enough common interests to be able to accept separate activities without anxiety. Only when companionship is insufficient or personal insecurity is excessive do separate activities cause conflict.

Individual talents need not atrophy just because the spouse does not share them. If the wife is a crack shot with a rifle but her husband is afraid of guns, she doesn't have to stay glumly at home nor must he drag himself around the countryside. If a musical man is married to a tone-deaf wife, she doesn't have to attend quartet rehearsals in order to prevent him from wasting his talents. Instead she can relax at home with her mystery story while he fiddles elsewhere—each enjoying their favorite activity without guilt—provided there are other things they do together.

Every couple consists of two separate persons—not one entity that must go everywhere together:

> *You have your friends and I have mine. Though we may enjoy our friends together, we still have our own separate connection with each of them. I can't speak for you with any of them and I don't want you speaking for me. If you get in trouble with my mother you'll have to bail yourself out, and I promise not to go around protecting you against her or her against you. If you need to confront my father don't say to me, "Will you ask your father not to . . ." or "Will you explain to your father that I can't . . ."*
>
> *And I say the same to my friends and my parents: "Don't ask me to be a go-between for you with Richard. It's your relationship and your battle. I don't want to carry that burden. And if I did, I'd just make it worse for all of us."*

Continuing individuality requires mutual respect for personal space:

> *When I come home at five-thirty, exhausted after an excruciatingly stressful day, I can't be loving and sensitive or listening to Yvonne's hard day, nor can I immediately by magic become a caring father for a bunch*

of tired children. She had to learn not to expect that of me. I appreciate her giving me that space for the first half hour and allowing me to be by myself, to rest and pull myself together before I can enjoy or contribute to the home scene.

Separate desks are a must for most couples and separate studies can make joint living easier. In our marriage:

> *Since Bob was the writer and teacher and counselor for so many years, he needed the big study downstairs. There was no room for my books and my magazines and my files, and my sewing machine, so they stacked up in our bedroom and were a constant source of irritation to Bob and me. I blamed myself harshly for not being more orderly, but the actual problem was no space for my things. One advantage of the empty nest was that I got a study too!*

Some couples prefer to have separate bedrooms so each has a place to rest, meditate, and meet different sleep or privacy needs. Most individuals want to open their own mail. Self-care requires that each partner pay attention to his/her own needs and not confuse this with "being selfish":

> *I need to protect my own space and make you understand that there are limits to my involvement with you. As an infant I was totally dependent on my mother's care. Now I am a grownup and need not be trapped in the illusion that any other person is absolutely necessary for my life. I want to be faithful to myself. I want to believe that there's life and strength in me that exists apart from your loving support. I am not totally dependent on you and your affection for my happiness. You are not responsible for my happiness. I am. I want each of us to live out our own truth, not to hide our own truth to please the other. That's being faithful to my life, and ultimately the only way we can be faithful to each other.*
>
> *Because I am your loved one does not mean that I can be with you constantly or that I have to listen sensitively and openly to your grievances against me when I am tired or feeling depressed or emotionally upset.*

Every person has a different energy level and self-care may involve saying no to some of my partner's demands for togetherness. I may need more time just to be quiet. We don't always have to get up at the same time in the morning to prove we are good spouses. If I am a slow starter, I may want to beg off from preparing breakfast or having to talk early in the day:

> *Both of us have a right to want good things from the other. Both of us have a right to ask for what we want. But I know you can't always be there for me. It's an illusion that two unique, alive, and growing persons can constantly be available to each other. Sometimes we hurt and frus-*

trate each other when we go our own ways. It seems like "betraying," but it's not. I want to free myself from having impossible expectations about our relationship.

Separateness versus Disengagement.   In Chapter 21, we describe "disengagement" as a major threat to marriage: drifting apart into separate ways. What is the difference between disengagement and separateness? How can one be harmful and the other beneficial when they sound so much alike? We suspect the difference is not in what couples do when they are apart, but in what happens when they come back together. Disengaged couples ignore each other. Couples still involved with each other bubble over with the events they have experienced apart. They have more to share because they have done something that the other doesn't know about. In communicating their separate experiences, they enable the partner to share in them vicariously. The horizons of life are stretched to cover the territory that each has explored alone. Such couples fulfill Martin Buber's phrase: "All life is meeting." For them, autonomous experiences revitalize their encounter. Their separate activities harvest resources to be brought home. Their marriage becomes wealthier than it would have been if they had confined their explorations to paths they could walk together:

> *I keep asking myself what love is—the love that makes it possible for me to keep wanting to struggle with you and find a meeting ground with you. The more I know myself and you, the more I realize how different we are. I realize that we are different from the persons we were and will continually differentiate as we grow. I want to respect my differences from you and your differences from me, and not demand that you agree with me at every moment. To love well is to be sensitive to each other's truth, not hiding it or being threatened by that truth when the other dares to share it. To express our differences need not mean to reject the other's.*
>
> *To develop this kind of presence-in-diversity is a deeply spiritual task. In daily life it must be undergirded by physical and emotional presence—sharing tasks and leisure and continuing to communicate. To dance together we must dance often. But each of us will want to develop skills, friendships, and interests that make it possible for us to feel confirmed and confident by ourselves without the constant support of the other. My existence does not depend only upon what you give me.*

Separateness in marriage—yes. But there must be togetherness, too. Too much separateness ends in divorce. Too much togetherness is smothering. Happy are those who maintain a flexible bond between growing personalities. For them, marriage is a liberating force and a creative achievement.

11 Extramarital Involvement

For some, there is a monogamy so entire that no other love ever touches it; but others "fall in love" time and time again, and must learn to make riches of their affection without destroying their marriage, or their friends (*Toward a Quaker View of Sex*, London, 1964).

Separateness and togetherness becomes an acute issue when it includes intimate involvement with persons other than the marriage partner. Intimacy may be emotional or physical or any combination of the two and, in the case of physical intimacy, may range all the way from kissing and hugging through sensual touching to sexual intercourse. Because the research literature deals primarily with complete sexual involvement and because that is for many couples the toughest question, we will concentrate on sexual involvement with persons of the opposite sex. Similar jealousy issues arise when the outside partner is of the same sex and when the involvement is emotional rather than physical.

We have already seen that happily married persons make new friends easily. Just as they were attracted to marry across sex lines, so they are attracted to friends of the opposite sex (as well as of their own sex). Unlike "authoritarian personalities," they are not prejudiced against the opposite sex or rigidly segragated in their social life (Adorno, 1950). They are not afraid of mixed company or embarrassed to find themselves the only man in a group of women, or vice versa.

The multiplicity of cross-sex friends for happily married individuals decreases the likelihood of overinvolvement with one friend. The greatest threat to the marriage occurs when a special friend becomes an ally against the partner:

When Harold and I were having trouble, he always ended up talking to Grace about it at her place. It made me furious that he couldn't deal with me directly without being shored up by her. Sharing our intimate affairs with someone else may have been natural and human, but I became terribly jealous of the confirmation he gained from her that I seemed unable to give him.

When a married wo/man complains about the spouse to a person of the opposite sex and seeks that person's sympathy, s/he destroys the "fiction of solidarity," revealing what Waller and Hill (1951) called "a master symptom of alienation."

The fiction of solidarity is also destroyed by persons who remove their wedding rings to date unsuspecting partners. This pretense requires the anonymity of an urban environment. In rural communities, public knowledge of one's comings and goings minimizes such behavior. But even in suburban apartment complexes, the deadend courtyard has been described as "the greatest invention since the chastity belt." According to Whyte (1957: 393–94):

> It's almost impossible to philander without everyone's knowing about it. One's callers are observed, and if neighbors feel there is anything untoward, suburbia's phenomenal grapevine will speed the news. This is not mere venom; in a web of relationships as delicate as that of a court, an affair can harm not only two marriages, it can upset the whole court applecart.

A web of relationships buffers marital stability. Attempts to escape this web through secrecy are a sign of trouble. As long as cross-sex friendships are openly conducted, there is less to fear.

Extramarital involvement may be either a separate activity (as in a secret affair) or a joint acitivty (as in couple-front swinging or group marriage). For many couples, separate sexual involvement with an outside party is the greatest challenge to their togetherness, but even joint involvement with others strains many marriages since it radically violates the traditional sexual exclusiveness.

THE INCIDENCE OF EXTRAMARITAL INVOLVEMENT

Extramarital involvement is not a new phenomenon. As long ago as the 1940s, Kinsey (1948, 1953) estimated that half the men and a quarter of the women in his sample appeared destined to have extramarital sex at least once in their lifetime. Since then, extramarital sex has come out of the closet in books on open marriage, organizations of swingers, and the like. Does this mean that extramarital involvement has become more widespread or just better known?

Table 11–1 suggests that at least half of the younger American men who were interviewed in 1974 would engage in extramarital intercourse

Table 11-1 Lifetime Experience in Extramarital Intercourse, by
Age of Men and Women

Age	Men	Women	Men/Women Ratio
18–24	32%	24%	1.3X
25–34	41%	21%	2.0X
35–44	47%	18%	2.6X
45–54	38%	12%	3.2X
55+	43%	15%	2.9X

Adapted from Hunt, 1974: 258, 261. *Source:* White men and women in 24
American cities who had ever been married. Reciprocal percentages of
persons in the particular age bracket had never had extramarital intercourse.

at some time during their marriage. The figures for women make prediction more difficult. Whereas in the older age brackets men were several
times as apt as women to have had outside sexual partners, in the younger
age groups the difference between the sexes was narrower. Indeed, the
youngest wives had already had the most experience. If the 18–24-year-
old women maintained their ratio as they grew older, probably more than
one third of them would eventually have sex with a man other than their
husband. These figures show that the double standard once governing
extramarital behavior was disappearing among the younger people in this
sample. Comparing his data with those of Kinsey a generation earlier,
Hunt concluded that the sexual revolution had affected young women
more than any other age group of either sex.

Important Factors in Getting Involved

Employment.   Contrary to the traditional assumption that working wives
are more apt to become involved with other men, Edwards and Booth
(1976) found in a Toronto study of married women with children that
those holding outside jobs were significantly *less* apt to have extramarital
intercourse than those who were not employed. Perhaps whatever opportunities for personal involvement arise with colleagues are more than
offset by the responsibilities women shoulder when they play the multiple roles of wife, mother, housewife, and wage earner. They are presumably too busy to add extramarital activity to all those other activities. In
any case, women who lack job contacts with men apparently have alternative ways of meeting them and becoming involved if they choose to do so.

Independence.   Whether individuals take advantage of opportunities for
extramarital involvement depends on how independent and courageous/
foolhardy they are. To challenge social convention requires a tough-
mindedness implied in Edwards and Booth's finding that both women

who dominated their husbands and men who dominated their wives were more apt to engage in extramarital intercourse. Perhaps because the taboos for married women are higher than for married men, the correlation between dominating the family and engaging in extramarital intercourse was particularly high for women.

Extramarital intercourse frequently requires one to venture outside the home into another physical space. Analogously, both the men and the women who had had extramarital intercourse in Edwards and Booth's study were apt to have threatened to leave home at one time or another. To think about the possibility of leaving home and to express that threat to the spouse exhibits an independence from the spouse that facilitates involvement with someone else. By contrast, husbands and wives who felt less love, felt more alienated, or had more arguments were not apt to engage in extramarital intercourse. Presumably, these persons felt so dependent on the spouse that they could not disengage themselves enough to create space in their lives for a secondary partner.

Timing. A historic change in extramarital behavior appeared in Hunt's finding that, whereas men and women age 35 or older had waited six to ten years, respectively, after marriage before their first extramarital involvement, younger men and women had waited only two to four years, respectively. These figures are biased by the fact that younger men and women hadn't been married long enough to have the opportunity to begin late; nevertheless, the extraordinarily rapid involvement of the younger persons suggests a revolutionary change. Moreover, Kinsey found that college-educated men and women particularly waited until middle age to become externally involved, but Hunt found such delays less common among educated men and women than they had been earlier.

This is not to say that extramarital involvement had become characteristic of American marriages by the time of Hunt's study. It does mean, however, that the barriers to such involvement for college graduates, for newly married persons, and even for actively religious persons (in data we have not cited) were substantially lower than they had been a generation before. As a result, extramarital involvement was more evenly distributed among the general population, even though it was nowhere near as widespread as premarital intercourse had become.

Duration. When men and women become involved in extramarital relationships, how long do those relationships last? For another book, Hunt (1969) interviewed 80 middle-class men and women who had been extramaritally involved. He found the typical duration was a good many months but less than a year. Only a small proportion were transient episodes of a week or less. Indeed, such brief episodes were even rarer in subsequent involvements than in the first one.

Most of the involvements studied by Hunt were secret, unilateral affairs. The fact that most of them lasted less than a year is curiously parallel to the duration of most communes and group marriages. Affairs, communes, and group marriages are all complex human relationships requiring heavy investments of energy. As long as they last, they may have high payoffs for the participants, but they tend to collapse of their own weight eventually, except for persons who are extraordinarily skillful in interpersonal relationships.

Although any given involvement tends to end, few men and women limit themselves to a single affair. In Hunt's experienced sample (1969), only one fifth of the men and a third of the women had one outside partner. All the rest had already had more than one extramarital partner. At the time they were interviewed, a majority of the women but less than half of the men had returned to a sexually exclusive relationship with their marriage partners, at least for the time being. Conversely, a majority of the men and more than a third of the women were still involved in outside relationships—in most cases, the latest in a considerable series. Hunt commented that for most of these persons with ongoing experience, extramarital involvement had become a "way of life" that they expected to continue as long as possible, hopefully until forced to retire by old age or by death.

Whether sexually open marriage becomes a continuing way of life as often as these largely secret affairs did remains to be seen. In any case we infer that whether extramarital involvement is unknown or shared with the partner, it seldom constitutes a single episode any more than Americans marry the first person whom they date. The most common pattern for those who venture outside their marriage seems to be a series of intimate involvements alongside a more enduring relationship with the marriage partner.

Bypassed Opportunities

In addition to the substantial number of people who engage in extramarital intercourse at some point after marriage, Table 11–2 suggests that many others encounter situations in which outside sex is available but choose not to take advantage of the opportunity. Johnson (1970) studied middle-aged couples in the Twin Cities, a relatively conservative section of the country, finding that almost twice as many women and more than twice as many men passed up opportunities for extramarital sex as became involved. Indeed, the typical husband had passed up the opportunity, whereas the typical wife had never had such an opportunity.

Contrary to the traditional assumption that the lesser exposure of women to opportunity reflects their confinement to the home, Johnson found that wives who were currently unemployed had had no fewer opportunities than those who were employed.

Presumably, the large proportions of men and women in the Twin Cities who failed to take advantage of opportunities for extramarital in-

Table 11–2 Opportunity for, and Actuality of, Extramarital Intercourse, for Middle-Aged Men and Women

Opportunity/Actuality	Men	Women
Actually had extramarital intercourse	21%	11%
Had opportunity but no intercourse	51	19
No opportunity	28	71
Total	100%	101%
Number of cases	95	95

Recomputed from Johnson, 1970: 451. *Source:* Middle-aged married couples in two middle-class suburbs of Minneapolis and St. Paul. Opportunity was defined as having "ever been in a position where you could easily have had sexual relations with someone other than your spouse."

volvement reflect the conservatism of a community that provided little support and much censure for such activity. In areas where extramarital involvement is more common, the resistance to taking advantage of opportunities is correspondingly less.

Marital Causes of Extramarital Involvement

Much of the motivation for extramarital involvement has nothing to do with marriage. A wish for adventure or a fear of growing old does not depend on the state of the marriage. But whether the marriages of persons who become involved are good or bad and whether their marital sex is good or bad will explain some of the connections between their marital and extramarital behavior.

Marital Dissatisfaction.   Traditionally, extramarital involvement has been blamed on the unhappiness of the participants' marriages. Several studies show that this assumption is not always correct.

Gilmartin and Kusisto (1973) studied couples where one partner had had an extramarital involvement and found that "there was no indication of any kind that the couples in these marriages were any less happy than those couples whose marriages had remained fully free from any form of extramarital coitus." Similarly, Johnson (1970) found no difference in the marital happiness of those who had or had not already engaged in extramarital intercourse or of those who said they would or would not like to do so in the future.

However, the more liberated women become, the more apt they are to seek outside involvements to compensate for dissatisfaction with their marriages. Bell, Turner, and Rosen (1975) studied an unusually liberated sample of women who were relatively young (average age 34), career oriented (69 percent employed), and highly educated (23 percent had been to graduate school and another 33 percent to college). They found that 55 percent of those who rated their marriage only "fair" or worse had already been extramaritally involved compared to only 20 percent of those who rated their marriage as "good" or "very good."

We conclude from these studies that extramaritally involved persons *may* be just as happily married as those who have sexually exclusive marriages. There is no simple correlation between marital happiness and extramarital involvement.

Sexual Dissatisfaction.   The liberated women in Bell, Turner, and Rosen's sample who had engaged in extramarital sex were generally dissatisfied with the sexual side of their marriages. They complained about not having sex often enough, which reflected the fact that they were highly sexually oriented (they liked fellatio, cunnilingus, anal intercourse, and masturbation). They lived in environments that supported their behavior (they had been exposed to pornography more than monogamous wives and were less apt to live in the conservative Mountain or Prairie States). Finally, they were more apt to have been married longer than five years. These data suggest that if a woman places a high value on sex and does not find sexual satisfaction at home, she is apt to grow impatient with her husband after a few years and turn elsewhere for sexual pleasure.

Similarly, Johnson found that extramaritally involved men were significantly less satisfied with the sexual aspect of their marriages than were uninvolved men, even though they were not less satisfied with their marriages as a whole. However, the involved women in his sample were not significantly dissatisfied sexually in comparison to the uninvolved women. Apparently, sexual dissatisfaction especially predisposes men to seek sexual involvement elsewhere (see Table 11–3).

Trends in American society include increasing opportunity for extramarital sex, increasing emphasis on the "right" to sexual fulfillment, and decreasing willingness to settle for sexual disappointment if the mar-

Table 11–3   Extramarital Sexual Involvement by Sexual Satisfaction in Marriage, for Husbands and Wives

	HUSBANDS		WIVES	
Extramaritally Involved	Sexually Satisfied	Sexually Dissatisfied	Sexually Satisfied	Sexually Dissatisfied
Ever	14%	40%	7%	16%
Never	86	60	93	84
Total	100%	100%	100%	100%
Number of cases	71	25	67	32

Recomputed from Johnson, 1970: 454. *Source:* Middle-aged married couples in two middle-class suburbs of Minneapolis and St. Paul. Sexually satisfied persons were those who described their sexual relationship with their spouse as "extremely enjoyable" or "very enjoyable." Dissatisfied persons found their sexual relationship only "somewhat enjoyable," "not too enjoyable," "dissatisfying," or "extremely dissatisfying."

riage partner is not satisfying. This is analogous to the decreasing willingness of American men and women to stay in unsatisfactory marriages rather than to get divorced. Extramarital involvement provides a potential alternative to getting a divorce, not necessarily permanently, but pending the time when one of those extramarital partners develops into a remarriage partner.

The converse of all this is that some people may be dissatisfied with their marriage, but not sexually oriented enough to be interested in extramarital sex. Likewise, others may be satisfied with their marriage, but so sexually oriented and exposed to sexual opportunity that they participate in extramarital activities that do not reflect on the satisfactoriness of the marriage.

The Comparative Satisfactoriness of Marital and Extramarital Sex. If sexual dissatisfaction is one motive for extramarital involvement, how satisfactory are the sexual experiences that people have with their extramarital partners?

Table 11–4 shows that the extramarital sex of the experienced minority of Hunt's sample was considerably less pleasurable than the marital sex of his sample as a whole. This lesser satisfaction was paralleled for women by a lower frequency of orgasm in extramarital sex compared to the orgasmic responsiveness of married women with their husbands. Men, similarly, more often experienced impotence and premature ejaculation in extramarital intercourse than in marriage.

Presumably, the reasons why extramarital sex is generally less satisfactory reflect some of the factors that we described in Chapter 9, namely, that sexual responsiveness between any two people has to be learned and that some extramarital sex is so fleeting that there isn't time for the partners to learn how to relate to each other sexually. Presumably, other obstacles to sexual satisfaction include moral scruples and fear of discov-

Table 11–4 Overall Pleasure of Marital and Extramarital Sex, for Men and Women

Overall pleasure	MEN		WOMEN	
	Marital Sex	Extra-marital Sex	Marital Sex	Extra-marital Sex
Very pleasurable	67%	47%	55%	37%
Mostly pleasurable	30	43	35	37
Neither	2	6	7	14
Mostly nonpleasurable	1	1	2	8
Very nonpleasurable	1	2	1	5
Total	101%	99%	100%	101%

Adapted from Hunt, 1974: 278. Source: All married respondents and all respondents who had ever had extramarital sexual experience.

ery, reflecting the social and spousal disapproval of this activity. We assume that only when extramarital partners have the consent of their primary partners, the support of their peer group and subculture, and the time and energy to work out their secondary relationship is their experience likely to become as sexually satisfying as marital sex generally is.

Even if extramarital sex is generally less satisfying than marital sex, this does not mean that persons who are dissatisfied with their marital sex will necessarily find extramarital sex even worse. Unfortunately, Hunt failed to restrict the information about marital sex in Table 11–4 to persons who had had extramarital experience. In the absence of such data we can only guess that for persons whose marital sex is poor, the probabilities are that extramarital sex will be better, especially if they take the time to work out a satisfying relationship with the new partner. On the other hand, for persons whose marital sex is satisfactory, the probabilities of extramarital sex being equally satisfying are low.

Perhaps an anology would be helpful. Persons whose marriages are so unsatisfactory that they choose to get a divorce usually like their next marriage better. Conversely, widowed persons whose marriages were satisfactory frequently hesitate to remarry for fear a new marriage would not measure up to the previous one. This reflects what statisticians call "regression toward the mean." The chances are that persons who have experienced either extremely good or extremely bad relationships in one situation will have more nearly average experiences in the next. So, the worse the present sexual deprivation, the greater the chances that extramarital sex will be an improvement. What we cannot say, on the basis of Hunt's data, is that extramarital sex is generally better than marital sex. Despite the myth of marital boredom, extramarital sex is on the whole less enjoyable than marital sex.

PATTERNS OF EXTRAMARITAL INVOLVEMENT

So far we have lumped extramarital relationships together as if they were all the same. But extramarital patterns vary enormously in the amount of togetherness or separateness that they create. We will look now at different types of involvement, focusing first on the question of whether only one partner or both partners are involved with others, and subdividing each category according to the knowledge or co-participation of each partner in the other's behavior.

Unilateral Involvement

A secret affair is the classic kind of extramarital involvement. Although both partners may coincidentally carry on affairs behind each other's backs, most often only one partner is active while the other is inactive.

Secret Affairs. Under this heading we will describe cases in which the active partner attempts either successfully or unsuccessfully to keep extramarital involvement secret from the partner. How often does the attempt succeed? In Gilmartin's study of California couples (1974), 31 percent of the husbands and 8 percent of the wives in the control group of couples who had never engaged in swinging had been unilaterally involved with extramarital partners, and practically all of them had successfully withheld knowledge of their activities from the spouse. Respondents reported that one of their primary motives for keeping the outside relationship secret was that they did not want to jeopardize their marriages by revealing this information.

Gilmartin found no evidence that these secret affairs undermined the marital happiness of the inactive spouse. In a careful cross-check, he found that unaware spouses of these extramaritally involved men and women rated their marriages just as happily as did the active partners. Apparently what the inactive partners didn't know didn't hurt them.

This runs contrary to the modern emphasis on openness of communication. It suggests that secret affairs and satisfactory marriages are not necessarily incompatible. Persons with an abundance of time and energy and with the ability to compartmentalize their lives may be able to enjoy their marriage and an additional relationship at the same time.

On the other hand, if a marriage is already poor, becoming involved in an outside relationship may impoverish it still further by draining off energy. The so-called satellite relationship may become the core one for someone whose investment in his/her own marriage is slight:

> *Alice and I are breaking up. I have decided that I can't bear her continuing dependence on me. Recently my long-time friendship with Barbara moved into a desire on both our parts for deeper intimacy and permanence. The problem is that Alice and Barbara are like sisters. If I tell Alice, it will be hell let loose. Her anger and sense of betrayal by both of us will make the months before our divorce excruciatingly painful. I want to keep it secret and test our compatibility on weekend visits to Barbara that Alice won't know about. Then I can get out of my marriage with the least strain and into my new relationship as fast as possible.*

The trouble with secret affairs is that, despite the best intentions of the participants, the inactive partner may somehow discover that s/he has been deceived. At that point the attempted secrecy boomerangs in feelings of betrayal and mistrust. Few inactive partners appreciate that the withholding of information may have been intended to protect them from hurt. Rather, negative reactions to discovered affairs are generally worse than those to voluntarily disclosed affairs. People who engage in unilateral affairs with the intent of keeping them secret have no guarantee that they will be able to achieve their goal of "getting away with it." And if they fail, they are in notoriously deep trouble.

Known Affairs.   We have pointed out the negative consequences of failure in attempting to keep unilateral involvements secret. Some individuals go to the opposite extreme and tell the spouse every detail of their outside involvements, partly in an attempt to live up to the contemporary ideal of openness, partly attempting to relieve the tension of trying to keep the secret, partly in the hope that the inactive partner will assent to the active partner's behavior and thereby relieve any guilt feelings.

The trouble is that listening to such "news" is frequently excruciating. Few persons can listen to such reports without feeling left out. Even if the inactive partner has no desire for similar experiences, it is difficult not to envy the spouse's enjoyment of the outside relationship, and difficult not to resent the fact that s/he was not spending that time and money and energy at home. Since few married persons have as much companionship and affection as they would like, it is difficult to hear how one's spouse has been giving those "goodies" to someone else.

For persons with such reactions, is there any way of avoiding the pain of having to listen to such recitals without falling into the perils of secrecy? Myers (1973: 356–57) proposed "the compartmentalization of marriage" to resolve this dilemma:

> I suggest that life for the married person can arbitrarily be divided into compartments. Compartment I is the time/energy spent with one's spouse; Compartment II is the time/energy spent on "family" matters with or without children) but specifically not with one's spouse. Compartment III is non-family time; time/energy spent at work, community projects, entertainment with friends, sports, and so on, when one is not accompanied by spouse or children, but time that is completely "open" to inspection: your spouse can know exactly what you are doing and with whom. Compartment IV is energy devoted to private time—time that according to traditional standards is "cheating" or at least "deceiving." It is the opportunity to do something that you do not want your spouse . . . to know about.
>
> . . . the acceptance of compartment IV can allow spouses to accept the possibility of extramarital relationships without demanding to know the degree of intimacy or sexual involvement. It can avoid direct confrontation with something that our traditional values uniformly condemn. It can help to eliminate irrational compulsion either to give or withhold information. It can allow each person to decide for her (him) self when everything or nothing may be communicated to the marriage partner.

Myer's proposal implies that a couple would recognize the freedom of either partner to become extramaritally involved as s/he sees fit. By recognizing this possibility in general terms, they remove it from the realm of secrecy and betrayal. Insofar as either partner acts privately on this mutual understanding, it is no longer a violation of the marriage contract but his/her privilege in terms of their revised contract. By defining the experience as private, it is not subject to interrogation by the inactive partner, who in turn is less exposed to the pain of hearing about the relationship. Except for persons who rejoice in a partner's enjoyment of outside relationships, the compartmentalized approach offers a possible compromise between secret and open unilateral affairs.

Another kind of relationship is found in what Ramey (1976) called "intimate friendships." According to his definition, "Intimate friendships include any and all of the various kinds of relationships, primary or not (including monogamous marriage), that involve some degree of social, emotional, sexual, intellectual, family, or career intimacy, wherein interaction between persons is more important than, but may include, sexual relations." These are not necessarily couple-to-couple activities, but occur spontaneously as liberated individuals develop friendships with persons to whom they are attracted. The spouses of such persons may have similar involvements, but because friendships are spontaneous rather than deliberately contrived it seems appropriate to classify them as unilateral. In Ramey's sample, most people felt that such friendships were so natural and so much a part of their lives that they told not only the spouse but other friends about them. Indeed, each friendship typically became part of a network of friends who were variously linked to one another.

To become intimate is not necessarily to become sexually involved. Table 11–5 is based on only one sample and must be viewed in the context of that study's emphasis on networks of intimate friends. It shows intimate friends engaging in a wide variety of activities and deemphasizing sexual intercourse as such.

Table 11–5 Percentage of Contacts with Intimate Friends during Which Specific Activities Occurred

Activity	*Probability of Occurring*
Social activity	72%
Cuddling, touching, caressing	49%
Discussion, problem solving	47%
Recreational activity	34%
Business activity	26%
Sexual intercourse	19%
Avocational activity	16%
Activity involving other family members	13%
Travel	11%
Community or political activity	6%

Adapted from Ramey, 1975: 25. *Source:* 380 upper-middle-class persons involved in heterosexual friendships with secondary partners with whom sexual intimacy was considered appropriate behavior by the participants. Reciprocal percentages of contacts with these friends did not involve the specified activity. Total adds to more than 100% since more than one activity could be engaged in on any particular occasion.

The most frequent activity for Ramey's secondary couples was sociable. Presumably, much of this sociability involved other members of the networks to which these respondents belonged. Physical intimacy was the second most common activity, but it was more affectionate and sensual than sexual in the sense that it was not focused on orgastic experience. By contrast, sexual intercourse occurred less than half as often as milder forms of intimacy, not quite every fifth time these couples got together. Just because sexual intercourse was permissible did not mean that it was their primary goal or that it necessarily ever occurred. Most married couples don't have sex every day. Likewise, most extramarital couples whose ongoing relationship is not restricted to secret rendezvous engage in a wide variety of pleasurable and practical activities of which sex may be a part but is not usually the main element.

As we assess the trends of extramarital involvement in American society, we foresee a gradual shift away from secret affairs and from affairs that are focused on sex toward the development of friendships that are open to the possibility of sex when this occurs naturally. Open marriage concepts and behavior seem unlikely to die out despite the threat they present to traditionally oriented persons. As more honest and caring relations evolve between all persons, fear that the sexual aspect of intimacy will run rampant may diminish. Wider expressions of affection may loosen up the marriage bond without threatening its richness and stability. Possibly future generations will see no necessity for husband and wife to compare notes on how many intimate friends each has. Such friendships would develop spontaneously and be spontaneously communicated to the partner.

Bilateral Involvement

When only one partner has intimate friends, the other frequently feels left out. Insofar as sexual and/or emotional intimacy is expected only in marriage, the inactive partner feels that the marriage vows have been broken. And if the active partner is seen as having fun, the nonparticipant may feel gypped.

To prevent such feelings, some couples try to even things up, saying that if either of us has outside relationships, we both should. Couples may require that the number of friends with whom they are separately involved be kept even. For others, even that much separateness is too scary—they prefer swinging exchanges with other couples or group sexual activities where they can monitor and share each other's activities. For a few couples, intimate friendships become so mutual and close that they bring the extramarital partners into the home to form a group marriage. Then, the boundaries between marital and extramarital relationships theoretically disappear or at least become blurred.

Separate but Equal.   People who have suffered the strain of trying to keep a unilateral relationship secret or the resentment of feeling left out of a known affair find those problems lessened when the inactive partner becomes active, too:

> I had been enjoying my friendships with other men but every time I came home from being with one of them, I had to put up with a lot of flak from Tom. Finally, he decided to go to a workshop on jealousy and try to figure out what he could do to cope with his negative feelings. He had such a good experience relating to the other women in the workshop that he decided he was missing something. He came home and made a luncheon date with one of the women in his office whom he felt good about but had never got to know personally. Now he understands how much I was getting out of my friendships because he has the same experiences himself. It is a relief not to have the flak any more.

When outside involvement shifts from unilateral to bilateral, the marriage achieves a balance that post–double-standard couples appreciate. Instead of one partner feeling left out, both feel in. Instead of feeling that marriage vows have been violated, the contract is revised to include sexual openness for both partners.

Nevertheless, emphasizing equality may create new problems. Just because a couple decide to be open to outside sexual relationships does not mean they will find partners equally fast. Knapp (1976) found that while slightly more husbands than wives suggested trying sexual involvements, the wives more often were the first to actually have the experience. Moreover, wives had more different partners than the husbands. These inequalities often created jealousy in the partner who lagged behind. Knapp reported "a tendency for greater stress to be present in marriages in which one partner had considerably more outside partners than the spouse had."

Partners under "separate but equal" conditions are likely to feel unhappy insofar as inequality develops between them. They may compete about the number of times each has intercourse with another partner, the number of different partners with whom each is involved, or the amount of time and money each spends with others. To reduce bad feelings, one couple gave each other a quota of one outside sexual experience a month. Some couples periodically evaluate their feelings (every three or four months seems to be a popular interval) to be sure both partners feel that a rough equality exists, even if they don't keep statistical records.

The more insecure a couple feels about outside involvements, the more stringent the regulations with which they bind one another. But the strain on the marriage from unequal outside relationships is seldom as severe as the strain from unilateral involvement.

Partner Exchange and Group Sex.   With the possible exception of group marriage, "swinging" is the kind of extramarital involvement most closely associated with marriage. When one couple exchanges partners with another, this joint recreational activity requires their cooperation, joint decision making, and joint participation. It may produce the same sense of togetherness as other joint leisure-time activities.

Whereas separate-but-equal bilateral involvement potentially threatens marriage by virtue of its separateness and because both partners are seldom equally involved at the same time, swinging is so structured that it suffers from neither liability. One couple we interviewed reported:

> *We felt a lot of anxiety while both of us were involved with separate partners. So we finally decided we would be better off if we developed friendships with other couples. We put an ad in the personal column of the* New York Review of Books *for couples who might be interested in developing an intimate friendship. We jointly interviewed ten of the couples who responded and developed warm friendships with several especially congenial ones. When these friendships came to include sex, we found it more enjoyable because we were relating to them as a couple ourselves. After about a year we got tired of relating to them sexually, but we still consider them good friends and see them occasionally. The main thing I want to say is how much closer Jan and I felt relating as a couple than when we had been off doing our own thing separately.*

Not all swingers want ongoing friendships. Patterns of swinging vary widely.

Bartell (1971) studied 280 white middle-class swingers in the Chicago suburbs. Almost half of the men were salesmen. The rest were small businessmen, engineers, chemists, lawyers, and other technically oriented men. Very few were in humanistically oriented vocations. Most of these people had few leisure-time interests other than swinging.

Bartell's couples had developed elaborate patterns of behavior that enabled them to swing frequently with minimal danger to their marriages. They placed ads in swingers' publications to meet couples with similar sexual interests. An elaborate etiquette of meeting and getting acquainted enabled couples to size each other up before deciding whether to become sexually involved. Given their relatively slight acquaintance, the couples' typical second meeting for sexual purposes was filled with tension that was only partly relieved by heavy drinking. Sexual technique and performance were stressed and performance failures were especially embarrassing when couples remained in the same room. For such reasons, most of Bartell's respondents preferred to have sex in separate rooms, especially during their early experiences.

Although Bartell's swingers were sexually involved with comparative strangers, they were careful not to become involved affectionally for fear that their marriages would be threatened. Emotional involvement was minimized by taboos on swinging with the same couple more than once and on having any social contact with former swinging partners. Especially taboo was affectionate language between swinging partners. Alternatively, swinging parties attended by large numbers of people were so impersonal that individual pairings were essentially anonymous.

Denfeld and Gordon (1970) found that swinging couples avoided single persons since they threatened the bilateral nature of their sexual involvement and undermined the emotional security felt when all persons participating in the exchange were married. These researchers also noted that a norm requiring all sexual activities of either partner to be communicated to the other gave couples a sense of co-participation and prevented them from feeling "cheated" on.

Bartell found that most of his respondents tired of swinging after a year or two, sometimes frightened off by the risk of venereal disease and vaginal or bladder infections in sexual contact with so many relatively unknown persons. Dropouts did not necessarily give up extramarital involvement, but settled down in ongoing relationships with couples whom they particularly liked.

In the New York suburbs, George and Nena O'Neill (1970) found swinging dominated by married couples in the same way as in Bartell's Chicago suburbs. In Manhattan, however, swinging was predominantly a singles activity, so that the married minority necessarily becomes involved with single persons. Half of the Manhattan respondents also broke another Chicago rule by socializing outside the swinging scene.

In the San Francisco Bay area, Lynn and James Smith (1973) noted that sexual relationships that originated in organized clubs and bars tended to be transient whereas private sex parties produced more enduring friendships. Among their respondents, half had never participated in any commercially oriented sex groups and preferred to develop intimate friendships (in contrast to the Chicago couples' rigid separation between sex and friendship).

In addition to the geographical differences that we have described, Varni (1973) found a generational difference in his San Diego sample. Older swingers were afraid of emotional involvement but younger swingers had less fear of ongoing relationships and preferred affectional intimacy with their swinging friends. This suggests that the severe restrictions described by Bartell represented an early phase in the history of swinging and that couples in the future may feel more comfortable with affectionate extramarital relationships.

The effects of swinging on the marriages of the participants are so complex that they are not easily assessed. Presumably, where one partner is coerced into participating and finds the experience unpleasant, the marriage suffers. Varni found that swinging was almost always initiated by the man and resisted by the wife:

> *Stan had been reading all the books he could find about swinging and was dying to have some new experiences. I was dragging my feet. During a camping trip with another couple, the other three began to relate to each other in ways that were repulsive to me because they were so unfamiliar. This touched off old memories of times when men had exposed themselves to me when I was a kid. I really hated Stan for moving so fast. Our marriage was already on shaky ground and this became a real sore point for me. He felt okay about that experience and wanted more. I kept being afraid he would do it again without my consent.*

Henshel found that more husbands than wives were the first to learn about swinging possibilities (often through their professional and business contacts) and were even more prominent in the decision making that led to taking advantage of these opportunities (see Table 11–6).

Even though men dominate the initiation, women frequently discover that they enjoy being pursued by other men. So the strain of the initial coercion may be replaced by enjoyment of the actual experience. Many researchers have noted that the greater freedom of women from homosexual hangups and their capacity for multiple orgasms enables them to enjoy group sex more than men.

Like the participants in most other forms of extramarital involvement, those who engage in partner exchange frequently claim beneficial effects. Varni (1974) found that half the couples in his San Diego sample reported greater warmth, closeness, and love between the husband and wife. These feelings were particularly strong when they returned to each other after sexual involvement with another couple.

Table 11–7 shows that swinging couples in another California sample rated their marriages generally happier than a carefully matched control sample. We cannot tell from this study how much of the difference resulted from the swinging and how much of it reflected the fact that only relatively happy couples felt their marriages were strong enough to dare

Table 11-6   Husband-Wife Involvement in Decision Making about Swinging, by Stage in Decision Making

Dominant Partner	First Learned about Swinging	First Suggested it	Reached Final Decision
Husband	46%	71%	67%
Both together	37	21	29
Wife	17	8	4
Total	100%	100%	100%
Number of cases	24	24	24

Computed from Henshel, 1973: 888. *Source:* Married women in Toronto (median age 30) who were engaged with their husbands in sexual exchanges.

Table 11–7 Marital Happiness of Swingers and Nonswingers, for Husbands and Wives

Marital Happiness	HUSBANDS		WIVES	
	Swingers	Nonswingers	Swingers	Nonswingers
Very happy	56%	43%	58%	49%
Happy	29	33	23	31
Fairly happy	13	20	15	18
Unhappy	2	4	4	2
Total	100%	100%	100%	100%
Number of cases	100	100	100	100

Adapted from Gilmartin, 1974: 310. *Source:* Suburban Los Angeles and San Francisco participants in sexual freedom groups and nonswingers matched for age, neighborhood, income, education, and number of children.

to swing in the first place. However, when combined with the enthusiasm of so many persons studied in so many parts of the United States, it is difficult to avoid concluding that exchanging sexual partners is at least consistent with being happily married and may contribute to a couple's sense of togetherness.

The O'Neills found in their Manhattan study (1970) that many couples returned to their own sexual relationship with a fresh appreciation for the sexual harmony they had achieved over time compared with the difficulties of having sex with new partners. Most couples also found that the joint decision making required by their venture into swinging opened up channels of communication benefiting many aspects of their marriages.

A majority of Bartell's suburban Chicago couples reported that swinging improved their relationship both sexually and socially. They became more interested in each other sextually as a result of their sexual experimentation. And the large amount of time that they devoted to swinging gave them an intensified feeling of companionship with each other.

Because swinging is socially disapproved, they also experienced the thrill of adventuring successfully in an uncharted wilderness. Negative experiences of the Chicago couples included feelings of sexual inadequacy for the men, venereal infection scares, and other problems affecting the participants' individual morale more than their marriages.

Denfeld (1974) found that many ex-swingers who were involved in marriage counseling reported that jealousy was the reason for dropping out of swinging and that jealousy was felt by more husbands than wives. Men worried because their wives were so popular, had a greater capacity for sustained sexual performance, and had more fun. However, in the total population of swingers, these reactions seem to be in the minority. On the whole, more couples who exchange partners with other couples feel that they benefit from the experience than regret it.

Our review of the research suggests that partner exchange is one of the least threatening and potentially most beneficial forms of extramarital involvement insofar as it is a joint activity engaged in with the consent and to the satisfaction of both partners. Most couples exchange partners with other couples intensively for a few months, after which they either return to sexual monogamy or settle down into less frequent involvement with others.

Group Marriage.   The ultimate form of extramarital involvement is group marriage. While such groups do not necessarily include any legally married couples, our focus will be on that particular form of group marriage in which a married couple invite one or more single persons or couples to move in with them. In extraordinary cases group marriages involve more than four persons, but the commonest forms consist of three or four people.

Larry and Joan Constantine (1973a) studied 26 group marriages and found two-couple marriages overwhelmingly predominant. Sixty-two percent of the total number were four-person marriages, followed by 23 percent that consisted of three persons, while the remaining 15 percent were equally divided between five-person and six-person marriages.

Presumably, this distribution of sizes is not accidental. The small number of cases involving more than four persons reflects the complexities of trying to relate intimately to a large number of people. The predominance of four-person marriages reflects the equality and balance of having equal numbers of men and women. It also reflects the fact that by age 30, when these group marriages typically began, a majority of adults are already coupled up and most socializing is with other couples. These couples already had been married about seven years and had several children, so that they were well ensconced in the world of the married by the time they enlarged their families to include additional adults.

The Constantines found that the typical group marriage consisted of a total of seven persons—four adults and three children. Within this family, the pair bonds of the two couples not only preceded the formation of the larger grouping, but predominated within the tetrad and outlived it after the household broke up. Among the adults, relationships between the two men tended to be weakest, whereas the two women felt like sisters and the cross-sex, cross-partner relationships were the strongest of the new bonds.

The members of these group marriages were unusually capable of relating intimately to others (which was one reason they wanted to expand their relationships). Most of them had experience in the human potential movement and found that living in an expanded family was like being in a marathon encounter group. This prolonged encounter facilitated enormous personal growth but consumed equally enormous amounts of time and energy. A large proportion of the persons involved were professionals who could control their work schedules to free up time to spend at home.

Although rotated sexual sharing and rotated housework were characteristic of these group marriages, financial sharing was frequently limited to household expenses with the surplus retained by those who earned it. Biological parent-child ties were stronger than ties with satellite parents and children. The commonest sexual rotation pattern involved switching partners every three or four nights. Group sex was a rare peak experience that happened more easily in three-person marriages than in larger groups. With more than three people, sexual activity tended to break down into pairs and triads even if all were in the same room. Given the greater taboos against homosexuality in men than in women, group sexual encounters were more common in triads consisting of two women and one man rather than vice versa.

Although these group marriages were based on the principle of sexual sharing, they were not immune to feelings of jealousy, either within the group or with respect to extragroup involvements. (See, for example, Clanton and Downing's case history [1975] of a triadic group marriage that suffered from external involvements.) The Constantines found that group marriages that still survived were significantly less likely to include outside sexual relationships than those that had already dissolved. Presumably, the intact groups kept themselves going by concentrating their time and energy on getting along with each other without the added complications of outside involvements. Internal jealousy was widespread when group marriages first formed, but tended to fade as the participants became more used to multilateral relationships.

Compared to the college students in Chapter 4 who were living together unmarried, a larger proportion of couples in group marriages told their parents about what they were doing and received a favorable or at least a tolerant response. Perhaps by the time people get to be 30 years old, their parents are less apt to treat them as children subject to condemnation or interference.

Living in a group marriage is so intense that it tends to exhaust the participants. Eventually, they return to the simplicities of living alone as couples or as single persons. Among the Constantines' groups, the typical duration was a little less than one year, although other experiments in group living had ended so quickly that they fell through their research net before they could be studied. To break up within a year resembles communes that typically collapse or turn over in membership from one year to the next—for similar reasons of conflict and complexity.

Despite the fact that most of these group marriages fell apart as a result of difficulties in getting along, a majority of the ex-partners remained good friends. A majority also felt open to the possibility of entering other group marriages in the future, though they emphasized the desirability of choosing subsequent partners more carefully. Most participants, especially women, felt they had grown and matured through the experience, no matter how painfully it ended. And although a minority of the original marriages broke up (frequently as a result of the growth that the individuals had experienced in the larger group), the surviving couples rated their marriages as significantly improved by what they had learned through the group experience. Marriages that grew were generally those that were already strongest beforehand. By contrast, couples who entered group marriages because they were having trouble getting along often found that the group experience exacerbated existing problems and accelerated the demise of their relationship (Constantine and Constantine, 1973b).

THE MARITAL CONSEQUENCES OF EXTRAMARITAL INVOLVEMENT

We have referred in passing to some of the consequences of extramarital involvement. Now we want to focus on a broad range of consequences, some negative, some positive. The chief negative consequences are jealousy and divorce. The positive ones are growth through struggle and enrichment of the relationship.

Jealousy

A secret affair is the classic form of extramarital involvement and jealousy is the classic response to suspected or known unilateral involvement of the spouse elsewhere. This is not to say that bilateral involvement does away with jealousy altogether, but that unilateral involvement provokes the strongest jealous reactions. Jealousy is one of the most painful human emotions since it is rooted in the vulnerability that accompanies intimate involvement with other human beings. Back of the risk of reaching out and responding to another lies fear of the withdrawal of the one related to, fear of losing his/her affection to another person. Though promises and commitments have been made, there is no guarantee that the special nature of this relationship will continue. When other friends become important, the inactive partner feels rejected and at the same time deeply anxious about how much can be risked without losing the love of the partner. Back of the fear of loss is shame at giving oneself without being wanted in the same special way. For both partners, there is hurt and fear of further hurt that makes honest dealing difficult. Active partners may feel hurt that they are not trusted to keep commitments they have made but at the same time feel afraid of betraying the other's trust. Outside parties complicate the scene with their own ambivalences, fears, and needs in relation to each of the married partners.

Fear of rejection and loss go back to infancy. Before they learn to talk, little children do not understand why their parents cannot always be present. With adulthood supposedly comes the ability to survive without constant attention from the partner. In varying degrees we learn to risk going our own way, taking responsibility for meeting our own needs, knowing we will not be demolished as our partner does the same. But the less those lessons are learned, the more vulnerable we are to feeling hurt when the partner's attention is turned toward another person.

Those who have been deeply hurt in earlier relationships fear being hurt again. The greater our sensitivity, the less we are able to deal directly with the partner for fear we will get hurt even more in the confrontation. At times it seems safer to turn off feelings, or to turn them inward, punishing ourselves and our partners with emotional depression or physical illness. Or we may feel a compulsive desire to punish the partner through aggressive and violent behavior.

The lower our self-image, the greater our predisposition to interpret the partner's involvement with another as intended to put us down or reject us. We keep defining ourselves in competition with the outside person and imagining that the partner views us unfavorably. So feelings of shame and worthlessness are added to the other emotions.

The first reaction of the jealous person is to try to best the competitor:

> *Does Kathy meet needs that I should be meeting? What do you like about her? Is she someone who is more affectionate than I? How much have I shown affection physically in small ways? Have I been preoccupied with other matters and failed to take time to show I care—to listen, to ask questions about your concerns?*
>
> *You have a need for understanding. Have I supplied enough support? Have I taken time to tell you I understand when you hurt? You need to feel important. Have I told you how proud I am of you and the way you give of yourself to your work and to your friends? I act as if they and I are in competition. Why do I put myself down?*
>
> *I feel inadequate, ashamed and threatened, fearing that Kathy is there for you in a way that I am not.*

Such awareness can stimulate efforts to strengthen the marriage which benefit a relationship that has suffered from lack of attention. But if the marriage improves, that does not automatically mean the extramarital involvement will be terminated. The harder the inactive partner tries to please the active one, the greater the disappointment if the outside partner is not abandoned. Jealous feelings are then apt to increase in fury.

Ambivalent feelings plague the jealous spouse. The desire not to be possessive, not to be suspicious, to understand and to trust, and not to block the other's freedom to act and love, these rational desires fight with the suspicion of betrayal, the fear of loss and the scary knowledge of his/her own affectional withdrawal from the active partner. This ambivalence, and the accompanying guilt and self doubt that follow muddy the waters of negotiation. Traditionally, jealousy was considered proof that the inactive partner loved the spouse. Today it is more often seen as a sign that s/he does not love the spouse enough to grant him/her the freedom to have his/her own friends:

> I'm in a real bind. I feel deeply rejected but I also feel I am rejecting what is most beautiful and good in you, your reaching out and giving yourself affectionately to friends. I feel alienated by your actions but I feel wrong in trying to keep tabs on you. I tell you, "If you loved me, you wouldn't hurt me this way," and then I play the victim role which sickens me. Guilt feelings separate lovers. The more I increase your guilt, the more you feel alienated from me. I want to protect the fragile trust we have built up but you perceive my response as interference. I mistrust my intuitional response. I am losing faith in our love, in your love for me, your integrity and your judgment. In all I do I seem to drive you away. I can't win. I feel pulled to pieces.

Jealousy as Crisis. Frustration at not working through jealousy or not persuading the partner to quit produces the most violent behavior that many couples have ever known and confronts them with an emotional and behavioral dilemma that must be taken seriously. Jealousy is an early warning system, a sign that something is wrong with the balance between the marriage and external relationships. An outburst of jealous feelings is a feedback mechanism warning the couple that they need to change their marital/extramarital system—either by strengthening the primary relationship, by weakening the secondary relationship, or both.

Jealousy may also indicate that the partner's behavior has changed too fast for the jealous partner to assimilate. The pace of change must be similar if husband and wife are to be able to journey together. There is no "right" or "wrong" speed for changing life-styles. If the eager partner slows down this may allow the reluctant partner to adjust more easily, thus reducing the fires of jealousy.

Larry and Joan Constantine (1971) found that jealousy was less of a problem for older participants in group marriages (those age 31 or older) than for younger participants. The latter may have felt personally insecure and less secure in their ties to their primary partners since their marriages were relatively new.

The question is often raised whether jealousy ever disappears. The Constantines found that jealousy was a major problem in more than half of those group marriages that were very new, but in none of those that had lasted a year or more. Moreover, 20 percent of their group marriages reported jealousy had been resolved as a problem—principally in the longer lasting groups. Living in a group marriage confronts the participants with jealousy-provoking situations so directly and so constantly that it may be resolved very quickly (within a matter of months). For couples whose extramarital involvements do not include living together, jealousy may take years to work through.

Larry Constantine (1977) reported from his experience in leading jealousy workshops that some sources of jealousy tend to persist whereas others gradually disappear:

> Even in the most mature individuals and relationships jealousy does not disappear altogether. Jealousy is still apt to be expressed over basic functional issues, such as need gratification, privacy, or time together, that is, over things which are functionally necessary for personal integrity and the maintenance of a healthy couple-system. In contrast, things which are more important for their symbolic content than their real effect on a person—status, sexual fidelity, and the like—tend to become less salient as triggers for jealousy as maturity develops.

Insofar as jealousy reflects a fear that the spouse will leave and never come back, repeated extramarital involvements pile up evidence that this outcome is unlikely. Among upper–middle-class persons in Los Angeles, Ziskin and Ziskin (1973) found that anxiety reactions were most severe initially, diminishing with experience: "For most couples, after there have been two or three affairs and they see no evidence that the spouse is about to pack up and leave, they settle down into a fairly comfortable state."

Typically, jealousy is most severe the first time around. While there is no guarantee that it will ever disappear, it is likely to become less acute as multilateral involvement becomes more familiar.

If repeated experience does not result in decreased jealousy, the pain may become so acute that it propels the inactive partner into the second major negative outcome of extramarital involvement, namely, divorce:

> *Bernie has decided that he needs to be free to have whatever outside relationships feel good and right for him. He does not see this as a rejection of me but, rather, as an enrichment of himself, which he believes can enrich our marriage. I tried to go along and see if it would work, but I just can't take it. I deeply resent his lessening attention to me and the children. Whenever I ask him for more love or more of anything, he sees it as possessive demanding to which he cannot respond. I feel angry and rejected. If I could join him it might work, but I don't have the desire. There just doesn't seem to be any way out of our differentness except to split.*

Divorce

Of all the legal and ecclesiastical grounds for divorce, extramarital sexual intercourse has been the most widely sanctioned. Churches and legal jurisdictions that have forbidden marital dissolution for any other reason almost always consider this a ground for divorce, because it so clearly violates the traditional marriage contract of sexual exclusiveness.

How often extramarital sex actually causes divorce is not easy to ascertain. That it does not do so universally is shown by the fact that it is frequently kept secret from the spouse. Among Hunt's respondents who had engaged in extramarital sex (1974), only one fifth reported that their marriage partners definitely knew about it, although considerably more had apparently suspected it. Even if the partner does not suspect it, it may contribute indirectly to divorce by diverting energy away from the marriage or by making the active partner tense and hard to live with. In other cases, an active partner may become a better spouse in order to compensate for his/her outside activity, or as a result of sexual or other personal rewards experienced outside and brought home to the marriage. How often outside activity will have negative effects and how often positive effects cannot be prophesied.

When we turn to persons who have already divorced and ask whether extramarital experience contributed to their break-up, we have more evidence. Hunt reported (1974) that a majority of the divorced people in his sample who had had extramarital intercourse admitted that their sexual involvement had precipitated the breakup of their marriage, even when it had not been the only cause.

Although communal living does not necessarily result in extramarital sexual relationships, moving into the same household with other people frequently destroys existing pair bonds, especially when those bonds are weak in the first place. Kanter, Jaffe, and Weisberg (1975) studied 35 urban communes composed mostly of single persons and found that 50 percent of all couples moving in split up within the first few months. On the other hand, primary relationships that were strong enough to survive the initial testing period of communal living seldom broke subsequently.

This suggests that living with other people generally threatens primary relationships, but some relationships are strong enough to withstand the strain. Exposure to alternative partners sometimes heightens a couple's awareness of the value of the existing partnership. In any case, joining a commune tests the meaningfulness of that partnership. According to Kanter, Jaffe, and Weisberg (1975: 437):

> One is testing the relationship when one enters a commune. There is always the possibility that the relationship will be totally replaced, or cease to be useful within a communal context. The commune removes barriers to temptation and change, and a relationship that cannot stand comparison will probably not stand up to communal living.

Sometimes extramarital involvement serves as an alternative to divorce. Roebuck (1967) found that the cocktail lounge of the best hotel in a West Coast city of 250,000 provided extramarital sexual contacts for business and professional men in their late thirties and forties. Most of the men were married but complained that their wives were too busy and too "cold" and that there were too many "family pressures" (which we infer means too many children). They seemed thoroughly disengaged from their wives, visiting the cocktail lounge ten times a week and preferring such segregated sports as hunting, fishing, and golf. These men did not divorce (1) because most of them were active Catholics and (2) because they believed in a double standard. At home, they claimed to be "good husbands and fathers" who loved their families and were loved in return. At the hotel, they satisfied their sexual needs by establishing temporary liaisons with young, good-looking, low-status single women (many of them divorcees). For both the men and the women, this was sex without love—it was generally understood that to become emotionally involved violated the rules of the game.

When extramarital sex becomes a group practice, it is frequently governed by group norms that restrict its threat to marriage (Slater, 1963). In the cocktail lounge, elaborate rules governed the behavior permissible in public, limiting the development of spontaneity. Likewise, when rendezvous are secret, their limitation to brief times and special places prevents the development of full-blown, multi-faceted personal relationships. So if extramarital involvement is socially restricted, this minimizes the marital instability it might otherwise create.

The preceding studies suggest that most Americans in the 1970s still considered extramarital sex dangerous enough to their marriages to deem it advisable to keep it secret from their partners, and that where this activity became known it contributed to the breakup of some marriages. This shows that extramarital involvement is risky, but we do not know how often and under what circumstances it directly causes divorce.

Growth through Struggle

We have seen that extramarital involvement creates problems for many couples, problems that are sometimes so severe as to terminate the primary relationship. But for relationships that survive in the face of problems, the result, in retrospect, sometimes seems positive. To struggle successfully with tough problems requires confrontation, communication, and negotiation, which may make the primary bond extraordinarily vital and resilient.

Whitehurst (1974) interviewed 35 open-marriage couples scattered throughout the United States and Canada. These couples represented the successful end of the outcome spectrum—they had not split over this issue, and many of them had been propelled into it by experiences in therapy groups that gave them a positive orientation toward expanding relationships. Opening up their marriages less often reflected deficits in the marriage than a utopian desire to extend their intimacy experiences. They were "active seekers of some more or less utopian ideal and willing to pay the price in uncertainty, anxiety and to commit themselves to high levels of interaction to attempt to accommodate problems."

The positive orientation of Whitehurst's couples did not prevent them from having problems when they opened up their marriages sexually. Many commented about the pain that they experienced. But none regretted making the change, since the pain stimulated them to grow both individually and in their marriages. Working together on their problems was a stretching experience. Stretching can be exhilarating, provided the bond does not snap.

Whether the struggle leads to growth or destruction depends on how the couple go about it. The more they blame, judge, and put each other down, the more the relationship will suffer. If they become violent, it may collapse swiftly. On the other hand, the struggle may benefit the relationship by bringing the couple into greater dialogue with each other, requiring them to take the time to tell each other where they are coming from, to share their feelings, to listen, and to negotiate. Couples who have drifted into prosaic patterns are jolted out of the doldrums by the crisis of extramarital involvement. Sometimes the enduring struggle is the most meaningful contact a couple have had in years. If they find the issue too hot to handle, they may turn to marriage counselors for help, and this may enable them not only to deal with the particular issue but to revitalize their marriage generally.

This crisis-induced review may help the couple appreciate things in their relationship that they have come to take for granted:

> *What can we do to heal the hurt, to bridge the gap? I need to have you tell me often how and why you love me. I think I'm going to have to be courted all over again.*
>
> *And I will need to focus on the many ways in which I love you because they have got covered over with my resentment and hostility. If we keep remembering the good things we have together it will make it easier for us to cope.*

Extramarital involvement is not unique in offering opportunities for growth through struggle. Any marital problem offers this opportunity, provided that it is difficult enough to challenge the couple to their utmost and to command their full attention. Extramarital involvement is scary enough to require more effort, more communication, more verbal sharing than almost any other problem that a couple could encounter. Therefore, it has this growth potential to a peculiar degree.

If extramarital involvement has the virtue of precipitating such struggles, it is important to recognize that the outcome of the struggle is not necessarily a continuation of the outside involvement. If struggle is to be productive, it must take into consideration the needs of both partners. Sometimes the solution to the trauma of unilateral involvement is for the active partner to give up the secondary partner and turn his/her attention to improving the relationship with the primary partner. Sometimes the solution is for the inactive partner to take responsibility for finding his/her own satellite relationships so as not to feel deprived. In any case, the outcome of the struggle is not predetermined by generalities, but by the particularities of each person. The most creative solutions reflect the circumstances of all the three or more individuals who are involved, and especially of the primary partners. Struggle may lead to acceptance, termination, or restriction of the outside involvement. Any of these outcomes may be beneficial, provided that both spouses communicate fully with each other and search for a solution to their dilemma that takes into account the reality of the total situation:

> Janine is a very loving person and doesn't like to limit the affection she feels. She finds it easy to integrate her intimate friendships with other men with the love she continues to hold for me. I have no similar inclination to become intimate with other women and have great difficulty in not feeling rejected and excluded.
>
> I became aware of how my desire to protect Janine and not interfere with her "pleasures" undercut a clean expression of my anger. I was able to get in touch with my anger and tell her how I felt that her affair was interfering with our relationship from my side, although I believed her sincerity in insisting that from her side it didn't. The constant struggle over the other relationship had begun to poison our times together. Facing the reality of my pain alongside the reality of her enjoyment and the reality of our increasing alienation, we each moved to find new ground, a place where we each gave a little and both were more comfortable.

Marital Enrichment

Despite the traumatic consequences that many couples experience when one or both partners become sexually involved with outsiders, not all the consequences of such adventures are negative.

Sexual Enrichment. Some couples report that their sexual relationship has been enriched by their sexual experience with others. For persons whose previous experience has been limited, having sex with a new partner may introduce him/her to new sexual practices that may be brought home to the primary relationship. Conversely, the more diversified the premarital sexual experience of the couple, the less likely they are to encounter new techniques with other partners.

A majority of a group of adults who had typically had three premarital sexual partners told Ramey (1975) that their extramarital intimate friendships improved the "quality" of sex with the primary partner. (For 55 percent the quality improved, whereas only 1 percent reported a decline and the remaining 44 percent reported no change.) Presumably, this improvement reflected the fact that these couples were generally comfortable with the openness of their relationships and viewed them as a positive feature of their individual and joint lives. Indeed, a majority of these couples discussed their outside involvements with each other in detail, and some found that the excitement of their own or their partner's outside sexual activity raised the energy level of their mutual activity:

> It is a "turn-on" to discuss potential relationships beforehand. Twenty-eight percent of the sample indicated that they always discussed any potential relationships at length before becoming involved because they enjoyed sharing the anticipation of a new relationship and weighing the advantages and disadvantages, not just from a self-protective point of view, but because it was a way of sharing the excitement of a new adventure (Ramey, 1976: 103—italics in original).

Parallel to this heightened quality of the sexual relationship is an increase in the amount of sexual activity of persons who are simultaneously involved with both primary and secondary partners. Ramey's respondents typically had intercourse as often as usual with the primary partner, at the same time that they were having sex with secondary partners. This reflects the fact that the total level of sexual activity in human beings is not a fixed quantity, but responds to increased opportunity and attraction. Perhaps if individuals were to become intimately involved with secondary partners short of intercourse, they would engage in sex even more often with their primary partners. In any case, extramarital involvement does not necessarily interfere with the marriage as far as frequency of intercourse is concerned:

> When I feel close to another person I get high. I feel a lot of confidence and a lot of excitement, as if I love the whole world and the whole world loves me. I get turned on to life. This emotional high increases my desire to have sex. The turn-on may occur in a group where there is lots of sharing or with another person with whom I can be very real, but I don't feel the necessity to relate sexually with any of this group or with this particular person. This charge wants to flow and I like it to be physically expressed with my husband. There's no feeling of betrayal because the turn-on to life happened out there. Likewise, I don't feel jealous when he is affected by the beauty of other human beings. I guess I'm old-fashioned in wanting us both to bring it home when it comes to being sexually expressed.

Independence and Intimacy.   We saw early in this chapter that people who become extramaritally involved tend to be more independent than those who stick with the spouse exclusively. Sometimes their independence becomes so extreme that they abandon the spouse. Short of that, however, extramarital involvement enhances the already substantial independence of the active spouse, but does not necessarily mean that intimacy between the primary partners is reduced. When going out is followed by returning home, some couples appreciate one another anew.

In his study of successful open marriages, Whitehurst (1974) discovered that greater apartness and greater closeness developed in the same marriages:

> To the average mind in the West, the [sexually open marriage] system appears as paradoxical, for it seems to give people what our common wisdom says is impossible, simultaneously a more intense and important pair-bond with the primary partner as well as more independence, freedom, and autonomy to interact with other significant others.

Perhaps independence and intimacy are not truly simultaneous. They may coexist in the same marriage as twin products of extramarital involvement, but they are not experienced at the same time. At one moment, the active partner exercises his/her independence by going out to personal friends. Coming home, s/he finds intimacy with the spouse enhanced. S/he moves between the two poles of the experience of intimacy and independence as s/he moves back and forth between the primary and secondary partners.

For an inactive partner, the same alternation occurs. Whenever the active partner leaves, the inactive one must face his/her own need for more independence. One cannot expect the other to be the only source of one's support and nurture. The active partner's absence forces the inactive one to take responsibility for his/her own good times rather than relying totally on the spouse. And if the spouse does return home with fresh appreciation and warmth, the inactive partner may also experience enhanced intimacy. Temporary absence *may* make the heart grow fonder.

Independence and intimacy, then, are sequential rather than simultaneous characteristics of open marriages. By definition, going outside the marriage increases the partners' independence of one another. Independence stimulates the growth and development of both partners as individuals. It need not be antithetical to a strong marriage, since the partner returning home may feel a renewed appreciation of the spouse after being away. There is no guarantee that extramarital experience will have these beneficial results any more than there is a guarantee that the couple's sexual life will be enriched by their additional sexual experiences, but some marriages *are* enriched in these ways—when the conditions are right.

CONDITIONS FOR CONSEQUENCES

We have seen that the consequences of extramarital involvement range all the way from divorce to enrichment. Whether the consequences will be negative or positive for a particular couple is not accidental. How a couple will be affected depends on various conditions, some of which can be created deliberately. By understanding these conditions, a couple may be able to foresee the outcome of various kinds of extramarital involvement and to choose more wisely whether to enter into such relationships and how to improve the cost/benefit ratio for their marriage if they do.

Disclosure/Privacy/Secrecy

One condition that profoundly affects the consequences of outside in- volvement is whether the spouse knows about it. We have seen that in many cases s/he does not know. Persons who fear the negative impact of disclosure may attempt to hide knowledge of their behavior from the spouse. When this attempt succeeds, the spouse may remain blithely ig- norant of what is going on behind his/her back but the secondary partner may rebel at the dishonesty:

> *Sidney and I love each other and want to grow. Neither of us has had an intimate friendship with anyone else since we were 18. We negotiated an agreement that we'd like to risk some outside friendships that may or may not involve sex. And suddenly along came Fred, for whom I had a tremendous attraction. But I couldn't feel right with a physical relationship with him, because he insisted on total secrecy with his wife about our friendship. I couldn't do that to her. It made me feel too guilty. Eventually, his double standard and inability to be honest with her turned me off. It poisoned our relationship. That kind of friendship held no goodies for me.*

This woman placed a high value on openness with all parties con- cerned. But in many outside involvements neither partner has such a commitment nor such an agreement with their own spouse. People who decide to be active and do not have a liberal arrangement with their partners may feel that discretion is better than valor. Believing that secret outside relationships won't harm the marriage, they may choose not to inform the spouse in the hope of enjoying their marriage and enjoying other relationships too.

Research tells us very little about the effects of secrecy on marriage. As long as the affair is not known, it cannot become the focal point of either jealousy or divorce. In that sense, the flamboyantly negative conse- quences of extramarital involvement cannot occur. Some relationships are subtly eroded by the diversion of energy into practicing the deception. Presumably, one cannot persistently lie to one's partner without impair- ing the spontaneity and transparency on which a good marriage depends.

The biggest problem with secrecy is not the subtle consequences of "living a lie," but the escalated consequences of discovery. Jealousy and resentment may be bad enough when the partner reports openly on his/her activity. But to discover that one's partner has been lying for months or years is to shatter not only one's sense of exclusivity but, far more bitterly, one's ability to believe anything the partner says subsequently. This loss of trust creates enormous barriers to rebuilding the primary relationship after it has suffered from betrayal. How is the innocent partner ever to know whether anything the errant spouse says is ever to be believed henceforth? How can contracts be negotiated when one never knows whether the other is negotiating in good faith? In this sense, unsuccessful attempts to deceive the spouse are the worst alternative. Hoping that one may avoid the usual jealous reactions, the risk of discovery may seem worth taking, especially to persons who are anxious and unassertive. The question is whether avoiding those consequences is worth the risk of the even worse consequences if the deception fails.

Secrecy prevents the benefits of growth through struggle. We have already suggested that the most likely result of deceiving the partner is the unspoken barrier between them. Being careful what *not* to say is the exact opposite of the direct encounter that an openly acknowledged relationship precipitates. Openness promotes dialogue, communication, negotiation, and potential revitalization of the relationship. Where the active person voluntarily initiates this encounter by disclosing the outside relationship, the partner's shock is likely to be mitigated by respect for the courage and honesty that it took to do the telling. The channels of communication between partners are not only left open but blasted open even wider by the news. Thus self-disclosure, especially about a first outside involvement, triggers intensified communication. There may be plenty of fireworks, but at least the partners have an opportunity to hear each other and to believe what they hear. All this is severely jeopardized by deception.

The potential enrichment of the primary relationship by whatever good experiences the active partner has with the secondary partner is hampered by secrecy. The active partner could theoretically bring those goodies home to the spouse—the new insights, new knowledges, new enthusiasms. But fear that the spouse might wonder where they came from leads deceptive spouses to hoard those goodies rather than to share them. This blocks the flow of energy from the extramarital relationship into the marriage.

It is one thing for couples to decide that they want to inform one another about outside involvements, and something else to decide how much information to communicate about the details of those experiences:

> How much privacy is good? How much openness? If I share my thoughts, feelings, and plans with you, you may resist them and seek to control my private space. If I don't, I become a traitor, disloyal to our togetherness. If you reveal your anger at my behavior, isn't this one form of controlling me?

How much self-revelation is good? If I reveal too much, I become vulnerable and risk your blame and judgment.

Growth through struggle may not require sharing everything. Every couple needs to negotiate about how much they want to hear and use discretion in monitoring that flow of information. Many couples find that questioning backfires, and end up agreeing that the returning partner will share only what s/he wishes to:

It's a crazy concept of faithfulness when I give you the right to know everything that goes on in my mind or my experience. I don't want to feel pushed to share feelings that I'm not even sure of myself and that you could misconstrue and take too seriously. This is not part of my contract, to feel guilty if I don't share everything, and if I don't, you have the right to accuse me of hiding something.

Raymond Lawrence (1974) advised against complete disclosure:

A common fallacy in marriage folklore is that real intimacy means full disclosure of one's thoughts, feelings and actions. I contend that an attempt at total openness is not a true form of intimacy. It is rather a naive form of dependency. Real intimacy is experienced in the rhythmical movement toward and away from another person. Real intimacy is experienced only when persons have the capacity and wisdom both to give and to withhold, both to move toward and to move away from, both to be close and to be distant. One who cannot be distant destroys the value of his being close. One who cannot be close negates the value of his distance.

As a pastoral counselor in Houston, Texas, Lawrence "found it to be almost invariably true that married persons do not want to hear any of the details of the exploits of their spouses with a third party." Lawrence's experience may have been affected by his professional role as a clergyman and by his geographical location in a conservative area. In nonchurch circles in places like metropolitan New York and southern California, full disclosure may be not only tolerated but expected. Thus, John and Mimi Lobell (1972) lived out a "free marriage" in New York City that involved telling each other everything and enjoying it:

I enjoy it when Mimi comes home and tells me about her night spent with another man. Conversely, Mimi enjoys hearing about what happens between me and another woman as real things that tell you what people are all about.

And in another place:

Her experience is not a secret from me, but something we share later as we share all of the interesting things that happen to us. Our sex with others and love for them is an adventure we ultimately have in common.

Carl Rogers (1972) cited a couple in their thirties:

> We use words to get close. We have an understanding that we each strive for complete openness with each other—in fact I try to share particularly those things I don't want to, because they are usually getting in the way of our really being close and growing together. Like if I'm angry or jealous or strongly attracted to another woman—if I don't open up these things to her and they are on my mind we will gradually feel separate. I find that if I shut off some things I begin to build a wall—I can't cut the flow on just *some* things—without blocking *many* things.

Although complete openness has certain payoffs for a couple who want it, less sharing works better for persons less prepared to cope with some of the information. In other words, agreeing on complete disclosure depends on giving complete consent to the behavior that is to be disclosed. In marginal behaviors that are neither completely taboo nor completely acceptable, some persons choose to turn their backs on the partner's behavior, preferring not to hear about it.

Rogers concluded that "this open, sharing of *all* of one's self nearly always, in my experience, leads to personal growth." Presumably, it also opens the door to the possibility of marital growth as well. Perhaps radical openness is an ideal policy that would enrich and revitalize marriages generally, provided both partners are prepared to commit themselves courageously to the twin tasks of telling all and hearing all.

When someone says, "I know you are relating to other people but I don't want you to tell me all the intimate details," that is very different from the partner saying to him/herself, "I am relating to other people but I have decided not to tell you because you would be too upset if I did." The first policy is voluntarily negotiated privacy—the second is unilaterally decided secrecy.

It is risky for one partner to assume s/he knows what is best for the other. To do so is to risk the loss of trust, the foundation of marriage. Where two partners care deeply about each other, there is no substitute for dealing honestly with intentions and behavior in this difficult area. To deal with reality keeps the channels of communication open. The inactive partner's wild fantasies about the other's secret intentions and behavior may be far more painful and destructive than the real thing.

Spousal Inclusion/Exclusion

The consequences of extramarital involvement depend not only on whether the spouse knows that it is occurring, but also on whether the spouse knows the particular person involved. Generally speaking, an unknown third party is more scary than a known one. Inactive spouses feel more excluded and more resentful when the third party is kept out of sight. An unsigned article on "Sexually Open Relationships" in the May 1975 Family Synergy *Newsletter* summarized the experience of many couples:

> Contrary to the way that closed relationships handle outside sexual and emotional involvements, it seems to minimize fears and the problem of jealousy when the "third party" is known to and well liked (or at least "approved of") by the person of the same sex in the couple. This provides support for that person in several important ways, including the fact that the known is usually less frightening than the unknown. The most important aspect, however, is probably that one can' depend more on a friend for the consideration necessary to avoid hurt than one can depend on a stranger.... Another advantage is that all involved are aware of the marital status, feelings, desires, and fears of everyone else involved.

The following anonymous letter from a woman "To My Lover's Wife" appeared in the September 1976 issue of the same *Newsletter* and portrays the "other woman's" attempts to include the inactive partner:

> I met you both the same evening. He and I enjoyed one another spontaneously, and I noticed his pride in introducing you. I was even more pleased when I saw that he not only had sex appeal but also character. We exchanged cards and I knew I'd see him again.
>
> In the intervening weeks, we communicated our intention to meet and recently we had a dinner date.
>
> My hunch was right—I do like him. He is for real. I was pleased and surprised that he agreed to spend the night. We had time and reason to talk about your relationship together, and he assured me that you had accepted the idea of the friendship we were beginning.
>
> Our second evening together, he again felt at ease to stay over. I was hopeful that I'd lucked onto a relationship in which we'd have all-around peaceful, easy feelings. It's been a couple of years since I've enjoyed such a relationship with a couple, and so I was delighted with your invitation to dinner.
>
> Since then, I know that you are experiencing confusion about us. I imagine that you had an agreement with yourself about how you hoped to react to his involvement with another woman. Now it seems your mind and body do not agree. You barely made eye contact with me. You stayed in your kitchen while I dined awkwardly with your family. When we went out, you drove yourself and sent him with me. During the evening, you shrank into the corner of the most distant seat.
>
> My attempts to contact you seemed ineffective. I was pushy about trying to make significant conversation, but I felt it was important for

us to communicate. We sure made a ghastly evening for each other, didn't we?

Anyhow, your phone call the next day was a beautiful offering. Your admission that you felt confused was believable. Your earlier statements that we should "do our thing," that you were not bothered—I was not convinced, as your body language said you were feeling tiny, helpless, and injured.

As the proverb says, "The truth shall make ye free—but first it shall make ye miserable." I am actually relieved that your mind and your body now agree. That we can work on.

. . . You said that trying to force a friendship with me would be artificial; if we become friends, it'll be on your terms, in your own good time. I guess this will depend on how long you want to nurse your fear.

Why should you want to be my friend?

. . . For one reason, you might like me. You could call if I were seeing him, ask to talk to him and get a friendly response. I recognize the importance of your primary bond, and acknowledge that to you both. You could be complimented by his good taste and joyous that he continues to share so much with you when he obviously has other attractive options. After all, who wants a partner that no one else desires?

. . . If you really know me, then you can operate from clear perceptions, rather than from fantasies about me. Then you can make a more reasonable judgment about his relationship with me. You have every right to express your wishes about that; if the bond between you is as real as I perceive, he'll be sensitive to your wishes.

If you still object to our relationship, you will be acting from a factual evaluation of your feelings rather than ignorance. Keep in mind that you have spent years together, whereas I've spent about 24 total hours with him. My relationship, therefore, does not seem terribly significant, while yours to him definitely is.

. . . Why should you open to the person who is causing your pain? So you can deal openly and ask her to stop. Like it or not, I am involved and may be able to help dispel your confusion. You are part of *my* relationship with him. This relationship is not yet deep. Until now, we've been "grinning a lot, acting silly and playing." However, your pain has a real impact on how we relate. In half a lifetime together, you have both developed some strong bonds; when you're hurting, he's also affected.

You might feel safer if I were married. Please know that my primary person is the best, healthiest man I've ever loved and my way with him is as intimate and committed as most legal unions.

If you believe this, you may wonder why I also want your husband. Because I want more out of life than one man can possibly give me. Loving one person does not make me blind to the beauty of others, just as loving one's firstborn does not mean you'll not desire another child. The argument might go, "Why not stay with the safety of what you have? The next child could be retarded or deformed. Besides, if you *really* love the first son, you won't need any other."

Having a good primary relationship facilitates my enjoyment of others. I do not expect to take another person like a vitamin pill to cover deficiencies. I love my partners for joys we share and can overlook things I do not love. In fact, I prefer my men to have strong relationships with other women. Their commitment to another helps me feel free to be wholly myself.

... I will not be seeing him [your husband] until I can be sure I will not be consciously contributing to your pain. If you are uncomfortable, any time we spend together cannot be really joyous.

I feel like we've made some beginnings. I await your response.

In the chapter on separateness and togetherness, we saw that undomesticated activities are a threat to the togetherness of marriage. To *domesticate* means to include within the family circle, to make the wild tame, the unfamiliar familiar, the scary acceptable. To bring another person within the circle of our love may tame my fears about my partner's affection for that person. To know him/her as another human being and not someone out to get my partner, take my partner away from me; to face, communicate, and share activities with him/her is to guard against distortion and face the reality rather than the fantasy of the situation. The reality may be as bad as or worse than the fantasy, but usually a triangle that has friendly connections is safer than one any of whose points are out of touch.

This involves two processes:

1. To domesticate a person—a new friend is transformed from being wild to being acceptable, human, tolerable.

2. To domesticate a new activity—a new way of relating openly and warmly and directly becomes part of our way of life as we are able to give to others the warmth we have found with each other.

We have suggested that bilateral involvement generally places less strain on a marriage than unilateral involvement because it reduces or obviates the sense of unfairness when one partner gets the firsthand benefits of multiple involvement and the other gets only secondhand benefits or disadvantages. This exclusion is partially relieved when the spouse has firsthand contact with the other wo/man. By bringing the other person home or by occasionally going out together as a threesome, the inactive partner and the third party have an opportunity to become friends in their own right. Insofar as the three partners have enjoyable experiences together, the so-called inactive spouse becomes an active participant, too. The two persons of the same sex may come to feel like brothers/sisters and to enjoy their own one-to-one time together. For individuals whose choice of a secondary partner grows out of satisfaction with the primary partner, the two chosen ones are likely to have much in common and are likely to become good friends. The net result of including the inactive partner is to change what was initially unilateral involvement into bilateral involvement with the same person. This includes three-person activities and one-to-one activities for both spouses with that person. Under these circumstances, the previously inactive partner no longer feels excluded but, rather, included in an enlarged circle of warmth and affection.

Spousal Consent/Opposition

If the spouse learns about an extramarital involvement, the consequences of that knowledge vary enormously, depending on whether s/he consents to the relationship or opposes it. To believe in sexual openness is to give one's generalized consent to the partner's right to sexual freedom. But holding a philosophical belief does not guarantee that one will be comfortable every time that freedom is exercised.

Substantial minorities of Ramey's participants in intimate friendships (1976) developed ground rules for guaranteeing that consent would be secured in particular instances. Twenty percent informed the primary partner before entering into a new intimate friendship, giving the partner an opportunity to veto the potential friend if s/he seemed dangerous. An even larger percentage (26 percent) agreed that any problems resulting from the friendship must be discussed with the spouse. This enabled couples to monitor the effects of their nonexclusive sexual policy. Consent must be given not simply to the establishment of a new relationship but to all subsequent developments:

> For awhile I tried to go along with Ray's experiment in sexual freedom. But then I found I couldn't stand it any more. I was too upset when he went away for a weekend. Before he left I would say, "Have a good time," but while he was gone I couldn't sleep and lost my appetite and was tense and nervous. His enjoyment turned out to be my pain. So I decided we had to confront whether it would be more painful for him to give up his sexual freedom than it was for me to try to live with it. I told him I was hurting so much I couldn't feel his love any more. His response was that my hurting mattered more to him than his sexual freedom, that I was his highest priority and that the sexual aspect of his friendships was not that important. He assured me that he loved me more than all the other women in the world!
>
> There's a lot of talk about pain bringing growth. But in my case it almost burned up our relationship.

In the June 1975 Family Synergy *Newsletter,* a woman recorded her thoughts on "Looking Back on an Open Marriage," projecting guidelines for a future primary relationship. Her marriage had just ended in divorce after four years of sexual exclusiveness and two years of nonexclusiveness. Several of her guidelines bear on the question of consent:

I will move slowly, checking out each move with my partner before I make it. Relationships are as fragile as each individual in them. We made ourselves extremely vulnerable to each other, very open to being hurt. My habit of following my impulses without fully considering the impact on my partner caused irreparable damage. Actions can't be recalled and although I was repentant and asked forgiveness, my partner felt betrayed. Trust destroyed is not easily rebuilt.

I won't deny my feelings. Feelings are not rational; they're not good or bad. They just ARE—and must be faced and dealt with when they occur. We found that our feelings lagged behind our intellectual acceptance by months. I had a tendency to suppress feelings that contradicted my theories because I wanted to be progressive and liberated. Jealousy and possessiveness are impediments to alternative lifestyles, but they're strong, real emotions, trained into us from birth and aren't reduced by denial.

I will make time to deal with my partner about problems. I won't enter into a difficult change in our lifestyle at a time when one or both of us is very busy with work or school. These complicated relationships are enormously consuming of time and energy.

One way of insuring consent between partners is to write down agreements in a contract. Writing down oral agreements minimizes the chances of misunderstanding. A couple we know who are not married but whose relationship is of primary importance to them both agreed as follows:

1. We will provide support for a mutual depth relationship for the duration of 12 months beginning March 1, 1976 and ending March 1, 1977.

2. This basic year commitment contains a re-evaluation of the terms every 4th month of the commitment.

The terms agreed upon March 1, 1976 are as follows:

1. Interpersonal freedom to have one's *own* friends and interests without hassle from the other. Facets other than the primary relationship will add richness and vicarious growth through the *sharing* of experiences.

2. It is possible to have *occasional* other relationships of a sexual nature, allowing for spontaneity and personal satisfaction. The number of relationships will be evenly paced and meet a *mutual* balance at the agreed upon re-evaluation period.

3. Other sexual partners will be dealt with on a *non-illusionary* basis. The main emphasis *before* any sexual situation arises should be honesty about the current commitment situation.

4. Sexuality of the dyad and activities with others (group sex) is dependent on *mutual* consent and assessment of the *situation*.

5. Individual space will be allowed even if the residence is the same. Separate sleeping spaces will be treated as a *personal* domain.

6. These rules will not be governed by penalties but by trust and belief in our commitment.

Noteworthy in this agreement is that, even though outside relationships are generally permitted, the couple required specific consent in group situations where both partners would be involved and also provided for periodic review of the contract. Consent, for this couple, was not a blank check. Their outside relationships were governed by specific limits that the partners felt were necessary to protect their relationship.

During our jealousy workshops, we ask couples to negotiate on the issues that are giving them the most trouble. We have written a complete description of these workshops in Blood and Blood (1977). One example of husband-wife negotiations completed during a jealousy workshop was as follows:

> The worst thing about Jack's visits with his friend was not the fact that he was spending the night with her but that he would just disappear without telling me where he was going. I kept worrying about what I would do if some emergency arose and I didn't know how to find him.
>
> I asked him to leave a phone number with me whenever he was going to be gone overnight so I would be able to reach him in an emergency. I promised him that I wouldn't phone him unless something really terrible happened. I trust I'll never have to actually use it but it makes me feel a lot more secure to have him agree to keep me informed on where he is.

Agreements calling for continued consent giving are not always easy to implement. For couples who have committed themselves to extramarital freedom in general, saying no may come particularly hard. An anonymous article in the January 1976 Family Synergy *Newsletter* reported that couples involved in multiple relationships frequently got into trouble "because people are frequently loath to exercise the veto power in those cases. Based on the results observed some of the time, this unwillingness is unfortunate. Problems get unnecessarily severe before they are brought up for resolution, too often, if vetoes are not exercised when they should be."

Consent needs to be both explicit and authentic if it is to minimize the chances of negative repercussions to extramarital involvement. Where the spouse cannot consent, opposition may be equally beneficial. The fruits of growth through struggle accrue chiefly to those whose explicit opposition precipitates a creative struggle and search for mutual solutions.

Gradualness/Abruptness

Most people find it difficult to change drastically all at once. Pushed too hard, they get their backs up, become paralyzed, resist all the more. Confronted with unwanted changes in the partner, they feel resentful, hurt, betrayed. When changes are sudden and dramatic, they feel as if they have been forced to swallow something whole without having a chance to chew it into little pieces.

We propose a "mastication" theory of change. If change comes in easy stages, it is more digestible. But if too much is attempted too fast, the result is gagging or indigestion.

Gradualness affects both the size and the speed of change. The smaller the increment and the slower the pace of successive changes, the greater the chance that they can be experienced gracefully rather than resentfully:

> I can change. I can be open to new things. I can become different tomorrow from what I am today if you will respect me as a person, if you don't ride roughshod over me and push me around. I need time to hear you and know what you mean and discover my own true response. I need unpressured time to come to see things in a new perspective. I need time for my feelings to catch up with my thinking. I need time to assimilate new experiences. The more patient you can be with me, the more rapidly I may be able to move.

When pressure for change is too heavy, it gets in the way of hearing and understanding the feelings. When demands for change in a marital life-style are expressed before feelings are heard and dealt with, the communication and integration process is sabotaged.

For the less interested partner, an open marriage is easier to accept intellectually than emotionally:

> My ideals frequently run ahead of my ability to put them into practice. I damage myself when I ask too much too fast of myself. In dreams this comes out in trying to mount ladders with some of the rungs missing or taking such large steps that I cannot manage them and keep my balance. I am learning to take a step at a time and let that step lead me to the next one when the time is right. I lose my integrity when I push myself beyond my limits for fear of getting left behind. Our marriage is not truly together when I try to force myself to go along with you when I am not really in step with you.

The implications of gradualness vary for different couples and different individuals. Some partners are threatened by any time their spouse spends elsewhere, reading it as rejection. One man refused to "allow" his wife to play in a string quartet if it interfered with time that he was free. Some persons feel threatened by any emotional involvement of the spouse with anyone else. Uneasiness needs to be taken seriously by both partners rather than damned as possessiveness. The roots of discomfort must be taken into account, and worked through to a mutual solution.

For many, the greatest fear is that the partner will become sexually involved. This may be interpreted by the inactive partner as the greatest affront to their marital intimacy. To be asked to accept sexual intimacy before s/he is used to having the spouse spend time away from home or become emotionally involved with others may be asking more than the individual can bear. For others, casual outside sex is more tolerable than emotional involvement.

Clarifying the meaning of the friendship to the partner can come only through sharing verbally. As a couple communicate their feelings about outside relationships, it may become evident that both have unreal fantasies and fears surrounding emotional and/or sexual involvement with others. Continuing to share those fantasies and fears may ease the panic and bring perspective, as well as affecting the actual behavior of each partner. Taking small steps in developing outside relationships may be the happiest approach for the security of the marriage. Brief intervals may gradually become longer times apart. Casual contact with others that gradually becomes more affectionate and intimate may eventually secure the partner's support:

> We need not be adversaries. Hopefully we can learn how to take this journey together, each understanding what the other is experiencing and feeling. If we explore this uncharted wilderness together, keeping in touch with each other's experience, maybe we can come out of the woods together. If you forge ahead, leaving me behind, I will get frightened and panic.

Some couples shift from insisting only on joint involvement—couple to couple—to freedom for one-to-one involvement. Some couples move from separate involvement behind closed doors to public involvement in a common room. Some move from involvement with one other person to involvement with more than one, either serially or simultaneously, as in group sex or a group marriage.

No particular sequence of involvement is easy. Reactions will vary with individual tastes and experience, as well as with the varying ability of the partner to be accepting. In general, gradual change provokes less jealousy and less risk of destroying the marriage. Struggle is necessary when one partner is more eager than the other for outside relationships, but the more gradual the change, the greater the likelihood that both partners will find the struggle enriching.

Personal Security/Insecurity

The consequences of extramarital involvement depend on both interpersonal and intrapersonal factors in the marriage.

How someone reacts to the spouse's involvement with another depends partly on his/her personal resources. Anyone who feels abundantly endowed with inner resources can tolerate the diversion of some of the partner's resources in other directions more easily than a person who feels so unsure that every bit of attention directed elsewhere seems like a deprivation.

The fewer the inner resources, the more acute the jealousy. Bringle (1975) found that jealousy was especially common among persons who grew up in unhappy families and were dissatisfied with their current lives (with few alternative sources of emotional support). Persons who thought poorly of themselves and felt they had little control over their own lives were also jealous. Such persons have heavy emotional needs and depend on the partner to meet those needs. When the partner gives attention to a third party their precarious emotional equilibrium is threatened:

> I worry a lot about what other people will think of you if they find out that you have been "unfaithful" to me. It is hard for me to stand apart from you and not feel ashamed. When I am feeling low I accuse you of wanting to end the marriage. I feel cut off from friends and relatives who would disapprove of you if they knew what you have done. It is hard for me not to feel swayed by what I know they would say about you.

Insecurity begins as an inner feeling but seldom ends there. An insecure person finds it easy to blame the partner for making his/her life more difficult:

> It is easier to blame you for feeling what I feel, to expect you to supply my happiness and to solve my problems, than to manage my own life. Are you responsible for my jealousy, or do I make myself jealous? You can do something one day and I won't feel jealous at all (or maybe only a little bit), whereas another day you can do exactly the same thing and I'll erupt all over the place. Days when I am not on an even keel, I'm especially vulnerable.

If blaming is met by the repeated provocation of a continuing outside relationship, a vicious cycle ensues that is liable to poison the primary bond:

> I want to be your only lover. I feel Audrey has violated my territorial rights! You claim that your "cup" runs over when you share your love with her, but I find that my cup is poisoned. I don't feel that what we have is special any more. I've lost trust in our relationship and I no longer desire to be intimate with you, knowing that you are intimate with her.

Persons who feel good about themselves and confident about their ability to stand alone are less apt to feel jealous. They find it easier to share their partner's gifts with others. For them, the extramarital involvement is less often seen as a personal threat and more easily seen as a sharing of riches. Just as a doctor's wife may appreciate her husband's giving to his patients, a secure person may appreciate the love that the spouse shares with a friend.

The range of responses to extramarital involvement extends all the way from threat to appreciation, depending partly on the personal equilibrium of the spouse.

Strength/Weakness of the Core Relationship

Perhaps the most significant condition affecting the consequences of extramarital involvement is the strength of the marriage itself.

The classic starting point of the traditional affair was a married man telling a single woman about his marriage troubles. The man seldom claimed that this would save his marriage but it often seemed good for his mental health to find a confidante.

In those days, a popular "solution" to marriage problems was for a couple to have a baby, since that would "tie them together" and give them "something in common." We now realize how often babies born in such circumstances became new bones of contention as well as added burdens on the couple's resources of time, energy, and money. Having a baby often accelerated, rather than prevented, the collapse of already troubled marriages.

So much have times changed that contemporary couples sometimes think an extramarital involvement will save a weak marriage. The theory goes that one cannot expect any one person (e.g., the marriage partner) to meet all of one's needs (true) and that if an additional involvement meets other needs, it will reduce the pressure on the marriage and thereby make it more tolerable. In actuality, a fragile marriage is more likely to be destroyed by an extramarital affair.

The weaker the marriage, the greater the danger than an external involvement will not supplement but displace it, the so-called secondary relationship becoming the primary one. The weaker the marriage, the greater the likelihood that an extramarital involvement will lead to divorce.

At the same time, the weaker the marriage, the greater the probability of intense jealousy. The weaker the marriage, the more rational it is to feel jealous, given the danger that the outside relationship will take over:

> *You say that you wish to continue our primary relationship and that your relationship with Jon will be partial. Suppose the joy of sharing with him increases! Suppose our love becomes less as the bitterness in me comes out? You say I am your first love—but what if your relationship with Jon destroys the love you say you cherish?*

If the core relationship is strong and if satellite relationships are formed because of their attractiveness and not because of dissatisfaction with the spouse, extramarital involvement may enrich the already good relationship. Good things come only to those who already have a good thing going.

Persons embroiled in the task of transforming a closed relationship into an open one sometimes imagine that it would be easier if they had started with a policy of sexual openness from the very beginning. While theoretically this would bypass the pain involved in opening up a previously closed relationship, the question is whether a primary relationship stands much chance of jelling in such a fluid environment. Bernard (1972) suggested that initiating a primary relationship takes so much energy that it leaves little or no margin for satellite relationships. Some years of concentrating on building an exclusive relationship are necessary before the core relationship is strong enough to coexist with satellite relationships.

A dramatic example of the difficulty of developing primary relationships in an open environment comes from Sandstone, the sexually permissive club that existed in the Los Angeles hinterland from 1967 to 1972. The co-founders of Sandstone told a conference at Kirkridge, Pennsylvania, in 1970 that it had taken four years of pain to transform their closed marriage into an open-ended one. Although their long-standing relationship not only survived but thrived in the midst of a "family" of nine adults and a club of 500, most of the single members of the core family failed to develop strong pair bonds. The Francoeurs (1974) commented that "most primary relationships have to go through a period of romantic, exclusive, possessive bonding to establish the security and trust essential to an open relationship." They noted that, for most Americans, moving directly from being single into an open relationship was overwhelmingly complicated. A key official at Sandstone commented to the Francoeurs that Sandstone was

> a very difficult environment to start a primary relationship in. Most of the couples that have lived here haven't taken the time to build a strong primary bond before experimenting outside that bond, so the outside relationships tend to weaken the primary.

Elsewhere in the same book, this informant commented on the problems encountered by two single members of the Sandstone family who tried to develop satellite relationships before they had cemented their core relationship:

> Marty was having a little trouble handling the whole thing of nonexclusivity because he and Sue hadn't been together long enough to really form much of a relationship. There has to be a period at the beginning of any relationship where the two people are totally

monogamous. This can last for any length of time, depending on the two people, but if either of them goes outside the relationship before that level of trust is achieved, it can be very destructive to that pair bond.

It is not necessary for a new couple to be ideologically committed to sexual exclusiveness in order to develop a solid relationship. All that is necessary is to concentrate their energies on creating their own intimacy before adding the complexities of intimacy with others. Perhaps the least pain is felt by couples who experience multiple relationships prior to marriage and who marry with the express hope that eventually they will be able to open up their relationship, but who suspend their outside friendships temporarily while they concentrate on building their identity as a couple. To try to move directly from being single to practicing a sexually free marriage is to risk that the marriage will never become firmly established. Conversely, an old established marriage that was previously committed to exclusivity may be able to survive the pain of becoming open provided that it has not degenerated into an empty shell, but has retained sufficient strength and vitality to cope with the stresses of profound change.

The Sandstone experiences illustrate the unlikelihood that a core relationship will be successfully formed when it has to compete on equal terms with other relationships. A monogamous space is necessary initially to allow a new relationship to become firmly enough established to compete successfully with the peculiar fascination of new involvements. And an old relationship needs to be strong to be able to coexist with a satellite relationship without the balance between the two relationships becoming upset.

Limits on the Satellite Relationship

The effect of extramarital involvement on a marriage depends on whether unlimited amounts of energy are poured into the satellite relationship or whether limits are imposed on it. Ramey pointed out that "the sum total of ancillary relationships, whether one or many, should not really threaten the primary relationship because it will always be growing so much faster than they will, since it receives the bulk of the couples' attention" (1976: 93). Presumably, the relationship between partners who live together has a structural advantage because their co-residence brings them together more consistently than friends who merely visit one another. Provided that the core relationship is strong, alive, and growing, its preeminence can almost be taken for granted.

Despite this bias in favor of the residential relationship, Ramey's respondents set ground rules to guarantee the continued primacy of the core relationship by setting limits on satellite relationships. Forty-three percent adopted a rule that "family obligations come first." This means that only leftover time is available to the secondary partner. Indeed, one way of defining the difference between a primary and a secondary partner is that when obligations conflict the primary partner is the one who wins.

Forty percent held that "the sum of all outside relationships is not allowed to impinge on the time or psychic territory of the primary relationship." This means not only that each outside person taken individually is less important than the primary partner, but that all outside partners combined must not take so much time and energy that the primary relationship is overshadowed.

Some kinds of secondary partners were avoided as likely to demand too much. Fifty-nine percent were either unwilling or extremely reluctant to become involved with persons who were looking for a primary partner or who were in therapy, a marriage crisis, or another unsettled personal situation. Such persons can be like sponges, soaking up unlimited time and energy. They are frequently dissatisfied with remaining in a secondary position and prone to maneuver for first place. They threaten a primary relationship more than intimate friends with primary partners of their own or who are secure in their singleness and able to be comfortable with a limited friendship with a married wo/man.

In one of our jealousy workshops, a young man worked through some of his frustration at always being a secondary partner:

> I always thought I had to be first or nothing. I'm beginning to see that there are other relationships that are important and meaningful. I don't need to feel sorry for myself, or deprived. I can learn and grow in a relationship that doesn't have long-term commitment. I can give and receive a lot. I can enjoy these relationships for what they are. I can take the love someone is willing to give without feeling that I'm inadequate because they can't give more. I can accept the limits someone else sets to our relationship without blaming myself or her.

For the outside person as well as for the couple, it is important to understand the distinction between the primary and the secondary commitment. This clarifies expectations and defines limits. It minimizes unreal fantasizing in the minds of all parties concerned.

Guidelines specifying the limits on satellite relationships assure the inactive partner that s/he need not worry about being eclipsed by the other wo/man. Nothing is ever completely guaranteed but, insofar as limits are negotiated between partners and carried out in practice, the riskiness in third-party involvement is reduced.

The problem of maintaining a balance between primary and secondary relationships is reflected in reports by Ramey's married subjects (1975) about some of the difficulties they experienced with their intimate friendships. Forty percent were handicapped by lack of time. Friendships take time to develop and maintain. But marriages, too, take time and so do children and jobs. Anyone who has a full-time job, a primary relationship, parental responsibilities, and a secondary relationship must divide him/herself at least four ways. Thirty-two percent of Ramey's respondents found it difficult to get babysitters to care for their children while they were away enjoying their friends. Presumably, this figure would have been even higher if it had been based only on parents of small children.

After an individual has managed to find free time for him/herself, there is still a question whether the secondary partner will be free at the same time. Since many of Ramey's respondents were involved with persons married to other primary partners, the friend often faced equally severe problems. To balance two sets of family responsibilities so as to be available at the same time may require extensive planning and seldom allows for getting together impulsively on short notice. Thirty-six percent of Ramey's respondents reported that scheduling time with their intimate friends had been a serious problem.

Serious for only twenty-one percent but most pervasive of all (experienced at least mildly by seventy-four percent) was the question of sleeping arrangements. If both persons have primary partners, neither is apt to have a private space where the secondary relationship can be physically accommodated. Even the temporary absence of a primary partner may not resolve this problem if the person feels that his/her psychic space would be violated by an intruder in the marriage bed. Some couples resort to hotels/motels as neutral territory. In this sense, extramarital friendship with a person who does not have a primary partner is logistically simpler, even though emotionally more dangerous.

In general, the problems experienced by persons attempting to be intimately involved with both a primary and a secondary partner reflect the complexities of multiple involvement and underline the need for limits on satellite relationships in order to safeguard the core.

This brings us back to the question of the balance between the two relationships. The weaker the marriage, the more severely an extramarital relationship needs to be curtailed. Conversely, the stronger the marriage, the fewer the limits that may be necessary, except the limits that define the difference between primary and secondary relationships and guarantee the priority of the core.

12 Occupational Involvement

Extramarital involvement is at best optional in American marriages. For at least one partner, occupational involvement is not optional but compulsory. Despite this difference, the marital consequences of outside sex and outside work are strikingly parallel. Both take the individual away from home. Both absorb time and energy that might otherwise be given to the partner. Both bring home resources. Both affect the marriage differently when only one partner is involved instead of both.

The legitimacy of occupational involvement makes it a more insidious threat to marriage. Individuals preoccupied with their careers can argue that the family benefits from their income and prestige to counter criticism that they are never home. But weak marriages suffer from occupational overinvolvement. So husbands and wives face the task of balancing the time they devote to their careers against the time they spend with each other.

Not all work takes place outside the home. Housework was traditionally the woman's responsibility while the man supported his family financially. Today, assigning either of these responsibilities to just one sex is widely questioned. In our marriage counseling practice, the failure of husbands to share the housework is an almost universal grievance of their wives. That criticism becomes most severe when the wives themselves share the financial burden through outside work while their husbands fail to reciprocate by sharing the inside work. Housework and outside work are twin tasks that couples struggle to accomplish with maximum satisfaction and minimum conflict.

HOUSEWORK

Persons who never live alone before they get married may never have done much housekeeping. While they lived at home, they depended on their parents for most of the tasks around the house. And if they lived in college dormitories or other institutional facilities, paid help provided the meals and other services. Those who "batch" it alone in an apartment learn what it takes to keep a household going—the shopping, the cooking, the cleaning, and so on. For them, the transition to marriage is eased by learning the necessary skills. The new question, when shifting from living alone to living together, is deciding who will do what when two people share the same space.

Tradition provided lists of "men's work" and "women's work." For women, the list was long: the food operation, the clothing operation, the housecleaning, the interior decorating, the child care. For men, the list was not only short (shoveling snow, mowing the lawn, taking care of the car, putting on storm windows and screens) but seasonal or intermittent. Women were saddled with most of the work while men's tasks were hardly burdensome in duration, although they might be strenuous as long as they lasted.

Has the women's movement changed all this? Has the fact that large numbers of women now work outside the home just as much as their husbands mean that the men now work inside the home just as much as their wives? Table 12–1 shows that as of 1971 most household tasks were still performed unilaterally by the wife while home repairs were still chiefly the province of the husband. Only one of the six tasks (keeping track of the money and bills) was shared more often than it was done by either partner alone; even that was more often done unilaterally than shared. Moreover, just because "both partners" performed any of these tasks, they did not necessarily do so equally often or do it together. All that "both partners" meant was that at least occasionally the other partner did it even though the traditional partner may have done it all by him/ herself most of the time. If we had combined the figures differently to show how often the traditional partner mostly or always did certain tasks, we would have found that 87 percent of the wives were washing the dinner dishes, while home repairs were mostly or always done by 80 percent of the husbands.

Housework, then, continues to be divided along traditional lines, the husband doing a few specialized tasks and the wife carrying the major burden. Genuine togetherness is rare. Lopata's Chicago-area housewives (1971) reported that few tasks were ever done together. The most togetherness occurred in shopping, which was done jointly by 20 percent of her couples. The only other tasks shared by appreciable minorities were financial tasks (15 percent), heavy cleaning (14 percent), and gardening (8 percent). At the low end of the scale, not a single couple reported cooking together regularly.

Table 12-1   Who Does What Around the House?

Who Does It?	Evening Dishes	Picking Up for Company	Husband's Breakfast	Grocery Shopping	Paying Bills	Home Repairs
Wife only	75%	65%	56%	47%	36%	7%
Both partners	24	34	15	46	41	29
Husband only	1	2	29	7	23	64
Total	100%	101%	100%	100%	100%	100%

Adapted from Duncan, Schuman, and Duncan, 1973. *Source:* 700 Detroit married couples.

What about child care? In a retrospective study of parents of college students living in Montreal, Westley and Epstein (1969) found that mothers had been responsible for almost all the child-rearing, including the notorious burden of getting up at night when the child cried. The only tasks that fathers performed more often than mothers were engaging in sports and working on hobbies with the child (presumably the most enjoyable tasks). Both partners helped with schoolwork. All other child-rearing was predominantly the mother's responsibility.

When the time devoted to housework other than child-rearing was totaled up, wives in a national sample did more than 90 percent (Converse, 1966). Husbands averaged a grand total of 25 minutes per day, 15 in unilateral tasks and only 10 working with their wives. Wives averaged more than five hours a day. The most time-consuming of their chores were cleaning (2.2 hours a day), cooking and washing dishes (1.7 hours daily), and the laundry (1.4 hours a day).

Many women find that their husbands are a net loss as far as housework is concerned: they create so much untidiness that their modest help only partially compensates. One half of all the middle-class housewives in a Manhattan study complained about their husband's messiness—his commonest fault (Mayer, 1966):

> When my husband comes home from work, he takes off his coat and drops it, then he pulls off his shoes and throws them about. He lets his clothes lie about instead of putting them in the hamper.

Another Mayer respondent said:

> He's untidy. When he eats in the living room, he leaves his plate right there. He doesn't throw his mail away after looking at it—he just leaves it lying around.

We mentioned earlier that evidences of liberated women doing less housework are difficult to find. Stafford (1975) concluded from examining student couples at the University of Nevada that liberated men sharing household tasks may initiate more changes than liberated women going on strike. Particularly among couples living together unmarried, the more committed the man was to the relationship the less gender-linked were the tasks he performed. This implies that as men's consciousness is raised about the sexist character of the traditional division of labor, they may volunteer to share household tasks more equitably with partners engaged in ourside activities such as going to college or working.

Repercussions of the Division of Housework

Just because the division of housework is one-sided does not automatically mean it is unfair. If one partner is unilaterally involved in outside work, it is appropriate that the other be unilaterally responsible for inside work. In most marriages, these roles are played by the man and the woman, respectively, although occasional househusbands reverse the pattern. Because at any one time most married women are not employed outside the home, we might expect them to be generally satisfied with the status quo. For Converse's national sample (1966), this was true. Only one fourth of the wives complained that the help that they got from their husbands was insufficient.

Ten years later, Chadwick, Albrecht, and Kunz (1976) polled a state-wide sample of Utah adults and found that housekeeping was an area of considerable difficulty. Compared with other family roles such as child-rearing and sexual, recreational, financial, and therapeutic activities, both men and women reported their spouses fell short of their expectations more with respect to housekeeping than anything else. Housekeeping was the most common source of marital disagreements for the men and second most common for the women. The husband's housekeeping performance was of prime importance to wives, being more highly correlated with their marital satisfaction than any other variable. Yet the men's resistance to doing more housework was particularly high—six times as many men reported that they completely or mostly disliked housework as disliked any other family role. These findings suggest that the era when American wives generally will be satisfied with an unequal division of housework may not last much longer, and may already have disappeared.

Blood and Wolfe (1960) found that women whose husbands never shared any tasks were least satisfied with their marriages. Similarly, Westley and Epstein (1969) found that marriages in which wives were saddled with the most housekeeping responsibilities were the least satisfactory in several ways: partners seldom engaged in sexual relations, were sexually dissatisfied, and felt little affection for one another, and the marriage often had a destructive effect on the partners' emotional health.

Pratt (1972) measured the extent to which husbands and wives participated in the same housekeeping and child-care activities, finding that the larger the number of tasks shared by both partners, the better the

health of both husband and wife. She interpreted this as a causal relationship, suggesting that sharing the responsibility for household tasks eases
the burden on both partners and creates a correspondingly healthier home
environment.

Sharing is not the modal way of getting housework done in American marriages, but the research suggests that there may be untapped opportunities here for meaningful forms of togetherness for couples who are
seeking more satisfying life-styles. In our case:

> *Believing I owed it to Bob, since he worked so hard to bring home
> the bacon, I allowed myself to be saddled with the major portion of the
> housework for the first 25 years. When I chose to set a higher priority on
> work outside the home, everything had to shift. I faced up to the reality
> that the time I had been spending all my married life on cleaning and food
> preparation was not satisfying, and that it was no gift to anyone for me to
> play the servant role.*
>
> *Tasks are now divided up differently. Bob gets the breakfast because
> he's more interested in starting the day earlier. He does the major vac-
> uuming while I fill in with the rest of the cleaning. I no longer feel that I
> must plan ahead for perfect meals. More often we decide together what
> we feel like eating, and get it on faster by working at it together. I'm still
> the chief cook so that makes Bob the chief dish washer. He helps me with
> the heavy gardening jobs and I help him with the leaf raking. Together,
> we make the bed and prepare for guests. This has brought an enormous
> change in how I feel about myself; mainly, I don't feel like a martyr
> anymore. Housework and yard work no longer seem overwhelming and
> dull, eating up all my time. Actually, they serve as a nice change from the
> other things we are involved in.*

New attitudes toward the division of housework affect not only who
does what but how that work is viewed. Most couples fall either into the
trap of strict sexist roles or into a hard-nosed emphasis on strict equality.
Alternatively, the emphasis could be on appreciating each person's contributions as gifts to the family that are given more gladly when they are
appreciated:

> *I don't like it when you assume that I am naturally the person to
> patch your pants or vacuum or do the dishes. I really loved it when a
> friend of mine told her husband she'd rather he'd assume it's his job to
> sew up his own pants and then he could enjoy a nice surprise whenever
> she made a gift to him of a beautiful patch on the knee.*
>
> *I wish we could both notice when either of us does something that
> improves the order and beauty of the house rather than notice when we
> fail because our priorities have led us to do other things. Each of us
> surprising each other and expressing gratitude to the other for caring to
> make our joint household a nicer place to live feels very different from*

each blaming the other for not doing more, or even being afraid to say thank-you because it makes me feel guilty that you've done something that was really my job.

UNILATERAL OCCUPATIONAL INVOLVEMENT

The employment of one partner away from home can strain the marital relationship. The severity of those strains varies substantially between occupations.

Occupational Differences in Marital Strain

Persons in high-status occupations generally have lower divorce rates than those in blue-collar occupations. Even though high-status occupations may be very demanding, they provide substantial rewards in income and prestige. But among high-status occupations there are wide differences in divorce rates.

Authors and reporters both engage in writing for a living. The high divorce rate for authors shown in Table 12–2 may result from the financial uncertainties of working free lance, the difficulties of attempting to write at home where family members are noisy and distracting, and the freedom that comes from being on one's own. Conversely, editors and reporters have regular salaries. They work for bureaucratic organizations on regular schedules and are tied down to their jobs rather than free to come and go as they please. Presumably, these circumstances both benefit their families and prevent them from having as much opportunity for involvement with alternative partners.

Social scientists and natural scientists also differed sharply in their divorce rates. We suspect that the interest of social scientists in human affairs opens them to extramarital interests whereas the stereotypical

Table 12–2 Divorce Rates by Profession

Profession	Annual Rate of Divorce Suits
Authors	2.9%
Social scientists	2.8%
Lawyers and judges	2.0%
Engineers	1.9%
Editors and reporters	1.7%
Accountants and auditors	1.7%
Natural scientists	1.6%

Adapted from Rosow and Rose, 1972: 589. *Source:* California divorce petitions filed in 1968. Reciprocal percentages of members of the specified profession were not involved in a petition for divorce in that year.

Table 12–3   Divorce Rates by Medical Specialty

Medical Specialty	Annual Rate of Divorce Suits
Psychiatry	1.9%
General practice	1.7%
Obstetrics/gynecology	1.4%
General surgery	1.3%
Urology	0.9%
Anesthesiology	0.6%
Preventive medicine/Public health	0.3%

Adapted from Rosow and Rose, 1972: 595. *Source:* California divorce petitions filed in 1968. Reciprocal percentages of physicians were not involved in a petition for divorce in that year.

natural scientists have their eyes glued to microscopes. Natural scientists are generally more socially conservative than social scientists, and this predisposes them to more stable marriages. Whether this difference reflects more successful relationships or simply greater willingness to make do with a mundane status quo is impossible to infer from these statistics.

Medical Marriages.   Even within a given profession, there may be enormous variations in divorce rates. Table 12–3 shows that, among California doctors, psychiatrists had a high divorce rate—perhaps reflecting the emotionally intimate and prolonged nature of their contact with their patients. For the remaining specialties, we note that whole–patient-oriented general practitioners had more divorces than body-oriented surgeons; and that male gynecologists with their women patients had more divorces than male urologists with their mostly male patients. Anesthesiologists have little or no contact with patients, since they serve as technical adjuncts to surgeons. And preventive medicine and public health are organizationally oriented specialties involving no patient contact at all. Indeed, one of Rosow and Rose's most significant findings was that the more time a specialist spent with patients, the greater the chances that s/he would be involved in a divorce suit.

In general, then, persons in humanistically oriented professions and specialties seem predisposed to divorce, either by easier involvement with alternative partners, by provoking jealousy of the time and attention they give to their patients, or by sensitization to qualities that may be missing in their marriages.

Clergy Marriages.   Just as there are differences between medical specialties in rates of marital failure, so there are differences between religious denominations in the extent to which the "calling" to the ministry takes precedence over family activities.

Table 12–4 shows that ministers in old established denominations almost always believed in keeping any commitments they might make to their families and deferring emergency demands for their services. Those

Table 12–4 **Priority of Occupation or Family, for Ministers Employed by Churches versus Sects**

Definite Time Scheduled for Husband to Be with Family for Companionship	TYPE OF ORGANIZATION	
	Church	Sect
1. Husband would leave family to call meeting of church board on request of important church official.	0	73%
2. Husband would leave family to give counsel on religious or ethical matter.	4%	88%
Number of cases	26	36

Adapted from Scanzoni, 1965: 398–400. *Source:* Protestant ministers and their wives in a metropolitan area. A church was defined as a denomination that accepts the social environment, whereas a sect rejects it. Reciprocal percentages of respondents said the husband should either postpone the job request or decide on the urgency of the particular request.

employed by smaller sects usually believed in putting unexpected vocational demands ahead of family commitments.

In the same study, Scanzoni (1965) found that the wives of the ministers reported that the demands of the church similarly interfered with their own companionship with their husbands and children. Eighty-two percent of wives in small sects served as "assistant pastors," helping with church music, religious education, women's groups, and so on. Conversely, only 19 percent of the pastors' wives in large denominations were involved in the church enough to interfere with their family life. The parallel between the two partners' active involvement in the sectarian congregations and lesser involvement in the "church" congregations suggests an agreement on values between husband and wife that probably minimizes marital friction in the sectarian case, even though family activities are interfered with. For both partners, the church takes priority over the family.

Executive Marriages. In 1952 Whyte noted the pervasive conformity pressures placed by many corporations on wives of rising corporate executives:

> One rule transcends all others: *Don't be too good.* Keeping up with the Joneses is still important. But where in pushier and more primitive times it implied going substantially ahead of the Joneses, today keeping up means just that: keeping up. . . . The good corporation wife . . . does not make friends uncomfortable by clothes too blatantly chic, by references to illustrious forebears, or by excessive good breeding. And she avoids intellectual pretensions like the plague.

Presumably, wives of "organization men" in such corporations either conformed to expectations and sacrificed their personal freedom or defied those pressures and suffered repercussions. A husband caught between an independent wife and a possessive employer may choose to sacrifice either his marriage or his job, but he is not likely to avoid feeling caught in the crossfire. Conversely, a wife caught between the demands of a possessive husband and her own authenticity is not likely to resolve her dilemma easily.

The Ambassador's Marriage.   For persons in the public eye, occupational pressures on both marriage partners are heavy. For ambassadors to a foreign country, the symbolic nature of their position (representing their country abroad) makes these pressures particularly acute.

Hochschild (1969) found that ambassadors' wives were not supposed to hold "controversial" jobs (such as practicing law or medicine or taking a business position). They were expected to clear with the embassy before joining organizations and to limit their entertaining to persons "whom your husband should know and with whom he works." In formal social situations, both partners were subject to severe restrictions:

> According to protocol, everyone rises whenever the Ambassador or his wife enters a room, even when many people are present. Chiefs of mission and their wives precede others in entering or leaving rooms. And no one should leave a function before the Ambassador and his wife leave. This means that, out of courtesy to restless subordinates, the Chief of mission and his wife usually leave fairly early, in order to allow their subordinates to go home.

In such a conspicuous position, neither spouse can be "just a person," but both must conform to the demands of the system. The need for social propriety may reduce the divorce rate for such persons below what it might otherwise be, but at the same time allows little room for personal intimacy and authenticity between the partners. Hochschild noted that most ambassadors' wives attended ten or more dinners, luncheons, or receptions every week. Involvement with so many people prevented them from getting to know very many individuals well. If this busy schedule prevents intimacy with potential friends, it seems likely to reduce intimacy with the spouse also. So, the quality of the marriage is affected by this very demanding occupation, even though the involvement of the partners is at least unofficially bilateral.

Separation from the Family

Save for those rare individuals who work at home, employment takes people away from home. We are so used to this phenomenon that we fail to recognize that going to work means leaving home, leaving the spouse, and engaging in a marital separation, no matter how brief.

Working Hours. How the marriage is affected depends on how long the separation lasts. Where one partner is gone a "normal" length of time, s/he may be missed, but is not likely to be charged with marital delinquency. But persons whose working hours are longer than usual often find their prolonged absence resented. When the partner can't be home for dinner or, worse yet, doesn't come home at all, the marriage suffers. Meals together, evenings together, and nights together are everyday opportunities for husband-wife interaction. The less one partner is present, the less opportunity there is for the marriage to maintain its vitality. Occasional absences are tolerable and may even introduce new vitality into the relationship. Regular or prolonged absence, may cause progressive alienation.

Some of our marriage counseling clients have had so little time together during the past week that they have not been able to discuss their agenda item for the next counseling session. Between the demands of their separate vocations and their children, they have had no communication in depth since the previous week in our livingroom.

Working hours may be normally long but abnormally inconvenient or irregular. Table 12–5 shows that the marriages of working-class men on the day shift were consistently better than those on any other shift in terms of the husband's satisfaction with his marriage, his success in avoiding friction with his wife, and his ability to agree with his wife on who does what activities around the house. Rotating from shift to shift every week most disastrously undermined men's ability to agree with their wives on who was going to do what around the house.

Being away from home evenings interfered most with companionship within the home and joint activities outside the home. Being on rotation also interfered with sexual relations (because they tend to become patterned in most marriages?), with decision making, and with maintain-

Table 12–5   Effects of Shift Work on Marriage

Aspect of Marriage	SHIFT			
	Day	Evening	Night	Rotating
Husband's marital satisfaction	Best	Third	Worst	Second
Avoidance of friction	Best	Third	Second	Worst
Coordination of family chores	Best	Third	Second	Worst
Number of cases	219	164	131	391

Adapted from Mott, Mann, McLoughlin, and Warwick, 1965: 126. *Source:* Blue-collar workers in continuous process industries in the east-central U.S. Generally speaking, the day schedule worked from 7:00 A.M. to 3:00 P.M., the evening shift from 3:00 to 11:00 P.M., and the night shift from 11:00 P.M. to 7:00 A.M. The rotating shift changed shifts each week.

ing understanding (presumably because both partners are confused about what is going on in their complex lives). The night shift interfered most with the husband's ability to protect his wife from prowlers. In general, then, marriage tends to suffer whenever anyone works an abnormal schedule, but alternative unusual schedules create correspondingly different problems.

Although most shift workers hold blue-collar jobs, some are engaged in professions that serve the public around the clock:

> Since Joe started working at the hospital on a different schedule every week, I've begun to feel like we are roommates rather than marriage partners. It's not his fault. The trouble is nobody wants to work at night and so he and his partners have resolved that dilemma by saying that each of them will have to take over the long night hours on an alternating basis. What it means for me, though, is that two thirds of the time he just isn't around when I have finished my day's work and would like to relax with him. We do the best we can, but it isn't very good. I could count on him more when we were single and he was a med student than I can now when he's married to his job!

Spatial Separation.   In some jobs, the problem is not when but where the work takes place. Commuting extends the separation into the crucial evening hours, and may so thoroughly deplete the commuter's energies that s/he has little energy left after finally getting home. Public transportation sometimes is comfortable enough to minimize this problem, but anyone who has driven home through rush-hour traffic is likely to become not only exhausted but grouchy. Tired and irritable, s/he may be in no mood for interaction with anyone after arriving home in body but not in soul.

Gans (1967) found that few Levittown husbands complained about commuting up to 40 minutes each way, but longer commutes were so wearing that wives also suffered. Commuting an hour or more did not prevent the average couple from spending as much time as they wanted with one another, but the husband arrived home so late that he saw less of early-to-bed children and couldn't relieve his wife of the children during the dinner-preparation crunch. Wives complained that men exhausted from the journey home were hard to live with. These research findings suggest the benefits that families may achieve by reducing the distance between residence and workplace.

Where work is not located in a remote office but in a territory that must be covered by traveling far from home by car or plane, the interference with family life becomes correspondingly severe. Traveling persons may be away from home for days at a time, leaving both partners on their own rather than dependent on one another for companionship and support. For the traveler who must spend his/her nights away from home, life can be pretty grim after hours. Alternative companionship for both the traveling spouse and the stay-at-home spouse may relieve that grimness but create problems of extramarital involvement. Such involvement is particularly likely for the traveling partner because s/he is deprived of the physical and emotional comforts of home and freed from the social pressures of the home community. No wonder, then, that one study of white-collar occupations found that traveling salesmen had the unhappiest marriages (Lang, 1932).

For persons faced with repeated and prolonged separations, correspondingly greater energy must be invested if the absence is to be compensated for:

> One of the pleasantest memories of my childhood was the Saturday noon luncheon. Because my father's work took him out of town a lot, we saw very little of him during the week. However, he always arranged to eat lunch with us on Saturdays and then do something special together for the afternoon. This weekly reunion was one of the things my mother, brother, and I always looked forward to. We gained a feeling of closeness by relaxing with my father for a few hours. We also worked harder all week so we could make him happy with our accomplishments.

Looking at the demands of a job upon people's energy and time makes us realize how much vocational patterns determine marriage relationships. Sharing affection and talking about separate experiences may be desired, but cannot be achieved without available time and energy. Most people feel they have no choice. In our situation:

> It was the bout with cancer that made me [Bob] face up to the fact that I could have more of what I wanted in life, and that was more meaningful human relations with those with whom I worked, with my wife and with friends. I quit teaching large university classes where no personal discussions could occur. I gave up research and the pressures that went with that. I gave up the time-consuming staff and committee meetings. I also gave up the myth of security. Margaret and I joined forces in the contributions we felt able to give to others professionally. Going free lance gave us the ability to determine our own schedule.
>
> The payoff has been tremendous individually and marriage-wise. We work at home, saving commuting time as well as providing a more informal and comfortable environment for our clients and workshop participants. We work together in counseling and group work and all the homework that these entail. Our contribution is richer because of our sharing during and between appointments. We can schedule all the free time we need to engage in joint or separate recreation. Because of our solid base of time spent together, other friendships are welcome and pose less of a threat.
>
> Before Bob had cancer, I[Margaret] thought we had a good marriage. I thought that what we had was all there was. I did not realize how

little I knew my "most significant other." Most of his energy poured into his vocation; most of mine into family, housework, and the usual volunteer concerns. There was little time left for sharing except as we overlapped in raising our children. As we have taken charge of our time commitments and the spending of our energy resources, we have chosen to spend more time together in rewarding activities that in turn have enriched our knowledge of and appreciation for one another.

The Marital Cost of Occupational Success

Thus far we have discussed some effects of the involvement of one partner in occupations with varying requirements. But most white-collar occupations do not have fixed requirements. They do not begin at a certain time and end at a certain time, punching in and out on a time clock. Most of the readers of this book will have considerable leeway in how their career is to be pursued. The most dramatic example in our own lives occurred when I (Bob) was first hired by the University of Michigan. The chairman of the Sociology Department took me aside and advised me: "If you want to become a full professor, you will spend your evenings and weekends doing the research on which promotion depends." I thanked him for the advice but vowed not to follow it. I spent my evenings and weekends with my family (and never became a full professor!). The net result was less income for the family but more time for them, which all of us preferred. Our experience illustrates the principle that, beyond a certain point, occupational success conflicts with marital success.

When occupation and family collide, a couple's values are tested. If they hold the same values, family solidarity is preserved, even if the family is subordinated:

I must admit that I am jealous of the fact that Mel has the luxury of an expense account and travels a good deal, and I do get irritated when he fails to call me and say he'll be late for dinner. But I realize that if he is to progress up the ladder of success, he will have to relinquish time at home in favor of the office. If he gets so engrossed in his work that he forgets to call me, it's a sign he's putting his heart and soul into his work.

Both the preceding case and the following one reflect congruent values. In the previous case, both husband and wife preferred a heavy occupational involvement. In the next one, both partners preferred a limited involvement:

I purposely chose a job with a company that I felt would not hold the tension and continuous pushing of a big corporation. I don't want to come home in the evening tense from the day's work and preoccupied with my job. Both Nancy and I feel that the family should be of first importance before my job. I intend to do my best in the engineering field and to strive to progress, but not to the point of sacrificing my time with my family. For example, I will take a lesser salary if it means being able to spend more time with my family or living in a territory where the children are happy with school and friends and Nancy and I are happy.

Even though both couples agreed on the occupational/family balance problem, this does not mean that their marriages were similar. The couple who put career ahead of family reaped such values as security, affluence, and prestige but sacrificed the possibility of companionship and dialogue. The couple who clamped limits on career demands sacrificed their standard of living for the sake of their relationship.

Although there is little direct evidence about the costs of occupational success, the indirect evidence turns up in a variety of ways.

Table 12–6 shows an enormous difference between the marital happiness of both partners in "successful" and "unsuccessful" careers. The happiest marriages were those where men remained in the same occupation and worked so little that their income declined relative to the cost of living. Conversely, the more effort men invested in changing careers and increasing their incomes the less happy their marriages were either for themselves or for their wives. This reflects the balance of investment in occupation and marriage. The more energy a man puts into his career, the less will be available for his marriage and the less satisfactory this marriage will be either for him or for his wife. Conversely, the less energy he puts into his career (within limits—all these men were in middle-class occupations and had enough money to live on), the greater the time and energy available for the wife.

So far we have noted the deleterious effect of occupational involve-

Table 12–6   Marital Happiness of Husbands and Wives, by Husband's Early/Mid-Career Financial Success and Career Changes

	EARLY/MID-CAREER INCOME CHANGE			
	Declined	*Stable*	*Increased*	*Greatly Increased*
Changed Careers?	No	Yes	Yes	Yes
Marital Happiness				
Husband's decreased	10%	53%	57%	62%
Wife's decreased	26%	52%	60%	71%
Number of cases	19	73	35	21

Adapted from Dizard, 1968: 61. *Source:* 400 middle-class Chicago couples originally interviewed by Burgess and Wallin in 1939 and reinterviewed in 1955–60. Husbands whose incomes increased greatly were defined as those whose incomes increased more than three times the increase in the cost of living. Career changes were defined as movement from a nonrisky salaried position to risky entrepreneurial, commissioned, or private practicing professional work (or in exceptional cases in the opposite direction). Reciprocal percentages of husbands and wives experienced either stable or increased happiness over the interval from early to middle marriage.

ment on marriages that persist, but in extreme cases wives neglected by their husbands decide to leave rather than suffer in solitude.

Table 12–7 shows that over half the recently divorced middle-class wives felt their husbands were overinvolved in their jobs, whereas only a few still-married wives made this complaint. Even after allowing for the possibility that divorced wives are more critical generally than still-married women, these percentages probably mean that unilateral occupational overinvolvement contributed to the failure of these marriages. The costliness of overinvolvement is especially noteworthy in view of the fact that none of the divorced wives complained that their husbands were underachievers. Incidentally, the divorced husbands seldom complained about their jobs, so the typical pattern was a man preoccupied and pleased with his work while his wife felt neglected and rejected.

Differing Values. We have suggested that marriage suffers from one partner's occupational overinvolvement, even if the other partner holds similar values. The preceding paragraph suggests, however, that marriage suffers most when the involved partner and the stay-at-home partner differ in their values. If husband and wife disagree, the employed partner's devotion (or lack of it) to work becomes a source of contention. Pressure to work harder may come from either partner. Usually it is the employed partner who devotes more time to his/her job than the stay-at-home partner thinks s/he should. The participant in the occupational system is exposed to incentives and competition. Successful business executives reach the top precisely through their willingness to subordinate their lives to the demands of the job. In the words of Henry (1949):

> All the successful executives have strong mobility drives. They feel the necessity to move continually upward and to accumulate the rewards of increased accomplishment.... All show high drive and

Table 12–7 Satisfaction with Husband's Job, for Married and Recently Divorced Women

	MARITAL STATUS	
Satisfaction with Husband's Job	*Married*	*Divorced*
Satisfied	87%	37%
Dissatisfied due to underachievement	4	0
Dissatisfied due to overinvolvement	9	63
Total	100%	100%
Number of cases	112	24

Adapted from Scanzoni, 1968: 453. *Source:* Middle-class sample of existing marriages and of women divorced less than two years in a large northern city.

achievement desire. They conceive of themselves as hard-working and achieving people who must accomplish in order to be happy. ... The executive is essentially an active, striving, aggressive person. His underlying personality motivations are active and aggressive. ... This constant motivator, unfortunately, cannot be shut off. It may be part of the reason why so many executives find themselves unable to take vacations leisurely or to stop worrying about already solved problems.

Achievement drive is prized by some partners as a source of pride and vicarious gratification. Nevertheless, by definition, a hard-working spouse is seldom home and even then his/her thoughts are liable to be elsewhere. LeMasters (1957) reported that General Motors provided its chief executive with complete living facilities near his office so he wouldn't have to go home except on weekends. A study of Protestant ministers found that half of them had not taken a single day off for recreation with their wives during the preceding month (Douglas, 1965). Many of the neglected wives felt alienated from their husbands. For a wife with high affiliation needs and low mobility aspirations, occupational devotion is distressing. She pressures her husband to stay home and take longer vacations. To accede to her values, he must sacrifice his own ambitions. In neither case are both partners satisfied.

Sometimes the ambitious partner is the wife and the familistic one the husband. Westoff (1961) found more young wives than husbands willing to make sacrifices so the man could get ahead. Specifically, more wives were willing to move to a strange part of the country, leave friends behind, send the children to a poorer school, and postpone having the next child. The biggest difference was in the partners' willingness to have the man spend less time with the wife and children. Two thirds of the wives but less than one third of the husbands were willing to sacrifice family companionship to vocational ambition.

Perhaps this willingness of wives to make sacrifices results from deference to what they think the husband wants. When a wife pushes her husband beyond his own ambitions, however, the result is conspicuously unhappy. Such a man may escape into fishing expeditions or fraternal lodges. Sometimes he makes halfhearted attempts to please, but since her values are not his, these efforts are not likely to last long. Even if they did, the compensation in prestige and promotion might not seem worthwhile to him. Indeed, since promotion brings increased responsibility, it might only make such a man feel trapped. Conflicting values never have easy solutions. Such couples are poorly matched. Theoretically, they never should have married in the first place. They may have to endure continuing conflict until the spouse retires from the outside world.

Kinship Costs of Occupational Success. Although less relevant to marriage, the effects of occupational success on kinship ties are analogous to the effects on marital ties. Presumably, persons who are occupationally successful will spend less time visiting with their relatives just as they spend less time interacting with their spouses.

Table 12–8 shows that business and professional men who moved up in the world above their fathers saw less of their relatives than men who were born into that occupational level. Ditto for wives married to husbands in higher status jobs than their fathers had held. Apparently, occupational mobility takes a toll of kinship ties as well as marriage bonds. Kin who were "left behind" occupationally might be replaced with neighbors at the new social level, but Stuckert found that mobile men and women also had fewer ties with neighbors. Apparently occupational mobility requires so much time and energy that less is left for informal social life of any kind.

Moving the Whole Family

Movement up the ladder of success affects the family indirectly, but when the breadwinner moves to another community the whole family must pull up stakes and go, too. Some moves mean at least a new location within the United States, but some more drastically uproot the family and plant them in an alien environment. Both moves, in varying degrees, exact a toll on members of the family and affect relationships among them for better or for worse.

Domestic Movement.   The burden of domestic moving falls mostly on the wife. Men often feel better about themselves after moving, especially when they move in order to better their careers. Wives often feel worse. The net result is that a given move is likely to strain the relationship between the partners because they have contradictory vested interests and correspondingly contradictory costs/benefits.

In a national sample, Butler, McAllister, and Kaiser (1973) found that men who moved were happier than those who stayed in the same place, but their wives were not. The biggest difference was in reported

Table 12–8   Visits with Kin, by Occupational Mobility of Husband and Wife

	PERCENTAGE WITH WEEKLY VISITS WITH OWN KIN	
	Occupationally Stable	*Occupationally Unstable*
Husbands	70%	42%
Wives	78%	43%
Number of cases	9	24

Adapted from Stuckert, 1963: 305. *Source:* Professional and corporate executive families in Milwaukee, Wisconsin, who had parents or relatives living in the area. Mobility was determined by comparing the occupation of the husband and his father and (for the wife) of the husband and *her* father. Reciprocal percentages visited with kin less than once a week.

symptoms of mental disorders: men who moved had fewer symptoms than men who stayed, but their wives reported more symptoms than wives who stayed put. The net result was a wide gap between husbands in mentally healthy condition and wives plagued by emotional problems.

Parallel to this divergence is Gallaway's finding (1969) that men generally moved to better-paying jobs. Working wives, by contrast, at best held their own financially and often lost income as a result of moving. Presumably, the women were involuntarily deprived of good jobs when their husbands decided to move and had to take whatever they could find in the new location.

The typical pattern is for married men to move because they want to and married women because they have to. The women's movement has not left this inequity unchallenged. As early as 1973 an Associated Press article by John Cunniff reported that about one quarter of the corporations questioned by Atlas Van Lines "were encountering increasing reluctance by employees to intercity transfers." Family objections were the chief reason why some men turned down opportunities to move to jobs paying more money and requiring more responsibility. Cunniff concluded that "it is the emancipated housewife who no longer is willing to take orders from corporate headquarters."

Wives' dissatisfaction with decisions to move can be substantially reduced through participation in decision making. Jones (1973) found that 36 percent of wives whose husbands decided unilaterally to move were unhappy with their new community, but only 21 percent were unhappy when they and their husbands decided jointly on the move. The more active the wife was in making the decision, the more satisfied she was. Wives who were consulted not only by their husbands but by his superiors and those who actually made an exploratory trip to the new community before deciding whether to move were the most satisfied of all. This suggests that the negative impact of moving on wives can be sharply reduced if they have an active, informed, and equal part in the decision.

The worst period is just before and just after the move. Jones (1973) found that women were particularly anxious and nervous during the fortnight prior to the arrival of the moving van. For two weeks after the move, they had trouble sleeping and felt depressed and lonely. For the whole month before and after the move, they were irritable and subject to crying spells.

Several aspects of family life suffered during this period, especially family recreation and relaxing at home with the husband. Children, on the other hand, received more than the usual emotional support, perhaps because mothers worried about their adjustment to the new community and about their problem of losing old friends and making new ones.

Transitional problems were especially severe for couples who had never moved before. The more often couples moved, the easier it became for them, and the more the wife took over. Whereas only 60 percent of wives moving for the first or second time saw themselves as the central figures in the moving process, 85 percent of wives who had moved 16 or more times played a central part. As moving became more familiar, husbands turned over responsibility to their wives.

Barrett and Noble (1973) found that for children moving became more difficult as they grew older. Half again as many children over age 10 found it difficult to change schools as did children age 6 to 10. Three times as many older children found it difficult to make friends. Young children are not so tied to either schools or friends as to find moving very difficult, but adolescents find it more disruptive.

The unsettling effects of moving on school-age children are seen in Table 12–9. The larger the number of communities that boys and girls had lived in after starting first grade, the higher the proportion who became delinquent. The negative impact of moving held even when analysis was controlled by rural-urban residence, socioeconomic status, and broken-unbroken home status. This suggests that, even under the best family conditions, moving from community to community is likely to affect school-age children adversely. So, not only wives but children tend to suffer when the family moves very often.

Moving is not all bad, although we have focused on the problems that wives and children face when the husband/father decides to move. Jones found that the emotion most commonly felt by movers was excitement and exhilaration. Also, moving drastically reduced the number of wives who were bothered by having time on their hands! But until couples have moved often enough to learn how to do it gracefully, they need to be sensitive to one another in making the decision to move and in implementing that decision. If they approach the issue carefully, they can reduce the costs to the family and increase the benefits.

International Movement. Domestic movement temporarily disrupts the lives of family members, but the consequences of an international move last longer. Any move severs old relationships and requires making new ones. But moving abroad also requires learning one's way around in a

Table 12–9 Adolescent Delinquency, by Spatial Mobility

	NUMBER OF COMMUNITIES ATTENDED SCHOOL		
Delinquent Behavior	*One*	*Two to Four*	*Five or More*
High	23%	30%	37%
Low	77	70	63
Total	100%	100%	100%
Number of cases	505	1,320	479

Recomputed from Nye, 1958: 63. *Source:* High school students from three small cities in Washington State. The sample consisted of approximately equal numbers of boys and girls.

new culture and learning a new language. So international moves require correspondingly longer and more strenuous adaptations:

> *With each move that we have been forced to make due to my husband's military career, I find myself less and less able to get excited about learning a new language or involving myself in the native culture. I also feel reluctant to make friends within the American community abroad because I know the time will come when those ties must be broken. It's too painful to make and break friends so frequently. With less affection available from family and friends, I have become more dependent on my husband's attention and find it harder to accept his commitment to his career. I've become increasingly lonely and depressed.*

Nash (1969) found that housekeeping for American women in a Spanish city was complicated by the unreliability of municipal utilities, the difficulty of getting appliances repaired, and "the hopeless struggle to turn the maid into an adjunct of the American way of life." (Presumably, many of their husbands experienced similar frustrations with their Spanish colleagues and employees.) Wives learned the hard way that maids and handymen seldom if ever did things when they said they would and that "mañana" did not mean literally "tomorrow" but some indefinite time in the future.

The impact on children of moving to Spain differed, depending on their ages. Young children made new friends and learned the new language easily. Emotional and behavioral problems occurred chiefly among adolescents, especially in families impaired by the absence of one or both parents or by a lack of harmony between the parents. The adolescents generally weathered the stress reasonably well, provided that their family life was rich and harmonious. Had it not been a large city with three English-language schools, however, they would have faced the more difficult adjustments of attending a Spanish-language school or having to leave home to attend a boardingschool elsewhere.

Despite these difficulties in coping with an alien environment—or rather, perhaps, because of them—the American families found themselves drawn more closely together. Husbands and wives were forced to rely on one another for assistance in cutting through the difficulties they encountered in the community, and the whole family typically spent their leisure time together because other English-speaking people lived too far away and their command of Spanish was too limited to enable them to enjoy their neighbors. Spanish culture provided a bonus via fiesta holidays when businesses and schools were closed and all members of the family could be home together. The customary three-hour siesta enabled working members of the family to return home for lunch. This combination of fiestas and siestas meant that the typical employed person was less occupationally involved than s/he would have been back home in the States. So, going abroad had certain advantages for these families at the same time that it challenged their adaptability.

BILATERAL OCCUPATIONAL INVOLVEMENT

All marriages require at least one person to bring in the income needed for the family to live on. Whether the spouse also goes to work is not compulsory, but an option that an increasing number of couples are exercising. Wives may not work continuously but drop out when they have children and reenter the labor market sometime later. An increasing minority, however, pursue their careers continuously, either because they choose not to have children at all or because they make other arrangements for the care of their children.

Among Chicago married couples in their middle years, Dizard (1968) found that nearly all wives had worked at some point in their marriage. Only 14 percent had never been employed outside the home, but only 28 percent were working at the time of the interview. This means that a majority (the remaining 58 percent) were dropouts who had worked at some time but then had quit.

That employment was not entirely optional for these wives is suggested by the fact that the chances that the wife was still working were directly related to what had happened to the husband's income. If his income had decreased since early marriage, the chances that she was working were fifty-fifty. But if his income had greatly increased, only 12 percent of the wives were working.

Career versus Children.

The chief reason why married women drop out of the labor force is to have children. How long they stay out depends on how committed they are to their careers. Poloma and Garland (1971) found that most professional women such as physicians, lawyers, and college professors interrupted their careers with the arrival of children and that this disruption typically lasted at least five years.

Eventually, many women return to work at least parttime. Table 12–10 shows the proportion of married women who were employed either part-time or full-time despite having children to care for.

Whether women ever return to work depends on how many children they have. If their first child is succeeded by a second one, the mother acquires the burden of infant care again. Each succeeding child reduces the chances that she will be employed. Table 12–11 shows the steady decrease in the proportion of women working with increasing numbers of children.

Hoffman and Nye note the irony that the larger the number of children, the greater the need for supplementary income but the less the mother is able to earn it:

While more children increase the need for income, that need is more than offset by the greater "costs" of work for women with large

Table 12-10   Part-time and Full-time Employment of Married Women, by Age of Youngest Child

Weekly Working Hours	AGE OF YOUNGEST CHILD					
	None	Under 1	1 year	2–5 years	6–11 years	12–17 years
None	36%	87%	84%	71%	61%	32%
1–29 hours/week	12	9	12	17	22	43
30+ hours/week	52	4	4	12	16	25
Total	100%	100%	100%	100%	99%	100%
Number of cases	42	130	137	239	194	28

Adapted from Walker, 1970: 9. *Source:* Syracuse, New York, housewives aged 25–39.

families. These costs include such things as child care if the children are of preschool age, and the greater amount of housework, child supervision, and other duties characteristic of large families. Women with large families may also encounter more adverse comment about "leaving their families" to take employment than do women with small families (1974: 21).

The Careers of Highly Educated Women.   Whether married women ever work, whether they continue to work during the child-bearing years, and how fast they return to work after dropping out to bear children are influenced by their education. By contrast with Dizard's middle-American women who had dropped out and not returned to work, Ginzberg's (1966) sample of highly educated women had nearly all returned to work. All of them had studied at the Columbia University graduate school for at least a year between 1945 and 1951. By the time they were interviewed in 1963, three-fourths of those with children had gone back to work. Nineteen percent had gone back while the child was still an infant, 39 percent while s/he was between 1 and 4 years old, and another 16 percent when s/he was 5 or older. Presumably, some of the remaining 26 percent who were still at home when interviewed subsequently returned to work, increasing even further the proportion who returned after the child reached school age.

Ginzberg's sample of women with the intellectual ability and the

Table 12-11   Proportion of Women Employed, by Number of Children

	NUMBER OF CHILDREN					
	None	One	Two	Three	Four	Five
Proportion employed	51%	38%	32%	32%	24%	14%
Number of cases	168	210	378	294	169	77

Adapted from Walker, 1970: 8. *Source:* Syracuse, New York, area sample. Reciprocal percentages of women were not employed.

career motivation to attend a first-class graduate school were so vocationally committed that they tended to marry late, to bear few children, and to pursue their careers relatively undisrupted even when they did have children. Their graduate degrees enabled them to find employment that was satisfying and financially rewarding.

Table 12–12 shows that even for these highly committed women, having children altered their work history, and the more children they had, the greater the interference. Whereas most of the childless women worked continuously, less than half of those who bore a single child managed to stay in the labor force without disruption. Having a second child shifted the modal pattern to interrupted work, while a third child prevented most mothers from returning to work despite their graduate training. These data suggest the difficulty of combining employment and childbearing when the latter occurs repeatedly.

Conflicts between Husbands' and Wives' Careers. In addition to problems in combining employment with childbearing, married women sometimes face conflicts between their careers and those of their husbands. These problems are most acute when both partners have professional or executive careers rather than more routine occupations.

Poloma and Garland (1971) found that most women physicians, attorneys, and college professors had subordinated their careers to their husbands' and children's needs. Being wives and mothers was their primary concern while being professional persons took second place. This was symbolized by their preference for being introduced in social situations as Mrs. _____ rather than Dr. _____. Most of them worked fewer hours than their husbands, brought less work home at night, and participated in fewer professional meetings. Even academic women whose advancement depended on mobility between universities routinely put the husband's career ahead of attractive job offers. Conversely, most of these professional women routinely followed their husband's job opportunities even though, in the case of physicians and attorneys, this meant the total loss of their clientele.

Table 12–12 Work History of Highly Educated Women, by Number of Children

Work History	NUMBER OF CHILDREN			
	None	One	Two	Three +
Continuous	83%	48%	29%	7%
Interrupted	15	29	39	40
Terminated at least temporarily	2	23	32	53
Total	100%	100%	100%	100%

Adapted from Ginzberg, 1966: 82. *Source:* Married women who had studied in Columbia University graduate school for at least one year between 1945 and 1951.

Poloma and Garland cited friends who had developed more egalitarian solutions to these problems "such as the husband and wife residing in different cities to maximize career opportunities, the husband and wife agreeing to alternate the right to accept positions out of town in case of job termination or job dissatisfaction, and even a case in which a young child was being cared for in another city by the husband while the wife completed research for a book."

A note from friends of ours reported:

> With job-hunting as hard as it is this year, we have felt lucky to get joint offers from the University of Wisconsin. This will be the first move in twenty-five years. We have been more reluctant to leave than eager to go to the new place. Tom will be developing a new administration program at the School of Social Work in Madison, and Nancy will be teaching at the environmentally oriented branch of the University of Wisconsin in Green Bay 100 miles away. With an apartment at each end of the line, we will be able to see each other only on weekends (weather permitting). Daughter Karen will continue in the School of Natural Resources here in Ann Arbor, and Jon will be a second grader staying with his father in Madison.

Helen and Vern Raschke were unwilling to split up their family by taking professional positions in different communities. As a result, they found their professional mobility severely handicapped. In Helen's words:

> When we were married, Vern was in his 3rd year of graduate school and I was in my first. We agreed in advance that we would have a dual career, equalitarian marriage in which both of our careers would be of equal importance and both of us would share equally in the housework and child care. It seemed like it would be the best of both worlds, especially for me because of the elimination of sex-role stereotyping in the home and in the work world.
>
> As a result of this agreement, Vern turned down an offer when he finished his Ph.D. and took a temporary teaching position so I could finish my coursework in graduate school. The next year he was offered another teaching position but would not take it until I had found a definite position in the same geographic area. Taking the one-year position hindered him somewhat because he could not start any research or really get anything accomplished in 9 months. However, from our "joint perspective," it was more important that I get my coursework finished prior to leaving the University.
>
> After the second year in our new jobs, we began to have doubts about staying permanently in the area and began serious attempts to find teaching positions elsewhere. From the very beginning of our job hunting, from the initial probing to the dead-earnest searching, we kept bumping into the invisible "brick wall" of interest by prospective employers in ONE of us but not the other.
>
> The school year 1975–76 was especially frustrating because I was

offered a very good position at a large university in a large metropolitan area, had 2 weeks in which to accept or reject the offer, and had to finally reject it because Vern could not find anything in the same geographic area. I was interviewed for a teaching position in another large metropolitan area but the Chairperson heard, via the grapevine, that prior to my going for the interview, Vern had called every college and university in a radius of 50 miles. Again, there were no openings and I have the intuitive feeling that I was not offered the position (after the interview) because the Chairperson knew I could not accept it unless Vern had a job and the Chairperson did not want to wait the 2 weeks it would take to offer and then probably have me refuse it. Vern interviewed for a position at a large university and "leveled" about my needing a job, also, in the same area. The Chairperson was very interested in Vern but there was only one opening at that university and nothing in the area that I could locate. These are examples of what happened all year—some staged a little differently but all ending the same.

From our personal vantage points, our careers are hindered by each of us not being free to take the best job offer without having to consider the other. Sometimes, I feel as if I have an albatross around my neck, holding me back, keeping me ever reaching out and up, but never grasping anything. On the other hand, even though we did not foresee these job difficulties, I feel my family life is valuable and the rewards outweigh the costs. I have thought about, but never seriously considered, taking what has become known as the "professional route." This is the husband and wife living in different geographic areas—where each can get the best job, and then commuting to see each other—distance and amount of spare money determining how often this happens. The couples we know who are doing this either have no children or one has a child or children from a previous marriage. Our children are adopted and very mischievous and energetic; I feel it would be most difficult to live separately (and expensive, given today's inflation). Therefore, this "professional route" does not seem very practical for us when the children are young.

Our careers are also hindered by neither of us having a "housewife" to take care of running our home and taking care of the children (ages 6 and 7). I wonder how many "known" women professors (or other successful career women) do not have outside help with housework and children. Even doing half the housework and child care is time consuming and exhausting when I have to rush to get it done to get my career work done.

At present, we are branching out into other areas so one of us will have some alternatives to teaching. In this era of tight academic jobs, we realize we need a broader "base" of skills. One of our problems has been that our specialties are the same but we have been working on going in different directions. Whether this will pay off remains to be seen.

We may be forced to reduce our standard of living so we can live on one salary, then whoever gets the best job offer, we will take that. The other will move to the area without a firm job commitment (against the principles of our marriage), either do research or writing or counseling, until something in the geographic area opened up. This could not be done except in a large metropolitan area.

None of the couples interviewed by Poloma and Garland in Akron had developed an equalitarian approach. Nor were equalitarian solutions always organizationally permitted even when they were wanted by a couple:

> Even in the case of the most egalitarian couple in our sample where both domestic and child-caring roles as well as breadwinning concerns were *shared* by both spouses, the university prohibited the couple from having equally successful careers. Being one of the few places that were willing to hire this professor team, the university employed the husband at a higher academic rank than his wife—in spite of the fact that both possessed equal qualifications. With the job offer otherwise being appealing, the couple was forced to accept this condition of the university (1971: 138).

Dual careers, then, are seldom equal careers, which means that bilaterally involved marriages are seldom symmetrical. Despite the movement for the liberation of women, most women and their husbands continue to treat the man as the primary breadwinner and the woman as the primary homemaker even when both are employed outside the home. However, those few couples who have made the leap to symmetrical, bilateral employment are pioneering a new way of living.

The Marital Consequences of Bilateral Occupational Involvement

In our earlier discussion of the consequences of unilateral occupational involvement, we saw that family life suffered when the employed partner was overinvolved in his/her work. Unilateral overinvolvement seldom means working as much as 80 hours a week, yet when both partners hold full-time jobs, that is precisely the number of hours they are collectively absent from the home. The drastic increase from 40 to 80 hours spent away from home when the second partner goes to work suggests how profound are the changes in family life. Because some wives (and occasional husbands) work only part time, the change is not always that dramatic. But most dual-career marriages involve full-time employment for both partners so that they differ sharply from one-career families.

Family Affluence. Two incomes are better than one. The most obvious consequence of the second partner's employment is the second paycheck. However, the second is seldom as big as the first. Indeed, for dual-career families as a whole, wives in 1971 generally earned less than half as much as their husbands (Hoffman and Nye, 1974).

How much the wife earns depends partly on whether she works full time and pursues an uninterrupted career line like her husband, or whether she drops out of the labor market during the childbearing and perhaps also the child-rearing years. The Rapoports (1971: 22) pointed out the adverse financial consequences of interrupting the woman's career:

> It is difficult for women to rise into positions of senior responsibility once they have dropped out for a substantial period however unprejudiced the work environment may be and however competent the woman may be. Whatever ambition she may have had prior to childbearing is often damped down in the experience of infant-care, and there are few with sufficient resilience to overcome not only the strains of re-entry into the competitive world of work but the extra effort required to make up for lost time, missed information and the development of expertise.

Conversely, if the woman is as dedicated to her career as the average man is to his, her income may bring a substantial increment to the family budget and move the family from a moderate- to a high-income level. Though such families have little leisure time, they can afford to dine at the best restaurants.

Some of the money earned by working wives disappears in income taxes. Some goes to meet the costs of working: meals out, working clothes, transportation (two cars instead of one), laundry, and babysitters. Despite the increased expenses, however, most working wives increase their family's disposable income.

What do two-income families do with their extra income? Hafstrom and Dunsing (1965) found that nonacademic employee families at the University of Illinois (married five to 16 years) spent more on recreational activities and equipment, clubs, education, books, magazines, records, and liquor. On the other hand, they spent less on vacations and weekend trips, perhaps because they could less easily spare time from their busy schedules. They spent more on expensive, durable purchases (20 percent more on houses, 23 percent more on large appliances, and 26 percent more on furniture). They bought more furnishings and new rather than secondhand cars, and replaced them faster. Indeed, they bought new things so fast that they went deeper into debt than one-income families. Perhaps they felt more confident about repaying installment credit with their double incomes. Finally, they spent 27 percent more on insurance premiums (their chief form of investment). Most of the extra insurance was taken on the life of the wife. Presumably, families that depend on the wife's earnings to repay installment indebtedness insure her to cushion themselves against the accidental loss of her income.

The more professionally oriented dual-career families in the Rapoports' study (1971) spent considerable amounts of their dual incomes on recreation to relieve the fatigue they experienced in carrying heavy work and family loads:

Many of the couples... indicated that the overloads experienced made it important to provide for leisure and holidays which may be relatively costly because of the need on such occasions to be looked after so that the marital pair can regenerate their energies. They work so hard in between that they often feel that they "deserve" to be pampered a bit on holidays, which eats still further into the incresse in family income that the extra worker provides (p. 297).

After all the direct and indirect costs of bilateral work have been absorbed, the increase in disposable family income is considerably less than the wife's salary figure suggests. Even so, most women who are employed in business and professional work commensurate with their training and ability gain so many satisfactions from their work that they would continue working even if they only broke even on the balance sheet of expenses and income. In actual practice, however, the increase in affluence is almost always appreciable, even if it is marginal in comparison to the husband's earnings.

Equal Power.   Although American families generally are more equalitarian than families in many other countries, major decisions (and especially financial decisions) tend to be controlled by the partner who is involved in the occupational system and who brings home the paycheck. Where both partners work outside the home, the balance of power shifts toward equality. In those rare cases where the wife works and the husband stays home, the balance shifts still further in the direction of wife dominance.

Table 12–13 shows that husbands in dual-career marriages in Detroit were less dominant than men whose wives were not employed. It also shows that the more fully the man was involved in his job, the more powerful he was at home. In Germany, Lupri (1969) found that the same was true for women: wives who worked full time gained more power than those who worked only part time. Similarly, the Detroit study showed that the more years a wife worked after marriage, the more equalitarian the marriage became. And studies in both Germany and France (Lupri, 1969; Michel, 1967) found that each partner's voice in family decision making

Table 12–13   Husband's Power, by Occupational Involvement of Husband and Wife

	WIFE NOT EMPLOYED			WIFE EMPLOYED		
	Husband Overtime	*Husband Full Time*	*Husband None*	*Husband Overtime*	*Husband Full Time*	*Husband None*
Husband's mean power	5.62	5.28	4.88	4.50	4.46	2.67
Number of families	195	218	25	44	57	3

From Blood and Wolfe, 1960: 40. *Source:* Representative sample of Detroit wives. A higher figure represents a larger share of marital decisions made by husbands.

was proportional to the size of the paychecks that s/he brought home. When both partners worked equal amounts of time but one brought home more income, that partner had the edge in family bargaining. Since few women earn as much as their husbands, equality in American marriages must be relatively rare. Even so, dual employment narrows the gap between the partners.

A shift in the balance of power does not automatically tell us whether dual-income couples make their decisions together or whether the husband simply surrenders certain areas of authority, creating equal–but–separate spheres of influence. Among government employees in Ghana, Oppong (1970) found that dual employment shifted the manner of decision making, not only away from male dominance, but also away from equal separateness. The larger the contribution that wives made to the family exchequer, the larger the number of couples who made decisions jointly.

Shared Housekeeping. When only one partner works outside the home, most of the housework is done by the stay-at-home spouse. But when both partners work away from home, getting the housework done becomes problematic and all members of the family must cooperate if the work is to get done.

Table 12–14 shows how the wife's share of the housework decreased when she went to work and as the husband had more time available. The only exception was that retired husbands did not help their stay-at-home wives as much as might be expected. The reason they helped out no more than full-time, working husbands seems to be that the wives could manage without their assistance. Circumstances did not pressure the couple to change a pattern that they had followed throughout their marriage. From a feminist point of view this was unjust, but when this study was made in the 1950s, neither men's nor women's consciousness had been raised enough to provide an ideological basis for shared housekeeping.

Even when both partners are employed, the shift toward shared

Table 12–14 Wife's Share of Housework, by Occupational Involvement of Husband and Wife

	OCCUPATIONAL INVOLVEMENT					
	Wife Not Employed			*Wife Employed*		
	Husband Overtime	*Husband Full Time*	*Husband None*	*Husband Overtime*	*Husband Full Time*	*Husband None*
Wife's share of housework	5.81	5.57	5.64	4.66	3.40	2.33
Number of cases	198	218	28	50	58	3

Adapted from Blood and Wolfe, 1960: 62. *Source:* Representative sample of Detroit wives. A higher figure represents a larger share of housework done by wives.

housekeeping seldom produces genuine equality. Blood and Hamblin (1958) found that husbands of nonworking wives did 15 percent of the total housework while husbands of working wives did 25 percent. This meant they worked almost twice as much as before, but they still fell short of equality.

The impact of the wife's employment on the division of labor in the home is complicated by the fact that wives who go to work generally have fewer children. Only when the age of the youngest child and the total number of children are taken into consideration is it possible to be sure that differences in the amount of work done by the husband and the wife reflect the wife's absence as such, rather than reflecting differences in family composition that reduce her need to stay home.

Walker (1970) found that the only difference between dual-career families and single-career families in Syracuse was that working wives did less housework. Neither their husbands, their children, nor their servants did any more to take up the slack. Detailed examination of her data shows, however, that the chief difference lay in child-care activities, presumably because employed women had fewer and/or older children than nonworking women.

Table 12–15 offers a partially controlled test of this problem by focusing on families with infants less than two years old. Because most of the wives who were "employed less than 15 hours a week" actually did not work at all, we will discuss Table 12–14 as if it compared nonemployed versus employed wives although the differences would presumably be even greater if we could select only those women who did not work at all and those who worked full time. The table shows that mothers resolved their problem by transferring some tasks to the infant's older siblings and more of them to the husband and other helpers (some paid, some unpaid). So adequately did the dual-career families reorganize

Table 12–15 Weekly Hours of Housework Performed by Specific Family Members and Other Helpers, by Wife's Occupational Involvement

| | WIFE'S OCCUPATIONAL INVOLVEMENT | |
Weekly Hours of Housework	Low	High
Wife	66 hours/week	52 hours/week
Husband	12	20
Children	4	8
Other helpers	4	12
Total	86 hours/week	92 hours/week
Number of families	181	16

Adapted from Walker, 1970: 12. *Source:* Syracuse families with youngest child under age 1. Low occupational involvement was defined as 0–14 hours/week (most of these women did not work at all). High occupational involvement was defined as 15 or more hours per week.

their housework that they increased the total hours of domestic service performed by everyone put together. Taking the husband/wife total alone, the husband's share almost doubled from 15 percent to 28 percent. The average husband in this group worked outside the home 53 hours a week, probably more than the average wife.

To sum up, bilateral occupational involvement shifts the balance of housework toward greater equality, but true equality is seldom achieved inside the home unless there is equal outside involvement and unless the total burden on the wife is so heavy that she is forced to appeal to her husband for help. Presumably, the more generously the husband responds to that call, the greater the wife's satisfaction will be with her dual-career marriage. In most cases, husbands respond only sluggishly, so the combined burden of inside and outside work on working wives is substantially greater than the inside working hours of wives who stay home.

Altered Socialization of Children.   The increased affluence, shared decision making, and altered division of labor that result from bilateral occupational involvement create a different environment for children. How they will be affected depends on so many intervening factors that the outcomes are less predictable than the marital consequences we have already discussed.

Much of the effect on children depends on how successful women are in integrating their outside work with their domestic tasks. This depends on their husbands' willingness to assist them. Bilateral employment in some cases creates an equalitarian environment of mutual respect and sharing between the father and mother from which children of both sexes benefit. In other cases, the wife's employment is seen by both parents as a consequence of the occupational failure of the father, with resulting demoralization of both fathers and sons.

Let us take first the adaptive situation and then turn to the general case. King, McIntyre, and Axelson (1968) found that the more the husband responded to his wife's employment by sharing the housework, the more both sons and daughters accepted the mother's employment. Vogel et al. (1970) found that children of working mothers not only saw their mothers as more competent but their fathers as warmer and more expressive, presumably because their fathers helped with child care.

Reflecting the employed woman's ability to integrate her outside and inside-the-home activities, Baruch (1972) found that daughters viewed bilateral occupational involvement positively only when their mothers succeeded in managing both roles to the mother's own satisfaction.

Given these findings, we can expect maternal employment to affect children adversely either when the mother is so heavily involved outside the home that she has little energy for her children, or when the father is so unresponsive that his passivity is resented by the rest of the family. The former problem can be alleviated by working part time rather than full time. The latter is resolvable only if the husband is willing to adapt to the changed circumstances of his family.

When children are very young, the most controversial question is whether a day care center is intrinsically inferior to house care. Kagan, Kearsley, and Zelazo (1976) conducted an exhaustive comparison between children cared for exclusively at home and children who had attended a group care center five days a week from 8:30 A.M. to 4:00 P.M. from the time they were 3½ months old until they were 30 months old. The center was staffed by mature, conscientious, and nurturant caretakers. Children who spent their daytime hours in the center were just as highly developed on a series of measures as were children who had been reared by their mothers. The only significant difference between the two groups was that children who had been in the center were less afraid of unfamiliar peers since they had had so much experience with strange children. Although well-qualified child-care facilities are difficult to find, this study suggests that group care under quality conditions can be just as satisfactory as home care.

Even when satisfactory day care has been found, a working mother of preschool children still has her hands full. Swartz (1976) described how she drove 40 miles each way to place her 30-month-old and 5-month-old children in the home of a woman near the place where she worked:

> We all had to awaken before 6 A.M. allowing enough time to dress, feed the children, and prepare for our long drive to the babysitter's home. On dark wintry mornings, it was especially difficult dressing the children in their heavy snowsuits and boots. It was a rare occasion when there was not a missing glove, boot, or hat!
>
> Our one-and-a-half hour commute provided daily hassles. Inevitably, both children in the back seat wanted the same fire truck at the same time. Ever try to negotiate a peace settlement in the back seat while driving 55 miles per hour in rush-hour traffic? Every gas station attendant on the route knew us for the needed emergency pit-stops after the cry "I need to pee!"
>
> While driving to work one morning, a strange noise erupted from the back seat. Looking through the rear view mirror, I noticed that the baby had just vomited all over himself and the seat. Almost losing control of the car, I finally managed to steer the car off the road and to clean him as best I could. If the children were too sick to take to the babysitter's, either I had to stay home or scramble to find a one- or two-day sitter to come to the house. One day, my babysitter informed me that my son had gashed his head; I had to leave work immediately to drive him to a nearby hospital emergency room for treatment.

The older children become, the more appropriate it is for them to be left alone. Indeed, by the time they reach adolescence, they may benefit from having their mother away from home part of the time. Douvan and Adelson (1966) found that daughters of part-time working mothers showed "an independence of thought and values generally rare among girls." Ordinarily, middle-class girls are liable to be oversocialized. If the mother works, this danger is minimized. If she works part time when her daughter is an adolescent, a nice balance is struck between family and vocation (see Table 12–16, items 9 and 10).

Just as mothers who worked part time were able to balance work roles and leisure roles, their daughters engaged in an unusual number of leisure-time activities. Nor was this time taken away from their families. They were even more apt to spend their leisure with their families than girls whose mothers were always home.

If the mother worked full time, however, the daughter was inducted into precocious maturity—going steady earlier, holding an outside job and carrying major responsibility within the home, all at the expense of recreational activities with her family or anyone else (except, perhaps, her steady date). Douvan and Adelson suggested that girls "form these extra family involvements in order to supply emotional needs which have not been met at home, perhaps because their mothers are overextended in their own commitments outside the home."

So far we have mentioned only daughters. Many effects of maternal employment on sons are the opposite of effects on daughters. Girls benefit from their mother's employment by identifying with her example of feminine achievement. As a result, daughters of working mothers more often choose them as their ideal. However, the improved morale of the employed woman reflects adversely on her sons insofar as they see their

Table 12–16   Effects of Mother's Employment on Adolescent Girls

	MATERNAL EMPLOYMENT		
Daughter's Activities	*None*	*Part Time*	*Full Time*
1. Major household responsibility	5%	17%	22%
2. Holds part-time job	70%	74%	81%
3. Goes steady at ages 17–18	27%	38%	45%
4. Belongs to extracurricular groups	75%	84%	69%
5. Highly active in leisure activities	39%	49%	35%
6. Spends leisure with her family	47%	52%	38%
7. Mother is her adult ideal	31%	43%	42%
8. Rated highly feminine in traditional sense	27%	15%	19%
9. Resists peer pressure to break promise to her parents	13%	28%	16%
10. Tends to reject adult authority	5%	16%	6%
Number of cases	769	158	235

Adapted from Douvan, 1963: 145, 150–51. *Source:* National sample of girls 11–18 years old. Reciprocal percentages of girls did not report the specified activities.

father losing power relative to her. Propper (1972) found that sons of working mothers were less apt than sons of nonworking mothers to choose their fathers as the person they admired most.

Like their fathers, both sons and daughters of working mothers are pressed into domestic service. However, the sexes differ again with respect to part-time jobs. Roy (1961) found that girls followed their working mother into employment whereas boys reactively worked less outside the home. The boys seemed to nurse a grudge against their absent mothers.

Perhaps such factors lie back of the increased juvenile delinquency that Gold (1961) found in sons of middle-class working mothers in Flint, Michigan. The less financially necessary the mother's employment, the more it is liable to boomerang on the male members of her family.

These studies suggest that significant questions to be considered by a mother in deciding whether to work are (1) how old are my children? (2) what sex are they? and (3) how many hours a week will I be away? The older the children, the larger the proportion of daughters, and the fewer the hours worked, the more likely it is that the repercussions will be positive.

Altered Marital Satisfaction. We have already noted that dual occupational involvement alters both the balance of power and the division of labor between husband and wife. What do these structural changes in marriage do to the partners' feelings for each other?

The answer is—It depends.

For one thing, it depends on whether the husband's satisfaction or the wife's is considered. We have seen that husbands lose power and add housework, and their sons are sometimes demoralized. It should not surprise us, therefore, to discover in some studies that husbands are less satisfied and working wives more satisfied with their marriages. Scanzoni (1970) found this complementary pattern for college-educated men and women: the husbands were less satisfied and the wives more satisfied with their companionship and with their empathy when the wife was employed:

> We found that in the pre-child period it was advantageous for the wife to work. The double salary can be used to equip the house of the newly married couple and the fact that the wife contributes to the making of the family makes the phrase "a home made by the two" more true for them. If a wife works, she will be able to understand her husband more—the kind of tensions and troubles he may encounter in his work, the degree of tiredness after work, and through her understanding, she can be a better companion and caretaker. A wife who does not work tends to make demands on her husband to entertain her, to take her out at night when he longs for the rocking chair. Through her work, the wife can keep up with her husband in intellectual and experimental development and thus make him a better companion. She will not bore her husband with small details of family life.

Burke and Weir (1976) found that Canadian engineers and accountants were less satisfied, but their wives were more satisfied, with their marriages when both partners were employed than when the wife was not. The husbands of working wives reported demoralization ("lower spirits") while the working wives were in higher spirits. This contrast in morale was reflected in contrasting mental and physical health—both the stay-at-home housewives and the husbands of the working wives had been to a doctor more recently and reported more worries. The authors commented that when the wife goes to work "the husband may have to deal with a diminished sense of self-worth in his dual-role relations with the family, whereas the wife's sense of self-worth is likely to be enhanced."

Just because Burke and Weir's husbands of working wives were demoralized does not necessarily mean that all men would be. Conceivably, engineering and accounting are not likely to attract men who would find it easy to adapt to the stresses involved in dual-career marriages, whereas men in humanistically oriented professions might find it easier and even challenging to make those changes. In this study, both partners in dual-career marriages agreed on the objective features of their marriages, even though they differed in their subjective reactions. Both reported that they communicated more with their spouses (especially about the wife's personality, the husband's parents, and their sexual relations); they found their sexual relations and social relations with friends more harmonious; and they were more likely to report that disagreements were resolved by mutual give and take rather than by one person giving in. These achievements reflect considerable success in developing a new life-style of heightened sexuality, increased communication, and shared decision making despite the bad feelings of the husbands about those changes. From the standpoint of the choice between growth and deterioration (which we will describe in Chapter 21), these marriages have a promising future, even though the husbands may not recognize it yet!

Second, it depends on how rewarding are the jobs. Some jobs are a net gain to the individual and secondarily to his/her partner, while some are a net loss. Ridley (1973) found that women schoolteachers in Tallahassee were more satisfied with their marriages if they liked their jobs. The most ambitious women benefited more from their employment than women who placed less importance on occupational success. The greater the importance attached to employment, the more important it is that the job be satisfying if it is to benefit rather than undermine the marriage.

If the wife works only because she "has" to rather than because she "wants" to, she is apt to be unhappy about her marriage. She will resent the occupational failure of her husband that forces her to go to work and her resentment at having to work will poison her whole marriage. Orden and Branburn (1969) found that wives who worked out of necessity and their husbands reported more tensions in their marriages or in dual-career marriages where the wife worked by choice.

Closely related is the question of whether the husband wants his wife to work. Scanzoni (1968) found that middle-class men generally (72 percent) approved of the wife's employment whereas only half of recently divorced men had been sympathetic with the idea of their wives going to work before their divorce. This implies that if the wife works despite her husband's disapproval, this may precipitate a divorce. To state it in another way, if the husband is so chauvinistic as to stand in the way of his wife's working, divorce may result.

In sum, couples where either partner feels badly about the wife's working are not likely to adapt their relationship very well to the changes that dual employment brings. This is suggested by the answers of Scanzoni's sample of divorced wives when they were asked why their husbands disapproved of their working: "he is embarrassed to have me working," "he is ashamed," "it hurts his pride," and "he feels the man should support the wife." Such traditionally minded husbands could not be expected to take their wives' employment gracefully or to respond very generously to the wives' need for help around the house:

> *Office hours for most offices are mostly the same. In the morning, if the wife works too, she cannot clean up the house. She has to leave the whole thing until after she gets home, and very likely that is when her husband will be home. Surely he would not like to see the house still in a mess. If the wife comes home even later than her husband, then things would be even worse. I am the type of man who insists that all housework should be done by housewives except those heavy tasks or mechanical tasks. Further, I would like to have the dinner ready as soon as I am back from the office, and I surely would not like to see my wife trying to clean up the home and doing the cooking simultaneously and both in a hurry. This kind of busy work will very likely change her into a hot-tempered person. Furthermore, it is very possible that she would meet or hear something unpleasant and when she comes back, seeing the house in a mess and that her husband is waiting for dinner (even if he is not hurrying her) and having to do everything in a bad mood, will certainly ruin the happy warm family image.*

The impact on the marriage depends on the number of hours the second partner works. We have already seen that adolescent girls thrive when their mothers neither stay home all the time nor work full time but, rather, hold part-time jobs. The same is true for both parents. Orden and Bradburn found that both partners were happiest when the wife worked part time; both partners were most satisfied specifically with their companionship under these circumstances. Going to work 40 hours a week may overload the wife and strain the marriage, whereas part-time employment can be more easily combined with family activities.

The converse of the extent of the wife's involvement in her job is the extent of her responsibilities at home. The lower those responsibilities, the less the danger that going to work will overload her and the greater the likelihood that it will relieve her from feeling bored. At points in the family life cycle when the burden of housework is particularly heavy, staying home may be the most adaptive. Orden and Bradburn (1969) found that both husbands and wives were happiest if the wife stayed home when there were preschool children in the home. Conversely, by the time the youngest child reached school age, the burden of child care had diminished so much that there was no longer any marital advantage in one parent staying home.

These findings suggest that the problem is to find a balance between meaningful activity in the home and outside the home. The best marriages are either where home responsibilities are so heavy that the stay-at-home partner is fully occupied with meeting them or where job responsibilities are just heavy enough to take up the slack at home but not so heavy as to overburden the marriage. Part-time employment may not only fill a gap in a person's life, but stimulate both partners to higher levels of marital and leisure-time interaction than if they were demoralized by insufficiently challenging responsibilities at home.

Toward Symmetrically Limited Bilateral Involvement

We have seen that for both partners to hold full-time jobs tends to overload married couples and undermine their marriages. The easiest way to resolve this problem is for the wife to work part time while her husband works full time. This solution suffers the disadvantage of asymmetry. It leaves the husband the primary breadwinner, even if no longer the sole one. Conversely, the wife remains the primary housekeeper, even though she may receive marginally greater assistance from her husband.

A symmetrical solution to this problem would be for both partners to work part time. We have known a few cases where both worked half time and both shared the housework and child care fifty-fifty. Unfortunately, such couples are so rare that they fail to appear in the research literature. Our hypothesis is that symmetrically limited bilateral involvement offers the maximum opportunity for couples to reach their highest potential: (1) It provides a structural basis for complete equality between the partners that encourages the development of each to their fullest potential and promotes mutual respect; (2) it provides an adequate level of economic support for the family without depleting the couple's time and energy. Because they have more than the usual amount of leisure time, they can invest that energy in developing their relationship to its fullest potential.

Teamwork in Shared Careers

While bilateral symmetry resolves the limitations of unilateral occupational involvement that have been so eloquently described by Grønseth (1971), and of asymmetrical bilateral involvement, it does not guarantee the maximum interaction between husband and wife. To insure that, couples must work in similar occupations or, better yet, work together as a team.

Parallel Careers.   Many couples meet in graduate or professional school and then practice their careers separately, either working for different employers or engaging in separate private practices. One partner may be a corporation lawyer and the other an attorney specializing in domestic relations or a judge hearing all sorts of cases. One may be a pediatrician and the other a surgeon. One may be a college professor and the other a professional writer in the same field.

Other couples may not have been trained in the same department but may be engaged in similar work. We know a psychiatrist working for a penal institution whose wife is a marriage counselor working in a small clinic:

> As in all things there are positive and negative aspects (yin and yang). Although Dave and I are in the same field, we were trained differently, he analytically and I existentially, so we've learned a lot from each other. During my graduate years (his residency) we fought a lot over approaches to therapy. Over the years we've mellowed into a middle ground where we can appreciate the other's point of view and find value in it. Dave is giving me gems all the time from his training—more diagnostic, and I am helpful to him in terms of marital work, particularly the systems approach. Very often we'll supervise each other. From the other side, being in the same field can make us desire a break—like sometimes we don't want to talk psychology "shop talk" and we both desire something different—thank God for friends.
>
> The aspect that is most compatible is our leisure time. We both work late afternoons and evenings. As we develop our practices we try to schedule the same times off. If one of us worked a regular eight-hour day while the other worked evenings and weekends, it would be tough. The traditional roles we have learned to both share. We both cook—he some nights, me others. Since we both earn income, I have help come in to do regular cleaning. The only chore neither of us likes (but I do it) is grocery shopping. If Dave invites company and I don't feel like fixing dinner, he'll do so. Usually, we work together on cooking.
>
> Decisions, I must admit to my dismay, are usually Dave's. If we ever utterly disagree, we each state our point of view until over time a compromise is reached. For instance, last year I wanted a vacation in Europe but he wanted to go up the coast of California, Oregon, and Washington. We went up the coast and this year hope to go to Europe.
>
> If Dave were offered another job, would I go? I'd like to think that if either of us had something we wanted to do which meant moving, the other would make arrangements. If that decision ever had to be made, I guess we'd have to see where each other's feelings were. I place my

relationship to Dave ahead of my career right now, so if I had to leave my present job, I imagine I would. That may change in time—you never know—but today, I think that's how it would be.

People's first response to finding we're both therapists is that we must analyze each other all the time. This seems to occur less frequently—we do go to each other when we need it and ask for it.

Joint Careers.   When husband and wife work at similar tasks in the same organization, they not only do similar work but do it together. The smaller the organization, the greater the sharing, with the maximum in those cases where husband and wife have their own firm or private practice that they conduct entirely by themselves. Then husband and wife are a team with all the benefits and problems that this implies.

Martin, Berry, and Jacobsen (1975) studied couples in which both partners were employed by the same department of sociology and found that the wives had more successful careers than other women sociologists in terms of completing their Ph.D.s and staying with their professional commitments longer. Unfortunately, the researchers failed to study the effects on the marriage of working in the same department.

One couple studied by the Rapoports (1971) were architects with a joint practice in their home. The authors commented on some of the effects of this way of sharing a career:

> While similar interests can encourage stimulation, it can also make for conflict, and in a situation such as the Bensons, it is obvious that tensions which develop in relation to work affect their husband-wife relationship very much. Consequently they have developed some mechanisms for avoiding or reducing conflicts. The Bensons recognize the importance of criticism to maintain standards. In the more orthodox architectural practice this is done by colleagues and the situation at work is segregated from the love relationship. However, in their case, the work relationship is the same as the marital relationship and therefore when criticism is necessary they feel that it should be made not as a fundamental attack, but "with love," constructively, and with help to find the way to better solutions.... Because both the Bensons are strong-willed and competent, they recognize that each has sometimes to give way when something is seen as important to the other. This stems from a recognition that there are limits to the degree to which they can complement each other, and there are some instances in which their wishes will not correspond (pp. 116–17).

The Bensons met in architecture school and practiced together continuously from that point on. Sharing a career is more difficult if one partner practices continuously while the other drops out for childbearing/rearing or, worse yet, joins the other belatedly, devoid of prior experience or professional credentials. In our case, Bob was a full-fledged sociologist and marriage counselor for 25 years before Margaret began teaming up as co-counselor and as co-leader of experiential workshops. This belated teaming up required a long process of renegotiating our working relationship and our marriage which Margaret describes as follows:

> Meeting in graduate school, we began our married life thinking of ourselves as a team. The demands of children and household duties on me and of professional life on Bob quickly divided our energy and attention. Though acting the martyr at times, I was mainly happy as mother and family caretaker until the children flew the nest. Then there were years of consternation as I faced my sense of helplessness, uselessness, and dependency. The task of renewing our marriage and sharing our growth with other couples led us gradually to team up as co-counselors and co-leaders of human relations workshops. In the beginning this was exciting and easy, as I brought untutored, spontaneous responses to Bob's confident, patterned skills developed over the years. I found it easier to feel equally useful when others told us how complementary our different personalities and temperaments were.
>
> An important aspect in shifting into a new mix was my struggle to give up half of the housework. While mouthing liberated notions, I clung to it because it was safe and familiar, and there I was the expert. Giving up my half freed me from latent resentment about being Bob's servant and released my time and energy for more creative tasks. It was not half as hard for Bob to take on cooking, cleaning, and washing dishes as it was for me to give it up.
>
> Sometimes I feel jealous and competitive. In co-leading a group, who gives way when both of us wish to act? Usually I feel relaxed and trust the natural passing back and forth of our leadership, but sometimes I get angry as Bob seems to take all of the space available. I've had to learn I can't expect him to open the way for me graciously. I can move into space and take it if I really want to and have something to give.
>
> Because of his head start and his status among professionals, I sometimes fear my dependency on him, craving to be absolutely equal, wanting to pull apart and prove myself by working separately from him. I have to watch that I don't confuse being supportive and assisting and complementing with being dependent. In fact, I have to let go of considering "dependency" a bad thing. We do depend on each other all the time.
>
> It is important for me to attend separate training courses that stimulate me to bring back something special. It is important that I develop my own clientele in counseling and body movement work. In my workshops and classes I am in charge and Bob plays a supportive role. If in the future I choose to work more separately, I will undoubtedly feel more independent in some ways—but I would be fortunate to find a "boss" or "coworker" elsewhere who would give me as much support, encouragement, and freedom to move as he does.
>
> As we have nurtured others, they have nurtured us and our mar-

riage. The enormous energy that flows between people in counseling and group sessions pours into our relationship. Struggling with others, we know more clearly our own sensitivities and insensitivities. Other couples' fears and failures to confront one another stimulate us to attend to our own foibles and follies. We lend courage; we take courage. Our relationship is richer because of our teamwork. The risks we take, the strains that are inevitable, toughen our marriage and make it grow.

Bob Barrus taught in a private residential junior high school winters and ran a summer camp jointly with Dot Barrus. Dot describes how they gradually turned their camp into a full-time joint career:

> *We have just completed our twenty-second year of camp, which we began to supplement Bob's teaching income, and which has grown into our full income. We run two camps, 60 children in three three-week sessions with a staff of 20 college-age counselors and cooks and another 15 to 20 high-school "helpers" in a work–camp-type situation. It is a farm-home camp, an extension of our year-round life here, so a lot of time and energy goes into our homestead: milking the cow, putting in a big garden, growing feed for the animals, and so on. Occasionally, we hire help for off-season work, but as a rule we do most of it ourselves.*
>
> *During most of this time a lot of Bob's energy has gone into his teaching, and as the camp grew I felt increasing frustration as we needed to confer on plans for the organization of camp, hiring of staff, and so on, and he was always too involved with school or too exhausted to give his attention to it. He began teaching part time, and then gave it up altogether two years ago when we increased the camp to its present size. While we always considered the camp an equal partnership, I carried the weight of the off-season responsibility, as Bob had another full-time job. Now that he is not teaching I continue to carry this, although we find the decision making much easier and more relaxed without the competition of the teaching. And we find that with the increased size of camp there is more need for one of us to travel in the spring, talking with camp families, and showing slides to groups. Also, more staff to hire. There are plenty of jobs for each of us, and although we are pretty good at substituting for one another, generally we have areas where we operate—and this refers to physical space as well as jobs. Actually, we're both pretty strong and tend to conflict if we try to work together on the same job too closely. (We each have our own pet ways of planting the garden or getting a meal, so it's best if we just get out of each other's way.)*
>
> *Up until about six years ago I had always looked to Bob as the main breadwinner, and felt that my role was to make things easier for him by taking over all I could of the household tasks, care of the children, and so on, as well as the off-season camp work. This was a pretty heavy load at times, as we often had as many as six junior high students boarding with us as well as our own youngest and our retarded daughter. Although we*

couldn't have predicted exactly how things would evolve, what has happened is that Bob has taken over a lot of the parenting (we now also have another retarded boy living with us) and a good deal of the household responsibility, thus freeing me to spend more time on the office work related to the camp organization. In a way this is an especially neat solution as he moves toward an early retirement and I will be in the role of being the main breadwinner. He's seven years older than I. With all this going, it's not going to be a "put up your feet and take it easy" kind of retirement, but I sense a real relaxation knowing that he no longer has to carry this weight by himself. And I feel challenged and happy with more freedom to do my best—and less weight of household tasks.

I have been mainly dwelling on our off-season life together, which, time-wise, is the biggest part of our life. We really like the flexibility that we have from being our own bosses, being able to flow along with the weather, and how we feel. We're pretty much tuned to each other's needs, so to take off and go rafting down the river one of these glorious fall days if one of us feels like it, or to have sex any time or in some new or exciting place, is something we just do when the spirit moves us.

I don't think we feel any competition. It seems there's always so much to do and so many challenges and demands on our time that we have always had to pull together. We respect each other's feelings and opinions—very much value the chance to bounce ideas off the other before taking action on them. We each value our right to have input in each decision, even though it might seem to be in the other's area of responsibility. All major decisions we make together, and we keep working at them until they are mutual. We often confer in bed in the hour before others rise—a great time when your mind is fresh and none of the day's distractions can press in upon you, and the skin contact seems to facilitate the decision-making process.

One of the big things that has helped us to make this into a happy working relationship is that we don't have any hangups about traditional sex roles. We've learned a lot from listening to younger couples where both are working at outside jobs. Bob never did have insecurity about his masculinity, but until we began with the Marriage Enrichment program we did have more of a traditional concept of the role of a wife as the homemaker. I'm glad it has changed.

During the nine weeks when camp is actually in operation things are much different. Neither of us does any housekeeping, and we function as an administrative team. Generally speaking, Bob handles the program area and I handle the human relations end of things, but we overlap, and we can easily take over for the other when fatigue sets in. We try to be especially supportive of each other during this time. People often remark about how well we work as a team—seems natural when we care a lot about each other. My partner's success is my success and, likewise, I suffer when he fails. I've noticed that we tend to overlook minor irritations during this intense time.

Maybe I could sum it all up by relating a special memory. Last summer when we were at our busiest, but feeling exuberant and stimulated by the success of our joint venture, we met in the hall, and Bob picked me up in joy and said, "It's great to run this camp with you!" And that was just the way I felt, too.

For couples who do not run their own business but work for an employer, the ultimate joint career is a shared job. Young (1976) described two faculty couples at the University of Michigan who split the husband's job in half so the wife could share it. These were not limited bilateral involvements, however, because both couples spent the other half of their time on scientific research. Since it is difficult to divide time between teaching and research, each person alternated between being a full-time teacher one year and a full-time researcher the next. By being on the faculty, each gained access to laboratory facilities and administrative machinery that enabled them to secure the research grants needed for their professional advancement. Said one husband:

> It is difficult to find a job that you like, that pays a good salary, is in a place where you want to live and has nice professional colleagues. That's a relatively low probability for one person—say a possibility of 10 percent. When you've got two people married to each other, then the probability is now 1 percent. That's the nature of the whole problem for married people.

The partners maintained their professional autonomy by securing separate research grants and developing separate areas of expertise. Young commented that "this independence is particularly important for the women, who are underdogs not only because they are younger than their husbands, but also because they must fight the traditional female stereotype." Despite this autonomy, couples sharing the same job benefited from having adjacent offices and labs. One benefit was professional:

> We're both thoroughly familiar with each other's projects and we spend a lot of time talking about science. It's like having another professional colleague always on call, always interested in what you're doing.
>   When you get a good idea and you're both in the lab, all you have to do is walk a few steps and tell him about it. When it's hot, then really good collaboration develops. Whereas, if I had to wait six hours until I go home, I might have forgotten about it.

A second advantage was that sharing a job created a structure that brought the husband and wife into proximity. Said the wife just quoted:

> One thing that's really nice is that we get to see each other fairly often. . . . I'm a lot luckier than a lot of couples we know where the man

is an assistant professor in science and the woman is not in science at all. At this stage in his career, a scientist is in his lab twelve hours a day, six days a week and somebody who's at home really isn't going to see him very much, whereas I can walk over to Dave's office on the other side of that wall and we can have lunch together.

Working in the same field gives couples a common language and an intense interest in each other's vocational problems and triumphs. We expect empathy and communication to reach high levels in such marriages. In the Protestant ministry, Douglas (1965) found that the happiest wives were those who saw themselves as "team workers" with their husbands. They found fulfillment in their semiprofessional "vocation" and felt close to their husbands through involvement in the same work.

When partners work together in addition to living together, they experience so much togetherness that they have to try to create enough separateness. In our case:

We figure that we spend 95 percent of our time together since we eat all our meals together, share the housework, and lead workshops, groups, and couple counseling together. Although we find this very stimulating and enjoyable, we need time apart. We usually go to professional meetings and training programs together, but sometimes one of us goes alone. Margaret spent several weeks two different summers in creative dance courses in Arizona—which gave both of us major breathing space. Sometimes she visits her relatives by herself. One of us will have lunch with a friend or go folk dancing or ice skating while the other stays home. We try to listen to our bodies in deciding whether to join the other in what s/he wants to do at a particular time. If the answer is that we don't want to do it together, the stay-at-home person gets to experience the peacefulness of having the house all to him/herself and the going-out person has the stimulus of relating to others.

OCCUPATIONAL INVOLVEMENT AND EXTRAMARITAL INVOLVEMENT

Occupational involvement turns out to be remarkably analogous to extramarital involvement. Both unilateral and bilateral involvement in careers or friends may be so extensive as to undermine the marriage. On the other hand, limited bilateral involvement in work and friends is not only consistent with marital vitality, but may enrich it by stimulating both partners to new levels of personal growth and interpersonal sharing.

The happiest marriages are not those where the husband and wife are so engrossed in each other that they have no room for friends and no investment in work. Nor are they where there is unrestricted freedom for extramarital or occupational involvement. In both dimensions, the maximum satisfaction comes from balancing the energy invested in the marriage with energy invested outside the marriage. To do this successfully requires limiting the involvement in friends and in careers. Part-time employment and limited friendships are particularly consistent with a strong marriage bond. Balance is more easily attained when both partners have outside involvements than when only one partner has outside friendships or employment while the other "languishes" at home.

Neither occupational nor extramarital involvement is beneficial or detrimental in itself, but under certain conditions the benefits of each can be maximized and the costs minimized. These conditions may be summarized as limited, symmetrical, voluntary involvement in personally rewarding activities outside the family with the knowledge and consent of both partners, combined with enough energy invested in the marriage to keep it strong and growing.

13 Relatives/In-Laws

Marriage is not just an individual affair. Parents and other relatives are vitally interested. Every partner acquired is a new recruit to the family. Both partners join each other's families. Henceforth they participate in two kin networks: the husband's and the wife's.

The most important links in these networks are between parents and children—that is, between the husband and his parents, the wife and her parents. Prior to marriage these are close ties, originating in the dependency of infants and the long years of nurture to maturity.

When there is more than one child, parents become the focus for continued association among adult siblings. Children who grow up together feel closer to each other than to other relatives. Cousins who never live together have weaker bonds. In Greensboro, North Carolina, Adams (1968) found that 75 percent of his respondents felt close to their parents, 48 percent felt close to their nearest-aged sibling and only 18 percent to their best-known cousin.

Marriage brings together individuals tied to their respective families of orientation. As they create a new family, there may be transitional problems, boundary problems, allocative problems, or problems of culture conflict. But almost always, beyond the problems, there are positive ties of sociability and help.

SOURCES OF CONFLICT

The word "in-law" is one with which to conjure. "Mother-in-law" has particularly negative connotations. In a free association test, students typically gave such responses as "fight," "bother," "terrible," "ugh," "hatred," and "hell." Mother-in-law is the modern incarnation of witchcraft, the butt of jokes and cartoons expressing the resentment of sons- and daughters-in-law.

Waller and Hill (1951) pointed out that "grandmother" is a positive word, even though mother-in-law and grandmother are the same person once children arrive. Yet not quite. From *my* point of view, *my* grandmothers are those women two generations removed who were kind to me as a child. However, *my* mother-in-law is this stranger, only one generation older, whom I acquired by marriage. Whereas grandparents are part of my birthright, parents-in-law intrude later in life and require getting used to. Hence the transitional problems in interfamily relationships.

Transitional Problems

Though less prevalent than other problems, in-law problems are uniquely concentrated at the beginning of marriage. Blood and Wolfe found disagreements over in-laws commonest in the honeymoon stage, declining steadily thereafter. Thomas (1956) found that in-law problems were prominent in Catholic marriages that broke up soonest, especially those that failed within the first year.

Cultivating relationships with in-laws is a task that is seldom completed by the time of the wedding. Both partners must work out their own relationships to the other's family. They may not succeed equally well despite their best efforts. When they do not, this is liable to strain the marriage unless the partner whose family is unloved is able to accept that failure gracefully:

> *You have your relationship and I have mine with our parents. I have to work out my relationship with your parents and they to me. You can't be responsible for what I do nor can I be responsible for you. I used to think if you can't love my family you can't love me. But that's crazy thinking. You do love me and you aren't fond of my family. I'm learning that I can accept your real feelings and not try to change them or feel guilty and apologetic about them to my family.*

Marriage is a relationship that develops as a man and a woman gradually depend more on each other and less on their parents. Some parents resist the "loss" of their dependents, and some children feel ambivalent about the realignment. Then parent-child ties vie with husband-wife ties in conflicts of loyalty.

Parental Possessiveness. When the difficulty is a parent's inability to allow children to grow up, the mother is especially likely to be the culprit. Rosen and d'Andrade (1959) found that men generally encourage independence. Women, however, are more apt to enjoy having others depend on them. If a woman's chief satisfaction lies in being a mother, the prospect of children leaving home may be frightening. Sometimes the first child's marriage provokes the strongest resistance. Sometimes the last child is the last defense against an empty life. In either case, Duvall (1954) found that mothers were most often blamed for "possessiveness."

In Leichter and Mitchell's Jewish families in New York City (1967) it was the husband's mother who was typically the focus of conflict. The reason was apparently that while the wife continued to keep in close touch with her mother, the husband less often kept in touch with his, so she felt neglected and jealous of her daughter-in-law. Mothers often accused their sons of disloyalty, fomenting competition between mother and wife.

Overprotective parents sometimes attempt to break up a child's marriage:

> Wendell and I have a difficult marriage but I want to stay with it. There are a lot of minuses, but there are more pluses for me and our four-year-old daughter. I only wish my parents would support me in my determination to stay and work it out, instead of constantly fearing for my safety because of his anger. They don't help when they urge me to get out. I need their love, not their anxieties.

Childish Overdependence. Overpossessive mothers produce overdependent children. The wife's mother is the usual focus of conflict in cases of overdependence. Since daughters are more sheltered than sons, wives are more apt, figuratively or literally, to "go home to mother" when tension arises between husband and wife (Stryker, 1955). Overdependence is commonest among those who marry young. It is one expression of immaturity and incomplete preparation for marriage. Blood and Wolfe (1960) found that the younger the bride was, the more in-law disagreements occurred. When youthfulness causes overdependence, time may solve the problem. In extreme cases, attachment between parent and child may need therapeutic intervention:

Jeff can never say "no" to his mother when she invites us over. Even when we decide again and again that our family time comes first, he gets pulled in that direction and I feel that the children and I are secondary. She has a powerful hold on him which I can't break. I despise her for interfering with our marriage and I despise him for his weakness in giving in to her. It's a real triangle.

Boundary Problems

Normally, a couple establish their autonomy vis-à-vis the relatives with little difficulty. Their collective identity is respected by both sets of relatives. But I [Bob—see Blood, 1969] found that excessive contact with kin threatened the autonomy of the nuclear family. If relatives dropped in unannounced, they invaded the couple's privacy and lessened their marital solidarity:

> Ever since Rich went into business with his father I feel his parents have had a hold on him and won't let go. Even though his father has retired, they keep their finger in all the decision-making and are constantly over there giving him advice. I'm terribly jealous of their closeness as I see him often going along with their decisions as opposed to the ones we have made together.

Figure 13–1 shows that contact with kin is consistent with marital satisfaction up to a point of diminishing returns. In this sample, excessive contact occurred when couples got together with relatives more than once a week. The same study detected similar boundary problems when the whole clan gathered more than once a month. Relatives are a supportive resource in moderation, but the nuclear family requires some autonomy to avoid being overwhelmed.

Even though most families enjoy visiting regularly or extensively,

Figure 13-1 Kin Visiting and Marital Satisfaction

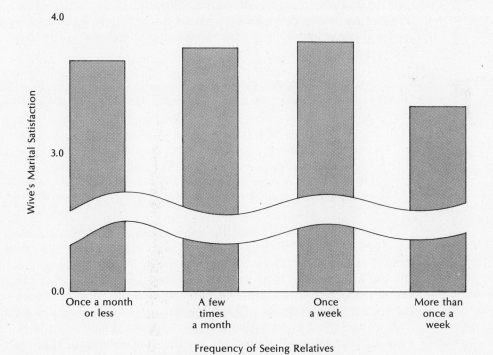

Adapted from Blood, 1969: 178. *Source:* Detroit wives, 1955.

every couple must find out for themselves what time limits are appropriate. In the following case, a combination of oversensitivity in the daughter-in-law and inflexibility in the mother-in-law made visiting difficult and required that visits be kept brief if they were to be enjoyable:

> My faraway mother-in-law always insisted that we come at Christmas and during the summer. But it was always horrendous after the first day or two. We never could work out a system for preparing meals that would satisfy her. I kept feeling she thought I was lazy. Our children's paraphernalia cluttered up her neat house and made me feel she thought I was sloppy. She constantly picked up our things and made me furious. She loved the babies but when they cried she couldn't stand it and wanted to upset my system of dealing with their crying. Over the years we discovered that three-day visits were the most any of us could stand without losing our cool.

Problems of Culture Conflict

Mixed marriages present special difficulties for in-laws insofar as the new son-in-law or daughter-in-law is categorically unacceptable to in-laws because s/he is seen as ineligible for membership in the family. How much trouble this causes depends on whether husband and wife unite against the family or whether one partner feels caught between loyalty to parents and loyalty to spouse:

> Because Marian is not Catholic, my mother has not yet been able to accept her or the children she brought to our marriage. Because I can't cope with mother's unhappiness and because I really felt sorry for her, the only way I could tell her I was going to get married was by mail rather than in person. It's going to take her a long time, and maybe she'll never really accept it. Marian gets angry that I don't stand up for myself and for the relationship that is most important to me. So my inability to deal directly with my mother is a big source of trouble between Marian and me.

Duvall (1954) found that the most common complaint against in-laws generally and mothers-in-law in particular was meddlesomeness. Parents have many reasons for intervening in the life of a young couple, but the most potent is a clash of cultures. Husbands and wives have enough trouble resolving their differences without reinforcements rushing in. Yet when matters of principle are at stake, restraint is difficult. Even in technical matters like cooking or keeping house, in-laws intervene all too easily, escalating the conflict and extending it beyond the issue at hand to questions of their right to get involved at all.

In Leichter and Mitchell's New York Jewish sample, the husband's relatives (especially his mother) caused conflict between husband and wife by interfering excessively. Most often, this interference took the form of criticizing the daughter-in-law for not keeping house properly or raising the children properly.

Every family has a culture of its own—distinctive ways of living that are deeply ingrained. One element is family ritual. Ways of celebrating holidays, of spending Sundays, or of putting children to bed are brought to marriage, along with peculiarities of etiquette, cooking, and keeping house. Whose culture is to prevail? Usually the wife's, since she is the chief housekeeper and child-rearer. Yet in the process wife and mother-in-law may come to verbal blows:

> I have a problem with Van's mother. We never had any trouble until the baby was born, but we had a big argument over the formula. She thought I was making it wrong, but I've been to prenatal classes so I know what I'm doing.

Conflict about how to raise the baby is common even between young mothers and their *own* parents. Yet when the trouble is with *his* mother, it snowballs into "in-law trouble." Whether beans should be cooked with ham or without, whether to say "either" or "eyether," whether to dress four-year olds in suits or playclothes—the possibilities of conflict are endless. In the first months of marriage, both sets of parents welcome decisions in favor of their own idiosyncrasies and bristle when their ways are snubbed. The fact that women are the chief bearers of family culture explains why they are the chief contenders in in-law conflict.

Table 13–1 suggests three principles of in-law conflict: (1) parents cause more trouble than siblings; (2) female relatives cause more trouble than male relatives; (3) wives are involved more than husbands. All three coincide in the relationship between wife and mother-in-law, making it crisis-prone.

Table 13–1 In-Laws with Whom Husbands and Wives Experienced Friction

	PERCENTAGE EXPERIENCING FRICTION	
In-Law	Husbands	Wives
Mother-in-law	9.0%	14.7%
Sister-in-law	3.4	3.8
Father-in-law	3.2	3.2
Brother-in-law	0.6	1.8
Two or more of the above	5.1	5.9
Total	21.3%	29.4%

Adapted from a study by Judson T. Landis of 544 couples in the early years of marriage (Landis and Landis, 1958: 406). Reciprocal percentages never experienced any friction with in-laws.

Allocational Problems

For exceptional couples with only one set of kin, allocational problems are minimized. They may still have to choose between different units of the network—which to visit when. But choices are easier within a given network than between networks.

In international marriages, only one network is accessible. If the bride moves to the husband's side of the world, her family ties are so weakened that they cease having much functional significance. International marriages, therefore, may have better-than-average relations with the remaining network—at least this was true of American soldiers with Japanese brides (Strauss, 1954).

Normally, however, both networks are accessible and compete for time and attention. Both families may want simultaneous visits from their children. Especially at Christmas or High Holy Days, the custom of gathering together the children (plus their spouses and the grandchildren) is felt with equal urgency. Only a Solomon could find a solution that would not disappoint one family (or both):

> At every holiday we always get invited out by both families. Maureen and I come from very close-knit families so, if we don't watch ourselves, we go right ahead and tell both, "Of course we'll be there." More than once we've separately committed the family to being in two places 100 miles apart for Thanksgiving dinner, and then there's general hair-tearing all around.

Both families may expect financial help in distress, frequent letters, visits from grandchildren, and other favors that tax the couple's resources. It would be a mistake to assume that all claims are initiated by the older generation. The fact that the husband and wife grow up in separate families makes each identify with their own network and push its claims. Even if both partners could be neutral, no couple can be in two places at once. So on family occasions choices must be made.

Despite the multiple sources of potential conflict that we have described, the most notable feature of Table 13–1 is that almost 80 percent of the husbands and more than 70 percent of the wives had no friction with any in-laws. This means that the average couple need not expect trouble. We saw in an earlier chapter that individuals who got along well with their marriage partner tended to get along well with friends. The same principle applies here. People who get along well in marriage are likely to get along well with their own parents and their partner's parents. Only in exceptional circumstances do in-laws become out-laws.

SOCIABILITY WITH RELATIVES

Most couples get along so well with their relatives that they spend a great deal of time with them more than with neighbors or other friends.

According to Table 13–2, the typical married couple in Detroit saw at least one relative every week. In rural Michigan a companion study of mine (Bob) showed that farm families got together with relatives even more often (and with other friends less).

In New York City, Leichter and Mitchell (1967) found that telephoning relatives was even more frequent than visiting, occurring about twice as often. Forty-seven percent of the married women and 15 percent of the men talked by phone with at least one relative every day. For many, the daily chat over the phone was a firmly established habit that was kept up even when it was inconvenient. Conversations typically included minute details of the lives of the persons on both ends of the line. Perhaps because phone calls occurred more often than face-to-face visits, phone conversations were less selective and more comprehensive than conversations during visits.

Visits go in both directions—from older to younger and younger to older, depending on ease of movement and facilities for hospitality. If more than one child lives in the same community, the house they grew up in is the natural meeting place.

Some visits to parents are motivated by a sense of obligation. (One of Firth's respondents made the wry comment that "relatives are the only people you can dislike but still be on good terms with!") Parents invest so much in their children that they create a debt children can hardly repay. Nevertheless, most visiting is voluntary. Most couples enjoy their parents and siblings more than other companions. They visit back and forth because they want to, not because they have to.

The 1956 Detroit Area Study found that families normally visited as total units. Husbands and wives rarely left their children behind (and then mostly because of conflicts with bedtimes or other responsibilities, rather than by choice). The spouse was even more rarely left behind. The husband does not participate in his kin group and the wife in hers, but both

Table 13–2   Visits with Relatives, Neighbors, Co-Workers, and Other Friends

	CATEGORY VISITED			
Frequency of Visits	Relatives	Neighbors	Co-Workers	Other Friends
Every day or almost every day	29%	20%	1%	3%
Once or twice a week	38	25	8	22
Once or twice a month	20	17	20	43
Less often	13	14	30	24
Never	0	24	41	8
Total	100%	100%	100%	100%
Number of families	728	723	723	726

Adapted from Detroit Area Study, 1956. *Source:* Representative sample of Detroit metropolitan area married women, 1955. Visits were to and/or from the specified parties.

participate in both. If relatives are equally accessible, they expect equal contact. Otherwise, long vacation visits to the distant family are expected to balance weekend visits to the nearer one.

Differential compatibility skews the frequency of visiting relatives. Nor are other factors equal. An only child visits home more often than a many-siblinged partner. A widowed or ill parent needs more visits.

Husbands and wives don't always agree on how much time they want to spend with parents. It strains the marriage if they try to force the spouse into the mold of what they or the parents expect as appropriate behavior:

> We were having terrible hassles about the way I behaved when her family came or when we visited them. After a while, my caring and interest gave out. I was supposed to stay there all the time she did because her parents would be offended if I didn't. But we are learning that quality time is more important than quantity time. If I push myself beyond the limits of what I am able to give authentically it doesn't pay off. In fact, we pay heavily for it the next few weeks in our own relationship.
>
> Mary and the kids want to stay there longer this Christmas than I do. In the past they always felt gypped when I forced them to leave. So this time we will take two cars so they can stay as long as they want and I can come home when I want to. I will take responsibility for excusing myself so she won't have to apologize for me.

Visits between parents and married children are as ritualized as other aspects of family living. In Table 13–2, the most popular frequency was once or twice a week. Many families get together every weekend, going to church or eating dinner like clockwork year after year.

Although gatherings of the clan occur less often, they also tend to be ritualized (see Table 13–3). Special days on the calendar and family events like weddings and funerals bring kin together. Christmas is the most popular time of year for family visits.

Taking relatives as a whole, in large numbers or small, Lopata (1971) found that the more special the occasion, the greater the likelihood that it would be spent with relatives rather than friends. The families included in Table 13–4 did not always see anyone else on the specified occasions, but when they did get together with others, it was more apt to be with relatives during a prolonged vacation visit than for a one-day holiday, and on Sunday rather than Saturday night. Indeed, for those Chicago families, Saturday nights and occasional weekends were the only times when they were more apt to be with friends than with relatives.

In the Twin Cities, Hill (1970) found that grandparent/parent/child chains of couples not only "almost always" spent at least one major special occasion a year together, but also "almost always" shared recreation and at least "sometimes" religious activities:

Table 13-3   Occasions for Large Family Gatherings in City and Country

	FAMILY RESIDENCE	
Occasion	City	Country
Family ceremonial occasions		
Family reunions	10%	42%
Birthdays	25%	31%
Weddings and engagements	14%	13%
Mother's Day, Father's Day	3%	18%
Anniversaries	9%	9%
Funerals	8%	9%
Children's religious rituals, graduations	7%	6%
Holidays		
Christmas	34%	37%
Other religious holidays	7%	37%
National holidays	43%	28%
Social occasions	28%	24%
None	24%	11%
Number of families	724	178

Adapted from Blood and Axelrod, 1955. Representative samples of married women in the Detroit metropolitan area and on southeast Michigan farms. Reciprocal percentages did not gather on the specified occasion.

Dad's family all got together nearly every holiday but especially at Christmas, at which time they just wouldn't allow anyone to be absent. Only Dad liked the Swedish food: lute fish, potato sausage, and raisin pudding. This caused conflict every Christmas because no matter how much Mother and we children wanted to do something different, Dad insisted that we not let his folks down.

This family quarreled over the diverse backgrounds of the parents. When parents share the same ethnic tradition, clan rituals produce cohesiveness and give a sense of continuity between past and future.

Table 13-4   Contact with Relatives versus Friends on Special Occasions

	OCCASION			
Spent with	Vacation Visit	Holidays	Sundays	Sporadic Weekend Contacts
Relatives	82%	74%	71%	43%
Friends	18	26	29	57
Total	100%	100%	100%	100%

Recomputed from Lopata, 1971: 329. Source: 571 Chicago area married women. These statistics are limited to those couples who saw either relatives or friends on the specified occasions.

Accessibility

Two types of accessibility affect kin sociability. Geographical distance is an obvious barrier, but social distance may also be a problem.

Geographical Distance. Typically, people marry within the same community, so their networks overlap. The custom that couples establish a new residence does not mean they go off to a new community, but to a new dwelling unit. The chief exceptions are teenage couples so strapped financially that they take advantage of shelter offered by parents. When emergency living arrangements are necessary, couples are more apt to move in with the wife's parents than with the husband's, thereby avoiding culture conflict between wife and mother-in-law (Glick, 1957).

Despite the high rate of geographical mobility in America, married couples typically live in the same community with their parents. (In one Indiana county, the median distance from both sets of parents was three miles [Locke, 1951].) Most couples prefer to live near their families and childhood friends. Moving away may improve vocational opportunities, but reduces family sociability. The greater the distance, the greater the reduction:

> *I find it very hard agreeing that we take that job in Seattle because it will mean leaving my parents. Our children have meant so much to them in their later years and I still feel unfinished in achieving an adult-to-adult relationship. The tie of loyalty and love to them is still strong for me. If we move I will feel a loss and also feel guilty about rejecting them.*

If husband and wife come from different communities, where is the ideal place to live? At first glance, equality suggests compromising midway. However, if the distance is great enough, sociability would be difficult with both families. More is gained by settling near one family (preferably the wife's) and visiting the other during vacations.

As would be expected, the farther couples live from their relatives, the less they see them (see Table 13–5). Couples tended to see relatives living within a three-mile radius of their home every week. Those living between 30 and 200 miles away were typically seen about once a year. And those living more than 200 miles away (especially those living overseas) were seen years apart, if ever. In addition to the several thousand relatives whom these 167 couples had seen during the past five years, a few hundred additional relatives had been in touch by letter or phone, but were not seen. By contrast, several thousand more were known of by name but never contacted. This shows that meeting face-to-face was the main form of contact for these couples, whereas writing or telephoning was infrequent with persons who were never seen. How heavily distance interferes with firsthand contact is strikingly apparent in these statistics.

Table 13–5 Frequency of Visiting Relatives, by Geographical Distance

Frequency of Visiting	GEOGRAPHICAL DISTANCE				
	< 3 miles	< 30 miles	< 70 miles	< 200 miles	200 + miles
Weekly	50%	8%	1%	0	0
Monthly	15	16	11	3%	0
Quarterly	9	16	19	14	2%
Yearly	15	26	35	42	25
Less often	11	35	34	42	73
Total	100%	101%	100%	101%	100%
Number of relatives	85	804	829	559	655

Adapted from Firth, Hubert, and Forge, 1970: 204. *Source:* 167 middle-class London married couples. This table is limited to relatives whom they had seen at least once in the last five years. The 200+ distance category includes relatives who live outside the British Isles but who had been seen during this period.

Social Distance. Cultural diversity strains kin relations the same way it strains husband-wife relations. Sociability suffers when marriages link diverse networks. Mixed marriages create impediments to easy sociability between the extended family and the "outlaw." As a result, visiting may be reduced or may not occur at all:

> *Nine months after the wedding, Joe gave up his childhood Catholicism and joined the Episcopal church that I belong to. He was the first member of his entire blood relation to buck tradition and leave the Church of Rome. This hit his parents hard. For 11 months they would have nothing to do with their son. Not until the baby was born did they come around, acting as if nothing had happened. By that time, however, permanent damage had been done. Joe and I both still feel resentment toward his parents. To this day visits are very infrequent (not more than three or four times a year), and we are not invited to any of the Mulligan family reunions.*

Social distance is created by social mobility as well as by intermarriage. When children move up the social scale (even with their parents' blessing), visiting usually becomes less congenial. On the other hand, parent-child ties may be so strong and parental enthusiasm over children's success so rewarding that visiting is not impaired.

In Greensboro, North Carolina, Adams (1968) found that upward mobile men kept in close touch with their fathers but had less contact with their brothers (see Table 13–6).

Table 13–6 shows that the kind of contact between mobile men and their nonmobile brothers that was most reduced was social activity outside the home. Perhaps when one brother belongs to the middle class and

Table 13–6   Contacts of Married Men with Nearest-Age Brother, by Social Mobility Status

	SOCIAL MOBILITY STATUS		
Contacts (3+/year)	Stable	Upward Mobile	Stable/ Mobile Ratio
Joint social activities outside the home	31%	18%	1.7X
Communication by mail or telephone	70%	55%	1.3X
Home visits	65%	59%	1.1X
Number of cases	113	44	

Adapted from Adams, 1968: 107. *Source:* Married men in Greensboro, North Carolina. Reciprocal percentages had less than three contacts per year of the specified kind.

the other to the working class, their leisure-time interests diverge too much to make it easy to agree on places to go and things to do. On the other hand, visits to one another's homes fell off less, perhaps because they require less choice making.

In an earlier book, I (Bob) discussed possible reasons why social mobility interferes with sibling contact more than with parent-child contact:

> Although parents take justifiable pride in the upward mobility of their children, siblings seldom sponsor each other's successes. Indeed, the rivalry of siblings within the nuclear family must be intensified when parents express pride in the superior achievements of a brother or sister. As members of the same generation, siblings indirectly compete with one another in school and the occupational system. They seem more likely than parents, therefore, to react negatively to losing out in that competition (Blood, 1972: 278).

Reduced contact between divergent families is an adjustive mechanism. Were such families to try to get together, they would experience tension and conflict. By avoiding one another most of the time, they reduce their difficulties and make it easier to maintain a minimum of contact.

MUTUAL HELP AMONG RELATIVES

The essence of kin contact is pure sociability. When emergencies arise, however, relatives are the first people to whom most couples turn for practical help.

Emergency Help

After a tornado in Topeka, Kansas, relatives were the main sources families turned to for that particularly intimate form of help—shelter (Drabek et al., 1975). Victims didn't even have to ask for help because relatives took the initiative in offering shelter to their kin who needed it. By contrast, the Red Cross offered help to only half the families, and many families aided by the Red Cross had to ask for it.

Litwak and Szelenyi (1969) found that the more burdensome a form of help was, the greater the chance that only relatives would supply it. Also, the longer the period of help required, the greater the chance of asking relatives rather than neighbors or friends.

Relatives, then, are a handy resource in time of trouble. And, the greater the need, the greater the likelihood that relatives will be chosen from the alternative resources available.

Ordinary Help

Taking all forms of help combined—in emergencies and under normal conditions—Hill (1970) found that almost three fourths of the help given or received by Twin Cities families was exchanged with relatives rather than with friends or through organizations. This figure may be higher than usual since all his families were parts of three-generation chains of married couples living within a 50-mile radius of Minneapolis/St. Paul. Nevertheless, this figure suggests how predominantly families turn to relatives when they are available.

When members of the oldest generation needed help, they turned first to their children. Members of the middle generation turned first to their parents and second to their children, while members of the youngest generation went to their parents. The middle generation did the most giving since both their parents and their children depended on them as their primary resources.

Table 13–7 shows that the oldest generation received more help than they gave in every area except child care (which they no longer needed). The middle generation gave more help than they received in every area except nursing care, where inflow and outflow were balanced. The youngest generation received more than they gave in child care and economic help but gave more than they received in the remaining areas. Hill labeled the grandparents "dependent," the parents the "patrons" of the other generations, and the children "reciprocators." It is important to note that reciprocation did not mean repayment in kind, but an exchange of services depending on what that generation needed, on the one hand, and could give, on the other.

The previous table shows the proportion of all aid of a given type

Table 13-7   Help Given and Received by Grandparents, Parents, and Married Children, by Type of Help

					TYPE OF HELP					
	Economic		Household Management		Child Care		Illness		Emotional Gratification	
Generation	Gave	Rec.	Gave	Rec.	Gave	Rec.	Gave	Rec.	Gave	Rec.
Grandparents	26%	34%	21%	52%	16%	0	32%	61%	23%	42%
Parents	41	17	47	23	50	23%	21	21	47	37
Married children	34	49	33	25	34	78	47	18	31	21
Total	101%	100%	101%	100%	100%	101%	100%	100%	101%	100%

Adapted from Hill, 1970: 67. *Source:* 321 families in three-generation chains in the Twin Cities. The grandparents were mostly in their seventies, the parents mostly aged 46–55, and the married children in their twenties.

that was given or received by a particular generation. When the question is revised to ask the relative frequency of various forms of aid, Sussman (1959) found that help during illness was the kind most commonly given.

Some couples feel that help from relatives threatens their marriages. In extreme cases it does:

> Ken's mother and father have always wanted to help us out finan-cially, first with the business, then with the house and now with the children's education. I feel the way he leans on them financially has kept him from feeling independent. I don't like the way he accepts their advice either. It has become a sore point between us.

In general, however, help is welcomed by most married couples. Blood (1969) found that the larger the number of kinds of help received, the more satisfied wives were with their marriages. Relatives usually strengthen those they aid rather than overwhelm them.

Help for Young Families.   Although parents are sometimes described as having "launched" their children when the latter have left home and gotten married, those married sons and daughters often need help in setting their course through unfamiliar waters. Periodically, young wives leave home to have babies. Then motherless households are rescued by mother substitutes.

When a substitute mother is needed, the wife's mother is the most likely person to respond. Table 13–8 shows that when a child was born in Detroit, the wife's mother was far more likely than the husband's mother to fill in. Only when the wife's mother lived elsewhere did the husband's local mother become the primary source of help, but even then some wives' mothers made the trek.

When children are young, child care is given even more frequently

Table 13–8 Help after Childbirth, by Residence of Wife's and Husband's Mother

Percentage Receiving Help from Specified Source	LOCAL RESIDENCE			
	Both Mothers	Wife's Mother Only	Husband's Mother Only	Neither Mother
Both mothers	9%	2%	8%	4%
Wife's mother	53	50	19	42
Husband's mother	11	5	28	8
Other relatives	4	15	15	12
Friends, employees	3	2	4	6
No help	20	26	26	28
Total	100%	100%	100%	100%
Number of cases	210	58	53	50

Adapted from Siddiqui, 1962. *Source:* Representative sample of white wives in Detroit who gave birth in July 1961.

when mothers are *not* ill. Professional babysitters cost more than most couples can afford as often as they wish. So nearby grandmothers release their daughters—and, to a lesser extent, their daughters-in-law—from bondage to young children.

Whereas child care may be supplied on a regular basis, especially when mothers are working, financial aid is seldom regular. In New Haven, Sussman (1953a) found that financial support for ordinary living expenses was supplied only when married children were still in school or in other training and not yet established in their occupations. Normally, money from relatives went for special purposes such as buying or building a home.

Care for Aged Parents.   Through most of the life cycle, help flows primarily from parents to children. But when parents get old and feeble, they may need personal attention even if they are financially independent. After one parent dies, the survivor is apt to find living alone difficult or precarious.

Table 13–9 shows that widowed parents of either sex received more financial aid and more housing aid than parents who were still married. It also shows that widows received more of every kind of help than did widowers. If the still married respondents were separated into married men versus married women, we would be able to discover whether the death of a spouse increases the flow of aid. But since the married sample consisted of men and women who were not married to each other, we cannot disentangle the effect of marital status from the effect of gender in influencing the amount of aid received. We assume, however, that elderly parents are more likely to be aided by their children when they are alone than when they still have one another to depend upon.

Dependent parents create a dilemma. Most Americans react nega-

Table 13–9   Help Received from Children by Older Parents, by Marital Status

Type of Help Received from Children	MARITAL STATUS OF PARENTS		
	Married	Widowers	Widows
Companionship	71%	46%	81%
Gifts	66%	34%	78%
Transportation	21%	20%	54%
Help with work	31%	23%	23%
Advice	17%	16%	25%
Money	8%	14%	20%
Place to live	5%	14%	23%
No help	20%	25%	6%
Number of cases	230	37	158

Adapted from Berardo, 1967: 23. *Source:* Residents over 65 years old in Thurston County, Washington. Reciprocal percentages of parents did not receive the specified type of help from children. The table was limited to parents with at least one living child.

tively to the idea of having older people live with their children. (Specifically, almost two thirds of a national sample were opposed [Morgan et al., 1962].) The older they got, the more often people were unqualifiedly opposed. For both generations, merging households is a last resort to be postponed as long as possible. Moving to the same community, the same neighborhood, or even a separate apartment in the same building is preferred as long as it is feasible. Living nearby makes contact easy without infringing on either family's integrity.

But, eventually, a surviving parent may need more care than can be provided in an independent location. If Grandmother can no longer safely cook her own meals, a separate apartment is no longer feasible. The ultimate choice lies between placing her in a nursing home and bringing her into the home of one of her children. That choice depends on both practical and personal factors: (1) How satisfactory are the alternative facilities? Does the family have a room to spare? Is there an attractive institution that the family can afford? (2) How warm is the relationship between the grandmother and her children? For reasons that by now are familiar, mothers move in with daughters more than with sons (by a ratio of 55 to 45 [Glick, 1957]). The wife may have to provide most of the care and sociability, and this happens more naturally with one's mother than with one's mother-in-law:

> One reason we've decided to move to Chicago is because Walter really feels he must be near his disabled mother. In her condition she needs a lot of physical and emotional support. And I resent that I'm the one that will have to carry that burden. He says he cares for his mother

but I've been the one who writes her. He'll visit with her but I'll be the one that has to clean up her house.

If and when an aged parent moves into a child's home, stress is minimized by mutual respect for the autonomy of the still separate "families." Grandmother's room needs even more to be her castle when she no longer has a house of her own. Conversely, she must respect the integrity of the family whose guest she is (Duvall, 1954).

Should senility wreak its worst havoc, even daughters may find the strain too much. When mental deterioration means that an aged parent no longer recognizes who is taking care of her, a nursing home may be no loss to her but a relief to the family.

When help for the aged involves financial support, all the descendants deserve to share according to their ability. The kin network is one place for pure communism: from each according to his ability, to each according to his need.

Inheritance

So far we have concentrated on the general flow of help during the older generation's lifetime. Whatever assets remain at death are bequeathed largely to the children in the form of inheritances. In Firth's London sample (1970), two thirds of the couples had inherited money, mostly from parents of either the husband or the wife, less often from both. In the great majority of cases, these inheritances were gratefully received and created no trouble with siblings or other relatives who were actual or potential beneficiaries of the same legacies. Satisfaction reflected either careful equality or allocation on the basis of generally accepted differential need.

In exceptional cases where disputes arose over an inheritance, kin ties were severely strained and often broken. The most troublesome disputes occurred when a parent had been divorced and remarried. Then the children of the first marriage often resented the second wife's diversion of their expected inheritance, or vice versa.

14 Conflict Resolution

Never for the sake of peace and quiet deny your own experience or conviction—*Dag Hammarskjöld*

Marriage inevitably involves conflicts. No two people can live together year after year without clashing—unless one or both decides it is best to give in rather than to confront issues. Even then the conflict exists subliminally and undermines the relationship.

MARRIAGE BREEDS CONFLICT

Marriage is a natural breeding ground for conflict. Individuals inevitably differ in their perceptions and expectations. Moreover, people and life situations constantly change. So, marriage necessarily involves disharmony, rather than unruffled living-happily-ever-after.

The Inevitability of Differences

Two people are two people, essentially different. They never have exactly the same perspective. Different experiences, needs, and values put them at different vantage points:

> *We just can't communicate. Joe keeps insisting that I am stubbornly resisting all his requests. I see these requests as demands to do it his "right" way. He can't seem to hear me when I am in a different place. Every difference becomes a battleground.*

Joe's response to his partner's difference makes living together intolerable. Many individuals think the problem exists in the other person rather than in the two partners' different experiences. One way of viewing the problem is as follows:

> *When I make a complaint or share a grievance, the problem is within me. I am the one who hurts. I am the one who is upset. You may be perfectly happy and feel okay about your behavior. If your behavior causes me to have a problem I must start with myself, owning my problem. Because our lives are intimately involved, it is important that you know when I have a problem. Your behavior may, or may not, change when you become aware of how it is affecting me.*

Another way of viewing the problem is that it exists between two people; it is not just one partner who is the "crazy one":

> *Because he had had psychiatric help before we met, we both had a way of saying that "his" problems were the cause of our clashes. I felt he had to be treated with kid gloves because he was so sensitive. I dared not talk about my own feelings because it might upset him. When we went into counseling, I began to discover that the problems weren't in him so much as between us. We both had to let go of the image of how he had failed to cope in the past and deal honestly and realistically with present issues and feelings. Earlier, he had convinced me that he couldn't relate to my family because he had a thing about parents arising out of his own unhappy childhood. With effort we found that my parents could be seen as different from his parents, and he could be released from those traps of the past.*

Since two people don't always perceive alike or find total agreement, they have to accept the essential difference and search for mutuality. The task is to see if we can find a mesh, or, failing that, if we can live side by side accepting the other's different approach, contributing to one another out of our differences rather than blocking one another.

Sometimes we can each occupy our own space. Exact commonality is not always necessary:

> *I [Margaret] care about food so I do most of the cooking and Bob enjoys eating it. We don't fight about whether we spend equal time in the kitchen. He tends to sail by rules, I by sensing intuitively. When he began to let me sail my way and learn through my own failures we had less conflict and more fun in sailing together. Sometimes his high energy irritates me (when I feel competitive). When I can accept that as okay for him and my lower energy as the way I am, what he gets done with his high energy benefits rather than threatens me, and sometimes my lower energy encourages him to be more relaxed than he would be otherwise.*

The way I define our differentness may affect the way I respond to you, which may in turn reinforce the very behavior I don't like from you. For example, if I perceive you as tyrannical and authoritative, I may respond by playing the role of victim, and thereby encourage you to fulfill the role of tyrant. A confirmed victim, would rather blame the partner than ask for change. Such hooks are prevalent in marriage, especially where partners label and devalue each other.

The Expectation Gap

Some conflicts emerge early in marriage from divergent expectations. The first task is to recognize what they are. The unconscious nature of many expectations makes this difficult. Many go back to parental models and childhood experiences. Discovering that the partner's behavior is not deliberately antagonistic removes much of the venom from the conflict. Even if the ancestry of conflicts is not immediately apparent, to see them as problems rather than as personal deficiencies makes them easier to tackle without defensiveness. The fault lies not in either individual, but in the lack of fit between the two.

The nature of the human computer makes us tend to generalize upon the basis of our experience. When you act and speak in certain ways, I "take you at your word" and expect you to think and behave the same way again. I begin to think I know exactly how you will respond to me. Rather than confront you or ask you directly about your opinion, I confront you in my head and come up with the "right" answer. This I sometimes call my intuition, or "knowing you better than you do." I insist that you be consistent and bind you to that consistency even though I may want you to change:

> Sometimes when I tell Bill I agree with him he will say, "I just don't believe you," which makes me furious. He defeats what he has just asked of me by mistrusting the positive response that I feel at the moment. Actually, he is right about my ambivalence, but he always assumes that the fearful, negative side of me is the whole of me.

Expectations formed in the early years of a relationship are not easily dislodged:

> Since Sue began her full-time job my home life has changed. I never expected to be carrying a full-time job plus half-time cook and housekeeper and babysitter responsibilities. It's logical and fair, but I can't help but envy my father relaxing at the end of a hard day.

When one person's expectations change, the partner often wants to hold on to the old pattern:

Maurice wants to open up our marriage. He says he no longer expects sexual monogamy for himself or for me, but my expectations are the same as when we first married.

Expectations and assumptions need to be constantly checked out. The reality of where I am and where you are is where it's at—not what's in my head or in your head about where the other ought to be or was in the past:

Before I met Dick I expected my husband to care for me the way my father did for my mother. But I also wanted to be independent. With the children in school, Dick is pushing me to share economic responsibility. It's been easier than it might have been because he made his expectation clear all along.

Incorrect expectations lead to feeling betrayed, to feeling hurt that you have not sensed my need and responded to it. I need to let you know what I really want, and not make you guess. I need to know what you really think before I blame you for something. I can't make you change to fit my expectations unless you participate in the decision to change:

My father never displayed outward affection for my mother so I really didn't expect Jim to show me any special affection. Yet I needed it. I had to reexamine my stereotype of men as incapable of being warm, and tell him I needed more. When I asked for it, I found he could be more affectionate than I ever dreamed possible.

Keeping in touch with expectations is a way of checking realities. False expectations built up and stored over the years become a source of shocking conflict sooner or later.

Vulnerability

I can help you to accept and open yourself mostly by accepting and revealing myself to you—*Powell,* 1969: 17

If I expose my nakedness as a person to you, do not make me feel shame—*Powell,* 1969: 10

Increasing affectional involvement usually accompanies increasing self-disclosure. At first it is easy and satisfying to share feelings, but when the feelings are critical of each other it becomes scary. And as negative reactions cause shock or disappointment, both partners begin to tread more warily. Self-disclosure does not guarantee an intimate relationship. The more I know of you, the more I may dislike you. To be open is to become vulnerable to criticism, judgment, and possible disappointment of my wishes. The riskiness of being open tends to generate the games of self-defense, protecting you (not wanting to hurt you), and covert manipulation.

Lack of directness is often rationalized as responding "sensitively" to the partner's needs. "Understanding" is seen as paying off more than honesty:

> *Because I was fragile I treated him too tenderly. I saw it as my good wifely role to smooth out the rough spots. What it meant in the end was that my irritation went underground.*

Does a spouse have the right to know all feelings and intentions? A classic statement of this right to know appears in Shakespeare's *Julius Caesar:*

> PORTIA: My Brutus, you have some sick offense within your mind which by the *right* and *virtue of my place* I ought to know of. And upon my knees I charm you by all our vows of love and that great vow which did incorporate and make us one, that you unfold to me, yourself, your half. Why are you heavy...?
> Within the bond of marriage tell me, Brutus, is it excepted, I should know no secrets that appertain to you?
> Am I yourself but, as it were, in sort of limitation, to keep with you at meals, comfort your bed, and talk to you sometimes?
> Dwell I but in the suburbs of your good pleasure? If it be no more, Portia is Brutus' harlot, not his wife!
> BRUTUS: You are my true and honorable wife, as dear to me as are the ruddy drops that visit my sad heart.
> PORTIA: If this were true, then should I know this secret.

How much privacy and how much revelation is good varies with each couple. The how much and when of self-disclosure must be experimented with if honesty is to be fruitful and not hurtful.

The Intimacy of Marriage.   People are on their best behavior in public. At home they let their hair down. The screens of privacy give way and the result is sometimes disgusting. Living together under the same roof, the partners are exposed to the seamy side of each other's lives. This strains any relationship that had been built on the prettier aspects of life. These intimacies involve facets of life where modesty or cleanliness was learned the hard way. Behavior that disgusts the partner revives childhood anxieties. Unconsciously, it arouses forgotten fears of parental punishment or loss of love.

The Cumulativeness of Marriage.   Stress is cumulative. Tension grows with prolonged exposure to an irritant. A child can tolerate a physical irritant for limited periods, but if exposed long enough will develop an allergy. Similarly, adults can stand irritating behavior a few hours or a few days but constant exposure makes them allergic. Unfortunately, most allergies are treated symptomatically. The real answer to an allergic reaction is to find the underlying stress that made the person overreact and alleviate that.

The Competitiveness of Marriage.   Envy and competition are as familiar in marriage as elsewhere. I may be jealous of your time spent elsewhere, of your devotion to your job, or of your relationship with one of our children. I may envy your success in your career, in making friends easily, in being comfortable at parties. I may even compete with you about getting up in the morning. (Your cocky crowing about being an earlybird implies that I am lazy when I lie abed later.)

Being human, husbands and wives compete for scarce resources whether they be money or affection or status. In a competitive society the need to win is socially reinforced and competition can go to extraordinary lengths. Many couples play a game of who can pile up the most hurt. As one expresses a grievance the other tops it with a bigger one, which is the equivalent of saying, "I'm more unhappy with you because you're more of a stinker than I am and I can prove it." Such couples might transform this game by giving points to the first partner who crosses the gap after a fight (the points being given by the one reached out to). In this game both win.

The Changeableness of Marriage.   If a businessman had to adapt so fast to changing circumstances, he would go crazy—or bankrupt. Yet hard-won solutions to family problems obsolesce with frightening speed. While the new "firm" is still shaky, it typically doubles in size and loses half its income. How can the "payroll" be met until the new "employees" finish their 20-year training? The tighter the financial strain, the tougher the decisions that will have to be made. Moreover, the original staff must do all the training alone, except for occasional assistance from retired executives of the parent firm. So labor as well as capital are in short supply for the crucial early decades of the new firm's existence.

No wonder the partners quarrel over how to spend their time and money. Frictions are inevitable. Some plans must be deferred, and strategies that worked this year will have to be revised next year as the trainees' skills and outside offers increase.

Conflict resolution, in short, is a never-ending process. It need not be painful. It may be effective. But it must be worked at constantly.

ABORTIVE ATTEMPTS AT CONFLICT RESOLUTION

Warfare and withdrawal are two ways of dealing with difference. Both can endanger the health of a relationship. Both can be self-defeating. Both are human responses, but can be tempered by learning how to communicate clearly and directly.

There are many ways to fight—fair and unfair, healthy and unhealthy. Some individuals learn toleration and adapt more easily than others. Most couples believe in rational discussion but get caught in debate and destructive argument. Some habitually avoid encounter, only to find that sooner or later resentment erupts. Whatever method is used carries its consequences for the relationship.

Coping versus Carping

One way of dealing with conflict is to learn to tolerate the other person. There is wisdom in toleration. Reminding myself that no one is perfect and that all persons are peculiar in some way, I come to you as you are with your limitations, a good exchange for asking you to accept me as I am.

Dirty socks on the bedroom floor, the cap left off the toothpaste, chronic lateness, forgetting an agreement—such trifling irritants can assume tremendous proportions. The solution may be to reduce expectations, accepting the fact that the difficulties are irremediable. Resignation may come through sheer exhaustion, but sometimes through self-insight as one discovers that sensitivity stems not so much from the grossness of the partner as from one's own anxieties learned in childhood. One may come to understand the partner's response mechanism to situations and accept the good intention, knowing how hard it is for the other to change. Love and time may ease the annoyance. What at first seemed revolting becomes a normal part of life. It is a good time in life when two people "mellow," when judgment is less harsh and mercy is more plentiful. I grow more tolerant of you because I don't demand perfection of myself.

Some critics decide that prolonging the war does more harm than good, so it's time to call a cease-fire:

> It really gets my goat to waste electricity. Every time I come home Jeanne has the house ablaze with light. Lately I've realized that Jeanne doesn't turn off the lights because I heckle her. So what's the use of causing all that trouble if it saves only a dollar a month on the electric bill?

Other critics adopt a do-it-yourself policy. With a fraction of the energy expended on a verbal barrage, all the switches in the house could be turned off. Developing immunity doesn't necessarily require learning to live with mass illumination or mass clutter. It only requires being able to live with the spouse. If her job is the livingroom and she has higher priorities than picking it up right now, I can do it myself. If I don't like the way he is discharging a responsibility, I can assume it myself. Maturity requires accepting the inevitable—providing the critic can really adapt and let go. To make concessions gracefully is beneficial, but to extend oneself grudgingly only causes more irritation, even if the task itself gets done.

Willingness to modify one's own behavior distinguished adjusted from maladjusted married couples (Buerkle, Anderson, and Badgley, 1961). For example, if a wife was bored with a party and wanted to leave but the husband was having a good time, a well-adjusted husband would tell his wife, "We'll leave, since you want to go," while she would say, 'I'll stay because you're enjoying yourself." Mutual deference to the other's feelings does not resolve conflict, since it doesn't specify whether they should stay or leave, but it transforms conflict from a clash of wills to an Alphonse-Gaston courtesy contest. The willingness of both partners to please the other is appreciated, no matter which solution is chosen. If both are willing to modify their behavior, compromise becomes a happy medium instead of a bitter necessity.

Patience, long suffering, and tolerance will smooth over many a rough spot, but to say "it's not that important" and "don't get so upset" may serve as rationalizations for pulling back, withholding one's energy as well as biting one's tongue.

Arguing

Having practiced businesslike discussions in school and clubs many married couples are thrown by not being able to resolve their differences rationally. Partners may resent each other for being either "too rational" or "too emotional." Both rationality and emotional-in-touchness are essential to resolving conflicts. The one who seems more rational may be unaware of the emotional grounds of his/her argument, using intellectual skills to prove points and trap the other. Such "rationality" avoids real issues because it avoids real feelings. Solutions thus found will be only temporary. True rationality finds ways other than arguing, since that involves trying to force you to agree with my "right" position. This is fighting, but not fair fighting. Unless both parties come up with a mutual agreement, the contract they make will probably not be kept, except at the expense of caring and trust.

Copping Out: Avoiding Confrontation

Avoiding an issue can hardly be called a process of conflict resolution, but it is frequently used to preserve "harmony." Such behavior may evolve from one (or both) partner's disgust with battles that bring no resolution. I may become discouraged about not being able to win over your rational arguments. If you always win (and I lose), why engage? If resentments are building, I can prevent further resentment (on my part, at least) by hiding out or withdrawing from the battleground. Lack of confidence, lack of a sense of self-worth, and little practice in assertiveness add to the reasons for not struggling.

The consequences of avoidance are escalated resentment, anger, and frustration, laying the ground for future violence, or on the other side increasing withdrawal, depression, and physical and emotional ill health.

Rarely is silent suffering beneficial. Only trifles are better endured than harped upon. But it takes maturity to handle irritation, and there is danger of displacing tension into covert aggression, making matters worse instead of better. The following situation illustrates the danger that unexpressed issues will be transmuted into hidden aggression, this time in resistance to requests:

> My husband is a regular slavedriver. He believes everyone should work hard, but he is never satisfied and never appreciates what I do. Often I have a terrible urge to walk across the room and slap his face, but I don't dare. I don't really do anything to get even with him, except that I do unenthusiastically the things he asks me to do.

If grievances are severe, holding them in will hardly improve things. Tension will build up until it explodes outwardly against the partner or inwardly in the form of ulcers or asthma. In Feldman's middle-class Syracuse marriages (1966), individuals who suppressed their responses to conflict situations were more aggressive toward their spouses. Keeping the lid on rarely works when real trouble is brewing. If the partner is perceptive, s/he will detect the tension. Once noticed, it is frustrating not to be able to come to grips with the issue because knowledge is deliberately withheld:

> I took to Wayne because of his calmness. It seemed to be a good balance for my excitableness. I've discovered since we've been married, though, that this means he'll go into his shell and not talk to me for a week. I never can find out the reason for his sulkiness until he finally gets over it. It's pretty exasperating to know he's got something against me but not be able to do anything about it since I don't know what it is.

Raush and his colleagues (1974) found that when a couple "suppress the hostile feelings and avoid overt conflicts, . . . resentments can build up and poison the relationship. The suppression of interpersonal differences and of the feelings attached to them means that less of each person's self gets communicated, and this can lead to erosion of trust" (p. 31).

Raush asked newly married couples to interact with one another around four role-playing scenes that were designed to provide for head-on conflict between the husband and the wife. Yet 15 percent of their couples

managed to avoid confronting each other directly. An even higher proportion of the husbands avoided confronting their wives in a scene where the
men had been instructed to express a wish to be alone. Instead of taking
responsibility for that wish themselves, 25 percent of the husbands
shifted the responsibility onto something outside themselves, most frequently blaming their jobs.

The psychologists conducting this study believed that these
avoiders wanted to elude the anxiety that they would have felt if they had
told the spouse directly of the wish to be alone. Even where the wish was
hinted at, it frequently was covered up by words or gestures of endear-
ment that masked the basic message and left the hearer bewildered and
confused. The higher the speaker's anxiety, the more s/he escalated the
avoidances by piling on innumerable denials. If the partner began to
suspect a hidden confrontation behind the denials, the speaker might
become even more deceptive by asking a completely irrelevant question,
such as "Did you feed the cat?" To interject such a question leaves the
partner bewildered and confused, feeling written off as a person since
his/her attempt to understand the cryptoconfrontation is ignored. To a
perceptive observer, the very irrelevance of the "cat" remark suggests that
the preceding dialogue was too close to the truth for comfort and was
deliberately diverted lest the feared confrontation occur. Humor often
serves as another means of derailing a threatened confrontation.

The researchers discovered that, in many marriages, copping out
was a cooperative endeavor: "Most often we found that partners colluded
with one another in avoiding interpersonal issues" (p. 79). When this
happens, the interchange frequently goes on interminably, getting
nowhere because the real issues aren't being dealt with. In several cases,
only the researcher's intervention brought the experimental dialogues to
an end. By themselves, the couples never seemed to get anywhere, and
could not even end their verbal exchange.

To avoid confronting one another may be a successful defense
against both partners' anxiety about conflict, but it prevents the growth
that can come only through struggle. A relationship cannot grow when
people avoid dealing with the issues that face them. To their surprise,
however, the researchers found that couples in such marriages were not
necessarily unhappy. Indeed, part of their pattern of denying problems
was to feel that everything was right with their marriages. Only those who
look at such couples from the outside are aware of what they are missing
when they avoid confrontation.

The Aggressive Use of Anger

Anger can be used deliberately to frighten off an opponent. Whether or
not the anger is "righteous," it is usually aggressive and provokes defen-

siveness in the partner. There are various degrees and forms of expressing anger, each bringing its own result. An individual who fears his/her own anger may fall into low-key nagging, blaming, and bitching. The traditional female stereotype is the wife whose tongue is like a faucet that drips and wears. The traditional male stereotype is the husband who" shouts and strikes and gets out his anger. Indirect anger goes around the edge of the partner's wall or even digs down and comes up unexpectedly on the opponent's ground. It is covert and manipulative. The partner who experiences the other's anger may feel put down, accused, blamed, condemned, guilty. Demoralized, s/he may paralyze and withdraw. The angry attacker may need to be curbed like a child:

> When I run my anger at Richard he has learned I need to have him make me stop. I will probably be offended and scream back louder and strike at him, but when he holds me and I can't strike I feel like a little child held to keep me from hurting myself and others. The rage turns into wrenching sobs until it's spent.

There is a difference between hiding anger and taking charge of anger. A friend of ours used to say to an angry friend, "I want you to take charge of your anger and help me to take charge of mine. I want to interrupt your pattern when you're dumping it on me and I want you to interrupt me when I'm running my anger. I can accept your angry feelings as real but I want you to trace them back to their cause and ask for what you need, now!"

Ashley Montagu (1953) speaks of aggressiveness as a deformed aspect of love, an attempt to compel love when feeling unloved. In counseling, we often see one partner who feels unloved and makes demands that alienate the partner even further. To demand affection rarely generates a caring response. Yet unmet wants and pent up grievances will eventually burst the gunny sack:

> I had to scream to make him hear me. He wouldn't listen until I exploded. It was horrible but we both felt better afterward.

Anger and aggression are human but are also dangerous, as they progressively build up over time and then blow off. The most loving person becomes a demon out of control. Potential violence exists in every family. Sooner or later, couples must learn to deal with anger, its causes and meaning. They must learn to be wary of its escalation, providing safe outlets, seeking help from one another and from others. Anger is pain crying for release. When listened to, it shows the way to needed change.

To resolve a conflict is not to withdraw from the battle. If the source of anger and frustration is not remedied, bitterness and resentment will still exist. Though some anger has been released, the issue, if not attended to, will arise again. If the bitterness and need to punish turn inward, depression and moodiness will ensue, clouding the relationship. Incapable of punishing you, I may sabotage myself and us.

Action and reaction across the battle lines are patterns that are hard to reverse but all is possible in love and war.

CONDITIONS FOR FAIR FIGHTING

Good loving and good fighting have to be learned by practice and experience. The definition of a fair fight, according to Bach (1969), is one in which there is no loss of esteem by either partner.

Conditions conducive to fair fighting include openness, ability to affirm the self and the partner, centeredness, and consent to dialogue. Openness involves the willingness to self-disclose negative as well as positive things. The how and what of self-disclosure must always relate sensitively to your feelings of worth. If I destroy your feelings of okayness, communication will be blocked by your defensiveness and pulling away. By continuing to confirm you, I make it possible for you to be self-assertive, that is, able to identify your own wants and needs and able to ask (without which there can be no true negotiation). Rollo May (1969: 146) defined self-assertion as

> a capacity to stand on one's own feet, an affirmation of one's self in order to have the power to put one's self into the relationship. One must have something to give and be able to give it. . . . If one is unable to assert oneself, one is unable to participate in a genuine relationship. A dynamic dialectical relationship . . . is a continuous give-and-take in which one asserts himself, finds an answer in the other, then possibly asserts too far, senses a "no" in the other, backs up but does not give up, shifts the participation to a new form and finds the way that is adequate for the wholeness of the other. . . . It is an assertion of one's own individuality in relation to another person. It always skates on the edge of exploitation of the partner; but . . . without it, there is no vital relationship.

How you feel about me is revealed in every word, gesture, and facial expression. The place where we meet is scary. Your attitude, your tone of voice, and your choice of words will affect my response.

If each of us comes out of a centered place within ourselves, we are more apt to meet one another with respect. If either or both are fatigued, frantic, "in pieces," we will find it hard to trust our own and each other's feelings and intuitions. We will project the unintegrated, negative parts of ourselves onto the other. I will be suspicious of your intentions and you of mine. As I doubt your motives, I will find it hard to believe that you can change. We may as well wait until we are more in tune with ourselves.

Consent

Bach and Wyden (1969) pointed out that one of the prime conditions for fighting fair is that both partners give their consent. No matter how urgent it may seem that an issue be dealt with, no matter how much a person may be hurting, nothing can be accomplished until the partner is ready to give his/her consent to resolving the conflict.

To be sure, the unready partner can pay enough attention to the eager partner's grievance to acknowledge that s/he is upset and to promise that the matter will be dealt with as soon as possible. Hopefully, the unready partner will give the spouse a "raincheck," promising to engage in dialogue at a particular time in the not-too-distant future. Such a promise is broken only at the peril of escalating the grievance still further. Many couples have a rule of thumb that postponements can be only until later on the same day. But the press of conflicting duties (such as job responsibilities) is frequently heavy, and a delay may not be just an excuse for avoiding the spouse. Sometimes the partner is too sick or too tired to do battle constructively:

> *Everytime Ruth gets mad at me she holds it until bedtime. Then she drops it like a bomb and insists we must deal with the hurt or else she'll never be able to sleep. The trouble is we're both too tired to be rational, so we go round and round getting nowhere and no sleep as well.*

In our marriage, we seldom are able to resolve conflicts late at night. As fatigue sets in, rationality gives way to irrationality and matters that could be settled expeditiously by the light of day escalate for us into disasters.

Saying no to a partner who wants to press an issue may, therefore, benefit both partners. It benefits particularly the no-sayer since his/her energy is simply not available at the time:

> *Laura and Ted have decided to set limits on how often they discuss heavies. She refuses to spend more than 20 minutes a day talking out problems that can add up to three hours a week. She agrees to take it all together or in 20-minute stretches.*

Both must give consent to dialogue, to pay attention, to stay with the ground rules or agreed-upon process. The time and place must be appropriate so there will be no interruption by children or other persons, where each can hear and speak honestly.

Many couples find it useful to clear the decks once a week, checking out how things are with the other and dealing with any unfinished business:

Since Bob and I [Margaret] work hard on weekends our evaluation time comes on Monday morning. We sit at either end of the couch, facing each other, legs touching in the middle.

Sometimes the one talking will close eyes and get into a soliloquy, avoiding the accusing eyes of the other who might be upset about something. Allowing the other fully to describe his/her feelings avoids the interrupting we used to do that prevented our hearing.

If the one listening can't take any more in and needs to respond, s/he holds up a finger to indicate readiness rather than jumping in. Taking turns keeps things cooler and more manageable—and pays off in feeling really heard, even if we can't find a solution at the time.

Meeting Face to Face

To meet is to face one another and to confront the issue that exists between us. We require couples who work with us to sit in chairs or cross-legged on the floor, turning their energy and attention to the other, giving eye contact if possible. This is a magic posture. It symbolizes and promotes presence, honesty, and support. If there is plenty of time and a lack of interruption, the environment is right. In our case:

We used to throw feelings and demands and accusations at each other across the room, across the dinner table, between rooms, or as one of us was on the way out the door. Sitting face to face brings out the best in us. I feel free, not forced, to respond because I have consented to deal with you. We are two adults leveling with each other, not parent talking down to child. I own I have a problem. I take myself seriously—my feelings, my needs, and my wants. This position indicates that I am not putting myself down, not backing off, not looking down on you or manipulating you from the side. I am grounded, feel my own strength. I take you seriously, hear you, am open to your input. I am here, willing to look for a solution with you.

Dealing with Negative Feelings

First, I need to remember that feelings of frustration, anger, anxiety, jealousy, sadness are not bad. They just are. And they are like physical pain, symptoms of something that's wrong and needs to be attended to, symptoms of unfulfilled wants and unfinished business.

Next I become aware of the feeling itself. I examine it. I may ask it questions. Who are you? Where do you come from? What color are you? What shape are you? Why are you here? What do you do for me? Every question I can think of will help me to analyze this feeling that burdens me. As I do this alone, I may be able to resolve my own burden. When I do it with you, I find that two minds are better than one and four ears can hear more than two.

What happens when I bring a load of negative feelings to you? If you are tired, you may not want to carry that load. Unless you can sympathize, you may react defensively. If I blame you, you are liable to respond in kind. Even if I don't, you may feel blamed indirectly. You may feel confused, not knowing how to respond. I may interpret your confusion as confirmation of your "guilt."

If my negative feeling has its source in outside activities, you may give me advice in which I am not interested. My irritated response to your "good advice" leaves you confused and wary. If you are silent, I may interpret this as uncaring or rejection. You may call my fears irrational, and try to argue me out of them, leaving me more frustrated than ever.

As these things happen, strange miscommunications occur. Each of us gets entangled in the other's negative feelings. One bad feeling generates another. Often the feeling itself becomes the issue: "I don't like your anger" or "I don't wish to hear your anger. "You're stupid to be angry." "You shouldn't feel guilty."

Bad feelings are a key to what is wrong. The pain will go away when the source is dealt with. Back of these bad feelings is a good desire—to protect and care for the self. When attention is focused on the expressed need—for clarification, for assurance, for support—the partner is better able to give a positive response.

Discharging Anger.   Couples who are angry or otherwise emotionally worked up can seldom resolve their problems as long as adrenalin is running around in their bloodstreams. Anger is an understandable reaction to many situations. It serves a useful function, signaling both partners that something is wrong. When one partner or both feel like beating each other over the head, they know emphatically that they have a problem. But beating each other won't solve it—it will most likely make things worse.

If releasing anger in physical aggression is destructive, what is to be done with it? We believe that ways can be found of discharging anger without hurting the partner. We personally like to push shoulders against one another, finding the balancing point where each of us is exerting maximum force without pushing the other up against the wall. When one of us feels frustrated, we sit facing one another, holding hands to symbolize that this is a cooperative endeavor in tension release, and roar at each other like lions. Other couples like to arm-wrestle, to pound on pillows, or to yell exaggerated obscenities at each other with the understanding that they are not to be taken literally. Each couple must experiment until they find a style that is right for them—one which is not hurtful, has no danger of escalating into violence, and leaves the angry partner(s) feeling relieved.

Couples unable to find any joint activity that is safe enough may resort to individual forms of tension release, such as chopping wood or running around the block. However, Thibaut and Coules (1952) found that people had less residual hostility when they were allowed to communicate their hostility toward the person at whom they were angry. For this reason we prefer more direct methods of discharge, provided that they turn out to be safe. Safety is more likely when couples practice these ways of discharging when they are not angry and agree to use them the next time they are angry.

We know that we have roared enough when we break out in laughter. Once the tension is broken, we can turn to the processes of conflict resolution with reasonable hope that they will be productive.

A word of caution is in order: Discharging anger is no substitute for rational problem solving, but only a preliminary to it. Also, unrestrained expression of anger can wreck any problem-solving process when it occurs in the middle of it. Straus (1974) found that unrestrained yelling and heated verbal exchanges between partners in the midst of fighting over issues often escalated into physical violence between them. The more verbally abusive couples became, the more physically abusive they were liable to be. This emphasizes that the discharge of anger must be conducted according to the rules of the game and separated from the rational problem-solving process itself.

Using I-Statements

The first rule for dialogue is to represent myself and to insist that you represent yourself. This, like the face-to-face posture, magically increases the ability to communicate. I, who know more than anyone else what I feel and think and believe, must speak for myself. To speak for you is to assume that I know more than you do. If I make assumptions about you directly or indirectly, we're off to a bad start and will soon slip into a vicious cycle of blaming and feeling blamed. Asking questions shifts attention from my own revelation to making you reveal your hand first. Questions tend to be leading ones that make you feel defensive. When I speak for myself, the words may be fumbling and unsure, but if I am patient and you are patient, what comes out will be real and unrehearsed. The very act of speaking my own truth increases my awareness of what I feel and want.

Gordon (1970) described "I-messages" as statements that do not begin with "You did this," but with "I feel upset." Criticism involves laying the problem on the partner. I-messages involve "owning" the problem myself, saying that "I am worried" or "I am afraid" or "I can't concentrate."

To be sure, I-messages often end with "when you do such and such". Nevertheless, when the intent is not to send a coercive message about what I want you to do but, rather, an informational message about how I am feeling, the partner is more open to hearing. Gordon noted that telling you that I have a problem does not impose a solution on you but leaves you free to choose how you would like to respond. Self-chosen solutions can be given more generously than other-imposed solutions can be accepted.

Active Listening

How can we be sure that we really hear each other? There are several ways that are worth practicing.

1. Tell me what you hear me saying: If you missed something, I will tell you what you missed. I like to be heard. When I hear you saying what my feelings are, I feel more clear and I feel supported by you (that it's okay to have those feelings). Accepting feelings does not mean accepting the logic of my case. I can trick myself in pure logic. I need your help in bringing my feelings into the picture.

2. Reverse roles: We can change chairs and get into the other's shoes, speaking for him/her what we have heard, speaking as the other person. Your words may not be identical with mine, but I know when you have identified with me and you know when I have been in your place. This is another magical exercise from Gestalt therapy.

When the exercise is simply to reflect the other's feelings, it is against the rules to put in one's own interpretation of what you are feeling or why you are feeling it.

Concentration

Few couples can solve more than one issue at a time, yet many couples drag in "everything but the kitchen sink." Bringing in other issues escalates the conflict to the point where it becomes too immense to be resolved.

Issues get diffused when the focus is broadened from the present to the whole length of the relationship: "You always do this," "You never do that." Raush and others (1974) discovered that "temporal expansion by one partner is perceived by the other as an attack"—and attacks lead to denials, not to solutions.

Issues are also expanded by dragging in the partner's family: "'Your mother' are fighting words for most of our couples, particularly though not exclusively at the newlywed stage, and they seldom fail to expand and escalate the original issue of conflict" (Raush et al., p. 97). To attack one's mother-in-law is a good example of what Bach and Wyden call "unfair tactics" because she is not present to defend herself. Since she is not, the spouse whose mother is attacked must do the defending, and again the opportunity to resolve the issue is lost.

The heaviness of an issue is escalated by what Raush et al. called "crucializing" it, that is, I tell my partner that s/he must capitulate to my demand "or else." The highest stakes involve putting the marriage on the line and saying, "If you don't do this for me, I'll get a divorce." Raush noted that the most common phraseology, especially favored by wives, was, "If you really loved me, you would . . ." Such tactics undermine the autonomy of the spouse, giving him/her a choice between compliance and disaster. Yet if compliance is not honest, it only breeds resentment. So to escalate the cost of disagreement is to run the risk of seeming to win but actually losing in the long run.

Some issues are crucial. In those cases, to tell you what I will do if you reject my demand is not only permissible but desirable, so that you will know what hinges on your choice. Crucializing, by contrast, means taking an issue that is not really crucial and pretending that it is. Crucializing commits me to the necessity of carrying out a threat if it doesn't succeed in coercing you. This tactic can end a marriage that might otherwise have survived:

> Every time I felt really low about myself and us, I would hit Ben with how I couldn't stand living this way any longer. In response, he would cordially agree that I could leave the marriage any time (that he wasn't going to be possessive with me), but that he preferred staying in the marriage since he loved me very much. I heard only the first part—before the "but." It annoyed me that he could let me go so easily! We found ourselves saying these same things every time the going got rough. One day we heard what we were doing and made an agreement that he would stop offering an easy out to me, provided I quit telling him the relationship was really intolerable. We decided not to put the marriage on the line as we struggled with a difficult issue. It not only was preventing us from solving the particular issue, but did not take into account the totality of the marriage.

EFFECTIVE CONFLICT RESOLUTION

Decision making is a critical skill. Some people are skillful enough to be able to concentrate on the content rather than on the method of dealing with a particular problem. But clumsy couples may have to pay more attention to the process. Effective problem-solving involves a series of stages. Raush and his colleagues (1974) specified six steps in the kind of decision-making process that not only resolves conflicts but solidifies the relationship between the partners:

1. identifying the problem
2. exploring alternative solutions
3. selecting the best alternative
4. implementing the decision
5. rebuilding the relationship
6. reviewing the decision-making process

Identifying the Problem

Some problems are hard to pin down because they are embarrassing. Sexual inadequacies may go undefined by squeamish couples. Ignorance of sexual terms may handicap effective communication. More often, the words are known but too emotionally loaded. Married men at Brigham Young University were more disappointed about their low frequency of sexual intercourse than about any other subject. But did they say anything to their wives? Sixty-five percent did not, preferring to "wait and see" what happened. Similarly, men disappointed with their wives' care of the home usually said nothing (Cutler and Dyer, 1965). Perhaps they felt their wives were doing the best that could be expected early in marriage, so they could reasonably hope for improvement in the future. Presumably, the longer a marriage has been in existence, the less appropriate it is to wait and see whether things will be better spontaneously. Moreover, even in this study only husbands were modally uncommunicative. Most wives broached their grievances directly.

Misleading cues are common. Symptoms mask underlying problems. Nagging and complaining—no matter how much they are blamed for marital unhappiness—are never the root of the problem. They are attempts to cope with deeper difficulties. What may be an issue in one marriage may be a symptom in another. Sexual problems are sometimes basic, but sometimes they reflect other dissatisfactions with the partner. Some couples say money is their problem, yet others thrive on the same income. Locating the fundamental problem may take considerable sleuthing.

If couples know *when* their bad feelings crop up but not exactly *how* the trouble originated, it may help to rehearse the order of events:

> *Carol and I both love books. When we got married we decided to put enough money in the budget for one book a month. Last month when we went to pick out our book everything seemed to go wrong. Both of us were disappointed about what should have been a pleasant expedition. After we got home, I said to her, "Let's go through the whole evening again and see where we went off the track." So right there in the living-room I pretended to go into the store and look around, all the while saying out loud what my thoughts had been. Then Carol did the same. It finally became clear that the crux of our problem lay in my desire to*

browse around and leaf through a lot of books whereas Carol wanted to find out whether they had certain books she'd already heard about, buy one, and then run home to start reading it. We haven't decided yet how to get together next time, but we're both relieved to know what the trouble was.

Stating the Problem.   It is not enough to know that something is wrong; it is necessary to state the problem before we can deal with it. When Raush et al. (1974) asked one partner to ask for distance and the other to ask for closeness, most couples failed to achieve closeness unless a specific issue was stated. The conflict was satisfactorily resolved in only 18 percent of the vaguely stated cases compared to 66 percent of the clearly stated cases. To state the issue clearly enables the partner to grapple with it effectively. To fail to state the issue leaves the partner feeling like s/he is shadow-boxing. Even when a clearly stated issue is not immediately resolved, couples at least find out where they stand with one another and the way is opened to subsequent solutions. Shadow-boxing gets nobody anywhere.

Each of us needs to take an uninterrupted turn, stating as clearly as possible how we see the issue from our side.

Exploring Alternative Solutions

Opening Statements.   After the issue has been identified and the feelings around the problem have been aired and heard, it is time for each partner to offer a proposed solution. Each takes a turn saying what s/he would like. This is not a final statement. The partner need not feel threatened because each has an opportunity to voice what seems good to him/her. This may be an offer from one partner, or it may be asking the partner to do something or to change in some way, or it may be a suggested solution to the problem. It represents taking responsibility for my own needs, letting you know what I want most. There is no guarantee that you will respond positively to what I ask you to do or be. You have a choice and without this freedom the asking becomes a demand that will boomerang in resentment.

Brainstorming.   The chief pitfall at this stage is incompleteness. Instead of thinking through all possible alternatives, only a few are considered. As a result, the best solution may be overlooked.

Because each partner has a preconceived answer, the fact that other solutions may be possible tends to be forgotten. If both partners have the same idea, they are even more likely to settle on it, regardless of its merits. If the television announcer has just made a persuasive plug for a loan company, shorthanded couples are apt to ignore less expensive alternatives. Only if neither partner has a ready answer will they be aware of the need to search for potential solutions.

Couples often make the mistake of combining proposing with evaluating. As soon as one solution is proposed, they discuss its pros and cons. Only when a given solution looks doubtful do they begin scavenging for another. With luck this system may work, but for best results, special attention needs to be paid to canvassing alternatives. Writing down proposals guarantees that no ideas will be forgotten. The initial order of alternatives depends simply on the accident of what pops first into someone's mind. Suggesting solutions gives both partners a sense of involvement in the final decision. More important, it widens the range of alternatives, thereby increasing the likelihood that the best possible solution will have been considered. The best means for this is brainstorming, with both partners suggesting items and neither partner commenting until the whole creative process is finished.

Postponing comments is difficult. Each partner must curb his/her reaction to the other's suggestions. Such restraint may not be necessary for couples able to approach their problems objectively. But for high-tension couples, stiff neutrality here may make the difference between successful problem solving and just another explosion.

At this stage it may be useful for each partner to fantasize what would happen if a feared alternative came to pass. Sometimes, facing the possibility of divorce lends perspective to the marriage itself and its problems. This may be followed by fantasizing the best that could happen. This in turn can lead to considering what we could do to change in whatever direction both of us want.

Making the Decision

Once the full range of possible solutions has been identified, we can begin deciding which is the best one. This process can be subdivided into a preliminary phase of evaluating each proposal on its own merits, moving on to the tougher problem of choosing one solution from the alternatives.

Evaluating the Alternatives.   Wherever two or more solutions are available, the first task is to measure them against each partner's values. After each partner has ranked them, the preferred alternatives can be compared to see how much agreement exists. Low-priority options can be abandoned and attention concentrated on each partner's preferences.

Some choices have such complex ramifications that both partners may feel ambivalent about the alternatives; both see gains and losses in each alternative. In such dilemmas, decision making may be expedited by jointly listing the values involved. For example, husband and wife might evaluate a job offer in another city:

Gains	Losses
1. Higher salary	1. Moving expenses
2. More challenging job	2. Changing schools in midyear
3. Greater opportunity for promotion	3. Loss of friends for the children and for us
4. More cultural advantages	4. Leaving our home
5. Closer to relatives	5. Pulling out of organizational responsibilities
	6. Longer commuting time

Sometimes the problem may be not to choose goals but the best means of achieving them. For example, husband and wife may agree that they need a new car, but have to choose among brands and models. Then evaluation requires research. Reading up on the subject, talking to others who've faced the same problem, and consulting with experts may be fruitful sources of information. Firsthand experimentation sometimes yields information no amount of study could give.

Once the list of gains and losses is complete, the weighing process can begin. How likely and how important is each? Moving costs must be compared with the salary increase, the husband's job satisfaction with the wife's regret in parting with her friends, and the like. Comparing gains and losses is not easy, but the weight of various factors will gradually emerge as each partner listens to the other. Understanding the partner's feelings is even more likely if each takes the place of the other, arguing in favor of the other's side and against his/her own. Switching places "should serve to increase empathy for the spouse and insight into one's own behavior" (Kimmel and Havens, 1966).

One pitfall is evaluating proposals as "right" and "wrong." These labels are too simple and too abstract. Calling a proposal right is another way of saying, "This is the answer I choose." Premature decision making short-circuits evaluation:

> Last week Ken and I were making plans for our vacation trip and he suggested that we write some of our friends and ask if we could spend the night with them. I felt pretty strongly that it wouldn't be right to do that and I told him so. He wanted to know why not, so I told him it was just the wrong thing to do.

Arguing that something isn't right because it is wrong doesn't get you anywhere. Concrete effects on the wife's feelings, on the prospective hosts, or on their friendship might contribute to evaluating this proposal.

So far we have written as though both partners know how they feel about the issue and as though each is clear about the solution that s/he advocates. But some issues are so complex and emotional that one or both partners may feel conflicted and ambivalent about them:

> I can't ask you for what I want or need if I don't know myself what I want. To be assertive with you I need to be together within myself. To come together, I need your help. Will you help me to do a Gestalt dialogue between the parts of myself over this issue? Ask me to choose two adjectives to describe the two parts of myself—adjectives like "Scared Margaret" and "Generous Margaret." Then listen while I introduce each Margaret to the other and carry on a dialogue between them, moving back and forth between two chairs facing each other as if I really were two persons. By the time I finish, I trust that I will discover where my energy is and then I will be able to tell you what I want. I could do all that dialoguing by myself but I would feel silly talking to myself in an empty room. If you sit by and watch you will provide the atmosphere in which I can take my dialogue seriously, and besides you will learn a lot by listening in.

Couples will find this way of facilitating one another easier after they have experienced it under the leadership of a Gestalt therapist. We recommend it as a powerful tool for couples in clarifying their own ambivalences.

Another process that helps couples deal with particularly sticky issues is writing down feelings in what might be called "position papers":

> If we can't agree on something, it helps enormously to put our opposing points of view on paper. That makes it easier for me to respect our difference and try and keep living with it. If we put our two worlds down on a sheet of paper, we will waste less time trying to figure out ways to pull the other over to our side. It will help us become more conscious of each other's needs and of our "blips" (sensitive areas).

Choosing the Best Alternative.   For a while there may be value in postponing the attempt to make a decision until the alternatives have been laid out and evaluated. But eventually each of us needs to state clearly and directly where we stand on the issue. The danger is that neither of us will disclose our true feelings because both will be tailoring our proposals to what we think the other wants.

Constantine and Constantine encountered this difficulty in the group marriages they studied. Their observations are equally relevant to conflict resolution in ordinary marriages (1970: 6):

> One group marriage ... became aware that many of their communication difficulties, especially in decision-making situations and in sensitive areas ... arose from conscious and unconscious attempts to give

what they termed "processed data." A processed statement is one which includes the speaker's attempt to take into account the perceived feelings and opinions of others rather than simply to express the isolated, spontaneous, individual feelings of the speaker. When most responses are processed, the group may never be able to . . . discern the real or "raw data" feelings and thus arrive at consensus, resolution or understanding.

Choosing the best solution cannot work unless each partner begins by stating his/her own individual preference. If the partners are lucky, they may discover that they prefer the same solution. In that case, they have arrived at a *consensus*. If consensus is achieved, no decision needs to be made. When consensus doesn't result from first-round evaluating, it may emerge by postponing the decision. As long as there is a tug of war between partners, consensus is difficult. Once the tension relaxes, agreement may unexpectedly appear. "Sleeping on it" often gives new perspective to both partners so that the next day each says, "Maybe you're right after all."

Consensus may involve one of the original alternatives. Or the differing preferences of the partners may be integrated in a creative synthesis that achieves the values of both. Not every dilemma lends itself to such creativity, but this is the most satisfying solution in situations important to both partners.

Reverting to our mobility dilemma, let us suppose that initially the husband wanted to change jobs but the wife wanted to stay where she was. Simple consensus would involve one partner becoming convinced that the other is right. A creative consensus might take the form of agreeing to stay in the home town but search for a new job there. If a promising opening could be found, the husband's vocational goals might be achieved at the same time that the wife's domestic goals were safeguarded. If both partners' values cannot be achieved through consensus, three alternatives remain: accommodation, compromise, or concession. (Voting is useless in two-person groups!)

Accommodation resembles creative consensus since it enables each partner to achieve his/her own goal. The difference is that consensus synthesizes separate alternatives into a mutually approved course of action. Accommodation means agreeing to disagree. Both alternatives are put into effect, but each applies only to its exponent. Each individual pursues his/her own goal unilaterally, regretting the failure of the partner to join in. Accommodation to mobility might see the husband move while wife and children remain behind. A split family illustrates the strain imposed by accommodation. Less extreme (but still stressful) accommodations characterize interreligious couples who maintain their separate faiths.

A *compromise* is midway between the partners' preferences. Neither partner achieves all s/he wanted nor loses everything. In black-and-white situations no intermediate alternative may be possible, but if shades of gray are available, equalitarian couples prefer this solution. Typical inter-religious compromises include Unitarianism for Jewish-Gentile couples and Episcopalianism for Catholic-Protestant couples. Contrasting with such *halfway compromises* are *sequential compromises* in which couples alternate between their preferences, achieving each partner's goal half the time. They take turns going to each other's churches or spend vacations alternately at the shore and in the mountains. Compromising maintains companionship whereas accommodation separates partners. Yet in matters like religion, compromise may be anathema, and in others it may be impossible. Moving halfway to a new job would hardly do, nor could the husband take turns working at the new job and the old one.

When neither consensus, accommodation, nor compromise is possible, the only way out is by *concession*. One partner loses all while the other gains all. The question is, who should do the conceding? Five approaches are possible. The concession may be forced, voluntary, rational, or delegated to either outsiders or chance.

Forced concession strains the husband-wife relationship the most. Whether the husband threatens to beat his wife or to deprive her of money, whether she badgers him verbally or deprives him of sex, the victory is costly. Force is not always physical. Stubbornness eventually forces the spouse to give in:

> *My husband is the stubbornest man you ever saw. I wanted to visit my folks this Christmas and he wanted to go to his. We argued for weeks about it until finally I suggested we draw straws. But he'd have none of it. He said we were going to his home or we wouldn't go anywhere. Finally I gave up. I figured if he was going to be that pigheaded, I couldn't win.*

Raush et al. (1974) found that individuals who attempted to coerce their partners or who made rejecting remarks suffered doubly negative outcomes. In the short run, they were less able to resolve specific conflicts; in the long run, their whole marriage tended to deteriorate. In the most discordant marriages in their sample, husbands more often used coercive tactics (and, conversely, less often rational statements) than men in the rest of the sample. Couples whose marriages ended in divorce manifested this highly coercive, deficiently cognitive pattern of behavior. It didn't matter what the wife did, whether she was rational, reconciling, or appealing, husbands in troubled marriages were roughly twice as coercive as the average husband.

Buerkle et al. (1961) discovered that well-adjusted couples were mutually willing to make concessions. Where intermediate solutions were possible, they often compromised. Where only one-side concessions were available, both partners competed for the privilege of making the other happy. *Voluntary concessions* were based on the desire of each individual to meet the other's needs.

If both partners are equally willing (or unwilling) or concede, other factors must be invoked. *Rational criteria* may provide an answer.

1. Are the partners equally involved in the situation? If one feels more strongly about his/her proposal, the nod should go to that person.

2. Will both partners be equally affected by the decision? If the issue is whether to buy a tank-type or an upright vacuum cleaner, the fact that it will be used primarily by the partner in charge of vacuuming means that his/her preference should have greater weight.

3. Are both partners equally well informed on the subject? If Bill has a green thumb but Mary is a greenhorn, Bill should decide what to plant.

4. Whose turn is it to win? Taking turns works wonders for three-year-old children and may do the same for three-year-old marriages. If the wife has made the most concessions before, it will be good for her morale to have her way this time.

If the couple remain deadlocked, can *someone else* cast a vote to break the tie? Labor and management sometimes choose an impartial arbiter; why not husband and wife? This rules out most relatives, since they're apt to be biased in favor of their own side of the family (or lean over backward in the opposite direction). A mutual friend may help or a professional consultant can be brought in. The outsider may prefer reopening the evaluation process to making an out-of-hand decision. If eventually s/he finds it necessary to cast the deciding vote, the couple will understand the steps by which the suggestion was arrived at.

Sometimes pros and cons are so evenly balanced that it doesn't make much difference which way the decision goes. A *flip of the coin* may be the quickest way out of the dilemma.

When couples have arrived at a major policy decision in a particularly controversial area, it may be useful to write down the agreement in the form of a contract governing that aspect of their relationship:

> *What is a contract? For us (the Bloods) it's a description of where we are at this time. It is not a guarantee that we will always feel or act as we are feeling and want to act right now. It will change as we and our situation change. When it no longer describes where each of us is, it will need to be brought up to date by renegotiating it.*

A friend commented on the value he found in written agreements:

> *I've got several more pages of agreements worked out with Marilyn. Even if agreements are not kept perfectly, it's better to discuss how they*

are not than to swear at and label each other. In the process of searching for agreements there is always the hope that we can change constructively, whereas when we castigate each other, the chance of anything constructive happening is close to zero.

Implementing the Decision

Choosing is the key phase of decision making. However, implementation is not automatic.

One advantage of joint decision making is that those who participate in making a decision feel more responsible for carrying it out. Lewin (1953) found that decisions arrived at by group discussion were more likely to be put into practice than concessions derived from being lectured at or otherwise manipulated. No matter how a decision is reached, however, problems may arise in carrying it out. Trouble can result from expecting immediate compliance. If deep-seated habits must be changed or complex skills acquired, individuals with the best intentions may learn only gradually. It takes time to learn new tasks. Rarely is perfection itself achieved. Much as a husband may want to remember to take out the trash, he is likely to forget when his daily schedule is upset, he doesn't feel well, or the boss comes to dinner.

Some plans of action include alternatives to be used in emergencies. The following couple recognized that their preferred plan would not always work, and knew what to do when circumstances demanded flexibility:

> *Five-thirty has been such a hectic time in our house that Cynthia and I decided something had to be done. From now on I'm supposed to relieve her of the responsibility for the children so she can concentrate on the cooking. Days when I feel too tired to cope with the children, I'll do the cooking myself.*

Reviewing the Decision in Operation.   When alternative solutions are being tried to test their implications, reviewing comes automatically. The only problem is, How much time is a fair trial? If the trial period is clearly understood in advance, griping can be avoided:

> *Leonard's family always read the Bible aloud before breakfast. In mine we preferred silent meditation. When we first got married, we agreed we'd try both methods and see which we liked best. The trouble was that we never did give my approach a sympathetic test. The very first day Len muttered about it being "barren and unstimulating," whereas I think if he had been willing to stick it out a few days longer he would have begun to discover its value.*

Even supposedly final decisions may have unanticipated consequences. Meditation might look good in theory, but noise from the next apartment may prove distracting.

Rebuilding the Relationship

In planning, executing, and evaluating the implementation of the decision, days, weeks, or months may go by. But immediately after a decision has been made, one partner is apt to feel that s/he "lost," even under the best of circumstances. Creative consensus is a rare stroke of good fortune. Choosing usually means that one partner's preference has been passed over, at least this time around. And that doesn't feel very good.

Raush and his colleagues (1974) found that many "winners" were aware of the partner's bad feelings and took specific steps to relieve them. This may involve verbal expressions of sympathy and/or nonverbal gestures of intimacy—moving closer together, comforting the partner, expressing loving concern in the language of touch. The traditional phrase for this is "kissing and making up" after a fight, and that phrase contains wisdom generated in the experience of innumerable couples.

It is not enough to choose an impeccably correct solution to a problem. The partners need to be concerned with each other's feelings, too. Emotional reconciliation insures that any damage done to the relationship is repaired as promptly as possible.

Beyond repairing damage, many couples take steps to strengthen their relationship by planning enjoyable activities that will enable the "loser" to forgive and forget the loss and enable the "winner" to experience this forgiveness concretely. The winner is especially apt to take the initiative in proposing a compensatory activity such as going out for dinner. However, since both partners stand to gain from putting rewarding activities into their life, either one may make the first move. Doing something together concretely and tangibly consolidates and reaffirms the value of the relationship to both partners.

We must beware of treating reconciliation as purely a task. Kissing and making up often happen spontaneously after the ordeal of combat. The fact that couples experience downs as well as ups contributes to the vitality of their relationship. When anger and hostility are aroused, even if the source of that anger is jealousy of other persons, this may revitalize the marriage. Anger initially creates a withdrawal, but withdrawal makes possible a return. Just as "absence makes the heart grow fonder," so a reunion following a struggle is especially sweet. The only qualification is that the struggle must have been waged successfully, that is, the partners must have fully encountered one another and worked the conflict through to a mutually-agreed-upon solution. They must beware of hastening into making love prematurely before their feelings for one another have revived. But the very fact that struggle requires investing a lot of energy is one reason why it can bring a couple into a fresh relationship, looking at one another in a new light, as if they hadn't seen each other before.

Reviewing the Decision-making Process

At some point after a particularly strenuous struggle, many couples in Raush's study took time to review how they had done. They valued the process of fair fighting as much as they valued the outcome in terms of a particular solution. They took satisfaction in their developing problem-solving skills. They enjoyed exploring ways in which they might deal with problems more effectively in the future. They appreciated sharing the subjective feelings that they had experienced during the struggle. In short, they found it stimulating and provocative to rehash the whole process and to plan for the future confrontations that they knew would inevitably arise.

Sometimes reviewing uncovers deficiencies that need remedying:

I used to feel that Ron dragged his feet in fulfilling a lot of our agreements. Then I discovered it was because I was so afraid that I wouldn't get my way that I had pushed too hard and fast, not really hearing how he felt. In the end I did not have his true consent—only a grudging acceptance. It boomeranged and in the end I didn't get my way after all. I felt he had broken a promise and we both felt resentful. We had to learn to take more time making even small decisions, time for each to state clearly how we felt before we began to negotiate. Where we differed we had to explore many possible alternatives until we found one that suited us both.

For such couples, conflict is a time when they discover things about each other, when they become more aware of each other's reality, when their relationship is tested and proven. In that sense, every confrontation is not simply a strain on the relationship, but a contribution to its growth and development. But only as that contribution is reviewed and discussed is it assimilated into the couple's behavioral repertoire most effectively.

Decision Making in Practice

No couple's decision making ever looks as neat as this outline. Instead of following a logical sequence, couples jump around, not finishing one stage and skipping the next. Over the years, most couples learn to solve problems with astonishing ease. Mere awareness that a problem exists may enable an empathic spouse to alter his/her behavior enough to solve the problem with hardly a word spoken. Couples build up repertoires of habits and skills that are called upon when new issues arise. For partners able to read between the spoken lines, condensed versions of the decision-making proces may suffice.

In Syracuse, the longer couples had been married, the less explosive their response to marital conflict became. They slammed doors less and criticized the partner less. They talked more calmly or forgot about their troubles rather than pressing them (Feldman, 1966). Perhaps they learned which issues could be pursued productively and which were best left alone. Nonpunitive responses to marital conflict (calm talk and/or forgetting about troubles) were correlated with marital satisfaction and with positive feelings after discussion.

Similarly, Raush and his associates (1974) found that over the first few years of marriage, couples increased the proportion of rational problem-solving behavior and decreased the proportion of rejecting behavior. This implies that with increased experience they learned better problem-solving methods. Apparently, this is one aspect of marriage where couples can hope to gain increased skill with added experience.

At the same time, Centers et al. (1971) found that husbands' power in decision making dropped fairly sharply after the first few years of marriage. This means different things in different marriages but, again, shows that couples change their decision-making after a trial period. Perhaps the initial male dominance represents a carryover from masculine initiative and influence prior to marriage, shifting to greater equality as wives become more sure of themselves and more secure in the relationship.

Adaptability to Changing Circumstances.   Decision-making patterns change not only from the learning and growth experiences of the partners, but from coming up against the repeated or catastrophic inadequacy of the old pattern. If the old decision maker no longer seems to know how to solve a couple's problems, it is appropriate for him/her to pass the leadership to the partner in the hope that s/he will do better. Failure of the old pattern requires trying a new one.

Bahr and Rollins (1971) tested young couples with a laboratory ball game. They found that relatively equalitarian couples (where the dominant partner made not more than two thirds of the leadership moves) switched leadership to the partner when the original leader's initiatives no longer succeeded in achieving the couple's goals. By contrast, in marriages heavily dominated by one partner, shifting power to the other partner seldom occurred even though the dominant partner's leadership was no longer successful. Indeed, Hill and Hansen (1964) pointed out that marriages dominated by a powerful leader may be so resistant to change that when a crisis becomes severe enough, the only alternative to the traditional leadership pattern is for the family to collapse in disorganization.

Thus, equalitarian decision making seems to be more efficient in times of crisis. According to Bahr and Rollins (1971: 365–66):

In couples with one very dominant partner, the weaker mate seems so overpowered or so used to relying on his (her) powerful mate that in a stress he continues to turn to his mate for guidance and leadership, even when the mate does not solve the crisis problem. The permanent patterns of interaction probably resist changes in power, even under stresses. In the couple that is not so dominated by one partner (equalitarian) the power structure is not rigid but fluid and flexible. Leadership roles are shifted and interchanged to meet the demands of a stressful situation. One partner is not dominated by the other but both partners are able to take charge of a situation when the need arises. Such couples give and take and help each other make decisions when the situation seems to demand it.

Growth through Struggle. In an earlier chapter we referred to growth through struggle as a potential outcome of conflict over extramarital involvement. Growth is equally possible as a result of struggling with any issue. As husband and wife wrestle with one another, they learn what it means to be human and what it means to be in relationship with a person who is unique in him/herself. This is a mind-expanding experience. Until I engage you in combat over our differences, I will never know what it means to be other than myself. As long as I keep to myself or interact with you only around our similarities, I will see the world only through my own eyes. But as you engage me and tell me about the different places you are coming from and the wishes you have that contradict mine, I will discover that I am not a universal person but unique too. Once we have discovered our uniquenesses, we can build a relationship that takes into account the rich diversity of both of us. To do that isn't easy. It takes a lot of energy, a lot of patience and persistence. It draws on my commitment to keep struggling with you to make our relationship as creative, as sensitive, and as growing as possible. And as we engage in that never-ending, always discovering task, each of us will be stretched beyond our own limits, will experience the pain and the exhilaration of growing into new awarenesses and new capabilities and new appreciations of each other, of ourselves, and of what it means to be alive and aware.

Decision-making Patterns and Marital Satisfaction

Power may be wielded equally or unequally in marriage. Equality involves either sharing all decisions or making an equal number of separate decisions. Traditionally, inequality yields dominance to the husband, but wives sometimes dominate.

Blood and Wolfe (1960) found that Detroit marriages on the whole were equalitarian. Especially at first, couples tended to be syncratic, talking over major decisions and arriving at joint solutions. However, some aspects of marriage were controlled separately, especially decisions linked to the division of labor. For instance, husbands usually made the final decision about their own jobs since "that's his own business," while wives made food purchasing and housekeeping decisions.

Because most couples enjoy doing things together, joint decision making should be the most satisfactory. Table 14–1 shows that this is indeed the case.

In general, the more husbands and wives share in making decisions, the healthier the marriage. Unilateral decision making may be quick and easy, but it is liable to allocate resources contrary to the wishes of the unconsulted partner. However, the unhappiest women are not the unconsulted wives of dominant husbands, but "deserted" wives left with the burden of making decisions alone.

We have described shared decision making as healthier for the marriage. Pratt (1972) also found that equalitarian decision making was literally healthier for the wife: that is, the physical health of wives was better if they shared power equally with their husbands than if they had either more or less power than their husbands.

Decision making at its best is not only equalitarian and shared but mutually deferential. Altruistic partners are willing to go more than halfway in meeting each other's wishes. Buerkle (1961) found that well-adjusted husbands had "deference and respect for the personal feelings of the wife." Their final decision was often a fifty-fifty compromise, but the willingness of both partners to concede more than half the battle meant that solutions were arrived at generously rather than grudgingly.

MARRIAGE COUNSELING—EMERGENCY RESOURCE

Whenever conflict is not resolved, it feeds upon itself. One quarrel leads to another, and the vicious cycle becomes difficult to break:

> We have emotional outbursts so often that something is going to have to be done or else we should call it quits. They follow a regular pattern. Julie makes a dig at me and I blow up. Since my feelings are hurt I just don't say anything to her for the next few days. She gets irritated at my coolness and then she blows up at the slightest provocation.

Table 14–1 Wife's Marital Satisfaction, by Decision-Making Pattern

			EQUALITARIAN	
	Joint	Separate	Husband Dominant	Wife Dominant
Wife's marital satisfaction	5.06	4.70	4.64	4.40
Number of families	120	187	120	91

Adapted from Blood and Wolfe, 1960: 258. *Source:* Representative sample of Detroit wives.

If conflict is chronic and the partners are powerless to stop it, outside intervention is needed if the marriage is not to be destroyed. Living within the confines of the same house, sharing the same bed, turns love to hate once interaction becomes vindictive. When attack leads to counterattack day after day, help must be imported to save the situation.

The Availability of Marriage Counseling

Of all the personal problems for which people seek outside help, marriage problems are the most common. In Gurin's nationwide sample (1960), only one person in seven had ever sought outside help, but of those who had, almost half had gone with a marriage problem. Specifically, almost 8 percent of the married individuals in his sample had sought help with a marital problem. An additional 6 percent reported that they could have used help with their marriage problems, but that they never contacted a professional person when they were in trouble.

Where do people take their marriage problems? Friends and relatives are the first resort. They are more accessible and infinitely less expensive than professional persons.

In young middle-class white families from Washington Heights in Manhattan, 21 percent of the wives were currently or had recently been in contact with professionals about their marriage problems (Mayer, 1966). Although this is higher than the national average, it is small in comparison with the number of friends and relatives to whom they had already talked. The average wife had shared at least some of her marriage troubles with 2.8 friends and 2.4 relatives. This means that sharing was not only widespread but diffused. For most wives, a best friend stood out as the chief confidante to whom she revealed more of her troubles than to any other person. For wives whose chief confidante was a relative, it was almost as often an in-law as a member of her own family. It was rarely a male relative, however. Normally, it was the wife's mother or mother-in-law, her sister or sister-in-law. Some wives felt closer to an in-law than to anyone in their own family. Mayer suggested that the use of bilateral kin for marriage counseling in these middle-class marriages reflected the strength of the marriage bond. The closer a woman was to her husband, the closer she felt to his mother and sisters.

Unfortunately, we don't know how effective these lay counselors are. They may have difficulty being as unbiased and objective as professionals are supposed to be. But even if their success rate is low, their aggregate service must be enormous.

Professional Resources.   When the exceptional couple seek professional help, where do they go?

Table 14–2 shows that clergypersons were the chief resource, exceeding medical specialists even when psychiatrists and other doctors

Table 14–2   Source of Professional Help for Marriage Problems

Source of help used	
Clergyperson	44%
Doctor	23
Psychiatrist	12
Marriage counselor	8
Other agencies	7
Lawyer	6
Total	100%

Adapted from Gurin, 1960: 309. *Source:* National sample of 2,460 adults (married and single). Percentages based on those who ever sought professional help for marriage problems (137 cases).

(mostly family physicians) are put together. The preeminence of ministers and family doctors reflects the ongoing relationship that most families have with one or both. A minister or doctor who is seen regularly for other purposes is available when marriage crises arise. Ministers, moreover, along with marriage counselors and lawyers, specialize in family problems. (People were more apt to take marriage problems than any other kind of personal problem to these three types of specialists.) Also, most couples were married by a minister, which makes him/her a legitimate resource in time of trouble.

By contrast, psychiatrists and marriage counselors are relatively rare and seldom known to the average layman. Gurin found that these specialists depended on referrals by other professionals. People had heard of marriage counselors and considered them appropriate resources but didn't know any. Hence, those interested in securing marriage counseling bulked large among those who wanted help but failed to obtain it.

Marriage Specialists.   Marriage counseling is a specialty practiced by increasing numbers of psychologists and social workers, some ministers, doctors, and family sociologists, and a few lawyers. The American Association of Marriage and Family Counselors is the chief national organization concerned with marriage counseling. Standards of membership are rigorous, including specialized graduate training and supervised experience. Members are concentrated in the metropolitan and academic centers of the country. Many engage in private practice at fees that resemble those charged by other private practitioners.

More accessible are the staff members of the Family Service Association of America, whose several hundred agencies are distributed throughout the urban United States. Staffed primarily by social workers, Family Service agencies minister to all social strata. Middle-class clients pay modest fees based on their ability to pay. Though not limited exclusively to marriage counseling, these agencies are an important source of such help. Unfortunately, they often limit their services to residents of the area covered by the United Fund or Red Feather campaign that subsidizes them.

Some reputable marriage counselors belong to neither of these national organizations, especially those whose profession is clinical psychology, psychiatry, and so on. An increasing number of states certify marriage counselors who are not already certified in another clinical profession. In case of doubt about the qualifications of a particular counselor, inquiring of his/her fellow practitioners usually helps.

Counseling Procedures

Because marriage counselors represent many professions, their methods vary widely. Although no surveys show which methods are most popular, they range all the way from client-centered counseling to highly directive counseling such as behavior modification. Some counselors emphasize childhood personal development whereas others concentrate on the present. Some focus on inner feelings while others stress overt behavior. Some recommend spontaneity, others planfulness, and still others avoid all recommendations. In short, methods depend on the counselor's training, experience, and philosophy.

The two of us have evolved a method of marriage counseling that we call "dialogic counseling." We ask the husband and wife to sit facing each other and talk to each other while we sit on the sidelines facilitating their communication. We encourage them to share their feelings, learning to listen to what the other is saying. We teach them how to ask for what they want and make proposals and counterproposals about solutions to their problems. We help them to negotiate solutions to particular problems and to make contracts governing the way they relate to each other.

Unlike some counselors, we focus on the present and the immediate future. We seldom allow our clients to deal with past events that cannot be changed. We are not interested in the childhood origins of current behavior. We are not interested in the history of the couple's relationship. Rather, we ask them to focus their attention on the ways they are interacting at present. When critical incidents occur during the course of the week, we ask that they reenact them, switching chairs to show the partner what would have been a more fruitful way of behaving.

Our main focus, however, is not on finding solutions to particular problems so much as enabling couples to learn how to communicate with one another and solve their problems more effectively. We use particular episodes as means of helping couples to learn better processes of dealing with one another. In this way, they acquire tools enabling them to deal with future problems.

The Time Required.   Interviews typically last an hour, once a week. Premarital counseling may require only a single interview. Where interpersonal tensions are involved, it takes longer to overcome them. And the longer the marriage has been in existence, the longer it takes to unravel the problems, or, conversely, the less the success that can be expected in a given length of time. In a major study of Family Service Agency clients throughout the United States, Beck and Jones (1973) found that couples married 12 or more years showed substantially less improvement during marriage counseling than couples who had not been married so long. They interpret this intransigence of longer-lasting problems as a reflection of

> an increase over time in role inflexibility, hostile and ineffective communication patterns, repetitive rationalizations and denials, valuation of secondary gains, and a general level of disenchantment and resignation—an attitude of "What can you do?"

Secondary gains occur when individuals get some kind of satisfaction out of the negative patterns they have developed toward one another, if only the satisfaction of feeling superior in putting the partner down. When couples find good in their bad stuff, marriage counselors have a tough assignment to break up the old patterns before new ones can replace them.

For the Family Service clients as a whole marriage counseling generally involved seven interviews, but that was not necessarily enough, as witnessed by the fact that almost half the clients terminated prior to the point where the counselor felt the service was completed. We estimate from our own marriage counseling practice that a dozen interviews are typically needed to carry the task through to a satisfactory ending—either in an improved marriage or in divorce. If personality disturbances are involved, correspondingly more time is needed to reconstruct not only the relationship but the mental health of the persons who are attempting to live together.

In the Family Service study, benefits increased substantially for persons who remained in counseling for 10 to 15 interviews and increased still further, although at a slower rate, for the next 20 interviews or so. Few clients showed any further improvement after 40 hours of counseling. This suggests that, from the standpoint of the investment of time and money, the maximum benefit is derived per unit from the first dozen interviews, and that for those with ample resources still further benefit can be derived from the second and third dozen, but eventually counseling reaches a point of diminishing returns where no further benefit is likely to be derived and the wisest course is for the couple to terminate.

As an alternative to the open-endedness implied in the preceding paragraph, some couples in some Family Service agencies went into marriage counseling as a planned short-term form of treatment. These couples averaged only nine interviews (compared to 13 for couples who went into open-ended counseling), yet found the short-term treatment more beneficial than the longer, vaguer setup. The researchers discovered that fewer couples dropped out of a limited schedule of interviews, husbands particularly welcomed the definiteness of the arrangement, and at the end of the original contracted-for period, clients and counselors could negotiate renewals of the contract as needed without losing the benefits of focusing on limited intervals of hard work together. Presumably, the maximum benefits are obtainable when counseling is entered into for specific periods of time and continued for additional periods as long as tangible gains are experienced.

Individual Counseling. One partner often seeks counseling without the other. But marriage counseling works best when both partners are seen. A few agencies refuse clients on any other basis. However, most begin working with the interested partner, hoping the other will come in later. The Marriage Council of Philadelphia reported: "In 65% of our cases, if the client has a good relationship with the counselor, the counseling is reflected on the partner so that he becomes willing to come despite his initial reluctance" (Mudd, 1951).

Although participation by both partners is ideal, counseling for one partner may enable him/her to become sufficiently objective and adaptable to restore the marital equilibrium.

Table 14-3 shows that while the greatest improvement occurred when both partners were seen, sizable minorities of husbands and wives improved in their behavior even when they were not counseled directly but simply benefited indirectly because their partners were in counseling. The counselors, by the way, were far less sure that these unseen spouses had benefited, but reports from the clients show that they felt that spouses unable or unwilling to participate directly had benefited indirectly.

Joint Counseling. Most marriage counselors prefer to work with all significant parties to a relationship rather than with only one client. This means seeing both husband and wife together. Joint sessions allow communication between the partners and opportunities for mutual decision making. Cookerly (1973) found that joint counseling was superior to bilateral or unilateral separate counseling in enabling couples to improve their marriages.

Table 14–3 Improvement in Husbands and Wives, by Who Was Counseled

	PERSON(S) COUNSELED		
Percentage Reported Improved	*Spouse Only*	*Self Only*	*Both Partners*
Husbands	41%	52%	60%
Wives	35%	61%	67%

Adapted from Beck and Jones, 1973: 99. *Source:* National sample of clients of Family Service agencies.

Marriage counseling is handicapped by the interpersonal nature of the difficulties involved. Gurin reported that individuals with marriage problems found professional help less useful than those with personal problems (see Table 14.4). He reasoned that marriage partners often blamed each other for their troubles and failed to seek help for their own part in the marriage. In any case, those who blamed someone else for their troubles were helped least of all, those who saw their problems as mutual somewhat more, and those who stressed their own involvement were helped the most. Beck and Jones (1973) also found that those who saw the problem in the spouse were helped least by marriage counseling whereas those who saw the problem in themselves were helped most.

The lesser effectiveness of marriage counseling is partly inevitable. Since marriage is a relationship involving interlocking behavior patterns, it cannot be changed as easily as an individual personality. Nevertheless, Gurin's findings have practical implications for marriage counselors and their clients. For counselors, they suggest the importance of involving both partners so that change can be initiated in both members of the dyad simultaneously. For clients, they imply that focusing on what's wrong with the partner will hinder progress. Since I control only myself, I must search for ways to improve my own behavior, confident that if I become a better husband or wife, my spouse is likely to respond positively.

Despite these handicaps, marriage counseling proves worthwhile to a substantial proportion of those who try it. Table 14–5 shows that three fourths of those with relationship problems found their professional contacts helpful.

Group Counseling. Groups of married couples provide an alternative strategy. As I listen to another husband argue with his wife, it may be easier to imagine what I look like to my wife. Or as I listen to another woman complain about her husband, the message may come close to home without creating as much defensiveness as if my wife were addressing me.

Groups widen the repertoire of behavior familiar to a couple. Mayer

Table 14–4 Helpfulness of Counseling for Marriage Problems and Other Personal Problems

Helpfulness of Counseling	Marriage Problems	Other Personal Problems
Helped, helped a lot	52%	71%
Helped (qualified)	14	17
Did not help	34	12
Total	100%	100%
Number of cases	133	174

Adapted from Gurin, 1960: 318. *Source:* National sample of adults.

Table 14–5   Helpfulness of Counseling, by Client's Perception of Locus of Problem

	PERCEIVED LOCUS OF PROBLEM		
Helpfulness of Counseling	Self	Relationship	Other Person
Helped, helped a lot	75%	60%	52%
Helped (qualified)	15	14	16
Did not help	10	26	32
Total	100%	100%	100%
Number of cases	71	97	77

Adapted from Gurin, 1960: 318. *Source:* National sample of adults.

(1967) noted that most people knew little about anyone's marriage other than their parents'. "As married persons in the group begin to learn about the marriages of other members, they may depend less on their memories of their parents." The wider their knowledge, the more flexibly a couple can adapt to new situation.

Burton and Kaplan (1968) did group counseling with married couples in which one partner was alcoholic. Despite the fact that many of the couples resisted going into group counseling, more of those in the group than in separate counseling (76 percent versus 57 percent) reported that they had gotten something out of it. While the most common gains in both types of counseling involved improved ability to communicate with the partner, some of the gains reported by group members were unique. Twenty-eight percent of the group couples gained insight into their own problems by hearing other couples talk about similar problems, and 23 percent felt better about their own situation after discovering that other couples had problems worse than theirs!

Nor need families in trouble learn only from each other. Landes and Winter (1966) brought their own families together with client families for weekends or whole vacations of work and play as well as talk. Staff families set examples of coping with frustration, communicating effectively and other methods of conflict resolution.

The Benefits of Marriage Counseling

Counseling offers therapeutic intervention to create the conditions for rationality, training and encouragement in rational behavior, and mediation of disputes.

Therapeutic Intervention.   Whenever the conditions for rational decision making are missing, counseling must begin by creating them. Insight into unconscious distortions, the development of maturity, and the restoration of love require substantial work. This is the most time-consuming form of marriage counseling, overlapping with other forms of psychotherapy.

Training and Practice. Sometimes decision making breaks down not because of emotional difficulties, but from deficiencies in technique or effort. Joint counseling enables couples to practice decision making under the counselor's watchful eye. Like an athletic coach, the counselor can point out inadequacies in method, demonstrate better methods, and provide moral support for continuing efforts when the "players" get discouraged.

One example of a successful six-session training program was conducted by Patterson, Hops, and Weiss (1975). In six sessions lasting one to one-and-one-half hours each, the researchers taught couples how to request changes specifically and nonbelligerently, how to negotiate and barter for reciprocal changes, and how to increase the positive reinforcement they gave each other during the change process. The training increased their ability to compromise, to arrive at positive solutions, to give approval, and to laugh and make positive physical contact while decreasing the amount of disruptive behavior such as criticizing, disagreeing, complaining, interrupting, and using putdowns. The overall result of the training program was increased marital satisfaction, as evidenced by greater pleasure and fewer unpleasant experiences in the relationship.

Mediation. Couples deadlocked over serious issues often want advice on how to solve them. Gurin found that advice was the most common benefit clients reported from therapy. Expert knowledge and detached judgment are major benefits available from marriage counseling. Given couples with reasonably healthy personalities and sound decision-making techniques, professional mediation resolves many husband-wife dilemmas.

Conflict is inevitable between separate growing people who are bound to have differences. Each day, each week and each stage in life bring new issues to resolve. The little child in us rises up again and again with fears of loss and rejection, jealousies, envies, feelings of frustration and helplessness. Two people can learn to deal patiently and openly with whatever the feelings are. There is a dynamic quality in a relationship where conflict is allowed and utilized as a vehicle of growth.

3

FAMILY LIVING

We turn now to family living with children. Though some couples, by conviction or lack of concern, allow children to come at random, most have preferences that they seek to implement (Chapter 15). The transition to parenthood in the nine months of pregnancy and the addition of the first child to the family brings into the woman's life even sharper changes than getting married (Chapter 16).

Once a couple become parents, they assume new responsibilities for raising children, divided here into closely related chapters on the rearing and education of children (chapters 17 and 18). This section concludes with an analysis of family living generally and family finances in particular.

15 Family Planning

Most couples want to have children. They vary considerably in the preferred number and spacing of those children. Knowing the factors involved in conception and in varied patterns of childbearing enables couples to plan their childbearing intelligently.

THE PHYSIOLOGY OF CONCEPTION

Conception occurs when sperm meets and fertilizes egg. This depends on many factors—knowledge of which is equally pertinent to those eager to achieve conception and to those who wish to prevent it.

The Woman's Contribution

Eggs are produced in the ovaries under the influence of hormones secreted by the anterior pituitary gland. Approximately halfway through the menstrual cycle, an egg breaks through the wall of one ovary into the body cavity. At the same time, the spot that the egg left (the follicle) enlarges into a corpus luteum that secretes the hormone progesterone. Under the influence of progesterone the walls of the uterus become spongy and fill with blood in preparation for the fertilized egg. If fertilization does not occur, the corpus luteum dwindles and the lining of the uterus sloughs off in menstruation.

Meanwhile, the egg is attracted to the entrance of the adjacent uterine tube. It travels slowly down the four-inch tube—the entire journey from ovary to uterus requiring about a week. Fertilization normally occurs

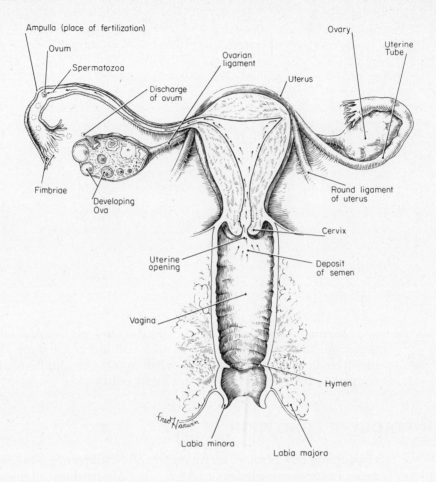

Figure 15-1 Female reproductive organs.

in the tube. Farris (1950) found that about 20 percent of the eggs of normal women were not capable of fertilization (though the range varied from practically zero in highly fertile women to more than 50 percent in women of low fertility).

The Man's Contribution

Whereas only one egg normally comes to maturity per month, several billion sperm are produced by a fertile man during the same period. Eggs are large enough to be barely visible, but an individual sperm is microscopic is size. Each has a small head containing the nucleus of the cell and a long, whiplash tail.

Sperm are produced in the testes—two glands in the scrotum that correspond to the female ovaries. As sperm are formed, they empty from each testis into the adjacent epididymis where they accumulate until ejaculation. During ejaculation, sperm from both epididymes pass through the seminal ducts. Near the base of the bladder, each duct receives secretions contributed by the seminal vesicles, the prostate gland and the bulbourethral glands. These contributions are indispensable to the vitality of sperm and provide them with a liquid environment.

The ducts pass through the prostate gland into the urethra at a point just below the bladder. (Though the urethra serves alternately as the passage for urine and semen, it cannot do so simultaneously since the blad-

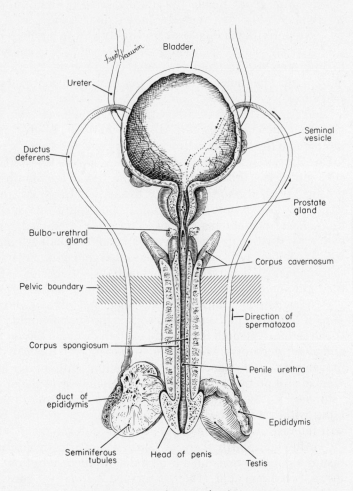

Figure 15-2 Male reproductive organs.

der outlet closes involuntarily during sexual arousal.) At the same time the blood vessels of the penis fill with blood, so that the erect, stiff penis is capable of penetrating the vagina. Impelled by muscular contractions at the climax, a teaspoonful of semen is ejaculated, normally containing several hundred million sperm.

Fertilization

Semen is deposited at the upper end of the vagina near the entrance to the uterus. Provided the sperm are not paralyzed by excessive acidity in the vaginal secretions of some women or prevented by contraceptives, they begin moving into the uterus, traveling one inch in eight minutes. The sperm swim about inside the uterus, some of them entering the tubes where fertilization may occur if an egg is present.

An unfertilized egg loses its vitality within a day or two after ovulation. The lifespan of spermatozoa is believed to be equally short. Conception requires several factors to coincide: a normal egg; a sufficient number of vigorous spermatozoa; and proper timing of intercourse in relation to ovulation.

Westoff (1961) found that the average wife conceived in about five months when no birth control methods were used. Couples who had intercourse three or more times a week conceived almost twice as soon as those who had intercourse less than twice a week (Westoff, 1963). Because conception is a hit-or-miss affair, the larger the number of shots, the greater the likelihood of hitting the target. However, this is true only within limits. Masters and Lampe (1956) found that successive ejaculations close together (as on the same night) declined rapidly in sperm count. Most valuable for conception is not frequent ejaculation but ejaculation when the wife is fertile. Intentional conception need not be a purely random matter. Westoff found that couples with correct information about the fertile period conceived much sooner than those less knowledgeable.

Masters and Johnson (1966) suggested several ways in which the pool of semen could be retained so that the sperm would have easy access to the cervix. The pool is located best if the woman lies on her back during and after intercourse. Loss of semen is reduced if the man ceases thrusting movements after ejaculation. Ejaculation without an orgasm for the woman and prompt withdrawal of the penis leaves the engorged lips as a "stopper" for the vagina, preventing the semen from running out. (Since rapid withdrawal interferes with the sexual pleasure of both partners, it will interest only couples who have difficulty in conceiving.)

After childbirth there is usually a medically prescribed delay in resuming intercourse and a brief delay in the resumption of fertility. As a result, Freedman et al. (1959) estimated the interval between birth of one child and conception of the next at eight months when no contraceptives are used. Added to the nine months' duration of pregnancy, this means the average mother would have a child every 17 months. Roughly every eighth conception ends in a miscarriage, reducing the total number of children who would theoretically be born without birth control to nine per family.

ABILITY TO HAVE CHILDREN

For some families, the problem is not how to prevent conception but how to achieve it. In Whelpton, Campbell, and Patterson's national sample of white women under age 40 (1966), 11 percent of all couples were definitely sterile. Twenty percent had experienced difficulty in having children.

When couples first marry, they seldom know their chances of having children. As they try and fail, they discover obstacles, many of which can be removed by medical treatment. As time passes, couples have illnesses or operations that interfere with their ability to have children. Consequently, the proportion of couples who know they are partially or completely sterile rises steadily.

Table 15–1 shows that by the time married women are in their late thirties almost half of them have had trouble bearing children. Part of this rising number of fertility impairments is a reflection of age, but part of it is a result of complications from previous childbearing. Older women marrying and attempting to conceive for the first time would not have as many fertility impairments as those shown for this cross-sectional sample of women, most of whom married in their early twenties. This difference is demonstrated by the fact that fertility impairments rise faster by length of marriage than by age.

Table 15–1 Fertility Impairments, by Age of Wife

	AGE OF WIFE			
Nature of Impairment	*18–24*	*25–29*	*30–34*	*35–39*
Operation preventing pregnancy	2%	5%	12%	18%
Recognized pathology	7	9	12	12
Long period without conceiving	4	7	13	17
Total impairments	13	21	36	47
Fertile women	87	79	64	53
Total women	100%	100%	100%	100%
Number of wives	513	600	624	677

Adapted from Whelpton, Campbell, and Patterson, 1966: 156. *Source:* National sample of white wives.

Table 15-2 First-born Infants Born Dead or Dying within Four Weeks, by Age of Mother

Death Rate	AGE OF MOTHER					
	15–19	*20–24*	*25–29*	*30–34*	*35–39*	*40–44*
Dead at birth	1.2%	1.2%	1.6%	2.7%	4.2%	5.6%
Dead within four weeks	2.0%	1.6%	1.6%	2.2%	2.8%	3.0%

Adapted from Shapiro, Schlesinger, and Nesbitt, 1965: 78–79. *Sources:* Fetal death rates, 1960–61. Neonatal death rates, 1950. Both are for the United States as a whole, limited to white women. Reciprocal percentages of infants did not die at the specified time.

In this national sample, 22 percent of the operations that prevented further pregnancies were vasectomies performed on the man. Half of the remainder were tube-tieing or cutting operations performed on the woman, chiefly for contraceptive purposes. The remainder were hysterectomies (removal of the uterus), 12 percent of which were due to cancer of the uterus, 82 percent due to other diseases of the uterus, and the remaining 6 percent for contraceptive purposes.

Of concern to couples is not only their ability to conceive an embryo, but to bear the child alive and to have it survive into healthy maturity. Table 15–2 shows the ability of children to be born alive or to survive for their first 28 days after birth. The latter is the crucial period for determining whether the child will survive and reflects its physical normality. Death rates were lowest for first children born to mothers in their early twenties. Other data show that older-aged mothers had the lowest death rates for children of higher birth orders. At most ages, infant deaths were lowest for second births, rising again with successive births, especially for young women who had their children so close together that the mother did not have time to recover her health between births. Conversely, for older women who spaced their children widely, deaths in later born children did not increase as much.

Mothers rarely die in pregnancy or childbirth. McCarthy (1966) reported that in 1963 the maternal death rate was lowest (14/100,000) for white women in their early twenties, and approximately doubled in each five-year age period after the late twenties so that it was more than ten times as high for women over 45.

Clearly, the risks to both mother and child of starting childbearing much past age 30 are appreciably higher, even though the chances for healthy outcomes are still better than fifty-fifty at all ages.

Artificial Insemination

If the husband is sterile and the wife is fertile, she may be able to conceive with sperm from an anonymous donor. The physician chooses a donor of proven fertility whose physical characteristics resemble the husband's.

The physician acts as go-between in conveying semen anonymously from donor to patient. Behrman and Gosling (1966) reported that careful gauging of insemination to the wife's fertile period produced conceptions even faster than the normal five-month interval for married couples.

Artificial insemination techniques may also be used when the husband's sperm count is low. By collecting and freeze-storing sperm from successive ejaculates, the equivalent of a highly fertile ejaculate can be secured for inseminating the wife (S. J. Behrman, M.D., in a newspaper interview, 1966).

Adoption

More common than artificial insemination is the adoption of children who are abandoned by their parents or whose parents have died or become incapacitated. Most adoptable children come from unmarried women who do not wish to keep them. However, older children are more apt to have been raised in poverty-stricken families that became unable to care for them after the death of one parent, after a divorce, or after the incompetence of the parents had led a court to take custody of the child. Often such children come from families so large that the parents' resources are overwhelmed by the number of children.

Kadushin (1970) studied 91 Wisconsin children who were adopted when they were between 5 and 12 years old. As far as he could judge, they turned out just as well as children who had been adopted as infants. Some parents feared more difficulties than they experienced—22 percent said it turned out better than they expected. Two thirds of the parents would definitely repeat the experience, but one couple in every eight found the experience so difficult that they would not repeat it if they had their lives to live over again. The only problem affecting more than half the families was that 55 percent were dissatisfied with the child's school achievement. Apparently, the intellectual consequences of being raised in an inadequate early home situation were not easily erased. Almost one in five children showed the results of their difficult early experiences in enuresis lasting months or years (and in some cases not yet resolved at the time of the followup). Smaller numbers of children committed thefts, set fires, were truants from school, were afraid of the dark, had nightmares, bit their nails severely, and so on. Presumably, these were caused not by being adopted, but by their pre-adoption experiences.

Most of the couples who adopted these older children had no alternative since they were typically unable to bear children of their own and were already in their forties, too old to adopt younger children. Nevertheless, for middle-class couples, such problems must have been painful. Both adoptive and natural parents take on heavy responsibilities when they acquire children.

Kadushin's parents found both advantages and disadvantages in adopting an older child. Most recognized that their own age made an older child appropriate. A minority were glad they didn't have to go through toilet training and other housebreaking tasks with an infant, liked the child's ability to communicate in English and take part in family activities from the very beginning, and were happy to avoid the trauma of telling the child that s/he had been adopted. Disadvantages included having to break old patterns and retrain the child into the new family's ways, having to cope with emotional difficulties inherited from the old family, and not understanding what had gone on in the child's past. Some parents regretted missing the experience of having an infant and felt jealous of the child's ties to his/her natural parents. On the whole, however, Kadushin came away from his research surprised at how well these older children and their adoptive parents had responded to one another.

Another innovation has been adoption by fecund parents concerned to aid children who would otherwise be homeless. As the world becomes more crowded, adoption has become an increasingly attractive alternative to bearing children.

BIRTH CONTROL METHODS

Rhythm and "the pill" may be used either positively or negatively, either to promote or to discourage conception. The remaining methods of influencing conception are exclusively negative in effect.

"The Pill"

As this was written, the most widespread method of contraception was "the pill." It was especially popular with college-educated women (Goldberg, 1967). Oral tablets contain hormones designed to inhibit ovulation. Most brands must be taken daily for approximately three weeks in the middle of the menstrual cycle. Several days after discontinuing the pill, menstrual bleeding occurs. One effect is to regularize the menstrual cycle. It may thereby aid the rhythm method of preventing conception or aid planned conception.

Behrman and Gosling (1966: 403–404) summarized the research findings about the pill as follows:

1. It is without question the most effective method of contraception currently available, and when used correctly, the only method that is 100 percent efficacious.

2. It reduces excessive menstrual flow in better than 63 percent of patients.

3. Eighty percent of women who previously had dysmenorrhea (menstrual discomfort) are relieved of this while on the medication.

4. By removing the fear of pregnancy, the enjoyment of marital relations is considerably enhanced.

The benefits of the pill are implied in Bumpass and Westoff's finding (1970) that women who switched to the pill increased their frequency of sexual intercourse, whereas women who stayed on other methods of birth control decreased their frequency over the same period (in line with the usual decline with age and length of marriage). Apparently, the security and unobtrusiveness of the pill create an attractive environment for making love.

Various unpleasant and potentially dangerous side effects have made medical supervision of the pill essential. Many women experience symptoms of pregnancy such as nausea and weight gain, especially during the first few months before they become acclimated to the dosage. Certain illnesses may be caused or masked by the use of hormones. This method is therefore inappropriate for women with certain medical problems.

Intrauterine Device (I.U.D.)

Various objects made of plastic, in a variety of shapes (coils, bows, loops, and so on) may be inserted by a medical specialist into the uterus and left there indefinitely. This does not prevent conception but prevents the fertilized egg from becoming implanted in the uterine wall. The mechanism is not entirely clear, but was reported by Dr. John Gosling to be an alteration of normal muscular functions so that the egg is propelled through the tube and uterus faster than usual. Unfortunately, the intensification of muscular functioning sometimes expels the device as well as the egg or causes painful uterine contractions during menstruation and excessive menstrual bleeding (especially in the first few months).

Next to the pill, this intrauterine device or I.U.D. was the most effective contraceptive method available at this writing. However, it was not 100 percent effective. Occasional pregnancies occurred with the device in place but were not harmed by its presence. The IUD has the advantage of being inexpensive and requiring no attention as long as it remains in place.

Diaphragm

The vagina contains few nerve endings. Hence, use of a diaphragm by the woman does not interfere with her enjoyment of intercourse. The diaphragm may be inserted before going to bed so that intercourse need not be interrupted. The diaphragm is a flexible rubber dome roughly two inches in diameter (the exact size determined through fitting by a physician). It is coated with spermicidal jelly, cream, or foam for added protection and inserted along the upper wall of the vagina to cover the cervix. It should be left in place six hours following intercourse—therefore relaxation after intercourse is not disturbed.

The fact that the diaphragm is worn internally is both asset and liability. It does not interfere with sexual intimacy but the woman must learn how to insert it properly, and both partners may doubt her proficiency. For neurotic wives with negative attitudes toward sex, any vaginal insertion was disgusting (Rainwater, 1960). A technical problem is that some women's internal anatomy is unsuitable for holding the diaphragm in position (Johnson and Masters, 1962).

Jelly, Cream, or Foam

The contraceptive jelly or cream used to coat the diaphragm may also be used separately. Inserted in the vagina a quarter of an hour prior to intercourse, it is intended to coat the surfaces of the vagina and cervix with a spermicidal chemical lasting six hours. However, Johnson and Masters (1962) found that some jellies and creams failed to distribute themselves evenly and might not be effective with early ejaculation. Jellies and creams were disliked by many women because they were messy. Aerosol foams were the least messy of these three substances.

Condom

The condom is a sheath made of rubber or animal membrane that fits over the penis during intercourse, retaining the ejaculated sperm. Provided condoms are properly manufactured (they should be tested by inflating before use), this method is fairly reliable.

A condom decreases the man's pleasurable sensations during intercourse and can be applied only to the erect penis, disrupting the spontaneity of sex play. For men who wish to delay their climax, dulled sensitivity may be advantageous.

The condom requires the man to assume contraceptive responsibility. Rainwater (1960) found that neurotic wives averse to sex generally, to handling their own genitals, or to contact with the husband's penis and semen liked the condom. Its visibility as an external device meant fewer fears about whether it was properly in place than with a diaphragm. Psychologically, however, it seemed to those who used it the most "unnatural" of mechanical methods, impairing the sense of intimacy in sexual union. One of Rainwater's male respondents described it as "like going swimming with your clothes on."

Chesser (1957) found that, even for the woman, "male methods" interfered with the enjoyment of intercourse more than "female methods." Hence, to minimize interference with the sexual relationship, most couples prefer other methods.

Withdrawal

Withdrawal is another method for which the man is responsible. It interferes with intercourse more than any other method because it requires him to withdraw prior to ejaculation. It is unacceptable to most couples on psychological grounds. Although better than no method, it breaks down due to leakage of semen prior to ejaculation and due to failure to withdraw soon enough. Roland commented that "withdrawal before ejaculation is a wholly unreliable technique (save for unusual men, who cannot recognize themselves as such before the fact) in which significant pleasure is sacrificed in the name of illusory protection against conception" (1973: 140).

Foams and Suppositories

Foam tablets and suppositories are inserted into the vagina and dissolve in contact with body heat and moisture. Many brands present timing problems, requiring insertion some minutes prior to intercourse and offering protection of such limited duration that another application must be made if intercourse is delayed an hour or more. Johnson and Masters (1962) found that tablets did not foam properly in some women until ejaculation provided additional liquid too late for contraceptive protection). Also, some women experienced unpleasant sensations from the foaming action. Suppositories had some of the same disadvantages as jellies and creams—uneven interior distribution and messy external dripping.

Douche

Douching involves washing sperm out of the vagina immediately after intercourse with a solution whose mild acidity is intended to kill the sperm. The necessity of getting out of bed immediately after the man's ejaculation is unpleasant. Physically, the method provides no guarantee against sperm entering the cervix where they are beyond reach of the douche. Rainwater found that it was liked chiefly by wives with negative reactions toward sex who felt "cleaner" after they had washed themselves out. Because of its unreliability, it is not medically recommended.

Rhythm

The rhythm method of family planning requires periodic abstinence from intercourse in order to reduce the likelihood of conception. In reverse, it may be used to increase the likelihood of conception by scheduling intercourse when the woman is fertile. In both cases the crucial problem is to discover when ovulation occurs.

Farris (1956) found that fluctuations in the woman's body temperature were an unreliable indication of ovulation. However, the rat test (in which urine from the woman is injected into young female rats, producing an ovarian reaction if the woman is ovulating) makes it possible to determine ovulation more accurately. From this information, Farris derived the following formula: ovulation is most likely to occur on the second day

Figure 15-3 Date of Conception by Length of Menstrual Cycle

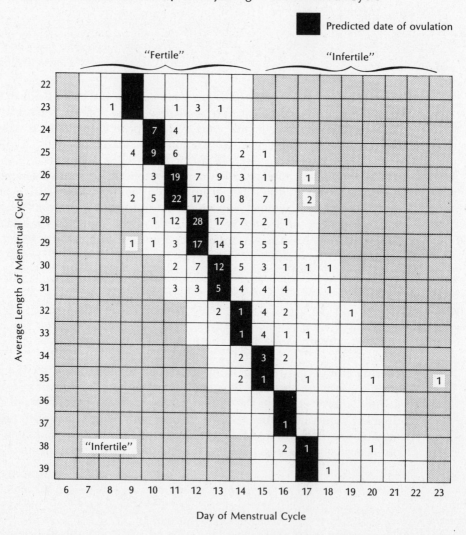

Adapted from Farris, 1956: 103. Figures show the number of conceptions resulting from artificial insemination on the specified day of the menstrual cycle.

prior to the midpoint of the menstrual cycle (the cycle is defined as beginning with the onset of menstruation). Using this formula as a guide to experimentation with artificial insemination or with once-a-month coitus, Farris charted the dates when conceptions occurred in several hundred couples.

Figure 15–3 shows the point in the menstrual cycle when semen was implanted in the wife resulting in conception. It can be seen that conceptions tended to cluster around the date of ovulation predicted from the formula. However, due to variability in length of the menstrual cycle, as well as in the viability of sperm and ovum, conceptions were dispersed over several days in the "fertile" interval.

Farris's research involved the positive use of rhythm to facilitate conception. Figure 15–3 suggests that, when used for family limitation purposes, unintended conceptions will be minimized if couples abstain from sexual relations for an eight-day period surrounding the midpoint of the woman's average menstrual cycle.

Irregular cycles make the prediction of ovulation difficult. The same pills that serve as contraceptives may also be used to regularize the menstrual cycle and thereby increase the effectiveness of the rhythm method. However, stabilization of the basic cycle does not prevent delays in ovulation occasioned by emotional stress or illness.

Rhythm demands self-discipline and alertness of those employing it. When the eight-day fertile period is added to the menstrual period, intercourse is unavailable up to a dozen days a month. If sexual desire and favorable circumstances could be relegated to the remaining days, the problem would be easier. But a couple's desire for intercourse cannot be expected to be so considerate.

BIRTH CONTROL IN PRACTICE

How widely are these family limitation methods used and how effectively do they prevent conception?

The Use of Birth Control Methods

Family planning—with rhythm or some other method—is almost universal in the United States. The methods chosen depend on the couple's desire and ability to have children, the number already born, their religious values, and their education. Contraception is discontinued by couples who discover that they have fertility problems. Conversely, it is used most diligently by those who have proven their ability to bear children.

Limiting Family Size

American families use contraception more to control the number than the timing of children. Especially with the first child, many let nature take its course. Because they are either unsure of their ability to have children or eager to have one as soon as possible, they postpone contraception until after the first child is born. Almost all fecund couples take precautions by the time they complete their preferred family size. Bumpass and Westoff found that 96 percent of couples in their later years were either using contraceptives, sterile, pregnant, or trying to become pregnant. They also found that as families approached or reached their desired size, they tightened up their use of contraceptives, taking fewer chances (especially outside of the "safe" period). The net result of more couples using some method, more using effective methods, and more using those methods consistently is that most of the women in Bumpass and Westoff's sample managed to prevent having more children than they wanted.

Religious Values and Birth Control Methods. Catholics and non-Catholics differ less in the proportion that attempt to limit their reproduction than in the methods used. To be sure, Catholics usually want larger families, and do not begin to shut down their reproduction as soon. Nevertheless, most Catholics eventually use rhythm and/or other methods to end their childbearing long before the potential nine children.

Table 15–3 shows that Catholic couples used effective methods less than non-Catholics. However, almost two thirds of them had already used methods other than rhythm by the time they were interviewed, and still more were likely to do so prior to menopause. Many began with rhythm but switched to other methods as their preferred quota of children filled up.

Table 15–3   Use of Effective Birth Control Methods, by Religion and Birth Interval

	BIRTH INTERVAL		
Religion	*Before First Child*	*Before Last Previous Child*	*Current Use*
Catholic	18%	30%	47%
Protestant	42%	62%	72%
Jewish	76%	87%	87%

Adapted from Bumpass and Westoff, 1970: 58. *Source:* National sample of metropolitan urban white married women. Effective methods included the pill, diaphragm, condom, or withdrawal. Reciprocal percentages were using ineffective methods such as the rhythm method or using no method.

The Effectiveness of Birth Control Methods

The various methods differ appreciably in their ability to prevent conception. However, the greatest source of unintended pregnancies is nonuse or misuse of methods. Few couples use any method consistently, so human factors are more important than technical factors in contraceptive failure.

The Human Factor in Contraceptive Failure. Rainwater (1960) found that willingness to practice contraception at all, as well as to practice it consistently, was closely correlated with sexual feelings. Couples who were neither afraid of sex nor disgusted with it, but treated it matter of factly and discussed it openly, used contraception more consistently. Babchuk and La Cognata (1960) found that unwanted pregnancies happened most to women with sexual problems or multiple marital problems, whereas those with few or no problems used the same methods more successfully. The ability to practice contraception depends on having a stable personality and a stable marriage.

Many couples who otherwise practice birth control faithfully take chances when they run out of contraceptive materials or don't want to be bothered. Especially after drinking too much, their normal controls against indiscretion are weakened. Though most couples "get away with it" the first time, the probabilities of conception are predictable. Hence, a substantial proportion of "accidental" pregnancies are not accidents but the inevitable consequence of taking chances.

Table 15–4 shows that the chief source of unintended pregnancies was failure to use contraception at all or to use it properly. In withdrawal the man failed to withdraw soon enough. Couples took chances with rhythm by narrowing the fertile intervale until the period was no longer "safe." Human failures were most common with contraceptive methods that required precautions "late in the game" of intercourse. But no matter what the method, chance taking introduced a lot of error.

Table 15–4   Cause of Unintended Pregnancies, by Method of Contraception

	METHOD OF CONTRACEPTION				
Cause of Unintended Pregnancy	Withdrawal	Douche	Condom	Diaphragm	Rhythm
Method not used at time of conception	75%	69%	57%	56%	46%
Method failed	25	31	43	44	54
Total	100%	100%	100%	100%	100%

Adapted from Freedman, Whelpton, and Campbell, 1959: 209. *Source:* Unintended pregnancies after first use of specified method by those who used only that method.

Technical Difficulties in Contraceptive Effectiveness. In Table 15–4 rhythm had a high rate of technical failure. Ovulatory variability is so great that couples often got caught in unintended conceptions when they thought they were safe.

Table 15–5 summarizes a variety of studies of the effectiveness of different methods of contraception. The first figure shows the lowest number of pregnancies per year per hundred women in any of the studies while the second figure shows the highest pregnancy rate in any study. This provides a crude rank ordering of methods in terms of their effectiveness in actual use. The table shows that withdrawal, douching, and rhythm produced high rates of failure whereas the pill and IUDs were markedly more effective than other methods.

Success in Family Planning. When these human and technical factors are combined, relatively few American families succeed in having just the number of children they want when they want them, though others profess not to care. Few couples plan successfully both the number and spacing of children. As of the 1960s, hardly more than a third of college-educated American wives achieved this. Some had fewer children than they wished because of fecundity impairments. Most of the rest either had "wanted" children at the wrong time or made no attempt to space their children. Relatively few confessed to having more children than they really wanted. Since that time, technical improvements may have increased the ability to plan successfully (Whelpton et al., 1966).

Table 15–5   Annual Pregnancy Rate, by Method of Contraception

Method of Contraception	Range of Pregnancies per Year per Hundred Women in Various Studies
The pill	0–1%
Intrauterine devices	1–3%
Diaphragm	2–30%
Jelly or cream	5–36%
Condom	6–28%
Foam tablets	6–49%
Suppositories	8–42%
Rhythm	14–35%
Douche	18–36%
Withdrawal	18–38%
None	50–100%

Adapted from Behrman and Gosling, 1966: 407; and Roland, 1973. *Sources:* Review of the literature on numerous studies of the actual experience of large numbers of women. The lower rates are a rough approximation of the effectiveness of the various methods when used consistently and carefully.

STERILIZATION

The previously described methods of birth control are useful for preventing the conceiving of the first child by couples who hope to begin later, and for spacing subsequent conceptions. They are widely used to limit family size to the maximum number a particular couple wishes to have. All of them suffer, however, from the risk of failure. Knowing that risk, couples who have reached that limit face three options. Either they may take the risk and plan to keep any unintended children who may be born; or they may take the risk and plan to terminate any unintended pregnancies by abortion; or they may have one partner sterilized and avoid the risk completely.

Vasectomy

A vasectomy is a simple operation that is normally performed in the doctor's office rather than in a hospital. Under local anesthesia, the seminal ducts that carry the sperm from the testicles to the penis are severed. The man may still attain an erection and ejaculate the fluids released by the glands at the base of the penis, but these fluids contain no sperm and are therefore incapable of causing conception. Although in some instances the operation may be reversed, there is no guarantee that the doctor will be able to reconnect the seminal ducts or that fertility will be restored even if s/he succeeds. For this reason, men who wish to protect themselves against disappointment if they change their minds may preoperatively deposit samples of their semen in a frozen semen bank that can be drawn upon for artificial insemination should the need arise.

In reviewing the research literature on the effects of vasectomy on psychological and sexual functioning, Cole and Bryon (1973) discovered that most vasectomized men and their wives would recommend this procedure to others. Nevertheless, some studies found a few cases of decreased sexual functioning (even though most studies showed that sexual frequency and satisfaction increased with removal of the fear of pregnancy). Rodgers et al. (1963) found that men who worried about their health or about their masculinity were apt to be adversely affected. Men who suggested the operation themselves were affected less negatively than those whose wives pushed them into it. Although negative emotional consequences may have decreased since Rodger's study with the trend toward smaller family size and toward this means of guaranteeing family limitation, there may be some men and some couples for whom vasectomy is not psychosexually advisable. For this reason, some physicians screen and counsel their patients before performing a vasectomy. In view of the frequent irreversibility of the operation, this is one case where "when in doubt, don't" may be an appropriate caution.

Female Sterilization

Several methods have been developed for sterilizing women. The traditional method of tubal ligation (tieing the Fallopian tubes) involved a sizable incision and required hospitalization. Newer tube-severing methods require only tiny abdominal incisions (chiefly through the navel in order to leave unobtrusive scars) and can be performed on an outpatient basis. The latter operation is similar in simplicity and only slightly more expensive than a vasectomy.

ABORTION

The legalization of abortion made this option available to women in the event of contraceptive failure. Even prior to legalization, more women who became unintentionally pregnant resorted to abortion than gave birth to the baby (Gebhard, Pomeroy, Martin, and Christenson, 1958). Since legalization, abortions have become safer and more accessible in doctors' offices, clinics, and hospitals.

As of this writing, abortions were performed by two main methods: suction and saline solution. Suction was used primarily in the first trimester (first 12 weeks) and removed the contents of the uterus by mechanical means. The introduction of saline solution into the amniotic membrane surrounding the fetus (used primarily in the second trimester) stimulated the uterus to expel the fetus by natural processes of contraction. Most suction abortions were performed on an outpatient basis whereas most saline instillation was done in the hospital because of the greater time required and the greater risk of complications in the later stages of pregnancy.

In a study of more than 40,000 legal abortions, Tietze and Lewit (1972) found that almost 12 percent of patients had physical complications following abortion, but most of the complications were "trivial" in nature, such as vomiting as a result of general anesthesia or having a fever for a single day. Table 15–6 shows that the earlier in the pregnancy the

Table 15–6   Major and Total Complications Following Abortion, by Length of Pregnancy

	LENGTH OF PREGNANCY (WEEKS)						
	Under 7	*7–8*	*9–10*	*11–12*	*13–14*	*15–16*	*17–20*
Major complications	1.6%	0.4%	0.6%	1.2%	1.5%	2.7%	3.0%
Total complications	8.9%	5.6%	6.2%	8.1%	15.7%	28.9%	26.7%
Number of cases	429	2706	4344	2845	921	863	1983

Adapted from Tietze and Lewit, 1972: 182. *Source:* Local hospital and clinic patients in 12 states who were followed up at least ten days later to discover postabortion complications.

abortion was performed, the fewer complications, except for the earliest period when the embryo is so small that the physician may experience difficulty in locating it.

No deaths were found by Tietze and Lewit to have resulted from abortions performed within the first trimester. Only one fatality was unmistakably attributable to the abortion as such among four fatalities for women in the second trimester, the remaining three occurring among women with heart trouble and other problems that would have made any operation risky. The overall death rate for the total sample was 9 per 100,000 or 0.009 percent, lower than the death rate for women in childbirth at full term. Especially in the earlier weeks of pregnancy, it is medically safer for a woman to have an abortion than for her to go through the full course of pregnancy. Only in the later stages of pregnancy do the risks of induced abortion exceed the risks of childbirth.

Taking all induced abortions together (most of them are performed in the earlier stages of pregnancy), Table 15–7 shows that for women of all ages the risk of death from abortions was less than the risk of death in childbirth. On the other hand, most contraceptive methods were even safer than abortions, except for the precipitous rise in mortality from the pill after age 40. From this as well as other standpoints, then, couples who do not wish to have children are better off attempting to prevent them by contraception and relying on abortion only if their contraceptive efforts fail.

In a study of Minnesota women (most of whom were single and whose average age was 23) who had had abortions, Bogen (1974) asked how painful the experience was physically and how they felt about it afterward. Thirty-four percent reported "a lot" of pain or discomfort, 40 percent "moderate," 23 percent "slight," and 5 percent none. After the operation was over, nearly all the women felt very relieved but 3 percent felt sorrowful and 2 percent depressed. In response to a separate question, 7 percent reported that they sometimes thought they had done the wrong thing, although none felt they had definitely made a mistake. Analysis showed that it was mostly Catholic women and actively religious women

Table 15–7   Death Rate from Contraception, Abortion, and Childbirth, by Age of Woman

	AGE OF WOMAN				
Death Rate/100,000	*20–24*	*25–29*	*30–34*	*35–39*	*40–44*
From IUD	1	1	1	1	1
From condom, diaphragm	1	2	3	4	4
From the pill	1	1	5	7	25
From abortion	2	2	5	9	6
From childbirth	5	7	14	19	22

Adapted from Tietze, Bongartz, and Schearer, 1976. *Source:* Computerized summary of numerous studies in the United States and Great Britain.

who had doubts. Again, as with sterilization, the implication may be "when in doubt, don't." Conversely, for women who view abortion as an acceptable solution to the dilemma of an unwanted pregnancy, the experience may involve some physical pain or discomfort but it is not likely to leave psychological scars.

A study by Butts and Sporakowski (1974) of white single women in the southeastern United States found that women who chose to bear an unintended child in a maternity home were considerably more likely than women having abortions to feel they had not made the right decision. Most of the women in the maternity homes placed their children for adoption, only 12 percent choosing to raise the child themselves. Twenty-nine percent of the maternity home women but only 3 percent of the abortion women said they would choose another way if they again faced an unwanted pregnancy. This indicates that abortion is not only chosen more often by contemporary American women, but that most single women find it more satisfactory than having an unwanted child.

For married women, abortion is less often the chosen solution. A considerable number of wives find it easier to decide that they want an "accidental" child than to have an abortion. Nevertheless, many married women utilize abortions as a fallback procedure after contraceptive failure. For wives unsure how they feel about abortion, the problem is more difficult than for single women in the same situation. The latter may bear the child and place it for adoption. Few married women find the latter a viable option. Therefore, they must choose between having a doubtful abortion and having a doubtful child. Since the latter requires almost two decades of child-rearing, choosing is a heavy responsibility.

CHILD-SPACING

Child-spacing involves both the interval between marriage and the birth of the first child, and the interval between successive children. The actual pattern of child-spacing by American families is shown in Table 15–8.

This table shows that women who desired a large family had each of their children (and especially the first two) very close together. At the opposite extreme, women who were bearing their last child waited especially long to have it. The typical pattern for the sample as a whole was to wait at least two years after marriage to have the first child and three years for each additional child. Only women who had outsized families of four or more children spaced them less than three years apart, and even such large-family-oriented women waited a full three years to have their last child if they planned on that number from the beginning of their marriage. Of particular interest is the fact that women who wanted only two children spaced them almost four years apart. Since two children subsequently became the American norm in the face of increased consciousness of the population explosion and increased liberation of women from

Table 15–8 Child-spacing, by Desired Number of Children

Birth Interval/Months	DESIRED NUMBER OF CHILDREN		
	Six +	Specified Number	Total Sample
Marriage to first birth	20 months	——	27 months
First to second birth	19	47 months	37
Second to third birth	26	41	37
Third to fourth birth	25	37	34
Fourth to fifth birth	26	36	32

Adapted from Bumpass and Westoff, 1970: 31. *Source:* National sample of 814 metropolitan urban white women. "Specified number" means that these women were having their last child.

being "just a housewife and mother," these women may represent the model for women in the future. These same women also waited the longest to have their first child (a full two and one-half years).

The trend, then, seems to be to have a small number of children at a relatively leisurely pace, allowing room for the marriage to be established emotionally and financially before having the first child and even more room for the first child to become established before having the second/ last child.

Needless to say, the larger the number of children a woman has, the larger the number of years she spends bearing them. Whereas Bumpass and Westoff's two-child women spent only four years having children, mothers with three children spent almost seven years, those with four children almost nine, and those with five or more at least ten years.

Readiness for Childbearing

The next chapter describes in detail the impact of children on parents. Here we need to preview the marital, financial, and emotional prerequisites for the transition from childless marriage to parenthood.

Marital Readiness. No matter how wealthy or well adjusted a man and woman may be, they are rarely ready to have children when they first get married. Learning how to be a good husband and wife is job enough for the first year without the complexities of parenthood. Living together without children provides a gradual transition from premarital activities. It also gives poorly matched couples a testing period in which to find out whether they can make a go of marriage. Otherwise, young parents may get trapped in unworkable marriages:

I've been trying to get away ever since I got married, but I've never succeeded. The children started coming too soon, and now I feel I have to stick it out for their sakes until they're grown up. If it hadn't been for them, I would have divorced Hank long ago.

For most couples, the question is not whether marriage will work but how soon they will be ready for pregnancy and parenthood. There is no set answer, but we suggest a minimum of one year prior to conception as a rule of thumb. In two American communities, Christensen (1962) found that the longer the delay from marriage to first birth, the lower the divorce rate. He believed this reflected greater readiness for parenthood and a lower proportion of unwanted pregnancies.

Women who marry late enough in life to be threatened by menopause may need to start having children sooner. On the other hand, couples who foresee a coming separation may be well advised to postpone children until the husband returns:

When I came back from overseas, the son I'd never seen was almost two years old. Of course, he didn't know who I was. My wife and he had come to depend on each other so much that I felt like an intruder. It didn't make coming home any easier to have to break into that charmed circle of theirs.

The first pregnancy and first child are such significant experiences that few husbands want to miss the opportunity to share them, and few wives want to miss the husband's emotional support.

Financial Readiness. How much does it cost to have a baby—and to keep it? Delivery and hospitalization expenses may be covered by insurance. Otherwise, the former reflects the patient's ability to pay, and the latter depends on the number of days in the hospital. In addition, there are the costs of prenatal and postnatal care. Medical expenses will total hundreds of dollars if they have to be paid out of pocket.

Once the baby arrives, its impact on the budget is felt gradually. As it grows older, its food and clothes cost more. If the family's income rises correspondingly, increased costs may be taken in stride. If not, long-range planning may be required. Tien (1961) found that couples struggling for upward social mobility tended to postpone their first child while they concentrated on training and equipping the husband for his career.

More critical than the cost of a child is the loss of the wife's income if she quits work. Then couples who have geared their standard of living to two incomes must cope with reduced income and increased expenses simultaneously.

Emotional Readiness. Those mature enough to be ready for marriage are usually mature enough two years later to be ready for parenthood. However, some couples marry prematurely, and others, skilled enough for marital interaction, are not ready for the complexities of childbearing and child-rearing. The emotional strain on the mother depends on how rapidly the children are born. Sears (1957) found that young mothers with several children felt overwhelmed and took out their frustration on their children by treating them coldly.

One sign of readiness is wanting to have children. The desire for children is almost universal, but not quite. Some women don't want to be bothered. Those wrapped up in themselves or embittered by their own mothers may be afraid to have children:

> *Shelly flatly told me that she would never under any circumstances have children and that if I would be unhappy without them, the wedding would be canceled. I thought her mind would change so the wedding ceremony was performed. We have been married six years, but to my great unhappiness she has not changed her feelings. In addition to thoroughly disliking children as such, Shelly takes great pride in her appearance and abhors the thought of losing her slim figure during and after pregnancy. She spends her days figure skating and playing tennis which she is loath to give up. She steadfastly maintains that having children is to end all independence.*

Whatever the reason a woman doesn't want children, she is wise to avoid them. To bear a child is no guarantee that she will love it. No one is more tragic than an unwanted child—except, perhaps, its guilt-laden mother.

Hardly less important is the husband's readiness. A man's impact on his children is as important as his wife's. And his help is crucial to her when the going gets tough.

The transition from readiness for marriage to readiness for parenthood is in some respects sharper for the man:

> *When I fell in love with Adrienne, I was very anxious to get married—and we did after a whirlwind courtship. We got along real well with each other and had a wonderful time that first year. Then Adrienne began to hint about wanting a baby. To tell the truth, I'd never thought much about it before. I'd had very little contact with kids and always felt a bit embarrassed when I had to deal with them because I didn't know how to behave. So it took me a while to get used to the idea. Eventually I came around.*

Comparing three aspects of readiness for parenthood, Westoff (1961) found the largest number of couples unready financially (41 percent), whereas 26 percent wished they had had more time to enjoy things together, and 19 percent felt they didn't have time to get adjusted to each other. Though most wives were satisfied with the timing of their first birth, twice as many felt it came too soon as too late and the most enthusiastic wives were those who waited at least two to three years.

Readiness for parenthood benefits the child as well as the parent.

Morgan (1962) found that children born into families that began childbearing prematurely ended up with less education than those born to parents of similar education, income, and so on, who had their children later. Educational impairment was particularly severe when the first child was born while the father was still a teenager. This suggests the value of postponing the birth of the first child at least two years after marriage. The younger the couple, the more urgent this delay.

Spacing Subsequent Children

Table 15–8 showed that American families typically had their second and third children at three-year intervals. Was this spacing ideal? Westoff's young respondents were most enthusiastic about second children born between two and two-and-a-half years after the first. The problem, as they saw it, was to balance their desire to provide a playmate for the first child against their desire to avoid having too many small children at once. With the third child, presumably, the playmate problem figures less than the need to limit the burden of childcare.

Ideal intervals between subsequent births may be longer than between the first and second. The farther apart children are born, the smaller the proportion who are considered born too soon. In four-child Detroit families, the minimum interval between second and fourth children necessary to reduce born-too-soon children to less than 0.5 per family was seven years (Freedman and Coombs, 1966). From this subjective standpoint, the minimum preferred spacing between children was two years from first to second child, three years from second to third, and four years from third to fourth.

Marital Consequences. The closer together children are born, the more overwhelmed the parents become with the responsibilities of caring for dependent young children. As a result, the less time and energy they have to give to maintaining their marriage. Hurley and Palonen (1967) found that marital satisfaction among graduate students at Michigan State University declined the closer together children were born. The larger the number of children born early in marriage, the more the marriage suffered.

Housekeeping Consequences. Child care is easier when children are spaced farther apart. A study by Wiegand and Gross (1958) of fatigue among mothers of young children showed that tiredness increased (1) the younger the child and (2) the larger the number of children. When these factors combine in a large number of preschool children, housekeeping and child care become difficult. Mothers of closely spaced children cannot do either their housekeeping, their child-rearing, or their loving as adequately as those with children spaced farther apart. When children are so closely spaced that their mothers are overburdened, fathers tend to be

Table 15–9   Division of Child Care Between Parents, by Child Spacing in Four-Child Families

	SPACE BETWEEN CHILDREN		
Child Care	*Under 20 Months*	*20–30 Months*	*30+ Months*
Wife primarily	64%	77%	86%
Husband/wife equally	29	20	9
Husband primarily	7	4	5
Total	100%	101%	100%
Number of cases	167	111	55

Adapted from Campbell, 1970: 51. *Source:* Four-child white women in Detroit metropolitan area.

pressed into service to help out with child care. Campbell (1970) found that in four-child families, the closer the children were spaced, the larger the proportion of fathers who did half or more of the work in caring for the children (see Table 15–9).

Despite the marginal tendency of husbands to come to the rescue of wives when the burden of child care is heaviest, mothers of very small children are frequently left "holding the fort." If their child-care responsibilities are sufficiently heavy, they may not be able to afford the luxury of going to see a doctor when they feel ill or have a temperature. Geersten and Gray (1970) found that the larger the total number of children and the larger the number of preschool children in particular, the more mothers grimly continued to fight the battle on the homefront rather than take time to get a medical checkup in the face of symptoms of illness (see Table 15–10).

Child-rearing Consequences.   Overtired parents cannot give children the attention they deserve. Fatigue is probably one reason why Sears (1957) found that mothers showed less warmth and affection toward closely bunched children, not only while they were infants, but as much as five years later. Sears also suggested that mothers still protectively attached to

Table 15–10   Mother's Failure to Seek Medical Assistance, by Family Size and Child Spacing

	FAMILY SIZE	
Child Spacing	*Under Four*	*Four+ Children*
Widely spaced	53%	57%
Closely spaced	62%	74%

Adapted from Geertsen and Gray, 1970: 642. *Source:* Mothers in a western state with at least one child under age 5. Closely spaced children were defined as two or more children under age 5. Reciprocal percentages of women would seek medical assistance when feeling ill or running a temperature of 100 or 101 degrees.

one child may have found it difficult to respond warmly to a new baby who arrived too soon. For parents as well as for prior children, a rapid succession of children creates more difficulty than does leisurely timing.

Since parental warmth is indispensable to successful child-rearing, (Chapter 17), any gain in warmth from wider child spacing is valuable to the child. Widely spaced children also receive more attention to their educational potentialities. Conversely, when too many children are born too close together to an immature woman, she can hardly give them the attention they need if they are to be motivated to achieve.

White (1975) studied the development of competence in young children and discovered that the birth of children too close together was the greatest interference with early development:

> Far and away the source of stress most difficult to deal with is from the behavior of a not-much-older sibling. Repeatedly, we find that when children are spaced less than three years apart families pay a significant price. To the extent that the gap is more than three years the consequences lessen, whereas narrower age differences lead to greater stress.

Nor did stress affect only the later-born child:

> A first child reared at home lives (usually) in a loving, protective atmosphere for most of his first two years. He rarely comes face to face with aggression or hostility. In contrast, a second child with a sibling a year or a year and a half older inevitably must cope with such forces day after day, once he begins to crawl about. The young infant finds this task very difficult; mothers often find themselves into at least twelve months of chronically unpleasant policing activities; and worst of all, the older child finds sharing his mother an unfair and unpleasant kind of existence (White, 1975: 263–64).

Sears and his colleagues (1957) suggested still another advantage in wider spacing—lessened sibling rivalry. Two-year-olds' language skills are too weak for them to be able to understand why they are being displaced. By three or four, sex education and loving orientation could help them anticipate the birth of the baby, reducing their resentment. We said earlier that naive young mothers in Westoff's sample were eager to have a second child soon after the first. They failed to realize that closeness in age makes sibling rivalry more likely at the same time that it makes companionship more possible. The problem is to space children far enough apart to minimize competitiveness without making companionship impossible. From this standpoint, three or four years apart is better than shorter intervals.

Financial Consequences. Having children "thick and fast" concentrates them early in the couple's careers when family income is low. Spreading them out delays the expense of later children until income has risen. The farther apart children arrive, the greater the family's opportunity to ac-

Table 15-11 College Attendance of Men and Women, by Spacing between Siblings

	SPACING	
Gender	Under Five Years	Five Years or More
Men	97%	83%
Women	86%	76%

Adapted from Adams and Meidam, 1968: 233. *Source:* White-collar two-child families in Greensboro, North Carolina. Reciprocal percentages of children never went to college.

cumulate financial assets: a home, car, savings, investments, and insurance. Freedman and Coombs (1966) found that Detroit families with four children born in the first five years after marriage averaged only $4,000 in assets, whereas those who spaced the same number of children over 12 years or more accumulated almost three times as much.

The burdens of child bunching intensify when children go to college. Most families depend on current income to meet their children's college expenses. If more than one child is in college at the same time, this is difficult. To avoid this problem, children must be spaced at least four years apart. Table 15-11 shows that children spaced five or more years apart were more apt to go to college than those born less than five years apart. The wider the spacing, the easier it is for parents to pay these costs.

FAMILY SIZE

During the 1950s and 1960s, most couples wanted at least two children and not more than four, averaging out at three. With the growing awareness of population problems and ecological problems and the growing orientation of women away from traditional domesticity in the direction of activities (especially employment) outside the home, the preferred number of children fell and the two-child family became increasingly popular. Radicals even advocated the social benefits of having only one or none in order to enable the population to stabilize sooner or perhaps even fall to a lower level that would consume less of the world's resources. Scientists estimate that if families averaged 2.1 children, population would stabilize. Every child above that level intensifies the world population explosion.

Competing Values

Career-oriented wives prefer to limit their childbearing. Table 15-12 shows how profoundly the family-size preferences of women in three midwestern cities were affected by their internal/external orientation.

Both partners may have alternative uses to which they wish to de-

Table 15–12   Desired Family Size, by Wife's Internal/External Orientation

Percentage of Wives with Desired Family Size	PERSONAL ORIENTATION		
	Domestic*	Equal	External/Companion†
Small family	7%	20%	63%
Medium family‡	21	45	16
Large family	72	35	21
Total	100%	100%	100%
Number of wives	14	20	19

Adapted from Rainwater, 1965: 191. *Source:* Middle-class married women, mostly in Chicago, some in Cincinnati and Oklahoma City.
*Solely oriented to children and home.
†Solely oriented to outside interests or to husband as companion.
‡A medium-sized family for Protestants was three children, and for Catholics four.

vote their time and money. Some occupations and avocations are difficult to integrate with parenthood. The economic cost of having children is substantial. In 1975 Dr. Thomas Espenshade estimated the cost of raising a child from birth to graduation from a public college at approximately $75,000, a figure that did not allow for subsequent inflation in the cost of living. The larger the number of children, the less spent per child. (In that restricted sense, they come "cheaper by the dozen.") The aggregate cost to the family, however, rises with the total number of children. Most families cannot afford both kids and Cadillacs, so except at extraordinarily high income levels, the parents' values will determine how they wish to allocate their money between children and alternative uses.

Religious Values.   For active Catholics, preferred family sizes run especially large. Bumpass and Westoff (1970) found that active Catholics preferred and actually had 4.3 children on the average, inactive Catholics 3.4, Protestants 3.0, while Jews preferred 2.7 and averaged slightly less in practice (2.6). In an earlier study, Freedman, Whelpton, and Smit (1961) found that these religious differences held even when couples were matched on socioeconomic characteristics such as education and income. Reflecting differences in contraceptive usage, Jewish women were most likely to achieve exactly the number of children they preferred whereas active Catholics most often failed. Failures just as often represented underachievement as overreaching goals. More than one fourth of the active Catholics in Bumpass and Westoff's sample wound up with at least two children fewer, or two more than they wanted.

"A Boy for You, A Girl for Me."   Because children come in two sexes, childbearing preferences are based on assumptions about the number of sons and daughters. Most couples prefer having both sexes so that families unlucky enough to have only one sex frequently raise their sights in hopes of breaking the spell. Bumpass and Westoff (1970) found that couples whose first two children were boys were 11 percent more likely to want additional children than those who already had a boy and a girl. If the first two children were girls, their desire for additional children was even higher (24 percent). Even couples with as many as four children of the same sex were substantially more apt to keep trying than couples whose four children included both sexes.

The Consequences of Family Size

Reed (1947) found that marital adjustment increased with success in controlling fertility according to the couple's own desires. Generalizations about ideal family size may be precarious, but the value of achieving one's own ideal is clear.

Having a lot of children infringes on the leisure time of both husbands and wives. Table 15–13 shows that shifting from having no children to having five or more children added an extra 14 hours per week to the work load of both men and women. For men, the major shift was an increase in the time required to support the additional mouths plus a modest increase in the time spent helping out at home. For women, there was an enormous increase in the time spent in housework (from 34 hours per week with no children to 61 hours per week in the largest families), which was only partially compensated for by working less outside the home. Thus, for both parents, having a big family is a big job.

One corollary of having large numbers of children is that some of them are apt to be unwanted. Table 15–14 shows that the larger the number of children born to women between 18 and 40, the larger the proportion who already had or who expected to have more than they wanted by the time they finished. Women who had one or two children were the only ones who generally expected to wind up with just the number they wanted, neither too few (as with most childless women) nor too many (as with a plurality of women expecting to have four or more children).

Table 15–13   Total Hours per Week Spent in Housework and Outside Work by Husbands and Wives, by Number of Children

Total Hours of Work/Week	NUMBER OF CHILDREN					
	None	One	Two	Three	Four	Five +
Husbands	57	64	66	64	67	71 hours/week
Wives	55	59	65	65	66	69

Adapted from Walker, 1970: 3. *Source:* 1,296 married couples in Syracuse, New York.

Table 15–14 Wanted and Unwanted Children, by Actual Number of Children Already Born

	ACTUAL NUMBER OF CHILDREN					
Expected Childbearing Outcome	None	One	Two	Three	Four	Five+
Fewer than wanted	52%	38%	25%	24%	12%	15%
Exactly the right number	48	57	56	44	43	37
More than wanted	0	4	19	31	46	48
Total	100%	100%	100%	100%	100%	100%
Number of cases	301	463	682	499	263	206

Adapted from Whelpton, Campbell, and Patterson, 1966: 66. *Source:* National sample of white women under age 40.

Child-rearing Consequences. The consequences of family size must be considered not only for the parents but for the children. Children benefit from siblings in some ways but suffer in others. In a national sample of adolescent boys, Bachman (1970) found that the larger the family, the lower the IQ, even when controlled on socioeconomic status. The same study showed similar declines with increased family size in academic achievement, political knowledge, occupational aspirations, and likelihood of going to college.

Table 15–15 shows that the college-impeding effects of family size affect daughters sooner than sons in view of the general bias in favor of sons if families can't afford to educate all their children. In that study, the education of daughters suffered when they had three or more siblings whereas for sons the decline set in when they had at least four siblings. This illustrates the general proposition that the larger the number of children, the less money there is per child at any given income level.

Achievement motivation declines as the family gets larger. All families start out small, but some last-born children must contend with larger numbers of siblings than others. The larger the number ahead of them in line, the less attention they receive from their parents. Consequently, last-born children in large families have less chance of acquir-

Table 15–15 College Attendance of Men and Women, by Childhood Family Size

	FAMILY SIZE (CHILDREN)					
Gender	One	Two	Three	Four	Five	Six+
Men	81%	86%	78%	89%	62%	33%
Women	86%	80%	82%	69%	57%	42%

Adapted from Adams and Meidam, 1968: 233. *Source:* White-collar families in Greensboro, North Carolina. Reciprocal percentages had not gone to college.

ing the motivation, the education, and the money to enter graduate and professional schools. In the University of Michigan Medical School, last-born children in two-child families were represented in the student body only two thirds as often as first-born children, in three-child families one third as often, and in families of four or more children one tenth as often (Cobb and French, 1966).

Belonging to a large family also affects older children adversely. When the father's occupational status was controlled, Blau and Duncan (1967) found that oldest children in families of five or more children were even more severely handicapped in occupational attainment than their younger siblings. Apparently, oldest children in large families often drop out of the educational system to help support their younger siblings. As a result, they are not able to get as good jobs as first-born children in smaller families. Regardless of birth order, the larger the number of siblings, the more children are handicapped in all sorts of educational and occupational ways by the inability of their parents to provide them with as much financial and moral support and encouragement.

Most women gradually tire of having children. Sears et al. (1957) found women less likely to breast-feed each succeeding child, more severe in weaning it, and clamping down more on the noise that children make. In another study, both fathers and mothers reported more obedience problems, aggression problems, and eating problems in families with larger numbers of children (Stolz, 1967). In families with five or more children, both parents reacted against the threat of chaos by stressing authoritarian control, obedience, manners, and orderliness. Nye, Carlson, and Garrett (1970) found that children were more apt to have been spanked and less apt to be reasoned with, if they had a large number of siblings. The larger the family, the more parents find it necessary to tighten up on the discipline problems that their children present.

Just as family income gets sliced into smaller and smaller segments, the larger the number of children, so parents' attention and affection gets divided into smaller and smaller bits. Nye, Carlson, and Garrett found that the larger the number of children, the less affection they received from their parents. Newson and Newson (1968) found that mothers with relatively few children were more likely to play with them than mothers with large numbers of children. The latter were too busy with housekeeping tasks to be able to play with their children.

Even among siblings, affection tends to be diffused and attenauated in large families (despite the myth that large families are close). Bowerman and Dobash (1974) found that adolescents with only one sibling were more apt to feel close to him/her than persons with a larger number of siblings. Thus, the larger the number of children, the smaller the share of love that each child receives not only from parents but from a given sibling.

For children, then, as well as for parents, family size must be limited for maximum satisfaction.

16 The Advent of Children

In some ways, the transition to parenthood is like the transition to marriage. Conception is like getting engaged; the nine months of pregnancy, the engagement period; childbirth, the rite of passage into parenthood; and the hospital sojourn, the honeymoon for mother and child.

PREGNANCY

Women are not aware that they are pregnant for several weeks after conception. The fertilized egg moves slowly down the tube to the uterus whose walls have become enriched with blood under the influence of two hormones, progesterone and estrogen. The embryo becomes embedded in the spongy tissues of the uterine wall. A week or two later the woman misses most or all of her menstrual flow because a hormone produced by the embryo retains the lining of the uterus. This hormone also inhibits the ripening of other eggs in the ovaries. Within five weeks, a hormone is produced in sufficient quantities to be detectable when urine specimens are injected into experimental rabbits, mice, or frogs. By the sixth week, the cervix has deepened in color enough to provide the physician with evidence of pregnancy.

Symptoms that *may* indicate pregnancy are skipped menstrual periods; nausea; excessive fatigue; tenderness, tingling, or enlargement of the breasts; or more frequent urination. Each of these may have causes other than pregnancy, and some of them (especially nausea) are not universally present. Nevertheless, the more signs there are, the greater the chances that the woman is pregnant.

Growth of the Fetus

At the end of the first month the embryo is still so small that it may not be recognized even on autopsy. In the fourth month the heartbeat becomes audible through the obstetrician's stethoscope, and in the fifth the mother can feel the baby kicking and stretching.

Fetal Deaths.   Pregnancies that end in death of the fetus prior to birth are popularly referred to as stillbirths, technically as fetal deaths or antenatal deaths. Most fetal deaths occur early in pregnancy, declining steadily in successive time intervals. In a comprehensive study on the Hawaiian island of Kauai, almost one fourth of all pregnancies (detected at four weeks after the last menstrual period) ended in fetal death (Bierman et al., 1965). The chances of a live birth rise, the longer the fetus survives in the uterus.

Most fetal deaths are less tragic than they seem. They usually involve defective germ plasm incapable of normal development. Guttmacher (1957) reported that more than two thirds of all spontaneously aborted fetuses were observably malformed. The tragic causes involve women who have trouble carrying any pregnancy to successful completion. Medical treatment with hormones, vitamins, and bedrest may enable them to retain a fetus long enough to improve its chances of survival.

Preterm Births.   The period of gestation is usually counted from the first day of the last menstruation (since that is more easily ascertained than the date of ovulation and conception roughly two weeks later). The American College of Obstetricians and Gynecologists arbitrarily defined the beginning of "viability" as 28 weeks of gestation. It defined low birth weight as less than five-and-one-half pounds. Both the age and size of the fetus determine its chances of survival.

Table 16–2 shows that even if a baby is born alive, its chances for

Table 16–1   Average Size of Fetus, by Monthly Intervals

Age	Length	Weight
One month	¼ inch	tiny fraction of an ounce
Two months	1¼ inches	$1/14$ ounce
Three months	3 inches	1 ounce
Four months	6–8 inches	5–6 ounces
Five months	10–12 inches	1 pound
Six months	14 inches	2 pounds
Seven months	16 inches	3 pounds
Eight months	18 inches	5 pounds
Nine months	20 inches	7–8 pounds

Adapted from Bowman, 1960: 403–405.

Table 16–2   Chances of Surviving at Least 28 Days for Newborn Babies, by Length of Gestation and Birth Weight

Birth Weight	LENGTH OF GESTATION (WEEKS)				
	Under 28	28–31	32–35	36	37+
under 2 lbs. 4 oz.	8.5%	17.1%	21.3%	57.1%	51.5%
2 lbs. 4 oz.	23.8%	44.0%	58.3%	62.2%	64.7%
3 lbs. 5 oz.	40.7%	65.4%	79.5%	85.7%	88.1%
4 lbs. 7 oz.	60.0%	81.2%	90.7%	95.0%	96.6%
5 lbs. 9 oz.	——	89.2%	94.9%	98.2%	99.0%
6 lbs. 10 oz.	——	94.4%	97.6%	99.2%	99.4%
7 lbs. 12 oz.	——	95.2%	98.9%	99.4%	99.5%
8 lbs. 14 oz.	——	——	——	99.0%	99.4%
9 lbs. 15 oz. +	——	——	——	98.6%	98.8%

Adapted from Shapiro and Unger, 1954: 18. *Source:* Nationwide data for white women, 1950. Reciprocal percentages of babies died within the first 28 days after being born alive. Blank cells had too few cases to be able to compute rates.

surviving for as much as four weeks are not very good if it is small or if it is very young. Conversely, the longer the child stays in the uterus before it is born and the larger it grows, the better its chances for survival.

Newton (1972) reviewed research findings that birth weight is adversely affected if the mother smokes tobacco. The more she smokes, the less the baby weighs. In addition to reducing infant birth weight, smoking causes other fatalities before and after birth. Research summarized in the January 29, 1973 issue of *Newsweek* showed that smoking increased the number of stillbirths and neonatal deaths by more than one fourth beyond that for nonsmokers. Increased mortality could be avoided by stopping smoking before the fourth month of pregnancy.

Table 16–2 shows a point of diminishing returns in weight. The optimum weight is around eight pounds, and oversized babies of nine pounds or more have a diminished survival rate. The table fails to show what happens to babies who remain in the uterus for more than the normal 266 days (that is, more than 280 days calculated from the last menstruation). Montagu (1971) reviewed the scientific literature on this subject and found that babies more than two weeks overdue tended to be too large to be born normally. As a result, twice as many had to be removed by Caesarean section and there were significant increases in severe abnormalities and in deaths occurring around the time of birth. Infants grow so prodigiously in the later weeks of gestation that if this period is prolonged, the baby's head is liable to become so large that it cannot travel down the birth canal.

Congenital Handicaps.   Not counting underweight babies, almost 11 percent of Bierman's Kauai babies were born with handicaps. These fell into four categories of about equal size:

1. Premature children requiring special care who matured into normal children by age two.

2. Children with minor physical defects and disorders that could be easily corrected.

3. Children with more serious disorders such as hernia or strabismus ("cross-eye"), which could be corrected with short-term, specialized care as by a major operation.

4. Children with handicaps requiring long-term medical, educational, or custodial care.

Typical among these last were congenital heart defects, severe mental deficiency (IQ below 70), or combinations of physical and mental handicaps. Bierman et al. (1965) commented, "Even with the best of care most of these children will be permanently handicapped in some degree."

Handicaps are not always detectable at birth. Many are noted only as the child begins to mature or if it receives special diagnostic study. Parents who have already had a normal child can tolerate an abnormal one more easily. But an abnormal first child produces not only unrelieved disappointment but anxiety about future children:

> We knew as soon as Mary was born that she wasn't normal physically, but it was only gradually that we realized that she was also mentally retarded. We could not love any baby more than we love her—normal or not. She is ours and when I feed her, stay up with her at night, and hold her tight, I'm sure I feel no different than a parent of any normal child. Yet there is no future in our relationship—she does not know either of us.
>
> When she was seven months old and we were quite sure she was retarded, we had long visits with my gynecologist. He assured us that Mary's condition is extremely rare and not hereditary and encouraged us to have another child. It was not the easiest pregnancy in the world, however, as I had many fears about the normality of the child I was carrying. I had seen so many abnormalities in Children's Hospital that I never knew existed. Even though I kept myself as busy as possible, it was a tremendous relief when the nine months of waiting were over and we finally had a healthy, normal baby.

Changes in the Mother

While the embryo is still too small to be felt in the abdomen, the mother's body chemistry is transformed to nurture it.

Physical Changes. The woman's body is marvelously adaptable to the needs of her growing child. Pregnancy is a natural state, not an illness or a medical "problem." Most expectant mothers experience no change in their general health. Among those whose health changed, three times as many mothers told Landis (1950) it improved as said it deteriorated. Some women's complexions bloom during pregnancy.

However, pregnancy does bring some physical problems to most women. Heinstein (1967) found that the most frequent physical complaint was feeling tired in the morning. Occasional nausea was typical in the first three months of pregnancy, but tended to persist beyond that point only for women who were reluctant to have the child. Rosengren (1961) found that some reacted to pregnancy as though it were an illness, worrying about the changes in their bodies, emphasizing the pain and suffering, feeling that they should be excused from normal duties, and relying on their doctor to help them "return to normal." Women who were generally unhappy or insecure were more apt to assume this "sick" role during pregnancy (for example, women married to less-well-educated husbands or whose husbands were downward mobile). Moreover, negative reactions intensified when pregnancy conflicted with other values (for example, aspirations for a home and furniture or the opportunity to continue working in an interesting job).

Robertson (1946) found nausea associated with disturbed sexual functioning, including lack of orgasm and dislike of intercourse. This applied especially to women with persistent, severe nausea and vomiting, illustrating the profound repercussions of social and psychological factors on physical well-being during pregnancy. Chertok (1972) found that women tended not only to feel nauseated but actually to vomit if they were caught in ambivalence about the prospective child (both wanting it and not wanting it), if they reacted negatively to the first movements of the fetus within their belly, and if their relationship to their husband was negative, creating an insecure environment into which to bring a child.

The Committee on Maternal Nutrition of the National Research Council found that an average weight gain of 24 pounds during pregnancy was most favorable for both mother and child (Newton, 1972). Excessive gains make childbirth more difficult. Even with normal weight gain, the baby presses inward on the intestines and bladder so that constipation and frequent urination may occur during the last weeks of pregnancy.

Emotional Changes. Provided that a woman has chosen to bear her child and is satisfied that her husband joins with her in this amazing adventure of creating a family and intends to continue to help care for the new life, a first pregnancy carries an emotional high similar to or even beyond the magic of falling in love. To experience the child growing within and to plan for its coming is to fulfill her womanhood. And to take responsibility for bearing a child is to take even more seriously her marriage commitment:

I can no longer do exactly as I please. I begin to experience in new ways what it means to be an adult and to take responsibility for another life that for many years will be totally dependent on me and us. It is frightening and at the same time awe-inspiring that I could love and trust you so much that we dare to bring a new life into this world, a baby who comes into being because of our love. In bearing this child, I join the stream of human life. Life is using my body as a channel. I become more aware of my body and its amazing functioning than ever before. The baby is growing and developing with little conscious effort on my part. My body knows how to care for it. I watch and observe with joy and gratitude this miracle occurring within my being.

Women who work only part time or not at all may use their leisure to prepare themselves physically, mentally, emotionally, and spiritually for the birth and for parenthood. They may meditate on the inner growth of their baby, read the latest literature on the care and rearing of children, attend prenatal classes with their husbands, exercise, plan and buy equipment for the baby. If natural childbirth is chosen as the method of delivery, there are more things to learn and practice in preparation for the event. These are tasks not simply to be endured but to be enjoyed, every moment.

Marriage during Pregnancy

Much of the woman's reaction to pregnancy depends on her husband's reaction (and his on hers). If he is happy about pregnancy, sympathizes with her problems, and does not regret her change of figure, her morale is reinforced. Except for insecure husbands married to narcissistic wives, most couples adapt easily.

Stott (1952) studied obstetrical patients and found that their actions didn't change much, but the partners' feelings toward each other notably improved. Half the couples said their love became deeper, and nearly two thirds said the prospective baby drew them closer together. Wives felt more appreciated and better understood.

Raush and his colleagues (1974) found that pregnant couples role-played conflict scenes differently from couples married equally long who were not expecting a child. The pregnant women were less rational, more emotional and more coercive in their verbal behavior. Presumably, another way of saying the same thing is that they became more demanding. Their husbands were remarkably empathic in response. They became more conciliatory. Rather than reacting to their wives' coerciveness in kind, they became less coercive and less rejecting. This suggests that pregnancy was understood by both partners as a time of unusual difficulty for the woman that requires extraordinary considerateness from the husband. These changes must make pregnant wives feel much loved by their husbands.

If the husband fails to respond to his wife's need for love and sympathy, she feels lonely and deserted. Faced with a new and perhaps scary experience, her loneliness is intensified by losing contact with her colleagues if she quits work. Fear of childbirth is so widespread (63 percent of the student wives studied by Poffenberger et al., 1952) that the husband has a crucial supportive role.

Sexual Changes.   During the first few months, the embryo is too small to be noticed. However, physiological changes affect the wife's sexual responsiveness. Masters and Johnson (1966) found that the normal swelling of the breasts during first pregnancy was painfully intensified for some women by vasocongestion under sexual stimulation. Nausea, sleepiness, and chronic fatigue depressed the sexual interest of more than three fourths of their first-pregnancy women during the first trimester. However, most women experienced none of these sexual handicaps in subsequent pregnancies.

In the middle trimester, the concentrated blood supply to the growing fetus accentuated vasocongestion in the genital area during sexual stimulation. As a result, many women were more sexually responsive and more interested in having intercourse than at any other time in their lives.

In the last trimester, both partners generally lost interest in having sexual relations as the fetus became more of an obstacle. During the last six weeks, most doctors prohibited intercourse for fear of infection. Masters and Johnson suggested that antibiotics made infection so easily curable that this risk was not significant. They recognized, however, that uterine contractions during orgasm might precipitate premature delivery by women with a history of miscarriages.

For a man to lose interest in having intercourse with his wife or to be forbidden to do so by her obstetrician does not mean he will lose his sexual feelings. Among Masters and Johnson's college-educated couples, almost one fourth of the husbands engaged in extramarital intercourse during the months just before and after childbirth when they were unable to have intercourse with their wives. Alternatively, the couple may explore the tremendous variety of ways in which two people can enjoy and care for one another's bodies without having to depend on intercourse. In the latter months of pregnancy, the wife will especially appreciate lower back rubs and total body massage. With restrictions on intercourse, she can masturbate her husband and give him the pleasure of orgasm in new ways.

Childbirth

Pregnancies vary greatly in length. The average date of delivery is 280 days from the last menstruation. However, the date of conception is not a fixed interval following menstruation, nor is the interval from conception to delivery standardized. Hence, considerable latitude must be allowed in predicting the date of childbirth.

Figure 16–1 shows that only one birthdate out of 25 was predicted correctly. The middle 50 percent fell within a two-week interval, but the remainder were more than a week off, and 10 percent were as much as three weeks early or late.

Labor

Labor usually begins gradually—especially for women who have never had a baby. Sometimes the bag of fluid surrounding the baby breaks first, precipitating labor. Sometimes the first sign is a thick, mucous, bloody discharge from the vagina. More often, the muscular contractions of the uterus begin first. Since there may be false starts, it is useful to keep track of the decreasing interval between contractions. When they come regularly as often as every ten minutes, the chances are that labor has begun, so the woman is likely to be asked to go to the hospital.

The first stage of labor involves dilation of the mouth of the uterus until it is open wide enough for the baby to pass through. The cervix consists of a band of circular muscles that have been contracted throughout the life of the woman. These muscles are potentially elastic, capable of

Figure 16-1 Duration of Pregnancy (from last menstruation)

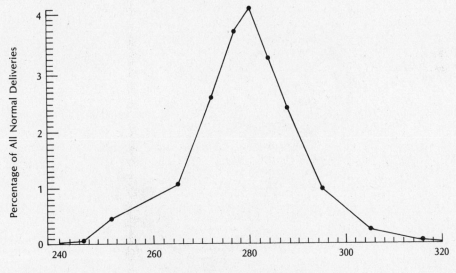

Number of Days from Last Menstruation

Adapted from Eastman, 1950: 198.

stretching until the head (usually the first and always the largest part of the baby) is ready to pass through (see Figure 16–2).

Relaxation is the circular muscles' natural response to being nudged by the baby when the longitudinal muscles of the uterine walls begin to contract. If the mother is tense and fearful her circular muscles tighten, blocking the baby and causing pain. The mother's task during this stage is to relax. When a contraction comes, lying back and consciously relaxing helps the dilation. Deep, slow abdominal breathing helps the baby rotate into position for passing out through the pelvic opening. The average duration of labor is twice as long the first time (12 hours) as in subsequent births because the first dilation is the hardest (ACOG, 1965).

Natural Childbirth. "Natural childbirth" emphasizes advance preparation for dilation. Dr. Grantley Dick Read (1944) believed that fear of the unknown tenses the uterine circular muscles. Fear is reduced by education and training for parenthood, giving the expectant mother confidence about the experience she will undergo. Trained mothers deliver faster than untrained ones. Thomas (1950) found that the time span from onset of labor to completion of delivery was 19 percent shorter for first deliveries by trained women.

Ease of dilation reduces the necessity of surgical cutting to enlarge

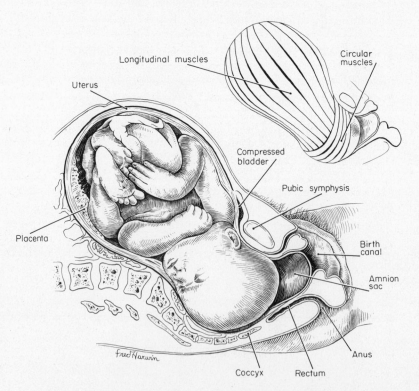

Figure 16-2 Fetus at full term and uterine muscles involved in birth.

the vaginal opening. Newton (1972) criticized the tendency of many obstetricians to perform episiotomies routinely, believing that training could enable most mothers to give birth without this surgical trauma.

Natural childbirth reduces the need for anesthesia by preparing women for the alternate pushing and relaxing that enables the baby to be expelled relatively painlessly. Vellay (1972) pointed out that mothers benefit from the nonuse of anesthesia by a reduction in postpartum depression. If they experience fully the extraordinary act of birthing a child and avoid the depressive effects of sedation, they are more likely to feel high rather than low during the ensuing days.

Natural childbirth benefits the child as well as the mother. Newton (1972) reported research findings that barbiturates and other sedatives administered to the mother during delivery passed into the bloodstream of the baby, leaving it drugged for up to five days after birth. One effect of this inadvertent sedation was that the baby tended to suck less well at the breast or bottle and therefore to consume less of the nourishment needed for survival in those crucial first days. For breast-feeding mothers, this lesser sucking provided less stimulation for initiating the flow of milk. Worse yet, Vellay reported that anesthesia given to the mother is a major cause of breathing failure and heart failure in newborn children.

Delivery

Having the husband present in the delivery room is an innovation that Bradley (1962) saw benefiting mother, father, and child. Wives appreciated the support and coaching of their husbands, had more rapid deliveries and fewer postpartum psychoses.

While the cervix is dilating, the baby begins moving through the vagina or "birth canal" (see Figure 16–3). Rhythmic contractions of the longitudinal uterine muscles force the baby out, a push at a time. The mother may aid this process by gently bearing down, reinforcing the uterine contraction. During each contraction she can take several deep breaths and hold her breath at the peak of the contraction. Her active cooperation with the birth process speeds up the delivery.

Movement of the baby through the birth canal stretches the vulva. Panting like a puppy during emergence of the head prevents pushing at this time and insures a gentler delivery. If the mother has not had too much anesthesia, the baby emerges wide awake, crying spontaneously so that its lungs fill with air and it starts breathing.

Discharge of the placenta along with the umbilical cord membranes is called the afterbirth. This occurs five to fifteen minutes after the baby is born. Usually it happens spontaneously. If not, the mother can contract her longitudinal muscles as in the second stage of labor.

Childbirth in Retrospect. Mothers who remain conscious during childbirth often describe it as one of the most significant experiences of

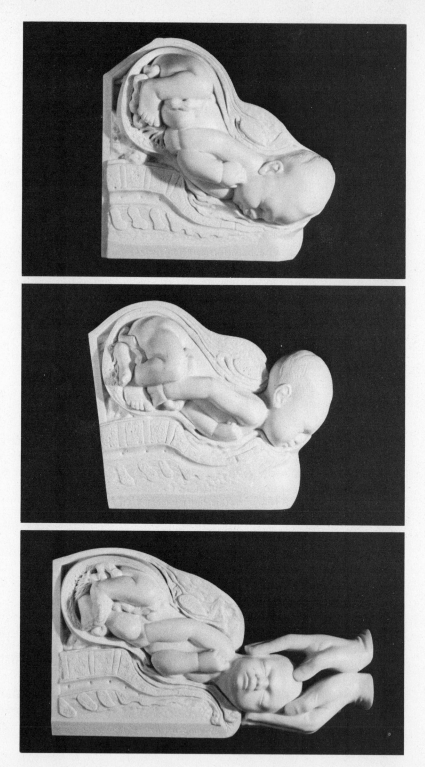

Figure 16-3 The birth process (photos copyrighted by Cleveland Health Museum, reproduced by permission).

their lives. Poffenberger et al. (1952) found that mothers generally viewed it in retrospect as less painful than they had anticipated.

Following childbirth, some women suffer a postpartum depression so severe that they have to be hospitalized. Jacobs (1943) reported that this psychosis accounted for more than 5 percent of all female admissions to mental hospitals. A mild depression in the form of a "blue day" is a common experience. However, the termination of the long period of expectancy and fascination with a child of one's own give most new mothers a honeymoon-like euphoria.

Room Arrangements

Mothers are encouraged to get out of bed within 24 hours after delivery. By that time they have slept off much of their fatigue from the exertions of labor and delivery. Physical activity revitalizes muscular tone, making it possible for most women to go home in three to seven days.

Many hospitals assign mother and child to separate rooms. The baby is placed in a central nursery that only the nursing staff enters. Much of the responsibility for the baby is assumed by the nurses. This is an asset to overtired veteran mothers but deprives novices of the opportunity to learn how to care for their infants.

Some hospitals have "rooming-in," placing the baby where the mother can have easy access to it in a bassinet beside her bed. Sometimes a tiny nursery is next to each hospital room so the mother can observe her child and retrieve it at will. Rooming-in helps new mothers gain self-confidence. If the mother carries the responsibility for the child from the beginning (with the instruction and help of the nurses), she gains skill in interpreting the child's needs. McBride (1951) found that phone calls to physicians from anxious mothers after they got home decreased by 90 percent after rooming-in was introduced at Duke University Hospital.

A baby that has the full-time attention of its mother instead of sharing nurses with the other inhabitants of a nursery is more likely to get attention when it wants it. The mother is able to feed, change, or cuddle the baby at will. This gives the baby a more comfortable transition from the uterine environment where its needs were met continuously. The mother is reassured to know that her baby's needs are not being neglected by harried nurses. Thoms (1950) found that breast feeding got off to a better start since the baby was fed when it was hungriest. Newton (1972) reported that breast feeding increased from 35 percent to 58 percent of all mothers when Duke University Hospital shifted from compulsory separation to compulsory rooming-in.

The Birth Crisis

What does it mean to the child to emerge from the uterus into the outside world? The prenatal environment was dark, quiet, enveloping, warm, and nourishing. How traumatic childbirth will be depends on the extent to which the postnatal environment duplicates the uterus. Leboyer (1975) developed a method of childbirth designed to smooth the transition. He darkened the delivery room by using a small night light. He required that everyone whisper rather than speak normally. He postponed severing the umbilical cord for five minutes after birth so that the baby could continue receiving oxygen while learning how to breathe. The tactile warmth of the uterus was duplicated by laying the child on the mother's belly and massaging it gently. After the umbilical cord was cut, the baby was placed in a body-temperature bath until fully relaxed. Then it was returned to snuggle with the mother where it was allowed to remain indefinitely. Leboyer reported that infants born in this manner cried less than those born into a less womblike environment. Presumably, their attitude toward life should be more positivbe as a result.

Touching.   Klaus et al. (1972) found that body contact between mother and child in the first few days affected the mother as well as the child. Mothers who were given an opportunity to hold their naked babies for one hour within the first few hours after birth and for five hours a day on the next three days learned how to mother their infants more intimately. One month later these mothers paid more attention to their babies while the latter were being examined by a physician, soothed and fondled their babies more, and gave their babies more eye contact than did a control group of mothers who had not had body contact with their babies in the hospital. Klaus believed that these maternal actions provided babies with greater warmth and stimulation.

Casler (1961) suggested that the characteristics of the womb have implications for subsequent care of the infant. Warmth is provided by body contact. (Infant monkeys prefer warm mother substitutes to cold ones.) Thus, babies need to be carried about on the mother's back or in her arms, or to sleep beside her. Petting and caressing provide tactile stimulation similar to the uterine environment. Leboyer (1976) advocated daily massaging with oil. The kinesthetic stimulation of the prenatal environment suggests the advantages of a cradle and rocking chair. Carrying the child also serves this purpose. Finally, the continuous feeding of the umbilical cord is approximated by demand feeding.

Montagu (1971) cited research that supports Casler's recommendations:

1.   Freedman, Boverman, and Freedman (1960) found that premature infants who were rocked for an hour a day gained weight faster than twin siblings who were not rocked.

2.   Sokoloff, Yaffe, Weintraub, and Blase (1969) found that premature babies who were stroked five minutes every hour for the first ten days gained weight faster than a control group who were given routine nursery care.

3. Salk (1960) found that tape-recorded heartbeat sounds (which simulated the uterine experience) not only promoted weight gain but produced deeper breathing, more regular heartbeat, and decreased respiratory and digestive difficulties. Although this may indicate the advantage of tape recorders as nursery equipment, the multiple tactile benefits of the parents cradling their child in their arms suggests that rocking, stroking, and cuddling the baby in a rocking chair might combine all these advantages in one, with the additional advantage for a nursing mother of feeding her child at the same time.

Observations of middle-class mothers and their infants at a country club pool impressed Clay (1968: 205) with how seldom most mothers touched their babies even when they were very young:

> When they cried, their mothers picked them up and fed them bottles or changed their diapers. Sometimes they were rocked or patted. When they slept, they were put back to bed (in their baby carriages).
>
> One of the patterns that the study dramatically shows is the separation of the bodies of mother and child that occurs in American culture. From the time the child is born he is kept away from the mother in things like cribs, carriages, and baby carriages. When the infant is in distress or when it is the "right time," the mother goes to him to perform her essential mothering services, after which she returns him to his bed or play area. American mothers largely omit the ... close bodily attachment ... when the mother's and the neonate's needs for sensory contact, sensory stimulation, and sensory communication seem to be the greatest.

Clay's observations suggest that only exceptional mothers are comfortable enough with their own sensuality to give their newborn baby enough touching to provide it with a physical environment that would minimize the birth trauma.

BECOMING PARENTS

As soon as the child arrives, life at home changes sharply. These changes are not necessarily resented, but they are more drastic than at most other turning points in life.

In a cross-sectional sample of Minneapolis parents of first-born children, Russell (1974) found that mothers tended to be affected rather differently than fathers. Table 16–3 shows that the mothers mostly had physical problems while the fathers had characteristically practical ones. Balancing these problems were such pleasures as enjoying the baby and having more things to talk about with the partner.

Russell found that problems were not evenly distributed among couples. The crisis was less if the pregnancy was planned, the delivery was easy, the baby was quiet and had few problems, and the marriage was

Table 16–3 Most Widespread Complaints about Having a Child, for New Mothers and Fathers

Mothers' Complaints	Fathers' Complaints
1. Fatigue and tiredness 78%	1. Interrupted sleep/rest 61%
2. Interrupted sleep/rest 76%	2. In-laws' child-care suggestions 54%
3. Worry about personal appearance 74%	3. Had to change plans 54%
4. Feeling emotionally upset 68%	4. Increased money problems 53%
5. Worry about loss of figure 61%	5. Increased work required at home 53%

Adapted from Russell, 1974: 296. *Source:* Cross-sectional sample of Minneapolis parents of first-born children at average age of 29 weeks. Reciprocal percentages did not experience the particular problem.

happy. Mothers who had been married a relatively long time and who were in good health were better able to cope. Fathers who wanted additional children and for whom being a father was important particularly welcomed their first child.

Dyer (1963) found that only fragile marriages were seriously endangered by the intruder. Some parents found the impact of the child less severe if they had taken courses in family life education, but most were surprised how much harder coping with an infant was than they had expected.

From Dyad to Triad

"Two's company, three's a crowd" symbolizes the difference between a pair able to give their attention to each other and a trio whose attention must be divided. Since a newborn infant is helpless and the parents are responsible for it, this trio lacks the symmetry of marriage. The child alters the power structure, the division of labor, and the personal relationship between the parents.

Revised Power Structure. If the wife withdraws from the labor force, she becomes more dependent on her husband. The younger she is and the more rapidly she acquires children, the more the husband dominates:

> As the mother of a new baby, she gives up her job and is confined to her home by the heavy demands of child-care. Not only is she cut off from contact with her fellow workers but even the opportunity to participate in recreational activities and organizational meetings is impaired by her baby-sitting responsibilities. Under these circumstances, parenthood brings a sudden loss of resources to the wife combined with increased need for husbandly support. It is no wonder, therefore, that the wife's dependence increases (Blood and Wolfe, 1960: 43).

Revised Division of Labor.   If the woman shifts from full-time work to full-time housekeeping, this brings corresponding changes in the allocation of domestic tasks. When the mother has just given birth to her first child and is learning how to care for it, she needs her husband's help. However, once she recovers her strength and masters new skills, the division of labor generally becomes sharper. Most husbands do less housework when their wives are home fulltime. Couples share fewer tasks and role specialization increases (Blood and Wolfe).

Revised Personal Relationships.   Once children arrive, the honeymoon is over. No longer can husband and wife enjoy each other's unlimited companionship, especially outside the home. Bott (1957) found that "before they had children, all couples had had far more joint activities, especially in the form of shared recreation outside the home. After their children were born, the activities of all couples had become more sharply differentiated and they had had to cut down on joint external participation."

A baby inevitably alters the husband-wife relationship. Where before the two could focus on each other, now there is a distraction. Or perhaps it should be called an attraction. Both parents turn their attention to the child. Its needs and interests compete with those of the partner. As more children arrive, each family member's slice of attention gets thinner. Never again is the change as drastic as with the first child.

Children disrupt many patterns:

> *Gracia and I made a big thing out of mealtimes. At dinner we'd have candlelight and silver and read to each other the letters we'd received from mutual friends. One Christmas when the mail was running heavy, we began to be vaguely aware that our reading wasn't getting across as well as it had before. Finally we realized that the baby was getting old enough to want his share of attention. We decided right then and there never to try to read mail at meals again—at least not until the children are old enough to understand what we are reading.*

Rosenblatt's observational study of heterosexual couples in public places was not limited to married couples. Nevertheless, it shows (see Table 16–4) how much less couples with children smiled at one another or touched each other. They even talked less to each other. This illustrates how parents going places and doing things with their children give less attention to the partner than parents who are unaccompanied by their children or couples who have no children.

Objectively, the husband is necessarily "neglected" by the wife. Half of Dyer's new fathers recognized that they were "sometimes" neglected and 12 percent more felt that they were "often" neglected in favor of the child. The more immature the husband, the more he resents this loss:

Table 16–4   Interaction between Couples in Public Places, by Presence or Absence of Children

	CHILDREN'S PRESENCE/ABSENCE	
Interaction between Couples	*No Children*	*Children*
Talking	66%	53%
Smiling	33%	6%
Touching	30%	6%
Number of couples	345	95

Computed from Rosenblatt, 1974: 752. *Source:* Male-female couples in a variety of public places in Minneapolis and St. Paul. Reciprocal percentages of couples were not engaged in the specified behavior during the observation period (walking through a 30-foot-long space as at a shopping mall or a beach).

> *Fred got pretty pouty when our first baby was born. I suppose he really was jealous of the attention I gave Sally. If I had to get up from the table to do something for her, he'd make a crack about having to eat all alone. If I didn't have his dinner ready on time because of a five o'clock feeding, he'd be irritable. I think his resentment has made him hard and demanding on Sally ever since.*

Lopata (1971) summarized the effects of the advent of children on the husband-wife relationship:

> Many features of the nine-month pregnancy and of the first few months after delivery are rejective of the young husband, especially during times when sexual relations are medically discouraged or when the wife is too tired to pay sufficient attention to his desires. The early months of a child's life require almost constant care, since its hours of wakefulness are unpredictable. Most young mothers are so very uncertain of themselves that the time when the baby sleeps is filled with worry about it or with preparation for the next episode of waking. This means that the mother has less time, energy, and psychological inclination to focus on the role of wife than she had before. In the meantime, the husband is not as directly involved in the care process and often feels left out of the basic mother-child unit. There is, further, a tendency of young mothers to feel that the baby is theirs, a possessiveness that excludes male ownership. Finally, the wife's needs in terms of the behavior and attitudes of the husband change as she becomes a mother.... The situation under which the [change] takes place is not conducive to quiet reformulation because of the anxiety and physical exhaustion of the mother while the father's ego is hurt and his sleep often interrupted (p. 198).

Paradoxically, Ryder (1973) found that young mothers in his Washington area sample felt even more neglected than fathers. Women with children complained that their husbands did not pay enough attention to them more often than women without children. This might mean either that new fathers diminished the amount of attention they gave their wives or that wives wanted increased attention, or that both changes might occur simultaneously. In any case, mothers of young children more often felt they were not getting as much love and attention as they wanted.

Ryder's findings parallel those of Raush et al. (1974) who found that the understanding, empathic way in which husbands dealt with pregnant wives ended when the child was born. New fathers ceased being conciliatory and became more cognitive and rational in their approach to marital problems. The researchers commented, "Apparently they no longer see their wives as needing special support when engaged in marital conflict . . . these husbands may be failing their wives just when support is most needed." Our guess is that one reason for this shift is that husbands are not affected directly by the changes of pregnancy and can afford to be generous with the troubles that uniquely face their wives, whereas once the child is born they too experience extra work and disrupted sleep, so that their main concern is with solving practical problems rather than merely expressing sympathy. While the shift may be understandable, it must be disappointing to wives to experience this withdrawal of emotional support at a critical time.

If both husbands and wives feel neglected following the birth of their first child, it should not surprise us to find that new parents are generally less satisfied with their marriages than are couples married the same length of time who have not had a child. Feldman (1971) found not only that the marital satisfaction of couples with a child was lower than that of couples without a child, but that before-and-after-childbirth studies of the same couples showed decreasing satisfaction. The only exceptions were that couples who had very little communication previously found that a child gave them something to talk about and made their marriage less unsatisfactory than it had been before. In this limited way, having a child redeemed these "bad" marriages. But for couples already in touch with each other, children generally got in the way of interaction.

Specifically, Feldman found that five-month-old children impeded their parents' sexual activity and interfered with the wife's ability to express her feelings to her husband (typically, she felt more nervous and "blue"). New fathers lost their sense of humor, and became more serious about life. Both partners were more concerned with emotional and financial security. Thus couples generally experienced a shift away from enjoying their relationship toward feeling burdened by the responsibilities of parenthood.

Responsibilities of Parenthood

The trouble with infants is that they are helpless. In time they become domesticated, and eventually self-sufficient. But their initial impact is critical precisely because they make such total demands. Since wives carry the main burden of these responsibilities in most marriages, it will simplify our discussion if we focus on what happens to the female parent.

Being Tied Down. A newborn infant can never be left alone and to some extent cannot even be entrusted to someone else. Most young parents have so little money that they can hire correspondingly few mother substitutes. Substitutes can stay with the sleeping baby and feed it too (provided it's on the bottle instead of the breast). If the cost of sitters comes too high, time out must be fitted to the baby's schedule or the spouse's: "I can't come then because she'll be asleep.... I'm sorry but that's when she's liable to need feeding.... It depends on whether Steve can be home that night."

Sometimes the baby can go out too—sleeping peacefully in a bassinet or breaking into the middle of the party with demands for attention. The problem may be solved by grandparents willing to help (if they live in the same town and enjoy *their* new role). Or husband and wife take turns sitting for the neighbors, replacing funds with barter.

The fact remains that social life must be curtailed, though the change has some compensations. The very fact of having a baby is a new activity—a kind of recreation as well as work. It is no accident that parents are often described as "proud." A baby is not only a task but an achievement. Every development is an event for the co-parent to hear about (and friends and relatives too). The first smile, first tooth, and first step highlight what is often a wearing but seldom a dull existence. If husband and wife go out less, they have more to stay in for. Instead of saying that social life is restricted, it's better to say it is revised.

We have assumed that the baby inhibits the mother's employment. No matter how interesting a child may be, adult companionship and outside stimulation are missed. Women who work right up to the last months of pregnancy and switch to staying home find the change especially drastic. Lopata (1971) found that for many women the shift to being a mother created an identity crisis similar to men's experience at retirement. The loss of career (for those who give it up), the reduction of social life, and other interferences with skills that the woman has found satisfying are apt to leave her feeling that parts of her self have been "lost" or put in cold storage.

At the same time that old skills become obsolete, new skills are required. So Lopata found that the changes in the self that came with children were partly losses and partly gains.

Disruption of Routines. In the uterus the baby was fed continuously, 24 hours a day, and slept when it wanted to, unaware of day or night. Getting adjusted to the routines of the adult world takes time. In the meantime, most babies are irregular and unpredictable. Only a lucky few wake up, take their feeding, and promptly go back to sleep. For every one of those, several ordinary babies want a middle-of-the-night feeding, fuss at odd hours, and change their "schedule" every few days. Worse yet are those whose "three-month colic" doesn't yield to treatment.

The average mother finds her sleep disrupted and her meals disturbed just when she is recuperating from the labors of childbirth. As a result, she is apt to feel chronically tired. In a Houston sample of college-educated couples, Dyer (1963) found the most widespread problems were tiredness, exhaustion, and loss of sleep, especially during the first two months—complaints that came from 87 percent of the mothers.

Expansion of Tasks. At the same time that her duties become unpredictable, they balloon in scope. Whereas during the last weeks of pregnancy there may have been hardly enough to do, suddenly there is too much. Now the time required by the family jumps to the highest it will ever be (save when subsequent infants are equally young).

Table 16–5 shows that the arrival of an infant more than doubled the housework responsibilities for both parents in dual-career families. Some of this burden eased by the time the baby was one year old, but even when the youngest child was a teenager, parents continued to have appreciably more household responsibilities than couples without children.

The key new task is feeding. To be sure, childless wives have themselves and their husbands to feed, but the complexities of feeding infants make adult requirements seem simple. Oral gratification is important to the child's early adjustment. Breast feeding, self-demand scheduling, and cuddling the baby during feeding are beneficial. Although there are potential values in each of these, Brody (1956: 319–21) found that going through the motions did not automatically provide the child with the intended satisfactions:

> Breast-feeding did not insure gentle procedures, intimacy or restfulness. . . . The endorsement of self-demand schedules was poorly related to satisfactory feeding experiences for either mother or infant. . . . Holding an infant did not necessarily enhance his comfort during feeding, and often it meant being held awkwardly or uncomfort-

Table 16–5 **Total Hours per Week Devoted to Housework by Both Parents Combined, by Age of Youngest Child, and by Wife's Employment**

	AGE OF YOUNGEST CHILD (YEARS)					
Wife's Employment	None	Under 1	1	2–5	6–11	12–17
Not employed	42	78	72	68	64	59
Employed	34	73	66	54	50	45

Adapted from Walker, 1970: 12. *Source:* Syracuse, New York, families. Figures show the total number of hours per week spent in household work (including child care) by the husband and wife combined. Figures for childless couples were for wives under age 25. A few "not employed" wives worked up to 14 hours a week. All "employed" wives worked at least 15 hours a week, most of them full time.

ably. . . . It appears that a mother may choose to breast feed, may try to give good physical support to her infant and may try to feed on a demand schedule—all . . . important criteria for adequate feeding—and yet she may unknowingly offer little satisfaction to her infant in the process.

This does not mean that methods of infant care do not matter, but that feelings are as important as methods.

Breast Feeding.   Heinstein's survey of California mothers (1965) found that college-educated women in metropolitan areas were more apt than any other segment of the populace to breast-feed their newborn children, apparently because they believed this was good for the child. However, these same women weaned their children to the bottle sooner than did less educated or rural women (most making the shift after only a couple of months of nursing).

Even brief nursing may be more valuable than none at all for mother and child. Immediately after birth, suckling at the breast promotes the discharge of the placenta and the contraction of the uterus to normal size. Montagu (1971) reported that the colostrum produced in the breasts during the first two days after birth prevents infant diarrhea and immunizes the baby against disease. He cited a longitudinal study of 173 children from birth to age 10 in which those who had not been breast fed had 4 times as many respiratory infections, 8 times as much eczema, 20 times as much diarrhea, 21 times as much asthma, and 27 times as much hay fever.

Hammarth (1960) emphasized the body contact between mother and child:

> Can you imagine being told that it would be just as satisfying to kiss rubber lips as it is to kiss warm live ones? . . . Even if bottle-fed babies are held for each feeding, the physical contact between the nursing infant and his mother cannot be duplicated. . . . It is not the quantity and quality of breast milk alone nor its value as a source of food that constitutes its importance. It is the exchange of energy between two live organisms which goes along with breast feeding that makes for the unique value of the experience.

For Hammarth, this reasoning implied not only the value of initiating breast feeding, but of continuing it until the child voluntarily relinquished it. Newton and Newton (1972) discovered that in most primitive societies breast feeding continued for several years rather than several months, as has been customary in America.

Newton (1971) noted major psychological and physical differences for both mother and child between "unrestricted" and "token" breast feeding. Unrestricted feeding typically involved as many as ten feedings a day during the early weeks, gradually diminishing to five or six feedings after six months. She concluded that unrestricted breast feeding was easier and more satisfying for both partners than feeding restricted to certain times or interfered with by premature administration of supplementary foods.

Newton and Newton (1972) reported that numerous psychological factors affect the mother's ability to nurse her child. Painful memories may get in the way of the mother-infant relationship. The more difficult her experience of giving birth to a particular child, the less likely the mother was to choose to breast-feed it (Jackson, Wilkin, and Auerbach, 1956). If extensive anesthesia was required to dull the pain, and if the obstetrician found it necessary to use forceps to aid the delivery, the mother was less likely to nurse her baby.

The attitudes of the mother toward breast feeding correlated with her ability to nurse her child. Women who expressed positive attitudes immediately after giving birth produced 68 percent more milk four days later and were three times as apt to be able to supply the baby with its entire food needs as women with negative attitudes. Those who were ambivalent toward breast feeding had almost as much difficulty as the purely negative women. This suggests that women with positive attitudes toward breast feeding can be optimistic about their ability to accomplish it.

Other factors that interfered with breast feeding included dislike of nudity (Newson and Newson, 1962) and discomfort with sexuality as evidenced by intolerance of children's masturbation and sex play (Sears, Maccoby, and Levin, 1957). Conversely, breast-feeding mothers valued exchanging affection with other people more than bottle-feeding mothers. These qualities reflect the fact that breast feeding requires baring the breasts, gives sexual pleasure to both mother and child, and provides an opportunity for intimate affectional interchange.

For the baby, the sensual/sexual aspects of breast feeding become more apparent with increased age. According to Newton and Newton (1972: 392):

> The total body shows signs of eagerness—rhythmic motions of hands, feet, fingers and toes may occur along with the rhythm of sucking. Erection of the penis is common in male babies. After feeding, there is often a relaxation that is characteristic of the conclusion of satisfactory sexual response.

Most mothers, according to Masters and Johnson (1965) found nursing sexually stimulating, sometimes to the point of orgasm. And the reduced tension in the breast as the milk supply is consumed was reported by many women as a pleasurable experience reminiscent of detumescence. The fact that men and women enjoy oral-breast contact so much in sex play testifies in another way to the sensual pleasure involved for both mother and child in breast feeding.

Experiments with infant monkeys suggest that the baby benefits from being held during feeding, regardless of whether it is breast fed or bottle fed (Harlow and Harlow, 1966). One danger with bottle feeding is that the baby may be provided with an inanimate bottle holder and abandoned in its crib.

Most babies settle down to fairly regular schedules. Even so, they sometimes wake up ahead of schedule and scream for their milk. At other times they don't wake up when they are "supposed" to feed. For a few babies schedules never fit. Some need food more often than others—the mother can determine this by observation (with clues from the doctor about what to look for). Just as adults occasionally feel hungry earlier or later than usual, it is natural for babies to vary from their usual pattern. Eating when s/he is hungry is more comfortable for both child and parent.

There are tangible benefits for both generations from demand feeding. Salber (1956) found that babies fed on demand gained weight faster than those fed on a schedule. Nursing mothers are more likely to find their milk supply enhanced when the child's sucking motivation is at its height than when the child is either not hungry enough or tired out from crying prior to being nursed.

Such complexities make infant care time-consuming. But long hours and difficulties do not mean that parents feel unrewarded:

> Let's be realistic, a baby is a helpless, uncivilized, and demanding creature. He requires a lot of work, acceptance and patience. I'm not exactly smiling after I change an active, husky baby's diaper, containing a special present, and he proudly grabs a handful and smears everything within reach. When he burps curdled milk, I can brush my dress off, but the sour smell remains. How long can I tolerate a baby's crying all night when he is teething, knowing there is nothing to stop him? And how much patience can I have for a child who is a very slow eater and spits out every other spoonful? Then, what about toilet training the little boy who thinks it much more convenient to wet and then has the exceptional talent of missing the deflector every time? And when I realize I am stuck for 24 hours every day, the picture looks pretty weary. However, it is not all black. Mornings are good times; a fresh start for us both. The baby's laughs revive me and there's constant joy in watching it develop physically and mentally. Despite the hassle, there is something about babies which is difficult to define but makes them just something wonderful to have around.

Anxiety. The heaviest responsibility of parenthood is not the time and money that must be invested but knowing what to do. Being responsible for a helpless infant often frightens mothers with their first child. In Houston, Dyer (1963) found that most new mothers felt inadequate and uncertain about whether they would be a good mother. In Chicago, Lopata (1971) found the typical young mother baffled and upset by her emotional reactions to the strains of living with young children:

She has been trained to handle problems rationally, systematically, without a show or even a strong experience of anger; to solve each in order and to proceed to a new situation. School and work teach her to be task-oriented, to measure accomplishment in terms of finished product, and to organize it in blocks of time within a specialized division of labor. The care of infants and the socialization of children are, however, highly emotional processes in this society . . . and there are no perfect procedures for them. In addition, American youths are expected to be handled emotionally, with "tender and loving care." Parent-child interaction, particularly in the pre-adult years, consists of many "episodes" laden with all forms of sentiment and high emotion. Constant interruptions make the work to be accomplished between these exchanges very difficult, and children often disorganize what mothers have just finished doing. The young mother . . . surrounded by anxiety, guilt, and frustration, often finds herself acting in ways she does not like and becoming angry at times when she wants to maintain calm. The emotional level of interaction appears "abnormal" to her when compared to prior life and training, and it often causes negative feelings toward herself (pp. 185–86).

Lopata noted that many mothers felt badly about their inability to be patient with their children and keep their cool despite the provocative and unpredictable frustrations.

The problem is intensified by the infant's inability to talk. When it cries, the cause could be hunger, wet diapers, diaper rash, too many blankets, wanting to be cuddled, or half a dozen other things. Worse yet is the fear that it is seriously ill. One function of the pediatrician is to provide support and reassurance but that telephone line is always busy.

Yet even the best support from doctor, husband, mother, or sister only partially allays anxiety. Brody (1956) found new mothers "conspicuously active but also erratic in their attentiveness, efficiency, and sensitivity. They quite sedulously governed their infants' actions by stimulating, restricting, or instructing them" (p. 266). Even though "experience itself did not necessarily provide mothers with sensitivity or consistency, experience was likely to increase the assurance, competence, and predictability of maternal behavior" (p. 271). Experienced mothers were not always *better* than inexperienced ones, but they were usually more relaxed.

Unfortunately, maternal anxiety is felt by the child, creating a vicious cycle—the mother's tension increases the child's tension, producing symptoms that aggravate the mother's anxiety, and so forth. Mussen and Conger (1956) noted that many research projects have found more nervous symptoms in first-born children than in later-born ones. One of the worst infant symptoms is colic, described by Lakin (1957: 7):

Attacks of colic usually begin suddenly with an agonizing, loud and more-or-less continuous cry. . . . The abdomen is distended with legs flexed on the chest. Fists are clenched. The paroxysms end abruptly after minutes or hours, sometimes only to begin again.

Although Lakin found that colic was not confined to first-born children, it was associated with maternal anxiety:

> Mothers of colicky babies . . . more often cited feelings of nervousness and tension in response to the infant's crying. They expressed greater inadequacy in attempts to interpret the demand or need which was the source of the crying. They also more often complained of feeling ill at ease in handling their babies (p. 29).

Paradoxically, mothers who had the most trouble with their infants got the least help from their husbands and mothers. Perhaps if they received more support, the vicious cycle could be broken.

THE IMPACT OF HANDICAPPED CHILDREN

The preceding sections pointed out the stressful impact of the advent of any first child. The previous chapter showed how these stresses intensify, the larger the number of children born and the more closely they are spaced.

All of that discussion assumed that the children were normal. But occasional children are not. When a child turns out to be mentally retarded or chronically ill, the dependency burden on the parents vastly increases. One handicapped child may be the equivalent of many normal children in terms of the burden on parents and siblings. If the handicap is permanent, the family may be saddled with the equivalent of an infant who will never grow up. On the other hand, if the handicap is severe enough, the family may free itself of the burden by placing the child in an institution.

Mentally Retarded Children

Fotheringham, Skelton, and Hoddinott (1971) compared Toronto families that institutionalized a retarded child with ones who kept it at home. They found that families were more apt to institutionalize a disruptive child if their own coping abilities were inadequate because of ill health in the parents or inadequate facilities for caring for the retarded child and its siblings.

Table 16–6 shows that conditions in families that retained their retarded child worsened more than twice as often as they got better over a one-year period. Generally speaking, the older the child grew, the greater the strain on the family. The researchers found that the mental and physical health of the child, the parents, and the normal siblings generally worsened over the year of stressful living together. The toll fell most heavily on mothers, secondarily on siblings, and least on fathers (perhaps because they were away from home more).

Table 16–6   Change in Family Functioning by Retention of Mentally Retarded Child in the Home or Placement in an Institution

	DISPOSITION OF CHILD	
Change in Family Functioning	Retained in Family	Institutionalized
Improvement	17%	78%
No change	47	8
Deterioration	36	13
Total	100%	99%
Number of cases	36	60

Adapted from Fotheringham, Skelton, and Hoddinott, 1971: 94. *Source:* Toronto families studied over a one-year period from time of institutionalization compared to families with a similar retarded child that did not place it in an institution.

By contrast, families that placed their retarded children in institutions almost universally improved their family life. By relieving themselves of the burden of caring for a mentally handicapped child, families recovered from the stress they had experienced and returned to functioning normally. In almost every case, they felt an enormous relief.

Physically Handicapped Children

Hewett (1970) compared families with a cerebral palsied (spastic) child with families with normal children of the same age and found that this physical difficulty affected family life less severely. As with all handicaps, the extent of the impact depended on the severity of the impairment. Some CP children had fits, temper tantrums, and mobility handicaps requiring special handling that made it difficult to find babysitters. Consequently, one or both parents were thoroughly tied to the child. In other cases, the impairment was mild enough so that family life was not far from normal.

Focusing on the marginal differences between CP and normal families, we find the following:

1.   CP families spent extra money on special clothes and equipment for their handicapped children.

2.   Extra time was required to give the child the care it needed at home and at specialized facilities.

3.   Sixty-one percent of the mothers felt depressed, many because they had to spend so much time with the handicapped child.

4.   Over half the mothers made special allowances for their handicapped child. They frequently expected less of the child and punished him/her

less severely (spanking less) when the child failed to live up to even those reduced expectations. For some families, this created problems with normal siblings who resented the favoritism toward the handicapped child.

5.   Cerebral palsied children had more temper tantrums (especially when their verbal skills were impaired) and more sleeping difficulties. Parents adapted to the latter by having the child sleep in the same room or in the same bed with one or both of them. This reduced the child-care problem but interfered with the sexual privacy of the parents.

6.   One third of the parents had been deterred from having additional children, either because they had their hands full with the CP child and any older siblings already born, or because of fear that subsequent children might be handicapped, too.

Presumably, other physical impairments in children create similar problems and responses. Having children is time- and energy-absorbing enough when children are normal, but correspondingly more absorbing when they are not. Or when they come in pairs, triplets, or other big doses.

17 Child-rearing

The child-rearing responsibilities of parents have so many facets that this chapter and the next can hardly do them justice. On the other hand, there may be virtue in simplicity.

Children are born with great potentialities but begin their lives undeveloped. Before I was born, I could not tell the difference between myself and my warm, dark environment. After birth, I still considered myself the center of the universe. I was not aware that other people were separate. Only gradually and painfully did the "Copernican revolution" dawn. First I discovered that my parents were not part of myself, then that my father was distinguishable from my mother. Later, I discovered they had needs of their own and other tasks besides mothering and fathering me. Finally, I learned that my role was not simply to receive but to give, and that I must temper my impulses to the needs of others. Only then was I fully human.

To the family, the stress of coping with an untamed creature comes early. No matter how great their tolerance, parents must curb their "little monster" if it is not to destroy their domestic tranquility. Every child is a potential "Dennis the Menace." Although socialization sometimes occurs so swiftly that the threat is not visible, its success is crucial.

To a child, being allowed to run wild seems delightful. But wild men end up in cages—either prisons or mental hospitals. Children who fail to learn conformity face a tragic future. For the child, most pointedly, socialization is indispensable.

LOVE IS THE FOUNDATION

Socialization begins with love. Although love is given concretely in food, clothing, and shelter, Bowlby (1969) suggested that social interaction is the crucial element in developing attachment between parent and child. The more readily a parent responds to an infant's crying and the more often s/he initiates social interaction with the baby, the stronger the bond becomes.

Ainsworth and Wittig (1969) suggested that parents encourage attachment when they soothe the baby's crying and provide it with warmth and security by holding it frequently and for long periods of time, especially during the first six months. The parents' responsiveness to the infant's signals and their ability to synchronize their interventions with its rhythms (via self-demand feeding and self-demand holding) also build attachment. Responsiveness to the baby's demands gives the child a sense of the consequences of its own actions. Ainsworth and Wittig predicted that when such conditions exist, parents and child will grow to love and find "mutual delight" in each other.

By the time children were four years old, Newson and Newson (1968) reported that many mothers and children found reciprocal companionship and enjoyment:

> Where there is no baby to limit their scope, mother and child are able to indulge in little outings together—to the shops, to the park, or on more ambitious expeditions to a cinema or into town—and it is difficult to say which of the two derives most pleasure from these trips, which sometimes seem to have an almost conspiratorial quality of enjoyment.

According to a University lecturer's wife:

> One thing I get tremendous pleasure out of is her capacity for enjoying little treats. And not necessarily treats for her—for instance, if I take her out shopping and we go to buy some clothes. It doesn't matter whether it's something for her or for me, and it doesn't matter whether it's a new dress or just a . . . pair of socks, she gets a thrill out of choosing and discussing and deciding (pp. 56–57).

Clay (1968) found, however, that when middle-class mothers and their children gathered in groups at a country club beach, the children were neglected. Because they belonged to the same club, the mothers knew each other and became so absorbed in chatting that their children were abandoned to the care of the lifeguard. What little physical contact mothers had with their children was initiated chiefly by the children themselves—the mothers generally responding passively, unattentively, and without feeling. They seldom touched their children playfully or affectionately. Physical contact was limited to the minimum necessary for keeping the children under control and taking care of their physical needs. When the children needed comforting, the mothers typically offered food to distract them rather than holding and soothing them. As a result, when many of the children were upset, they didn't ask their mothers for comfort, but sucked their thumbs or clung to objects like beach towels or soft toys.

Clay's observations suggest that in some social situations, mothers' energies may be so diverted that they hardly provide the love necessary for attachment. When they are alone with their children, however, and especially when their children are relatively young, mothers are more affectionate. In any case, the more affectionate parents are, the more successful their child-rearing is likely to be.

Sears, Rau, and Alpert (1965) found that American parents viewed attachment more positively for girls than for boys. The mother is normally the chief parent to whom young children attach themselves. When a daughter forms a close relationship with her mother, she is seen as following in the mother's footsteps. For a little boy, attachment creates problems. Insofar as men and women still have differentiated roles, parents feel uneasy when they see a boy attached to his mother. For this reason, boys face more parental ambivalence than girls in acquiring the foundation of love.

Note how problematic the attachment was between this young woman and her parents:

> My parents suppressed any physical display of affection toward us children. I believe that young children treasure the physical, the tangible above the less tangible, implied emotional love. Certainly a small baby cannot, in words, be made to understand that her parents love her. I recall moments of doubt as to whether my parents were actually my real parents or whether I was in reality an adopted child. To make matters worse, my father liked to tease and trouble me by saying that the babies in the hospital were mistakenly switched and the wrong baby was brought home. I know now that this is not true but there was a stage in my development when these worries were magnified to a terrifyingly disturbing height and at that time my father unfortunately contributed to the uncertainties that were already imbedded in my childish mind.

What is the evidence that attachment is the first step in raising children? One index of successful socialization is the absence of antisocial behavior (such as delinquency), not simply because children are afraid of being punished but because they believe in social norms. Three major research projects dealt with these factors. Bandura and Walters (1959) and Glueck and Glueck (1950) compared adolescent boys who were respectively aggressive versus nonaggressive and delinquent versus nondelinquent. Sears, Maccoby, and Levin (1957) compared five-year-old children with high and low consciences. From the previous discussion, we expect attachment to be greater in children who are not aggressive, not delinquent, and have high consciences.

Sears and his colleagues found that five-year-olds of both sexes developed stronger consciences if they were dependent on their parents.

Moreover, conscience development was accentuated when attachment resulted from warm, accepting behavior by the mother. Children who clung desperately to mothers who basically rejected them did not develop high consciences. Only when attachment sprang from a positive mother-child relationship did consciences develop successfully.

For girls in Sears's sample, conscience development was especially smooth. Their tie to their mothers was more often accepted by the mother and respected by the father. For boys, on the other hand, attachment to the mother was often criticized by the parents as sissified. Fathers unsure of their own masculinity pushed their sons toward detachment and punished them for attachment. Such boys developed attachment anxiety; they became afraid to be close to anyone because dependence had been punished in the past. With their attachment needs throttled, they were unlikely to emulate the parents' behavior. Though the parents hardly intended it, frustrating their children's attachment wishes alienated them and left them at the mercy of their impulses.

For Bandura and Walters's teenage boys the pattern was similar. Normal boys sought help, companionship, and praise from parents, teachers, and peers, showing that they were not afraid of close relationships. These attachment abilities had originated in childhood, when their mothers and especially their fathers expressed warmth toward them. By contrast, boys who became aggressive had been punished for seeking help from their parents, so they felt rejected and resisted their help and their companionship.

Table 17-1 Nondelinquency Rate, by Parental Love and Discipline

Percentage Not Delinquent, by Parental Relationship to Son	Father	Mother
Affection		
Warm	66%	57%
Indifferent	27%	14%
Hostile	16%	13%
Supervision		
Suitable	——	90%
Intermediate	——	43%
Unsuitable	——	17%
Discipline		
Firm but kindly	91%	94%
Erratic	30%	38%
Lax	40%	17%
Overstrict	25%	27%

Adapted from Glueck and Glueck, 1950: 113–31. Reciprocal percentages were delinquent. *Source:* 500 matched pairs of delinquent and non-delinquent boys, ages 11 to 16, Boston area, 1940. For the total group of 1,000 boys, the delinquency rate was ipso facto 50 percent (much higher than the community-wide rate).

Table 17–1 shows a similar pattern when the criterion for successful socialization was the prevention of delinquency. Attachment-producing warmth was provided by successful parents, especially fathers. From mothers the chief danger was not too little warmth but too little discipline. Many mothers of delinquent boys were warm, but indulgent to the point of laxity, allowing them to run wild.

INFLUENCING BEHAVIOR

Loving lays the foundation for children's social development. But if parents only loved them, their children would never grow up, remaining dependent and infantilized forever.

Beyond loving, parents must somehow enable their child to change from an infant into an adult. This requires an enormous amount of learning. So the principles of learning theory must be applied if children are to learn well.

Modeling

The example that parents set by their own behavior has a powerful effect. Insofar as I loved my parents, they acquired a secondary reward value for me, and so I wanted to be like them. When I was small, my attempts to imitate their behavior were not always successful, but the older I became, the more skillfully I followed their example. This does not mean that I became a carbon copy of either my father or my mother, but that a fundamental influence on my growing up was the example they set by the way they lived.

Bandura (1964) conducted experiments to compare the effectiveness of modeling with reinforcement in enabling children to learn new behaviors. He found that modeling was far more powerful. Reinforcement is fine once the desired behavior occurs, but modeling gives children a picture of the behavior they are supposed to learn. The value of modeling is revealed when parents do not practice what they preach. Under those contradictory circumstances, children are more apt to follow their parents' example than their instruction.

Children in happy families naturally enjoy imitating their parents. When parents play role-reversal games, the learning process becomes all the more fun. Newson and Newson (1968: 52) gave several examples of four-year-old children imitating their parents and other adults. Both child and parent enjoyed the child's practice in behaving like an adult.

Factory manager's wife:

> I play with her a lot as I'm going round the house. I'm the little girl,
> and she's the Mummy. We get through a good morning like that.

Sales manager's wife:

Well, this morning she had her cookery set out and a box of chocolate beans, and she was making cakes and we all had a party, with paper hats and all that, and I was doing the ironing but I sort of joined in and that.

Cycle worker's wife:

Just before you [the researcher] came, she was you. She went out and knocked on the door, and she says "I'm the lady with the taperecorder." So I says "What can I talk to you about?"

Setting Standards

To learn to conform to social norms, children must discover what those norms are. In addition to learning from the parents' example, children learn from what their parents tell them about behavior that is appropriate and inappropriate.

Firmness. Some parents are so permissive that their children get the idea that anything goes, while others kindly but firmly set standards for their children and see to it that their children live up to them. Some parents naively believe that they must put up with nuisances in order to protect their children's personalities from being damaged. Noise, messiness, destructiveness, interference with their privacy, inordinate demands, and dangerous behavior, may be tolerated in the hope that their children will grow up uncontaminated. To be sure, they will grow up naturally, but naturalness will look like wildness to everyone else. Parents do not need to sacrifice their own peace and quiet to their children.

We saw in Table 17–1 that firm but kindly discipline prevented children from becoming delinquent, whereas both laxity and overstrictness failed. Baumrind (1966: 905) noted:

Authoritarian control and permissive noncontrol may both shield the child from the opportunity to engage in vigorous interaction with people. . . . To learn how to dissent, the child may need a strongly held position from which to diverge and then be allowed under some circumstances to pay the price for nonconformity by being punished. Spirited give and take within the home, if accompanied by respect and warmth, may teach the child how to express aggression in self-serving and prosocial causes and to accept the partially unpleasant consequences of such actions.

High standards, vigorously asserted, provide the child with a climate for social learning and development.

Standards facilitate the child's learning, not only when particular behaviors are taught but when broader realms of achievement are advocated. Holding out high hopes for children pays off in giving them the motivation to control their own behavior in specific situations.

Sears, Rau, and Alpert (1965) found that parents with high achievement standards produced children who resisted the temptation to violate the rules of the game in several experimental situations. Chein and his colleagues (1964) found that parents of young adult heroin addicts in New York City had had unrealistically low aspirations for their sons compared with parents of nonaddicts in the same neighborhood. A majority of the addicts' parents (and almost none of the nonaddicts' parents) held standards that were vague and inconsistent. Conversely, high, clear standards enabled boys to grow up normally rather than to participate in the drug use that was rampant in their neighborhoods.

Even more generally, parental convictions about the importance of good behavior rub off on children in terms of greater consciousness of social norms and rules. Sears and his associates (1965) found that parents who believed in teaching about right and wrong had children who at age four were more capable of resisting temptation. They were more emotionally upset and more readily confessed when they gave in to temptation and broke rules.

The most temptation-resistant girls in Sear's sample had fathers who not only believed in teaching right and wrong but who put pressure on their daughters to understand this difference and expressed continuing, nonpunitive dissatisfaction when they fell short. In other words, successful fathers invested a lot of energy in conveying their standards to their daughters and in seeing to it that the daughters practiced what they were taught.

Consistency. If norms are to be effective, they must be understood. Clarity requires consistency. Norms presented consistently over time not only by parents but by others will be clearly understood. Conversely, a norm is blurred if one parent says one thing and does another, or wobbles in his/her behavior from time to time. Confusion arises if two parents advocate contradictory norms, one strict, the other permissive. If parents with different norms are not always present, standards will fluctuate with their comings and goings:

> While my father was gone, my mother had to rely on herself and she was always afraid she was making mistakes. She'd be very permissive for a time and then suddenly become very restrictive. Because we didn't know exactly what was expected, we became more unruly. We beat up the house and each other but couldn't look to Mother for justice. We could persuade her into most anything relatively easily. Whoever could talk fastest and most convincingly won out. When my father was home, our family was in a confused permissive-authoritarian atmosphere. We

*knew he demanded obedience, so on the rare occasions that he told us to
do something, we were afraid to talk back. But Mother usually let us do as
we pleased, although on certain occasions she was also irrationally firm.*

Peck (1958) found that consistent parental control produced a
stronger ego (emotional maturity), a stronger conscience, and willingness
to conform to social norms. Conversely, Bandura and Walters (1959: 205)
found that mothers of aggressive boys failed to expect obedience consistently:

> The mothers of the aggressive boys made fewer demands for obedi-
> ence and were more inclined to overlook non-compliance. Con-
> sequently, their sons had become inclined to ignore their mothers and
> to obey only at times when extra pressure had been brought to bear.
> The mothers' mounting anger usually served as the cue that they ex-
> pected compliance and that they would brook no further delay.

Consistency here involved not *what* behavior was advocated but
whether the standard was to be taken seriously. Clarity requires consistency in both senses: a single standard and certainty that parents mean
what they say.

Participation in value-oriented organizations reinforces the socialization process. Nye (1958) found that the more often parents went to
church, the less delinquent their adolescent children were. The church
bolstered the parents' social norms and provided for the whole family a
support system that took those norms seriously.

Support from relatives and friends helps parents socialize their children. Zimmerman and Cervantes (1960) found that if parents surrounded
their children with relatives and friends who shared the same social
norms, the impact of those norms was reinforced. Conversely, neighborhoods and social circles whose norms conflicted with those of the parents
undermined parental teachings, leaving the child unsure where s/he belonged or what was expected.

Feasibility.   The goal of socialization is to produce mature adults. This
can't be done overnight. Expecting too much is just as fatal as expecting
too little. If standards were low, I would not be encouraged to progress. If
they were high, I would become discouraged because I could not attain
them. Standards needed to be tailored to my age and readiness to learn.
This is more easily said than done. Expectations had to be revised upward
as I grew older. As I attained each goal, I needed a higher one. Moreover,
what was appropriate for me would not fit a sibling of different ability.
Appropriate standards stimulated each of us to move ahead as fast as
possible.

Reasoning

There are two ways of imposing standards: authoritarian or rational. When I was a child, I challenged each new norm with the question "Why?" Why must I abandon old ways? Why must I curb my impulses? Why must I act differently? The easy answer would have been, "Because I said so." It is short and swift. It requires no thought. And it allows no room for argument. Yet research proves that taking the trouble to reason with a child pays off in the long run. Bandura and Walters's socialized boys were reasoned with more than their aggressive boys. Nye (1958) found that parents of nondelinquent teenage boys and girls more often explained the reasons for any punishment they administered and the reasons for any behavior they required than did the parents of delinquent adolescents. Reasoning also promoted conscience development among Sears's kindergarten-age children. How does this happen?

Authoritarianism creates a power struggle between parent and child. At first the contest is uneven. When a child is young, it is at the mercy of its parents. Nevertheless, it instinctively rebels, and the older it gets the more successful the rebellion. Adolescent rebels do the opposite of what their parents demand, just because they demand it.

Authoritarianism fails because it is external. It depends on the parents' say-so. When they are not around, the child has no basis for controlling its own behavior. Parents are not portable. But portable standards are precisely what is needed. If a child is to function independently, it must control its own behavior. Nothing external can do that. The child needs something internal.

Reasoning takes the emphasis off parental coercion and puts it on the facts of the situation. Reasoning describes the circumstances in which particular actions are appropriate. It shifts attention to the thoughts and feelings of those around. It develops empathy, sensitivity, and awareness of the needs of others. It helps a child understand how it would feel if it were in their shoes.

When parents take the trouble to discuss issues, the child realizes that demands are not imposed as punishment or because the parents are mean. When whys are answered, the child senses the parents' respect, so their ideas deserve respectful consideration. By contrast, how would you feel if your parents stretched their authority beyond the bounds of truth, as in the following passage from Sears et al. (1957: 353).

CHILD: Mother, why can't I go out and play?
MOTHER: It's raining, dear, and I don't want you to catch cold.
CHILD (looks out the window): But it *isn't* raining, mummy. It just stopped.
FATHER (overhearing interchange): Young lad, if your mother says it's raining, it's raining.

Listening. Reasoning involves not only talking to the child but listening to his/her responses. By listening, I (the parent) can find out whether you understand what I have been saying. Listening opens the door to reciprocal reasoning. Sometimes my demands will seem unreasonable to you and so you will want to give your own reasons for not wanting to do what I have requested or will propose an alternative to my demands. If I take your counterproposal seriously, you will learn how to resolve conflicts.

The older you become, the broader your experience will become, and the greater the wisdom you will bring to the negotiating table. Eventually, when you become an adult, you and I will confront one another essentially as equals. The earlier this mutual reasoning begins, the more rapidly we will reach that goal.

Nye (1958) found that nondelinquent adolescents were more apt to be allowed to explain their behavior, whereas delinquent children's parents seldom listened to their side of the "story." Presumably, the delinquent children sometimes felt unfairly punished by their nonlistening parents, which undermined their respect for the parents' attempts to control their behavior.

Coopersmith (1967) found that fifth- and sixth-grade sons held themselves in high esteem if their mothers had the following attitudes: (1) A child has a right to question the thinking of the parents; (2) A child has a right to his own point of view and should be allowed to express it; (3) There is no reason parents should have their own way all the time any more than children should have their own way all the time; (4) Children should have a say in family planning. These attitudes suggest an atmosphere of mutual respect between parents and children, which produces children with self-respect.

Parents who used reasoning and discussion to obtain cooperation produced children with higher self-esteem than those who relied on force and other autocratic means. Table 17–2 shows that a majority of reasoned-with boys had high self-esteem whereas an equal proportion of coerced boys had their self-esteem crushed.

Table 17–2 Son's Self-Esteem, by Parents' Use of Reasoning or Autocratic Means of Securing His Cooperation

	PARENTS' USUAL PROCEDURE FOR SECURING COOPERATION	
Son's Self-Esteem	*Reasoning, Discussion*	*Force, Autocratic Means*
High	55%	21%
Medium	19	24
Low	26	55
Total	100%	100%
Number of cases	47	33

Recomputed from Coopersmith, 1967: 214. *Source:* Fifth- and sixth-grade boys in public schools of two New England towns.

Respect for the Child's Autonomy. Even when children are too young for dialogue and when the issue is the unphilosophical one of whether they should eat particular foods, imposing parental authority may be counterproductive, whereas respect for children's right to control their own bodily intake is valuable. Apley and MacKeith (1962) commented, "As parents hope the child will become an adult with discriminating tastes in all fields, it seems reasonable to treat these preferences with some respect. . . . The less there is of attitudes of victory and defeat (on either side), the sooner the problem of food refusal or dawdling will clear up." Parents can no more force food than behavioral standards on their children without danger that they will choke.

When parents let their children choose their own bedtime on the basis of how tired they are, the children benefit from this respect for their control over their own bodies. Table 17–3 shows that when parents of fifth- and sixth-grade boys allowed their sons to choose their own bedtimes, sons were more apt to have high self-esteem than when parents decided for them. Presumably, this self-respect stemmed from the boys' experience of their parents' respect for them in allowing them to make their own decision.

Here is Larry Constantine's description of what happened when he and his wife, Joan, decided to allow six-year-old Joy and four-year-old Heather to take charge of their own bedtimes:

> Since I do have a right not to be on call all evening, the deal we worked out left the kids free to choose when to go to bed, but after 8:30 they had to do it by themselves. Joy rapidly tuned in to her own sleep needs; Heather continued to underestimate hers. With time, Joan found it increasingly hard to resist falling back into the old routine of being responsible for the girls, except the hours became later and less regular. I, on the other hand, found it easier to resist and so became the "meany." It wasn't working for any of us and Joan requested a Sunday morning meeting to reconsider the whole issue.
>
> Heather announced, "I don't like having to tell me to go to bed." Joy said she did like deciding for herself but missed the "goodnights"

Table 17–3   Son's Self-Esteem, by Whether He or His Parents Decide on His Bedtime

	PERSON DECIDING CHILD'S BEDTIME	
Child's Self-Esteem	*Child*	*Parents*
High	60%	33%
Medium	20	22
Low	20	46
Total	100%	101%
Number of cases	25	55

Recomputed from Coopersmith, 1967: 213.

when she stayed up late. We all accepted a fixed bedtime for Heather with a "no-hassle" agreement from her. Joy goes to bed when she pleases with the understanding that if she is big enough to stay up late she is big enough to manage the details. It was her suggestion that she could come to us to say goodnight when she went to bed late (Constantine, 1975: 14–15).

Coopersmith's finding about bedtime and self-respect is an example of the general principle that parents teach their children two lessons—by the content of the standard that they set and by the way they deal with the issue. Allowing children to choose their own bedtimes may not teach them to go to bed early, but it does produce high self-esteem. By contrast, Newson and Newson (1968) found that mothers who were "very concerned" about toilet training as early as age one were more apt to have children who were reliably trained at age four than mothers who were only mildly concerned or unconcerned, but the very concerned mothers probably produced children lower in self-esteem than the mothers who were less anxious. High expectations and early expectations produce conformity at an earlier age, but respect for children's autonomy produces greater self-respect.

A related question has to do with when children will be expected to do something. Newson and Newson asked their respondents, "Suppose you asked (your four-year old) to do something for you, and he said 'No, I can't do it now, I'm busy.' What would you do?" Over half of the mothers would either withdraw their request or defer it until the child was ready to comply. An additional fraction would accept the delay but criticize the child's unwillingness to comply immediately, making such comments as: "I wouldn't make her, but I'd tell her she was naughty if she wouldn't help me, I'd say that Holy God would not love her," or "I'll p'raps say, 'Oh, you're an old meanie—all right, if you don't love your Mummy you needn't bother, I'll do it myself,' and he'll do it straight away then." The remaining mothers (almost one third) insisted on immediate obedience. The researchers commented:

> The question deliberately suggested a situation in which the child seeks a right of autonomy which in an adult would normally be respected: moreover, it is a situation which in almost every home occurs the other way round at least occasionally, often daily, when the mother puts off the child's demands in these same words. What this question is testing, then, is the mother's recognition of reciprocity in her dealings with the child: her willingness to allow the issue of fairness and democratic rights to prevail over her wish to maintain authority (Newson and Newson, 1968: 394).

By definition, then, heavy-handed insistence on parental authority is unreasonable.

By the time children reach adolescence, they need to be autonomous in decision making if they are to flourish. Rehberg and his associates

(1970) classified families as autocratic if the parents almost always told their teenagers what to do. Democratic families gave children of the same age at least "considerable" opportunity to make their own decisions after dialogue between the generations. Table 17–4 shows that those raised in a democratic environment were more apt than those from autocratic homes to plan to go to college.

More detailed analysis shows that democratic parents were more apt to have high educational expectations for their children (resembling the high opinion they had of their children's ability to make decisions). They also were more apt to praise their children for their educational achievements. Given these differences, it is surprising that so many children from autocratic homes wound up interested in going to college. Our guess is that their college expectations often represented mere conformity to their parents' model rather than genuine aspirations for themselves. This is suggested by the fact that few working-class children from autocratic homes expected to go to college.

In short, democratic families provide an atmosphere in which adolescents feel inspired to develop their potential.

For my socialization to be successful, the standards set by my parents had to be adopted by me as my own. They had to be internalized so that I no longer conformed because my parents told me to or because they would have punished me if I didn't or rewarded me if I did, but because I felt that I should. The better my parents' reasoning, the faster this happened. Reasoning involved interpreting the benefits to be gained by adhering to norms. In the process, these standards came to make more sense and were eventually adopted as my own philosophy.

Table 17–4 Adolescent College Expectations, by Family Authority Pattern

	FAMILY AUTHORITY PATTERN	
Expect to Go to College	*Democratic*	*Autocratic*
Yes	70%	60%
No	30	40
Total	100%	100%
Number of cases	1,093	419

Recomputed from Rehberg, Sinclair, and Schafer, 1970: 1023. *Source:* High school freshman sons of white-collar fathers in seven communities in the southern tier of New York State. To the question "How are most decisions between you and your parents made?" democratic answers included "I usually can make my own decisions, but my parents would like me to consider their opinions," "My opinions usually are as important as my parents' in deciding what I should do," and "I have considerable opportunity to make my own decisions, but my parents usually have the final word." Autocratic answers included "My parents listen to me, but they usually make the decision" and "My parents usually just tell me what to do."

Reinforcing Learning

Learning theory indicates that responses must be rewarded if they are to be reinforced. Some rewards come automatically. When I imitated my parents I felt grownup, "like Daddy or Mommy." When I responded to requests, I could anticipate their pleasure (which made me feel good). When I responded to reasoning, I had already been rewarded by their attention as they discussed the problem with me.

How my parents responded affected the speed of my socialization. If they paid no attention to how I behaved, my incentive to learn would have been weakened. If they treated me the same whether or not I tried, why try? They had to find out whether I performed as requested, and needed to alter their behavior depending on how well I did. The better their response fit my performance, the faster I learned.

Supervision and Trust. Their first job was to gather information. If I was supposed to make my bed, they had to take the trouble to inspect the job, or be sure I reported back when I finished. One way or another, they had to learn whether I did it or not. Table 17–1 showed that the better the mother's supervision, the more successful the socialization.

When children are small, supervision tends to be fairly constant. Newson and Newson (1968: 51–52) describe the situation:

> Most mothers . . . take care to be in more or less constant touch with their four-year-old: they like to be certain where he is at any time; they listen with half an ear for any alteration in the familiar sound-pattern of his play, ready to investigate the deviation which suggests mischief; and if the child is quiet on its own for more than half-an hour or so, the mother will usually go and check that everything is well.
>
> In practice, however, such checks will not often be necessary, since the child himself takes the initiative in keeping tabs on his mother. He too likes to know where she is and what she is doing; he too is alerted by a change in the background noise pattern of her work, and will come running to investigate anything which might be of interest. Problems and complaints are naturally brought to the mother; she is expected to arbitrate in quarrels, to reassure him in fear, and to minister to his hunger, thirst, cold or pain. Many children make a constant companion of their mother, following her round the house as she cleans and tidies, helping her in her housework or using her continually as an adjunct to their own play.

The older the child becomes, the more supervision shifts from direct observation to self-reports on personal behavior. By adolescence, checking up too much implies that the child isn't expected to behave. By contrast, trust creates a feeling that the child tends to respond to. Not wanting to violate an agreement made with one's parents becomes a powerful incentive to good behavior. Peck (1958) found that mutual trust between parents and children was even more influential than consistency in producing socialized behavior:

> *My parents and I spent a lot of time discussing when I should be in at night. I hated to have them tell me when I had to be in, each time that I went out. At first, they did. But soon they did not say anything more about what time I should be in when I left to go someplace. I knew what time I should be home, according to where I was going (which I always told them), and I was home on time. If I hadn't they would have immediately stepped in. In other words, I still came home at an appropriate hour, but I felt more like an adult because they had not nagged me.*

Trust is a fragile matter between parents and children and must be constantly nurtured. Open sharing about expectations and open negotiation leading to clear agreements to which all parties give their consent produces less frustrated parents and less rebellious children.

Trust should not be confused with conformity to parental expectations:

> *When I was in high school my parents were really uptight about the drug scene and my mother kept saying, "I trust you, John." That didn't help much when my friends were putting a lot of pressure on me to behave in ways that I wasn't sure about. I needed to talk to my parents but they never gave me a chance to let my hair down with them. If they had been honest, they would have said, "We're scared about what you might do but we expect you to do the right thing, which is, of course, not to get involved with drugs." Actually, they didn't trust me at all—they just expected me to conform to their wishes.*

Despite the importance of trust, it must not be confused with laissez-faire. Parents need both clear standards and adequate enforcement if children are to be socialized effectively. Coopersmith (1967) found that when parents carefully and consistently enforced rules, most children felt high self-esteem, whereas when parents enforced rules only moderately or even less often, a majority had low self-esteem. Enforcement begins with supervision and moves next to differential parental response to the child's behavior depending on what the parent discovers.

Reward versus Punishment.   When I did well, I deserved to be rewarded. Rewards increased my sense of accomplishment, compensated me for my trouble, and made me want to repeat the act.

My parents needed to react according to my behavior, gauging the reward to the accomplishment. When I behaved poorly, I should not be rewarded—provided that the cause was lack of effort. Where performance was poor despite earnest effort, they might have expected too much, and needed to coach me on how to proceed.

If the problem was not the standard but me, if my failure stemmed from laziness or disobedience, was nonreward enough? Should I be punished? The answer is no, at least in general. Sears et al. found that conscience developed slowest when punishment was frequent. Bandura and Walter's aggressive boys came from families who used many kinds of punishment, especially taking away privileges, punishing physically (in early childhood), nagging, scolding, and ridiculing.

Punishment usually makes matters worse. Why?

1. It hurts (either physically or psychologically) and creates resentment. Resentment interferes with the confidence and trust essential to socialization.

2. It undermines self-confidence, lowering morale so that children feel discouraged. At worst, they think of themselves as bad, unable to do right, expected to misbehave.

3. It is perceived as aggression. Especially physical punishment. When parents use their hands to spank, children learn to use their fists. Becker (1962) found that physical punishment produced more conduct problems and made children aggressive both at home and elsewhere. Sears found that severely punished children responded with aggression against their parents and displaced onto others.

4. From the standpoint of learning theory, it is a poor way to teach desired behavior. Sears recognized that in certain circumstances punishment (or the threat of it) is the quickest way to halt undesirable behavior. But controlling is not the same as motivating problematic behavior in the present or good behavior in the future:

> The permanent elimination of changeworthy behavior, and its replacement by more desirable and mature forms, i.e., the control of learning, offers a different problem. To effect elimination of a response requires that it no longer be rewarded, i.e., that it not be followed by a satisfying state of affairs. The strengthening of desirable behavior can occur only when a satisfying state of affairs does follow. It has been found that the introduction of punishment into the *learning* process (as distinct from action control) creates some difficulty, for punishment *after* an undesirable performance breaks up the child's activity but does not give direction toward any specific new behavior, and may produce an emotional state that interferes with the learning of the desired substitute behavior. Usually, punishment provides a fairly inefficient means of non-rewarding the changeworthy actions, and offers a strong sanction that tends to impel some new (but not specified) kind of action, perhaps mainly an avoidance of the punisher (1957: 318).

Despite the fact that punishment often backfires and makes matters worse, parents use it frequently, especially when their children are small. Table 17–5 shows that daughters seldom were punished much before the

Table 17-5 Frequency of Punishment, by Age of Daughter

	AGE OF DAUGHTER (YEARS)				
Frequency of Punishment	*Under 1½*	*1½–3*	*3–4*	*4–5*	*5–6*
Daily	14%	37%	31%	27%	5%
Several times a week	14	29	37	28	27
Once a week	5	16	16	25	30
Rarely	17	15	13	19	30
Never	51	3	3	2	8
Total	101%	100%	100%	101%	100%
Approximate number of cases	89	113	56	56	56

Adapted from Heinstein, 1965: 44. *Source:* State-wide California sample of preschool children.

age of 18 months (especially when they were tiny), but between the ages of 18 months and three years they were modally punished every day. This age span includes the notorious "terrible twos" when children test the limits of their parents' tolerance for misbehavior and parents lose their tempers and inflict punishments of all sorts. Parents and children get locked in a power struggle that is important to the child in discovering his/her autonomy and important to the parents as an anxiety-laden loss of control.

By the time of the "trusting threes," punishment in Heinstein's sample had modally ebbed to every other day and by kindergarten age to once a week or less. Indeed, a small but notable growing minority of parents had resolved their conflict with their children by that age and abandoned punishment for good. Parental resort to punishment, thus, peaked around age two and declined thereafter. One can almost hear parents and children alike breathing sighs of relief once the worst was over.

For Heinstein's boys, however, the experience was worse. Conspicuously more of them were punished daily at the lowest and highest ages (26 percent and 19 percent instead of the 14 percent and 5 percent for girls), and the decline with age was not only slower but less regular. So parents and children (and especially parents and sons) have trouble with each other that results in frequent punishment.

Physical versus Psychological Sanctions. Both rewards and punishments may be subdivided into physical and nonphysical categories. Physical rewards include pay and gifts. The commonest physical punishment is spanking. Praise is a verbal reward, ridicule a verbal punishment. Earlier we saw that reasoning aids socialization by facilitating the internalization of standards. The same principle applies here: Psychological sanctions promote socialization more than physical ones.

Figure 17-1 is not a statistical table but a diagram of the relationships between the variables that we have discussed: rewards versus

Figure 17-1 Effectiveness of Various Methods of Discipline in Socializing Children

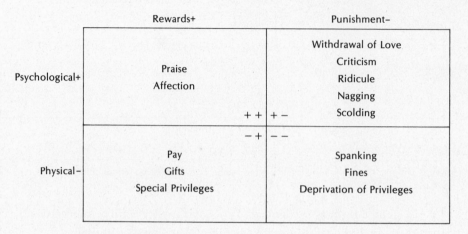

punishments and physical versus psychological sanctions. It suggests that psychological rewards are the most effective and physical punishments the least effective (or the most harmful) sanctions.

Spanking boomerangs as the child learns from the parents' example to use his/her fists to get what s/he wants from other children. In a review of the research literature, Slater (1962) pointed out that numerous researchers have found that "strict, punitive parents, particularly in the sense of heavy reliance on physical punishment, tend to produce impulsive, 'acting out,' extrapunitive children." In other words, parents who lose their tempers and lash out at their children produce protégés who act impulsively and beat up their peers or children weaker than themselves. Like father, like son! As one writer describes it:

> Fortunately, more and more professionals are calling a spade a spade and describing corporal punishment for what it is: legalized, socially sanctioned violence, assault and battery on people who are smaller and weaker. The fact that there are extremes of brutal child abuse in no way excuses or mitigates the lesser violence of a 5'8" person spanking or slapping a 4' person (Constantine, 1975: 12).

Newson and Newson (1968: 422) found that another disadvantage of physical punishment was that it tended to escalate:

> Once a mother accepts spanking as a means of discipline suitable for many occasions, and begins to use it often, she thereby debases her own currency of methods of control: that is to say, if spanking is the response to everyday 'naughtiness,' she has nothing in reserve for more serious misdemeanours. Because, every now and then, the child will do something which the mother feels needs a special mark of her

disapproval, she will therefore tend gradually to increase the severity of her blows, either by hitting harder, or by moving to a more vulnerable part of the body—from legs and bottom to the face, for instance. Most mothers have certain taboos about where they will 'draw the line' . . . but once the current taboo has been broken, and spanking has escalated to a new level, even for one occasion, that new level has a much better chance than before of becoming the mother's normal practice. This is why frequent spankers are also likely to be objectively hurtful spankers (edited to replace the British "smacking" with the American "spanking").

Once a child experiences his/her parents as sources of hurt, the parent-child relationship and the whole child-rearing process become impaired.

Just as we saw that Heinstein's California parents frequently punished their preschool children, Table 17–6 shows that those same parents most often punished physically and more specifically spanked their children. The percentages in the table show how many children in the sample were spanked or slapped. If we disregarded children who were not punished at all and asked what proportion of all punished children were spanked, the percentages would be even higher.

From what we saw earlier about the frequency of punishing two-year-olds, it is not surprising to find that corporal punishment is also most frequent in the two- to three-year-old age bracket. Presumably, if Heinstein had separated the two-year olds from the three-year olds, he would have found an even higher frequency of spanking concentrated in that critical year. Table 17–6 suggests that the crisis is more acute for mothers than for fathers (perhaps, especially for mothers who are home all day) and conspicuously acute for mothers in relation to hard-to-control boys. But even fathers (who spank their daughters relatively seldom) have a notable peak when their children are at that same difficult age.

In Detroit, Duncan and his associates (1973) found encouraging

Table 17–6   Mothers' and Fathers' Use of Spanking as Their Usual Method of Punishment, by Age and Gender of Child

	AGE OF CHILD (YEARS)		
Parent/Child	*Under 2*	*2–3*	*4–5*
Mother/Son	51%	68%	44%
Mother/Daughter	52%	54%	42%
Father/Son	34%	57%	43%
Father/Daughter	24%	53%	34%

Adapted from Heinstein, 1965: 52–53. *Source:* State-wide California sample. Reciprocal percentages of children were either not punished at all or were punished in other ways (principally by isolation, censure, or coercion).

changes between 1953 and 1971 in the kinds of punishments and rewards that parents used. Although there was no decrease in the proportion using physical punishment, there was a substantial decrease in scolding, warning, and threatening children and an even larger increase in the proportion who did not punish at all but responded constructively by reassuring a child in trouble. When it came to rewards, the same study showed major shifts from material to psychological rewards. 1971 parents less often rewarded their ten-year-old children with money or gifts and more often praised them or were affectionate toward them. In 1953 only 1 percent of parents loved or kissed their children when they were good, whereas in 1971 18 percent were overtly affectionate.

Thus, although many parents still punished generally and spanked in particular when their children misbehaved (especially when children were small), the trend of child-rearing practices was away from punishment toward positive reinforcement, particularly toward verbal and affectionate ways of reinforcing good behavior.

Transitional Methods. Although research demonstrates that psychological methods of discipline are generally more effective than physical methods, this does not mean that the latter are never useful. When children are young or are developmentally retarded, physical rewards may change behavior. Oakland and Wulbert (1969) used physical rewards in behavior modification programs with mentally retarded and otherwise handicapped children. They gave money to reward a five-year-old child of borderline intelligence. With the money he bought toys that appealed to him. They helped a seven-year-old boy afflicted with spina bifida overcome his dallying in coming to meals by making his dessert contingent on eating the rest of the meal promptly. They commented, however, that behavior modification seldom rests on physical rewards alone. From the beginning they paired physical rewards with praise and aimed toward eventually relying on praise alone. Physical rewards have a transitional value with certain children but psychological rewards are ultimately more useful.

Hamblin and his associates (1971) found that children with serious behavior problems (such as hyperaggressive or autistic children) were unresponsive initially to psychological reinforcements that worked well with normal children. But if such children were hungry enough, they responded to food as an incentive for giving up their hyperactivity or for learning to speak. In giving food or other material rewards, the therapists routinely said "thank you" or "that's correct" or gave a pat or touch. These psychological rewards eventually became sufficiently reinforcing to support the children in maintaining the new behavior. Those particular children were so damaged that they required tangible rewards to get them started learning new patterns.

One disadvantage with food is that it works only when children are hungry. Sooner or later hunger becomes satiated and then some other reinforcer is needed. For this reason, Hamblin and his associates used food only for crucial learning tasks, relying otherwise on tokens that could be exchanged for toys, admission tickets to movies, and other goodies. Unlike food, tokens may be given in the midst of a learning situation without distracting the child from the task at hand—and cashed in later when the lesson is finished.

Conscience—the Goal of Discipline

The goal of discipline is not to teach children that if they conform to norms they will be rewarded by their parents, but to instill norms that will control them from within. Internalized norms operate via anxiety and guilt.

Anxiety. After I had internalized a parent-imposed norm, my anxiety was aroused whenever I was tempted to misbehave. Unconsciously, I felt a negative emotional reaction that was the legacy of previous disapproval. I no longer thought of my parents but only of the wrongness of the act. As a result, I disregarded my temptation and inhibited the action.

Anxiety prevents individuals from engaging in antisocial behavior. Lack of anxiety to inhibit delinquent behavior was one deficiency in Bandura and Walters's aggressive boys. They were particularly blasé about sexual misbehavior.

For some neurotics, anxiety is excessive, preventing not only antisocial behavior but ordinary social interaction. It is possible to "oversocialize" children, especially when parents fail to use reasoning to enable them to understand the difference between tabooed and proper behavior.

Guilt. Closely related to anxiety is guilt. If conscience is not strong enough to prevent antisocial behavior in the first place, it may create guilt feelings afterward. Guilt feelings have two uses: (1) they make people less likely to repeat their behavior; (2) they encourage them to undo their "crimes." Guilt feelings are a self-punishment that makes deviant behavior less likely to recur. If restitution is possible, guild-ridden individuals may attempt it even if no one knows what they have done.

Poorly socialized children feel less guilty than well-socialized ones, even though the former's crimes are more gross than the latter's. Bandura and Walters's well-socialized teenagers felt guilty and ashamed in the few instances when they were aggressive toward parents, peers, or teachers or after they committed minor delinquencies. On the other hand, aggressive boys felt little guilt even after flagrant misdemeanors.

Guilt, like anxiety, causes trouble in excess. Some people need psychotherapy to reduce their anxiety and guilt. However, if parents fail to inculcate a conscience strong enough to produce anxiety and guilt, psychotherapy can accomplish relatively little. In appropriate amounts, guilt and anxiety are signs of a successfully developed conscience.

Behavior Control—Pending the Growth of Conscience

What to do until conscience develops is one of the problems faced by parents when children are young. The problem is difficult because toddlers lack not only conscience but the ability to understand language. Hence reasoning and praise are ineffective.

Infants are no problem, because they can't get into trouble. Once they begin to crawl, however, and especially after they learn to walk, they can create serious trouble for themselves and others. How can they be handled during the period between walking and talking?

Distraction. I didn't learn when I was distracted. I simply turned from one activity to another. When the distraction was skillful, I did not even realize anything was wrong with my behavior. When I was young, incapable of understanding or learning, distraction was the easiest way to shift me from undesirable to desirable behavior. The only danger was that the distraction might be so rewarding that I would learn to repeat precisely what I wasn't supposed to do! After I learned to understand English, distraction became obsolete. Henceforth, my parents and I could confront issues head on, rather than bypass them.

Isolation. Sending me to my room might have either a punitive or a therapeutic intent—with correspondingly different effects. As punishment, isolation would come close to rejection. I would feel unloved and excluded from the family. My natural response would be to kick and scream, or weep and mope. My objection to confinement would testify to my need to reestablish contact with the family. If my desperation increased my parents' determination to isolate me, a vicious cycle would ensue.

Some children need isolation at certain times. Those who are highstrung get overstimulated in groups. They talk louder and act more wildly until they lose control. When children get "high," removal from the group provides a chance for calming down. If parents recognize what is building up, they may intervene before children lose their temper. Firmly but calmly, they may get across the feeling: "This is not punishment but an opportunity for you to recover your equilibrium." Communication is enhanced by going with the children, explaining what is being done and why. Brevity reduces the chances of making matters worse by slipping into an argument. Though the children may not respond immediately, interesting playthings may distract them from thinking about the group they have left. In such ways, the point may be made that isolation is not rejection.

In families who use isolation therapeutically, children learn to appreciate their need for cooling off. As they grow older, they recognize their oversensitivity and withdraw when others threaten their equanimity.

Environmental Control. While distraction and isolation may solve problems that have already arisen, some situations are so dangerous that they must be prevented. Physical safety is the main problem—how to keep children away from fire, water, and moving automobiles. Sears found that most parents relied on environmental controls for this purpose. They put up fences, locked doors, hid matches and poisons. They supplemented preventive measures with constant vigilance, since the most innocent-appearing situations can be exploited by youthful ingenuity in unexpected ways. Some hazards, however, cannot be removed. Hot stoves are the traditional example. To teach a preverbal child to avoid such hazards, spanking has dramatic value. Like distraction, however, environmental control obsolesces with the advent of language.

FATHERS AND MOTHERS

The main tasks for parents are providing love and imposing discipline. Historically, these were assigned to different parents—love to the mother and discipline to the father. Research by Moulton (1966) suggested that differentiation reduces the parents' influence. Paternal discipline tends to become coercive and maternal love seductive. Only discipline from loving parents can be accepted and internalized. Only love from parents concerned with children's progress toward maturity can avoid infantilizing them. Hence, fathers and mothers ideally unite both love and discipline. One parent's behavior cannot differ greatly from the other's if their childrearing is to be effective.

Kohn found that middle-class fathers and mothers in Washington, D.C., lived up to this ideal in most cases: "The middle-class pattern is for both mothers and fathers to play an active part, not only in the imposition of constraints but also in the provision of support" (1969: 119–20). This indicates that, ideally, the traditional pattern of stern fathers and warm mothers has been replaced by parents of both sexes who are warm and at the same time concerned about their children's behavior.

Collaboration

Dual parents are advantageous not only to children but to the parents themselves, as those who bear the burden alone know all too well. A second parent provides support, consultation, and relief.

Support. We have already mentioned the confusion children feel when parents hold conflicting standards. To have no spouse is better than to have one who disagrees over disciplinary methods or standards. Battles occur easily because children raise so many issues. Indeed, Blood and

Wolfe found that when children were preadolescents and adolescents, their parents quarreled over them even more than over money.

When parents work together, two parents are better than one. If only one takes a stand, it can be dismissed as a parental quirk. When both say the same thing, the message is more impressive.

Consultation.   Parents don't always know what stand to take. When problems are new and complicated, a consultant in the home is a valuable resource. To be able to talk the situation over with someone who knows it equally well provides perspective.

Relief.   Parents generally come to each other's rescue when the energy of one ebbs and patience wears thin. Since children have more energy than adults, they need two parents to keep up with them. Being a good parent means being sensitive not only to the child's needs but to the partner's. Especially when one parent is having difficulty imposing discipline on a recalcitrant child, the other can take a fresh approach.

Living with Children

Important as discipline is in handling critical situations, it would be a mistake to think of it as the chief way that parents guide their children. The time devoted to discipline is a small fraction of the total. More often parents and children interact spontaneously with no thought of methods or goals. Most of the time children simply live as members of a family, inevitably but unconsciously influenced by the behavior of the father and mother.

The parents' example and activities with the child are far more influential than their occasional disciplinary interventions. As long as the tone of the parent-child relationship is positive, children automatically absorb the parents' way of living, their values, and their philosophy. The largely automatic nature of this process reduces the pressure on parents. They don't have to shape their children deliberately all the time. They can have faith in the future. If they are emotionally mature, their children will grow to maturity too, through the guidance that human beings spontaneously give each other.

Adolescents often seem to reject their families, disagreeing on political and social issues. Yet early experiences with parents and grandparents strongly affect their values and behavioral priorities. In our own case:

> *My [Margaret's] relatives may be shocked by the radical life-style of our sons but beneath the surface of their particular witnesses I see the stream of my parents' and grandparents' ideals flowing and being expressed: idealistic devotion (absolutist at times) to solving the problems of*

society, faith in democratic processes, equalitarianism, not wanting to spend more than their share of the world's resources (frugality and charity, my parents used to call it), and gentleness and caring in personal relations. These values run as deep in my sons as in us, their parents, and in the grandparents on both sides, though finding unique expression in each person in their particular time.

18 Educating Children

As civilization becomes more complex, the tasks of parents enlarge. No longer is it enough to teach children not to misbehave. The opportunities of modern life are too rich to be missed. Yet missed they will be unless children are introduced to them and motivated to take advantage of them. This chapter focuses on the parents' opportunity to teach children what they know and to motivate them to learn even more than they know.

PARENTAL ASPIRATIONS AND CHILDREN'S POTENTIALITIES

Just as parents set standards for behavior, they set goals for learning. If children are to achieve their full potential, goals must be high (else they are not goals), but not so high as to discourage effort. Parents may betray their children in either direction—by underestimating or overestimating their ability. If parents aim too low, children will be satisfied with less than their best. If they aim too high, children may not try because both generations will be disappointed.

The task is to encourage children to do their best. This is easier to express in attitudes—of conscientiousness, diligence, and ambition—than in concrete goals. Nevertheless, goals are more tangible than attitudes, so as children grow older, parents may suggest goals as well: learning to typewrite, making first chair in orchestra, or going to college.

In a study of 10,000 graduating high school seniors in public and private schools in Wisconsin, Sewell and Shah (1968) found that 57 percent of those whose parents wanted them to go to college intended to do so whereas only 6 percent of those whose parents did not care intended to do so. Even after controlling by social status and intelligence, parental aspirations determined whether children planned to go to college or not. Among intelligent high-status seniors (the most likely college prospects in terms of their intellectual and financial ability), less than one-fourth of those without parental encouragement intended to go to college, whereas 84 percent of those encouraged by them expected to go.

Among tenth graders in New Jersey, Sandis (1970) found that 91 percent of those whose mothers expected them to finish college planned to do so, whereas only 21 percent of those whose mothers did not aspire so high for them expected to graduate. Table 18–1 shows that some of the latter were stimulated indirectly to think about college when their parents provided them with culturally enriching experiences such as lessons outside of school, trips to museums, or going to concerts or plays. Conversely, mothers who talked about college plans but did not provide supportive experiences gave their children a double message so that they were appreciably less apt to take those aspirations seriously. In general, parents influenced their children's college aspirations chiefly by their own expectations, but cultural enrichment significantly supplemented talking up a college education.

Developing the motivation to achieve is one element in successful socialization. Rosen and d'Andrade (1959) found that parents of highly motivated boys were more interested in their sons' performance and set higher goals for them.

We have already mentioned the danger of overestimating children's abilities. Morrow and Wilson (1961) found a difference between "encouraging" and "pressuring" with respect to achievement. High school boys did better when their parents encouraged achievement but didn't "overinsist" on it. If parents push too hard, children are miserable. If parents always "harp on" grades and insist on studying, children are apt to rebel. Indeed, Pearlin and his associates (1967) found that children

Table 18–1 Percent of Adolescents Who Expect to Graduate from College, by Mother's Educational Encouragement and Cultural Enrichment Experiences

Number of Types of Cultural Enrichment Experiences	MOTHER'S EDUCATIONAL ENCOURAGEMENT	
	Less than College Graduation	College Graduation
None	9%	78%
One or two	24%	90%
All three	29%	94%

Recomputed from Sandis, 1970: 207. *Source:* 418 tenth-grade students in eight northern New Jersey communities. Types of cultural enrichment experiences included (1) extracurricular lessons in art, dancing, dramatics, or music; (2) trips to museums; (3) concerts, ballet, opera, or theatrical performances. Reciprocal percentages of students did not expect to graduate from college.

pressured to succeed not only failed to learn what the parents wished but actually learned unintended negative lessons. Fifth-grade children in an Italian city who were pressured by overambitious parents learned to cheat when faced with a laboratory task so difficult that success was almost impossible. Conversely, children whose parents put less pressure on them were more able to resist the temptation to cheat.

Parents who overinsist are usually self-centered. They want children to fulfill their own dreams, to accomplish what they didn't, to become adults of whom they can be proud. Rosen and d'Andrade found that it was particularly easy for *fathers* to crush their sons. Mothers were less dangerous, perhaps because they were more apt to combine pressure with love.

Parents need to encourage their children to do well. But in the last analysis, the children must do the achieving. They are not likely to try very hard unless they choose the courses, avocations, and vocation to which they are to devote their time. Parents must respect children's autonomy at the same time that they express high hopes for them and support efforts to reach whatever goals the children finally adopt.

PARENTAL RESPONSIVENESS

One of the saving graces in children is that they have their own drives. They are not clay, dependent on the potter to be fashioned. They are alive and growing. Children are blessed with boundless curiosity. Especially little children. As soon as they can talk, they want to know what makes things tick. They ask so many questions that parents tire of answering.

The Cultivation of Curiosity

Children are curious because they know so little. They haven't learned yet not to ask questions. When my parents told me to stop pestering them or when they paid no attention to my questions, I learned all too soon that it doesn't pay to be curious—it gets me into trouble or it wastes my breath. Curiosity is a priceless asset, worth more than all the encyclopedias, atlases, and dictionaries a family could buy. Educational resources will never be used if the spark of curiosity is quenched with parental cold water.

The best way to cultivate curiosity is to reward it—which means taking the trouble to answer every question. With examples from religious education, here are several principles designed to keep curiosity alive:

Nonpostponability.   How seriously parents take each question determines whether children will come back for more. Children whose questions are brushed aside will turn to playmates for answers. Or they may decide that asking questions is fruitless and lose the eagerness to learn that is essential to growth. Hence, when Johnny asks, "Where is God?" it pays to answer.

Sometimes parents are so busy they can't spare the time. But they should give their reasons for not answering. Provided these excuses are genuine and rebuffs do not come too often, curiosity should survive. To some extent, parents can count on questions coming up again if they're not answered now. But only partially. Those who want the best for their children will seize every opportunity for discussion. It's too easy to say, "I'm busy now—come back later." "Later" may never come. Not only may children hesitate to ask again, but their attention span is so short and their distractability so great that they can hardly be relied on to use rainchecks.

Appropriateness.   Answers must be geared to children's ability to understand. This is partly a problem of vocabulary. Children are capable of learning complicated concepts, but new words must be defined as they are used. It doesn't do much good to talk about "salvation" without explaining what it means to the parent. Sometimes a shorter word does just as well and saves time.

Honesty.   Does appropriateness mean that religion must be brought down to the children's level? Must God be depicted as a bearded patriarch so children can "picture" Him? Not unless that is the parents' conception. Settling for anything less than the parents' own beliefs is misleading in the same way the birds and bees mislead in sex education. Parents can share what they believe to be the truth, no matter how difficult it is to explain. Children will hear the personal meaning for the parent more than the words. Parents' attempts to explain their honest point of view are appreciated by children, no matter how little they understand at the moment.

Turning from curiosity about religion to inquiries in general, White (1975: 264) described parents whose preschool children developed most competently:

> They were available to the child several hours each day to assist, enthuse and soothe when necessary. They used a particular style in responding to overtures. They would usually respond promptly even if only to delay action. They would pause to consider the baby's purpose of the moment. They would provide what was needed with some language, on target and at or slightly above his level of comprehension. They would add a related idea or two and they would not prolong the exchange longer than the baby wanted.

White labeled this the "consulting" function of parents. Nonpostponability and appropriateness are the key elements in the kind of responsiveness that enables children to learn now and to want to come back for more information in the future.

Parental Elusiveness

Sometimes the problem is not the complexity of the subject but its uncomfortableness. For instance, race or death or sex.

Some parents try to avoid the problem by putting off answers or waiting until the child is "old enough." Even then, Goodman (1952) found parents tongue-tied over how to explain, confused over the terminology to use, and unwilling to use certain words at all.

Black parents in a prejudiced community know their children are going to discover eventually that they are second-class citizens. On the theory that well-balanced individuals can take a lot of punishment, some try to postpone the day of disillusionment.

But children soon discover prejudice and ply their parents with excruciating questions. Beyond admitting the facts of prejudice and discrimination, parents can reassure their children of their love and appreciation. Without condoning it, they can share their understanding of the causes of prejudice and help children see whites as human beings like themselves.

These tasks are difficult but not impossible. Parents who take a growing child into their confidence establish a we-feeling that can hardly be equaled as a base of operations in a bewildering world.

Black parents would have fewer problems if more white parents discussed human relations with their children:

> I told my boys very early (two years on) that the world has many countries in it besides our own. Each country has its own people. There are people of various colors of skin, hair, eyes, and so forth. They speak many languages and differ in their dress and ideas about things, but certain things are common to all people and important to everyone on earth—being treated kindly, having enough to eat, enough money for necessary things for each family, roads, schools, homes, and care for the sick.
>
> We've had hundreds of short discussions in the evenings about aspects of these topics and talked about the importance of the different countries and peoples learning to get along without bombing each other. By the time the boys reached school age, they both had an orientation to their place in the world and some of the crucial issues of our day—war and peace, racial discrimination, population problems, and ecological issues. I didn't use big words. We talked about things in daily life that relate to the big problems—neighborhood quarrels, black schoolmates, overcrowded city streets, and polluted rivers not safe for swimming. Talking about these things has given the boys ideas of which kinds of work they may want to take up, which problems they'll want to attack.

How about death? Some parents try to protect their children from knowing about the death of a neighbor or pet. Yet the fact of death is no more avoidable than the "facts of life." Better for parents and children to discuss it openly than for children to feel something is hush-hush, too terrible to mention.

No matter what happens in the world outside, children who are loved feel secure. Studies in Great Britain during World War II showed that those who stayed in bombed-out London with their parents were less afraid than those evacuated to country estates away from their families (Freud and Burlingham, 1943). As children hear of war, crime, and death, they want to know how their parents feel about these scary events. Precisely how parents interpret such things counts less than children's sense that "we're in this together." This sense of security provides a basis for living in a world where one can never be entirely sure what the next minute will bring.

Elusiveness about Sex.   Faced with embarrassing questions, most parents find excuses for not answering. Sears and his associates summarized parental policies toward five-year-olds' sex questions under the heading of "information control." Parents whom they studied generally believed in *not* satisfying their children's curiosity:

> Some mothers were clearly antagonistic to what they called the "modern doctrines" that they felt were advocated in some child-training books and newspaper columns. . . . When a mother was opposed to giving any sex information to children, however, she had to be able to give the child some other explanation when a younger sibling was born. One said to her son, "Gee I'm getting fat. I guess I'll have to go away for a week or so and go on a diet. . . ." Others spoke of "putting in an order for a baby at the hospital."
>
> Most of the mothers were willing to tell their children a little more than that about the reproductive process, however. At least, they described the presence of the new baby inside the mother. Mothers who had tried to be completely free and open in their information-giving usually found, however, that there was a point beyond which they were unwilling to go in answering the child's questions. . . .
>
> It is safe to say that not one family in our sample was completely free and open in the discussion of sex with their young children (1957: 190–92).

Closely related to parents' reluctance to answer questions was their tendency to avoid sexual terms. Sears called this "avoiding labels." Most parents gave as little information as their children would let them get away with:

> Many families got along without any names for the genital area, using vague terms of reference like "it" or "there." . . . When communication was necessary between parent and child, one of the babyish toileting terms current in the family was used, as in a child's "Mommy, my wee-wee hurts." . . . Despite the absence of explicit language, however, mothers and children seemed to be able to communicate with each

other fairly effectively about some events in the intellectual shadow-
land of sex, as was illustrated in the following interchange between
mother and son:

The mother saw the boy rubbing his penis. She said:

"Johnny, what are you doing?"

"Nothing, Mummy."

"Well, stop it, then."

"O.K." and he stopped.

While some parents avoided any sort of labeling in the area of
sex, some did provide their children with names for the genital parts
of the body. We did not encounter anyone, however, who helped the
children to identify the *emotional* states related to sex. Many mothers
said to a child something like: "You're angry and upset now. We'll talk
about it when you're calmer." But none, as far as we could tell, said:
"You're feeling sexy, that's why you're acting like that" (1957: 189–
90).

Information control and nonlabeling were part of a pattern of avoiding the issue: the same parents used (1) distraction rather than discipline
to curb unwanted sexual behavior and (2) indirect, nonsexual arguments
for conforming to sexual norms (telling children they would catch cold if
they didn't get dressed when the real issue was nudity). In England,
Newson and Newson (1968) found that parents expected their children to
be modest but were unwilling to explain about modesty because the subject was too embarrassing.

In Iowa, Burchinal (1960) found that less than half the parents were
willing to reply fully and frankly to their daughters' questions about sex.
Sons tend to be even worse off than daughters. Table 18–2 shows that
both boys and girls learned the facts of life chiefly from their peers. However, mothers were considerably more active than fathers. Indeed, Hunt
reported that fathers not only were seldom the *main* source of information, but typically *never* talked about sex with either their sons or their
daughters. Just over half the mothers talked with their daughters at least

Table 18–2 Main Source of Sex Education, by Gender

Main Source of Sex Information	Men	Women
Father	6%	1%
Mother	3	16
Teachers, other adults	9	9
Reading	20	22
Friends	63	52
Total	101%	100%
Number of cases	982	1,044

Adapted from Hunt, 1974: 122. *Source:* Adults aged 18 and over in 24
American cities.

once. Most parents who ever talked with their children got around to it so belatedly that they told them nothing they didn't already know. Among the youngest adults in Hunt's sample a somewhat larger proportion had discussed sex with their parents, but those talks had been no more informative than in earlier generations. College-educated parents in Hunt's sample provided their children with the facts of life no more often than less educated parents.

If more parents did communicate with their children about sex, the chances are that they would convey attitudes reflecting the generation gap in sexual attitudes. Libby and Nass (1971) asked parents in Manchester, Connecticut, what they would do if they discovered that an 18-year-old daughter was having sexual relations. Four percent would force her to get married; 17 percent would force her to stop by breaking up the relationship, punishing and restricting her; 43 percent would express disapproval and try to convince her that she was wrong. Some parents weren't sure what they would do, 5 percent saying it would depend on the circumstances, and 16 percent would seek help from a professional person such as a minister or counselor. Only 10 percent would try to understand and be supportive and a mere 5 percent would give contraceptive advice. When Libby and Nass subdivided the parents into those with generally democratic and authoritarian ideologies, the so-called democratic parents were just as repressive as the authoritarian parents.

These studies suggest that sex education is so touchy a topic that adults who in other aspects of their lives are thoughtful become paralyzed and tongue-tied. One cannot expect either parents or children to find sex as easy to talk about as other topics. Nevertheless, the question remains: How much *should* parents respond to their children's sexual curiosity?

Responsive Sex Education

Some parents are less reticent. Chesser (1957) found that parents with the happiest marriages were more apt to tell the truth about sex, whereas unhappily married parents brushed off their children's questions or responded with untruths. Sears and his colleagues (1957) found that mothers who were emotionally warm and seldom spanked their preschool children were more permissive about sexual problems.

Children who receive their sex education from their parents conform more to social norms than those whose parents neglect them. Table 18–3 shows that parent-educated British women had the happiest marriages, reading was next best, followed by other adults, leaving friends the worst source. Vincent (1961) found that unmarried mothers especially often received their sex information from companions rather than from their mothers or teachers. They generally had less information and more negative attitudes toward sex than did other women.

Butman and Kamm (1965) found that pregnant high school girls

Table 18–3 Marital Happiness, by Main Source of Sex Education

Marital Happiness	Parents	Reading	Other Adults	Friends
Very happy	77%	69%	62%	53%
Fairly happy	19	27	29	36
Unhappy	4	4	9	11
Total	100%	100%	100%	100%
Number of cases	325	136	248	443

Adapted from Chesser, 1957: 176. *Source:* Women patients of British physicians.

knew less about sex in general and contraception in particular than classmates who were not engaging in sexual intercourse (see Table 18–4). On the other hand, girls who were involved in sexual relationships without becoming pregnant knew the most about sex and contraception. Presumably, these girls put their contraceptive knowledge to good use in preventing conception.

Because parents often feel tongue-tied, it may be useful to illustrate possible responses to sex questions. For children, the question "Where did I come from?" is innocent enough. They are oblivious to the connotations stirred up in their mother's mind. All they want is the answer to another question—like the one they just received to "Where did this book come from?" The most useful answers are simple and direct. There is no one "best" answer, but it must satisfy the questioner and be accurate.

The following answers to typical questions are not prescriptions but samples:

Q.: Where did I come from?
A.: You grew inside of me/your mother.

Q.: Where? (One question leads to another—soon or late.)

Table 18–4 Sexual Knowledge, Contraceptive Knowledge, and Adults as Major Source of Sex Information for Pregnant, Sexually Active, or Sexually Inactive Adolescent Girls

		SEXUAL ACTIVITY	
	Pregnant	Sexually Active, Not Pregnant	Sexually Inactive
Sexually knowledgeable	0	48%	22%
Contraceptively knowledgeable	0	44%	15%
Adults chief source of sex information	33%	37%	49%
Number of cases	9	27	279

Adapted from Butman and Kamm, 1965: 137–41. *Source:* 15–17-year-old white girls in a midwestern city. Most of those who had gotten their sex information from sources other than adults had relied on peers. Reciprocal percentages had not received the specified sexual information.

A.: In a special place called the uterus. (References to tummy or stomach are apt to create images of being eaten.)

Q.: Where is the uterus?

A.: Inside here. (At this point a simple diagram of female internal anatomy may help. If the parent is not an artist, s/he may use an encyclopedia or a biology book.)

Q.: How did I get there?

A.: Mommy had a tiny egg that joined with a tiny sperm from Daddy and grew into a baby.

More drawing may be needed to show where the egg came from and so forth. Some parents wonder how soon the man's part should be introduced. Describing reproduction is difficult enough without having to discuss intercourse. Yet this is another discovery that can be made most easily when the issue first arises. Most children are satisfied with brief answers and pursue the question further only at intervals. On the other hand, a barrage of questions signifies an inquiring mind that deserves to be answered. The answers, however, should fit the questions. One about reproduction need touch off no more detailed a lecture than one about automobile production. Yet neither lecture involves any danger of "overdosing" children. As soon as they are tired, they will turn their attention elsewhere. Answers too complex to be understood do not harm children. They just waste the parents' energy.

Hunt reported that men and women "remembered with deep gratitude" parents who had provided them with books, answered their questions, initiated talks, or "even drawn pictures for them and explained things with ease and naturalness" (1971: 125). Parents who overcome their reluctance to share with their children in this difficult area can expect not only to help their children develop their sexual knowledge and understanding, but to increase the openness between them and their children.

PARENTAL STIMULATION

Parental stimulation begins the day a child is born. Casler (1961) noted that research on child development underscores the value of stimulating all the senses: seeing, hearing, tasting, smelling, and feeling. As infants get older, they need freedom of movement and toys that they can manipulate. These experiences enable them to learn with their bodies.

Parents set a persuasive example for their children. If they enjoy hiking in the woods, their children become aware of wildflowers, birds, and sunsets. If they go to ball games, sports become salient. If they play classical music, their children acquire a musical repertoire by osmosis. Most home learning is a by-product of living in a particular environment.

Schramm and his colleagues noted a similar process with television tastes (see Table 18–5):

> If a parent views educational television, then the child is almost sure to do so; and if neither parent does view educational television, then the child is almost sure not to do so. This is a very potent kind of influence. We venture to say also that if parents use the Sunday press conferences and discussions, then the children are almost sure to do so when they come to be old enough. Example is the best persuader (1961: 182).

Other resources in the home are toys and play equipment. Perceptiveness and creativity develop as children experiment with paper, cardboard, building blocks, crayons, paint, paste, clay, and tape for assembling them.

Parental Initiative

Although most of what children learn is accidental, learning can be intentional. Parents concerned to enrich their children's lives can involve their children in educational activities at home and expose them to educational resources elsewhere.

Education at Home. Bossard and Boll (1960) stressed the impact of family conversations on children who sit around the dinner table day after day, year after year. They suggested that "in many respects, family table talk may be likened to a university seminar on family culture that continues for a number of semesters." During meals, parents ask about school, discuss the news, conduct quiz games, share the mail. These conversations transmit the family culture from generation to generation.

Parents must take the initiative in discussing sex if children do not. Responsiveness is fine as far as it goes, but it must be replaced by responsibility when questions cease. Sex teaching must be done by precept

Table 18–5   Child's Viewing of Educational Television, by Father's Viewing of Educational Television

Child Views Educational Television/week	FATHER VIEWS EDUCATIONAL TELEVISION/WEEK		
	One Hour or More	Less than One Hour	Never
One hour or more	46%	16%	15%
Less than one hour	38	73	4
Never	16	10	81
Total	100%	99%	100%

Adapted from Schramm, Lyle, and Parker, 1961: 279. *Source:* 182 fathers and their 442 "younger" children in San Francisco.

rather than by example. Because the sexual side of marriage is private, sex education cannot rely on interpreting the meaning of events but must be undertaken deliberately.

Parents seldom teach their children explicitly about marriage. But when everyone has a good time raking leaves, conversation about the satisfactions of working helps children realize why the afternoon has been fun. When parents have a scrap, children profit from observing it and being told how the trouble developed in the first place as well as how it was resolved.

Television as Teacher.   Parental initiative requires not only exposing children to desirable influences but shielding them from undesirable ones. Children need both positive and protective intervention in their televiewing. Blood (1961) found that high-status parents encouraged their children to watch educational programs (even beyond their usual bedtime) and controlled the types of programs watched. Crime and violence were especially forbidden.

In our own family during the child-rearing years, these were our provisions governing use of television:

Location: out of the livingroom to avoid interference with other functions

Time limits: not before 5:00 P.M. weekdays
    not more than 5½ hours on Saturdays (to insure outdoor exercise and other activities)

Program controls: all crime and horror programs banned
    cowboys limited to 7 per week (to avoid overstimulation)
    not more than 2 hours at a time (to avoid fatigue)

Conflicts over program choice: between children—majority rules or take turns
    between parents and children—parents take precedence since children watch more than parents do

Such restrictions are exceptional, however. As of 1972 the Nielsen survey found that the average American home had their television set(s) on more than six hours a day. In homes with a preschool child, televiewing was even more omnivorous since young children have no schooling to interfere. Looney (1971) found that preschool children were glued to the tube almost eight hours a day, which he figured was almost two-thirds of their waking time.

The enormous number of hours devoted to television by the average child reflects the fact that the average parent makes no attempt to control it. Steiner (1963) found that even parents who were critical of television's influence on their children usually did little if anything about it.

Not only do few parents limit the quantity of viewing, but few attempt to influence the programs that their children see. Musgrave (1969) found that most parents of 11-year-old children never prohibited any programs. To Bronfenbrenner (1970), this meant that parents were not spending as much time with their children as their predecessors did, having by and large abandoned them to "the seductive power of television for keeping children occupied" (and, incidentally, to their peers). Parents had abdicated much of their responsibility to the models provided by actors on the television screen.

Television Violence and Children's Aggressiveness. We have often noted how children imitate their parents. Bandura (1963) found that they also imitate actors and even cartoon figures portrayed on film. Table 18–6 shows that although live actors stimulated aggressive behavior the most, film actors came a close second. Even cartoons about an aggressive cat increased children's aggressiveness in comparison with a control group.

These findings indicate that filmed violence affects children profoundly. They disprove the notion that fictional violence provides cathartic release of aggressive impulses. Rather, it is a contagious model of aggressiveness.

Whether children exposed to violent television programs will behave aggressively depends on the consistency between the televised model and the parental model. Dominick and Greenberg (1971) concluded from a study of Michigan children in grades four to six that the parents' attitude was more influential than television programs in determining how children behaved. Television violence stimulated violent behavior in children whose parents felt ambivalent about violence. In that moral vacuum, children reacted to violent programs with increased willingness to use violence and to suggest violent solutions for conflict situations.

McLeod, Atkin, and Chaffee (1971) found that the effect of television violence depended on the model that the parents presented in their child-rearing behavior. Parents who were violent (that is, who punished their children physically or verbally or by taking away privileges) produced children who reacted to televised violence with increased aggressiveness. On the other hand, parents who explicitly advocated nonviolence

Table 18–6 Aggressive Behavior of Children in Response to Portrayals of Aggression, by Gender

Ratio of Stimulated/Unstimulated Aggression by Gender	PORTRAYAL OF AGGRESSION			
	None	Cartoons	Filmed Actors	Live Actors
Boys	1.0X	4.1X	6.1X	7.3X
Girls	1.0X	4.3X	5.0X	7.9X

Adapted from Bandura, Ross, and Ross, 1963: 6. *Source:* 96 children enrolled in the Stanford University Nursery School, all of whom were subjected to a common frustrating situation before being observed for aggressive behavior imitative of what they had seen.

and who behaved nonpunitively produced children who were relatively immune to violence.

Even so, Bronfenbrenner (1970: 114) believed that the effect of televised violence on American children as a whole was disastrous:

> Given the salience of violence in commercial television, including cartoons especially intended for children, there is every reason to believe that this mass medium is playing a significant role in generating and maintaining a high level of violence in American society, including the nation's children and youth.

Television Stereotypes.   Children learn many things besides aggressiveness from television. DeFleur and DeFleur (1967) found that 6- to 13-year-old children who watched television became familiar with occupations they had never seen firsthand. They knew about judges, lawyers, reporters, head waiters, butlers, and bellhops—all of whom had been portrayed on television programs in the preceding six months. However, their knowledge of these occupations was highly stereotyped because the television scripts portrayed them that way:

> Lawyers were very clever, and usually legally unorthodox. Members of artistic professions were almost always temperamental and eccentric. Police officials were generally hardened, and often brutal. Private investigators were always resourceful and clearly more clever than the police. Nurses were cold and impersonal. Salesmen were glib. Journalists were callous. Taxi, bus and truck drivers were burly and aggressive (DeFleur, 1964: 71).

Schramm and his colleagues (1961) noted the contrast between the world of television and the real world:

> There is no doubt that television's picture of the world includes an abnormally high proportion of sexy women, violent acts, and extralegal solutions to legal problems. There is some reason to think that it contains also an overrepresentation of inadequate fathers, of get-rich-quick careers, and of crooked police and judges. If this is the case—if a child is absorbing a markedly erroneous picture of adult life—then obviously this is no positive contribution to socializing him, and may require some very hard adjustments later. (This) picture of adult life . . . should cause parents . . . to query whether they are doing enough to give the child some counterbalancing insight into adult life (Schramm, Lyle, and Parker, 1961: 155).

Parents whose children watch television extensively can expect their children to pick up lots of information, but it will be distorted by the limitations of this medium. To take their educational responsibilities seriously, parents will need to engage in an ongoing dialogue with their children about the differences between what they are seeing and the nature of the world as the parents understand it.

Benign Programing. Positive programing may be just as beneficial as negative programing is detrimental. Stein and Friedrich (1971) studied the effect on nursery school children of an educational television children's program that emphasized cooperation, sharing, sympathy, affection, understanding the feelings of others, delayed gratification, learning to accept rules, and coping with frustration. Children who had seen the educational program were able to stick with rules, tolerate delay, and persist in tasks under frustrating circumstances. Television can either aid or undermine parental efforts to educate their children, depending on the programs watched.

External Resources. Many community resources are available only upon parental initiative: concerts, plays, museums, libraries, or travel. Other resources are extracurricular activities in schools and lessons—music lessons, art lessons, and so forth.

How much initiative should parents take? With formal schooling, parents don't wait for children to express interest but insist that they attend. The fact that school is compulsory makes it more acceptable.

In optional areas, parents must exert stronger pressure. When they insist on music lessons, they are doing them a favor (which in the long run children will probably appreciate). To be sure, parents cannot force their children to be educated against their will. They must make learning as attractive and as rewarding as possible. Nevertheless, parental initiative legitimately includes extracurricular learning.

Parental Structuring of Learning

Homework and practicing cause friction in many families. Friction can be reduced by minimizing distractions, providing encouragement, and rewarding achievement.

Minimizing Distractions. Parents must safeguard children's opportunity to study. Peace and quiet are necessary. To find them, children may need special places for study or times when younger siblings and even parents are not allowed to make distracting noises (even if those noises are labeled "music").

Television is a powerful distractor. Televiewing and studying cannot go on in the same room at the same time. Most parents, as we have seen, make no attempt to control the amount of time their children spend watching television. Bailyn (1959) found that schoolchildren (6 to 16 years old) spent an average of 22 hours a week watching. This is almost as much time as they spend in school and eats up an enormous proportion of the free time that might otherwise be available for studying, for extracurricular learning experiences, or for active recreation.

Despite the fact that most parents abdicate their socialization responsibility with respect to television, some children by the time they reach adolescence switch from television watching to reading. Table 18–7 shows that children who had a good relationship with their parents tended to watch television less (and also listen to the radio less and go to movies less) and read books and magazines more. Conversely, those who got along badly with their parents tended to rely on the hot media at the expense of the cool ones.

Providing Encouragement.   Getting started is easier when it is ritualized. If homework always comes right after dinner, less struggle is necessary. Routine scheduling provides a framework within which lessons get done more easily.

Except for providing suitable conditions, parents must beware of taking too much responsibility. It is easy for parents to nag about getting started, but nagging stiffens resistance. When other activities interfere with the usual schedule, parents may ask children when they plan to do it instead. This gives them a choice and yet commits them to a specific objective.

By and large, homework is a solitary business. Sometimes collaborators are needed and parents can help coach. When an exam is pending, parents can ask review questions. When children are stumped, parents can help them find their way through unfamiliar problems. But only sometimes. The farther they go in school, the harder it is for parents to keep up. Perhaps both generations can search together. As long as children share in the learning process and don't have work done for them, they learn along with the parents.

Bee (1971) found that mothers who taught their children how to solve problems enabled their children to solve problems on their own. By

Table 18–7   Children's Use of Mass Media, by Degree of Conflict with Parents

Use of Mass Media	CONFLICT WITH PARENTS			
	None	Moderate	High	High/Low Ratio
Radio listening per school day (minutes)	78	86	102	1.3X
TV watching per school day (minutes)	159	174	187	1.2X
Movies attended per month	2.5	2.9	3.1	1.2X
Magazines read per month	4.3	4.1	3.8	0.9X
Books read per month	3.2	2.8	2.6	0.8X
Number of cases	549	312	114	

Adapted from Schramm, Lyle, and Parker, 1961: 292.

contrast, mothers who told their children exactly what to do or solved problems for them robbed their children of the opportunity to learn for themselves. Bee concluded that an ideal mother "(a) guides the child sufficiently so that his attention is focused on relevant portions of the problem, or on important strategy decisions, but then (b) leaves the decisions and the action to him."

Music practicing benefits from collaboration more than homework. Even in studying the piano, four-hand duets are sociable. If neither parent can play, one is still a welcome companion on the bench. For other instruments, accompanists are valuable. Few instruments sound pleasant alone the first year or two. Stringed instruments sound awful at first. Parents can make the early stages more satisfying by supporting children's feeble notes with rich chords.

Rewarding Achievement. When parents and children practice together, learning is intrinsically rewarding. Children relish companionship. Of course, parents will have to hold their tongues when tempted to criticize. They must be supportive if they are to be helpful.

Regardless of whether parents help actively, the previous chapter suggests the importance of rewarding children if they are to continue trying. To sustain a high level of motivation, parents must be interested in what children do. As they progress, parents must reward their achievements with warmth and applause. When the orchestra gives a concert, parents must be in the audience. When a project is brought home from school, they must take the trouble to look at it. When the Scouts hold a Court of Honor, they must attend. Whatever talent they want to encourage, they must invest themselves as well as their money. How parents react—whether indifferently or attentively—determines whether children's interest will be discouraged or encouraged.

19 Family Living

A family is not only an instrument for rearing children. It is a group of people living together.

FACILITIES FOR FAMILY LIVING

Family living is eased by a suitable environment—inside and outside the home.

Housing the Family

The home either encourages or limits activities. The amount of space, the allocation of rooms, and the kind of furniture affect the way in which the family lives. Needs for space and furniture change over the life cycle. Couples shoehorned into tiny apartments often move to larger quarters during their child-rearing years. Hill and his associates (1970) found that newly married Twin Cities couples typically stayed in their first residence at least a year but moved during the second year, when their first child arrived. If we turned the data around and asked how many couples move to larger quarters during the pregnancy/childbirth year, the answer would probably be the great majority.

The same study found that the original residence was typically a one-bedroom furnished apartment, followed by an unfurnished apartment in the following year, a two-bedroom apartment in the third year, and buying a house in the fifth year of marriage. In making these moves, the average couple increased the percentage of their income that they spent on housing from 16 percent the first year to 19 percent in the fifth year and 22 percent in the sixth to tenth years. Although increased expenditures and frequent moves provided steadily larger facilities, these couples had children so fast that in their sixth year of marriage they still felt pinched and hoped to acquire an even larger house with more bedrooms and baths before they expected to be satisfied.

Gans (1967) found that couples who had bought a home in Levittown, New Jersey, got along better with each other because added space meant they got in each other's way less often. Another result was spending more time at home, fixing up and taking care of the house and grounds.

After children grow up, the need for space and the energy to care for it diminishes, so some families return to smaller quarters. Furniture needs also vary over the life cycle. Newlyweds tend to buy furniture that is comfortable and stylish. They install wall-to-wall carpeting, soft upholstery, and fragile lamps. For a year or two they enjoy beauty and comfort. Then comes the baby, dumping food on the carpet, knocking over the lamps, and scarring the furniture—not because it is vicious, but because it is young, adventurous, and clumsy.

Child-proofing the Home. Wear and tear can be decreased by child-proofing a home. Given children of specified ages and vigor, the damage wreaked depends on the vulnerability of the environment. Washable paint and scrubbable wallpaper can protect the walls. Smart upholstery may be covered by washable slipcovers to catch spilled food and grimy fingerprints, or replaced by plastic or leather. Coiled springs in easy chairs and sofas are notorious invitations to bouncing when nobody is looking. Foam rubber cushions are more durable. When the baby pulls itself up to a standing position, it fingerprints white drapes or tears fragile curtains but not rugged, figured materials.

Even the wooden surfaces of tables and chairs are vulnerable. Polished dark wood shows scars and dents from weapon-wielding hands. Blood (1952) found that parents with "traditional" child-rearing philosophies preferred mahogany furniture, but that "developmental" parents preferred the lighter woods and rougher finish of colonial furniture. As one mother expressed it, "The more beat up our pine coffee table gets, the more lived-with it looks."

Loose articles in prechild livingrooms may be stored away "for the duration." Bric-a-brac sometimes frequent flat surfaces accessible to climbing youngsters: potteryware, glassware, and other smashables. One-year olds cannot be expected to leave such objects alone or handle them safely. A few years on the shelf leaves children and parents less worried and breakables intact for the day when children will be old enough to live with them.

White (1975) found that when parents child-proofed their home, they contributed to the development of competence in their children by enabling them to explore their physical environment more freely and thereby to enlarge their mental capacities:

> Designing the living area: They protected the child from the dangers of the home (safety proofing), and they protected the home from the child (childproofing), usually ahead of time. They then provided maximum access to the living quarters. They particularly made the kitchen safe and useful. They made kitchen cabinets and safe utensils, etc., available for play (p. 264).

When infants are allowed to roam freely and play with the objects they encounter, they acquire a mastery of spatial relations and creativity that stands them in good stead throughout their lives. Much of the imaginativeness and flexibility of the human brain is developed in early childhood and a child-proofed home provides an environment within which those capacities can be developed.

Anyone can store decorative objects, but few families can afford to replace their furniture when children come. Hence, couples need to anticipate the consequences for themselves, the furniture, and their children when they embark on interior decorating. As one parent stuck with handsome but impractical furniture said, "If I had only known then what I know now about children!"

> *At first my fiancé and I were not planning our home around the children we are hoping to have. We had been thinking about a French Provincial house with a recreation room in the basement for the kids. I never stopped to think that the children won't want to be in the basement all the time and would be hard on the kind of livingroom we had planned. Now, however, we are planning somewhat more sturdy furniture for the first part of our married life, and perhaps when our children are old enough, we can have our French Provincial.*

Picture windows can't be stored away, but anxiety about baseballs can be alleviated by insuring them. No matter how heavily insured or how indestructible the house, parents need to teach children to respect property, not to spill food, not to write on walls. The purpose of child-proofing is not to eliminate the need for property socialization, but to minimize the consequences of the inevitable failures.

> *When we built our house, the four Blood boys were still small. We expected them to use the basement "recreation" room for their trains and blocks and games, but it never worked out that way. They preferred to play in the center of things and that meant in the livingroom. Later we hoped they would retire to their own rooms for studying, but they always preferred to do it right there with the rest of us—in the livingroom. So we were glad our livingroom was big enough and had the kind of floor and furniture that didn't require constant "no-nos."*

Parents don't want to live in a gymnasium. They have needs, too. Hence, even a small house may need reserved space for parental hobbies, relaxation, and writing. Also, common rooms may contain concessions to adult comfort and grace that limit childish boisterousness.

Insulating Competing Activities. As long as multiple family members share the same house, they are liable to come into conflict. Conflicts can be minimized by strategic architecture and planned room use and equipment acquisition:

> Conflict in the American home often centers around use of scarce physical facilities. The current trends to a second car, a second television set, and a second telephone result ... in decreased tension for family personnel who can now use parallel facilities simultaneously instead of having to compete for control of single channels. Similarly, the recreation room provides the rest of the family with a retreat when daughter decides to throw a party in the living room, taking the tension off competition for "the only room in the house where I can entertain my friends" (Blood, 1960).

Some conflicts intensify as children get older. They result not from failures in socialization but from the normal development of adolescent interests. A 1957 survey of adolescent girls by the Gilbert Youth Research Company found that conflict over the telephone was almost universal if only one line was available. Since the average teenager used the phone more than an hour a day, the demand on facilities outran the supply when the whole family was home. The larger the family, the larger the number of bottlenecks, with bathrooms at 7:30 A.M. another prime example.

Conflicts may be reduced by zoning the house. Noises that would antagonize someone reading the newspaper or doing homework are tolerable when muffled by closed doors. Contrary to the theory that "open planning" creates sociability, kitchens without walls and rooms that "flow" into one another are more apt to create irritability. The din of kitchen machinery (dishwasher, disposal, washer and dryer) needs to be segregated by walls and closed doors from the rest of the house. The sound of music needs segregation, too, especially when it is being practiced by a student in the early stages of learning an instrument. A soundproofed music room can protect the frayed nerves of a mother napping in another room. If family members want to play records and watch television simultaneously, equipment must be dispersed in separate rooms. A "music room" equipped with stereo, television, and piano is fine for a single person but prevents parallel musical activities for families of more than one.

Space Enough for Group Activities. Where people need to be in the same place at the same time, conflict is reduced by ample space. Although the livingroom is an obvious example, the kitchen is more apt to be skimped.

Some architects recommend an "efficiency" kitchen in which stove, refrigerator, and sink are placed close together to save steps for the cook. The trouble is that children like to play there and families to eat there. Efficiency kitchens either make multiple-person activities impossible or fray nerves as people bump into one another. Foote (1960) found that almost no one (with the possible exception of childless newlyweds) preferred small kitchens, and most people who criticized their kitchens wanted more space for preparing and/or eating meals.

Choice of Neighborhood

Neighborhood interaction may be so intense that choosing neighbors is a bit like choosing a marriage partner. Just as mixed marriages encounter special problems, so do mixed neighborhoods.

Rosenberg (1965) found that it made little difference whether children lived in a completely homogeneous neighborhood or in a balanced neighborhood. For example, Protestant children in half-Protestant neighborhoods had just as much self-esteem and just as few psychosomatic symptoms as those who lived in all-Protestant neighborhoods. But Table 19–1 shows that when children were a minority (25 percent or less) in a "foreign" neighborhood, their emotional health suffered. Rosenberg reported that children in alien neighborhoods were more often teased, left out of things, or called names by other children.

As bad as uncongenial friends, however, are no friends at all. Neighborhoods go through cycles in age composition. New subdivisions swarm with preschool children who don't have enough babysitters to care for them. Ten years later there is a surplus of babysitters. A decade more and the teenagers are gone, leaving middle-aged parents behind. If a fam-

Table 19–1 Self-Esteem of Protestant, Catholic, and Jewish Children, by Ethnic Composition of Neighborhood

	ETHNIC COMPOSITION OF NEIGHBORHOOD		
Percent with Low Self-Esteem	Nondissonant	Dissonant	Dissonant/ Nondissonant Ratio
Protestant children	25%	31%	1.2X
Catholic children	29%	40%	1.4X
Jewish children	17%	29%	1.7X

Adapted from Rosenberg, 1965: 67. *Source:* 1,021 juniors and seniors in New York State public high schools. Nondissonant neighborhoods had at least 50 percent children of the same faith as respondents while they were in grade school. Dissonant neighborhoods had three-fourths or more children of a different faith. Reciprocal percentages of respondents held themselves in medium or high esteem.

ily with young children moves in at this point, there may be scarcely a playmate for blocks around. Choosing a house entails choosing playmates and schools for the children: Small children make extraordinary demands upon the attention and energy of parents when no other children are available as playmates.

Gans (1967) found that although the principal reason for moving to Levittown, New Jersey, was the nature of the house, most families also explored the schools and recreational facilities for their children. Less than half, however, inquired about the people they would find in their neighborhood, which suggests that families typically left the supportiveness of the neighborhood up to chance.

FAMILY PROBLEM SOLVING

Although problems can be reduced by appropriate facilities, an occasional clash of wills is inevitable. The intimacy and intensity of family relationships make conflict more likely than in casual groups.

Some parents (and grandparents) think it is their responsibility to worry about each other and spend long hours discussing and making decisions about their children's lives:

> My parents' bedroom was next to mine and I could hear my father endlessly going round and round with my mother about what my brother or sister was doing wrong. Some discharge was probably necessary, but the feelings were never spoken to the right person. My father developed migraine headaches, which I'm sure grew out of the load of hassles that were never resolved.

Family conflict is complicated by the changing ages of the children. Initially, children are nonself-governing, subject to parental authority since they can't understand language. Between the ages of 2 and 18, they must become completely self-governing while parental authority is completely relinquished. Just as the liberation of a colony from an imperial power is seldom accomplished without a struggle, the liberation of children from their parents is not likely to take place peacefully. The continually increasing abilities of the children require constant readjustment by the parents during the entire time that the two generations live together.

Family conflict is complicated by the fact that children in the family are not all the same age. The balance between parental control and youthful autonomy appropriate for one child will not be appropriate for an older or younger sibling.

Intergenerational conflict is intensified by the rapidity with which society changes. If parents could simply treat their children the way they were treated by their parents 25 years ago, raising children would be easier. But children live in a world quite different from the one their parents knew, subject to different peer pressures, exposed to new values, and faced with new options. The new morality, the sexual revolution, communal living, and the drug scene confront parents with issues different from those they faced when they were young. Those social changes depart from traditional values. They lead children to want to do things their parents did not do in their own adolescence. Some are things the parents have never experienced as adults. This split between parental authority and the insurgent demands of children creates a generation gap.

Blood (1953) found that the more permissive the parents, the more noise and clutter per square foot. No one "issue" is most troublesome, but frictions pile up into emotional tautness. Parents interact with their children at the same time that they try to keep up with the laundry, cleaning, cooking, and dishwashing. Explosions come when so many demands coincide that not all can be met:

> Last night Dan came home late to supper. The kids were hollering for their dessert and he wanted his supper, so I felt like an automat. He wanted me to sit down and hear about his troubles, but I had to tell him we'd talk about it later. He said, "I can see that you're not one bit interested in me. All you think of is the kids!" Then I blew up and told him off. I told him that if he had to go through everything I had, he wouldn't feel like listening to someone else's troubles either.

Parental tensions infect children too, making them quarrelsome and irritable. Family crises are common on that bane of every mother's existence: rainy days. Parents long for the end of school vacations, house-confining colds, and dreary weather so children can leave for a while.

Resolving Conflict over Scarce Facilities

Where facilities cannot be enlarged, families may establish priority systems:

> If the bone of contention is the television set, a schedule for the whole week, born of a major showdown, may take the place of petty conflict "every hour on the hour." If the scarcity has been financial, the record of decisions takes the form of a budget. Here the mutual recriminations sparked by overdrawn bank accounts can be obviated by advance planning about where the money is to be spent (Blood, 1960).

Priority systems determine which family member has precedence. The hardest working members of the family may be given first choice of recreational activities, the rarest viewers of television the chance to watch what they wish, the newest swimmer the choice of where to go. Taking turns may be fairest when competing interests are equally strong. Even for interests that are unpredictable, systematic solutions are sometimes available. For example, answering the next phone call may be the job of whoever received the last one. Whatever the problem, systems diminish conflicts once they are agreed on.

Adult Priority.   Historically, families were governed by a caste system. Parents were the privileged caste. "Little children should be seen and not heard." Children were expected to conform to adult wishes, work hard, and beware of bothering their parents. As long as everybody practiced it, the caste system worked.

Today family patterns differ. Parents who seek to perpetuate their priority must contend with their own and their children's knowledge that the rights of parents have gone the way of the "divine right of kings." Parents can no longer wield authority arbitrarily without misgivings.

Meanwhile, children have discovered that they have rights too. Hence, parental authoritarianism is at least resented, if not resisted:

> *Mother and I had a showdown last week because she insisted on reading my letters from Dave. She maintains that no matter how old I am— whether 21 or 31—I should still confide everything to her. She is my mother, and I don't want to flout her. But I'd feel more like confiding if she didn't insist on everything.*

The Child Is King.   As often happens in history, the pendulum moved from one extreme to the other. Rebellious children resolved to do better by their children and sensitive experts defended the rights of infants.

If parents were not also persons, breadwinners, housekeepers, and husbands or wives, they could devote themselves to serving their children. But since parents have other roles, putting children first creates role conflicts. Children's demands are often insatiable:

> *The children always want something different from what they get— it's most frustrating and I have no patience with them. I hate people who swear, but I say under my breath, "Damn those kids!" One busy day last week Jane wanted me to wash her doll's clothes. That wasn't so bad, but after that she insisted that I sit down and mend a frayed hem on the doll's dress. At that, my patience just gave out.*

When parents abandon their other responsibilities to their children's desires, trouble results. When children become tyrants, parents feel like martyrs. The more time and energy they spend on their children, the more they begrudge the sacrifice of their own interests. Their grudge is nursed during moments of despair and wielded against their children in moments of anger: "Look at all we've done for you—and you don't appreciate it!" Such diatribes confuse children after what seemed to be enjoyable times together. The end result is parent-child tension.

Substituting tyrannical children for authoritarian parents does not improve the situation.

The Person-Centered Family.   Priority need not be assigned to either generation. Every person can be important. This means that children's interests are limited by parental interests and vice versa. A happy medium can be found between the children's desire to keep their parents home and the parents' enjoyment of social life. In adult-centered families parents go out whenever they want, limited only by their babysitting budget. Child-oriented parents feel it is their duty to stay home. Compromise lies somewhere in between—not so much in a fixed quota of nights out, as in a working balance between the parents' and children's wishes. With no priority for either generation, families must find other ways of resolving intergenerational conflicts.

Our friend, Malinda McCain, patiently negotiated with her nine-year-old daughter to find a balance between her own need for quiet and her daughter's need for sound:

> *Janine was watching TV. It was turned on loud enough that I was distracted from my conversation in another part of the house.*
> MALINDA: *The TV sounds really loud.*
> JANINE *(turning it down some)*: *How's that?*
> MALINDA: *Still sounds pretty loud here.*
> JANINE: *I don't think I can hear it if it's lower.*
> MALINDA: *How about turning it down more, and if you can't hear it, turn it back up?*
> *Janine turned it down more and left it down.*

Comment: Both persons' needs were met by the final solution.

Person-centered families have an extraordinarily different atmosphere from traditional families. I (Bob) will never forget the annual meeting of the National Council on Family Relations where Joy Constantine, aged six, led a roundtable for professional adults on the rights of children. Larry, her father, presented a paper at the same meeting in which he described his relationship with Joy, her four-year-old sister Heather, and his wife Joan:

> In talking about my own family I have often found that listeners have assumed I live in a communal family with three women. Joy and Heather, the younger members of our family, are people I like, people I find interesting and enjoy being with. My very tone of voice seems to convey that I regard them as friends and respect them as persons. In a visit to our house, one might well find Joy doing some parentally solicitous caretaking of me, or Heather pointing out the error of Joan's ways. Even this assumption of ostensibly parental roles is in no way the rule, for all of us seem to have the flexibility and family approval to be "masculine" or "feminine," "parental" or "child-like" as fits the

mood and moment. No one has the full burden or the trap of any such role. Completely on their own, Joy and Heather have taken to doing role reversals to learn more about each other's and even our points of view (Constantine, 1975: 13).

In his paper, Constantine also compared his family to the O'Neills' open marriage (1972) in its emphasis on honest and open relationships, equality among parents and children, and a commitment to the growth of each family member as an individual. Open families are committed to adaptability, emotional sharing, responsiveness, and authenticity. Interdependence develops as families make decisions based on consensus and persuasion, dialectic and dialogue. "Individual differences and mutual negotiation rather than role prescriptions determine each member's participation in family tasks.... Everyone expects to learn from everyone else and no one has the impossible burden of always being right." Instead of waiting for the conflicts that trigger explosive changes, Constantine's family attempted to "monitor their own process closely, reassessing how well family goals are being met, how well the family is working for every member, whether goals need to be modified." Changes in relationships, rules, and privileges were sensitive to individual needs and were chosen rather than forced.

Sibling Rivalry over Parental Affection. Some of the toughest conflicts are between siblings. Jealousy is almost universal at certain ages. In families where it is not apparent on the surface, it often crops up in fantasies and dreams. Jealousy originates in a child's resentment at being displaced by a new baby. Previously (if s/he was the only child), s/he was the center of attention, but now an intruder gets the attention. "Losing" the mother creates bitterness. Sears et al (1957) found that first-born children were usually aggressive toward their parents. Younger siblings, in turn, attacked the next oldest child. In each case, rivalry focused on the adjacent child as chief competitor.

Sibling rivalry cannot be prevented entirely. However, the traumatic consequences of sharing parents with a stranger can be minimized. Children who are informed of the impending arrival may get used to the idea through role playing. Parents can give a displaced child extra time and affection to allay his/her fears of losing their love.

Every child needs to feel accepted. All parents are occasionally accused of favoritism, but they can do much to make this accusation undeserved. Most important is unreserved affection for all their children. Beyond this is fairness and appropriateness in dealing with each child.

Because siblings differ in age, equal treatment is not always appropriate. Suppose a six-year-old boy would like to be able to stay up like his nine-year-old sister. He can be assured that he too will be able to stay up when he is nine. In practice, however, older children often "run interference" for younger siblings in securing age-graded privileges. Parental resistance weakens by the time later children come along. Such changes are often begrudged by the older child:

> *When Paul and I were both in our teens, he would often go to my parents saying, "You never let me do that when I was his age." I know that I was allowed to do more things at an earlier age than he was. However, I did not like him to say such things to my parents. We always got along best when they were not at home, for when they were around we vied for their attention.*

Some parents tighten up with subsequent children, reacting against earlier permissiveness. Whichever way they change, the child who is treated more strictly is likely to complain. If parents communicate to each child that they care even though they cannot satisfy every demand, conflict diminishes.

Rivalry is more or less inevitable. Like any conflict, sibling rivalry provides opportunities for learning how to resolve friction and to share—in short, how to get along with other people This cannot be learned easily. But when parents approach their children with fairness, flexibility, and understanding, lessons in human relations are derived from sibling squabbles.

Parental Intervention.   To intervene or not to intervene in a rising dispute—that is the constant question:

> *Kristin, age 3, joins Louis, age 4½, as he puts together the new wooden track for his train. Louis grabs the track out of her hand and glowers fiercely. Kristin squints nervously and then quietly gives him another piece of track. Louis relaxes and both build on the two ends of track.*

An intervening adult might have talked about property rights or told Louis that he ought to share his toys. But such preachments are irrelevant to Louis's experience of being threatened and discovering that Kristin and he could play together after all:

> *Too often I rush in and fan the flames. Yet to come in before the heat builds and encourage my two boys to hear what the other is really saying helps them find their own solution. Sometimes I serve as an interpreter, suggesting words that are not so loaded and that communicate better what each really wants or needs.*

Back of most anger is some kind of fear. When parents learn to be aware of and deal with their own feelings, they panic less about their children's eruptions:

Max is an efficiency expert who spends half of every week advising business executives out of town. When he returns home, he upsets the whole family by his authoritarian interference. He is eager to make up for lost time and interferes pontifically in the systems that we have worked out in his absence. He is beginning to realize that he faces the same challenge at home as he does in his work—that of being a facilitator rather than a dictator, one who can provide objectivity and perspective.

Our friend, Malinda, reported how she helped her boys resolve a conflict over the dishes.

Brian and Kevin were scheduled to do the dishes. They negotiated about who would wash and who would rinse. Kevin wanted to rinse because he had a sore hand. Brian wanted to trade halfway through, saying that only this provided an equal sharing of the work since rinsing is "cinchy." Kevin insisted he didn't want to get his sore hand wet.

BRIAN: *You'll get your hands wet rinsing anyway.*

MALINDA: *I hear Kevin saying he can probably rinse with one hand but that washing would mean getting both hands wet.*

BRIAN: *Not if he wore rubber gloves.*

KEVIN: *Wow—fine—that sounds like fun!*

Comment: Malinda did not settle the argument for her children but participated supportively in their dialogue until they resolved the conflict themselves.

Children frequently use a parent to settle their conflicts. This entangles the adult and places him/her in an authority position that prevents the children from dealing with each other and with the real issue. The parent becomes a judge handing out a solution. Usually it is not a question of which child is right or wrong but of conflicting interests. Parents can help their children pay attention to the issue, clarifying it (rather than blaming one or both opponents) and helping them to negotiate or find mutual ground. Children are closer to their feelings than hardened game-playing adults and can learn to stay with a scary antagonist. Each time they break through an impasse, they learn self-reliance, self-respect, and faith in the humanness of others. In attempting to avert violence between children, parents produce a forced withdrawal and inhibition that breaks down self-worth and undermines the child's ability to take care of him/herself in future differences with others.

Family Decision Making

Caring in the family grows out of learning how to share feelings, activities, and decision making. This takes awareness and effort. It will occur between particular family members, but daily or weekly sharing times of the whole family are important as well:

> *The best period of our family life was when we used suppertime as an opportunity for each child to share without interruption, something new and good or something that was upsetting during the day. It kept us in touch with what was happening inside and outside the home.*

A less direct way of sharing feelings is to post lists on the refrigerator with headings such as "Gripe of the Week," "Anger of the Week," or "Joy of the Week" (Constantine, 1975). A family with small children put up a long sheet with plenty of room for family members to draw the leaves of a "Nice Feeling Tree" (Kessler and McLeod, 1976). Another family posted a sheet entitled "Winners Not Losers" on which members gave points to anyone who came out of a grump on their own and took the initiative in reaching across a gap to reconcile hurt feelings.

Family meetings may have to be scheduled regularly to be sure they happen. Meetings may need to begin with clearing away accumulated hurts and grievances. If unattended to, these will frustrate the family's ability to achieve any consensus on practical issues. Sharing information about coming events and giving everyone a chance to choose whether to participate or not will save time and prevent feelings of being left out. When parents talk about their need to go out and enjoy themselves, children will more easily accept the babysitter or the responsibility of caring for themselves. Visits, trips, holidays, and parties enlist more cooperation when all share in the planning. Brainstorming by everyone about what we can do together is easier than one or two having all the bright ideas and the rest dragging their feet.

Having everyone present take a turn at making an uninterrupted opening statement of how s/he sees a difficult issue is a magical way of involving everyone from the beginning and preventing battle lines from forming prematurely. Otherwise, one family member is liable to make a pitch for a particular point of view, hoping to sell those less prepared and less motivated. This usually puts everyone else on the defensive. If the others give their assent grudgingly, they may sabotage the activity by halfhearted or resentful participation:

> *Our oldest child was a sharp debater. He knew what he wanted and brought a well-thought-out position to every meeting. His preparation was admirable but no one would buy his plan. We all just bristled and dug in to resist him.*

Some of the conditions under which family conflict may be most fruitfully resolved include:

1.   Willingness to listen on the part of both generations, suspending judgment until each person has finished his/her entire statement, allowing space for the others to express·everything that they need to say. We saw this happen dramatically in one of our parent-teen workshops when a suspicious mother finally heard her 16-year-old daughter's reasons for wanting to spend the night at a girlfriend's house and the daughter finally heard her mother's anxiety and was able to reassure her.

2.   Willingness to communicate on both sides, to share honestly what is inside, to self-disclose.

3.   Openness to changing one's own views, to learning from the other generation, to discovering truth from any source—no matter how old or how young. Combined with openness to retaining one's views where they seem right after considering the alternatives.

4.   Reluctance to impose one's views on others. Especially as children grow older, respect for the other's right to differ.

5.   Patience in negotiation. Recognition of the value of allowing time to elapse as making it easier to change one's views.

6.   Involvement of all the affected parties. Decision making by the whole family about issues that affect the whole group.

7.   Use of special techniques for dealing with difficult situations:

—role playing and role reversal to practice new approaches and prepare for a potentially threatening situation
—gestalt dialogues for dealing with ambivalence—the same person playing both sides of him/herself
—nonverbal ways of struggle: boxing with gloves under an umpire, wrestling, pushing, "roaring"
—doubling: speaking over the shoulder of another family member
—parent-teen workshops
—family therapy

Families that use such processes can hope not only to live together creatively, but to provide their members with an extraordinary opportunity for personal growth through struggle.

SHARING RESPONSIBILITY FOR HOUSEWORK

Ray and Mary grew up in homes that made few demands on what they could contribute. They feel deprived and hope to inculcate better work habits in their children. The children have little motivation to fulfill their parents' hopes that they will learn how to work. Neither pecuniary rewards nor withdrawal of privileges seems to be effective. Ray and Mary find themselves screaming at one another as each screams at the children. Nothing seems to work.

How can parents inculcate responsibilty? How can they motivate children to want cleanliness and order when the children do not share this value? Family members have different needs and values. To live together, they must accept the separateness of each member. Togetherness requires sharing feelings and negotiating among the members. There is no short cut to communication and community. When the compulsion to achieve perfect neatness, precise equality of effort, or complete parental authority supersedes the value of group process, the chance for responsible participation by family members is undermined.

Wants, needs and values change. With this change must go a continuing process of renegotiating agreements about what family members can expect of one another. If the desire to make a go of some project exists only in some family members, it will not work until all are sold on it. Responsibility cannot be taught by threats or pressure. It can only be modeled. Only as parents respond to their children as they are at any moment can there be a meeting of minds in a common effort:

> *The model for me [Margaret] as a child was that my mother or the maid did all the work. We children did not feel needed. Work was something we did to "learn how to work" or to "learn how to earn money so that we could learn how to put it in the bank and save it." Always there was someone around who could do it better and who I felt would be dissatisfied with the quality of my work.*

If husband and wife are clear that all who belong to this family share the housework and they behave this way themselves, they will be more apt to gain the cooperation of their children. Since most people prefer to do their own thing rather than to cook, clean, pick up, wash dishes, buy food, or do the laundry, family tasks must be organized:

> *When I [Margaret] didn't organize the family chores, I ended up doing everything and feeling a resentful martyr. I needed Bob's help since he is a great organizer. But if I had it to do over, I'd want the whole family meeting together to carry the responsibility for working out a system of chores.*

The first step in dividing household responsibility is clarifying what needs to be done, followed by negotiating who will do what and being sure that all understand their part. A family meeting fails if it is no more than an undercover manipulation by parents mouthing democratic principles. It can generate a spirit in which there is satisfaction for all in planning and carrying out what needs doing for all of us, rather than just for parents. As all family members begin to do their share, an enormous amount of energy is freed up that had been wasted in endless bickering about who will or won't, who did or didn't, and what to do about it. Punishments can be junked as whips to get the work done. Taking away privileges is a drag on the family spirit that belongs with the obsolete patriarchal/matriarchal practice of exacting work out of unwilling young slaves.

Reward systems must never be confused with giving or withdrawing love. Constantly labeling cooperative and uncooperative behavior as "good" and "bad" teaches children that they are loved only when they do right. When their own sense of rightness conflicts with their parent's, children may sell theirs short in exchange for strokes from adults. When this response becomes ingrained in children, there is no joy in work or in accomplishment, only anxiety about pleasing.

Working together can be more fun than working alone, and the work goes faster. Family "work parties" to plant or weed the garden and to rake the leaves can be fun. Cooperation is rewarding when experienced as collective power.

Compulsive mothers and fathers spend too much energy interfering with the private space of their children. In a person-centered home, each person is responsible for his/her own property and room. When bedrooms are shared and cleanliness standards differ, this is one more issue that must be negotiated:

> *I hate it if anyone else picks up my desk, and yet for years I had no respect for my children's private space. When I failed to get them to do it willingly, I would feverishly and resentfully pick up every toy, book, or piece of clothing, satisfying my own sense of orderliness. Doing it for them didn't teach them orderliness. Only as they wanted it for themselves did it come. I might have spared my own irritation and theirs by leaving their rooms alone.*

FAMILY RECREATION

Weekends are family times for special projects, picnicking, swimming or skating, and visiting friends and relatives.

Nye (1958) found that children benefited from almost every kind of family recreation—the larger the number of family activities, the smaller the proportion of teenage children who were delinquent. Only 22 percent of those who did things with their parents at home more than once a week were delinquent, compared to 42 percent of those who never had any fun at home. Similarly, going to ballgames and going on picnics with parents resulted in closer parent-child relationships and less delinquency.

Rituals

Families develop patterned ways of doing things that give continuity to family living. For students at San Diego State College, the most important family rituals when they were children had been having dinner together at Christmas, Thanksgiving, Easter, and other holidays; opening Christmas presents and decorating the tree; and exchanging gifts and cards or attending parties to celebrate birthdays, Mother's Day, and Father's Day (Klapp, 1959).

Other recreational rituals include television programs that everyone anticipates, and family night at gym or swimming pool. Many families develop bedtime rituals. In our family:

> When Larry was three, he always wanted the same songs in the same order: "Little Boy Blue," "Twinkle, Twinkle Little Star," and "Rockabye Baby," while Alan prescribed 15 kisses and one bear hug.

Rituals sometimes arise spontaneously. Some are consciously invented. Some are handed down from generation to generation. The ritual-produced piling up of pleasant memories contributes to family integration and family pride. Klapp found that families with the most rituals were the most cohesive.

> We Bloods had our share of sibling rivalry but we also remember high times together—reading, making music, playing games, and traveling.
>
> I [Margaret] will never forget our intense collective involvement in the adventures of E. B. White's Stuart Little and Charlotte's Web; Robert McCloskey's Homer Price; and Holling C. Holling's Tree in the Trail and Paddle to the Sea.
>
> Drama and games peaked during preschool birthday celebrations. Peter's fourth anniversary turned into a grand circus with everyone taking turns being ringmaster, horses, and elephants, or sideshow fortune-tellers, magicians, and tricksters while others cheered. His fifth birthday was a spectacular space party with imaginary rockets taking off and great feats of jumping over houses on the moon. Alan played the leading role at his fourth birthday dramatization of Alladin and His Lamp with all assembled guests appropriately costumed.
>
> Music has been a joy from singing nursery rhymes and Christopher Robin songs through playing Mozart piano quartets to the excitement of joining the orchestra and chorus in a Christmas Messiah Sing, which originated in our basement and grew into an annual community event. With our grown children, family reunions include singing folk songs accompanied by guitars, fiddles, banjo, and penny whistles.
>
> Trips included annual pilgrimages to grandparents in New Hamp-

shire and Kentucky, biennial visits to the ocean at Cape May Quaker gatherings, and a grand American "roots" tour to Williamsburg, Monticello, and the national capitol. Two sabbaticals in Japan prompted camping across the West, shooting the waterfalls in Hawaii, and an omnivorous tour of Eastern and Western Europe. More sober rituals were several family treks to Washington, D.C. to stand together with other Quakers around the Pentagon in vigil against the war in Vietnam.

Parent-child Companionship

Families contain too many ages and sexes to make community of interest always possible. Subgroups can have a special closeness that the whole group seldom achieves;

> *I'll never forget the time Dad came to visit me at Wellesley. He'd bought a new suit and overcoat, which was very unusual for him. He was a real Dad to me and we had a fabulous time. The girls in the dorm just loved him. He took several of us to a cabin in the mountains for the weekend with no idea of the money involved. We went on hikes and played cards and stayed up all hours. I wish he'd done that sort of thing more often when I was growing up.*

Among Tallahassee teenagers, swimming, movies, fishing, and picnics were enjoyed by many combinations of family members. Fathers and sons went to ball games and went hunting together. Mothers and daughters enjoyed going shopping or cooking special dishes (Connor et al., 1955).

Balance

Some families wear themselves out trying to do too much. Especially when children are old enough to participate in outside activities, the demands on parents for chauffeuring are notorious. Hawkins and Walters (1952) found that parents who did the most with their children also entertained most, attended the most social functions, and engaged in the most activities away from home. Perhaps because they overdid things, they reported the most family tensions:

> I never see my children any more. They're out for something every night in the week. Monday is Scout night, Wednesday the band rehearses, and Thursday the senior play. Of course, on Friday and Saturday there are social activities. It's gotten so we don't have any family life any more.

Parents cannot expect growing children to spend all or most of their time at home. Even special family times need escape clauses. Many adolescent crises are caused by insistence on a routinized family activity to which exceptions might be granted.

RELIGION IN FAMILY LIVING

According to the billboards, "Families that pray together, stay together." Religious families have fewer divorces than nonreligious families. Locke (1951) found that couples whose marriages subsequently failed attended church less than those whose marriages were happy.

We do not know, however, how much of this lower divorce rate for churchgoing families reflects their greater reluctance to get divorced and how much, if any, involves a qualitative strength in the family life of religious people. Many studies have shown that church attenders rate their marriages more happily than do secular people, but a devastating study by Edmonds, Withers, and Dibatista (1972) demonstrated that neither religious activity in general nor church attendance in particular was related to marital happiness, once the tendency of religious people to overstate the happiness of their marriages was discounted.

Even though we must remain agnostic about the effect of religiosity as such on marriage, we can be sure about the difference between unilateral and joint participation in church activities. We saw in Chapter 3 that interreligious marriages suffer from the diversion of their energies in different organizational directions. A similar strain on marriage occurs when one partner is religious and the other is not.

In Table 19–2 we can discount the difference between the happiness of those who go to church regularly and those who go occasionally as a reflection of the inflation process we have already described. But the difference between wives who occasionally go to church with their hus-

Table 19–2 Marital Happiness of Wife, by Husband's and Wife's Church Attendance

	CHURCH ATTENDANCE			
Wife's Evaluation of Marriage	Both Regular	Both Occasional	Both Never	Wife Occasional, Husband Never
Exceptionally or very happy	91%	79%	62%	55%
Fairly happy	8	19	32	33
Unhappy or very unhappy	1	2	6	12
Total	100%	100%	100%	100%
Number of cases	120	479	269	170

Adapted from Chesser, 1957: 279. *Source:* Women patients of English physicians.

bands and those who go alone is another matter. Unilaterally involved marriages are worse off than marriages in which neither partner goes to church. Religion is a divisive force when it involves either differential or unilateral activity.

The conventionalism of religious people has certain payoffs for their children: they are less apt to engage in unconventional behaviors such as dropping out of college or committing juvenile offenses. Morgan (1962) found that the children of parents who attended church at least twice a month stayed in school and college longer than those whose parents attended less often (even after holding constant parental education, income, and a dozen other factors). Parents with no religious preference had especially unsatisfactory results. Morgan was puzzled about the cause, but suggested that the educational achievement of children from religious families may have been "an indication of strongly held values such as family responsibility." Zimmerman and Cervantes (1960) found that arrest rates for juvenile delinquency were higher for children of parents with no religious affiliation than for homogamous marriages of any religious faith.

Thus, religious activity promotes parental conformity to the norm of marital stability and children's conformity to a variety of social norms. We know very little about the precise ways in which specific religious activities affect family life, but in the absence of research findings we suggest the potential contributions of two dimensions of religious activity—in the home and in the community.

Religious Activities in the Home

Religious rituals offer rich contributions to family living.

Grace at Meals. Wynn (1961) found that the most frequent ritual was grace before meals. For some, grace means silent meditation, holding hands around the table. For others, it means singing together, a timeworn recital, or a spontaneous prayer. The most tangible consequence is to coordinate family eating. To be sure, grace-less families may taboo eating until all are seated. However, grace promotes coordination. When all eat together, the possibilities of conversation around the dinner table increase. The cook, especially, is integrated into the family circle when others wait until s/he finishes serving before even the hungriest child may plunge in.

Festival Celebrations. Just as High Holy Days bring to synagogues those who otherwise never attend, so families that otherwise have no religious activities at home, ceremonialize festive seasons. Traditions for celebrating Christmas and Easter or Hannukkah and Passover add interest and variety to family living.

Participation in Religious Organizations

Church participation promotes family welfare in three ways: (1) participation is a joint family activity; (2) the church provides a supporting network of primary relations; (3) the clergyperson is a therapeutic resource in times of trouble (as we saw in Chapter 14).

Church Attendance as a Family Activity.   Any joint activity strengthens the family, provided it is mutually rewarding. When families leave their home base and go out into the community together, they sense their group identity. The more regular and frequent the expeditions, the greater the benefit.

Institutional Support for Family Life.   Church participation links families with similar values. In minority faiths and small, intimate congregations, family friends tend to be drawn from the church (Zimmerman and Cervantes, 1960). When friends interact throughout the week as well as on Sundays, they reinforce each other's values. This network of primary relationships provides social control, encouraging good behavior and discouraging irresponsibility.

For mobile families, "often the church constitutes the one familiar spot in an otherwise strange community" (Fairchild and Wynn, 1961). It provides an entree into the community for new families.

Even large, impersonal congregations promote commitment to familistic values. Hence, both informally and formally, as a group and as an institution, the church provides external support for families.

THE CYCLE OF FAMILY LIVING

Family relationships change as each child grows older. At first a baby is helplessly dependent. As it learns to walk and talk, it begins asserting its identity, culminating in the two-and-a-half-year old's delight in discovering that it can say no. During the preschool years, family interaction is at its peak, and children spend most of their time at home, participating in everything.

The Grade School Years

When the oldest child leaves for school, the family enters a new era, less involved internally, more involved with the school and other organizations.

Most families cooperate with the school. Regular contact makes problems easier to deal with. All children have occasional problems.

Teacher personalities differ so much that the same child may love school one year and loathe it the next.

The classroom seldom has the same rules as the home. Strict parents may be disturbed by the flexibility of an open classroom. Permissive parents may wonder how their child can accept school routines. Though the temptation may be great, parents can rarely reform the teacher. His/her methods reflect personality, training, and experience. Discrepancies between home and school seldom disturb children as much as parents fear. Well-adjusted children will adapt to the situation. They see what is expected and act accordingly. Children who delight in freedom at home may conform at school (or vice versa).

One reason that children adapt well to school is their admiration for the teacher. In our case, when Miss O'Piela said children should brush their teeth *before* breakfast, nothing we could say persuaded Peter to wait till afterward.

When a child is having difficulty, parents can often supply information that makes it easier for the teacher. We helped Alan's teacher to see in kindergarten restlessness his eagerness to learn to read and write like his big brother.

Adolescence

In the grade-school years children begin making friends outside the family. Yet their parents remain special people with whom they enjoy doing things. With adolescence, parents lose status as the discrepancy narrows between their adulthood and the adolescent's "near adulthood."

Adolescent Ambivalence. Adolescents often feel caught between the dependence of childhood and the independence of adulthood. Although they long for independence, they fear it. They waver between resentment of parental controls and fear of losing their parents' love. Often they are dissatisfied with their parents, no matter what they do:

> When I finished high school, I was lost in a world of freedom and completely unable to cope with the situation myself. My parents suggested a trip to South America, but I interpreted the offer as a ruse to try to run my life. I refused and became secretive, evasive, and quite remote from the folks. They tried to reason with me but it did no good. Then they decided that to put me on my own would help, so they said I would have to straighten myself out. This idea filled me with resentment and I stubbornly took the challenge and set off for New York where I lived according to my own dictates, and succeeded only in making matters worse. I went from one job to another and from one trouble to another.

When children resent both freedom and control, parents are baffled. One moment teenagers want protection, while the next they want to be "treated like an adult." Mood swings are sudden and unpredictable. Faced with this dilemma, many parents don't know what to do. Panic sometimes leads them to reinstate long-abandoned controls:

> *It seems, as I look back on that not-too-far-removed time, that I could do nothing to please my parents—everything was wrong and there was much open conflict between them and me. They reverted to my childhood days in being extremely overprotective and not allowing me to do anything.*

Parental Ambivalence.   Parents have their own mixed feelings, which make it hard to be objective. They are proud of the increased skill of their offspring. However, they mistrust their children's judgment and worry about the tragedies that befall other adolescents—the auto accidents, pregnancies, and drug addictions. It is difficult to let go when pain may ensue. Moreover, some parents have frustrated ambitions that they would like to realize through their children.

These motives lead some parents to override children's wishes and map out their lives. Such parents choose colleges and careers for their children. This "guidance" is rationalized as interest in the children's welfare, but parental welfare may outweigh the child's.

Adolescent Rebellion.   When parents apply pressure, they intensify their children's dilemma, increasing the need to rebel. But their attitude makes rebellion tantamount to betrayal. Caught between powerful forces, adolescents may be afraid to rebel because of the bitterness it will create, yet reluctant to give in when it frustrates their deepest desires. Those who rebel turn against whatever their parents try hardest to teach them. If the parents are religious, they will spurn religion (or vice versa).

Table 19–3 shows that adolescents who were locked in conflict with their parents differed from them politically if the parent was politically interested. If the parent had little political interest, they were no more apt to hold a different political viewpoint than adolescents from low-conflict homes. Conversely, teenagers who had a congenial relationship with their parents were especially apt to hold the same viewpoint as their parents if political issues were important to the parent. The saliency of political issues for men in our society is reflected in the fact that political rebellion was greatest between boys and their fathers, somewhat less for boys and their mothers, but for girls was not a means of rebellion against either parent, no matter how great the conflict. Presumably, girls found social/sexual deviancy more potent for defying their parents.

Although adolescent revolt makes parents feel rejected, it may pave

Table 19–3 **Adolescent Divergence from Parental Political Position, by Parent's Interest in Politics and Intergenerational Conflict**

	FATHER'S INTEREST IN POLITICS	
Percent of Sons Diverging from Father by Intergenerational Conflict	*High*	*Low*
High	64%	48%
Low	34%	54%

Adapted from Eckhardt and Schriner, 1969: 498. *Source:* Junior high-school boys in a rural Ohio community. Reciprocal percentages of boys held the same political position as their fathers on a scale ranging from "extremely liberal" to "extremely conservative." Intergenerational conflict was measured by the frequency of conflict in nine areas such as dating, clothes, cars, and friends.

the way for adult-adult relations. Going away to college provides an opportunity for emancipation:

> *When I transferred to State, my parents were far enough away so that they couldn't dominate me as easily. I was much happier since I could be independent and express myself as an individual. I deliberately stayed away from home for a whole year, and they gradually got used to the idea that I loved independence. After that, we grew closer as a family, but on a new plane. All along I basically loved both my parents, but I could not accept them under the conditions they imposed. This made me feel guilty. Under the new conditions, however, we could again become friends and I was much relieved. My parents were proud of my achievements, yet they felt left out and were worried about the breach. Our new level of acceptance was different than before. It was a mutual respect and a realization of each other's needs. My father began to ask my advice on family and business matters, and I began to take them into my confidence about my aspirations and goals. My parents and I are now very close.*

Mutual Reticence.   Although some parents and their teenagers engage in open conflict, others are so wary of one another that they break off communication. Hubbell (1963) found that the most avoided topic was family finances (which fathers were especially reluctant to talk about). Teenagers did not talk about their friends and neither generation talked about sex. These topics were avoided because of personal embarrassment, a desire to maintain privacy, and anticipation by teenagers that their parents would disapprove of their ideas if they expressed them. Both generations split in their attitudes toward these topics, half wishing they could talk about them, and the other half glad that they had successfully avoided talking about them because open conflict might ensue if they were broached.

Granted that these topics are not easy to discuss, families who avoid them miss an opportunity to discover where they are as persons. When children reach adolescence, the time has come for parents and children to listen to each other without feeling that they have to achieve consensus on every issue. Even if agreement cannot be reached, to be able to understand where another person is coming from and what s/he has experienced in life is a valuable learning experience for both generations. To avoid talking about some of the most important issues in life is to feel alienated from the other members of one's family. Breaking through the barriers of fear and mistrust on these touchy subjects offers the possibility of bridging the generation gap and achieving respect and affection.

Chronic avoidance of crucial topics makes it impossible for families to solve problems. Westley and Epstein (1969) found that families who evaded or denied emotional problems piled up more and more unresolved problems. Seventy-five percent of the children in families who failed to talk about emotional problems were emotionally disturbed. By contrast, in families who talked about things that were emotionally important to them, only 12 percent of the children were emotionally disturbed.

Reticence between parents and children cuts off the flow of communication that is necessary for solving problems and expressing warmth and empathy. Parents who fail to talk are apt to have rigid personality structures. They are afraid to let themselves go with their children, and afraid to face the problems in their midst when their children's behavior disappoints them. Westley and Epstein found that none of the parents with emotionally disturbed children showed any awareness of those disturbances, so thorough was their avoidance and denial.

Family Flexibility.   Sensitive parents can keep up with changes in their children's needs and capacities. Long before adolescence, family consultation builds self-confidence. As children grow older, their ability to participate in decisions develops with use.

Adolescents are in training for adulthood. They can be expected to make mistakes. They will sometimes be bewildered by the choices they have to make—hence, open to suggestions. When the going gets rough, they may appreciate reassurance. As trainees, they need opportunities to gain experience under supervision.

Malinda gave her 12-year-old son a free hand in making a decision, advancing only procedural suggestions:

> *Kevin had planned a vacation with his grandparents for the week ending with Labor Day. Then we learned that school would start before Labor Day, meaning he would miss the first three days. Starting junior high school for the first time, Kevin felt those days could be important. I suggested he make a comparison chart, showing pros and cons of both alternatives. This laid the issue out clearly, but he was still uncertain. He decided he wanted more information, so he talked to two people. The first was a friend of his who is both a teacher and a parent of several school students. She made no recommendation but gave him some in-*

formation about the kinds of things that probably would happen during the first school days. The second person was the principal of the new school who placed no pressure on Kevin to start on time. Kevin decided he could catch up adequately, and took the vacation.

Adolescents need a flexible combination of support and release:

> *My parents have always treated me as an individual and considered me a mature person in accordance with my age. They are always willing to listen to my side of the issue. They never close their minds to my viewpoints and they do not draw conclusions irrationally, but reason things out with me. If I am right, they admit it as readily as I admit being wrong. They have never been overly strict with me but allowed me to date as soon as I felt I was ready to. They never told me who not to date, but felt that I was the best judge of the type of person I would like. They never gave me a curfew, as they felt I had enough sense to know what was a reasonable time to be home. But if, due to unexpected circumstances, I found I would be home so late that they might worry, I would call home and tell them. This way I was given a certain amount of responsibility, which I did not abuse. I therefore justified my parents' opinions of my capabilities and gained their respect.*

A flexible approach lessens intergenerational conflict. Among high-school seniors in the state of Washington, Landis and Stone (1952) found that "democratic" parents functioned quite differently than "authoritarian" parents. Democratic parents

1. allowed their children to go out as many evenings as they wished
2. never criticized where they went on dates
3. were "fairly generous" with allowance money
4. usually gave reasons for requests
5. discussed family problems with their children
6. respected their opinions and judgment "at least half the time"

Democratic families can afford to be permissive because their children have internalized appropriate standards of conduct. Free rein is good for teenagers who are ready for it. More basic, however, to smooth-running family living is discussion that enables parents to communicate their own standards at the same time that they find out their children's views.

Table 19–4 shows that democratic families had appreciably fewer problems. Conflicts with parents occurred less often and wishes to leave home diminished even more.

Westley and Epstein (1969) found that college students who came from families that respected the right of every member to make his/her

Table 19–4   Adolescent Difficulties, by Family Authority Pattern and Gender

		FAMILY AUTHORITY PATTERN	
Problem	Gender	Democratic	Authoritarian
Trouble getting along with parents	Boys	6%	17%
	Girls	8%	24%
Wants to leave home	Boys	2%	9%
	Girls	3%	12%
Number of cases	Boys	769	396
	Girls	537	533

Adapted from Landis and Stone, 1952: 24–25. *Source:* High-school seniors in Washington State, 1947. Reciprocal percentages of students did not have the specified problem.

own decisions were almost always emotionally healthy. Conversely, in families that gave little autonomy to any member of the family (so that even the parents were dependent on each other), teenaged children usually became emotionally disturbed. In families lacking in autonomy, adults as well as children fail to become self-governing persons. They are locked into overdependence on one another and trapped in correspondingly difficult emotional problems.

Kandel and Lesser (1972) found that adolescents who felt they had enough independence from their parents turned most to their parents for counsel and advice. Almost half of those with enough freedom talked over their problems with their parents, compared to less than one fifth of those who didn't get enough freedom. Those given freedom of choice were more apt to respect their parents' opinions and would voluntarily stop seeing friends to whom their parents objected. Conversely, those who felt they didn't have enough freedom said they would go on seeing forbidden friends if they could get away with it.

Kandel and Lesser found that the opposite extreme produced equally negative reactions, namely, parental permissiveness. Teenagers in the latter families felt especially distant from their parents and talked with them least of all. Apparently, permissiveness is often a synonym for neglect and rejection. Conversely, democratic parents who combined interest in their children with respect for the children's autonomy produced the most responsive children and had the warmest intergenerational relationships.

Parents and Peers.   When children reach adolescence, they waver between relying on their parents or their agemates for advice and guidance. As members of different generations, parents and peers are likely to hold different viewpoints, both because they have been socialized to different values in a changing society and because they occupy different social statuses. Turning to peers for advice and guidance means potentially rejecting parents' values for alien ones.

Table 19–5 shows that American adolescents in Kandel and Lesser's sample actually sought their peers' advice about relatively few issues. One issue was problems with their parents, where by definition parents are largely ineligible. Presumably, teen-agers who relied on their parents consulted one parent about how to get along with the other. If the problem involved both parents, they necessarily had to turn elsewhere for advice. The only other topic on which adolescents asked friends more than parents was what to read—hardly a major issue. By contrast, parents were preferred with respect to morals and values. Even the choice of the friends to whom teenagers might alternatively turn for advice was influenced by parents in most families. The table suggests that parents are more influential than peers with respect to most of the major issues where value clashes might potentially arise.

Kandel and Lesser observed that two major processes minimize adolescent-parent conflict: (1) parents supervise the selection of friends by their children, and (2) teenagers choose friends who hold the same values as their parents. As a result of these dual processes, parents and peers in most families reinforce one another with respect to most major issues. Thus, it may not matter very much whether a teenager turns to parents or to peers for guidance because s/he is likely to receive similar advice from either source.

Presumably, it is to the adolescent's advantage to choose friends who are congenial to his/her parents. Then there is less personal strain with which to contend. But this does not always happen. Some adolescents reject their parents (frequently in response to the parents' own rejection of

Table 19–5   Adolescent Reliance on Parents and Peers for Advice, by Type of Problem

	PERSON UPON WHOM ADOLESCENT WOULD RELY		
Type of Problem	Parents	Peers	Parent/Peer Ratio
College	30%	5%	6.0X
Career plans	40%	7%	5.7X
School grades	20%	5%	4.0X
Morals and values	51%	23%	2.2X
What clothes to buy	57%	39%	1.5X
Choice of friends	50%	40%	1.2X
Dating	49%	46%	1.1X
Personal problems not involving parents	42%	43%	1.0X
Personal problems with parents	27%	41%	0.7X
What books to read	14%	32%	0.4X

Consolidated from Kandel and Lesser, 1972: 119. *Source:* 1,057 U.S. high-school students. Peers included both friends and siblings. Residual percentages would turn to teachers, guidance counselors, clergypersons, and so on.

them) and turn to peers who are different. Under those circumstances, Condry, Siman, and Bronfenbrenner (1968) found that sixth-grade children engaged in more antisocial behavior such as teasing other children, lying to their parents, truanting from school, and committing illegal acts. Since most parents disapprove of this behavior, it follows that children who are oriented away from their parents toward peers are more apt to engage in disapproved behavior.

When parents find their children involved in alien groups, how can they respond? The child's problem is rarely solved by demanding permanent withdrawal from the group Severing group ties is too traumatic. Better to work for change in the group itself. This may seem difficult, and it *is* for a solitary parent. However, other parents may have the same desires. When children are young, consultation among parents often suffices to change the situation. By adolescence, joint meetings of both generations offer opportunities to talk over problems and search for neighborhood solutions. Change is always easier if everyone changes together.

In exceptional cases, parents and peers clash over major issues. One circumstance is where parents represent an ethnic way of life whereas peers are Americanized. Rosen (1955) found that conflicting pressures undermined parental efforts to "keep kosher" in communities where Jews were a small minority. In general, where peers and parents disagree, adolescents take the easy way out, especially when the dominant pattern is easier. To be caught in the middle is too difficult to endure for long.

Fortunately, crises are not the general pattern of adolescence. When parents tolerate the idiosyncrasies of the group or collaborate to control them, teenagers don't have to choose. Peers play an important role in the social development of the average person. Whereas families provide interaction with one or more siblings of varying ages and with parents from an older generation, peer groups provide experience with equals in age, strength, and skill. Like families, they give a sense of security. Each is a special group among the hundreds or thousands of fellow students in school. Identification with this group reduces emotional dependence on the parents as persons. The emancipation essential to readiness for marriage is assisted by this shift in personal ties from parents to peers.

Terminal Stages

Couples enter the postparental stage when their children leave home. Table 19–6 suggests that for many couples, the departure of children makes possible a revitalization of the marriage. Husbands in the same study reported a less dramatic increase in the proportion who rated their marriage "very happy" after the children's departure, but they too were more apt to feel enthusiastic about their marriage after the last child had left home.

Table 19–6 Marital Happiness of Middle-aged Wives, with and without Children at Home

	CHILDREN AT HOME	
Wife's Marital Happiness	Yes	No
Very happy	46%	71%
Fairly happy/unhappy	54	29
Total	100%	100%

Adapted from Glenn, 1975: 108. *Source:* National Opinion Research Center, representative U.S. sample of wives aged 50–59.

Deutscher (1959) examined in detail some of the ways the departure of children facilitated marriages. His "empty nest" couples felt more carefree than they had at any time since the advent of children. They were freer to go places and do things without children. Travel was easier. Entertaining was easier. Going out at night was easier. They could talk confidentially at the dinner table, and not just in the privacy of the bedroom. So, the marital dyad that in so many ways goes into eclipse during the child-rearing years reemerges when those years are over.

The opportunity to do things together receives a further boost when both partners retire. Then neither children nor jobs get in the way of doing what the couple wish to do. Prior to retirement, only self-employed persons have that much control over their own lives.

To be free provides an opportunity for marriages to flourish anew. But it is also a test for marriages that have gone sour. Townsend (1957: 74) found for working-class couples in London:

> Retirement produced frustrations in men, because they could not fill in their time and because they felt they were useless, and it also produced frustrations in women, because they had been used to a larger income and to a daily routine without interference from the husband. Friction could not always be dispelled by a new formulation of the division of occupations. A wife said of her retired husband, "It's different with him at home. Because he's at home he wonders what you're doing. Before that he wasn't here and you could get on with things. Now he's asking you what you're doing this for and what you're doing that for."

If the most important thing in life is to "get on with things," a retired spouse may well be a nuisance. But if companionship matters most, questions can lead to sharing household tasks and to understanding each other's life. In Chapter 21 we will return to the choice that all marriages face between growth and deterioration. Retirement poses this choice most squarely.

20 Family Finances

Despite some of the highest incomes in the world, Americans quarrel over money more than over anything else. Perhaps they have too much. Poor people have no choice. Their money must go for bare necessities. As income rises, options and financial disagreements increase. On the other hand, if couples get rich enough, they no longer have to choose. Both partners can have what they want. (Blood and Wolfe found financial disagreements most common among couples with incomes just above the median, where discretionary funds were available but not inexhaustible.)

Table 20–1 shows the conspicuousness of financial conflicts when American wives recalled the main disagreements they had ever had. Other studies find the same thing: money is the chief bone of contention between husbands and wives.

Why so? (1) Families rely on money for the goods and services they consume. (2) Occupationally involved partners earn most of the money but stay-at-home partners spend most of it, leaving the former wondering where it went. (3) American marriages are equalitarian enough to make both partners feel they should participate in decisions. When discretionary funds are limited, decisions won by the other side deplete one's own chances for implementing one's values in a "zero-sum game." One-sided power structures may not produce happier marriages, but they prevent conflict because it takes two to quarrel. (4) Whereas in-law problems are concentrated at the beginning of marriage and child-rearing problems in the middle, financial conflicts spread over the whole life cycle, taking new forms as circumstances change. (5) Financial problems are more tangible than most. If one partner buys a new car, it visibly reminds the other that s/he was not consulted.

Table 20–1   **Areas of Disagreement in Urban Families**

Area of Disagreement	PERCENTAGE OF WIVES MENTIONING	
	First	At All
Money	24%	42%
Recreation, companionship	16	30
Children	16	29
Personality characteristics	14	28
In-laws	6	10
Roles	4	7
Miscellaneous (religion, politics, sex)	3	5
None, or not ascertained	17	17
Total	100%	168% *
Number of families	731	731

Adapted from Blood and Wolfe, 1960: 241.
*Total adds to more than 100% because wives could report more than one area of disagreement.

CURRENT EXPENSES

How much does it cost to live? The answer varies with changing circumstances and depends on how efficiently the family spends its money.

Life-cycle Crises

Newly married couples with both partners working are remarkably prosperous. Though they begin with little equipment, they have only two mouths to feed. Each income may be low, but the combined income often exceeds what either partner alone might be able to earn for many years. If the man's promotional prospects are dim, family income may never be as high again if the woman drops out of the labor force.

On the heels of this prosperity comes the deepest depression. Disagreements about money are commonest in families with children (see Figure 20–1). Many families give up the wife's income just when they add the children's food, clothing, medical, and housing expenses, creating the severest strain they are likely ever to experience.

Lansing and Morgan (1955) found that financial disagreements jumped from minimum to maximum in response to this squeeze. Liquid assets dropped sharply, most families went into debt, and their satisfaction with their standard of living sagged to a low ebb. The larger the number of children and the faster they arrived, the deeper the crisis.

Lansing and Morgan found that children became even more expensive as they got bigger, but most family incomes rose with experience and seniority. Consequently, the strain eased gradually during the child-rearing years, save for the college crisis. Paradoxically, the average per-

Figure 20-1 Financial Disagreements, by Stage in Family Life Cycle

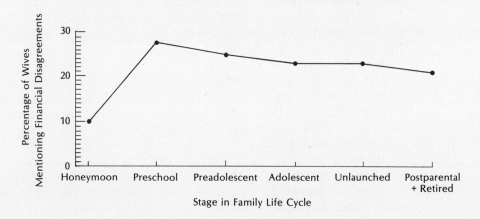

Adapted from Blood and Wolfe, 1960: 247.

son's earnings peaked around age 50, too late to benefit the children since the last child had normally left home. By then a sufficient inventory of family equipment had accumulated to reduce overhead expenses. Consequently, optional expenditures rose. Subsequently, retirement brought a second cut in income, the severity of which depended on retirement savings.

This analysis discloses three critical intervals: the childbearing years, college education years, and retirement years. Conversely, there are typically two eras of plenty—at the beginning and just before the end.

Allocation of Financial Resources

How do families spend their money? The answer depends on how much money they have, how many children they have, and their stage in life.

The more money there is, the larger the proportion they can spend on luxuries. The U.S. Bureau of Labor Statistics (1957) compared college-educated men at three income levels. As income rose, people didn't smoke much more, eat much more, get sick oftener, or get more haircuts, so fixed-cost items shrank percentagewise. Housing and utility costs also declined proportionately. Transportation remained a relatively standardized cost, provided it was confined to local travel.

Allocation to discretionary areas increased. More money went to operate the household, buying services to relieve the couple of house-keeping tasks. More emphasis went to clothes, recreation, and education. More money was saved in many forms, including personal insurance. The biggest change was increased generosity to persons and organizations outside the family. Low-income families spent most of their money on themselves. As income rose, gifts to relatives, friends, and worthy causes became more feasible.

Table 20–2 shows the effect of children on the standard of living and the distribution of expenditures. With the addition of four or more children to the family, educational expenses more than tripled. Food and clothing expenses went up 40 percent and the cost of utilities and recreation for the family rose disproportionately. Most other expenditures decreased about 20 percent. In part, these were adult luxuries: eating out, reading, smoking, drinking, and especially travel. But large families had to make do with spending proportionately less on such necessities as housing and medical care.

Analysis over the life cycle showed that childless couples made heavy down payments on cars and houses. The advent of children accentuated the need for household furnishings and equipment. The child-rearing years raised the costs of clothing, food, recreation, reading, education, medical care, and insurance. As children got older, families spent more for transportation, perhaps on multiple automobiles for husband and wife and eventually for children old enough to drive. The departure of the last child freed the budget for increased housekeeping services (much appreciated in old age) and contributions to the happiness and welfare of others. At 65 there was a last-minute spurt of insurance investment for the retirement and widowed years.

Table 20–2   Family Expenditures, by Number of Children

	NUMBER OF CHILDREN					
Expenditure	None	One	Two	Three	Four	Large/ Small Ratio
1. Education	0.5%	1.3%	1.5%	1.6%	1.6%	3.2X
2. Food at home	18.0	18.4	19.8	21.4	24.3	1.4X
3. Clothes	8.7	10.6	11.2	11.9	11.8	1.4X
4. Utilities	4.6	4.3	4.4	4.6	4.9	1.1X
5. Recreation	3.6	4.1	4.4	4.6	4.0	1.1X
6. Personal care	2.9	2.9	2.9	2.8	2.9	1.0X
7. Eating out	4.9	4.9	4.5	4.4	4.3	0.9X
8. Household operations	6.2	5.8	5.8	5.6	5.3	0.9X
9. Housing	14.4	13.4	12.9	12.4	11.9	0.8X
10. Furnishings and equipment	5.7	5.5	5.0	5.0	4.7	0.8X
11. Medical care	7.6	6.5	6.3	6.0	5.7	0.8X
12. Reading	1.0	0.9	0.9	0.8	0.8	0.8X
13. Smoking, drinking	3.8	3.3	3.2	3.2	3.2	0.8X
14. Miscellaneous	2.4	2.1	2.3	2.2	1.8	0.8X
15. Automobile	13.6	14.4	13.4	12.1	11.4	0.8X
16. Travel	2.2	1.6	1.4	1.2	1.4	0.6X
Total	100.1%	100.0%	99.9%	99.8%	100.0%	

Adapted from U.S. Bureau of Labor Statistics, 1964: 11. *Source:* National sample of urban American families.

Decision Making about Expenditures.   Though categories of families differ only marginally in their allocation patterns, individual families vary widely. Transportation costs are sharply reduced for those who do not own a car. The cost of ownership increases with the car's expensiveness, newness, and frequency of replacement. In clothing, style consciousness and the growth of children produce rapid obsolescence. Housing costs rise to provide space for family recreation, hospitality for friends and relatives, or offices for writing books like this.

Like other choices, financial decisions reflect personal values. These differ between husbands and wives as well as between families. Conflict may focus on a particular purchase or on the whole pattern of expenditures (for example, when couples feel that their total expenses are too high or that too little money is available for a particular purpose). When the whole pattern is questioned, budgeting offers a systematic method of decision making.

Budgeting.   A budget is a plan for allocating financial resources. It records decisions about how money is to be spent during a forthcoming interval. Usually plans are made a year at a time, especially if salaries change yearly. Any period is appropriate during which income and expenses are stable or predictable. For couples whose income fluctuates wildly, a budget can chart a conservative minimum, treating any surpluses as windfalls to be decided about later.

Half the families in Morgan's 1965 Detroit sample were budgeting at that time. Somewhat more had budgeted or expected to budget at critical points in life. Leavitt and Hanson (1950) believed that "only two groups of persons of necessity should plan and keep a detailed budget: (1) newly wedded couples who have not yet had a chance to test their ability to live within their incomes; and (2) married couples ... who find themselves in financial difficulties or who think they should save more of their incomes." We would add (3) newly divorced persons whose expenses suddenly rise as they establish separate households and incur legal fees. Budgeting is needed most by those in danger of bankruptcy, but is useful to anyone who wishes to allocate expenditures rationally. Couples who want to get the most for their money (spending it in accordance with their needs and values) find budgeting a means of seeing their financial picture as a whole.

Budgeting strikes a balance between income and various possible expenditures. Fixed obligations such as mortgage payments determine budgetary allotments in advance. Whyte noted a trend toward "budgetism," increasing the proportion of expenditures that were contractually scheduled:

> This does not mean that they actually keep formal budgets. Quite the contrary; the beauty of budgetism is that one doesn't have to keep a budget at all. It's done automatically.... Just as young couples are now paying winter oil bills in equal monthly fractions through the

year, so they seek to spread out all the other heavy seasonal obligations they can anticipate: Christmas presents, real-estate taxes, birthdays, spring cleaning, outfitting the children for school. If vendors will not oblige by accepting equal monthly installments, the purchasers will smooth out the load themselves by floating loans (1957: 356–57).

No matter how committed a couple are to fixed costs, they always have marginal areas that are discretionary: food, clothing, recreation, and contributions can vary widely and are usefully planned in advance—not in terms of what is to be bought, but of how much is to be spent in each category.

The first budget is the most difficult. Planning the first year of marriage requires shooting in the dark. What guidelines can new couples use? Previous expenditures for personal items may not change much with marriage. The costs of keeping house can be learned better from others who have just set up housekeeping than from parents who've long since equipped their houses and moved into higher income brackets.

Even couples of the same age and income provide hardly more than a point of departure. Each couple's values shape their distribution of money. No one need adhere to a standard plan. If they choose to sink money in a particular direction, that's their privilege.

Every couple must work out their own financial destiny. Lists of "proper" percentages can be more hindrance than help if taken as inflexible rules rather than as suggestive guides. Even the budget's categories should reflect personal predilections. Those with a passion for photography or music will need separate categories for their hobbies, while others can lump these costs under recreation. From year to year, as interests wane and new needs arise, categories will change accordingly. A good financial plan allocates (1) to those categories that are significant to the couple, (2) those amounts of money that will yield the maximum satisfaction.

Few budgets pinpoint just what the money in each category must be spent on. Rather, they guarantee that "X" dollars a month will be there to spend as the food buyer sees fit. There is still freedom to decide whether to have chicken or pork chops tomorrow. Persons limited to $200 a year for clothes may still choose between summer or winter clothes. The fact that they can't afford both reflects their income more than the budget. The budget just makes their limits unmistakably plain.

Those who wish to maximize their freedom can specify a "miscellaneous" item or personal allowances, spendable will-o'-the-wisp:

> Sylvia is terribly frugal about records. She thinks it's wonderful the way you can borrow them from libraries. I like to buy lots of them and get a keen pleasure out of coming in the room and seeing that long shelf of records, even though I may not play any one of them very regularly. Since I haven't been able to sell her yet on the value of buying records, we put

fat $25 a month personal allowance in the budget, which gives me a chance to go ahead and buy them whenever I want to.

Though plans are usually made a year in advance, they can always be revised to meet new circumstances. Especially the first year, revisions must be expected. Beginning planners typically overlook Christmas and wedding presents, vacation trips, newspapers and magazines, dry cleaning and shoe repairs, lunches away from home, liquor and tobacco, entertaining, contributions, and savings for emergencies. These need not be separate items, but the budget should provide somewhere for these "little" costs that can add up to so much.

Although making a budget takes a lot of work, it saves subsequent spats. To apply it requires keeping records to show where the money has gone so far. Tallying up the month's expenses takes time, but filling out an income tax long form depends on such records. Until couples get on their feet, the dividends of budgeting are likely to be worth the investment.

A budget is not a panacea. Couples who lack the prerequisites for rational problem solving will probably violate it. Even for disciplined couples, it is never more than a prediction of how money will be spent. Inevitably, actual expenditures will differ from the prediction. But any forecasting is better than none, especially for people subject to impulse buying:

> *When we first got married, Tom would cash his monthly paycheck, pay the bills, and buy things with very little thought of how we would meet the expenses of the last half of the month. We would eat quite well the first two weeks and skimp the last two. I would accuse him of being stupid when it came to handling money. I urged him to budget our money but he said he couldn't—it made him nervous. Finally we came to realize that he definitely is not a mathematician. So we agreed that I should take over the responsibility of budgeting our money to meet all the demands. This way he isn't frustrated by a task he isn't temperamentally suited for, and I have a free hand to use my skill for the benefit of the whole family.*

With increased experience, many couples gain a "feel" for money that requires less detailed control. The more rapidly their income rises, the less the danger of bankruptcy. Hence the need for planning gradually decreases. In changing circumstances, however, and especially when change is for the worse, systematic decision making helps prevent disaster and maximizes returns from limited resources.

Specific Plans. Budgeting is the most comprehensive form of planning. Regardless of whether a couple budget their routine expenses, it is useful to plan unusual expenditures. When a major appliance or new car is to be bought or the house is to be redecorated, planning is more efficient.

In a study of three generations of families in the Twin Cities, Hill (1963) found that the larger the proportion of planned actions, the more efficient the financial decisions. Efficiency rose with planning for a particular time rather than for a vague "sometime" in the future. Long-range planning frequently suffered from imponderables. The most definite planning was geared to the short term—the next step to be taken, given the known facts.

Consumer satisfaction was enhanced most by rational decision making:

1. securing information about costs of the desired object and of alternatives

2. considering the long-range consequences as well as the immediate effects of the purchase

3. conferring with the family so that all affected persons' views were considered

4. securing a family agreement on the action to be taken

Families that took the time to plan their expenditures were less likely to regret their purchases later.

Hill found that the better a couple communicated, the more effective was their "consumership." However, most couples got sloppier as time went on. At first they shopped around and planned together, but as the years went by they bought more impulsively. In a later report from the same study, Hill described these progressive changes as follows:

> As a marriage begins, the couples have much to learn about each other. Facing the necessity of planning together they begin through discussion to achieve marital consensus (one of the components of marital integration). As the marriage seasons, the couples having the highest consensus have less need to articulate a plan before taking action because they have at hand long term policies on which actions are based. Thus, high marital integration will appear increasingly associated with low pre-planning of actions, and low marital integration will be associated with the necessity to pre-plan because the couples dare not risk taking action without having first made out a plan (1970: 216).

In other words, as time goes on couples in touch with each other can afford to risk buying spontaneously because they can guess each other's reactions. Similarly, high-income couples in Hill's sample planned less than low-income couples because they could afford to make mistakes and preferred to save time rather than money.

These findings suggest that planning and budgeting are most urgent for newly married couples with modest incomes who cannot afford the spontaneity of planless buying. For other couples, planning may be less urgent; nevertheless, Hill found that couples under all circumstances were more satisfied with their consumer expenditures the more rational and less impulsive they were. So planning always has at least a marginal payoff.

Allowances

Most families give their children an allowance that they can use for spending money. In our family, each son's allowance went up automatically on his birthday, and all four boys were subject to the same formula. In those preinflation days, the formula was five cents times the number of years of age. Having a general formula meant everyone recognized the impartiality of the system, even though at any one time each boy's allowance was different from all the others. The allowance could be spent on anything. In adolescence, a supplementary allowance was earmarked for clothes, so each boy took responsibility for buying his clothes with that weekly sum.

Table 20–3 shows that adolescent girls were more apt to spend money on clothes than on anything else. This may reflect both the importance of clothes in their value system and a transfer of responsibility for clothes buying from the parents. That transfer was seldom complete, however, since less than one fourth of the 61 percent of 17–18-year-olds who spent money on clothes bought all or most of their clothes. The decline in recreational spending after age 16 presumably reflected increased dating paid for by their partners.

Nye (1958) found that impartiality was important to the girls in his sample. Girls were more apt to become delinquent if they thought their

Table 20–3 Spending of Own Money, by Age of Girl

	AGE OF GIRL		
Expense	Under 14	14–16	Over 16
Clothes	40%	57%	61%
Recreation	40%	40%	25%
School expenses	18%	19%	29%
Personal expenses	10%	11%	13%
Gifts, contributions	16%	8%	10%
Savings	20%	14%	12%
Number of cases	844	922	259

Adapted from Douvan and Kaye, 1956: 87. *Source:* National sample of secondary school girls aged 11 to 18. Figures refer to the percentage of girls of that age who spent any of their own money for the specified purpose. Totals add to more than 100% because respondents could name more than one category of expenditure. "Own money" included allowances, gifts, and earnings.

mothers sometimes or often gave more money to their siblings than to themselves. For boys, delinquency was triggered when the father seemed stingy compared to the fathers of friends. Either situation led young people to feel gypped and to rebel in delinquent acts. This does not mean that the most generous parents had the best relationships with their children. Children of both sexes, especially boys, were more apt to become delinquent if their parents gave them relatively large allowances or if they had money at their disposal from outside earnings. Nye believed that having lots of money enabled boys to buy cars and get into trouble when they were away from home. If this interpretation is correct, money was not so much the intrinsic source of trouble as having a car. Nye's analysis of the latter factor showed that 40 to 43 percent of boys and girls who owned cars were delinquent compared to 24 to 25 percent of those who never had access even to the family car.

MAJOR EXPENSES

Budgeting and budgetism take care of routine expenses. Items too large for current income require special arrangements. We have already mentioned college education and retirement expenses. Others arise earlier— buying a car and buying and equipping a house. Since couples usually buy a car, furniture, and appliances first and their house later, we will consider them in that order.

Automobile Ownership

In urban areas with mass transit, automobile ownership is optional. But for most families, owning at least one car is a necessity. Options lie chiefly

Table 20-4   Depreciation, by Size of Car and Year of Ownership

Year of Ownership	SIZE OF CAR			Standard/ Subcompact $ Ratio
	Standard	Compact	Subcompact	
First	25%	14%	12%	3.2X
Second	15	13	11	2.1X
Third	13	12	11	1.8X
Fourth	10	11	11	1.4X
Total	63%	50%	45%	2.2X

Computed from Liston and Aiken, 1976: 13–15. *Source:* Depreciation in the value of cars driven 10,000 miles per year in suburban Baltimore. The totals show that at the end of four years, standard cars were worth only the residual 37% of their original purchase price, whereas subcompacts were still worth 55% of their original purchase price.

in the size and vintage of car to be purchased and in the length of keeping it before trading it in.

Table 20–4 shows that standard cars depreciated faster than smaller ones. Not until the fourth year did depreciation for any size shrink to a level commensurate with the increased age of the car.

Families buying large cars pay a heavy premium if they trade that car in every year. In this study the original price of standard cars was 1.6 times that of subcompacts. When the higher price and faster depreciation of standard cars were taken together, they depreciated three times as much during the first year as subcompacts. This means that persons who buy large, expensive cars must hold them a relatively long time if they wish to escape the heavy cost of early-year depreciation. By contrast, owners of smaller cars can trade them in more frequently with less loss.

Equipment for Family Living

Most newly married couples live in apartments. The easiest place to begin keeping house is in an apartment already equipped with major appliances and furniture. Renting furnished enables couples to concentrate on buying cars for access to jobs and recreation. Many couples move next to an unfurnished apartment or house, buying furniture and appliances if they don't already own them.

Hill (1970) found that young married couples in the Twin Cities generally purchased a range, refrigerator, washer, radio, and sofa during their first year. Practically all couples owned these by the time they had been married five years. A vacuum cleaner and television were usually next on the list, but not bought until the second year and not by quite as many couples. Next came carpeting, a sewing machine, a coffee maker, and a dining table, owned by 56 to 79 percent of the group and purchased within the first couple of years. These dozen items constituted a typical inventory (aside from a car and smaller items) of couples who had been married five years or so.

The larger the number of durable goods a couple bought, the worse off financially couples felt at the end of the year, presumably because they bought so many on credit and went deeply in debt. The most urgent requirement for buying appliances was buying a home. Home buyers bought six times as many items as usual during the three-month interval in which they moved into their first house.

Buying on Credit.
One element in Whyte's "budgetism" was buying on credit whenever possible. Most families used credit in buying houses and cars, but only a minority did so for smaller items. The more expensive the item, the fewer the families able to pay cash. The lower their income or the higher their expenses, the less the couple will have left over with which to make payments on a given item, so the longer the period over

which they will need to spread repayment in order to afford it. But Table 20–5 shows that the longer the repayment period and the lower the monthly payment, the greater the total interest cost becomes, and therefore the greater the cost of purchasing on credit.

Some families use credit even for inexpensive items. But installment buying is a costly alternative to paying cash:

> A mythical couple we will call the Frugals decide to defer all but necessary purchases for enough months to accumulate an extra $500. They will then have a revolving fund of their own which they can use for cash purchases, and instead of paying a fixed amount each month in installment loans, they will use these sums to replenish the $500.
>
> Now let's take a normal couple. The Joneses, with precisely the same income, don't put off purchases, but instead commit themselves to a combination of installment loans and revolving-credit plans. At the end of ten years the Joneses would have paid out somewhere around $800 in interest. The Frugals, by contrast, would have earned interest—roughly $150. Not counting the extra benefits they would have reaped by being able to buy for cash, they would be, in toto, almost a thousand dollars better off (Whyte, 1957: 360–61).

In these days of discount stores selling only for cash, the benefits to the Frugals are likely to be even greater.

Credit is expensive (see Table 20–6). Sometimes, as in buying a house, it is worth the cost. In every case the cost must be weighed against the loss suffered in postponing the purchase until cash could be accumulated. The lower the cost and the less urgent the purchase, the greater the advantage of waiting to pay cash.

> *When Peter was little we read a story about a family who moved to the country. First they bought a cow and then they waited awhile, saved up their money until they seemed to need a pig, and after that they waited again until they really did want some chickens and a rooster. Later it was some sheep for wool and finally a horse to ride. Each time they really wanted it and needed it and between times they had time to get acquainted*

Table 20–5   Monthly Payments and Total Cost of Purchase, by Number of Payments

Cost of Repaying $360 at 17.5% Annual Interest Charge	NUMBER OF MONTHLY PAYMENTS		
	12	*18*	*24*
Monthly payment	$ 32.83	$ 22.77	$ 17.73
Total interest	$ 34.00	$ 49.87	$ 65.62
Total cost ($360 plus interest)	$394.00	$409.87	$425.62

Adapted from Household Finance Corporation, 1970: 31.

Table 20-6   Interest Rates for Consumer Loans, by Source

Source	Limitations	Annual Interest Rates
Life insurance companies	Cash value of policies held	5–6%
Credit unions	Loan to members only	9–12%
Commercial banks		
(a) Passbook loans and other secured loans	Limited to savings on hand or value of collateral	8½–12%
(b) Unsecured loans	For home improvements, car purchases, etc.	11–18%
(c) Credit card plans	Limit depends on credit rating of customer	15–18%
Consumer finance companies	Specialize in small loans	15–36%

Adapted from Household Finance Corporation, 1970: 20–21. Note that although interest charges may vary in subsequent years, the rank order of rates for these sources is likely to remain stable.

and enjoy the newly purchased animal and after each acquisition the whole family agreed that their family seemed just right for then.

That was a metaphor to me for the way I felt about our household purchases. Each new purchase came only after we had thoroughly integrated the last one. Each addition was very special. We never bought on credit, only what we could afford. I felt like a pioneer at times and was proud that we were never in debt. I kept thinking if we had had it all at once there would be nothing to look forward to.

Housing for Family Living

Low down payments on mortgages make it possible to buy a house sooner after marriage. Low down payments have one disadvantage, however. The lower the down payment, the higher the monthly payments. To ease the strain on the child-rearing years, it is desirable to have monthly payments as small as possible. Hence, it is valuable to make the largest possible down payment. To protect savings toward this purpose from disappearing in current expenditures, they need to be transferred from a couple's checking account to a savings account (where they will have the added advantage of earning interest).

At any particular time, families may not have any choice about the interest rate they will pay since rates in a given community tend to be uniform. Table 20-7 shows how higher interest rates affect the size of the monthly payment relatively little, but affect the proportion going toward interest much more. The main factor determining how much interest a family eventually will pay is not the interest rate, however, but the length of time for which the money is borrowed. The faster the rate of repayment,

Table 20–7   Monthly Payments and Total Interest Charges on $20,000 Mortgage, by Interest Rate and Repayment Period

| | ANNUAL INTEREST RATE | | | |
| | 7% | | 9% | |
Repayment Period	Monthly Payment	Total Interest Charge	Monthly Payment	Total Interest Charge
10 years	$232	$ 7,866	$253	$10,402
15 years	$180	$12,359	$203	$16,513
20 years	$155	$17,214	$180	$23,188
25 years	$141	$22,408	$168	$30,352
30 years	$133	$27,902	$161	$37,931

Adapted from Household Finance Corporation, 1971: 31. Monthly payments include principal and interest only. Taxes and insurance costs would be additional.

the less the total interest. Table 20–7 shows that at 7 percent interest the cost of a $20,000 mortgage loan is doubled in less than 25 years, while at 9 percent it is doubled in less than 20 years and almost tripled if the repayment extends over 30 years. Particularly noticeable is the staggering increase in total interest cost for a marginal lowering in monthly payment when the repayment is extended over 30 years instead of 25. This suggests the wisdom of paying mortgages off as fast as practicable, rather than taking a mortgage out for the longest period to which a lender is agreeable.

Higher Education for Children

Paying for children's college educations is one of the most difficult tasks faced by families, especially if their children are spaced so closely together that more than one is in college at the same time. As early as the 1950s, almost half the parents of college students felt they were not helping their children enough (Lansing, 1960). The lower the family income and the larger the number of children, the larger the proportion of parents having difficulty. For the academic year 1959–60, parents paid for 61 percent of their children's total expenses, students earned 23 percent, scholarships provided 9 percent, and miscellaneous sources the remaining 7 percent. Where did parents get their share?

Table 20–8 shows that less than half the families saved any money in advance. For those who did, the college years were less difficult. (In 1959, Roper found that only 39 percent of parents expecting to send children to college had begun saving.)

Theoretically, borrowing money fits the life cycle better than saving it in advance. If the average family has a financial surplus *after* children

Table 20–8 Sources of Funds for Children's College Expenses

Source of Funds	Percentage of All Parents of College Students
Saved money in advance	48%
Current income, reduced expenses	44
Mother worked more	19
Father worked more	8
Borrowed money	8
Total	127%

Adapted from Lansing, 1960: 52. *Source:* National sample of parents of students in college 1955–60. Total adds to more than 100% because some families used more than one method.

go to college, it should be easier to repay borrowed funds than to set aside savings during the lean years while children are growing up. Most families could secure thousands of dollars by refinancing the mortgage on their home.

Table 20–8 shows that borrowing was rare. It was chiefly an act of desperation by those in the greatest financial difficulty. Extra work by the father or mother, similarly, was forced on those whose past or present incomes were not adequate for setting aside the necessary amounts.

Advance saving was the most popular method of financing. Where was it saved? Parents invested their college savings in the following places (in order of frequency): (1) savings accounts; (2) endowment insurance; (3) government bonds; and (4) common stocks (interpolated from Lansing, 1960, and Roper, 1960).

Savings Accounts.   The most popular investment was in savings accounts. This relies on parental self-discipline to put money in the account and to leave it there. Roper's respondents listed as one of the major "advantages" of a savings account the fact that it could "be used for other things" besides education. This liquidity means savings accounts are frequently multipurpose affairs, not restricted to educational purposes. They are often raided in family crises, leaving the children lucky if their educational funds survive intact.

Endowment Insurance.   An insurance policy designed to mature when the child reaches college age provides for regular payment whenever the bill arrives. It insures against the premature death of the breadwinner provided the policy is written on the life of the parent with the child as beneficiary. (Unfortunately, the child's life is often insured instead.)

Some form of insurance is necessary to protect a child against the death of the parent before college funds have been accumulated. Families that invest their savings in more profitable directions should insure the parent enough to cover the interval during which savings are accumulating. Decreasing term insurance (see below) is especially appropriate for this purpose.

Government Bonds. "Safety" was the chief appeal of government bonds. Where payroll-deduction, bond-a-month plans exist, they also have the forced payment advantages of endowment insurance. However, since they come in small denominations, there is more temptation to cash in "just one" bond than to liquidate a whole insurance policy. Like insurance policies, government bonds carry maturity dates that discourage the raiding to which savings accounts are subject.

Common Stocks. Rarest of the four methods of investment was the purchase of common stocks, either directly or through mutual investment funds. Unlike the fixed return from the other three methods, stocks bring a fluctuating return correlated with the fate of the economy. When the economy declines, stocks do too. Conversely, they gain during inflationary periods. A study by the University of Chicago showed that the average annual income in capital gains with dividends reinvested on all stocks on the New York Stock Exchange was more than 9 percent per year over the 40-year period between 1926 and 1965. This high rate of return is remarkable in view of the fact that this period included the Great Depression when the stock market fell to record lows.

Common stock is especially lucrative when held long enough to amortize the broker's fees over ten or more years. Like other piecemeal investments, it requires supplementary insurance. King (1954) recommended that reliance not be placed exclusively on fluctuating investments, but on a combination with fixed-return savings to provide a hedge against deflation. The long-run trends in the United States are inflationary. Hence families should investigate the higher returns and the hedge against inflation that Roper's stock purchasers valued.

For a few families, real estate investments served the same purpose. Though a poor market may make it difficult to liquidate by selling out, real estate (like most forms of saving) can be used as collateral for borrowed funds.

Retirement Income

The problems of retirement income are similar to those with college expenses. In both cases many years are available for accumulating the necessary reserves. For retirement income, Social Security provides a cushion but must be supplemented. The investments discussed for college savings are also available. However, if college expenses 20 years hence are difficult to predict, retirement has the added enigma that death is even less predictable. The starting date for retirement can be planned but the end cannot. It is necessary, therefore, to rely on annuities (insurance policies that will yield income as long as the beneficiary lives). Such policies spread the risk of longevity among a large enough group to be able to support even those who "survive to one hundred and five." They guarantee support not only to the couple after retirement, but to the widow for the decade or more by which the typical wife outlives her husband. Many companies have compulsory retirement pensions. For families who have not previously saved enough, launching the last child is a signal to set aside a major portion of income.

INVESTMENT

Much of what has been said about investing savings toward special purposes applies to general investment as well. Once the major costs of family living have been met, affluent families have a margin to spare. By investing in stocks directly or through mutual funds, buying rental property, and so on, such families augment their annual income.

Table 20–9 shows that most couples had some liquid assets from the beginning of marriage, and that the proportion without savings decreased the longer they were married. Savings accounts in banks and other financial institutions were the preferred depository for liquid assets, partly because of accessibility and partly for ease of withdrawal. The next most popular investment was government bonds. But as time passed, more couples moved into the stock market (and more held all three types of investments).

We are impressed with the ability of these families to accumulate diversified liquid assets during the early years of marriage when they were also buying furniture, buying houses, and having babies. The fact that they were able to do so many things simultaneously must have re-

Table 20–9 Liquid Investments, by Year of Marriage

	YEAR OF MARRIAGE					
Liquid Investment	*1*	*2*	*3*	*4*	*5*	*6–10*
Savings only	42%	38%	40%	41%	44%	48%
Government bonds with/without savings but no stocks	24	26	30	27	26	19
Stocks with/without savings and/or bonds	3	6	8	6	7	18
None	31	30	22	26	23	15
Total	100%	100%	100%	100%	100%	100%
Number of cases	102	97	85	74	61	46

Adapted from Hill, 1970: 127. *Source:* 102 couples under age 30 in the Twin Cities area of Minnesota.

quired considerable financial planning. Hill reported that accumulation of liquid assets was facilitated for many couples by participation in systematic savings programs such as payroll deduction plans.

Dividends, rents, and other investment income may be plowed back into a pyramiding estate or used to supplement earned income. The latter enables people to take risks in changing jobs or occupations. It frees them to go back to school, to travel, or to volunteer their services for the public welfare.

INSURANCE AGAINST CATASTROPHE

The purpose of most forms of insurance is to spread the cost of unpredictable catastrophes among large numbers of people, so that the unlucky few who get hit can be reimbursed by the contributions of the lucky many who escape.

Property Insurance

Though the chief risk of losing a home is from fire, "extended coverage" for storms and other threats costs little more than fire insurance alone. Comprehensive home insurance policies cover liability for damages incurred on the property and theft of personal belongings. Package policies are less expensive than separate ones covering the same risks.

In an era when the value of houses appreciates due to inflation rather than depreciates with wear and tear and obsolescence, one problem is that the value of insurance tends to fall behind the rising value of property. Some insurance companies have responded to this problem with provisions for automatic annual increases in the amount of coverage to reflect the rising value of the insured property.

Cash buying, as usual, saves installment costs. Families thrifty enough to pay for insurance annually pay less than the cost of more frequent installments.

Automobile Insurance

The chief threat of economic disaster in owning an automobile is not what others may do to my car but what I may do to them. If I have a new or expensive car, I may wish to protect myself against having to replace it. Indeed, if I don't own the car outright but am only buying it piece by piece, the finance company may require me to protect *its* investment by carrying collision insurance.

Otherwise, it is more economical to bear the collision risk myself, especially for cars whose value has depreciated. Even for new cars, the insurance problem is how to pay for big bumps, not little ones. It is cheaper to choose deductible clauses that insure against damage above a certain amount (such as $100). Nondeductible insurance is exorbitant because rates must be high enough to cover the cost of processing petty claims.

Liability insurance is another matter. An automobile can wreak destruction on life and property totaling thousands of dollars in damage suits. Liability insurance protects me from bankruptcy should I incur such a financial obligation, and protects my victims by guaranteeing sufficient resources to meet that obligation.

Health Insurance

The cost of medical care has risen faster than the cost of living. As medical science becomes more specialized and medical equipment more elaborate, the possibility of disastrous medical bills multiplies. As with collision insurance, there is little need to cover everyday medical costs. These can be budgeted almost as predictably as other current expenses. The insurance problem involves the rare but catastrophic long illness or major surgery that costs thousands of dollars.

"Major medical insurance" has a thrifty deductible clause for bills under $100 or so per family member. When bills run sky high, major medical insurance takes over.

Life Insurance

The worst thing that can happen to a family financially is to lose a parent while the children are young. This means losing hundreds of thousands of dollars of potential income, compared to which losses through illness, fire, or auto accidents are trifling. The chances of any given parent's premature death are small, but the consequences are so severe that this risk deserves to be spread by means of insurance.

Life-cycle Changes in Insurance Needs. The purpose of insurance is to provide money for recouping economic losses or meeting expenses that could not otherwise be met.

To lose a child will not bankrupt a family. After burial expenses have been met, the burden on the family income is reduced by one less dependent. Hence, insurance need not be taken on the life of a child.

Losing a spouse is costly. To be sure, if there are no children, the survivor could take care of him/herself again so childless couples have no need for life insurance. However, a stay-at-home mother of young children is less easily dispensed with. The father cannot stay home to care for the children, so there would be babysitting and housekeeper expenses. If the husband's life were adequately insured, there might be some point in insuring the wife's, too, during the years when she is caring for dependent children.

Where both partners are employed and the family is dependent on both their earnings, life insurance needs to take into consideration the consequences of the loss of each partner's income. Would there be any decrease in the family's cost of living with one less adult to maintain? If so, the loss of one partner's income may not need to be replaced fully by insurance. Would Social Security provide benefits to surviving dependent children? Again, insurance needs are reduced accordingly. Once the rock-bottom survival needs of the family are computed, it may make sense to insure both partners' lives proportionately to their incomes. If one partner earns twice as much as the other, this implies putting two thirds of the insurance coverage on that one and one third on the the other.

Few families insure their breadwinners adequately. As of 1973, the Institute of Life Insurance reported that the average family carried enough insurance to replace the family income for only two years. To be sure, Social Security provides almost half the average husband's income for the duration of the children's dependent years, but where is the other half to come from after the insured four half years are used up? The average American family would suffer at least a 50 percent cut in its standard of living should the breadwinner die early. (The higher the family income, the greater the loss, since Social Security benefits are proportionately smaller.) To prevent this hardship, families need enough insurance to close the gap between Social Security and their normal living costs until the youngest child reaches maturity. If this gap were $10,000 per year and the youngest child had 20 years to maturity, a family would need $200,000 worth of insurance (disregarding the complexities of compound interest). Although $200,000 would be needed the first year, only $190,000 is necessary the next year, and so on, until nothing is needed after the last child leaves home.

The basic life insurance needed by a family begins at zero in the honeymoon phase but hits higher peaks with the birth of each succeeding child. After the last child is born, the need declines to zero when s/he leaves home.

The most insurance is needed just when family economic resources are lowest. Hence the average family needs insurance that is as inexpensive as possible and that declines in value from year to year. Only one type of insurance offers these features.

Types of Life Insurance. The following list (adapted from Morgan, 1955: 163) shows the approximate annual cost of insurance with an initial value of $200,000 purchased at age 30:

20–year endowment	$9,230
20–payment life	$6,180

Ordinary life insurance (paid up at 85) $3,880

20–year term insurance $1,470

20–year decreasing term insurance $ 780

"Decreasing term insurance" is the only form that most families can afford during the child-rearing years and the only one that decreases from maximum value at the beginning to zero at the end. Any form of term insurance is pure insurance with no investment. Like fire insurance, which repays only in the event of fire, it pays off only if the owner dies during the term of the policy. Decreasing term comes under a variety of names, often called"mortgage protection" insurance since it decreases at a rate similar to a mortgage loan. Or it may be called "income protection" insurance. For pure insurance geared to the child-rearing phase of the family life cycle, it is the best buy. It must be supplemented, however, by other means of saving for educational and retirement expenses (in case the parent survives).

All other forms of insurance are so expensive that they limit most buyers to too little coverage in the early years when need is greatest. On the other hand, they would provide more coverage than necessary in the later years if they were taken out in adequate amounts at the beginning of childbearing. As a result, most young families have too little insurance and many middle-aged couples have too much.

Other forms of insurance cost more because they return more—more than the minimum needed for protecting children against the premature death of the parent. Families who can afford it may wish to buy these "extras." But extras should not take precedence over the basic requirement of providing enough pure insurance.

"Ordinary life insurance" is the commonest form. Premiums are paid as long as the individual lives (or up to a certain age, such as the 85 shown in the list). Whenever the individual dies, the beneficiary gets the face value of the policy. In the meantime, the policy gradually increases in loan value or cash surrender value, since it combines savings with death protection.

"Variable life insurance" provides a guaranteed minimum death benefit, but offers the possibility of increased death benefits if the insurance company's investments in the stock market pay off in increased earnings. In times of rising stock prices, this kind of insurance brings increased earnings that offset the erosion in the value of insurance that otherwise comes with inflation. Another way of coping with inflation is a cost-of-living rider that some insurance companies make available to purchasers of conventional life insurance. This provides for the addition of enough one-year insurance each year to the original policy to compensate for increases in the Consumer Price Index that have occurred in the meantime. This guarantees that the purchasing power of the owner's death benefits will not erode as a result of the rising cost of living. The cost of the additional term insurance is added to the customer's annual bill for the total insurance package.

"Twenty-payment life" insurance is limited-payment insurance. At the end of 20 years, the policy is completely paid for and remains in force for the life of the insured. If I wanted to buy insurance at age 45, I might choose this kind so my payments would be completed before I retired.

"Twenty-year endowment" pays full value should the insured die during the 20-year interval. If s/he survives, the company pays the face amount to the beneficiary at that time. This is primarily a savings program with the insurance feature added. It is the most popular form of insured savings for children's college expenses.

"Family income" insurance combines ordinary life with decreasing term insurance. The Household Finance Corporation (1973) reported that it was less expensive than buying the two types of insurance separately.

Group insurance is not a different type of coverage but a different means of purchasing it. Individuals who are employed by a company or belong to a professional association or other common interest group that has made arrangements for all their members to be eligible to purchase insurance from a particular insurance company are able to secure that insurance more cheaply than if they were to purchase it on the open market as individuals. Buying insurance on a group basis is preferable to buying it separately.

Families who rely on insurance policies to cover both their protection and savings needs often combine different types of policies in varying amounts. Families seeking higher returns on their savings may use decreasing term insurance for maximum protection at lowest cost while they invest their savings in stocks and other equities.

One option in most forms of insurance is a disability waiver of premiums. If the parent is disabled and cannot work, the family is in a fix. The fix can be relieved slightly by policy provisions that waive the necessity of paying further premiums in case the insured is unable to work. Such provisions cost slightly more but provide added protection.

Theoretically, it would be desirable to carry insurance that would provide family income in the event of the parent's disability. Unfortunately, Morgan (1955) concluded that such insurance was too expensive and too hedged with limitations to be worthwhile.

4

CRISES AND OPPORTUNITIES

Although we have dealt with problems before, most of this book has been written with the attitude that they can be solved if only couples will go at them sensibly. But in an era when large numbers of families are falling apart, to assume that problems will be solved is over-optimistic. We will end this book, therefore, by examining the ways in which marriages end and in most cases are replaced by subsequent marriages.

Before we reach the point where some marriages fall apart, we need to pay attention to the more widespread process by which most marriages go downhill. In acute cases, deterioration leads to divorce. In less acute cases, it saps the vitality that led couples to get married in the first place, which they had assumed would stay alive throughout their marriage.

Deterioration is natural, but this doesn't mean it is inevitable. Alternatively, some marriages progress and mature year after year after year. This growth is the alternative to deterioration.

21 Growth or Deterioration

We suggested in the introduction to this section that deterioration is the usual fate of marriage. Evidence comes from numerous studies and manifests itself in numerous facets of marriage—subjective and objective. In this chapter, we will first portray the declining interaction that most couples experience and the corresponding disappointment that they feel. This poses a challenge to marriage, which we hope will alarm our readers and stimulate them to invest energy in keeping *their* marriage alive and growing. We will then analyze some of the things that couples can do to counteract the normal corrosions of time, which can turn a long-term relationship into a source of personal growth.

DETERIORATION

The average marriage coasts downhill. The longer it lasts, the lower it sinks. Partly the decline is psychological, an ebbing enthusiasm for the partner. But it is also pragmatic in the sense that partners become disengaged from one another. Some marriages fall apart. Others not only resist decay but grow and develop. In between are the bulk of marriages—superficially intact but steadily less cohesive.

Disenchantment

Most couples lose their enthusiasm. Although they prized the partner at first, each gradually takes the other for granted and sees him/her more prosaically. Not that the marriage necessarily turns sour, but the taste goes flat.

Figure 21–1 shows that Detroit wives found their marriages less satisfactory as time went on. Fifty-two percent were "very satisfied" during the first two years of marriage, but only 6 percent were after 20 years. In the same groups, the proportion of "very dissatisfied" wives jumped from zero to 21 percent of those still married (after the loss of the divorced).

Gurin (1960) also found that older married couples were less enthusiastic than younger couples. This might mean only that marriages were getting better with the passing decades, since neither of the previous studies dealt with the same families over time. However, Pineo (1961) studied the same couples over a 20-year interval and found that husbands and wives declined significantly in their love for each other and in their confidence in the permanence of their marriage.

People tend to rationalize this disenchantment, saying that love doesn't matter—after it is gone. Feldman (1966) found that older couples valued sex, having children, feeling needed, and being in love less than young couples. But this devaluation of interpersonal relationships seems to us precisely the result of disenchantment.

Two factors contribute to this waning enthusiasm: the transition from anticipation to fulfillment and the transformation of a new relationship into an old one.

From Anticipation to Fulfillment. In earlier chapters we suggested that much of the excitement of falling in love comes from anticipating new experiences. Marriage is the culmination of earlier hopes. Competitive insecurity changes to committed security.

Figure 21-1 Wife's Marital Satisfaction, by Length of Marriage

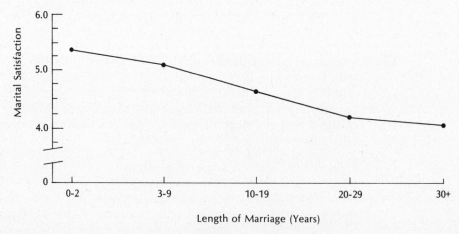

Adapted from Blood and Wolfe, 1960: 264. *Source:* Representative sample of Detroit married women.

Many years ago, Levy and Munroe labeled this process "disillusionment" and gave a classic illustration three years after marriage:

Mary Jane's frock for mornings at home looks a little frayed and faded. Her apron has definitely seen neither Lux nor a harsh washing soap for several days. She scrapes dispiritedly at the breakfast plates, slightly repulsive with congealed egg yolk and slimy cold bacon grease. For the fourteenth time she exhorts Junior to stop dawdling and eat his cereal. She is not at the moment enjoying her marriage very much. Why should she? Washing dishes day in and day out is not the same thing as canoeing in the moonlight with your heart's beloved.... She is remembering five o'clock with Jim waiting at the corner, [thinking] of dinner and dancing, of going to the movies, or a concert, or the theater, or just a long ferryboat ride. Of the difficult goodnight kiss and the ecstatic knowledge that soon she would have Jim all the time for always. She is thinking rather wryly of how entrancing, how full of promise this battered dishpan looked when it first emerged from pink tissue paper at the shower the girls gave her. She may even think, a little cynically, as she surveys the gray grease-pocked surface of her dishwater, of the foaming pans of eternally virgin suds she expected from her perusal of the advertisements. Well, she's married now. She has her own house, her own dishpan, her husband, and her baby. All the time and for always. She doesn't even go to the movies any more because there's no one to stay with Junior. She speaks so crossly to the child now that his tears fall into the objectionable cereal. Why on earth won't Jim let her get Mrs. Oldacre in to stay evenings? He'll be earning more soon; Mr. Bayswater practically told him he would be put in charge of the branch office as soon as old Fuzzy retired. Five dollars a week savings—much good that does anyway. Mary Jane's thoughts about her husband become quite definitely uncharitable. "If he only had the least understanding of the kind of life I have, but all he notices is Junior's shoes are scuffed out and he wouldn't even try that Bavarian Cream I fixed yesterday. It's all very well for him to think Jimmy Junior's cute when he sneaks out of bed—he doesn't have him all day and all night and nothing but Jimmy Junior" (1945: 59–61).

Mary Jane was disillusioned because her marriage was not what she expected it to be. Naivete about what marriage will be like accentuates disenchantment. But even hard-headed realists who don't expect marriage to be all "canoeing in the moonlight" encounter a change of pace between going together and being married. Whereas dating gains intensity from its uncertainty, marriage loses intensity when it seems secure. Married persons make the mistake of thinking they have arrived and find the goal less exciting than the struggle to get there.

To think of getting married as having arrived is to disregard the fact that marriage is a process of endless change. Jourard (1975: 199) suggested that two widespread fallacies led couples to ignore the necessity of change:

One is the myth of the right partner. The other is the myth of the right to act so as to ensure peace, joy, and happiness. People believe, or are led to believe, that if they just find the right partner, the right answer to the riddle of their existence will be found. Once having found the right person and the way of relating that is satisfying at this time, the partners try to do everything to prevent change. That's tantamount to trying to stop the tide. Change, indeed, happens, but it happens underground, is concealed, and then it's introduced and experienced as a catastrophe. Instead of welcoming it, the partners find it devastating. Each may then seek to find someone who will not change, so that they never need face the need to change themselves.

Marriage partners become familiar only in the superficial sense that the other person still has the same name and looks about the same. For couples who fail to look below the surface and discover the inner changes that are at work in each other, marriage may seem to be in a rut. But the corrosion of time is sure to be going on unless they engage in constant dialogue to update their relationship.

From Novelty to Familiarity. Disenchantment takes place not only between dating and marriage but during marriage itself. Gradually the average person treasures the partner less (and takes him/her more for granted). At the beginning, the contrast is sharp between having a marriage partner and never having had one. Everything s/he does is appreciated. S/he is appreciated as a person. The newly married person is sensitive to the other's presence, aware of him/her as a new element in life. They miss each other when they are apart and look forward to seeing each other when they return.

By contrast, after enough years elapse, the spouse seems as familiar as a piece of furniture. Taken-for-grantedness is one way of describing the security of marriage. But, less happily, it means loss of appreciation. Familiarity breeds contempt not so much in the sense of downgrading the partner as ignoring him/her. The husband at breakfast with his head buried in the paper is the classic symbol of disinterest. Luckey (1966) found that the longer people had been married, the fewer favorable qualities and the more negative ones they saw in each other. Among the virtues that faded were affection, consideration, cooperation, gratefulness, and friendliness. Instead the spouse was increasingly perceived as selfish, bitter, touchy, hardhearted, cold, and unfeeling, and as always expecting others to admire them. Luckey's older respondents recognized more selfishness in themselves, too, but not as much more as they saw in their partners.

Accumulated Resentments. Time not only allows love to wither; it allows resentments to pile up. Some people hoard unresolved irritations and grievances in a store of ammunition that escalates new conflicts into irrational proportions. Any hope for future progress can be blocked by being stuck in the past. As the gunny sack of unresolved grievances grows heavier, good times never have a chance to materialize. Fear that past hurts will be repeated creates suspicion and mistrust. Only as two persons stay in the present can they keep clear of the muck that will contaminate their relationship.

Disengagement

Parallel with disenchanted feelings are disengaged practices. Ongoing marriages tend to see less and less interaction between partners. Disengagement begins all too soon. Within limits, it may be a good thing. In Chapter 10, we recognized that togetherness may be excessive. If husband and wife are to bloom individually, they cannot do everything together.

The trouble is that after most couples have been married very long, they do too little together. After the intimacy of the honeymoon comes the estrangement of marriage. Instead of stopping at the right point, disengagement goes too far. We have already seen in Chapter 9 that couples disengage sexually faster than is physiologically necessary. A similar decline affects most kinds of marital interaction.

Pineo (1961) found that most couples spent less leisure time together in the middle years of marriage than earlier. This decline especially affected outside activities—the kind that brought them together in the first place. If Mary Jane, three years after marriage, already recalled canoeing with nostalgia, how much more regret is she likely to feel 20 years later? In Pineo's sample, almost three-fourths of the middle-aged Mary Janes confessed that "dating" had fallen off. Similarly, Feldman's couples (1966) had fewer "gay times together" outside the home as they got older. Joint use of leisure declined, despite the fact that relatively few couples changed their preferred activities. Most continued to like the same things but did them less often together. Not only the amount but the proportion of shared to nonshared activities declined, suggesting that couples became disengaged from each other faster than from the rest of life:

> We have not had to work very hard at loving each other in our marriage. It's been almost too easy. Things that are easy aren't as good as they might be. Each of us is being drawn into more whirling circles, separate circles—his business work, his increasing responsibilities with the advancement of the Republican party, his public speaking. In each of these he has gained confidence and in each of these he feels needed and gains satisfaction. I too have gained new confidence in my talents and skills and could easily be swept into more and more responsibilities and friendships. So our energies are increasingly spent apart from each other.

If disengagement occurred only outside the home, it would be less serious. Yet it happens inside the home as well. As time goes by, couples pay less attention to each other, even when they are in the same room.

Figure 21–2 shows that the average Detroit husband reported back to his wife almost every day during the first few years of marriage. During the child-rearing years he shared things only a few times a week, and after the children grew up less than once a week. After retirement he had understandably little to say. Up to that point the decline was not due to changes in the amount of information at his disposal, so much as in his readiness to share it.

Lest it be thought that husbands are the only ones who disengage themselves, it should be acknowledged that wives do too. Blood and Wolfe found that new wives "usually" told their troubles to their husbands, whereas postparental wives did so only half the time.

Feldman (1966) found that the time spent in discussion and the frequency of discussing anything declined the longer couples were married. Topics like sex and in-laws, which demanded attention at the beginning of marriage, disappeared as relationships were worked out. Some new topics partially replaced them: repairs for aging houses, religion, and outside events—news, sports, and culture. In a later report on the same couples, Rollins and Feldman (1970) reported sharp declines in the frequency with which couples engaged in positive interaction—laughing together, calmly discussing something together, having a stimulating exchange of ideas, or working together on a common project. Whereas more

Figure 21-2 Frequency Husband Tells Day's Experiences, by Family Life Cycle

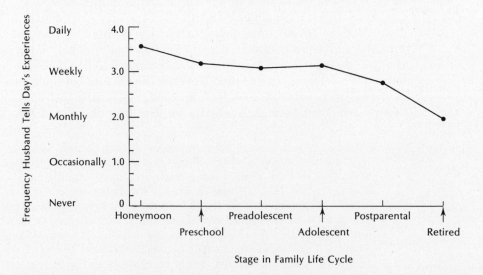

Adapted from Blood and Wolfe, 1960:158. *Source:* Representative sample of Detroit married women.

than 70 percent of childless young couples reported such interchanges at least once a day, less than half were still interacting daily after the first child arrived, and hardly more than a third of the couples who had been married longer than that.

Dizard (1968) found that as couples moved from the early to the middle years of marriage, they shifted from shared decision making to domination by either the husband or the wife. Similarly, Blood and Wolfe (1960) found that the longer Detroit marriages existed, the greater the trend toward making decisions separately. As time passed, husbands and wives talked less about decisions, leaving power in the hands of the partner with the greater interest. Since wives were interested in family affairs more consistently than husbands, decision making tended to become wife-dominant. Wives seldom seized power, but husbands often abdicated it.

Dizard found that as one partner came to make most of the decisions, the dropout partner was apt to resent that his/her views were not represented in those decisions. One result of the shift to unilateral decision making was that agreement between the partners on how to handle money, children, and in-laws declined. This decrease in consensus left couples unsure about whether they wanted to stay married.

Parallel to this decrease in joint decision making is a decrease in joint housework. Figure 21–3 shows that couples in the later stages of the family cycle shared fewer tasks than newly married couples. At first, keeping house together is fun. Newly married couples enjoy being together and care about one another so that they help each other out. As time wears on, however, the novelty of sharing wears off and each partner

Figure 21-3 Task Sharing, by Stage in Family Cycle

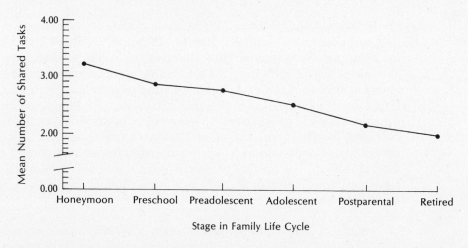

Adapted from Blood and Wolfe, 1960:70. Average number out of a total of eight tasks which are performed by both the husband and the wife at least occasionally.

tends to fall into a rut of doing certain tasks and leaving others to the spouse. Presumably, such specialization is efficient, but it undermines the togetherness of early marriage and alienates the partners from one another.

Thus, marriages that at first involve shared decisions and work tend over time to become segregated and specialized. This might not have caused problems if couples adapted their attitudes to their changing circumstances, but Dizard found that attitudes and practices increasingly diverged. While their marriages were becoming more traditional as they shared less in decision making and other activities, their attitudes toward marriage were becoming less traditional. No wonder, then, that they became increasingly dissatisfied with their marriages.

Apparently, disengagement is mutual and pervasive. One cause is the boredom that comes with experience. Some activities are attractive when new but less interesting after the novelty wears off. When sexual intercourse is new, couples explore and experiment. Once they have tried everything, intercourse becomes less intriguing. The incentive to engage in it diminishes. The same with talk. At first everything one partner encounters at work is new to the spouse. But as information is relayed from day to day, the partner's knowledge increases. Most of what might be said resembles what has been heard before. Maybe it should be said anyway, but the urgency wanes. My mother once told me (Bob):

> When we were first married, Dad told me about his patients. He was just getting started in practice and every new patient was another triumph on the road to success. I heard about every operation and struggled with all the diagnostic problems. Even though I didn't understand half of what he was talking about, it was exciting to sit there and listen to him. Now I hardly hear about it even if my best friend has cancer.

The Distraction of Children.   Children complicate a relationship. Usually they were wanted. Parents are glad to have them, wouldn't give them up for anything. Nevertheless, they interfere with marital interaction. We have already seen in Figure 21–2 the waning reports from husband to wife after the advent of children. Taking all topics together, Feldman (1960) found that the birth of the first child cut conversation time almost in half. Whereas newly married couples averaged two hours a day, young parents managed hardly more than one. Moreover, the content of discussion shifted from themselves and their relationship (inner feelings and sex) to their children. They became primarily parents, and only secondarily marriage partners. Feldman blamed this reorientation on having a young child in the house:

> During this period the couple's attention is focused almost constantly on the baby. They have little time and energy left over for each other.

Meals are hurried and irregular and often husband and wife eat separately while one or the other performs some domestic chore. With little opportunity to go places and see people, there's less to talk about. The main topic is children. In the evening, when they finally have a few moments together, they're exhausted, physically and mentally.

Husbands and wives do so many things with their children that they are rarely alone together. The intimacy of a one-to-one relationship cannot flourish in the presence of chaperones, no matter how young. The larger the number of children, the less the opportunity. According to Blood and Wolfe, few husbands and wives with more than three children were able to concentrate on each other enough to keep their love unimpaired.

To expect that we can lose sleep night after night with small children and keep our warmth (much less our cool!) is asking too much of the human body. Loving, caring, listening, and supporting take energy. When the well is empty, there's no more to drink. When the candle burns down, the flame goes out.

The need for rest is as essential as the need for interaction. In my case (Margaret):

> When the children were small their nap time was my only time alone. I wanted it and needed it to do so many things. But my body needed rest too. Too often I made demands unmercifully upon myself to keep going, to get all those things done that needed doing, to show that I was not a sloppy housekeeper, to show myself and Bob that I could be something more than "just a housewife."

From a graduate student couple who didn't plan to have children we heard:

> It's not that we don't want to be together and share good things like we used to do before the twins arrived but we have no choice any more. When we faced the reality of our priorities we found that the babies came first, our schoolwork second, housework third, and our time together limped into fourth place. Because the first three take so much out of us, we have little or no energy left to encourage and support and enjoy each other—much less for sex. We don't like our increasing irritability. How can we survive these days, much less our marriage survive?

There are times in the family cycle when we can't have what we want. We have to pare down our expectations. We don't have enough energy to be the best student, the best boss/employee, the best father/mother, and the best husband/wife. The marriage doesn't have to go down the drain. Accepting the reality of the pressures, not blaming myself or my partner or the children for not being perfect relieves some of the burden and sense of hopelessness. But no couple can be pressured forever without damage. Couples, like individuals, must review their priorities, letting the least important elements go.

The Impact of Aging. Physiological capacity declines from birth to death. Most conspicuously, energy sags. Every mother knows how strenuously preschoolers play, how exhausting the pace that they maintain. Even young adults, by comparison, are sedentary. The older we become, the less energy we have for anything, and the more attractive rest and passive entertainment become. As our pace slows, we do less and less, even things as easy as talk.

The Transformation of Love

Whoever expects a continuous high in marriage expects too much. But love grows and deepens through the vicissitudes of marriage.

Honeymoon intensity cannot last but there are new highs that are different: the first house, the first baby, the first crisis weathered. Each experience contributes its own meaning. And there are surprises too, the unexpected good things that come out of bad things or out of nowhere at all. In our marriage:

> When we became more aware of our own feelings and could deal more openly with one another, we began to see our relationship as a spiral. We kept running into the same issues, but looking back we could see we'd made some progress and were a bit further ahead.

Each stage of life brings new experiences that were not possible before:

> When I [Margaret] look at pictures of myself as the mother of four small children, I see little sparkle and a lot of fatigue. I wonder how Bob could have loved me (since I certainly didn't love myself very much). Twenty-five years later there are no demanding children and I have more energy, enthusiasm, compassion, and understanding. At 30 I sadly gave up practicing the piano as little hands got in the way. Today I enjoy accompanying while Bob plays his cello. At 40 bike riding seemed too hard and I quit. Now that I have bought a new bike and lost 20 pounds, I can bike farther at 60 than I ever would have tried 20 years ago. Eight summers at our cabin have brought something different each year—new flowers, birds, weather, friends.
>
> I anticipate more good things in the future. But they don't just happen. We have to pay attention and plan ahead for those far out "impossible" things. Bob is a good planner and once he says (as with going to

Japan) "Why not?", it always seems to come off. I used to regret having seen so little of England. Then one day my sister asked me to go with her and Bob said "Go!" I went without him and what a time we had afterward sharing my adventures and dreaming about going again together! The same way he has urged me to take summer dance workshops in the West. Earlier in our marriage, resources were scarce. Now they are everywhere and we take advantage of them—separately and together—to enrich our lives and our relationship.

Married love gains in breadth. The reach of memory widens as husband and wife share events. Their knowledge of each other deepens as they learn to recognize barely perceptible cues to mood and desire. Symbolic of this cumulative knowledge is the increasing proportion of the husband's friends whom Blood and Wolfe found that the wife considered her friends too.

Although the average couple in Pineo's 20-year study became disenchanted, there were exceptions. Among the minority of husbands whose love was still "intense," 90 percent would marry the same partner again and 97 percent had no regrets about their marriage. The inevitable transformation of love does not mean the inevitable destruction of the feeling that marriage is meaningful.

Nor is disengagement inevitable. Ninety-five percent of Pineo's "best" husbands still kissed their wives and confided in them as frequently as 20 years before. Only with respect to outside activities did Pineo's marriages almost universally slow down.

Deterioration is not inevitable. Keeping a relationship alive is not impossible. But it takes sustained effort.

EMOTIONAL SUPPORT

From day to day, both spouses encounter many challenges. Problems and opportunities tax their resourcefulness. Marriage increases each one's resources as the partner stands in the wings encouraging his/her performance.

Career Support

The marriage partner benefits from the paycheck that the spouse brings home, and therefore is vitally interested in hearing about vocational successes and failures. Beyond this economic stake, however, each partner provides support for the other's vocational odyssey. When things are going badly, it's helpful to let off steam at home and receive solace there. We will describe the latter process more fully under the heading of "therapy for emotional stress." Meanwhile we wish to focus not on the emotional benefits of marital therapy, but on the career benefits of marital support.

Western culture is replete with sayings such as "behind every great man there stands a woman." At the very least, there is considerable anecdotal evidence that behind American presidential candidates there stands a woman who has agreed to forego companionship in order to give her husband the time for campaigning.

Career support once was unidirectional, from behind-the-scenes women to out-in-the-world men. With the increased employment of married women, husbands too have opportunities to give support. Presumably, the more precarious either person's occupational venture is, the greater the benefit. One example of occupational precariousness can be found in persons who are so physically or mentally handicapped that they need vocational rehabilitation. Balswick (1970) found that handicapped persons were more successful in getting jobs the more they and their marriage partner ate meals together, relaxed together, or went to public events together. Both men and women benefited vocationally from companionable support. However, only women benefited from psychological forms of support—from husbands who expressed concern about their handicap, who talked over their vocational plans, and who encouraged them in their work. Men, by contrast, were *less* successful vocationally when their wives treated them this way. However, highly educated men reacted less negatively to psychological support. Perhaps it is possible for men to become emancipated from their traditional supersensitivity and to learn to respond just as positively to emotional support as women do. In the meantime, feminine "advice" remains problematic in American marriages.

Support for Community Activities. The less routine the situation, the more useful moral support becomes. The saying about the woman behind every great man reflects the encouragement needed by those who push ahead of their peers and stick their necks out. Lesser persons need encouragement when venturing into roles new to them, even though not to the world at large:

> John still is sometimes hesitant about meeting people or trying new ventures, but he has gained much more self-confidence. Whenever he feels incapable of meeting a situation, I bolster up his ego by pointing out to him his other successes. Somehow, when I say, "You can do it!" I can see his eyes light up in anticipation. It's very rewarding for me to build up his enthusiasm and his confidence in his own worth.

Moral support in either direction bolsters achievement in nonmarital roles. The husband-wife relationship then becomes a source of strength for both partners.

Therapy for Emotional Stress

What if the partner doesn't get promoted? What if s/he gets fired instead? What if a culinary masterpiece falls flat in the oven? Then what?

Frustration produces emotional stress. The natural reaction is aggression, designed to demolish the source of the frustration. But civilization inhibits this sequence. Children may be aggravating, but parents are not supposed to beat them. When employers cause trouble, retaliation would only make matters worse. Yet adrenalin has surged into the bloodstream, impelling the body toward aggressive action. Either partner may be short-tempered with the spouse when everything has gone wrong. External stresses create crises at home or intensify milder difficulties.

Therapeutic Utilization of the Partner. When I am emotionally upset by an external crisis, I may turn to my partner or to some other resource for help, or handle it myself. The choice depends on the nature of the problem and differs between the sexes.

Table 21–1 shows that a large minority of men and women reacted passively to problems. They slept them off or ate or drank them away. They forgot about them by watching television, going to the movies, or engaging in other recreation. Few dealt directly with problems, solving them on their own. The remainder sought outside help.

Where do people take their troubles? In Table 21–1, we saw that most people didn't go anywhere. Nevertheless, a minority did seek help from other people. Table 21–2 shows that informal resources were used much more than professional resources.

When men and women turned anywhere for help, they utilized their closest relationships. The spouse was a major resource for those who had one (only three-fourths of Gurin's sample), provided s/he was not the cause of the difficulty.

Blood and Wolfe asked married women how often they told their

Table 21–1   Usual Way of Handling Worries and Unhappiness, by Gender

Usual Way of Handling	WORRIES		UNHAPPY PERIODS	
	Men	Women	Men	Women
Passive reaction	38%	30%	26%	20%
Prayer	8	23	22	40
Informal help-seeking	22	28	19	21
Direct coping reaction	21	9	9	4
Miscellaneous	11	10	24	15
Total	100%	100%	100%	100%
Number of cases	1,077	1,383	1,077	1,383

Adapted from Gurin et al., 1960: 372, 374. *Source:* National sample of adults (married and single).

Table 21–2 Other Persons Utilized in Handling Worries and Unhappiness

Chief Source of Help	Worries	Periods of Unhappiness
Informal		
Spouse	59%	19%
Parents or children	7	15
Other relatives	1	18
Friends, acquaintances	17	38
Formal		
Clergyman	4	6
Doctor	4	4
Total	99%	100%
Number of cases	689	545

Adapted from Gurin et al., 1960: 368. *Source:* National sample of adults (married and single). Limited to those who ever used any outside help.

husbands their troubles after a bad day. Most Detroit wives told their troubles selectively. Few always told their husbands, and few never did. Telling "half the time" was especially characteristic of college-educated wives. Perhaps the reason they were selective was not that they were so well educated but that their husbands were so busy.

Selectivity may be forced on some couples, but it doesn't make the most cohesive marriages. In Detroit, wives who always told their troubles were most satisfied with their marriages (Blood and Wolfe, 1960). Nor is this just a feminine reaction. In Tokyo, both sexes were most satisfied with marriages in which both always told their troubles (Blood, 1967).

To abandon selectivity about *whether* to tell one's troubles need not mean lack of selectivity about *when* to do so. Some times and places are more conducive than others. It may be easier to listen after dinner than before. Distractions such as small children need to be out of the way. Sooner or later, though, a time can be found if couples try hard enough.

Whether it is wise to tell you my troubles is sometimes difficult to judge if you seem preoccupied. But if I take the initiative in asking about your life, I am more apt to know where you are and how I can help. Michel (1970) found that Parisian wives whose husbands usually asked them how they had spent their day were especially satisfied with his under-standing. But the most satisfied wives of all had marriages in which communication was reciprocal—that is, where both partners shared their emotional troubles and financial difficulties, and withheld no problems from one another. The best marriages, then, have the most communication from husband to wife and from wife to husband.

Floyd Mann reported that bank executives saw two values in getting their wives to talk:

First, it is diagnostic for the listener; second it is therapeutic for the spouse. Getting the tense and nervous person to talk is a necessary first step if the listener is to decide what part, if any, he should play in the situation. The listener can learn how the other sees the situation, make his own assessment, and can then decide what course of action to take. Getting the other person to talk is therapeutic in that frustrations get formulated into words so that they are no longer free floating and tension maintaining. The very process of trying to explain what is bothering or what has happened helps the tense person to organize all of the facts of the situation and this can lead the person who is upset to see the problem in a new perspective (pp. 7–8).

When my partner is unavailable, friends and relatives are alternatives. When stress is mild, I may be able to cope with it without burdening anyone else. Short of full-blown therapy, a sense of humor takes the edge off emotional tension and prevents it from becoming contagious. In our own marriage:

> *Every once in a while during those first few years, I'd come home grumpy from the office. After a while, Margaret got so familiar with these moods that she kiddingly said I was "acting like a bear." After that, all I had to do was growl and she knew I was nervous or anxious. The growling was so silly it made us both laugh instead of getting teed off at each other.*

The problem is to prevent external stress from setting off internal aggression and counteraggression. To prevent mutual recrimination, awareness of where the feeling comes from is enough. Whether this information is conveyed by factual reporting, private signals, or facial expression does not matter as long as the message gets across. Once it does, the spouse can put on the proverbial kid gloves and mobilize his/her therapeutic responses.

Response to the Partner's Troubles.   The first task is to understand. This requires listening—not as easy as it sounds, especially when children are around. Husband and wife have to compete with other family members for attention. Even without children there are competing attractions— household tasks, the day's mail, the evening paper, television. Yet, without attention, it is impossible to respond appropriately.

Listening is intrinsically therapeutic. Emotional catharsis requires only an interested audience for pent-up grievances. However, to be most effective, listening demands response. The appropriate response depends on the problem. Taking all sorts of bad days together, the men in Blood and Wolfe's study responded as shown in Table 21–3.

The most common reactions of Detroit husbands were sympathy and advice. Passive listening is hardly a reaction, yet even it was better than

Table 21-3   Comparative Effectiveness of Therapeutic Responses

Husband's Response When Wife Told Troubles	Percentage of Total Husbands	Mean Effectiveness*
Help in withdrawing from situation	3%	3.80
Sympathy and affection	32	3.63
Advice and discussion of how wife could solve problem	23	3.53
Help in solving problem	7	3.31
Passive listening	20	2.92
Dismissal as unimportant	8	2.79
Criticism and rejection	7	1.89
Total	100%	
Number of cases	643	

Adapted from Blood and Wolfe, 1960: 206. *Source:* Representative sample of Detroit wives (excluding those who never told their troubles).
*Code: Wife felt much better   4 points
         A little better   3 points
         Sometimes better, sometimes worse 2 points
         About the same   1 point
         Worse   zero

reacting negatively—brushing off the wife's troubles or criticizing her for getting into them in the first place or for bothering him with them.

Among the positive responses, help in solving problems did not relieve the wife's feelings immediately, but in the long run left her most satisfied with the husband's understanding of her problems and feelings. The quickest relief came when husbands helped her forget her troubles by taking her out to dinner or to some other distracting activity. Since bad days usually occurred at home, leaving "the scene of the crime" reduced tension fast. Sympathy and affection provided emotional support, whereas advice and discussion were pragmatically oriented toward resolving the problem or preventing it from arising again.

Mann found sharp differences between the responses of engineers and their wives. If a man arrived home at five-thirty to confront his stay-at-home wife in the midst of her troubles, he could choose between taking her away from it, helping her on the spot, advising her how to proceed, and so on. If he had troubles at work, however, his wife could not respond directly, only indirectly:

> I put the dog in the basement, turn on the stereo, give a wink to the children, and after a quick dinner, wait until he's ready to discuss the problem. I make sure the dinner conversation is light and casual with no complaints about anything.

Mann commented, "The wife's first task is therapy, not diagnosis . . . she sees it as her job to establish a therapeutic environment for the husband—one in which he is enveloped, protected from further onslaughts, and one in which the natural process of recovery can function to restore his sense of well-being" (p. 22). This is not easy at a busy time of day, but many wives provide this service skillfully.

It is self-defeating to burden the partner beyond his/her ability to cope. Better not to rely on him/her at all than to bludgeon him into negative reactions. Once the limit is reached, outside resources may ease the load on the marriage circuit and prevent blowing a fuse.

The spouse, too, must beware of becoming too entangled in the partner's troubles and taking excessive responsibility for resolving them or preventing them. In our case:

> When I [Margaret] find myself getting overanxious about the conflicts you get into with your family or with persons at work or with one of your friends, I need to disengage. At one point I became aware of how my own identity was threatened when you "failed." Too often I wanted to protect your image against criticism. And who was I protecting? Myself, I suspect. It feels better now, not hovering over you, letting you manage your own relationships, not feeling responsible for you anymore, letting you learn through your failures like I did with the children. But it isn't easy to see you hurt (because I don't like to hurt).

Therapy for Physical Stress

We know little about the nursing care that marriage partners give each other when they are sick. The problems are analogous to those raised by emotional troubles. In fact, the two overlap since half of all physical illnesses are psychogenic. If my husband breaks his leg skiing, it is easy for me to be sympathetic (provided I don't think he was a fool to attempt that trail). But if he wakes up with a headache and wants to be taken care of like a little boy, then what? Some wives (and husbands) believe sympathy is dangerous:

> Every once in a while, Alex refuses to get up in the morning. He mutters some excuse about his back acting up again and wants me to bring him a heating pad and serve him breakfast in bed. He exaggerates his ailments and puts on such an act that it makes me mad. I may bring him a little something, but I am careful not to overdo it because I don't want to spoil him when he acts so childish.

Such behavior is childish. It is also a plea for sympathy and nurture. To withhold it only makes matters worse, creating tension between husband and wife where originally only the sick individual was tense. Paradoxical as it may seem, the patient is likely to get well faster if the illness is accepted. After s/he has had enough nursing, however, the time may come when s/he will need to be encouraged to resume his/her normal life.

Parsons and Fox (1952) believed that this combination of "permissive-supportive and disciplinary facets of treating illness is peculiarly difficult to maintain in the kind of situation presented by the American family." Hence they felt professional care was often needed for physical illness. Nevertheless, even if the patient is hospitalized for primary care, the partner's sympathy or hostility will hasten or delay his/her recovery. In any case, the partner's attitude determines whether illness strengthens or weakens the marriage.

Menstrual Stress. Many couples go for years without illness, but few avoid the tensions of menstruation until they disappear at menopause. Filler and Lief (1963) stated that "Some degree of discomfort at the time of the period is well-nigh universal." Most men are aware that women generally have this problem. But they cannot support their wives unless they know when the difficulty arises. Few men can be expected to keep track of the calendar. So wives must communicate their condition. Once husbands are aware, they can provide sympathy, massage, and relief from children and can make allowances for the predictable irritability. Empathy and understanding can relieve the woman's troubles, replacing the sand in the gears of marriage with lubricating oil.

GROWTH

What can a couple do to keep their marriage alive and well? Fortunately there are many things, often seemingly insignificant, and requiring small bits of effort more than major bursts. There are familiar pleasures: a kiss in the morning, tea in the livingroom after dinner, or the right sauce with the broccoli. And there are unexpected ones—a cartoon clipped and brought home, a joke remembered to share, or flowers bought on a whim. Unexpected gifts demonstrate thoughtfulness and sensitivity. Expected gestures reinforce satisfying and happy memories.

Commitment to Growth

By now it is apparent that one of the main reasons why marriages go downhill is because people are too involved in their jobs, their children, their friends, or their personal pleasures to spend the time and energy needed to make their marriage flourish. Liberated wives and husbands may react against their parents' overdependence on one another with excessive apartness as each goes his/her own way in career and leisure. Two full-time careers plus "doing my own thing" recreationally leaves little time to be together.

Most of the couples who come to us for counseling are in trouble because their marriage has been low priority. The hour or two spent in counseling each week is often the only time they talk. And it's not enough to reenergize their marriage.

Carl Rogers was skeptical of commitment to the institution of marriage, but he saw a great deal of value in commitment "to working together on the changing process of our present relationship because that relationship is currently enriching our love and our life and we wish it to grow" (1972: 201).

Sidney Jourard (1975: 204) emphasized the importance of dynamic change in the relationship between partners:

> Marriage is not an answer, but a search, a process, a search for life....
> Yesterday's marriage or way of being married is today's trap. The way
> out of the trap is to resume the dialogue, not to end it.

We, too, have discovered the value of commitment to struggling with our problems. Although we have been greatly enriched by the positive experiences that we have enjoyed, we have grown the most from the struggles to resolve our crises. We have discovered that crises are not simply threats to what we already have but arenas in which we learn to fashion new dimensions of understanding, appreciation, and resiliency. The process is never finished. No matter how long we are married, there are always new opportunities for our relationship to grow:

> *When I [Margaret] say that I am committed to our continuing growth, that is not just a statement of hope. I am aware of your having grown and my having grown. I can look back and see where I, you, and we have come from. I know I can trust the aliveness and durability of our marriage because I have experienced it for so many years. I am committed to dealing with you and experience that process as healthy and not destructive; fulfilling and not dehumanizing. I intend to continue to reach out toward you, to struggle to find the mutual ground that nurtures and fulfills us. I am excited about discovering that there is always more to explore and find. I believe that we will keep on finding new things in our relationship, that the possibilities are infinite.*

Personal Growth.   The growth of our relationship is tied to our growth as individuals. We cannot struggle together without changing personally. No other experiences in life have stretched us more than the confrontations we have been through with one another.

Likewise, personal growth sparks marital growth. Rogers (1972: 209) described this under the heading of "Becoming a Separate Self":

> Perhaps I can discover and come closer to more of what I really am
> deep inside—feeling sometimes angry or terrified, sometimes loving

and caring, occasionally beautiful and strong or wild and awful—without hiding these feelings from myself. Perhaps I can come to prize myself as the richly varied person I am. Perhaps I can openly be more of this person. If so, I can live by my own experienced values, even though I am aware of all of society's codes. Then I can let myself be all this complexity of feelings and meanings and values with my partner—be free enough to give of love and anger and tenderness as they exist in me. Possibly then I can be a *real* member of a partnership, because I am on the road to being a real person. And I am hopeful that I can encourage my partner to follow his or her own road to a unique personhood, which I would love to share.

For us, the key word is "authenticity." Our marriage is meaningful as each of us manages to keep in touch with his/her own feelings and expresses them, listening and responding to the other. Each of us is first and foremost an individual person engaged in a life journey. We have decided to journey together so our life careers are what Farber (1964) called "mutually contingent." But the contingency is secondary, the individual journey primary. As I pursue my own journey, follow my own light, develop my potential as a human being I become a valued companion to you:

> Earlier we limited ourselves by imaging you [Bob] as the rational, logical, intellectual mamber of the family and me as the intuitive, sensitive, feeling member—masculine and feminine stereotypes. Gradually, I found that a rational side existed in me also, and you began to allow your feelings to be expressed. Now I feel more comfortable with you, knowing that you too feel deeply and you make mistakes and can admit them. You too are human!

People change. Kelly (1955) found that between young adulthood and middle age, men and women became more religious in their values and more masculine in their interests. After 20 years, his couples had changed 52 percent of their values, 55 percent of their vocational interests, 69 percent of their personality characteristics, and 92 percent of their answers to attitude questions. These sweeping changes suggest that couples will have much to talk about if they are to grow together rather than apart.

Marriage cannot be static. If it attempts to stand still, it will regress. As each partner changes, couples face the challenge of what Foote (1956) called the "matching of husband and wife in phases of development." Matching requires husbands and wives to carry on a continuing dialogue.

Separate experiences renew a marriage when they stimulate the growth of the individual and are shared vicariously through conversation. Too many husbands and wives are bored with each other because they are bored with themselves. To invigorate their lives through mind-stretching and feeling-stretching experiences renews their attractiveness to the partner. Love does not thrive on the disrespect that comes with awareness that the partner's life is empty.

Meaninglessness especially plagues stay-at-home mothers. Tied down to routine housework and cut off from contact with the outside world, they get depressed. Retaining intellectual vitality and a sense of identity is difficult but critical. Even mothers of very young babies need to find time for an occasional get-together, a visit, or a phone call to a friend. Employment at home may provide a diversion that can be set aside when the baby wakes up. The activity doesn't matter as long as it revitalizes the person.

Dream Work in Marriage.   In our marriage, one of the most valuable ways we have facilitated one another's growth is by doing Gestalt work on each other's dreams.

> *For me personally [Bob], it has been a great relief to work with Margaret on my nightmares. As she has asked me to "become" each of the feared characters in the dream—the murderer, the gun, even the bullet—my terror has diminished. I have experienced the acceptance and reintegration of these alienated parts of my personality. As I have gotten into these alienated parts, I have dared to say things that ordinarily I would repress. Through facilitating my dreams Margaret has come to know me more deeply than I could have shared with her directly. Moreover, I have discovered things about myself that I didn't know before. As a result, we feel closer to each other than we could have otherwise.*

It is not necessary to be trained professionally in order to facilitate a partner's dream work. It does help to have participated in a workshop to see how dream work is done. We learned how to work on each other's dreams by observing how others did it. The crucial contribution of the facilitator is to be an attentive audience to the dreamer. Simply by being present, s/he provides a setting within which the verbalization of the dream can take place. By asking the dreamer successively to become each of the characters and objects in the dream, the listener provides an opportunity for him/her to allow the dream to develop its full potentialities, for the conflicts in an aborted dream to become resolved, and for the characters within the dream to engage in fruitful dialogue with one another. We commend it as a powerful tool for personal growth and for growth in understanding between partners.

New Experiences

Because one basis of disenchantment is the replacement of novelty by familiarity, new experiences are anticorrosive.

Children, from this point of view, offer advantages (as well as disadvantages). To the perceptive observer, they provide an endless stream of sayings and accomplishments. As they develop, they confront parents with challenges and revive childhood memories to be shared. Beyond these intrinsic novelties lie countless opportunities to be grasped or neglected, depending on the parents' ingenuity.

Apart from children there are chances for travel, for making new friends, for stretching oneself in reading and service. Outside the home there are jobs to be done, organizations to be joined, new posts to be filled in old organizations, and new tasks to be undertaken in old posts.

Some new experiences come unbidden. Life crises provide an occasion for reviewing priorities and for making fresh beginnings. In our case, one turning point was a physical crisis:

> Bob's cancer was frightening but it brought a whole new realization to him and to us that we weren't living the way we really wanted. His job wasn't satisfying and fulfilling. As a result, we decided to simplify our life and give up our financial security by going free lance. We found new satisfaction in our vocational and married life. If it hadn't been for the cancer, we'd still be in that rut.

For many men and women, the forties and fifties bring abrupt changes in life-style and values. Turning to a new cause, a new faith, a new way of relating may satisfy deep human needs that have been unmet.

After children leave home, stay-at-home women must face the fact that they are no longer needed. They must fill the void with a new job, activity, or deeper relationship. If the husband is occupied elsewhere and the children were their only bond, the marriage will be in crisis. At the same time, a husband who has given his all to his vocation may crave a deeper relationship with his wife, only to find that she is now deep in a new career with all of its pressures. Whether the marriage can be saved depends on how much the two are willing to face honestly what they want for themselves and from each other. A whole new marriage may emerge.

At all stages of the journey both partners must cherish and develop their independence. Changes in affection, accidents, sickness, death can intervene at any time. Both partners must be prepared to go it alone emotionally as well as financially. Sooner or later the separation of bereavement is inevitable. Those who have found wholeness within themselves are better able to bear the ending of their marriage, which comes to every survivor either by divorce or by bereavement.

Marriage Enrichment Workshops. Couples need not rely only on their own resources for new experiences. An increasing number of organizations provide intensive and ongoing workshop experiences available to couples. They come under such labels as marriage encounters, marriage retreats, couples workshops, and couples groups. A national organization with the acronym ACME (Association of Couples for Marriage Enrichment) promotes these opportunities for couples. We recommend that every couple participate in such a workshop at last once a year. Leading these workshops has enormously enriched our own marriage.

Although workshops differ in style, their greatest value lies in providing a structured setting in which couples can examine their relationship, appreciate what is positive in it, and explore possibilities for making the changes they wish. The group provides a sympathetic audience for the individual couple's work, enhancing their sense of the significance of the occasion, and provides a chance to learn from observing their work.

Separation and Return.   For some old married couples, sheer separation may introduce the novelty that they need to revitalize their relationship. The reason for leaving may not be personally revitalizing—it may be as mundane as a business trip or as harsh as military service. But when couples have lived in the same place in the same way for so long that they have gotten into a rut of conventionality, to be separated for a while may bring them back together with renewed appreciation.

Slater and Woodside (1951) found that British women who had been married a fairly long time experienced an improved sexual relationship when their soldier husbands returned home on occasional leaves during World War II. Similarly some couples take separate vacations in order to be able to come back together with renewed appreciation. In our case:

> *Making ourselves take separate vacations has never been easy because we both enjoy the security and the dependency we have in our closeness. And yet we have found that days and sometimes weeks apart benefit us both. In the early days when Bob went alone to professional conferences, the usual family routines would shift. I'd teach the children piano. They'd help more in order to take his place. With him gone, the children and I felt closer. Though I missed him, I was glad to get those extra household and personal things done that I had been putting off for so long. Some of my happiest memories have been the coming-home times, when he came down the walk and through the door—how good he looked and felt! There was always so much to talk about and to catch up on. Later, when an ill parent called one of us out of town, we could make our peace with that aging parent alone better than as a couple.*
>
> *Because we now share a joint career, time apart is necessary. We need to be away from each other just as we need to be away from the house where we work. Separate assignments and training workshops mean testing ourselves in new ways and bringing home new skills and insights to enrich our common work. We write long letters, recapture our romantic feelings, and find ourselves expressing appreciation for things we've been taking for granted. At these times it's good to know I miss him, and it's good to be assured how much he misses me.*

Intensive Interaction

In Chapter 7 we noted that love tends to evaporate when prolonged separation prevents interaction. It evaporates just as fast when partners are together but fail to interact. When the proverbial newspaper—rather than half a continent—separates husband from wife, the effect is just as disastrous. Indeed, the husband's unwillingness to interrupt reading the paper "for brief expressions of affection at the wife's approach" was one of the chief disappointments of wives interviewed by Ort (1950).

Companionship. Interaction involves more than laying down the newspaper. It requires doing things together, especially talking and listening. Conversation at the end of the day is as important as letters between partners who are geographically separated.

Many couples who have lost touch with one another find their way back by actually making dates with each other and writing the time on their calendar—a time after the children are in bed for sharing about their work, about the children, about the coming vacation, about grievances. If they want real sharing time, they must create an environment in which this is possible—no interruptions, television off, facing each other on the couch or in adjacent chairs.

Levinger and Senn (1967) found that couples whose unhappy marriages had propelled them into marriage counseling disclosed almost as many unpleasant feelings but substantially fewer pleasant feelings than matched couples not involved in counseling. Disclosure by one partner tended to promote sharing by the other partner. And the higher the rate of disclosure of all feelings, but more especially of pleasant feelings, the happier people rated their marriages.

This study suggests that marriage may be enhanced more by selective disclosing than by indiscriminately communicating everything. Indeed, Levinger found in a related study (1965) that satisfied spouses were less apt to bitch about their partners than dissatisfied spouses, but more apt to talk about outside troubles similar to the "bad day" troubles we discussed earlier. He also found that the more important a topic was to a couple, the greater their tendency to share positive feelings in that area and the more circumspect they were about disclosing negative feelings in that especially touchy area. These findings suggest that communication is especially beneficial when it is so positive that it promotes the morale of the partner or so externally oriented (if the content is negative) that it evokes the partner's sympathy. Negative communication about the partner, on the other hand, can be damaging if it involves indiscriminate attacks that go unresolved, especially if those attacks concern vital areas.

Navran (1967) found that certain types of communication enabled couples to keep their marriages in good shape. The biggest difference between happily married and unhappily married couples was that the happy ones more often talked about pleasant things that had happened during the day. They were also more apt to discuss shared interests and to talk about their "most sacred beliefs" without restraint or embarrassment. Conversely, they were less apt to break off communication by sulking or pouting. These differences are partly circular in the sense that happily married couples have more good things going on between them and fewer things to pout about. Nevertheless, they suggest the value not simply of having good things going, but of taking the time to talk about them.

We suspect that in the best marriages, sharing bad feelings about the partner may be less dangerous than it seems in these statistical studies. The crucial question is probably not the frequency with which but the way in which bad feelings are broached. In our marriage counseling we are well aware of the destructive effect of dumping bad feelings on the partner, attacking the partner, or putting down the partner. Such "communication" understandably corrodes the relationship.

But when I "own" my feelings, when I share my bad feelings as an act of disclosing something to you about myself, I give us the opportunity to explore the sources of those feelings and their resolution. It may be that my bad feelings say more about my fatigue, my menstrual cycle, or my childhood upbringing than they say about you, even though something you have done has triggered a "blip" on my electronic screen. As I share my bad feelings, you may discover that there is something you want to do in response—either to respond therapeutically to my condition or to change your behavior. The outcome is not predetermined. But the possibility of change arises when I share my feelings with you and you listen nondefensively. In any case, when problems arise, every couple must communicate about them or they will never be resolved.

Interaction is more than just talk. It is doing things together. Chapter 10 documented the crucial role of companionship in American marriages. Yet we have already encountered Pineo's report that this aspect of marriage fades fast. Effort is particularly needed to sustain joint use of leisure. As children grow up and leave, a whole new stage of life opens up in which the range of potential leisure-time activities is as broad as couples want to make them: camping, mountain climbing, ice skating, cross-country skiing, bicycling on country roads, hiking in the woods, exploring all kinds of new terrain physically and geographically as well as personally and emotionally. More time and energy and money are available to most postparental couples.

Kindness.   It's an old-fashioned word, but kindness is an important component in marriage. Kindness comes to stay when two people learn that marriage has limits, love has limits, and anger has limits and when two persons living together through the thick and thin of life can have mercy on themselves and on one another, not expecting perfection, not expecting constant gratification, knowing that the imperfections don't have to limit the understanding.

Romantic Activities.   Not all activities need to be romantic. But when they are, they indicate the specialness of the partner. The daily goodbye and hello-again kiss is the most widespread ritual of romance. In Japan, the whole family bows the husband out the door and in again at night. Farewell and welcoming rituals symbolize the daily disruption and reestablishment of relationships.

Love is enhanced by little extras—candles on the table, flowers, gifts, a poem, dressing up. These may be only symbols of love, but they express it more visibly than words.

A walk under the stars, moonlight swim, or toasting marshmallows in the fireplace enable couples to rise above their everyday level, even though the next day must resume its normal course. In the words of Levy and Munroe (1945), "Glamour in marriage cannot be continuous, but it needn't be absent. The morning after does not destroy the reality and value of the night before."

Opportunities for Intimacy.   That children distract their parents is inevitable. It does not, however, have to be perpetual. During the decades when couples are living with children, they need opportunities to be alone. Before marriage, privacy for uninhibited talk and affection is sought. After marriage, couples may think they have privacy, but a closer look is apt to disclose the interfering presence of others. The older children get, the later they stay up, whittling the private segment of parental lives. The only solution is to get rid of the children. Intervals of undistracted companionship require that children be shifted to someone else. Grandparents, babysitters or cooperative neighbors must be used until children grow old enough to care for themselves. The task is to get away from children and for nonemployed wives to get away from the house too, since it's their never-done workplace. How long parents can leave their children depends on their funds for child care and external activities. The well endowed can manage whole weekends away. The rest may have to settle for occasional evenings.

Even at home, enclaves of privacy can be created in the midst of family living. Parents who feed their children early or in a separate room gain opportunities for conversation or for reading their mail together.

The activity need not be romantic or even recreational. Maybe the couple go on business trips together or circulate petitions together. The essential factor is time.

Renewed Commitment

Anniversaries are occasions to re-create old times, revisit the scenes of falling in love, replay old love songs. If marriage is worth celebrating originally, it is worth recelebrating. The original commitment of marriage can be reaffirmed, but now the couple have more to celebrate than the first time—all the life they have shared since the wedding day.

But if marriage changes, then anniversaries become more than simply a time to reaffirm the old. In an address to the National Council on Family Relations, Sidney Jourard (1975) said he didn't know how many times he had been married, but that "I am married at the present time to a different woman of the same name in ways that are suited to our present stage of growth as human beings."

On our thirty-first anniversary, we were very aware that we were embarking on our "third marriage" to each other. We wrote a new contract which specified what that new relationship was. We bought a new wedding ring to symbolize that new relationship.

On their tenth wedding anniversary, our friends Bill and Marcy Litzenberg invited in three couples whose friendship was especially meaningful to them and exchanged the following vows to mark the beginning of their "second marriage" to each other:

I am here to confirm my commitment to you with a marriage ritual.

I welcome this ritual as an opportunity for me to explain what our marriage means to me. For I believe that when you understand the extent of my commitment you will know the depth of my love.

Life with you is fun and challenging for me: it offers me opportunities which you encourage me to take. Life with you is also warm and secure: it offers me shelter from challenges when I need a rest.

I believe nobody could care about me more than you do. You help me feel worthwhile and encourage me to be kind to myself. I can be honest with you, knowing that you will listen to me and understand.

I feel tender and loving toward you, and helping you be happy is very important to me. I feel complimented when you let me help. For when you share your hopes with me I see that I am trustworthy. When you come to me for comfort I see that I am kind.

From all of these things I have learned what love is. I know that I love you, and I know that you love me.

I recognize the hard work that love requires, but it is worth it to me. You can count on me always to try.

I will never turn my back on you.

I will be open and honest with you so that you can know what is important to me and what I hope for.

I will listen to you and how you feel so that I can know what is important to you and what you hope for.

I will do my best to stay in touch with my own thoughts and feelings. I am the keeper of my own happiness.

I will encourage you to do things to further your happiness.

I will take responsibility for what I think and do, accepting both my strengths and weaknesses as part of me.

I will try to help you accept your strengths and weaknesses, and especially to help you see the good in you.

I offer to help you stay in touch with your feelings, trying never to assume that I know how you feel.

I will not judge you. I will respect your right to think and feel differently from me.

I happily and willingly enter into this second marriage with you. What was good before will still be there, and what is new will build upon that strong foundation. I realize that my promises may be difficult to fulfill, but with you to love I know I can fulfill them.

None of these couples—the Jourards, the Bloods, or the Litzenbergs—had ever legally divorced each other (although some of us had gone through separations or crises as we moved from one phase to another of our successive marriages). For all of us, the process of rethinking our marriages and committing ourselves anew to the old/new partner has been profoundly meaningful. In our own case, we prize this activity so much that we now recommit ourselves to one another for a year at a time so that we will have the opportunity at every anniversary to express our appreciation for one another and to revise and update our contract for another year. Sometimes that's a heavy process, but it is never perfunctory! To define what my commitment means this time around is a useful anniversary task:

Commitment to you right now is not based on past promises and intentions. Trying to fulfill some past intention, hope, or understanding that was more or less clear 10 or 20 or 30 years ago would be irrelevant to the new place where you and I are today. I commit myself to you as a person, the real you—not the you that I concoct in my imagination, or the you I might need at any particular time. I commit myself to the everchanging, ever new you, where you are now, this year, this month, this day.

22 Divorce and Remarriage

For persons whose relationship is destructive, divorce and remarriage offer an alternative path to achieving the values they sought when they married the first time. The turning point occurs when one partner concludes that the chances of achieving those values are greater in a future marriage than in the present one, or that the present relationship costs more than it is worth.

THE INCIDENCE OF DIVORCE

Almost half of all recent marriages ended in divorce, but these statistics include both first divorces and subsequent ones. Since remarriages have a higher divorce rate than first marriages, the divorce risk for first marriages is correspondingly less.

When Divorce Occurs

Despite jokes about the "Seven-Year Itch," more marriages break up in the first year than in any other single year (see Figure 22–1). At the very beginning, the worst incompatibilities become apparent. Clark and Shulman (1937) found that over one-third of all causes of divorce emerged in the first year of marriage, even though most couples did not dissolve their marriages until years later. The alienation that eventuates in divorce often begins at the outset. Kephart (1954) and Goode (1956) found that sexual problems and personality clashes led to particularly quick dissolutions.

Figure 22–1 shows how large a proportion of marriages that failed

Figure 22-1 Duration of Marriage before Predivorce Separation

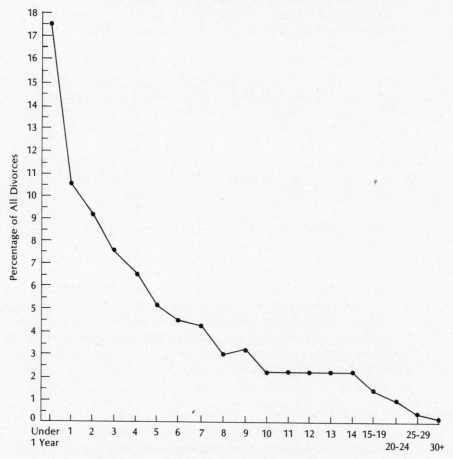

Number of Years between Date of Marriage and Date of Separation

broke up in the first years. The process is analogous to oil refining. The most volatile marriages crack up first and then the worst of the remainder, until after ten or twenty years most of the marriages still intact are capable of surviving indefinitely.

When husband and wife separate, the marriage for all practical purposes ends. Because of legal complications (including compulsory "cooling off" periods and crowded legal dockets), the interval between marriage and divorce is longer. In California (Figure 22–1), the median interval from marriage to separation was 4.8 years and the typical divorce decree did not come through for another 1.7 years. In 1969 the total interval from marriage to divorce for 26 states was 6.9 years (NCHS).

Customarily, the wife sues for divorce, accusing the husband of having wrecked the marriage (though most marriages fail because of mutual incompatibility). Besides chivalrous protection of the woman's reputation, feminine lawsuits enhance the wife's chances of gaining custody of the children. In exceptional cases (less than 27 percent in 1965), the husband is the plaintiff. Such husbands often seek custody of their children, contending that the wife is an unfit mother. Some judges grant custody to the wife even if her husband was the plaintiff, and most are reluctant to take children from the mother unless she is flagrantly alcoholic, mentally ill, or delinquent.

CAUSES OF DIVORCE

It is difficult to pin down the causes of divorce. The official causes (the legal grounds on which judges grant the decree) tell us little. Most divorces are granted for "cruelty," a notoriously vague term. Most of the rest are based on desertion (leaving unnoted the reason why the spouse left home), nonsupport (which frequently overlaps with desertion), or "indignities."

With the enactment of no-fault divorce in California and Arkansas in 1969 and in an increasing number of states since then, even the legal grounds for divorce disappeared. The California statute grants divorce on the basis of "irreconcilable differences which have been caused by the irremediable breakdown of the marriage." Similar terminology in the no-fault legislation of the various states either abolished the granting of divorces based on the "fault" of one partner or provided an alternative to divorce based on fault. Robbins (1973) commented that no-fault divorce "has gone a long way to alleviate some of the trauma and suffering usually associated with finding guilt and placing before the public eye the alleged marital indiscretions of spouses." Fisher (1974: 103) pointed out other benefits of no-fault legislation:

> It makes divorce easier to get since it allows couples to split up without first proving one is to blame for the breakup. Custody, visitation, and property settlements create most bitter court battles. As who gets custody, visitation rights, and property settlements become less contingent on who is at fault in the breakup of the marriage, the likelihood of precipitation of a court battle for divorce is diminished.

Despite the fact that divorce is less often based on a single fault by one party only, couples vary in the issues over which their relationship founders. It is possible to learn something about such issues by asking lawyers or their clients to name them. Table 22–1 compares the opinions of Idaho lawyers about the "real" causes in cases they handled with the

Table 22-1 Causes of Divorce, According to Lawyers and Divorced Women

IDAHO LAWYERS		DETROIT DIVORCED WOMEN	
Cause	*Percentage*	*Cause*	*Percentage*
Financial problems, nonsupport	20%	Consumption problems, nonsupport	21%
Adultery	19	Triangle	6
Drunkenness	18	Drinking	12
Basic incompatibility	11	Personality clashes	11
Irresponsibility	6	Lack of interest in home life	9
Immaturity	5	"Drinking, gambling, helling around"	12
Cruelty	5	Authority problems	12
Cultural differences	4	Conflicting values	8
Sexual incompatibility	4	Sexual problems	1
Desertion	3	Desertion	3
In-laws	3	Relatives	2
Miscellaneous	2	Miscellaneous	3
Total	100%		100%
Number of cases	282		425

Adapted from Harmsworth and Minnis, 1955: 320 (Idaho), and Goode, 1956: 123 (Detroit).

opinions of Detroit divorcees about the causes of their own difficulties. The latter picture is biased from the feminine point of view, underestimating the wife's own contribution. Table 22-1 lists the lawyers' opinions in order of frequency, giving equivalent categories from Goode's study (1956). Economic problems were conspicuously prominent. Families depended so heavily on the husband's income that inadequate or wasted earnings had disastrous repercussions on family solidarity. Adultery and drinking would have ranked higher for the divorcees if Goode's complex of "drinking, gambling, helling around" with other women had been subdivided. Authority problems involved attempts by husbands to dominate their wives (only roughly equivalent to cruelty). Sexual problems ranked low on both lists, leading Goode to conclude that "as every serious survey has shown, sexual problems do not form any large proportion of the 'causes' for marital disruption." Relatives were seldom a major problem, save at the very beginning of marriage.

THE EFFECTS OF DIVORCE

If marriage counseling cannot reconcile a couple in trouble, both partners and the counselor eventually recognize that continuing the marriage would only prolong the agony. If continuing together only creates tension, why go on? The costs for everyone (children as well as parents) are great when a mutually destructive relationship drags on.

Effects on the Children

In 1967, three-fifths of all U.S. divorces involved one or more children (an average of 2.2 each). Were those children better off or worse off after their parents split than if they had stayed together? Ideally their parents would have been happily married, but that option was not open. The only choice was between an unhappy home and a broken one. Table 22–2 shows that losing one parent was preferable to living with two unhappy parents.

Children of divorce had fewer personal and family problems than children of parents unhappy enough to make divorce relevant. Perhaps there should be more divorces for the sake of the children rather than so many marriages prolonged for their sake.

Rosenberg (1965) found that children of divorce had low self-esteem in certain situations: (1) the stronger the religious or ethnic taboos against divorce (as for Catholics and Jews); and (2) the younger the mother when she was divorced. The first correlation may reflect the fact that the stronger the taboos, the worse a marriage had to be before it was broken. Rosenberg suspected that young divorcees had particularly difficult life circumstances and that young children were particularly impressionable. The Nye study suggests that even in these circumstances, the children might have been worse off if their parents had continued living unhappily together.

One effect of divorce is that children have less contact with their paternal grandparents than with their maternal grandparents. This reflects the fact that mothers with custody of the children are their chief link

Table 22–2 Effect on Adolescent Children of Parental Unhappiness or Divorce

Adolescent Child's Characteristics	MARITAL STATUS OF PARENTS		
	Unhappy	Separated/Divorced	Unhappy/ Divorced Ratio
Child disagrees with mother about values	47%	26%	1.8X
Child feels rejected by father	69%	40%	1.7X
Child disagrees with father about values	53%	34%	1.6X
Psychosomatic illness	50%	31%	1.6X
Child rejects father	55%	37%	1.5X
Delinquency	48%	39%	1.2X
Child feels rejected by mother	55%	44%	1.2X
Child rejects mother	42%	35%	1.2X

Adapted from Nye, 1957. *Source:* Students in three high schools in Washington State. One-sixth of all homes were broken by divorce, but most parents were remarried by the time of the study. An equal number of unhappy homes were selected for comparison on the basis of marital unhappiness, quarreling between parents, attempted domination of each other, and lack of mutual activities or interests. Reciprocal percentages of students did not exhibit the specified characteristics.

with the older generation. When a father without custody loses contact with his children, they have less chance of contacting his parents. Anspach (1976) found that when divorced women remarried, children tended to have more contact with their stepfather's parents than with their father's parents. So children change relatives both when their parents divorce and when the custodial parent remarries.

Table 22–3 is not limited to grandparents alone, but includes aunts and uncles as well. It shows how markedly the former spouse's kin are excluded from contact, and replaced by the new set of step-kin in case of remarriage.

We know a couple who don't believe that their divorce has been all bad for their kids and who refuse to accept the myth that former spouses can't continue to be friends and co-parents:

> Though Ken and I found it impossible to stay in our marriage, we wanted to be able to stay in close enough touch geographically and emotionally to fulfill our commitment to our mutual parenting. Counseling helped us through the toughest time. In the beginning we all agreed it was best for me and the children to live separately from Ken in a nearby city, close enough for frequent week-end visits from Ken and by the children to the old house in the country where he continued to live. But a part-time father wasn't enough so we moved closer, which allowed more frequent visits and help with child care during the week. As the interaction between the three children became difficult, we all discussed things and decided that Judd would move in with Ken. Father and son developed a new closeness as they kept house together. Summer came and the other two insisted on their vacation in the country. My financial situation made payments on my house in town very difficult. Talking it through we decided that it made sense for me to move into the old house with Ken and the children, not as a wife and sexual partner, but as a co-parent and friend. People thought we were confused and mixed up, but we all feel glad for the experience we've had together this summer.

Table 22–3 Contact with Relatives, by Mother's Marital Status

	MOTHER'S MARITAL STATUS		
Relatives Seen	*Married*	*Divorced*	*Remarried*
Mother's relatives	81%	83%	90%
Father's relatives	72%	33%	29%
Stepfather's relatives	——	——	72%
Number of cases	35	47	37

Adapted from Anspach, 1976: 326. *Source:* Women with one or more dependent children in Portland, Maine. Reciprocal percentages had no contact with the specified relatives during the preceding week.

I've gotten over my fear of returning to the old house. New memories have replaced old, bitter ones. I appreciate Ken in new ways as a friend and father. We enjoyed taking Parent Effectiveness Training together and have experienced our best family meetings yet. I feel we can still be good parents helping the children establish their priorities, helping them make decisions about buying their own clothes and about visiting friends and grandparents. I no longer dread the teen years, nor do I dread the possible dependency of children upset by our divorce. This fall we'll have a new combination. We all fantasized at a family meeting where we would most like to be if we couldn't all be together. Judd feels good about going with me to the city again, while Rachel and Ted want to be near their friends in the country and have a special time with their father. They do not feel rejected by my leaving as long as we all continue to make frequent week-end visits and write often. The different combinations seem to keep all of our relationships alive and growing. I am pleased with their growing independence and confidence in themselves, which means they do feel loved.

Hill and Rodgers (1964) described the family as an evolving system that can adapt to changing requirements as it passes through the family life cycle. The above family has continued this evolution even though the relationship between the parents changed drastically. There is no final decision as to where the children will live. They continue to make adjustments to the changing needs of everyone. Though the marriage has ended, the family continues.

Effects on the Husband and Wife

Most divorced persons feel glad they terminated their marriage. The worse the marriage, the greater the relief when it ends. Nevertheless, divorce is not a painless process. Expenses include legal fees and court costs. It costs more to operate two residences than one. Hence, it takes courage to file suit. One source of support may be the marriage counselor whose attempt at marital rehabilitiation failed, and who now becomes the partners' divorce counselor, supplementing their attorneys.

Despite the pain of getting a divorce, the pain of staying married would have been worse.

Table 22–4 shows that unhappily married women (regardless of whether they were in their first or second marriage) were the most depressed. Even women who merely separated benefited from leaving their husbands. Those who went a step further and got divorced found their depression relieved still further. Those who remarried successfully following a divorce were almost as rarely depressed as those who were happily married the first time. This reaffirms our view that the most

Table 22–4 Depression, by Marital Status and Marital Success by Race

Percent Depressed	White	Black
Happily married	7%	4%
Unhappily married	32%	22%
Separated	27%	19%
Divorced	18%	10%
Happily remarried	10%	5%
Unhappily remarried	32%	24%

Adapted from Renne, 1971: 342, 346. *Source:* Representative sample of 3,537 women in Alameda County, California. Reciprocal percentages of women were not depressed. The remarried women were all previously divorced.

painful thing an unhappily married person can do is to stay in an unhappy marriage. Nor does it matter whether that person is a man or woman; Renne's study showed the same pattern for men as for women.

Even pain may be beneficial. One divorcee felt her bitter experiences had deepened her understanding of life. She was impressed by others who had been through the same travails:

> It's strange how much you can question once the structure of all the things you've taken for granted is thoroughly shaken. Personally, I find the most sensitive, tolerant, self-knowing, honest, and wide-minded people and those most loving are divorced. They are people who grew and changed over the years, often going through counseling or intensive psychotherapy in the process. They see the world differently, less innocently, but with more compassion; and they understand more of their own human nature and that of the people around them than those whose lives have traveled straighter paths.

THE PREVENTABILITY OF DIVORCE

A significant but unknown percentage of divorces could be prevented by more careful mate selection. Better compatibility testing, courses in preparation for marriage, premarital instruction and counseling, and waiting periods prior to marriage might reduce the number of divorce-prone marriages. However, some marriages are so destined to failure that no effort by the couple or by experts could salvage them. In extreme cases (the doctor married to the go-go dancer, the old man and the teenager, the rich woman and her chauffeur), everybody knows they are bad risks except the couple themselves.

On the borderline between unworkable marriages and compatible ones are marginal cases where divorce is not inevitable. Sometimes the period between filing for divorce and coming to trial is sufficient to produce second thoughts:

> *I've been doing quite a lot of thinking, and I've decided divorce wouldn't be such a good thing. I wouldn't want to have some stranger taking care of my baby because he'd probably feel like he had two mothers. I enjoy being with him so much I'd feel pretty bad about having to go to work. I've been disappointed with Paul's low income, but I'm afraid divorce would mean even less money and more expenses.*

Many states require predivorce waiting periods in the hope that reconciliation will occur spontaneously. Some communities take advantage of this interval to see what can be done to engineer a reconciliation. Particularly where children are involved, referral to a marriage counselor may be mandatory. Late as it is, such counseling salvages enough marriages to warrant enthusiasm on the part of courts that have tried it.

We have counseled many couples who looked like sure candidates for divorce on their first visit, but who turned their marriages around within six to twelve sessions as they learned how to communicate. Their very despair over the hopelessness of their situation served as motivation for change. Once both partners committed themselves to putting energy into changing instead of blaming, the negative cycle turned into a positive one. If there is still any caring left in a relationship, miracles can happen as a couple discover new ways to deal with their grievances.

DIVORCE COUNSELING

While divorce counseling is mandatory in some jurisdictions for some couples, it is potentially available to couples wherever professional marriage/divorce counselors are located. Even if neither partner has any doubt about the desirability of the divorce, counseling is useful.

For many couples on the verge of divorce, one or both partners feel some ambivalence. For ambivalent persons, a Gestalt dialogue between the two parts of themselves—the part that wants the divorce and the part that doesn't want it—may help them discover which side the bulk of their energy is on. The first task is to discover whether there is any hope that the marriage might be reconstructed on a mutually acceptable footing. Just as some divorce suits are withdrawn because couples change their minds, some couples in divorce counseling discover that their marriage has possibilities after all and wind up getting marriage counseling instead. However, most couples who enter counseling this late decide to go ahead with the divorce.

Sometimes one partner wants out while the other hangs on, reluctant to end a marriage that was intended to be life long. If we as counselors are convinced that the partner who wants a divorce has no affection for the other and no willingness to put energy into making the changes that would be necessary to save the marriage, we share our conviction that it takes two to make a marriage. Given the unwillingness of the first partner to consent to the continuation of the marriage, our task is to see whether the second partner can consent to its termination.

This requires the latter to listen to the cold reality of the disillusioned partner as well as having a chance to express his/her own shock, dismay, hurt, frustration, and rage. When feelings have been heard on both sides, consent comes more easily.

With some, the fight to keep the marriage is a way of retaliating against the rejecting partner. To divorce without consent creates bitterness and terrible hurt that comes with a legal battle. If consent is achieved, two persons can divorce more amicably.

Arriving at a definite decision not only relieves some of the anxieties involved in taking such a fateful step but helps couples understand why their marriage failed. In some cases, they realize that they never should have married in the first place, because they were too incompatible to be able to make a viable marriage. This may help each partner learn what kind of person to look for the next time and how to avoid getting into the same trap again.

In other cases, the problem lies not in the choice of partner but in destructive interaction patterns. For these couples, divorce counseling points up behavior that will need to be avoided in future relationships. Both partners may learn to recognize danger signals indicating that they need to take time out to work on their relationship, and signs that their coping procedure is inadequate so that they need to go to a marriage counselor before their relationship reaches the breaking point. Divorce counseling may debrief a couple about their dying relationship and prepare them to do better in subsequent informal and formal relationships.

Near the end of the divorce counseling, we ask a couple to express appreciation to one another for the good things they remember from their marriage. It is a rare individual who has no good memories, no matter how bitter the marriage has become. Sharing those memories helps each partner to realize that the marriage was not a total loss and that his/her own efforts were not totally wasted.

Finally, we ask the couple to negotiate the kind of relationship they wish to have after the divorce. A couple who have discovered that they cannot stand to live together may nevertheless want to resume the friendship they had before they got married. They may choose to de-escalate their relationship instead of terminating it altogether.

The Separation

If a couple are still living in the same house when they come to the counselor, an early task will be to decide about separating.

1.   When should the separation take place? Is there any reason to keep the family together until after an expected visit from relatives, until the end of the school year, or until the lease expires? If not, how soon can the departing spouse find a place to live?

2.   Who should leave? If there are children, the husband usually moves out, but this needs to be agreed upon by the particular couple. If there are no children, the question which partner stays and which one leaves is less easily decided.

3.   After the separation, will the old home be retained? Since living in two places costs more than sharing one place, it may be impossible to keep up the payments on the old one. Both partners may need to find new accommodations. Alternatively, some divorced persons seek out new housemates to help with the financial burden of staying in familiar surroundings.

4.   Many of the property questions that must be given final answers in the divorce decree must be given temporary answers as soon as the couple separate.

5.   If there are children, a sticky question for many parents is how and when to tell them. Parents usually assume that the decision to separate and divorce will come as a shock to the children. But children usually sense the tension between their parents, even if they have not witnessed overt battles. They may understand the miserableness of the marriage, even if they feel torn by the prospect of losing daily contact with one parent. Where parents are able to sit down together with their children and inform them that this has been a joint decision arrived at regretfully but decisively, children are more able to accept the decision than when they hear about it from only one parent at a time. Although there may be reasons for delaying telling children in some cases, the "reasons" usually advanced for delay have more to do with the parents' reluctance to go through an emotional ordeal than with any benefits to the children from postponement. The danger in postponement is that the children will either suspect or discover that their parents are making decisions behind their backs, and that their confidence and trust in their parents will be undermined. The same factors argue in favor of telling the couple's families early on.

The central phase of divorce counseling involves a search for agreement between the partners about the terms of the divorce settlement. This counseling is frequently provided by attorneys, and ultimately must be codified in legal language. But many attorneys prefer to work in an adversary system of justice, where they represent the interests of one partner in conflict with the other partner who is represented by a different attorney. Even attorneys who are comfortable with the role of mediator may be too busy to sift patiently through a couple's complicated feelings about the common property and children who must somehow be divided between them. So divorce counselors who are not legally trained may provide preliminary services that will enable the couple to go to their attorneys better prepared to tell them what kind of agreement they want.

The Property Settlement

Most childless couples accept the principle that their common property and financial resources should be divided equally. (Where children are involved, the question of what principle to go by in allocating financial resources is more complicated.) First, the couple must make an inventory of their assets. This may require having the value of property appraised. Dividing up liquid assets (investments, insurance policies, and the like) is normally easy enough. But tangible property is less easily divided. Gifts to the couple may have sentimental value. If they have come from one partner's family or close friends, they normally go to that partner. Where both partners have sentimental reasons for wanting to keep something irreplaceable that they have acquired jointly (art objects are classic examples), they may need to make separate priority lists of their preferences and bring them to the divorce counselor for negotiation.

After divorce, each partner is normally responsible for his/her own support. Alimony payments for ex-wives have largely gone out of style as a result of the increased employment of women.

Child support, however, is another matter. The principle of equality suggests that both parents contribute to their children's financial support proportionately to their ability. If the parents' earning power is equal, the noncustodial parent should regularly supply enough money to cover half of their expenses. Where their earning power is not equal, the noncustodial parent's responsibility is correspondingly greater or less as the case may be. In actual practice, most custodial parents get stuck with a disproportionately large share of the financial burden either because support payments fail to be revised upward with the increased cost of living or because the supposedly required payments are not paid on time or in full.

Arrangements for Children

We have already seen that in more than 70 percent of all cases, the mother gains custody of her children. During divorce counseling, the parents seek to agree on the custody arrangements that they prefer. Perhaps some children will go with one parent and some will stay with the other. Splitting the children may make sense in large families where the strain of child care would fall heavily on a single parent. In families where sibling rivalry has been intense, this may offer a way of separating siblings who have as much difficulty getting along as their parents do! Some couples decide to continue exercising joint responsibility for their children through "joint custody." This does not mean that the children live with both parents once the parents have separated, but that both parents must be consulted about major decisions affecting them. Unless the divorce has been unusually harmonious, joint custody opens the door to the same kinds of battles that led the parents to split up in the first place. Even if parents are reasonably cooperative, having to consult one's absent "ex" before being able to make decisions about the children who live in one's house is cumbersome at best.

Just as persons involved in multiple relationships need to sort those relationships into a primary partner and one or more secondary partners, children involved with multiple parents need to know which is their primary parent and which is their secondary one. This principle applies not only to decision-making responsibility but to where the children will live. Despite the temptation to try to achieve equality by shuttling children back and forth between parents at regular intervals, most children are better off having a primary home with one parent while the other parent's home is a place to visit.

Some men fear losing contact with their children when their ex-wives gain custody. Actually, many noncustodial fathers develop a higher quality relationship with their sons and daughters outside the marriage than they had in it. Planned visits that involve giving full attention to one another bring rewards to almost every parent-child relationship.

There is no neat formula for visiting patterns since circumstances vary enormously. At best the secondary parent will be visited summers, holidays, and weekends. But since the primary parent normally wants to have some special time with their children, holidays and vacations need to be divided up too:

> Jean and I agreed that she would have the children up through Christmas Day every year and then they would come to my house for the rest of their vacation, starting with our own Christmas celebration on the 26th. She and I will take turns having them for Thanksgiving one year and Easter the next.

For couples who stay in the same community, there may be a lot of negotiating to do about Saturdays, Sundays, and so on.

Not every couple is able to agree on all these issues during divorce counseling. But when they have gone as far as possible in arriving at mutual agreements, they are ready to turn to their lawyers to formalize their agreements in legally binding terms.

The Legal Process

The more thoroughly the husband and wife agree on the terms of their divorce, the less necessary it may seem to hire two lawyers. Yet Fisher

(1974) reported that employing only one lawyer violated the Code of Professional Responsibility for lawyers:

> Having one lawyer for both husband and wife is not proper although both consent; such an arrangement is deemed against public policy. Since the practice of law is still partisan, it is considered truly impossible for one attorney to draw an agreement fair to both parties. With respect to people in limited circumstances, it is proper for a lawyer to put in writing that he represents the wife only, draw an agreement satisfactory to her, and send it to the husband with a letter telling him to take the agreement to another lawyer to look over and sign, or possibly with that warning the husband may sign without a lawyer (p. 98).

The point of Fisher's comment is not that every couple must employ two attorneys, but that if they choose only one s/he must declare which partner is his/her client and not claim to represent both partners.

If the partners cannot agree on the terms of their divorce, they will need two attorneys to help them negotiate a fair settlement. If that negotiation fails out of court, ultimately the judge will have to decide between the contending parties.

GRIEF WORK

When a marriage ends in the death of one partner, the survivor receives support and sympathy in his/her bereavement. When a marriage ends in divorce, both survivors are largely left to flounder. Family and friends often feel too ambivalent to know what to say. There are few equivalents of the funeral ceremony. And so the grieving that both partners need to do to work through their pain over the ending of their marriage is not easily accomplished.

Informal Sharing

It may help to talk. Although relatives and friends hesitate to bring up the subject of divorce, they will usually listen when the divorced person initiates a conversation. To talk about resentments and broken dreams helps the individual sort out his/her feelings and begin to let go of the pain about what happened. Talking also reduces the sense of alienation from the person addressed.

Formal Sharing

Some persons whose ties to their religious community are especially meaningful have experimented with ceremonial equivalents of funeral services to mark the end of their marriage. Ellie Carnes and Artie Yeatman came to us for counseling and went back to their Friends Meeting determined to share their decision to separate with their friends in the meetinghouse. Here is Ellie's report of that event.

We announced one Sunday that we were having a special meeting the following Sunday at nine-thirty to explain our separation—a separation we both felt good about. Frowns and whispers. I got up and told them I could appreciate their dismay; we knew they wanted to know why, and although we were quite willing to talk about why, we preferred to wait to do that until we were in the extraordinary context of a meeting for worship. Three men came up afterward and hugged me, shook Artie's hand, and said they'd be there. I felt awful, and if I had needed warning I certainly had gotten it; society was not going to make it easy for us.

Sunday I arrived late with the kids. When I saw the number of cars pulling up, I was just quivering; my knees wouldn't work. Artie was already seated in one of the two chairs placed before the meeting. I joined him and the children sat behind me on the facing bench. About 100 people were there. Terror. I couldn't breathe. Artie got up and spoke. Beautifully. Much like he would build something, one thing upon another, no extras, short words, slow words:

"A little over two years ago, Ellie and I stood right here in a meeting for worship with our families and friends and promised to love each other as long as we both shall live. Today we have again called a special meeting for worship with our family and friends, this time to share with you our decision and our plans to make a major change in our marriage."

"As you all know, Ellie and I have very different temperaments. We also have different ideals and desires for the fulfillment of our individual lives. I would like to live a frugal, conservative, self-sustaining, domestic life-style. Ellie, on the other hand, has an intense desire to discover her whole self, psychologically, and to go wherever that may lead her. Neither of us is willing to devote the time necessary to be a full partner to the other in achieving these goals. And in our situation, why should we try to change our true personalities just to achieve a conventional marriage?"

"And so, in order not to stifle our personal initiative, we plan to live in separate homes and manage our finances separately. I would like to find a place as near here as possible so that I can continue to be a father to our baby because I love her very much, and also so I can keep in contact with Ellie, socially, sexually, intellectually, to whatever extent we both desire. This will allow Ellie to continue living on her farm, which she dearly loves."

"This all sounds pretty gruesome, which is exactly how I don't want it to sound, because really, I am happy and excited about some of the possibilities this opens up for me, such as living in some sort of community with other people, not necessarily in the same house, but perhaps with common property."

"So now I would like to say to you, Ellie, that I do still love you and I feel certain that you still love me, and I see no reason why we can't continue to uphold our marriage vows. And to our friends, I hope you will understand us and even rejoice with us as we embark on our new relationship."

Again silence. Artie's sister began to cry. Then I got up.

"Artie has spoken for me. I have been searching my deepest feelings, and hope I can share them with you now for I am thinking about marriage, and the belief that what is bound on earth is also bound in heaven; that our marriages are symbolic of the world continually creating itself out of chaos, and therefore marriage is a mystery, and can be a sacrament. When I married Artie, my promises were good-faith promises. For I love you, Artie. But I hadn't acknowledged the ultimate truth of change: that what is bound will be loosed. Change had impressed itself on me so deeply that I couldn't any longer live within the framework of marriage as we know it—something quick and fluid was smothering in me, and yearned to be free."

"So Artie and I are experimenting with our marriage. We are opening ourselves radically to the truth of change, trusting it, stretching our relationship, knowing it might break, not wanting it to break. I need your love and understanding as much as I did two years ago when I married in this room. I want you to understand that I love Artie more, if such a thing is measurable, than I ever did, because I now know him. I want you to understand that our children understand. I want you to know that I am aware of the myriad negative effects possible from such experimentation, but I embrace them, I salute them; because of the growth which is their sure accompaniment."

I sat down. And then, one by one, our friends stood up and said "yes" to us. One man spoke of the saying "ye shall know the truth, and the truth shall make you free." The meeting ended and we were overwhelmed with the physical affection of our meeting. Artie's Uncle Bro, a man in his late seventies, put his arm around me so tenderly, kissed me once, twice, on the mouth, no words; his wife Dottie saying "Bless you, bless you. I had a prayer half-born, perhaps it will speak itself in meeting." Other people came in and about five minutes later meeting proper began.

Like the slow movement of a symphony, that meeting for worship began to deal with the feelings generated by our meeting. One after another stood and spoke of their pain, their lost hopes, their marriage compromises, their appreciation and even gratitude, joy released, for our honesty, their belief in the rightness of what we had done. When the meeting was almost over, and all had spoken on top of each other, a woman got up whom I fear. She is one of the older members, strong-willed and demanding—she began to speak about self-immolation. We should do this, we ought to feel this and that. More and more, her voice getting harsh, high, haranguing, trailing off into prayer, getting back on the scent.

"We should all do as Christ did, remembering that he said 'the finest thing one can do for another is to lay down his life for him.'"

I stood up. "I am anguished," I cried. "Die! Who can say that is what another ought to do? I feel the pain in this meeting; forgive me if I have activated it. I am sorry for our pain, for your pain. Indeed, we can cry for our humanness, for that is what we are, unperfected-seeming. But I love myself, I can't help it."

The meeting absorbed this, a kind of murmuring silence, and then, one after another, three people spoke about courage, about loving oneself first, about joy in ourselves, about rejoicing. Artie's brother got up, a silent man. He stood there with his hand on my shoulder. "I have never spoken in meeting," he said, "but I hope the words come, I must speak." Terribly long silence, he was breathing heavily. "I believe in these people," he said, "I love their truth. This is what Quaker Meeting should be and what we are, sometimes—times to remember." Meeting broke. It felt good, very good to Artie and me and the children and many—most—others. A time of learning, healing, grief, and affection.

Individual Therapy

Professional therapy provides an opportunity for grief work, too. When family and friends are not available or are too biased to be good listeners, a professional person can provide a divorced person with an opportunity to work through those painful feelings until they diminish to the point where life seems bearable again. For persons who have used a marriage/divorce counselor, it is natural to continue working with that same resource person during postdivorce counseling.

If grief work is blocked for divorced persons by the lack of social mechanisms for facilitating it, it is blocked even more for persons who do not know whether their spouse is lost or not, namely, where the spouse is missing and may or may not return. Boss (1975) found that wives of military men who were missing in action in the Vietnam war struggled with uncertainty about whether to cling to the hope that their husbands might return or whether to give up hope and begin building a new life. Professional counseling reduced these women's unrealistic hopes for their husbands' return and helped them discontinue organizing their family activities around the long-absent men.

Group Support

One of the most useful sources of relief is the support of other persons going through the same mourning. In workshops for separated and divorced persons, an intensive weekend or a series of meetings can provide an opportunity for individuals not only to share their own feelings, but to listen to others and discover their commonality. Fellow sufferers often develop a strong caring for one another.

National organizations such as Parents without Partners and We Care provide group support. Weiss (1973) studied a 600-member Boston chapter of PWP and noted that it provided a sustaining community, friends in the same boat, support for a sense of worth, and opportunities to form new relationships with persons of the opposite sex. These services combined the opportunity to mourn the loss of the old relationship with a place for beginning life as a single person again. Hunt (1966) quoted a PWP officer who conceded unofficially that "the primary motive of nine-tenths of the incoming members is to look for eligible partners." Hunt commented that organizations for formerly married persons are especially useful sources of new partners because they bring eligible people together in a place where they can unobtrusively look each other over and decide whether they wish to date.

ON BEING SINGLE AGAIN

To be single again in one's late twenties or early thirties, after being married for five or ten years, is a difficult transition. When the divorce comes later in life—in one's forties or fifties after 20 or 30 years of marriage—the shock is even more intense. Even though there may be a sense of relief with the ending of the hassles of marriage and a sense of freedom to do what one wants to do, there are still losses in giving up the old and fears in encountering the new.

Since most couples have a complementary division of labor rather than shared tasks, divorce requires the separated partners to take over all the tasks that the missing partner performed. For men, the most difficult problem is learning to cook. For women, house repairs, automobile repairs and maintenance, income tax returns, and other financial operations may have to be learned. Technical experts, to be sure, could perform any of these functions, but they cost money and money is less available than it was before. One of the virtues of equalitarian marriages is that both partners are prepared to cope with any emergency that may arise, including the emergency of divorce.

For wives who have not been working, divorce frequently requires becoming self-supporting. Even though most divorce settlements provide that the absent father must pay child support, this seldom supplies enough money to enable the mother to stay home. So, with or without children, most wives must go to work when they become single again. For women who have never acquired marketable skills or whose skills have become obsolete, finding any job may be difficult. When a job is found, it is likely to be low paying and uninteresting. Conversely, wives who have worked throughout their marriage can make the transition to being single with less strain.

For the parent with custody of the children, there is the task of raising children singlehanded. Even if the "ex" wasn't a very active parent, having him/her around to fill in during emergencies was useful. And having a co-parent to consult with when the children were unmanageable was a relief. Few former spouses were total losses so that the absence of even minimal services is acutely felt when parent-child battles erupt and when parental fatigue sets in.

Fortunately, most children are adaptable. If a divorced mother sits down with her children and explains how tired she is, they are likely to be touched and to come to the rescue. They may even take over some of the missing father's chores and prove real assets in a difficult situation.

Relationships with the Opposite Sex

For many divorced persons, the most painful aspect of being single again is no longer having a partner in leisure. Even bad marriages usually had some residual companionship in going places and doing things, some residual sexual and sensual pleasure. To be single again is to be acutely alone in ways that children hardly satisfy for the parent without custody.

Loneliness is especially acute on sentimental occasions like anniversaries and birthdays, and on family holidays like Thanksgiving and Christmas. Mealtimes are painful for a childless person who must eat alone and bedtimes are lonely for one accustomed to a warm body in a double bed.

Sociability.   Fortunately, for every divorced man there is a divorced woman—and vice versa. So the problem of loneliness is theoretically remediable. All that is necessary is for each divorced person to make contact with someone else's ex. Hunt (1966) found that many divorced persons spent their first dates telling one another about their ex-marriages. This sharing frequently created a sense of closeness between strangers:

> Since instant intimacy requires a sense of kinship and a fund of common experience, many of the Formerly Married find that dating never-married or widowed people is far less satisfactory than dating other FMs. Among the people I queried, fellow-FMs were preferred as dates about two to one over the other two categories of unattached people combined; this preference was particularly marked among people in their upper thirties and above (pp. 122–123).

One of the men whom Hunt interviewed told him:

> I know what a divorced woman is all about—and she knows what I'm all about. I can count on certain things in her. She's far better able to reply and respond to me and my feelings than the single girl (p. 124).

This awareness comes only when a formerly married person begins to date, rather than being known in advance.

The potential companions are there, but finding them and reaching out to them is more easily suggested than accomplished. Many divorced people feel that they have lost their sociability skills during the years they were married. They have forgotten how to encounter strangers of the opposite sex, how to disclose themselves and how to ask for what they want. They have also mercifully left behind the experience of risking rejection of their overtures and risking disappointment when an overture accepted turns out to be less satisfying than hoped. The skills and effort and risking that we discussed in our opening chapter are again called into play, and for many divorced persons they are resumed reluctantly.

For those people whose earlier dating involved playing games, there may be an understandable reluctance to revert to behavior that now seems distasteful. But dating in one's thirties need not be a carbon copy of teenage behavior. Hopefully, the intervening years will have taught one how to be more assertive, more open, more direct, and therefore more effective in relating to others. After so many years have elapsed that life seems shorter, after so many responsibilities have been acquired that leisure time seems precious, divorced persons are understandably reluctant to waste it on chitchat and playing games. They want to move swiftly into meaningful relationships, even if they hesitate to move into committed relationships.

Once they feel ready to start moving, they are likely to have the knowhow to develop relationships more quickly than before. If they do not find these skills within their repertoire, singles organizations and workshops provide classes and laboratory situations in which those skills can be studied, practiced, and learned.

The more acrimonious the marriage, the greater the danger that the divorced person will find it difficult to trust any member of the opposite sex. Trouble with one man may diffuse into prejudice against all men—ditto with women. Mistrust and resentment may bar the way to dating in the first place or mess up new relationships whenever anger against the old partner is triggered by the new one, however innocently. Even if the new partner commits an offense that justifiably evokes a negative reaction, contamination with the old hatred may produce an overreaction that bewilders the new partner and jeopardizes the relationship. Although overreactions may be forgiven when they are discussed and understood (especially if the partner is also a divorced person with similar proclivities), they may sabotage relationsips so much that something needs to be done to minimize or prevent their recurrence. Personal therapy may mop up the residual mess of the old marriage, so the divorced person can move unencumbered into new relationships.

Much of the trial-and-error character of postmarital sociability is also therapeutic. Through new relationships of varying intensity, the individual gradually learns to trust again. At first, becoming emotionally involved may seem too threatening in view of the fact that the prior involvement ended in divorce:

> The Formerly Married's hunger for love is greater than ever, because to love and be loved again would be the most healing of all experiences, the most positive of all proofs that he is a worthy human being; at the same time, however, he is inordinately fearful of trusting those feelings which have so grievously betrayed him and proven so unreliable. And not only does he mistrust his own feelings, but those of anyone who cares for him, for he built his life upon them once, only to find them not a rock, but sand (Hunt, 1966: 174–75).

Having had their fingers burned once, divorced persons may limit themselves to emotionally superficial relationships at first, since this is all they are ready for. In Hunt's analogy:

> Perhaps, as with alpinists, they must rest at these way-stations in order to acclimate themselves to the altitude before climbing farther. It may be only through loving partially that the Formerly Married can become more nearly capable of loving completely (1966: 174).

Among Boss's military wives (1975) whose husbands were missing in action, those who gave up the search for their husbands and turned to building a relationship with another man found that their emotional health improved. In a study of factors affecting adjustment after divorce, Raschke (1974) found that social participation "was by far the most influential variable in alleviating postdivorce stress." There is no cure for the trauma of ending an old relationship like beginning a new one! Despite the uncertainties, postmarital sociability almost always brings some rewards and frequently is deeply therapeutic.

Sexuality. Many divorced persons especially miss physical closeness, the sensuality of touching and being touched, the excitement of sexual arousal and orgasm. The sexual aspect of marriage may have dwindled and even disappeared before the couple split. Many divorced persons face an interval of sexual deprivation between the termination of their marital sexuality and the beginning of their postmarital sexuality.

But not for long. Hunt (1974) found that five-sixths of the divorced persons in his sample reactivated their sexuality within the first year after they separated from their spouses. Once they resumed sex, they almost never voluntarily quit. In Hunt's total sample of persons who had been divorced varying lengths of time, all the men had had intercourse at least once during the preceding year, as had nine-tenths of the women. Thus, divorced men and women almost universally engage in at least occasional sexual activity.

How often do divorced persons manage to have sex? We might expect that they would not get around to it very often in view of the barriers to sociability that we discussed earlier. Except for unusual persons who move in with a new partner, they don't, after all, have a built-in sexual partner. We expected, therefore, to find that divorced persons have sex substantially less often than married persons. But we were wrong. Hunt's divorced men typically had sex more than twice a week—more often than married men of the same age. And while the rate for divorced women was slightly less than twice a week, even that was just as frequent as for married women.

Given the efforts required to date new partners, these data suggest that divorced men and women put an enormous effort into filling the loneliness in their lives and that they succeed remarkably well in filling it with sexual activity. They also imply—although they do not prove—that having sex has become a standard part of dating for formerly married men and women. Hunt found in his interviews that many divorced men felt dutybound to make sexual overtures to prove their "normalcy" and many women felt dutybound to accept those overtures in order to compensate the man for his "investment" in the date. In his earlier study of formerly married persons, Hunt (1966) found that divorced men typically made a "pass" at a new partner on their first or second date, estimating that about half of those overtures were accepted. A number of his respondents told him that they felt it was impossible to date a woman more than four or five times without feeling obliged to approach her sexually if they were not to be considered abnormal.

These reports suggest that all is not well with the postdivorce sexual scene. It is not just an arena of mutual enjoyment, but to some extent one of compulsive and unwanted sexual activity. Some divorced persons need to learn how to say no when they want to, to pay more attention to their own wants and less to social expectations, and to be able to negotiate more successfully with the particular partner. These skills may be learned in singles workshops.

These appear to be exceptional stresses rather than the general experience. Most of Hunt's divorced respondents found their sexual experiences highly pleasurable. Indeed, he concluded that postmarital sex involved just as much physical pleasure as marital sex. Clearly it involved more variety. The typical divorced man in Hunt's sample had eight different sexual partners in the previous year and the typical woman four different partners. Both men and women had engaged in a wider variety of sexual practices with those partners than had even the youngest, most sexually liberated group of married couples. Nor did this seem to be forced experimentation since not one respondent said s/he would prefer any less variety than s/he was having.

If there is any shortcoming in postmarital sex, it seems to be the instability of relationships. Insofar as sex takes place between persons who have just picked each other up or are trying to prove something to one another or feel pressured into having intercourse, it lacks the spontaneity, the resonant overtones, and the joyousness that sex attains in a loving relationship. On the other hand, the very newness of postmarital relationships gives them an adventurousness and excitement that marriages allowed to run downhill often lack.

Sexual experience is widely available to divorced men and women, who generally take advantage of this opportunity. The pervasiveness of postdivorce sexual activity suggests that it is one of the major ways in which divorced persons try out new partners and find someone whom they wish to marry. Hunt (1966) pointed out that a large proportion of the divorced persons whom he interviewed used sex as a first step in redeveloping their capacity to love:

> Casual or uninvolved sexual liaisons are another and very important stage in the process of redefining the self, repairing the ego, and rediscovering the meaning of one's manhood or womanhood. The (Formerly Married's) casual sex activities are not so much a denial of love as a step in learning to love again (pp. 153–154).

Gebhard (1971) found that divorced women differed sharply from widowed women in their sexual behavior. In any given age bracket, hardly more than half as many widows as divorcees had any sexual experience, and of those who ever had sex at all, the widowed women did so much less frequently.

Gebhard believed that the lesser sexual activity of widows was related to the fact that more of them attended church regularly and presumably held moral scruples against nonmarital intercourse. Correlatively, they were less apt to have engaged in extramarital intercourse, whereas many divorced women had had sexual relations with other men prior to ending their marriages.

Gebhard's sexually active widows were much like their divorced counterparts in other respects. A majority of both groups had sexual relations with more than one partner and both groups were highly sexually responsive. Indeed, among young women in their twenties, widows had significantly more orgasms than divorced women of the same age. Either the divorced group included women who had gotten divorced because of their sexual unresponsiveness or they had been so traumatized by the early failure of their marriage that their responsiveness was impaired with subsequent sexual partners. This difference disappeared after age 30. Curiously, almost as many widows as divorced women reported that they were having more orgasms postmaritally than they had had with their husbands. Perhaps the same improvement would have occurred if their husbands had remained alive since orgasmic capacity tends to improve with age. In any case, widows who had sex with other men were seldom disappointed physically with what they experienced.

Finally, although substantially fewer widowed than divorced women in Gebhard's sample remarried, the proportion of sexually active women who remarried was similar in the two groups. Sixty-three percent of the sexually active widows and 57 percent of the sexually active divorced women remarried. While this does not prove that only sexually active women remarried, Gebhard commented that "the more sexually motivated and responsive females tend to marry." So while there may be individual exceptions, those divorced and widowed women who are most socially and sexually active are most apt to marry one of the men with whom they are intimate.

REMARRIAGE: ESTABLISHING A NEW RELATIONSHIP

Divorced people are disappointed with their first marriage but rarely disillusioned with the idea of marriage. Frequently, they are more eager than ever to marry before they get any older. Most Americans feel a happy marriage is their birthright. If they don't achieve it on the first round, they hope to do so on the next.

The Incidence of Remarriage

Carter and Glick (1970) found that more than 80 percent of all divorced men and over 70 percent of all divorced women eventually remarry. Although these rates are not as high as the proportion of the population who ever marry at all (over 92 percent), at any particular age proportionately more divorced than single persons marry.

The picture given for women in Figure 22–2 is identical with that for men. At any age, divorced persons were the most apt to remarry and never-married persons least likely, while widowed persons fell in between. These data suggest how strongly divorced people are motivated to remarry. Most widows and widowers have pleasant memories to live on, but divorced people have unpleasant memories, hopefully to be erased by remarriage.

To be sure, eligibility affects the chances of remarriage. The younger a divorced woman, the better her chances. One study showed that a divorcee's chances of remarriage remained better than fifty-fifty until she was 45 years old, whereas for widows the turning point was 33 and for single women 30 (P. Landis, 1950).

Divorced women with children need to remarry in order to solve their financial and child-rearing problems. Glick (1957) found that they succeeded in marrying, age for age, almost as well as women without children, suggesting that children were only a slight handicap.

If remarriage is ever to follow the first marriage, it tends to come soon. Figure 22–3 shows the interval between marriages for men and women who remarried in the early 1950s.

For postdivorce marriages in 1969 the median interval to remarriage was 1.1 years, for postbereavement marriages, 2.8 years. The dif-

Figure 22-2 Probability of Marrying, by Age and Marital Status, for American
Women

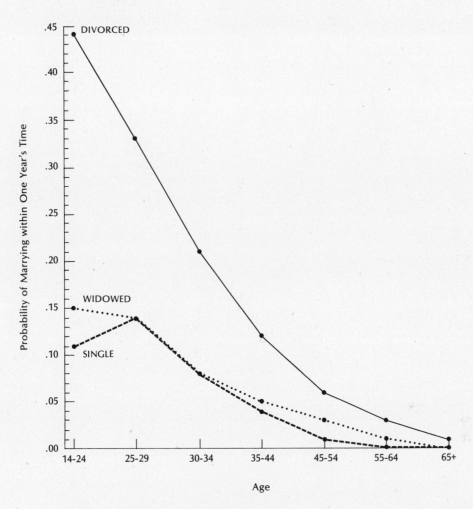

ference may reflect the taboo on hasty marriage after bereavement out of
respect for the memory of the loved one. Divorced persons, by definition,
have nothing to respect. Moreover, their first marriages normally ended in
separation many months before the divorce decree was final. If an extramarital relationship motivated the divorce, the foundation for the new
marriage was laid before the termination of the old one. In a study of high-
status Americans, Cuber and Harroff (1965) found the most frequent
reason for divorce was "finding a mate who seemed better to fit the man's
or the woman's needs and wants—an engaging alternative to the lack-
luster of one's present circumstances." Whether one wishes to call the
discovery of a new partner a *reason* for divorce, it is unquestionably an
occasion for divorce and prompt remarriage.

Figure 22-3 Interval between Divorce or Bereavement and Remarriage

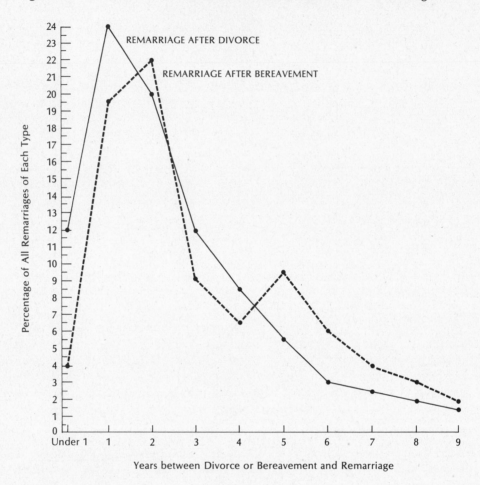

REMARRIAGE AFTER DIVORCE

REMARRIAGE AFTER BEREAVEMENT

Percentage of All Remarriages of Each Type

Years between Divorce or Bereavement and Remarriage

Adapted from Glick: 1957, 139.
Source: Current Population Surveys of remarriages occurring 1950-53.

When divorced persons remarry, they most often choose someone who has also been divorced. In 1969, national statistics showed that 55 percent of divorced persons married other divorced persons. When both partners have been through a divorce, they can more easily empathize with one another's experiences.

The Success of Remarriage

There is little reason to question the general success of postbereavement marriages, but the marriages of divorced persons are another matter. Given the fact that 100 percent of their first marriages failed, by sheer chance we would expect some to select better partners the next time. When we add the maturity gained in the interval between the beginning of the first marriage and the second, and the wisdom gained from previous experience, we would expect even more second marriages to succeed. On the other hand, some divorced people are incapable of living with anyone. The most unsuitable may not even try to marry again (or at least not find a willing partner). Of those who do remarry, those who are emotionally impaired constitute a growing proportion with successive marriages. Hence the success rate declines when second marriages are compared with third marriages, and so forth. Figure 22–4 shows the incidence of divorces involving remarriages (after divorce and bereavement combined), using divorces following first marriages as a base line. The larger the number of previous marriages, the greater the likelihood of divorce.

Figure 22-4 Probability of Divorce, by Marriage Order

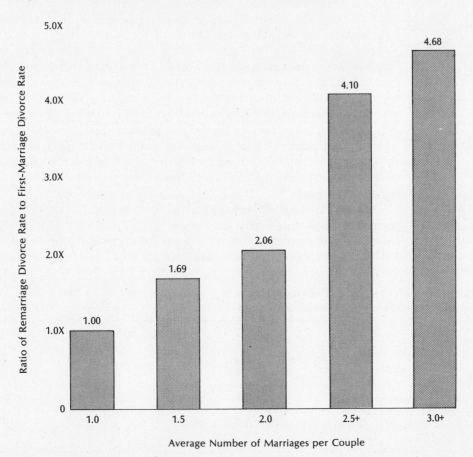

Adapted from Monahan, 1952: 287. *Source:* Number of marriages and number of divorces for state of Iowa in 1948-50, by average number of marriages for husband and wife combined.

This illustrates the increasing proportion of divorce-prone partners in multiple remarriages.

Not only are remarried persons more apt to get a divorce than persons marrying for the first time, but remarried persons who become dissatisfied with their new marriages split up sooner than first-marrying persons. Table 22–5 shows that the larger the number of remarriages involved in a given partnership, the more rapidly couples separated and legalized that separation in a divorce.

Presumably, persons who marry for the second time and find that they have failed again become easily discouraged. Their previous experience in terminating an earlier marriage enables them to move more quickly through the dissolution process.

Many second marriages are stable in the sense of avoiding another divorce, and the individuals involved are usually delighted with the contrast between the new marriage and the old. Eighty-seven percent of Goode's remarried women found their new marriage "much better" than the first. Almost as many credited their experience in the first marriage with making the second one easier.

Preparation for Remarriage. If divorced individuals are to benefit fully from their previous marital experience, professional counseling is needed. Just as children from unhappy homes need "remodeling" in preparation for marriage, persons from unhappy marriages need remodeling, too. Divorce counseling can help each individual explore the reasons why the first marriage failed. Realizing that s/he will probably remarry, the client can explore qualities to look for in a new partner and means of making remarriage work. Later on, "pre-remarital" counseling can serve the same purpose.

Preparation for remarriage may also occur informally through "trial marriage" with a new partner. Berger (1974) studied couples who had lived together unmarried in noncollege settings and found that almost half of them included at least one partner who was divorced. Many of

Table 22–5 Median Duration of Marriage Prior to Separation and Divorce, for First Marriages and Remarriages of Husbands and Wives

Duration	Husband's: Wife's	MARRIAGE/REMARRIAGE (YEARS)			
		First First	Second First	First Second	Second Second
Wedding to separation		4.9	4.4	2.7	1.7
Separation to divorce		5.6	5.0	3.9	3.4
Wedding to divorce		10.5	9.4	6.6	5.1

Adapted from Carter and Pratt, 1958. *Source:* District of Columbia vital statistics.

these divorced persons were hesitant to remarry, and found that living with a new partner for some months or years enabled them to work through their fears of remarriage.

With life so short and the second chance for marital success likely to be the last, remarriage after divorce deserves extra preparation. Given that preparation, the chances of finding a satisfactory partner and building a rewarding second marriage are fairly good.

Children and Remarriage

Although most adults are enthusiastic about their remarriages, their children are less positive. Rosenberg (1965) found that children of remarried mothers had lower self-esteem and more psychosomatic symptoms than children whose divorced mothers never remarried. Similarly, Nye (1957) found that children felt closer to a mother without a partner than to one with a new partner. Apparently, from the child's viewpoint, to have one's mother remarry is not to restore one's family to normalcy but to lose the remaining parent to a stranger. Bad enough to lose one parent through divorce—worse yet to lose the other by "desertion."

On the other hand, just as adoption works best with young children, the younger the child when it changes parents, the better the adjustment to the new parent. Perhaps if stepparents courted children as effectively as they court their new spouse, the new family would be better integrated. Without such effort, broken families may disintegrate further from the invasion of a stranger.

When widowed parents who still have children living at home remarry, they face greater problems than single parents who have been divorced. Bowerman and Irish (1962) found that teenagers who acquired a stepfather after divorce were slightly more apt to feel affectionate toward him than those whose fathers had died. The difference was bigger in the case of stepmothers. Teenagers who were living with their father following divorce were far more affectionate toward a new stepmother than children whose bereaved fathers had married a new woman. Presumably, adolescents who either chose to live with their fathers or were given into the custody of their fathers because their mothers were unfit were as open to acquiring a new and better mother as their fathers were to acquiring a new and better wife. So stepmothers in the postdivorce situation were relatively welcome. Stepparents of either sex, on the other hand, faced a difficult task when replacing a loved parent who had died.

Regardless of how the marriage ended, Bowerman and Irish found that stepparents were accused by their stepchildren of discriminating unfairly among siblings and of rejecting their stepchildren more often than natural parents. Stepchildren wished that they lived in a different family more often than did children living with both natural parents.

Stepmothers, especially, were resented by their stepchildren. While step-parents may to some extent provoke this resentment by discriminatory behavior, we suspect that it is extremely difficult for a new parent to come into most families and be viewed with much affection. To be a latecomer is to be handicapped in ways almost impossible to overcome.

Remarriage after Bereavement

We have already seen that widowed persons differ from divorced persons in many of their remarriage patterns. They are less apt to remarry at all. If they do remarry, they take longer to get around to it, remarrying only if they find an attractive successor to their first spouse rather than with the urgency that generally afflicts divorced persons. Having already been successfully married before, their second marriages almost always turn out well—but not always. We can learn some lessons that may be valuable not only to widowed persons but to divorced persons contemplating remarriage by comparing the factors involved in successful and unsuccessful remarriage after bereavement.

McKain (1972) studied a representative sample of widowed persons who were at least 60 years old when they remarried. He found that older persons faced a special problem when they wanted to remarry—their children sometimes attempted to dissuade them for fear that the remarriage would interfere with their expected inheritance. Children also viewed second marriages as betrayals of the memory of their deceased parent and found it difficult to sympathize with the surviving parent's desire for companionship, affection, and sex. Social pressure against remarriage was so strong that at least one-fourth of McKain's respondents almost gave up their plans to remarry, and the great majority downplayed their second wedding and honeymoon so they would not offend their critics.

We should not jump to the conclusion that children's and friends' opposition is necessarily either self-centered or irrelevant. Table 22–6 shows that remarriages receiving the blessing of the children of the bride and groom were more successful. We do not interpret this as a cause-and-effect relationship (that the children's support improved the marriage) so much as evidence that the children saw the potential trouble spots in the remarriage. As in first marriages where parental opposition is frequently a premonition of trouble to come, children and other outsiders may spot potential trouble in a remarriage.

The participants themselves were less apt to regret marriages to someone they had known a long time. Most of McKain's couples had known each other before either of them was widowed. Many were neighbors, members of the same church, social acquaintances, siblings-in-law, or childhood sweethearts. Those who had known each other for a decade or more prior to marrying seldom regretted their choice.

Table 22–6 Success of Remarriage, by Attitude of Children

	CHILDREN ENCOURAGED REMARRIAGE	
Marital Success	*Yes*	*No*
Successful	80%	59%
Unsuccessful	20	41
Total	100%	100%
Number of cases	115	27

Adapted from McKain, 1972: 68. *Source:* Representative sample of Connecticut marriages of widowed persons aged 60 and over, five years after remarriage.

One way of responding to children's fears about their inheritance would be for remarried couples to keep separate financial accounts. While this may improve the parent-child relationship, it is not good for the marriage. Almost half of the remarriages in McKain's sample failed when couples kept separate accounts, compared to less than 13 percent of couples who pooled their finances.

Another problem in remarriage is the question of where the couple will live. McKain found that inequality between the partners was inauspicious. If one partner owned a home and the other partner moved in (literally taking the place of the deceased spouse), half the marriages turned out badly. Ownership by only one partner caused no trouble as long as the couple didn't attempt to live there. Presumably, moving into the old house prevents a couple from giving their remarriage a fresh start. The new partner needs to be seen in his/her own reality, not distorted by memories of the lost partner. Such memories die hard in a house that the ex-couple shared.

Remarriages versus First Marriages

Remarriages, regardless of whether they follow divorce or bereavement, differ qualitatively from first marriages.

We have already seen that second wedding ceremonies of older widowed persons are less pretentious than first weddings. Although McKain attributed this to the desire to avoid offending children and friends, we suspect that much of this inconspicuousness is due simply to the fact that, having got married once before, remarrying couples are less excited about weddings. Hollingshead (1952) found that persons marrying for the second time were less apt to have an engagement ring, a church wedding, a big wedding, or a honeymoon. Like first intercourse, a first wedding marks a bigger transition than subsequent ones.

Once they are married, second-round couples treat each other differently as well. Centers and his colleagues (1971) found that remarried husbands were less domineering than men in their first marriages. Perhaps the failure of their first marriage leads them to approach decision making more gingerly. Crockett and his associates (1969) found that remarried persons were more apt than people in their first marriages (84 percent versus 54 percent) to change their religious affiliation—a difference reminiscent of their having changed their marital affiliation. Remarried persons who changed churches were less apt than first-married changers to change toward a common faith (57 percent versus 83 percent of those changing faiths). Thus, remarried persons were not only more changeable, but more independent of their new spouse in making those changes. This means that they less often provided themselves with the external support that is conducive to marital stability.

Rosenthal (1970) found that Iowa Jewish persons remarrying after divorce were more apt than those marrying for the first time to wed Gentiles. Where neither partner had been married before, the percentage of intermarriages was only 35 percent, whereas where both partners had been divorced, the percentage of mixed marriages was 76 percent. The larger the number of previous marriages, the higher the rate of intermarriage became. This lesser ethnic conformity is analogous to the lesser religious conformity of Crockett's respondents who remarried following a divorce. These studies suggest that remarried persons emphasize separateness in their new marriages more than first-marrying couples generally do.

These are some of the differences between remarriages and first marriages. But as with all generalizations, they describe only marginal differences. The biggest differences are not between remarriages and first marriages, but between couples, regardless of the number of times they have been married. In any marriage what matters most is the energy and sensitivity that the two partners bring to their relationship.

References

NOTE: Multiple works by the same first author are listed chronologically by year of publication. Multiple works in the same year are listed alphabetically by title.

Adams, Bert N. 1968. *Kinship in an Urban Setting*. Chicago: Markham.

Adams, Bert N., and **Miles T. Meidam.** 1968. "Economics, Family Structure, and College Attendance." *American Journal of Sociology* 74: 230–39.

Adorno, T. W.; E. Frenkel-Brunswik; D. J. Levinson; and **R. W. Sanford.** 1950. *The Authoritarian Personality*. New York: Harper.

Ainsworth, M. D. Salter, and **B. A. Wittig.** 1969. "Attachment and Exploratory Behaviour of One-Year-Olds in a Strange Situation." In *Determinants of Infant Behaviour*. Edited by B. M. Foss. New York: Barnes and Noble. Cited in Bowlby, 1969.

American College of Obstetricians and Gynecologists (A.C.O.G.). 1965. *Manual of Standards in Obstetric-Gynecologic Practice,* second edition. Chicago: ACOG.

Angelino, H.; E. Edmonds; and **E. Mech.** 1958. "Sex-expressed 'First' Sources of Sex Information." *Psychological Newsletter* 9: 268–69.

Anspach, Donald F. 1976. "Kinship and Divorce." *Journal of Marriage and the Family* 38: 323–30.

Apley, John, and **Ronald MacKeith.** 1962. *The Child and His Symptoms*. Oxford: Blackwell. Cited in Newson and Newson, 1968.

Ard, Ben N., Jr. 1974. "Premarital Sexual Experience: A Longitudinal Study." *Journal of Sex Research* 10: 32–39.

Athanasiou, R.; P. Shaver; and **C. Tavris.** 1970. "Sex." *Psychology Today* 4, no. 2: 37–62. Cited in Smith and Smith, 1973.

Atkeson, Paula. 1970. "Building Communication in Intercultural Marriage." *Psychiatry* 33: 396–408.

Babchuk, Nicholas. 1965. "Primary Friends and Kin: A Study of the Associations of Middle Class Couples." *Social Forces* 43: 483–93.

Babchuk, Nicholas, and **Angelo La Cognata.** 1960. "Crises and the Effective Utilization of Contraception." *Marriage and Family Living* 22: 254–58.

Babchuk, Nicholas; Harry J. Crockett, Jr.; and **John A. Ballweg.** 1967. "Change in Religious Affiliation and Family Stability." *Social Forces* 45: 551–55.

Bach, George R., and **Peter Wyden.** 1969. *The Intimate Enemy: How to Fight Fair in Love and Marriage*. New York: Morrow.

Bach, George R., and **Ronald M. Deutsch.** 1971. *Pairing.* New York: Avon.

Bachman, Jerald G. 1970. *The Impact of Family Background and Intelligence on Tenth-grade Boys.* Ann Arbor, Mich.: Institute for Social Research, University of Michigan.

Bahr, Stephen J., and **Boyd C. Rollins.** 1971. "Crisis and Conjugal Power." *Journal of Marriage and the Family* 33: 360–67.

Bailyn, Lotte. 1959. "Mass Media and Children: A Study of Exposure Habits and Cognitive Effects." *Psychological Monographs* no. 471.

Balswick, Jack O. 1970. "The Effect of Spouse Companionship Support on Employment Success." *Journal of Marriage and the Family* 32: 212–15.

Bandura, Albert. 1964. "Behavioral Modification through Modeling Procedures." In *Research in Behavior Modification.* Edited by L. Krasner and L. P. Ullman. New York: Holt, Rinehart, and Winston.

Bandura, Albert, and **Richard H. Walters.** 1959. *Adolescent Aggression: A Study of the Influence of Child-training Practices and Family Interrelations.* New York: Ronald Press.

Bandura, Albert; Dorothea Ross; and **Sheila A. Ross.** 1963. "Imitation of Film-mediated Aggressive Models." *Journal of Abnormal and Social Psychology* 66: 3–11.

Bartell, Gilbert D. 1971. *Group Sex: A Scientist's Eyewitness Report on the American Way of Swinging.* New York: Wyden.

Baruch, G. K. 1972. "Maternal Influence upon College Women's Attitudes toward Women and Work." *Developmental Psychology* 6: 32–37. Cited in Hoffman and Nye, 1974.

Bates, Alan. 1942. "Parental Roles in Courtship." *Social Forces* 20: 483–86.

Bauman, Karl E., and **Robert E. Wilson.** 1974. "Sexual Behavior of Unmarried University Students in 1968 and 1972." *Journal of Sex Research* 10: 327–33.

Baumrind, Diana. 1966. "Effects of Authoritative Parental Control on Child Behavior." *Child Development* 37: 888–907.

Bayer, Alan E. 1972. "College Impact on Marriage." *Journal of Marriage and the Family* 34: 600–10.

Beck, Dorothy Fahs, and **Mary Ann Jones.** 1973. *Progress on Family Problems: A Nationwide Study of Clients' and Counselors' Views on Family Agency Services.* New York: Family Service Association of America.

Becker, Wesley C.; Donald R. Peterson; Zella Luria; Donald J. Shoemaker; and **Leo A. Hellmer.** 1962. "Relations of Factors Derived from Parent-Interview Ratings to Behavior Problems of Five-Year-Olds." *Child Development* 33: 509–36.

Bee, Helen L. 1971. "Socialization for Problem Solving." In *Family Problem Solving.* Edited by Joan Aldous, Thomas Condon, Reuben Hill, Murray Straus, and Irving Tallman. Hinsdale, Ill.: Dryden.

Behrman, Samuel J., and **John R. G. Gosling.** 1966. *Fundamentals of Gynecology,* second edition. New York: Oxford University Press.

Bell, Robert R. 1967. *Marriage and Family Interaction.* Homewood, Ill.: Dorsey.

Bell, Robert R., and **Jack V. Buerkle.** 1962. "The Daughter's Role During the 'Launching Stage.'" *Marriage and Family Living* 24: 384–88.

Bell, Robert R., and **Jay B. Chaskes.** 1970. "Premarital Sexual Experience among Coeds, 1958 and 1968." *Journal of Marriage and the Family* 32: 81–84.

Bell, Robert R., and **Janet Connolly.** 1973. "Noncoital Sex in Marriage." Paper presented at annual meeting of National Council on Family Relations, Toronto.

Bell, Robert R.; Stanley Turner; and **Lawrence Rosen.** 1975. "A Multivariate Analysis of Female Extramarital Coitus." *Journal of Marriage and the Family* 37: 375–84.

Benson, Purnell. 1955. "The Common Interests Myth in Marriage." *Social Problems* 3: 27–34.

Berardo, Felix M. 1967. *Social Adaptation to Widowhood among a Rural-Urban Aged Population.* Pullman, Wash.: Washington Agricultural Experiment Station Bulletin no. 689.

Berger, Miriam. 1974. "Trial Marriage Follow-up Study." Unpublished manuscript, Jamaica, N.Y.

Bernard, Jessie. 1972. *The Future of Marriage.* New York: World.

Bernhard, Yetta. 1975. *Self Care.* Millbrae, Calif.: Celestial Arts.

Besanceney, Paul H. 1962. "Unbroken Protestant-Catholic Marriages among Whites in the Detroit Area." *American Catholic Sociological Review* 23: 3–20.

Bierman, Jessie M.; Earl Siegel; Fern E. French; and **Kenneth Simonian.** 1965. "Analysis of the

Outcome of All Pregnancies in a Community." *American Journal of Obstetrics and Gynecology* 80: 37–45.

Bigman, Stanley. 1957. *The Jewish Population of Greater Washington in 1956.* Washington, D.C.: Jewish Community Council of Greater Washington. Cited in Gordon, 1964.

Blatt, Carol, and **Ray Blatt.** 1970."An Evolutionary Theory of Social Interaction." Unpublished manuscript,

Blau, Peter M., and **Otis Dudley Duncan.** 1967. *The American Occupational Structure.* New York: Wiley.

Blazer, John A. 1964. "Married Virgins—A Study of Unconsummated Marriages." *Journal of Marriage and the Family* 26: 213–14.

Blood, Robert O., Jr. 1952. "Developmental and Traditional Child-rearing Philosophies and Their Family Situational Consequences." Ph.D. dissertation, University of North Carolina, Chapel Hill.

Blood, Robert O., Jr. 1953. "Consequences of Permissiveness for Parents of Young Children." *Marriage and Family Living* 15: 209–12.

Blood, Robert O., Jr. 1956. "Uniformities and Diversities in Campus Dating Preferences." *Marriage and Family Living* 18: 37–45.

Blood, Robert O., Jr. 1960. "Resolving Family Conflicts." *Conflict Resolution* 4: 209–19.

Blood, Robert O., Jr. 1961. "Social Class and Family Control of Television Viewing." *Merrill-Palmer Quarterly* 7: 205–22.

Blood, Robert O., Jr. 1963. "The Husband-Wife Relationship." In *The Employed Mother in America.* Edited by F. Ivan Nye and Lois W. Hoffman. Chicago: Rand McNally

Blood, Robert O., Jr. 1967. *Love Match and Arranged Marriage: A Tokyo-Detroit Comparison.* New York: Free Press.

Blood, Robert O., Jr. 1969. "Kinship Interaction and Marital Solidarity." *Merrill-Palmer Quarterly* 15: 171–83.

Blood, Robert O., Jr. 1972. *The Family.* New York: Free Press.

Blood, Robert O., Jr., and **Morris Axelrod.** 1955. Unpublished data from Detroit Area Study and companion rural research project.

Blood, Robert O., Jr., and **Robert L. Hamblin.** 1958. "The Effect of the Wife's Employment on the Family Power Structure." *Social Forces* 36: 347–52.

Blood, Robert O., Jr., and **Donald M. Wolfe.** 1960. *Husbands and Wives: The Dynamics of Married Living.* Glencoe, Ill.: Free Press.

Blood, Robert O., Jr., and **Margaret C. Blood.** 1977. "Jealousy Workshops." *Jealousy.* Edited by Gordon Clanton and Lynne Smith. Englewood Cliffs, N.J.: Prentice-Hall.

Bogen, Iver. 1974. "Attitudes of Women Who Have Had Abortions." *Journal of Sex Research* 10: 97–109.

Bohannan, Paul, ed. 1971. *Divorce and After: An Analysis of the Emotional and Social Problems of Divorce.* Garden City, N.Y.: Doubleday Anchor.

Bolton, Charles D. 1961. "Mate-Selection as the Development of a Relationship." *Marriage and Family Living* 23: 234–40.

Boss, Pauline. 1975. "Psychological Father Presence in the Missing-in-Action (MIA) Family System: The Testing of a Theory on Father Interaction." Paper presented to National Council on Family Relations,

Bossard, James H. S., and **Eleanor S. Boll.** 1950. *Ritual in Family Living.* Philadelphia: University of Pennsylvania Press.

Bossard, James H. S., and **Eleanor S. Boll.** 1960. *The Sociology of Child Development.* New York: Harper.

Bott, Elizabeth. 1957. *Family and Social Network.* London: Tavistock.

Bower, Donald W. 1975. "A Description and Analysis of a Cohabiting Sample in America." Unpublished master's thesis, University of Arizona.

Bowerman, Charles E., and **Donald P. Irish.** 1962. "Some Relationships of Stepchildren to Their Parents." *Marriage and Family Living* 24: 113–21.

Bowerman, Charles E., and **Rebecca M. Dobash.** 1974. "Structural Variations in Inter-Sibling Affect." *Journal of Marriage and the Family* 36: 48–56.

Bowlby, John. 1969. *Attachment.* New York: Basic Books.

Bowman, Henry A. 1960. *Marriage for Moderns.* New York; McGraw-Hill.

Bradley, Robert A. 1962. "Fathers' Presence in Delivery Rooms." *Psychosomatics* 3: 1–6.

Bresler, Jack R. 1961. "The Relation of Population Fertility Levels to Ethnic Group Backgrounds." *Eugenics Quarterly* 8: 12–22.

Bringle, Robert G. 1975. "Prospectus on a Social Psychological Study of Jealousy and Envy." Unpublished research proposal, Department of Psychology, Indiana University/Purdue University at Indianapolis.

Brody, Sylvia. 1956. *Patterns of Mothering.* New York: International Universities Press.

Bronfenbrenner, Urie. 1961. "Toward a Theoretical Model for the Analysis of Parent-Child Relationships in a Social Context." In *Parental Attitudes and Child Behavior.* Edited by John C. Glidewell. Springfield, Ill.: Thomas.

Bronfenbrenner, Urie. 1970. *Two Worlds of Childhood: U.S. and U.S.S.R.* New York: Russell Sage Foundation.

Brown, Gwen; Brack Cottle; Fred Denooy; Cynthia Daiboch; and **Mike Murphy.** 1975. "Heterosexual Cohabitation among Unmarried College Students at San Diego State University." Unpublished master's thesis, School of Social Work, San Diego State University.

Buber, Martin. 1958. *I and Thou.* New York: Scribner's.

Buerkle, Jack V.; Theodore R. Anderson; and **Robin F. Badgley.** 1961. "Altruism, Role Conflict, and Marital Adjustment: A Factor Analysis of Marital Interaction." *Marriage and Family Living* 23: 20–26.

Bumpass Larry L., and **Charles F. Westoff.** 1970. *The Later Years of Childbearing.* Princeton, N.J.: Princeton University Press.

Burchinal, Lee G. 1960. "Sources and Adequacy of Sex Knowledge among Iowa High School Girls." *Marriage and Family Living* 22: 268–69.

Burchinal, Lee G., and **Loren E. Chancellor.** 1963. "Survival Rates among Religiously Homogamous and Interreligious Marriages." *Social Forces* 41: 353–62.

Burgess, Ernest W., and **Leonard S. Cottrell, Jr.** 1939. *Predicting Success or Failure in Marriage.* New York: Prentice-Hall.

Burgess, Ernest W., and **Paul Wallin.** 1953. *Engagement and Marriage.* Chicago: Lippincott.

Burke, Ronald J., and **Tamara Weir.** 1976. "Relationship of Wives' Employment Status to Husband, Wife, and Pair Satisfaction and Performance." *Journal of Marriage and the Family* 38: 279–87.

Burton, Genevieve, and **Howard M. Kaplan.** 1968. "Group Counseling in Conflicted Marriages Where Alcoholism Is Present: Clients' Evaluation of Effectiveness." *Journal of Marriage and the Family* 30: 74–79.

Butler, Edgar W.; Ronald J. McAllister; and **Edward J. Kaiser.** 1973. "The Effects of Voluntary and Involuntary Residential Mobility on Females and Males." *Journal of Marriage and the Family* 35: 219–27.

Butman, Jean W., and **Jane A. Kamm.** 1965. *The Social, Psychological, and Behavioral World of the Teen-age Girl.* Ann Arbor, Mich.: Institute for Social Research, University of Michigan.

Butts, Robert Y., and **Michael J. Sporakowski.** 1974. "Unwed Pregnancy Decisions; Some Background Factors." *Journal of Sex Research* 10: 110–17.

Campbell, Frederick L. 1970. "Family Growth and Variation in Family Role Structure." *Journal of Marriage and the Family* 32: 45–53.

Carter, Hugh, and **William F. Pratt.** 1958. "Duration of Marriage Prior to Separation and Divorce: A Study Based on Vital Records." Paper presented to American Sociological Society. Cited in Carter and Glick, 1970.

Carter, Hugh, and **Paul C. Glick.** 1970. *Marriage and Divorce: A Social and Economic Study.* Cambridge: Harvard University Press.

Casler, Lawrence. 1961. *Maternal Deprivation: A Critical Review of the Literature.* Child Development Monograph no. 80.

Centers, Richard; Bertram H. Raven; and **Aroldo Rodrigues.** 1971. "Conjugal Power Structure: A Re-examination." *American Sociological Review* 36: 264–77.

Chadwick, Bruce A.; Stan L. Albrecht; and **Phillip R. Kunz.** 1976. "Marital and Family Role Satisfaction." *Journal of Marriage and the Family* 38: 431–40.

Chambliss, William J. 1965. "The Selection of Friends." *Social Forces* 43: 370–80.

Chancellor, Loren E., and **Thomas P. Monahan.** 1955. "Religious Preference and Interreligious Mixtures in Marriages and Divorces in Iowa." *American Journal of Sociology* 61: 233–39.

Chancellor, Loren E., and **Lee D. Burchinal.** 1962. "Relations among Migratory Marriages and Civil Weddings in Iowa." *Eugenics Quarterly* 9: 75–83.

Chein, Isidor; Donald L. Gerard; Robert S. Lee; and **Eva Rosenfeld.** 1964. *The Road to H: Narcotics, Delinquency, and Social Policy.* New York: Basic Books.

Chertok, Leon. 1972. "The Psychopathology of Vomiting of Pregnancy." In *Modern Perspectives in Psycho-Obstetrics.* Edited by John G. Howells. New York: Brunner/Mazel.

Chesser, Eustace. 1957. *The Sexual, Marital and Family Relationships of the English Woman.* New York: Roy.

Chilman, Catherine S., and **Donald L. Meyer.** 1962. "Educational Achievement of Undergraduate Married Students as Compared to Undergraduate Unmarried Students, with Analysis of Certain Associated Variables." Cooperative Research Project no. 961, Syracuse University, Syracuse, N.Y. Cited in Marshall and King, 1966.

Christensen, Harold T. 1962. "A Cross-cultural Comparison of Attitudes towards Marital Infidelity." *International Journal of Comparative Sociology* 3: 124–37.

Christensen, Harold T. 1963. "Timing of First Pregnancy as a Factor in Divorce: A Cross-cultural Analysis." *Eugenics Quarterly* 10: 119–30.

Christensen, Harold T., and **Hanna H. Meissner.** 1953. "Studies in Child-spacing: III. Premarital Pregnancy as a Factor in Divorce." *American Sociological Review* 18: 641–44.

Christensen, Harold T., and **George R. Carpenter.** 1962. "Value-Behavior Discrepancies Regarding Premarital Coitus." *American Sociological Review* 27: 66–74.

Christopherson, Victor A.; Joseph S. Vandiver; and **Marie N. Krueger.** 1960. "The Married College Student, 1959." *Marriage and Family Living* 22: 122–28.

Clanton, Gordon, and **Chris Downing.** 1975. *Face to Face to Face: An Experiment in Intimacy.* New York: Dutton.

Clanton, Gordon, and **Lynne G. Smith, eds.** 1977. *Jealousy.* Englewood Cliffs, N.J.: Prentice-Hall.

Clark, Charles E., and **Harry Shulman.** 1937. *A Study of Law Administration in Connecticut.* New Haven, Conn.: Yale University Press. Cited in Monahan, 1962.

Clay, Vidal S. 1968. "The Effect of Culture on Mother-Child Tactile Communication." *The Family Coordinator* 17: 204–10.

Cobb, Sidney, and **John R. P. French, Jr.** 1966. "Birth Order among Medical Students." *Journal of the American Medical Association* 195: 172–73.

Cohen, David B.; F. J. King; and **Willard H. Nelson.** 1963. "Academic Achievement of College Students Before and After Marriage." *Marriage and Family Living* 25: 98–99.

Cole, Steven G., and **David Bryon.** 1973. "A Review of Information Relevant to Vasectomy Counselors." *The Family Coordinator* 22: 215–21.

Comstock, George A., and **Eli A. Rubinstein, eds.** 1971. *Television and Adolescent Aggressiveness.* Washington, D.C.: U.S. Government Printing Office.

Condry, John C., Jr.; Michael L. Siman; and **Urie Bronfenbrenner.** 1968. "Characteristics of Peer- and Adult-Oriented Children." Unpublished master's thesis. Department of Child Development, Cornell University.

Connor, Ruth, and **Edith Flinn Hall.** 1952. "The Dating Behavior of College Freshmen and Sophomores." *Journal of Home Economics* 44: 278–81.

Connor, Ruth; Theodore B. Johannis, Jr.; and **James Walters.** 1955. "Family Recreation in Relation to Role Conceptions of Family Members." *Marriage and Family Living* 17: 306–309.

Constantine, Larry L. 1975. "Open Family: A Life-style for Kids and Other People." Paper presented at annual meeting of National Council on Family Relations, To be published in *The Family Coordinator.*

Constantine, Larry L. 1977. "Jealousy: Techniques for Intervention." In *Jealousy.* Edited by Gordon Clanton and Lynn G. Smith. Englewood Cliffs, N.J.: Prentice Hall.

Constantine, Larry L., and **Joan M. Constantine.** 1970. "Counseling Implications of Comarital and

Multilateral Relations." Mimeographed version of paper later published in condensed form, co-authored with Sheldon K. Edelman in *The Family Coordinator* 21 (1972): 267–74.

Constantine, Larry L., and **Joan M. Constantine.** 1971. "Sexual Aspects of Multilateral Relations." *Journal of Sex Research* 7: 204–25.

Constantine, Larry L., and **Joan M. Constantine.** 1973a. *Group Marriage: A Study of Contemporary Multilateral Marriage.* New York: Macmillan.

Constantine, Larry L., and **Joan M. Constantine.** 1973b. "Sexual Aspects of Group Marriage." In *Renovating Marriage: Toward New Sexual Life-styles.* Edited by Roger W. Libby and Robert N. Whitehurst. Danville, Calif.: Consensus.

Converse, Philip E. 1966. Data from national survey conducted by Survey Research Center, Institute for Social Research, University of Michigan, Ann Arbor.

Cookerly, J. Richard. 1973. "The Outcome of the Six Major Forms of Marriage Counseling Compared: A Pilot Study." *Journal of Marriage and the Family* 35: 608–12.

Coombs, Robert H. 1962. "Reinforcement of Values in the Parental Home as a Factor in Mate Selection." *Marriage and Family Living* 24: 155–57.

Coombs, Robert H. 1966. "Value Consensus and Partner Satisfaction among Dating Couples." *Journal of Marriage and the Family* 28: 167–73.

Coombs, Robert H., and **William F. Kenkel.** 1966. "Sex Differences in Dating Aspirations and Satisfaction with Computer-selected Partners." *Journal of Marriage and the Family* 28: 62–66.

Coopersmith, Stanley. 1967. *The Antecedents of Self-esteem.* San Francisco: Freeman.

Cottrell, Ann Baker. 1973. "Cross-national Marriage as an Extension of an International Life-style: A Study of Indian-Western Couples." *Journal of Marriage and the Family* 35: 739–41.

Cottrell, Ann Baker. 1975. "Outsiders' Inside View: Western Wives' Experiences in Indian Joint Families." *Journal of Marriage and the Family* 37: 400–407.

Crockett, Harry J., Jr.; Nicholas Babchuk; and **John A. Ballweg.** 1969. "Change in Religious Affiliations and Family Stability: A Second Study." *Journal of Marriage and the Family* 31: 464–68.

Croog, Sydney H., and **James E. Teele.** 1967. "Religious Identity and Church Attendance of Sons of Religious Intermarriages." *American Sociological Review* 32: 93–103.

Cuber, John F., and **Peggy B. Harroff.** 1965. *The Significant Americans: A Study of Sexual Behavior among the Affluent.* New York: Appleton-Century.

Cutler, Beverly R., and **William G. Dyer.** 1965. "Initial Adjustment Processes in Young Married Couples." *Social Forces* 44: 195–201.

Cutwright, Phillips. 1970. "Income and Family Events: Getting Married." *Journal of Marriage and the Family* 32: 628–37.

Danziger, Carl, and **Mathew Greenwald.** 1973. *Alternatives: A Look at Unmarried Couples and Communes.* New York: Institute of Life Insurance.

DeFleur, Melvin L. 1964. "Occupational Roles as Presented on Television." *Public Opinion Quarterly* 28: 57–74.

DeFleur, Melvin L., and **Lois B. DeFleur.** 1967. "The Relative Contribution of Television as a Learning Source for Children's Occupational Knowledge." *American Sociological Review* 32: 777–89.

Denfield, Duane. 1974. "Dropouts from Swinging: The Marriage Counselor as Informant." In *Beyond Monogamy.* Edited by James R. Smith and Lynn G. Smith. Baltimore, Md.: Johns Hopkins University Press.

Denfeld, Duane, and **Michael Gordon.** 1970. "The Sociology of Mate Swapping: Or the Family That Swings Together Clings Together." *Journal of Sex Research* 6: 85–100.

Dentler, Robert A., and **Peter Pineo.** 1960. "Sexual Adjustment, Marital Adjustment and Personal Growth of Husbands: A Panel Analysis." *Marriage and Family Living* 22: 45–48.

DesRosiers, Mary, and **Richard Kleinschmidt.** 1973. "Contemporary Marriage Contract." *Friends Journal,* November 15.

Detroit Area Study. 1956. *A Social Profile of Detroit.* Ann Arbor, Mich.: Institute for Social Research, University of Michigan. Annual series of research reports.

Deutscher, Irwin. 1959. *Married Life in the Middle Years: A Study of the Middle Class Urban Postparental Couple.* Kansas City, Mo.: Community Studies.

DeVos, George. 1959. "Personality Patterns and Problems of Adjustment in American-Japanese Intercultural Marriages." Unpublished report, School of Social Work, University of California, Berkeley. Cited by Wagatsuma, 1973.

Dewees, Lovett. 1947. "Premarital Physical Examination." In *Successful Marriage.* Edited by Morris Fishbein and Ernest W. Burgess. Garden City, N.Y.: Doubleday.

Dizard, Jan. 1968. *Social Change in the Family.* Chicago: Community and Family Study Center, University of Chicago.

Dominick, Joseph R., and **Bradley S. Greenberg.** 1971. "Attitudes toward Violence: The Interaction of Television Exposure, Family Attitudes, and Social Class." In *Television and Adolescent Aggressiveness.* Edited by George A. Comstock and Eli A. Rubinstein. Washington, D.C.: U.S.G.P.O.

Douglas, William. 1965. *Ministers' Wives.* New York: Harper and Row.

Douvan, Elizabeth. 1963. "Employment and the Adolescent." In *The Employed Mother in America.* Edited by F. Ivan Nye and Lois W. Hoffman. Chicago: Rand McNally.

Douvan, Elizabeth, and **Carol Kaye.** 1956. *Adolescent Girls.* Ann Arbor, Mich.: Institute for Social Research, University of Michigan.

Douvan, Elizabeth, and **Joseph Adelson.** 1966. *The Adolescent Experience.* New York: Wiley.

Drabek, Thomas E.; William H. Key; Patricia E. Erickson; and **Juanita L. Crowe.** 1975. "The Impact of Disaster on Kin Relationships." *Journal of Marriage and the Family* 37: 481–94.

Duncan, Otis Dudley; Howard Schuman; and **Beverly Duncan.** 1973. *Social Change in Metropolitan Detroit: The 1950's to 1971.* New York: Russell Sage Foundation.

Duvall, Evelyn. 1954. *In-Laws: Pro and Con.* New York: Association Press.

Dyer, Everett D. 1963. "Parenthood as Crisis: A Restudy." *Marriage and Family Living* 25: 196–201.

Eastman, Nicholson J. 1950. *Williams's Obstetrics,* tenth edition. New York: Appleton-Century-Crofts.

Eckhardt, Kenneth W., and **Eldon C. Schriner.** 1969. "Familial Conflict, Adolescent Rebellion, and Political Expression." *Journal of Marriage and the Family* 31: 494–99.

Edmonds, Vernon H.; Glenne Withers; and **Beverly Dibatista.** 1972. "Adjustment, Conservatism, and Marital Conventionalization." *Journal of Marriage and the Family* 34: 96–103.

Edwards, John N., and **Alan Booth.** 1976. "Sexual Behavior In and Out of Marriage: An Assessment of Correlates." *Journal of Marriage and the Family* 38: 73–81.

Ehrmann, Winston W. 1952. "Student Cooperation in a Study of Dating Behavior." *Marriage and Family Living* 14: 322–26.

Ehrmann, Winston W. 1955. "Influence of Comparative Social Class of Companion upon Premarital Heterosexual Behavior." *Marriage and Family Living* 17: 48–53.

Ehrmann, Winston W. 1959. *Premarital Dating Behavior.* New York: Holt.

Elder, Glen H., Jr. 1969. "Appearance and Education in Marriage Mobility." *American Sociological Review* 34: 519–32.

Ellis, Albert. 1949. "A Study of Human Love Relationships." *Journal of Genetic Psychology* 75: 61–71.

Eshleman, J. Ross, and **Chester L. Hunt.** 1967. "Social Class Influences on Family Adjustment Patterns of Married College Students." *Journal of Marriage and the Family* 29: 485–91.

Fairchild, Roy W., and **John Charles Wynn.** 1961. *Families in the Church: A Protestant Survey.* New York: Association Press.

Farber, Bernard. 1964. *Family: Organization and Interaction.* San Francisco: Chandler.

Farber, Bernard. 1971. *Kinship and Class: A Midwestern Study.* New York: Basic Books.

Farris, Edmond J. 1950. *Human Fertility and the Problems of the Male.* New York: Author's Press.

Farris, Edmond J. 1956. *Human Ovulation and Fertility.* Philadelphia: Lippincott.

Feldman, Harold. 1960. Preliminary research report entitled "Why Husbands and Wives Can't Talk to Each Other," written by John Kord Lagemann, *Redbook,* December 1960.

Feldman, Harold. 1966. "Development of the Husband-Wife Relationship: A Research Report." Mimeographed. Ithaca, N.Y.: Cornell University.

Feldman, Harold. 1971. "The Effects of Children on the Family." In *Family Issues of Employed Women in Europe and America.* Edited by Andrée Michel. Leiden: Brill.

Feldman, Saul D. 1973. "Impediment or Stimulant? Marital Status and Graduate Education." *American Journal of Sociology* 78: 982–94.

Filler, William, and **Harold I. Lief.** 1963. "A Psychologic Approach to the Gynecologic Patient." In *The Psychological Basis of Medical Practice.* Edited by Harold Lief, Victor Lief, and Nina Lief. New York: Hoeber.

Firth, Raymond; Jane Hubert; and **Anthony Forge.** 1970. *Families and Their Relatives: Kinship in a Middle-class Sector of London.* New York: Humanities Press.

Fisher, Esther Oshiver. 1974. *Divorce: The New Freedom—A Guide to Divorcing and Divorce Counseling.* New York: Harper and Row.

Foote, Nelson N. 1956. "Matching of Husband and Wife on Phases of Development." *Transactions of the Third World Congress of Sociology* 4: 24–34. London: International Sociological Association.

Foote, Nelson N.; Janet Abu-Lughod; Mary M. Foley; and **Louis Winnick.** 1960. *Housing Choices and Housing Constraints.* New York: McGraw-Hill.

Fotheringham, John B.; Mora Skelton; and **Bernard A. Hoddinott.** 1971. *The Retarded Child and His Family: The Effects of Home and Institution.* Toronto: Ontario Institute for Studies in Education.

Francoeur, Robert T., and **Anna K. Francoeur.** 1974. *Hot and Cool Sex: Cultures in Conflict.* New York: Harcourt, Brace, Jovanovich.

Freedman, D. G.; H. Boverman; and **N. Freedman.** 1960. "Effects of Kinesthetic Stimulation on Weight Gain and Smiling in Premature Infants." Paper presented to American Orthopsychiatry Association. Cited in Montagu, 1971: 135.

Freedman, Ronald; Pascal K. Whelpton; and **Arthur A. Campbell.** 1959. *Family Planning, Sterility, and Population Growth.* New York: McGraw-Hill.

Freedman, Ronald; Pascal K. Whelpton; and **John W. Smit.** 1961. "Socioeconomic Factors in Religious Differentials in Fertility." *American Sociological Review* 26: 608–14.

Freedman, Ronald, and **Lolagene Coombs.** 1966. "Childspacing and Family Economic Position." *American Sociological Review* 31: 631–48.

Freud, Anna, and **Dorothy Burlingame.** 1943. *War and Children.* New York: International Universities Press.

Fromm, Erich. 1956. *The Art of Loving.* New York: Harper.

Fujisaki, Sumi. 1970. "Senso Hanayome no Higeki we Ima mo nao" ("Still Continuing Tragedy of War Brides"). *Fujin Koron* (September): 218–24. Cited by Wagatsuma, 1973.

Gallaway, Lowell E. 1969. "The Effect of Geographic Labor Mobility on Income: A Brief Comment." *Journal of Human Resources* 4: 103–109.

Gans, Herbert J. 1967. *The Levittowners: Ways of Life and Politics in a New Suburban Community.* New York: Pantheon.

Gebhard, Paul H. 1966. "Factors in Marital Orgasm." *Journal of Social Issues* 22: 88–95.

Gebhard, Paul H. 1971. "Postmarital Coitus among Widows and Divorcees." In *Divorce and After.* Edited by Paul Bohannan. Garden City, N.Y.: Doubleday Anchor.

Gebhard, Paul H.; Wardell B. Pomeroy; Clyde E. Martin; and **Cornelia V. Christenson.** 1958. *Pregnancy, Birth, and Abortion.* New York: Harper and Hoeber.

Geertsen, H. Reed, and **Robert M. Gray.** 1970. "Familistic Orientation and Inclination toward Adopting the Sick Role." *Journal of Marriage and the Family* 32: 638–46.

Geiger, Kent. 1955. "Deprivation and Solidarity in the Soviet Urban Family." *American Sociological Review* 20: 57–68.

Gersuny, Carl. 1970. "The Honeymoon Industry: Rhetoric and Bureaucratization of Status Passage." *The Family Coordinator* 19: 260–66.

Gibran, Kahlil. 1923. *The Prophet.* New York: Knopf.

Gilmartin, Brian G. 1974. "Sexual Deviance and Social Networks: A Study of Social, Family, and Marital Interaction Patterns among Co-Marital Sex Participants." In *Beyond Monogamy.* Edited by James R. Smith and Lynn G. Smith. Baltimore, Md.: Johns Hopkins University Press.

Gilmartin, Brian G., and **Dave V. Kusisto.** 1973. "Some Personal and Social Characteristics of Mate-Sharing Swingers." In *Renovating Marriage.* Edited by Roger W. Libby and Robert N. Whitehurst. Danville, Calif.: Consensus.

Ginzberg, Eli. 1966. *Life-Styles of Educated Women.* New York: Columbia University Press.

Glenn, Norval D. 1975. "Psychological Well-being in the Postparental Stage: Some Evidence from National Surveys." *Journal of Marriage and the Family* 37: 105–10.

Glick, Paul C. 1955. "The Life Cycle of the Family." *Marriage and Family Living* 17: 3–9.

Glick, Paul C. 1957. *American Families.* New York: Wiley.

Glick, Paul C. 1960. "Intermarriage and Fertility Patterns among Persons in Major Religious Groups." *Eugenics Quarterly* 7: 31–38.

Glick, Paul C., and **Hugh Carter.** 1958. "Marriage Pattern and Educational Level." *American Sociological Review* 23: 294–300.

Glick, Paul C., and **Hugh Carter.** 1970. *Marriage and Divorce: A Social and Economic Study.* Cambridge, Mass.: Harvard University Press.

Glueck, Sheldon, and **Eleanor Glueck.** 1950. *Unraveling Juvenile Delinquency.* Cambridge, Mass.: Harvard University Press.

Gold, Martin. 1961. *A Social-psychology of Delinquent Boys.* Ann Arbor, Mich.: Institute for Social Research, University of Michigan. Data reprinted in Hoffman, 1963.

Goldberg, David. 1967. "Our Falling Birth Rate: Fact and Fiction." Paper presented at meeting of Planned Parenthood/World Population in Denver, May 5.

Goldsen, Rose K.; Morris Rosenberg; Robin M. Williams, Jr.; and **Edward A. Suchman.** 1960. *What College Students Think.* Princeton, N.J.: Van Nostrand.

Goldstein, Sidney, and **Calvin Goldscheider.** 1966. "Social and Demographic Aspects of Jewish Intermarriages." *Social Problems* 13: 386–99.

Goode, William J. 1956. *After Divorce.* Glencoe, Ill.: Free Press.

Goode, William J. 1959. "The Theoretical Importance of Love." *American Sociological Review* 24: 38–47.

Goodman, Mary Ellen. 1952. *Race Awareness in Young Children.* Cambridge, Mass.: Addison-Wesley.

Gordon, Albert I. 1964. *Intermarriage: Interfaith, Interracial, Interethnic.* Boston: Beacon.

Gordon, Thomas. 1970. *Parent Effectiveness Training.* New York: Wyden.

Gronseth, Eric. 1971. "The Husband Provider Role: A Critical Appraisal." In *Family Issues of Employed Women in Europe and America.* Edited by Andrée Michel. Leiden: Brill.

Gross, Gary. 1976. Summary of incomplete master's thesis at San Francisco State University, reported in *Cohabitation Research Newsletter* 5: 18.

Guittar, Edea C., and **Robert C. Lewis.** 1974. "Self-concepts among Some Unmarried Cohabitants." Paper presented to National Council on Family Relations,

Gurin, Gerald; Joseph Veroff; and **Sheila Feld.** 1960. *Americans View Their Mental Health.* New York: Basic Books.

Guttmacher, Alan F. 1957. "Abortions." In *Modern Marriage and Family Living.* Edited by Morris Fishbein and Ruby Jo Reeves Kennedy. New York: Oxford University Press.

Haerle, Rudolf K., Jr. 1969. "Church Attendance Patterns among Intermarried Catholics: A Panel Study." *Sociological Analysis* 30: 204–16.

Hafstrom, Jeanne L., and **Marilyn M. Dunsing.** 1965. "A Comparison of Economic Choices of One-Earner and Two-Earner Families." *Journal of Marriage and the Family* 27: 403–409.

Hamblin, Robert L.; David Buckholdt; Daniel Ferritor; Martin Kozloff; and **Lois Blackwell.** 1971. *The Humanization Processes: A Social, Behavioral Analysis of Children's Problems.* New York: Wiley.

Hamilton, G. V. 1929. *A Research in Marriage.* New York: Boni.

Hammarth, Alice Kahn. 1960. "Breast Feeding and Bottle Feeding Compared." *Balanced Living* 16.

Harlow, M. K., and **H. F. Harlow.** 1966. "Affection in Primates." *Discovery,* January.

Harmsworth, Harry C., and **Mhyra S. Minnis.** 1955. "Nonstatutory Causes of Divorce: The Lawyer's Point of View." *Marriage and Family Living* 17: 316–21.

Harris, Dale B.; Kenneth E. Clark; Arnold M. Rose; and **Frances Valasek.** 1954. "The Relationship of Children's Home Duties to an Attitude of Responsibility." *Child Development* 25: 29–33.

Haskell, Martin R. 1973. *The Psychodramatic Method.* Long Beach, Calif. California Institute of Socioanalysis.

Hawkins, Harold, and James Walters. 1952. "Family Recreation Activities." *Journal of Home Economics* 44: 623–26.

Heer, David M. 1974. "The Prevalence of Black-White Marriage in the United States, 1960 and 1970." *Journal of Marriage and the Family* 36: 246–59.

Heinstein, Martin I. 1965. *Child Rearing in California.* Berkeley, Calif.: California Bureau of Maternal and Child Health.

Heinstein, Martin I. 1967. "Expressed Attitudes and Feelings of Pregnant Women and Their Relations to Physical Complications of Pregnancy." *Merrill-Palmer Quarterly* 13: 217–36.

Heiss, Jerold S. 1960. "Premarital Characteristics of the Religiously Intermarried in an Urban Area." *American Sociological Review* 25: 47–55.

Heiss, Jerold S. 1961. "Interfaith Marriage and Marital Outcome." *Marriage and Family Living* 23: 228–33.

Heiss, Jerold S. 1962. "Degree of Intimacy and Male-Female Interaction." *Sociometry* 25: 197–208.

Hennon, Charles B. 1975. "Conflict Management within Pairing Relationships: The Case of Nonmarital Cohabitation." Paper presented to North Central Sociological Association,

Henry, William E. 1949. "The Business Executive: A Study in the Psychodynamics of a Social Role." *American Journal of Sociology* 54: 286–91.

Henshel, Anne-Marie. 1973. "Swinging: A Study of Decision Making in Marriage." *American Journal of Sociology* 78: 885–91.

Hewett, Sheila. 1970. *The Family and the Handicapped Child: A Study of Cerebral Palsied Children in Their Homes.* Chicago: Aldine.

Hicks, Mary W. 1970. "An Empirical Evaluation of Textbook Assumptions about Engagement." *The Family Coordinator* 19: 57–63.

Hill, Reuben. 1949. *Families under Stress.* New York: Harper.

Hill, Reuben. 1963. "Judgment and Consumership in the Management of Family Resources." *Sociology and Social Research* 47: 446–60.

Hill, Reuben, and Donald A. Hansen. 1964. "Families under Stress." In *Handbook of Marriage and the Family.* Edited by Harold T. Christensen. Chicago: Rand McNally.

Hill, Reuben; Nelson Foote; Joan Aldous; Robert Carlson; and Robert Macdonald. 1970. *Family Development in Three Generations: A Longitudinal Study of Changing Family Patterns of Planning and Achievement.* Cambridge, Mass.: Schenkman.

Hobart, Charles W. 1956. "Disagreement and Nonempathy during Courtship." *Marriage and Family Living* 18: 317–22.

Hochschild, Arlie. 1969. "The Role of the Ambassador's Wife: An Exploratory Study." *Journal of Marriage and the Family* 31: 73–87.

Hodge, Marshall B. 1967. *Your Fear of Love.* Garden City, N.Y.: Doubleday.

Hoffman, Lois W. 1963. "Effects on the Children: Summary and Discussion." In *The Employed Mother in America.* Edited by F. Ivan Nye and Lois W. Hoffman. Chicago: Rand McNally.

Hoffman, Lois Wladis, and F. Ivan Nye. 1974. *Working Mothers: An Evaluative Review of the Consequences for Wife, Husband, and Child.* San Francisco: Jossey-Bass.

Holling, Holling C. 1941. *Paddle to the Sea.* Boston: Houghton Mifflin.

Holling, Holling C. 1942. *Tree in the Trail.* Boston: Houghton Mifflin.

Hollingshead, August B. 1952. "Marital Status and Wedding Behavior." *Marriage and Family Living* 14: 308–11.

Household Finance Corporation. 1970. *It's Your Credit—Manage It Wisely.* Chicago: Money Management Institute.

Household Finance Corporation. 1971. *Your Housing Dollar.* Chicago: Money Management Institute.

Household Finance Corporation. 1973. *Your Savings and Investment Dollar.* Chicago: Money Management Institute.

Howells, John G., ed. 1972. *Modern Perspectives in Psycho-Obstetrics.* New York: Brunner/Mazel.

Hubbell, Anne. 1963. "Barriers to Communication between Parents and Teenagers." Paper presented to annual meeting of Midwest Sociological Society,

Hunt, Chester L., and **Richard W. Coller.** 1957. "Intermarriage and Cultural Change: A Study of Philippine-American Marriages." *Social Forces* 35: 223–30.

Hunt, Morton. 1966. *The World of the Formerly Married.* New York: McGraw-Hill.

Hunt, Morton. 1969. *The Affair.* New York: New American Library.

Hunt, Morton. 1974. *Sexual Behavior in the 1970s.* Chicago: Playboy.

Hurley, John R., and **Donna P. Palonen.** 1967. "Marital Satisfaction and Child Density among University Student Parents." *Journal of Marriage and the Family* 29: 483–84.

Ivey, Melville E., and **Judith M. Bardwick.** 1968. "Patterns of Affectional Fluctuation in the Menstrual Cycle." *Psychosomatic Medicine* 30: 336–45.

Jackson, E. B.; L. C. Wilkin; and **H. Auerbach.** 1956. "Statistical Report on Incidence and Duration of Breast Feeding in Relation to Personal-Social and Hospital Maternity Factors." *Pediatrics* 17: 700ff. Cited in Newton and Newton, 1972.

Jacobs, Betty. 1943. "Aetiological Factors and Reaction Types in Psychoses Following Childbirth." *Journal of Mental Science* 89: 242. Cited in Newton, 1955: 30.

Jacobson, Alver H. 1952. "Conflict of Attitudes toward the Roles of the Husband and Wife in Marriage." *American Sociological Review* 17: 146–50.

Johnson, Michael P. 1969. "Courtship and Commitment: A Study of Cohabitation on a University Campus." Master's thesis, State University of Iowa, Iowa City.

Johnson, Michael P. 1973. "Commitment: A Conceptual Structure and Empirical Application." *Sociological Quarterly* 14: 395–406.

Johnson, Michael P. 1975. "Premarital Cohabitation on Campus." Unpublished manuscript.

Johnson, Ralph E. 1970. "Some Correlates of Extramarital Coitus." *Journal of Marriage and the Family* 32: 449–56.

Johnson, Virginia E., and **William H. Masters.** 1962. "Intravaginal Contraceptive Study: Phase I. Anatomy." *Western Journal of Surgery, Obstetrics, and Gynecology* 70: 202–207.

Jones, Stella B. 1973. "Geographic Mobility as Seen by the Wife and Mother." *Journal of Marriage and the Family* 35: 210–18.

Jourard, Sidney M. 1975. "Marriage Is for Life." *Journal of Marriage and Family Counseling* 1: 199–208.

Kaats, Gilbert R., and **Keith E. Davis.** 1970. "The Dynamics of Sexual Behavior of College Students." *Journal of Marriage and the Family* 32: 390–99.

Kadushin, Alfred. 1970. *Adopting Older Children.* New York: Columbia University Press.

Kagan, Jerome; Richard B. Kearsley; and **Philip R. Zelazo.** 1976. "The Effects of Infant Day Care on Psychological Development." Paper presented to American Association for the Advancement of Science, Boston, February 19.

Kandel, Denise B., and **Gerald S. Lesser.** 1972. *Youth in Two Worlds: United States and Denmark.* San Francisco: Jossey-Bass.

Kanin, Eugene J. 1957. "Male Aggression in Dating-Courtship Relations." *American Journal of Sociology* 63: 197–204.

Kanin, Eugene J. 1967. "An Examination of Sexual Aggression as a Response to Sexual Frustration." *Journal of Marriage and the Family* 29: 428–33.

Kanin, Eugene J. 1969. "Selected Dyadic Aspects of Male Sex Aggression." *Journal of Sex Research* 5: 12–28.

Kanin, Eugene J., and **David H. Howard.** 1958. "Postmarital Consequences of Premarital Sex Adjustments." *American Sociological Review* 23: 556–62.

Kanin, Eugene J.; Karen R. Davidson; and **Sonia R. Scheck.** 1970. "A Research Note on Male-Female Differentials in the Experience of Heterosexual Love." *Journal of Sex Research* 6: 64–72.

Kanin, Eugene J., and **Karen R. Davidson.** 1972. "Some Evidence Bearing on the Aim-Inhibition Hypothesis of Love." *Sociological Quarterly* 13: 210–17.

Kanter, Rosabeth Moss; Dennis Jaffe; and **D. Kelly Weisberg.** 1975. "Coupling, Parenting, and the Presence of Others: Intimate Relationships in Communal Households." *The Family Coordinator* 24: 433–52.

Karen, Robert L. 1959. "Some Variables Affecting Sexual Attitudes, Behavior, and Consistency." *Marriage and Family Living* 21: 235–39.

Keaough, Dale. 1975. "Without Knotting the Tie." *The Arizona Republic*, July 27.

Keiser, Steven D. 1974. "Cohabitation: A Preliminary Analysis." Unpublished paper, Department of Sociology, Southern Illinois University, Edwardsville, Ill.

Kelly, E. Lowell. 1955. "Consistency of the Adult Personality." *American Psychologist* 10: 659–81.

Kemper, Theodore D. 1966. "Mate Selection and Marital Satisfaction According to Sibling Type of Husband and Wife." *Journal of Marriage and the Family* 28: 346–49.

Kephart, William M. 1954. "Some Variables in Cases of Reported Sexual Maladjustment." *Marriage and Family Living* 16: 241–43.

Kerckhoff, Alan C. 1964. "Patterns of Homogamy and the Field of Eligibles." *Social Forces* 42: 289–97.

Kerckhoff, Alan C., and **Keith E. Davis.** 1962. "Value Consensus and Need Complementarity in Mate Selection." *American Sociological Review* 27: 295–303.

Kieffer, Carolynne M. 1972. "Consensual Cohabitation: A Descriptive Study of the Relationships and Sociocultural Characteristics of Eighty Couples in Settings of Two Florida Universities." Master's thesis, Florida State University, Tallahassee.

Kimmel, Paul R., and **John W. Havens.** 1966. "Game Theory Versus Mutual Identification: Two Criteria for Assessing Marital Relationships." *Journal of Marriage and the Family* 28: 460–65.

Kimura, Yukiko. 1957. "War Brides in Hawaii and Their In-Laws." *American Journal of Sociology* 63: 70–79.

King, Francis P. 1954. *Financing the College Education of Faculty Children.* New York: Holt.

King, K.; J. McIntyre; and **L. J. Axelson.** 1968. "Adolescents' Views of Maternal Employment as a Threat to the Marital Relationship." *Journal of Marriage and the Family* 30: 633–37.

Kinsey, Alfred C.; Wardell B. Pomeroy; and **Clyde E. Martin.** 1948. *Sexual Behavior in the Human Male.* Philadelphia: Saunders.

Kinsey, Alfred C.; Wardell B. Pomeroy; Clyde E. Martin; and **Paul H. Gebhard.** 1953. *Sexual Behavior in the Human Female.* Philadelphia: Saunders.

Kirkendall, Lester A. 1955. "A Concept of Interrelationships Applied to Premarital Behavior." Unpublished manuscript.

Kirkendall, Lester A. 1956. "Premarital Sex Relations: The Problem and Its Implications." *Pastoral Psychology* 7: 46–53.

Kirkendall, Lester A. 1960. "Circumstances Associated with Teenage Boys' Use of Prostitution." *Marriage and Family Living* 22: 145–49.

Kirkendall, Lester A. 1961. *Premarital Intercourse and Interpersonal Relationships.* New York: Julian Press.

Kirkpatrick, Clifford, and **Theodore Caplow.** 1945. "Courtship in a Group of Minnesota Students." *American Journal of Sociology* 50: 114–25

Kirkpatrick, Clifford, and **Charles Hobart.** 1954. "Disagreement, Disagreement Estimate, and Nonempathetic Imputations for Intimacy Groups Varying from Favorite Date to Married." *American Sociological Review* 19: 10–19.

Kirkpatrick, Clifford, and **Eugene Kanin.** 1957. "Male Sex Aggression on a University Campus." *American Sociological Review* 22: 52–58.

Klapp, Orrin E. 1959. "Ritual and Family Solidarity." *Social Forces* 37: 212–14.

Klaus, Marshall H.; Richard Jerauld; Nancy C. Kreger; Willie McAlpine; Meredith Steffa; and **John H. Kennell.** 1972. "Maternal Attachment: Importance of the First Postpartum Days." *New England Journal of Medicine* 286: 460–63. Cited in Newton, 1972.

Knapp, Jacquelyn J. 1976. "An Exploratory Study of Seventeen Sexually Open Marriages." *Journal of Sex Research* 12: 206–19.

Kohn, Melvin L. 1969. *Class and Conformity: A Study in Values.* Homewood, Ill.: Dorsey.

Koller, Marvin R. 1951. "Some Changes in Courtship Behavior in Three Generations of Ohio Women." *American Sociological Review* 16: 366–70.

Komarovsky, Mirra. 1973. "Cultural Contradictions and Sex Roles: The Masculine Case." *American Journal of Sociology* 78: 873–84.

Komarovsky, Mirra. 1974. "Patterns of Self-disclosure of Male Undergraduates." *Journal of Marriage and the Family* 36: 677–86.

Kovar, Mary Grace. 1968. "Employment during Pregnancy." *Vital and Health Statistics* 22, no. 7.

Lakin, Martin. 1957. "Personality Factors in Mothers of Excessively Crying (Colicky) Infants." Monographs of Society for Research in Child Development no. 22.

Landes, Judah, and **William Winter**. 1966. "A New Strategy for Treating Disintegrating Families." *Family Process* 5: 1–20.

Landis, Judson T. 1960. "Religiousness, Family Relationships, and Family Values in Protestant, Catholic, and Jewish Families." *Marriage and Family Living* 22: 341–47.

Landis, Judson T.; Thomas Poffenberger; and **Shirley Poffenberger**. 1950. "The Effects of First Pregnancy upon the Sexual Adjustment of 212 Couples." *American Sociological Review* 15: 766–72.

Landis, Judson T., and **Mary G. Landis**. 1958. *Building a Successful Marriage*, third edition. Englewood Cliffs, N.J.: Prentice-Hall.

Landis, Paul H. 1950. "Sequential Marriage." *Journal of Home Economics* 42: 625–28.

Landis, Paul H., and **Carol L. Stone**. 1952. *The Relationship of Parental Authority Patterns to Teenage Adjustments*. Pullman, Wash.: Washington Agricultural Experiment Station.

Lang, Richard D. 1932. "A Study of the Degree of Happiness or Unhappiness in Marriage as Rated by Acquaintances of the Married Couples." Master's thesis, University of Chicago. Cited in Burgess and Cottrell, 1939.

Lansing, John B., and **James N. Morgan**. 1955. "Consumer Finances over the Life Cycle." In *Consumer Behavior*, Volume 2. Edited by Lincoln H. Clark. New York: New York University Press.

Lansing, John B.; Thomas Lorimer; and **Chikashi Moriguchi**. 1960. *How People Pay for College*. Ann Arbor, Mich.: Institute for Social Research, University of Michigan.

Lawrence, Raymond. 1974. "Toward a More Flexible Monogamy." *Christianity and Crisis*, March 16.

Leavitt, John A., and **Carl O. Hanson**. 1950. *Personal Finance*. New York: McGraw-Hill.

Leboyer, Frederick. 1975. *Birth Without Violence*. New York: Knopf.

Leboyer, Frederick. 1976. *Loving Hands: The Traditional Indian Art of Baby Massages*. New York: Knopf.

Leichter, Hope Jensen, and **William E. Mitchell**. 1967. *Kinship and Casework*. New York: Russell Sage Foundation.

LeMasters, E. E. 1957. *Modern Courtship and Marriage*. New York: Macmillan.

Lenski, Gerhard. 1961. *The Religious Factor*. Garden City, N.Y.: Doubleday.

Levine, Lena, and **Mildred Gilman**. 1951. *Frigidity*. New York: Planned Parenthood Federation of America.

Levinger, George. 1965. "A Comparative Study of Marital Communication." Unpublished paper cited in "Disclosure of Feelings in Marriage," by George Levinger and David J. Senn, 1967, *Merrill-Palmer Quarterly* 13: 237–49.

Levinger, George. 1966. "Systematic Distortion in Spouses' Reports of Preferred and Actual Sexual Behavior." *Sociometry* 29: 291–99.

Levinger, George, and **James Breedlove**. 1966. "Interpersonal Attraction and Agreement: A Study of Marriage Partners." *Journal of Personality and Social Psychology* 3: 367–72.

Levinger, George, and **David J. Senn**. 1967. "Disclosure of Feelings in Marriage." *Merrill-Palmer Quarterly* 13: 237–49.

Levy, John, and **Ruth Munroe**. 1945. *The Happy Family*. New York: Knopf.

Lewin, Kurt. 1953. "Studies in Group Decision." In *Group Dynamics*. Edited by Dorwin Cartwright and Alvin Zander. Evanston, Ill.: Row, Peterson.

Libby, Roger W., and **Gilbert D. Nass**. 1971. "Parental Views on Teenage Sexual Behavior." *Journal of Sex Research* 7: 226–36.

Libby, Roger W., and **Robert N. Whitehurst, eds**. 1973. *Renovating Marriage: Toward New Sexual Life-styles* Danville, Calif.: Consensus.

Lind, Andrew W. 1964. "Interracial Marriage as Affecting Divorce in Hawaii." *Sociology and Social Research* 49: 17–26.

Liston, L. L., and **C. A. Aiken**. 1976. "Cost of Owning and Operating an Automobile." Washington, D.C.: U.S. Department of Transportation.

Litwak, Eugene, and **Ivan Szelenyi.** 1969. "Primary Group Structures and Their Functions: Kin, Neighbors, and Friends." *American Sociological Review* 34: 465–81.

Lobell, John, and **Mimi Lobell.** 1972. *John and Mimi: A Free Marriage.* New York: St. Martin's Press.

Locke, Harvey J. 1951. *Predicting Adjustment in Marriage: A Comparison of a Divorced and a Happily Married Group.* New York: Holt.

Locke, Harvey J.; Georges Sabagh; and **Mary Margaret Thomes.** 1957. "Interfaith Marriages." *Social Problems* 4: 329–33.

Looney, G. 1971. "The Ecology of Childhood." In *Action for Children's Television.* New York: Avon Press. Cited in Rue, 1974.

Lopata, Helena Znaniecki. 1971. *Occupation: Housewife.* New York: Oxford University Press.

Lu, Yi-chuang. 1952. "Predicting Roles in Marriage." *American Journal of Sociology* 58: 51–55.

Luckey, Eleanore B. 1961. "Perceptual Congruence of Self and Family Concepts as Related to Marital Interaction." *Sociometry* 24: 234–50.

Luckey, Eleanore B. 1966. "Number of Years Married as Related to Personality Perception and Marital Satisfaction." *Journal of Marriage and the Family* 28: 44–48.

Luckey, Eleanore B., and **Gilbert D. Nass.** 1969. "A Comparison of Sexual Attitudes and Behavior in an International Sample." *Journal of Marriage and the Family* 31: 364–79.

Lupri, Eugen. 1969. "Contemporary Authority in the West German Family: A Study in Cross-national Validation." *Journal of Marriage and the Family* 31: 134–44.

Lyness, Judith L.; Milton E. Lipetz; and **Keith E. Davis.** 1972. "Living Together: An Alternative to Marriage." *Journal of Marriage and the Family* 34: 305–11.

Macklin, Eleanor D. 1972. "Heterosexual Cohabitation among Unmarried College Students." *The Family Coordinator* 21: 463–72.

Macklin, Eleanor D. 1974. "Unmarried Heterosexual Cohabitation on the University Campus." Unpublished manuscript.

Macklin, Eleanor D. 1975. "Review of Research on Nonmarital Cohabitation in the United States." Paper presented at Symposium on Current and Future Intimate Life-styles, Connecticut College, New London, Conn.

Maier, Joseph, and **William Spinrad.** 1958. "Comparison of Religious Beliefs and Practices of Jewish, Catholic, and Protestant Students." *Phylon Quarterly* 18: 355–60. Cited in Gordon, 1964.

Manheim, Henry L. 1961. "A Socially Unacceptable Method of Mate Selection." *Sociology and Social Research* 45: 182–87.

Mann, Floyd C. N.d. "The Handling of Job Tensions." Unpublished manuscript, Survey Research Center, Institute for Social Research, University of Michigan, Ann Arbor.

Marshall, William H., and **Marcia P. King.** 1966. "Undergraduate Student Marriage: A Compilation of Research Findings." *Journal of Marriage and the Family* 28: 350–59.

Martin, Thomas W.; Kenneth J. Berry; and **R. Brooke Jacobsen.** 1975. "The Impact of Dual-Career Marriages on Female Professional Careers: An Empirical Test of a Parsonian Hypothesis." *Journal of Marriage and the Family* 37: 734–42.

Maslow, A. H. 1953. "Love in Healthy People." In *The Meaning of Love.* Edited by Ashley Montagu. New York: Julian Press.

Maslow, A. H. 1954. *Motivation and Personality.* New York: Harper and Row.

Masters, William H., and **E. H. Lampe.** 1956. "Problems of Male Infertility, II. The Effect of Frequent Ejaculation." *Fertility and Sterility* 7: 123–27.

Masters, William H., and **Virginia E. Johnson.** 1966. *Human Sexual Response.* Boston: Little, Brown.

Masters, William H., and **Virginia E. Johnson.** 1970. *Human Sexual Inadequacy.* Boston: Little, Brown.

Masters, William H. and **Virginia E. Johnson.** 1974. *The Pleasure Bond: A New Look at Sexuality and Commitment.* Boston: Little, Brown.

May, Rollo. 1969. *Love and Will.* New York: Norton.

Mayer, John E. 1957. "The Self-restraint of Friends: A Mechanism in Family Transition." *Social Forces* 35: 230–38.

Mayer, John E. 1961. *Jewish-Gentile Courtships.* New York: Free Press.

Mayer, John E. 1966. *The Disclosure of Marital Problems: An Exploratory Study of Lower and Middle Class Wives.* New York: Community Service Society.

Mayer, John E. 1967. "The Invisibility of Married Life." *New Society,* February 26.

McBride, A. 1951. "Compulsory Rooming-in in the Ward and Private Service of Duke Hospital." *Journal of the American Medical Association* 145: 625–27. Cited in Newton, 1972.

McCarthy, Mary A. 1966. "Infant, Fetal, and Maternal Mortality, United States, 1963." *Vital and Health Statistics* 20, no. 3.

McCloskey, Robert. 1943. *Homer Price.* New York: Viking.

McKain, Walter C. 1972. "A New Look at Older Marriages." *The Family Coordinator* 21: 61–69.

McLean, Norman. 1953. "A Study of Catholic-Protestant Marriages." Paper presented at Groves Conference on Marriage and the Family, Ohio State University.

McLeod, Jack M.; Charles K. Atkin; and **Steven H. Chaffee.** 1971. "Adolescents, Parents, and Television Use: Adolescent Self-report Measures from Maryland and Wisconsin Samples." In *Television and Adolescent Aggressiveness.* Edited by George A. Comstock and Eli A. Rubinstein. Washington, D.C.: U.S.G.P.O.

Menninger, Karl. 1935. *Love against Hate.* London: Kegan Paul, Trench and Trubner.

Metropolitan Life Insurance Company. 1963. "The Changing Economic Role of Women." Reprinted from their *Business Economics* house organ.

Michel, Andrée. 1967. "Comparative Data Concerning the Interaction in French and American Families." *Journal of Marriage and the Family* 29: 337–44.

Michel, Andrée. 1970. "Wife's Satisfaction with Husband's Understanding in Parisian Urban Families." *Journal of Marriage and the Family* 32: 351–59.

Michel, Andrée, ed. 1971. *Family Issues of Employed Women in Europe and America.* Leiden: Brill.

Milne, Alan A. 1925. *Fourteen Songs from "When We Were Very Young".* New York: Dutton.

Monahan, Thomas P. 1952. "How Stable Are Remarriages?" *American Journal of Sociology* 58: 280–88.

Monahan, Thomas P. 1953. "Does Age at Marriage Matter in Divorce?" *Social Forces* 32: 81–87.

Monahan, Thomas P. 1973. "Some Dimensions of Interreligious Marriages in Indiana, 1962–67." *Social Forces* 52: 195–203.

Montagu, Ashley. 1953. *The Meaning of Love.* New York: Julian Press.

Montagu, Ashley. 1971. *Touching: The Human Significance of the Skin.* New York: Columbia University Press.

Montgomery, Jason P. 1973. "Commitment and Cohabitation Cohesion." Paper presented at National Council on Family Relations, Toronto.

Morgan, James N. 1955. *Consumer Economics.* Englewood Cliffs, N.J.: Prentice-Hall.

Morgan, James N. 1965. "A Pilot Study of Economic Decision Making in the Family." *Research Forum,* Institute of Life Insurance 3: 5–30.

Morgan, James N.; Martin H. David; Wilbur J. Cohen; and **Harvey E. Brazer.** 1962. *Income and Welfare in the United States.* New York: McGraw-Hill.

Morrow, William R., and **Robert C. Wilson.** 1961. "Family Relations of Bright High-Achieving and Under-Achieving High School Students." *Child Development* 32: 501–10.

Mott, Paul E.; Floyd C. Mann; Quin McLoughlin; and **Donald P. Warwick.** 1965. *Shift Work: The Social, Psychological, and Physical Consequences.* Ann Arbor, Mich.: University of Michigan Press.

Moulton, Robert W.; Eugene Burnstein; Paul G. Liberty, Jr.; and **Nathan Altucher.** 1966. "Patterning of Parental Affection and Disciplinary Dominance as a Determinant of Guilt and Sex Typing." *Journal of Personality and Social Psychology* 4: 356–63.

Mudd, Emily H. 1951. *The Practice of Marriage Counseling.* New York: Association Press.

Musgrave, P. 1969. "How Children Use Television." *New Society* 13: 277–78. Cited in Rue, 1974.

Mussen, Paul H., and **John J. Conger.** 1956. *Child Development and Personality.* New York: Harper.

Myers, Lonny. 1973. "Marriage, Honesty, and Personal Growth (Reflections on Upper–middle-class Urban Marriages)." In *Renovating Marriage.* Edited by Roger W. Libby and Robert N. Whitehurst. Danville, Calif.: Consensus.

Nash, Dennison. 1969. "The Domestic Side of a Foreign Existence." *Journal of Marriage and the Family* 31: 574–82.

National Center of Health Statistics (N.C.H.S.). *Vital and Health Statistics.* Washington, D.C.: U.S. Department of Health, Education and Welfare.

Navran, Leslie. 1967. "Communication and Adjustment in Marriage." *Family Process* 6:173–84.

Newcomb, Theodore M. 1961. *The Acquaintance Process.* New York: Holt, Rinehart and Winston.

Newson, L. John, and **Elizabeth Newson.** 1962. "Breast Feeding in Decline." *British Medical Journal* 2: 1744ff. Cited in Newton and Newton, 1972.

Newson, L. John, and **Elizabeth Newson.** 1968. *Four Years Old in an Urban Community.* Chicago: Aldine.

Newsweek. 1969. "Honeymoon Havens." *Newsweek,* June 23, pp. 90–91. Cited in Gersuny, 1970.

Newton, Niles A. 1955. *Maternal Emotions: A Study of Women's Feelings toward Menstruation, Pregnancy, Childbirth, Breast Feeding, Infant Care, and Other Aspects of Their Femininity.* New York: Hoeber.

Newton, Niles A. 1971. "Psychologic Differences between Breast and Bottle Feeding." *American Journal of Clinical Nutrition* 24: 993–1004.

Newton, Niles A. 1972. "The Point of View of the Consumer." Address given at National Congress on the Quality of Life, Chicago.

Newton, Niles A., and Michael Newton. 1972. "Lactation—Its Psychologic Components." *Modern Perspectives in Psycho-Obstetrics.* Edited by John G. Howells. New York: Brunner/Mazel.

Nye, F. Ivan. 1957. "Child Adjustment in Broken and in Unhappy Unbroken Homes." *Marriage and Family Living* 19: 356–61.

Nye, F. Ivan. 1958. *Family Relationships and Delinquent Behavior.* New York: Wiley.

Nye, F. Ivan. 1974. "Emerging and Declining Family Roles." *Journal of Marriage and the Family* 36: 238–45.

Nye, F. Ivan, and **Lois W. Hoffman, eds.** 1963. *The Employed Mother in America.* Chicago: Rand McNally.

Nye, F. Ivan; John Carlson; and **Gerald Garrett.** 1970. "Family Size, Interaction, Affect and Stress." *Journal of Marriage and the Family* 32: 216–26.

Oakland, James A., and **Margaret K. Wulbert.** 1969. "The Shaping of Handicapped Children's Behavior by Mothers." Paper presented at annual meeting of National Council on Family Relations.

O'Brien, John E. 1971. "Violence in Divorce Prone Families." *Journal of Marriage and the Family* 33: 692–98.

Olday, David E. 1976. Preliminary results from Ph.D. Thesis at Washington State University. *Cohabitation Research Newsletter* 5: 38.

O'Neill, George C., and **Nena O'Neill.** 1970. "Patterns in Group Sexual Activity." *Journal of Sex Research* 6: 101–12.

Oppong, Christine. 1970. "Conjugal Power and Resources: An Urban African Example." *Journal of Marriage and the Family* 32: 676–80.

Orden, S. R., and **N. M. Bradburn.** 1969. "Working Wives and Marital Happiness." *American Journal of Sociology* 74: 392–407.

Ort, Robert S. 1950. "A Study of Role-Conflicts as Related to Happiness in Marriage." *Journal of Abnormal and Social Psychology* 45: 691–99.

Parsons, Talcott. 1959. "The Social Structure of the Family." In *The Family: Its Function and Destiny.* Edited by Ruth Nanda Anshen. New York: Harper.

Parsons, Talcott, and **Renée C. Fox.** 1952. "Illness, Therapy, and the Modern Urban American Family." *Journal of Social Issues* 13, no. 4: 31–44.

Patterson, Gerald R.; Hyman Hops; and **Robert L. Weiss.** 1975. "Interpersonal Skills Training for Couples in Early Stages of Conflict." *Journal of Marriage and the Family* 37: 295–304.

Pearlin, Leonard I.; Marian Radke Yarrow; and **Harry A. Scarr.** 1967. "Unintended Effects of Parental Aspirations: The Case of Children's Cheating." *American Journal of Sociology* 73: 73–83.

Peck, Robert F. 1958. "Family Patterns Correlated with Adolescent Personality Structure." *Journal of Abnormal and Social Psychology* 57: 347–50.

Perlman, Daniel. 1974. "Self-esteem and Sexual Permissiveness." *Journal of Marriage and the Family* 36: 470–73.

Peterman, Dan J.; Carl A. Ridley; and **Scott N. Anderson.** 1974. "A Comparison of Cohabiting and Noncohabiting College Students." *Journal of Marriage and the Family* 36: 344–54.

Peterson, Donald R.; Wesley C. Becker; Donald J. Shoemaker; Zella Luria; and **Leo A. Hellmer.** 1961. "Child Behavior Problems and Parental Attitudes." *Child Development* 32: 151–62.

Pickford, John H.; Edro I. Signori; and **Henry Rempel.** 1966. "The Intensity of Personality Traits in Relation to Marital Happiness." *Journal of Marriage and the Family* 28: 458–59.

Pineo, Peter C. 1961. "Disenchantment in the Later Years of Marriage." *Marriage and Family Living* 23: 3–11.

Plateris, Alexander A. 1970. *Increases in Divorces, United States, 1967.* Washington, D.C.: National Center for Health Statistics, U.S. Department of Health, Education, and Welfare.

Plateris, Alexander A. 1973. *Divorces: Analysis of Changes, United States, 1969.* Washington, D.C.: National Center for Health Statistics, U.S. Department of Health, Education, and Welfare.

Poffenberger, Shirley; Thomas Poffenberger; and **Judson T. Landis.** 1952. "Intent toward Conception and the Pregnancy Experience." *American Sociological Review* 17: 616–20.

Pollis, Carol A. 1969. "Dating Involvement and Patterns of Idealization: A Test of Waller's Hypothesis." *Journal of Marriage and the Family* 31: 765–71.

Poloma, Margaret M., and **T. Neal Garland.** 1971. "Jobs or Careers: The Case of the Professionally Employed Married Woman." In *Family Issues of Employed Women in Europe and America.* Edited by Andrée Michel. Leiden: Brill.

Powell, John. 1969. *Why Am I Afraid to Tell You Who I Am?* Niles, Ill.: Argus.

Pratt, Lois. 1972. "Conjugal Organization and Health." *Journal of Marriage and the Family* 34: 85–95.

Pratt, William P. 1965. "A Study of Marriages Involving Premarital Pregnancies." Ph.D. dissertation, University of Michigan, Ann Arbor.

Price-Bonham, Sharon. 1973. "Student Husbands Versus Student Couples." *Journal of Marriage and the Family* 35: 33–37.

Prince, Alfred J. 1961. "Factors in Mate Selection." *Family Life Coordinator* 10: 55–58.

Propper, Alice M. 1972. "The Relationship of Maternal Employment to Adolescent Roles, Activities, and Parental Relationships." *Journal of Marriage and the Family* 34: 417–21.

Rainwater, Lee. 1960. *And the Poor Get Children.* Chicago: Quadrangle Books.

Rainwater, Lee. 1965. *Family Design: Marital Sexuality, Family Size, and Contraception.* Chicago: Aldine.

Ramey, James W. 1975. "Intimate Groups and Networks: Frequent Consequences of Sexually Open Marriage." *Family Coordinator* 24: 515–30.

Ramey, James W. 1976. *Intimate Friendships.* Englewood Cliffs, N.J.: Prentice-Hall.

Rapoport, Rhona, and **Robert N. Rapoport.** 1964. "New Light on the Honeymoon." *Human Relations* 17: 33–56.

Rapoport, Rhona, and **Robert N. Rapoport.** 1971. *Dual-Career Families.* Baltimore, Md.: Penguin.

Raschke, Helen J. 1974. "Social and Psychological Factors in Voluntary Postmarital Dissolution Adjustment." Ph.D. dissertation, University of Minnesota, Minneapolis.

Raush Harold L.; William A. Barry; Richard K. Hertel; and **Mary Ann Swain.** 1974. *Communication, Conflict, and Marriage.* San Francisco: Jossey-Bass.

Read, Grantley Dick. 1944. *Childbirth Without Fear.* New York: Harper.

Reed, Robert B. 1947. "The Interrelationship of Marital Adjustment, Fertility Control, and Size of Family." *Milbank Memorial Fund Quarterly* 25: 383–425.

Rehberg, Richard A.; Judie Sinclair; and **Walter E. Schafer.** 1970. "Adolescent Achievement Behavior, Family Authority Structure, and Parental Socialization Practices." *American Journal of Sociology* 75: 1012–1034.

Reiss, Ira L. 1967. *The Social Context of Premarital Sexual Permissiveness.* New York: Holt, Rinehart, and Winston.

Renne, Karen S. 1970. "Correlates of Dissatisfaction in Marriage." *Journal of Marriage and the Family* 32: 54–67.

Renne, Karen S. 1971. "Health and Marital Experience in an Urban Population." *Journal of Marriage and the Family* 33: 328–40.

Ridley, Carl A. 1973. "Exploring the Impact of Work Satisfaction and Involvement on Marital Interaction When Both Partners Are Employed." *Journal of Marriage and the Family* 35: 229–38.

Robbins, Norman N. 1973. "Have We Found Fault in No Fault Divorce?" *Family Coordinator* 22: 359–62.

Robertson, G. G. 1947. "Nausea and Vomiting in Pregnancy." *Lancet* 2: 336. Cited in Newton, 1955.

Rodgers, D. A.; F. J. Ziegler; and **P. Rohr.** 1963. "Sociopsychological Characteristics of Patients Obtaining Vasectomies from Urologists." *Journal of Marriage and the Family* 25: 331–35.

Roebuck, Julian. 1967. "The Cocktail Lounge: A Study of Heterosexual Relations in a Public Organization." *American Journal of Sociology* 72: 388–95.

Rogers, Carl R. 1972. *Becoming Partners: Marriage and Its Alternatives.* New York: Delacorte.

Roland, Maxwell, 1973. *Response to Contraception.* Philadelphia: Saunders.

Rollins, Boyd C., and **Harold Feldman.** 1970. "Marital Satisfaction over the Family Life Cycle." *Journal of Marriage and the Family* 32: 20–28.

Roper, Elmer, and **Associates.** 1960. "Parents' College Plans Study." New York: Education Program, Ford Foundation.

Rosen, Bernard C. 1955. "Conflicting Group Membership: A Study of Parent-Peer Group Cross-Pressures." *American Sociological Review* 20: 155–61.

Rosen, Bernard C., and **Roy d'Andrade.** 1959. "The Psychosocial Origins of Achievement Motivation." *Sociometry* 22: 185–218.

Rosenberg, Morris. 1965. *Society and the Adolescent Self-image.* Princeton, N.J.: Princeton University Press.

Rosenblatt, Paul C. 1974. "Behavior in Public Places: Comparison of Couples Accompanied and Unaccompanied by Children." *Journal of Marriage and the Family* 36: 750–55.

Rosenblatt, Paul C., and **Linda G. Stevenson.** 1973. "Territoriality and Privacy in Married and Unmarried Cohabiting Couples." Unpublished manuscript, University of Minnesota, St. Paul.

Rosengren, William R. 1961. "Social Sources of Pregnancy as Illness or Normality." *Social Forces* 39: 260–67.

Rosenthal, Erich. 1970. "Divorce and Religious Intermarriage: The Effect of Previous Marital Status upon Subsequent Marital Behavior." *Journal of Marriage and the Family* 32: 435–40.

Rosow, Irving, and **K. Daniel Rose.** 1972. "Divorce among Doctors." *Journal of Marriage and the Family* 34: 587–99.

Rosser, Colin, and **Christopher Harris.** 1965. *The Family and Social Change: A Study of Family and Kinship in a South Wales Town.* London: Routledge and Kegan Paul.

Roy, Prodipto. 1961. "Adolescent Roles: Rural-Urban Differentials." *Marriage and Family Living* 23: 240–349. Reprinted in Nye and Hoffman, 1963.

Rubenstein, Richard L. 1963. "Intermarriage and Conversion on the American College Campus." In *Intermarriage and Jewish Life.* Edited by Werner J. Cahnman. New York: Herzl.

Rue, Vincent M. 1974. "Television and the Family: The Question of Control." *Family Coordinator* 23: 73–81.

Russell, Candyce Smith. 1974. "Transition to Parenthood: Problems and Gratifications." *Journal of Marriage and the Family* 36: 294–302.

Ryder, Robert G. 1973. "Longitudinal Data Relating Marriage Satisfaction and Having a Child." *Journal of Marriage and the Family* 35: 604–607.

Salber, E. J. 1956. "Effect of Different Feeding Schedules on Growth of Bantu Babies in First Week of Life." *Journal of Tropical Pediatrics* 2: 97ff. Cited in Newton and Newton, 1972.

Salk, Lee. 1960. "The Effects of the Normal Heartbeat Sound on the Behavior of the Newborn Infants: Implications for Mental Health." *World Mental Health* 12: 1–8. Cited in Montagu, 1971.

Sandis, Eva E. 1970. "The Transmission of Mothers' Educational Ambitions, as Related to Specific Socialization Techniques." *Journal of Marriage and the Family* 32: 204–11.

Scanzoni, John H. 1965. "Resolution of Occupational-Conjugal Role Conflict in Clergy Marriages." *Journal of Marriage and the Family* 27: 396–402.

Scanzoni, John H. 1968. "A Social System Analysis of Dissolved and Existing Marriages." *Journal of Marriage and the Family* 30: 452–61.

Scanzoni, John H. 1970. *Opportunity and the Family.* New York: Free Press.

Schmidt, Gunter, and **Volkmar Sigusch.** 1970. "Sex Differences in Responses to Psychosexual Stimulation by Films and Slides." *Journal of Sex Research* 6: 268–83.

Schmitt, Robert C. 1969. "Age and Race Differences in Divorce in Hawaii." *Journal of Marriage and the Family* 31: 48–50.

Schnepp, Gerald J., and **Agnes Masako Yui.** 1955. "Cultural and Marital Adjustment of Japanese War Brides." *American Journal of Sociology* 61: 48–50.

Schoen, Robert. 1975. "California Divorce Rates by Age at First Marriage and Duration of First Marriage." *Journal of Marriage and the Family* 37: 548–55.

Schoenfeld, Eugen. 1969. "Intermarriage and the Small Town: The Jewish Case." *Journal of Marriage and the Family* 31: 61–64.

Schofield, Michael. 1965. *The Sexual Behavior of Young People.* London: Longmans, Green.

Schramm, Wilbur; Jack Lyle; and **Edwin B. Parker.** 1961. *Television in the Lives of Our Children.* Stanford, Calif.: Stanford University Press.

Schroder, Ralph. 1963. "Academic Achievement of the Male College Student." *Marriage and Family Living* 25: 420–23.

Scott, John Finley. 1965. "The American College Sorority: Its Role in Class and Ethnic Endogamy." *American Sociological Review* 30: 514–27.

Sears, Robert R.; Eleanor E. Maccoby; and **Harry Levin.** 1957. *Patterns of Child-rearing.* Evanston, Ill.: Row, Peterson.

Sears, Robert R.; Lucy Rau; and **Richard Alpert.** 1965. *Identification and Child Rearing.* Stanford, Calif. Stanford University Press.

Seligson, Marcia. 1973. "The New Wedding." *Saturday Review of the Society* 1 (March): 32–38.

Sewell, William H., and **Vimal P. Shah.** 1968. "Social Class, Parental Encouragement, and Educational Aspirations." *American Journal of Sociology* 73: 559–72.

Shaffer, James D. 1963. *Financial Aspects of Undergraduate Student Life at Michigan State University, 1961–62.* East Lansing, Mich.: Office of Institutional Research, Michigan State University. Cited in Marshall and King, 1966.

Shapiro, Sam, and **Jeanne Unger.** 1954. "Weight at Birth and Survival of the Newborn, United States, Early 1950." *Vital Statistics—Special Reports* 39, no. 1.

Shapiro, Sam; Edward R. Schlesinger; and **Robert E. L. Nesbitt, Jr.** 1965. "Infant and Perinatal Mortality in the United States." *Vital and Health Statistics—Analytical Studies* 3, no. 4.

Shipman, Gordon. 1968. "The Psychodynamics of Sex Education." *Family Coordinator* 17: 3–12.

Shuttlesworth, Guy, and **George Thorman.** 1973. "Living Together Unmarried Relationships." Unpublished manuscript, University of Texas, Austin.

Siddiqui, H. R. 1962. "Patterns of Help at the Time of Crisis." Unpublished paper analyzing data from Detroit Area Study under professors Ronald Freedman and David Goldberg, Department of Sociology, University of Michigan.

Siegel, Alberta E.; Lois M. Stolz; Ethel A. Hitchcock; and **Jean Adamson.** 1959. "Dependence and Independence in the Children of Working Mothers." *Child Development* 30: 533–46. Abridged in Nye and Hoffman, 1963.

Sigusch, Volkmar, and **Gunter Schmidt.** 1973. "Teenage Boys and Girls in West Germany." *Journal of Sex Research* 9: 107–23.

Simon, Rita James; Gail Crotts; and **Linda Mahan.** 1970. "An Empirical Note about Married Women and Their Friends." *Social Forces* 48: 520–25.

Slater, Eliot, and **Moya Woodside.** 1951. *Patterns of Marriage: A Study of Marriage Relationships in the Urban Working Classes.* London: Cassell.

Slater, Philip E. 1962. "Parental Behavior and the Personality of the Child." *Journal of Genetic Psychology* 101: 53–68.

Slater, Philip E. 1963. "On Social Regression." *American Sociological Review* 28: 339–64.

Smith, Charles E. 1966. "Negro-White Intermarriage: Forbidden Sexual Union." *Journal of Sex Research* 2: 169–77.

Smith, James R., and **Lynn G. Smith, eds.** 1974. *Beyond Monogamy.* Baltimore, Md.: Johns Hopkins University Press.

Smith, Lynn G., and **James R. Smith.** 1973. "Co-Marital Sex: The Incorporation of Extramarital Sex into the Marriage Relationship." In *Critical Issues in Contemporary Sexual Behavior.* Edited by John Money and J. Zubin. Baltimore, Md.: Johns Hopkins University Press. Reprinted in Smith and Smith, 1974.

Sokoloff, N.; S. Yaffe; D. Weintraub; and **B. Blase.** 1969. "Effects of Handling on the Subsequent Development of Premature Infants." *Developmental Psychology* 1: 765–68. Cited in Montagu, 1971.

Solomon, Philip. 1955. "Love: A Clinical Definition." *New England Journal of Medicine* 252: 345–51.

Springer, Joel, and **Suzanne Springer.** 1972. "Three Programs Designed to Improve the Dating Behavior of College Students." *Marriage and Family Counselors Quarterly* 7: 17–23.

Springer, Suzanne; Joel Springer; and **Rob Selvage.** 1974. "Evaluation of Premarital Dating and Courtship Experience in Relation to Marital Adjustment: Implications for Premarital Counseling." Paper presented at National Council on Family Relations, St. Louis.

Stafford, Rebecca. 1975. "The Division of Labor Among Cohabitating and Married Couples." Paper presented at National Council on Family Relations, Salt Lake City.

Stein, Aletha Huston, and **Lynette Kohn Friedrich.** 1971. "Television Content and Young Children's Behavior. In *Television and Social Learning.* Edited by John P. Murray, Eli A. Rubinstein, and George A. Comstock. Washington, D.C.: U.S. Government Printing Office.

Steiner, G. 1963. *The People Look at Television.* New York: Knopf.

Stolz, Lois Meek. 1967. *Influences on Parent Behavior.* Stanford, Calif.: Stanford University Press.

Stott, Leland. 1952. Report on Pregnancy Research Project at Merrill-Palmer Institute, presented at annual meeting of National Council on Family Relations.

Straus, Murray A. 1974. "Leveling, Civility, and Violence in the Family." *Journal of Marriage and the Family* 36: 13–30.

Strauss, Anselm. 1954. "Strain and Harmony in American-Japanese-War-Bride Marriages." *Marriage and Family Living* 16: 99–106.

Strong, Emily; William Wallace; and **Warner Wilson.** 1969. "Three-filter Date Selection by Computer." *Family Coordinator* 18: 166–71.

Stryker, Sheldon. 1955. "The Adjustment of Married Offspring to Their Parents." *American Sociological Review* 20: 149–54.

Stuckert, Robert P. 1963. "Occupational Mobility and Family Relationships." *Social Forces* 41: 301–307.

Sussman, Marvin B. 1953a. "The Help Pattern in the Middle-Class Family." *American Sociological Review* 18: 22–28.

Sussman, Marvin B. 1953b. "Parental Participation in Mate Selection and Its Effects upon Family Continuity." *Social Forces* 32: 76–81.

Sussman, Marvin B. 1959. "The Isolated Nuclear Family: Fact or Fiction." *Social Problems* 6: 333–40.

Sussman, Marvin B. 1975. "Marriage Contracts: Social and Legal Consequences." Paper presented at International Workshop on Changing Sex Roles in Family and Society.

Swartz, June Bagdade. 1976. "A Working Mother—Hassled, But Happy." Unpublished manuscript, Needham, Mass.

Talmon, Yonina. 1964. "Mate Selection in Collective Settlements." *American Sociological Review* 29: 491–508.

Terman, Lewis M. 1938. *Psychological Factors in Marital Happiness.* New York: McGraw-Hill.

Thibaut, J. W., and **J. Coules.** 1952. "The Role of Communication in the Reduction of Interpersonal Hostility." *Journal of Abnormal and Social Psychology* 47: 770–77. Cited in Raush et al., 1974.

Thomas, John L. 1951. "The Factor of Religion in the Selection of Marriage Mates." *American Sociological Review* 16: 487–91.

Thomas, John L. 1956. *The American Catholic Family.* Englewood Cliffs, N.J.: Prentice-Hall.

Thomason, Bruce. 1955. "Marital Sexual Behavior and Total Marital Adjustment: A Research Report." In *Sexual Behavior in American Society.* Edited by Jerome Himelhoch and Sylvia Fava. New York: Norton.

Thoms, Herbert. 1950. *Training for Childbirth.* New York: McGraw-Hill.

Thorman, George. 1973. "Cohabitation: A Report on the Married-Unmarried Life Style." *Futurist,* pp. 250–54.

Thorpe, Alice C. 1951. "How Married College Students Manage." *Marriage and Family Living* 13: 104–105, 130.

Tien, H. Yuan. 1961. "The Social Mobility/Fertility Hypothesis Reconsidered: An Empirical Study." *American Sociological Review* 26: 247–57.

Tietze, Christopher, and **Sarah Lewit.** 1972. "Interim Report on the Joint Program for the Study of Abortion." *Journal of Sex Research* 8: 170–88.

Tietze, Christopher; John Bongartz; and **Bruce Schearer.** 1976. Article published in February issue of *Family Planning Perspectives,* summarized in *Newsweek,* March 1, p. 60.

Townsend, Peter. 1957. *The Family Life of Old People: An Inquiry in East London.* Glencoe, Ill.: Free Press.

U.S. Bureau of Labor Statistics. 1957. *Study of Consumer Expenditures, Incomes, and Savings.* 18 volumes. Philadelphia: University of Pennsylvania Press.

U.S. Bureau of Labor Statistics. 1959. *How American Buying Habits Change.* Washington, D.C.: U.S. Department of Labor.

U.S. Bureau of Labor Statistics. 1964. *Consumer Expenditures, 1960–61. Washington, D.C.: U.S. Department of Labor.*

Varni, Charles A. 1973. "Contexts of Conversion: The Case of Swinging." In *Renovating Marriage.* Edited by Roger W. Libby and Robert W. Whitehurst. Danville, Calif.: Consensus.

Varni, Charles A. 1974. "An Exploratory Study of Spouse Swapping." *Pacific Sociological Review* 15, no. 4. Reprinted in Smith and Smith, 1974.

Vellay, Pierre. 1972. "Painless Labor: A French Method." In *Modern Perspectives in Psycho-Obstetrics.* Edited by John G. Howells. New York: Brunner/Mazel.

Vernon, Glenn M., and **Robert L. Stewart.** 1957. "Empathy as a Process in the Dating Situation." *American Sociological Review* 22: 48–52.

Vincent, Clark. 1961. *Unmarried Mothers.* New York: Free Press.

Vogel, S. R.; I. K. Broverman; D. M. Broverman; F. E. Clarkson; and **P. S. Rosenkrantz.** 1970. "Maternal Employment and Perception of Sex Roles among College Students." *Developmental Psychology* 3: 384–91. Cited in Hoffman and Nye. 1974.

Vreeland, Rebecca. 1971. "The Changing Functions of Dating: Dating Patterns of Harvard Men, 1960–1970." Paper presented at annual meeting of American Sociological Association.

Vreeland, Rebecca, and **Alan Austin.** 1971. "Some Aspects of the Sexual Revolution: Dating Patterns of Harvard Men, 1960–1970." Paper presented at annual meeting of Pacific Sociological Association.

Wagatsuma, Hiroshi. 1973. "Some Problems of Interracial Marriage for the Japanese." In *Interracial Marriage: Expectations and Realities.* Edited by Irving R. Stuart and Lawrence E. Abt. New York: Grossman.

Walker, Kathryn E. 1970. *Time-Use Patterns for Household Work Related to Homemakers' Employment.* Washington, D.C. U.S. Department of Agriculture.

Wallace, Karl. 1960. "Factors Hindering Mate Selection." *Sociology and Social Research* 44: 317–25.

Waller, Willard. 1938. *The Family: A Dynamic Interpretation.* New York: Cordon.

Waller, Willard, and **Reuben Hill.** 1951. *The Family: A Dynamic Interpretation.* New York: Dryden.

Wallin, Paul. 1950. "Cultural Contradictions and Sex Roles: A Repeat Study." *American Sociological Review* 15: 288–93.

Wallin, Paul. 1957. "Religiosity, Sexual Gratification, and Marital Satisfaction." *American Sociological Review* 22: 300–305.

Walsh, Robert H.; Mary Z. Ferrell; and **William L. Tolone.** 1976. "Selection of Reference Group, Perceived Reference Group Permissiveness, and Personal Permissiveness Attitudes and Behavior: A Study of Two Consecutive Panels (1967–71; 1970–74)." *Journal of Marriage and the Family* 38: 495–507.

Weiss, Robert S. 1973. "The Contributions of an Organization of Single Parents to the Well-Being of Its Members." *Family Coordinator* 22: 321–26.

Weller, Leonard; Orah Natan; and **Ophrah Hazi.** 1974. "Birth Order and Marital Bliss in Israel." *Journal of Marriage and the Family* 36: 794–97.

Westley, William A., and **Frederick Elkin.** 1957. "The Protective Environment and Adolescent Socialization." *Social Forces* 35: 243–49.

Westley, William A., and **Nathan B. Epstein.** 1969. *The Silent Majority: Families of Emotionally Healthy College Students.* San Francisco: Jossey-Bass.

Westoff, Charles F.; Lee F. Herrera; and **P. K. Whelpton.** 1953. "The Use, Effectiveness, and Acceptability of Methods of Fertility Control." *Milbank Memorial Fund Quarterly* 31: 291–357.

Westoff, Charles F.; Robert G. Potter, Jr.; Philip C. Sagi; and **Elliot G. Mishler.** 1961. *Family Growth in Metropolitan America.* Princeton: N.J. Princeton University Press.

Westoff, Charles F.; Robert G. Potter, Jr.; and **Philip C. Sagi.** 1963. *The Third Child: A Study in the Prediction of Fertility.* Princeton, N.J.: Princeton University Press.

Whelpton, Pascal K.; Arthur A. Campbell; and **John B. Patterson.** 1966. *Fertility and Family Planning in the United States.* Princeton, N.J.: Princeton University Press.

White, Burton L. 1975. "Critical Influences in the Origins of Competence." *Merrill-Palmer Quarterly* 21: 243–66.

White, Elwyn B. 1945. *Stuart Little.* New York: Harper.

White, Elwyn B. 1952. *Charlotte's Web.* New York: Harper.

Whitehurst, Robert N. 1974. "Open Marriage: Problems and Prospects." Unpublished manuscript.

Whyte, William H., Jr. 1952. "The Wife Problem." *Life,* January 7, pp. 32–48.

Whyte, William H., Jr. 1954. "The Web of Word of Mouth." *Fortune,* November.

Whyte, William H., Jr. 1957. *The Organization Man.* Garden City, N.Y.: Doubleday Anchor.

Wiegand, Elizabeth, and **Irma H. Gross.** 1958. *Fatigue of Homemakers with Young Children.* East Lansing, Mich.: Agricultural Experiment Station, Michigan State University.

Willmott, Peter, and **Michael Young.** 1960. *Family and Class in a London Suburb.* London: Routledge and Kegan Paul.

Winch. Robert F. 1958. *Mate Selection.* New York: Harper.

Women's Bureau. 1962. *Fifteen Years after College.* Washington, D.C.: U.S. Department of Labor.

Young, Laurie. 1976. "Sharing a Career as Well as a Marriage." *Michigan Daily,* October 17.

Young, T. R. 1964. "Recreation and Family Stress: An Essay in Institutional Conflicts." *Journal of Marriage and the Family* 26: 95–96.

Zerface, J. P. 1968. "Relative Effectiveness of Psychological Counseling and a Program of Social Interaction for College Males Fearful of Dating." *Dissertation Abstracts International* 23: 468–72.

Zimmerman, Carle C., and **Lucius F. Cervantes.** 1960. *Successful American Families.* New York: Pageant.

Ziskin, Jay, and **Mae Ziskin.** 1973. *The Extramarital Sex Contract.* Los Angeles: Nash.

Index

AUTHOR INDEX

SUBJECT INDEX